Lords
and
Lepers

✳

Corinne Jeffery

 FriesenPress

Suite 300 - 990 Fort St
Victoria, BC, V8V 3K2
Canada

www.friesenpress.com

ISBN
978-1-5255-1822-5 (Hardcover)
978-1-5255-1823-2 (Paperback)
978-1-5255-1824-9 (eBook)

1. FICTION, HISTORICAL

Distributed to the trade by The Ingram Book Company

Lords
and
Lepers

*

To - Kevin,

Delight in meeting
the engaging foursome
of friends. Lorraine.

May 12,
2019

Jeffrey

To my grandson,
Aidan Edward Jeffery—A.J.,
as you prefer—for your enlightenment about
how the youth of today are coming of age.

*

"Oh, just go away!" Carole hissed, glaring at Francine as if she were confronting a toad.

Whoever had coined the perfidious phrase "sticks and stones may break your bones, but words will never hurt you" had never met twelve-year-old Francine Stonehenge. Carole's derisive command made Francine feel as if she had just been spewed with the other girl's regurgitated lunch. She bolted upright from the coveted corner of the rickety outdoor skating rink, where the three high school students gravitated during every lunch hour and recess, and, holding her head high, walked back toward the old two-storey brick schoolhouse.

Wanting neither Carole nor Susan to see her sitting forlornly on the front steps, Francine decided to see if she could find Adele. Unfortunately, she was in the midst of a game of "guards and prisoners" with most of the other older students. Given the way she had been treating Adele since the beginning of the school term, Francine could barely blame her former classmate of five years if she no longer wanted anything to do with her.

Instead, she chose to embark upon a solitary walk that would take her the entire length and breadth of the large schoolyard before the bell rang for the afternoon class. In fact, if the school grounds had not been encircled by a grove of caragana trees, Francine might well have continued to amble off to regions unknown, so deep in thought was she.

*

What was happening already this fall? Francine had spent the entire summer looking forward to being in grade seven and racing up the flight of stairs to join the other high school students, especially Carole Martin, who was a year older and a grade ahead of her.

Three months before she had turned seven years of age, Francine had arrived at Hartney School as a new pupil to begin grade two and had instantly become fond of Carole when, for some reason, the elder student had taken her under her wing. The only other girl in Francine's class in the small country schoolhouse was Adele Perkins, and since she and Carole had been born and raised in the district, they had known each other and played together from infancy.

However, long before she could understand her immature feelings, Francine quickly came to resent their childhood friendship. She soon realized that she wanted to have Carole all to herself, and finally, this year at the end of June, Lady Luck had come to her assistance. Adele had failed grade six and subsequently would be required to remain downstairs with the students in the lower classes rather than vaulting to the higher echelons of learning on the second floor.

Not once throughout the protracted months of July and August did Francine feel the slightest hint of sympathy for Adele, although the mere thought of having to repeat a grade in school would have caused her to be prostrate with humiliation. Similarly, it had never occurred to her that Carole was not awaiting her arrival with the same anticipation, since she was the only girl progressing up the stairs to join her.

The month of September passed in its entirety before Francine came to terms with the undeniable fact that Carole was much more interested in Susan Smith, a tall, slender red-headed beauty with emerald eyes who was in grade eleven, the highest grade taught in the school.

Naturally, Francine had seen Susan during school assemblies, Christmas concerts, and other scheduled activities, but she had always held her in such awe that she could not imagine talking to her. Nor, for that matter, could she believe Carole considered she would become her friend. Susan was so much older, prettier, and wiser in the ways of the world than either of the two younger girls. Although they might aspire to be just like her, it was inconceivable that she would deign to grace them with her presence.

Remarkably, however, from the first day of the fall term, Susan had singled Carole out during the two scheduled recesses and lunch hour, and more often than not, they had their heads together in secretive discussions. Not knowing what to make of the unlikely friendship, Francine had tagged along, at first simply content to be seen in the company of the ever-elegant Susan. As the days passed, and her confidence grew, she ventured to contribute to their conversations whenever the opportunity presented itself.

It was soon apparent even to Francine, who was awestruck, that it was Carole, more so than Susan, who was becoming increasingly irritated by her uninvited and decidedly unwelcome participation in their tête-à-têtes. For the most part, Susan tolerated Francine's interruptions, seeming to listen with a modicum of graciousness not faintly shared by Carole. Still, every now and then, when the belle of the high school lifted her eyes skyward, Francine caught a glimpse of her cloaked condescension. Susan Smith was very aware that she had more and others had less and, therefore, that made them less.

On the Friday afternoon at the beginning of October, from the moment Carole had ridiculed Francine in front of Susan, the shadow of an oppressive idea began to take shape within Francine's young mind. Fortunately, the subsequent week was filled with preparations for Uncle Daniel and Mother Pat's Thanksgiving wedding, and Francine gave little thought to her fair-weather friend's utterance.

Nonetheless, Francine could not forget the incident. It began to consume her day and night, dredging up her suppressed feelings of culpability that eventually triggered terrifying recurring dreams. As the nightmares persisted throughout her adolescence, Francine started to believe she was subservient to most other people, a sentiment that haunted her for years before she wholly grasped how her deep sense of oppression stemming from her legacy of guilt was impacting her life.

*

Francine was an only child, and then suddenly, before the age of six, she became an orphan. One fine Indian summer Sunday while she was happily playing with her close friend, Margaret Dwyer, at her home in Cavendish, Francine's parents decided to boat along the vulnerable shoreline of Prince Edward Island's beautiful national park.

As the two young girls amused themselves in the safety and quiet of the Dwyer's sheltered basement, a severe storm whipped up on the unpredictable Atlantic Ocean. When the gale blew itself out, and the sun reclaimed the sky, Helen Dwyer had expected her childhood friend, Catherine, to arrive at any moment to collect her daughter. As she busily prepared supper, she planned to ask Catherine and her husband, Jake, to share the three lobsters her husband, Scott, had found in the trap early that morning.

Glancing frequently out the small kitchen window, Helen was at first surprised, and then alarm permeated her anxious mind when the sun began its descent below the horizon, and still there was no sign of Francine's parents. It was not like Catherine and Jake to be late, especially when it came to gathering their cherished only child.

Finally, becoming fearful, Helen went downstairs to bring the girls up for supper and suggested to her daughter that she ask Francine to stay for a sleepover. Francine's delight with the unexpected surprise invitation on an evening before a school day obliterated any question of the whereabouts of her mother and father, and after a quick meal, they hurried into Margaret's bedroom to begin their pyjama party.

Concern was even beginning to show on Scott Dwyer's usually

benign countenance. After he had eaten, he suggested to his son, Paul, that they walk the four blocks to the Stonehenge home. Noticing immediately that the house was in darkness, they hastened to the small pub on Main Street to ascertain if anyone had seen Catherine or Jake.

In their hamlet, every villager knew and cared about one another, and soon, equipped with large flashlights, several of the men headed toward the shore. Many hours later, in the early light of the dawning day, Jake's small fishing vessel was discovered washed up along the coast midway between scenic Covehead Bay, and the red sandstone dunes of North Rustico Harbour.

The bodies of Catherine and Jake Stonehenge were never found.

Francine was far too young to understand why her mummy and daddy were never coming back to take her home, but in a flash, the crippling seeds of guilt were sown. If only she had not stayed over with Margaret instead of returning to their cozy little cottage at the edge of the village, they surely would not have gone away. They must have been very angry with her. While she was laughing and having fun curled up with her friend under the comfortable quilt on Margaret's three-quarter bed, they would have been searching for her. When they could not find her, they had gone out to sea.

That had to be it. Daddy never took Mummy fishing with him, and when he did go, he waited until the sun had come up over the horizon. Then, every night he came back home to be with her and Mummy before the sky turned dark. Both Mummy and Daddy had always warned Francine that she must never go down to the ocean shore without one of them. Now Auntie Margaret and Uncle Scott were trying to make her understand that both of her beloved parents had gone to their watery graves, leaving her behind.

*

Every inhabitant of Cavendish and the surrounding small fishing communities was devastated by the senseless tragedy. Both Catherine and Jake had been born and raised in the unincorporated hamlet, situated approximately twenty-one miles northwest of Charlottetown. Other than making an occasional bus trip to the island capital, they had been content to remain in their two-bedroom cottage, visiting with their lifelong friends in the district.

Francine had arrived later in their marriage, long after they had given up all hope of ever having a child, and she was the highlight of their simple lives. Their daughter was constantly with them, and it was not until the autumn when Francine had started grade one that anyone could remember seeing either Jake or Catherine without her happily skipping along beside them. Still, her only playmate was Margaret Dwyer, and the older members of the community often mistook the two little girls for their respective mothers as they reminisced about how they too had been constant companions in their youth.

Neither Jake nor Catherine had any family in Prince Edward Island. Jake had been raised in an endless number of foster homes, and Catherine's mother was most surprised when, at her change of life, she had found herself once again with child. Her twin sons were nearly fifteen years older than her baby daughter, and now the first person to even recollect their existence was Helen Dwyer, although the two boys were all but grown up when she was Catherine's playmate.

Once Helen reminded them, others also began to remember the identical twins, Daniel and Darrin McGregor, and how when first their father and then, not three years later, their mother had passed on, they had chosen to leave their only sister in her new husband's care and to venture west during the Great Depression. It was known that they had eventually arrived and settled near the small town of Hartney, Manitoba, where they were operating a sheep farm. With their memories refreshed, at a town meeting, the villagers almost unanimously agreed that they were obligated to inform Catherine's brothers about her demise and the subsequent plight of their young niece.

Ironically, the only person hesitant about the decision was Helen. When she initially mentioned Daniel and Darrin, she had certainly expected that they should be advised about their sister's death, but she had given little consideration to any possible consequence of telling them about Francine. Scott had readily agreed with his wife that they would raise the girl with their own two children, and the family had settled, as much as possible after the devastating misfortune, into a routine when the letter arrived.

Opening it, Helen felt a sudden surge of fear, and when she perused the epistle, she discovered her apprehension was well-founded. The brothers wrote of their sorrow at the untimely death of their younger sister and of their deep regret they would never have the opportunity to see her again. However, they were not about to spend the rest of their lives without getting to know Catherine's only child, and the following summer, at the end of the school year, they would return to Cavendish to bring Francine back to Manitoba with them.

*

When Helen and Scott circulated the news around the close-knit community, no one could believe that Daniel and Darrin would cross the vastness of Canada for their small niece. But then, none knew of the abject loneliness and isolation of the brothers' existence since leaving Prince Edward Island because of their firmly held belief that it was the only way for them to survive during the hungry years of the Depression.

As autumn turned into winter, and finally spring was in the air, most of the islanders had forgotten about the impending return of the McGregor twins. Even the Dwyer family had long ceased to fret about the proposed departure of a girl who had become one of them, and as the end of June approached, they became busy with plans for the summer.

For months after Catherine and Jake's demise, Helen and Scott had consoled Francine, most often during the night, taking turns patiently calming her after she awakened screaming with yet another nightmare. Finally, she had begun to cope with her parents' death, although no amount of reassurance seemed to convince Francine that she was not to blame, that her mummy and daddy had gone out on the ocean and perished in the sudden summer storm. Subsequently, the last thing Helen and Scott Dwyer were going to tell the child was that her unknown uncles were coming to take her away to Manitoba.

✳

The twins arrived on the early evening bus from Charlottetown. They had journeyed day and night by train and by boat to bring the young niece they had never met back to Manitoba. It was perfectly natural for the brothers to return to the house in which they had been born and raised. After their parents had died and they decided to go west, they had left the family home to Catherine and Jake. Still, it was surreal to them that their sister and her husband would not be welcoming them back to their beloved isle.

The new owners of the Stonehenge cottage were surprised when two identical strangers knocked on their door in the gathering twilight. Nonetheless, the twins were ushered in and offered a meal and a place to sleep; such is the hospitality of the islanders.

The next morning after breakfast, while Daniel and Darrin ambled about the hamlet of their youth, every person they encountered greeted them with an air of detachment. There was very little indifference, however, when Scott and, shortly after, Helen arrived to answer the door of their home and the realization of the identity of their callers dawned upon them.

Slowly, they recovered from their incredulity, and remembered their manners, as Scott, five years older than his wife, was the first to recognize Daniel and Darrin. Dear God, were the McGregor twins really going to whisk Francine halfway across the country to some dreary sheep farm in Manitoba? Perhaps they had simply come to honour Catherine and Jake with a memorial service. When they realized that Cavendish was the only home Francine had ever known and that the islanders loved and cared for the petite child with her beautiful hazel eyes and brunette hair, the uncles would surely depart without her. Then they could all return to their ordinary lives.

However, the bonds between kin are more powerful than the ties of friendship, and over a cup of coffee, the brothers, after thanking Helen and Scott for their hospitality toward their niece, inquired if Francine could be ready to leave with them on the evening bus for Charlottetown. Their hosts were stunned into silence, aghast that Daniel and Darrin could be so insensitive to the trauma of such an abrupt departure. Eventually, it did occur to Scott that since Francine must go, it might be preferable for her to leave while she, as well as the rest of them, was cloaked in the numbness of shock.

As the gloom of dusk descended upon Cavendish, all 133 inhabitants clustered around the depot, with most of them having spent some time during the day expressing their farewells to Francine. She was dazed by the sudden attention she had been receiving, the reason for which she had not in the slightest begun to comprehend. Since she had never seen identical twins, the two middle-aged gentlemen who were the spitting image of each other beguiled Francine, and fascination diverted her attention as Helen began the heartbreaking task of packing her belongings.

It was not until Francine was ushered up the short flight of stairs into the bus while the entire village stood about and waved, all the women wiping their eyes with snow-white handkerchiefs, that she began to suspect she was expected to leave with the two adult strangers dressed exactly the same. As she stared vacantly at the sea of faces, crippling fear gripped her, and for many years to come, Francine would shudder whenever she remembered how all the people whom she had known and loved throughout her young life had cast her off the island that was her home.

✳

Waiting for the ferry at Charlottetown Harbour, Francine began to weep. She continued to sob as they crossed Northumberland Strait. Sadly, she would never be able to recall a single aspect of being on a boat that seemed like a ship compared to her father's small fishing craft. Francine persisted with her deluge after they reached the mainland, and when they were on the bus headed to Moncton, her uncles had not the slightest idea what they should do.

When they arrived at the train station, they bought her food and juice, although Helen had packed enough for all of them to journey most of the way to Manitoba. Francine refused to eat or drink, and much later, only the rhythm of the repetitive clickety-clack of the metal wheels on the track seemed to soothe her. Eventually, she was lulled into a fitful repose. Every now and then, she cried out in her sleep, and in the morning when she awoke, she had dark circles under her eyes. Sitting up with a start, Francine was totally at a loss as to where she was and what she was doing there.

Seeing her confusion, a man sitting across from her gently said, "Good morning, little Francine. I'm your Uncle Daniel, remember? If you take hold of my hand, I shall walk with you to the lavatory, so you can wash your hands and face before we have breakfast."

Glancing out the window to try and get her bearings, she noticed the greenery speeding by, and then Francine gratefully took her uncle's proffered hand. She was desperate to use the facility and did not want to fall as she shakily walked the length of the passenger car. She was also hungry and thirsty, but more than anything, she wanted to touch, to reach out to someone, anyone, to determine if what was happening to her was real. Somewhat to her surprise, Uncle Daniel's hand was soft and warm, and when they reached the small room at the back of the passenger car, she was reluctant to release it.

"Don't worry, Francine, I shall stand right outside the door and wait until you're finished. Then your Uncle Darrin and I are going to take you to the dining car for a hot breakfast. We usually just have something to eat in our seats, but we thought it would be a nice treat for you."

Hearing the kindness in his voice, tears started to well up in Francine's eyes once more, and again her distress threatened to engulf her. Nonetheless, for the moment, her physical need was more pressing. Stifling the urge to weep, she hastily entered the small washroom. It was some time before she reopened the door and meekly reached out to take her patiently waiting uncle's hand.

When they reached the dining car, they joined Darrin at a table covered with an ivory linen tablecloth and silver cutlery. The waiter immediately began to make a fuss over his young diner, offering her blueberry pancakes with maple syrup and savoury back bacon. Nodding in agreement, Francine was soon devouring the attractively served meal placed in front of her. She was famished, and when Uncle Darrin offered her one of his pieces of bacon, she nodded readily in assent.

After washing her breakfast down with the sparkling glass of freshly squeezed orange juice, Francine spoke for the first time since she had boarded the bus. "Thank you both for bringing me to the dining car. Now, can we go back home to Cavendish?"

After sharing a furtive look with his brother, finally, Daniel hesitantly replied. "Let's make our way back to the passenger car, and we'll talk about what we wrote your Auntie Helen to tell you about us."

He rose from his chair and extended his hand again to his niece, who eagerly clasped it. Upon settling back into their seats, to his astonishment, Francine snuggled up beside him, and he placed his arm around her in a tentative hug.

Sitting across from them, Darrin suddenly exclaimed, "Oh, Francine, you don't know how much you remind me of your mother. You look just like her. She used to take turns cuddling with Daniel and me from the moment she was able to climb up beside us on the sofa. We've missed her so much. Then, when the letter arrived, we knew we had to come for you. We realized it would be very hard for you to leave your home, but we thought it might be easier if you were prepared. That's why we waited an entire year, to give Helen and Scott a chance to tell you more about us and why we are so eager for you to be with your family. It breaks my heart that I never saw your mummy again."

"Auntie Helen didn't talk about you. She never told me that you were coming to get me," Francine said with the characteristic frankness of children.

"Surely she read our letters to you about how Darrin and I were travelling all across the country to bring you home to our sheep farm in Manitoba," Daniel replied.

"No, she never read any letters to me. Auntie Helen and Uncle Scott only said that when Mummy and Daddy went to heaven, I could live with them. Margaret is my best friend, and now we're sisters, and she shares her bedroom with me."

"Dear child, you can't mean you don't know that we are your mummy's twin brothers, and we want you to come live with us?" Darrin said, voicing the unthinkable possibility that no one had told Francine about their pending arrival and their plans for her.

"Nobody has ever said anything about you, except my mummy. She always talked to me about having two brothers, and every year, she read your Christmas cards and gave me the money you sent to buy a gift. So, why do you both keep asking me the same questions, and why do you wear the same clothes? I'm tired, and I want to go back to Auntie Helen's right now," Francine whimpered with a mixture of irritation and desperation.

Glancing stealthily over her head at his dumbfounded brother, Daniel softly said, "Rest your eyes for a minute, Francine, and later we can talk about what we are going to do." Whether it was because of her fitful sleep on the first night of their journey or the satisfying breakfast she had consumed, she was soon curled up in his comforting arms fast asleep as Daniel silently mouthed to his still-aghast brother, "Dear God, what have we done?"

✳

It was well into the afternoon before Francine stretched and opened her slumbering eyes. Daniel had sat immobilized in the same position for the entire time, not wanting to disturb her. Francine periodically emitted shuddering sighs as she slept, and the brothers quietly conversed about what they would do now that they understood their niece had not been informed about her relocation.

"We have been so selfish," Darrin said dejectedly.

"Yes, we were only thinking about what we wanted. Never once did we consider what it would be like for Francine," Daniel replied, speaking in tandem as they had done throughout their fifty years of life. "I guess that since we're underway, the best we can do now is make her train ride as eventful as possible and see how Francine reacts once we arrive home."

"Maybe we could keep her for the summer, and if she is still despairing when it's time to start school, one of us can take her back to Cavendish, regardless of how much sorrow it causes us. Oh, how could Helen and Scott not tell the poor child that we were coming for her? We must have written them at least six or seven letters."

"And when you were outside doing the evening chores as I was making supper, I also wrote several short notes to Francine and mailed them when you were otherwise busy in town," Daniel confessed.

"Oh, did you now? I wonder what we thought we could say privately that we could not convey from both of us, because I have to own up to sending pretty little cards to Francine while you were buying the groceries. You know, it might be the first time in years since we have acted independently, and all to try and gain the love of a little girl!" Darrin chuckled.

"I was just reflecting on that very thing. We have spent our entire lives together, doing what the other does, and even after fifty years, still dressing the same just because our mother likely started it from the day we were born. It never really occurred to me before we received that letter about Francine becoming an orphan how being an identical twin has probably limited both of us from fully developing our own personalities. It was always easier just to depend on one another than go our separate ways, although we did have each other to rely on when times were hard. But now I want Francine to know me as an individual, not only as your twin brother."

"Well, aren't you the pensive one. But we certainly did receive astonished looks from most of the villagers, because we still wear the same clothes. But I can't say that I have ever given much thought to what I would be like if you weren't my twin. I just know that I might not have survived the terrible years of the Depression if I had been alone, so I don't understand why you consider that having one another to lean on has been harmful to us. If it will make you happier though, when we return to Virden, we can go shopping for different clothes. Come to think of it, Francine might feel better if she can tell us apart. I guess it could be confusing for a little girl to try and sort out who is who."

"I do want to know which one of you is Uncle Daniel and which is Uncle Darrin." Francine sat up yawning and unfurled herself from Daniel's arms. "Now I'm hungry. Can we go back to the dining car?"

"Sure, but when Uncle Darrin takes you to wash your hands and face, I'll go to the other washroom and put on a different shirt, so you can tell us apart."

✳

Francine became weepy again as evening approached and then burst into heart-rending sobs when it was time to settle for the night. Although the conductor had found a little pillow and a soft blanket to make a bed for her on the wider seat at the rear of the car, she was inconsolable. Suddenly, Darrin remembered the rag doll that his friend Alice Webster had made for her and sent along with them, and he quickly pulled his valise out from under the seat.

Kneeling down beside her, he cradled the doll as if it was his cherished toy, and when she ceased crying for a minute, he gently offered it to her. Continuing to stroke the doll, he soon laid his large weather-worn hand on Francine's head and began to hum soothingly until her eyes closed and, once again, she escaped into sweet repose.

✳

The next morning, Francine was calmer and immediately asked to have breakfast in the dining car. Over the years, the brothers had prospered, and although they maintained the frugality that had enabled them to survive during the Great Depression, their parsimony would soon be challenged. Francine loved going to the dining car, where she became the centre of attention with the young waiters. After eating voraciously, she would sedately return to the passenger car.

Daniel and Darrin were loath to waste all the food Helen had sent with them, but deciding it was far more preferable to please their niece, they opened the basket and offered its contents to the other passengers. Francine became more relaxed as the days passed, particularly when she realized that her uncles were prepared to entertain her. The colouring book and crayons Mrs. Webster had purchased as a welcoming gift for Francine soon lost their appeal when she saw her uncles playing with the bright green and red pegs that they placed in a wooden board. They patiently taught her how to play cribbage and rummy, and when she tired of card games, they kept her occupied by taking turns regaling her with stories about her mother when she was a little girl.

Notwithstanding that Daniel and Darrin had rarely been around children since they had left Prince Edward Island, the fond memories of playing with their baby sister were slowly revived, and their enjoyment of amusing Francine was genuine. Given their stature of six feet and burly build, the twin brothers, previously always attired in the same bright plaid shirts and black denim trousers, could best be described as gentle giants. They had tended to their ewes and lambs for more than twenty years, seldom raising their voices and never expressing a cross word to each other or to any other person. Their neighbours considered them to be two of the most affable men to reside in the district, most having been the recipient of their generosity at one time or another.

Little children often share a remarkable similarity with small domestic animals of being able to readily recognize humans who are kindly disposed toward them. Should those individuals be prepared to respond to their essential physical and emotional needs, affection soon follows, and Francine was no exception. By the time their long train journey came to an end, she was feeling increasingly more comfortable in the presence of her uncles, and to think less and less about the people she had so abruptly left behind in Cavendish.

*

On a Sunday evening shortly after receiving the dreaded epistle announcing the untimely death of Catherine and Jake, Daniel and Darrin had been invited to Malcolm and Alice Webster's for supper. At first, they had been sorely tempted to decline, but later they agreed that it might assuage their sorrow if they were able to share the terrible news with their friends. If anyone in the community would understand, it would be Alice, and perhaps she might be able to give them much-needed advice about what they should do regarding Francine.

In addition, the brothers had always appreciated the welcome change of having a woman prepare dinner for them, especially given Alice's flair with food. However, when neither of them was tucking into the baked ham and scalloped potatoes with their usual gusto, Alice remarked, "What's wrong, guys? Did you leave your appetites at home?"

"We almost didn't come because of the terrible news we received earlier in the week. Our only sister and her husband had a boating accident and have been presumed drown off the Atlantic coast somewhere between Covehead Bay and North Rustico Harbour. It has been over twenty years since we last saw her, and although we always intended to return for a visit, the time just never seemed right. Now Catherine and Jake are gone forever and have left behind their young daughter."

"Oh, Daniel and Darrin, we're so sorry. Why didn't you tell us sooner? I know there is precious little one can say during such a tragedy, but by now, you must surely know that we will do whatever we can to help. How heartbreaking for your niece; she must be nearly six, if I remember correctly." Alice's eyes suddenly filled with tears of grief for the bereaved twins and especially for the unknown child, as her husband nodded his solicitude.

"Thank you, Alice and Malcolm," Daniel said. "We did consider that it might help if we came tonight and told you what has happened. Francine will celebrate her sixth birthday in November, and she will not have any family to be with her. Actually, we want to see what you think about our idea of bringing Francine here to live with us. We are her only relatives, and we believe that it is our obligation to raise her. Since the accident, Helen, Catherine's school chum, has been caring for her, but we've been discussing the notion of returning to Cavendish next summer to fetch her. Do you think that we two old men could properly care for our young niece?" As was often the case during their shared meals, it was Daniel and Alice, making sure she was not seated on the side of his deaf ear, who did most of the talking, with Darrin and Malcolm quite content to eat and listen.

"You are in the prime of life. I have always thought that both of you take such good care of yourselves, and I can see how you would feel responsible for Francine. Did your sister and her husband leave a will?"

"Helen didn't mention it in her letter, but all the islanders know that Darrin and I are her only blood relatives, so it seems pretty straight-forward to us. I don't think they had much, and, of course, we don't expect any of it. Whatever Jake and Catherine left would be put in trust for Francine."

"I was reflecting more on whether they had made any plans for Francine, not on any earthly goods. I'm glad though that you're waiting until next summer, because it will give her time to adjust to the loss of her parents in familiar surroundings and you the chance to prepare for her arrival."

"That's exactly why we decided to come tonight, other than for your delicious meal. We have no idea what we need to do before we bring Francine to live with us, and since you have raised your own family and are now a grandmother, who would know better than you?"

"I would be only too happy to arrange some of the preparations for Francine's coming to live with you, and my eight-year-old grand-daughter will be delighted to help me. We shall start as soon as possible. Malcolm and I will come over tomorrow, and together we can decide what construction to do inside your house. I think your upper half-storey loft with the alcove could be converted into a charming good-sized bedroom, precisely the kind of private place a young girl would love to call her own."

Heartened by Alice's assurances, for the first day during that grievous week, Daniel felt the return of his appetite, and he began to devour the delicious food heaped on his plate. In the back of his mind, he had been expecting Alice to discourage them, certain that she would consider them far too old to embark upon the challenging endeavour of raising a child. Instead, in her characteristic manner, she was offering her assistance and, no doubt, already forming a picture in her head about how she would decorate the bedroom in their loft.

As far as the brothers were concerned, they were prepared to give their friends full rein to make whatever changes they appraised to be necessary, knowing that Alice was as creative as Malcolm was handy when it came to making renovations to any house. Subsequently, over the next several months, Daniel and Darrin were only required to provide the construction materials, as the husband-and-wife team worked diligently during their spare hours to remodel the interior of the brothers' old brick home until it was scarcely recognizable to them.

*

The following summer, Alice's prediction rang true. From the moment Francine climbed the seven steps to the small landing before turning right and vaulting up the last four stairs into the wide-open loft bedroom, she loved it. Instantly envisioning sleeping on the sofa bed, which was thoughtfully built in along the alcove, she planned to unlatch the large bay window on balmy evenings and study the stars. Then, when Francine noticed the four-poster double bed covered with a duvet made from the same fabric as the curtains on the bay window and two smaller windows in the room, she could hardly believe her eyes.

Standing on either side of the bed were two white wooden night tables with the tops the same colour as two of the musty-rose painted walls and the front panels of the otherwise snowy white five-tiered chest of drawers. The matching floral wallpaper, interspersed with pastel pink, blue, and yellow butterflies, on the adjoining walls were the prettiest combination of colours Francine had ever seen. A full-length desk was tucked into the entire span of a slanted nook on the opposite side of the room with bookshelves on either side of the middle opening, where a reading light and chair were waiting for her. The room was lit with three Tiffany lamps, one on each table and in a recessed corner an upright lamp beside a comfortable lounge chair and ottoman, an ideal niche for escaping into an enthralling book.

Although she had had her own cozy bedroom in the cottage in Cavendish, Francine never expected that she would have such a spacious and exquisitely decorated room to call her own. As she had more than once during their long train journey across the country, Francine again glimpsed the lengths her uncles were prepared to go to please her. She felt like a princess being welcomed into their home.

Strangely, within a month of living on the sheep farm in Manitoba, Francine began to recover from the sadness that had permeated her existence since her parents had died. Or was it the guilt? Time had passed so quickly; it seemed like only yesterday since Malcolm and Alice, along with their granddaughter, Cassandra, had met them at the train station in Virden. They had arrived in the late afternoon, and when Malcolm had assured the brothers that their herd of sheep had already been attended to, they all went to the Virden Café for an early supper.

At first, Alice had considered taking them back to the farm for one of her home-cooked meals, but then she decided that she wanted to enjoy Francine and hear about their journey rather than running back and forth into the kitchen. However, it was fortunate that Cassandra was loquacious, because other than saying hello, Francine was much too reserved to express another word, and even Daniel was unusually quiet. They were surely all very tired, and after a good night's sleep in comfortable beds, they would feel more sociable and ready to share some of the details of their eventful trip.

During dinner, the adults agreed that when they arrived at the McGregor farm, Daniel and Darrin would take Francine into the house, which was to become her home, but once she had been shown around the main level, Cassandra would have the honour of giving her the tour of her loft. In addition to assisting with all the decorating and selecting the furniture, Alice had assiduously orchestrated having Cassandra visit with her grandparents for the initial two weeks of Francine's introduction to Manitoba. Her parents readily understood the merit of having a girl close to her age to ensure that Francine formed a favourable first impression of her new home and community.

At any rate, Cassandra had begged to return to the Bible camp at the little Hartney church, which she had attended the previous year, and Alice, with her usual aplomb, had arranged with the minister for both girls to be included in the week of activities and fun. No doubt, some of the other members of the congregation would complain that since Cassandra lived in Brandon, the space that she occupied should be given to a local child, but Alice could be one of the most persuasive individuals in the neighbourhood when she set her mind on accomplishing a goal.

Alice would dearly have loved to observe the expression on Francine's face when she saw her loft bedroom, but she knew that Cassandra was chomping at the bit to show every intricacy of their accomplishment to the timid little girl from Prince Edward Island. One of Alice's Christmas presents to her only granddaughter the previous year had been *Anne of Green Gables* by Lucy Maud Montgomery, and once they had read it together, she insisted on having the other seven books in the *Anne* series.

Although Alice and Cassandra had not finished reading all of them, Cassandra was quite convinced that since Francine came from Cavendish, she would be just like Anne, and she had been so excited about meeting the train that it had taken her hours to fall asleep the previous evening. Besides, Alice knew that she would hear every last detail of Francine's reaction to her new home the minute they were in the car returning to the Webster farm. Cassandra had the memory of an elephant and was nothing if not thorough. In addition, she delighted in the art of storytelling.

✳

Sure enough, Cassandra was bent on starting right from the beginning, and she continued long after they had returned home and should have been getting ready for bed.

"Oh, Grandma, you should have seen the surprise on Francine's face. She hardly said a word! She just sank down onto the soft pink carpet and closed her eyes. She thanked Jesus for giving her such a beautiful bedroom. Then she went to gaze out the bay window for the longest time. I've never seen anyone look so sad. She said she has to wait until she goes to heaven before her mummy and daddy can hug her again. I think that's why she's so shy. She's all alone, but I'm going to be her very best friend. It doesn't matter that I live in Brandon, because I will come to visit you lots, Grandma. And we'll always have Francine come over to stay with us, won't we?"

"Yes, darling, I'll include Francine until it seems like I have two granddaughters, and now it is long past time for you to go to sleep.

First thing tomorrow morning, right after breakfast we'll drive back to the McGregor farm, and you can show Francine around outside."

＊

By the end of the first week, the two girls had become inseparable. Cassandra rode her bicycle to the McGregor house every morning, and within three days, her uncles had taken Francine to Souris to purchase a shiny blue bicycle, so she could ride back and forth to the Webster farm. The following week, when they attended the Bible camp, Cassandra introduced her new friend to the other young girls in the district, proceeding in her assured manner to make it abundantly clear that Francine was to be included in their group long after she had returned to Brandon.

Then when her parents arrived to take her home, Cassandra explained to them that she needed to remain with her grandparents for at least another week to give Francine more time to become comfortable with living in Manitoba. After all, she was only just beginning to overcome some of her timidity and to feel confident about sharing her feelings and secrets with her and Grandma. Alice heartily agreed with her granddaughter, unable to believe the changes that Cassandra had wrought with the diffident six-year-old, and the die was cast for an extension of Cassandra's sojourn.

＊

During that initial summer, a confluence of forces converged, and Francine was quick to prove the resiliency of children. Daniel and Darrin came to love her beyond measure, as if their lonely existence had been predestined solely to await her arrival. In addition to her uncles doting upon her, Alice ensconced Francine with grandmotherly affection and attention, although none would ever dispute that Cassandra had been a godsend.

But, unknown to any of her new family and friends, it was the vast prairie that ultimately healed Francine. Suddenly, the world was still. For the first time in her life, she could no longer hear the incessant cadence of the ocean crashing against the shore. As soon as Cassandra took her into her bedroom, Francine had rushed to the window, eager to listen to the peace of the rolling hills of her uncles' pastureland, and every day she awakened and raced down the stairs to revel in another quiet misty Manitoba morning.

The pristine silence of the prairie was balm to her spirit, its silken breezes soothing, and its horizon seemingly stretching into forever. As the plaintive sounds of the ebbing and flowing of the tide slowly receded from her memory, Francine's overpowering sense of guilt began to fade away, and she would go for long blissful days without morbidly remembering that she had been responsible for her parents being swallowed by the sea.

Ere long, none of them could recall how life had been prior to Francine's arriving. The McGregor twins, their close friends, and all their neighbours soon forgot that the courageous little lass had not always resided with her kind-hearted uncles in their close-knit community. Even the lambs invariably rushed to the front of the pen bleating for her every morning. Then Francine would caress her new pets' heads and softly tell them how she was going to spend the day.

Francine had instantly learned that it was Uncle Daniel who did the cooking and most of the household chores. As soon as she had washed and brushed her teeth, she skipped into the kitchen to set the table and pour the cereal. One morning in late August, Daniel said, "Good morning, Francine. Did you sleep well?"

"Oh, yes, Uncle Daniel. I always sleep soundly, just like our lambs in the soft hay lying beside their mummies. I love my bed, and as

Cassandra says, I'm so lucky to have such a cozy loft bedroom."

"We're so glad that you like your new home. Your Uncle Darrin and I were talking earlier about driving into Souris right after all of us have finished our chores. First, we'll have lunch at the café, and then we'll go shopping for your school supplies and perhaps some new clothes."

"That sounds like fun, but don't forget Grandma Alice and Cassandra took me with them last week to buy new dresses, slacks, and blouses. But I still need to get scribblers, pens, and all the other things on the list that Miss Rose gave me when I met her at the Bible camp. Don't you think her name suits her? She's as pretty as a bouquet of flowers. I just know I'm going to like her."

Daniel gazed fondly at the child, who had become the light of his life. "I'm sure that Miss Rose will be happy to have you in grade two. She told me she was very pleased with your report card from last year, and seeing how fast you read the books Cassandra gave you for your library, Uncle Darrin and I believe you will be a good pupil. Now, since we're going out for lunch, we won't bother with toast this morning."

✳

Later, walking down the main street of Souris, the brothers beamed with pride whenever any of the townsfolk stopped them requesting to be introduced to their niece. The news of Francine's arrival had spread throughout the entire district, and the most apparent change brought about by the new addition to the McGregor family was in relation to the twins' mode of dressing. After wearing identical attire for more than twenty years, Daniel and Darrin suddenly appeared bent upon dressing quite the opposite of each other. If Daniel wore black trousers and a plaid shirt, Darrin could be seen in khaki pants and a plain-coloured shirt and vice versa.

Nonetheless, which one was Daniel, and which was Darrin remained a mystery to the majority of people, other than to Francine, who could quickly deduce their identity by their respective roles. Since it was Daniel who she saw first every morning, she would commit to memory what he was wearing for the day, and then when Uncle Darrin came in for breakfast, she could readily tell them apart. Recalling her brusque remark that first evening on the train, Francine had been amazed at how quickly her uncles had heeded her about wearing the same clothes, and she had thanked them umpteen times for dressing differently.

*

School could not begin soon enough for Francine. It was different from the feeling of excitement she had experienced the previous September, when she and her mother had walked down the road to meet Helen and Margaret Dwyer. The two friends had been planning for that first day throughout the summer, right down to the minutest detail of what each of them would wear as they went off hand in hand to the little red schoolhouse at the end of the street.

During the initial month, becoming a schoolgirl had been everything and more than Francine had expected. She was awake at the crack of dawn, dressed, and down the stairs, ready to return to the classroom before her parents were out of bed. In fact, it was not uncommon for Francine to forget when it was Saturday morning, and she could not go to school. Then she moped around until her mother rang Helen to ascertain if Margaret was available to play.

School became Francine's ultimate escape, initiated that Thanksgiving weekend when her parents decided to go boating and never came home. As much as she felt loved by Margaret and her family, books soon became Francine's only true relief from the devastating reality that she would never see her mummy and daddy again. It was only when she was engrossed in reading and studying that she was free from the terrifying demons that had unwittingly entered her life.

*

For a child suddenly aged beyond her years, that autumn was a new beginning. France wanted to prove to the exquisite Miss Rose that she was an adept student. When she had realized over the summer that although Cassandra was two grades ahead of her in school, Francine was the superior reader, she was determined to become Miss Rose's star pupil. She had met many of her classmates during the summer at Bible camp and felt confident that they would heed Cassandra's admonishment to welcome her into the school. But even if they chose to ignore her new friend's warning, and she did not have a single playmate, it would not matter, because Francine knew she would be seeing Miss Rose every day.

Furthermore, she had many friends on the farm—her lambs; Sam, her uncles' old sheepdog; and, the grove of conifers on the southwest edge of the old brick farmhouse. She had counted them when she first arrived and had excitedly told Daniel and Darrin that the circle of seventeen evergreen trees was a perfect spot for her to have a playhouse. Of course, they helped her carry out two folding chairs and a small table she had found in the basement, and whenever Cassandra came over, the friends would arrange afternoon tea within the confines of her imaginary abode.

Initially, the McGregor twins were concerned by how Francine treated every tree in the yard as if it were a living being. She spoke regularly to them, gave each one a name, and often could be seen hugging them. When their disquietude began to heighten, they talked to Alice about their niece's unusual behaviour. Needless to say, they were considerably relieved when their wise friend heartily assured them that Francine was a bright solitary child with an overactive imagination; surely, little harm could come from her respecting all of God's creation.

*

Fortunately, on one of his daily strolls around the pasture to check on the sheep, shortly after they returned to the farm with Francine, Darrin realized there could be an inherent danger in allowing his niece to befriend all the spring lambs. How would she feel when, come the fall, several of their neighbours came to purchase one of them, and they had to take the others to the slaughterhouse?

That evening, once Francine had gone to bed, the brothers decided the next morning they would take her to the sheep pen to select two of the lambs, a ewe and a ram, and give them to her as a welcoming gift. Thereafter, she would be responsible for their care, all their offspring would belong to her, and eventually, she could decide what to do with her increasing herd of adult animals.

It was well known that the only sheep farmers in the district did not eat mutton or lamb. Over the years, an increasing number of their neighbours and friends had routinely arrived every fall to buy one or two of the spring lambs for consumption during the winter months. They praised the brothers for the quality of the meat, often expressing that they had come to prefer the delicate taste of lamb to that of beef or pork. Neither Daniel nor Darrin had ever experienced the slightest inclination to sample the flesh of the animals they had delivered in the spring and tenderly nurtured until autumn.

Now, with Francine helping them every day with their care and watching the sweet young animals mature, it was unthinkable that they could butcher one of them for Daniel to prepare for the dinner table. Ironically, they never felt any similar scruples about eating the chickens and ducks they raised or when they purchased half a porker from Malcolm Webster. Both brothers enjoyed a T-bone steak as much as the next man, but it would have been sacrilege for them to consume lamb, regardless of how frequently they were chided about their paradoxical behaviour.

Before long, Patricia Rose, who had lived for almost thirty years in the Hartney area and had heard all about the quaint identical twin brothers from the Maritimes, began to believe that Francine came by her eccentricities quite naturally. The new girl in the school had not been in her classroom more than a month when Miss Rose recognized that Francine was an unusual child and was as bright as a shiny new penny. She was serious, sensitive, and enigmatic. She was also a voracious reader and eager to tackle any book in the two-room schoolhouse's library, even those that challenged Miss Rose's grade six students.

At first, Miss Rose had fully expected that Francine would be sedentary, but as soon as the bell rang announcing recess or lunchtime, Francine was out the door ready to participate in the extracurricular activities. She especially enjoyed the game "guards and prisoners," which had been played in most country schoolyards from when Patricia Rose was a student years earlier. The large circular groove of trees with the long open space at its centre lent itself to the pastime, in which the students chose two teams, and then each player attempted not to be caught away from home base by an opponent. In neutral territory, if touched by a rival, that particular student was captured and then held under guard until a teammate managed to break through the enemy's lines and run the full distance yelling, "Home free!" to release all the prisoners.

More than any other pupil, Francine loved the game, which had been made up by unnamed students long ago. Of all the many other contests they played outdoors during clement weather, she seemed to be inordinately delighted with "guards and prisoners." Whether it was because Francine could run like the wind or due to her proclivity for being stealthy, her opposition seldom caught her before she had safely arrived at her home base. Soon, her abilities were noticed, and she was often the first person to be selected by whoever won the toss. Although everyone was becoming familiar with her sneaky ways, Francine was still rarely touched before she reached her destination.

Even when the older students from the secondary grades deigned to grace the lowly elementary pupils with their presence in the game, they could not always thwart Francine from her quest. Certainly, they could usually capture her if they saw her, but she was so proficient at hiding in the trees until the most opportune moment that she was usually well on her way home before anyone caught sight of her. Eventually, Francine's success with the game began to reveal an aspect of her nature she had never before suspected: she was highly competitive, and in time, this characteristic would set the stage for her unhealthy lifelong tendency to draw comparisons between herself and others.

Ever conscious of the necessity of not showing favouritism, Miss Rose struggled on a regular basis with Francine in her class of twenty-eight students, ranging from age six to twelve through grades one to six. Never before, in all of her years as a schoolteacher, had she been blessed with such a precocious child, and every day, she found it increasingly difficult to conceal her joy of having Francine within the realm of her pedagogy.

Try as she might, Miss Rose realized she was on the verge of forfeiting her long-held practice of not displaying partiality toward any student the day that she had discovered Francine sitting in a quiet corner engrossed in reading the dictionary. Patricia remembered how, as a child, she had been enthralled with *Roget's Thesaurus*. The thought flashed through Miss Rose's mind that she would give Francine a copy of the *New Roget's Thesaurus* for Christmas.

Of course, the school administration frowned upon a teacher

singling out any student with a gift, and if her classmates ever learned of what Miss Rose had bestowed upon her, Francine would be branded as "Teacher's Pet," not that Francine would pay heed to any of the taunts her classmates might fling at her.

✳

Miss Rose had readily comprehended that Francine perceived the world differently, seeing what others did not, and missing the obvious, which was right in front of her eyes. She never seemed to notice what she was wearing, and even though the other girls made fun of her eclectic attire, she simply walked away without comment. It was hardly that Francine could not have had the latest trends in children's clothing; her uncles would have purchased the moon for her, had she asked. But she rarely did, and although Alice took her shopping, Francine had limited awareness, and even less interest, in how to coordinate her new clothing.

Furthermore, during the ensuing winter months, Miss Rose often provided her own toque and mitts, so Francine could go outdoors during recess, because, as repeatedly happened, she had dashed off for school without proper seasonal wear. On the other hand, Francine was so attuned to the fragility of nature that if Francine saw that a tree had a broken branch, she would immediately remove it, so the tree did not waste its energy attempting to heal its damaged limb.

However, it was during a resplendent Indian summer afternoon when Patricia Rose observed Francine standing motionless, lost in the splendour of the autumnal colours, that she clearly perceived it was beauty that filled Francine's eyes with wonder and stillness that imbued her insouciant soul with peace.

✳

Francine was so like Patricia when she had been a young girl.

Patricia was the second of four children, her mother's first of three daughters, and one son. Natalie Rose loved her children, and had it not been for their subversive father, they might have had a happy family life.

Terence was neither a drinker nor a philanderer; in fact, he earned an honest living working as a trainman for the railway. But, for reasons that were never clarified to Natalie or any of their children, Terence felt compelled to undermine his wife at every turn. Nothing she did was ever adequate. She did not keep their three-bedroom house clean or tidy enough, the meals were seldom sufficiently tasty, and the children were mishandled until his constant and deliberate sabotage wore away her confidence. As the years passed, so destroyed was Natalie's self-esteem by her husband's persistent complaining that she became increasingly unable to function. Had her three daughters not grudgingly assumed the majority of the household responsibilities, the home would have come to a standstill, and their father would have had even more grievances when he returned from work.

Soon, his son Matthew followed in his footsteps, until when Patricia did come out of her daydreaming or reading, she wondered what it was about the male gender that, firstly, expected everything to be done for them, and then when it was not to their liking, they had an undeniable right to complain. Patricia was much less bothered about the state of the house, what they ate, or what she wore to school than either of her younger sisters, Martha and Bella, far preferring to lose herself in her inner world with books and nature. She tried to do her share of the chores, but if anyone of the family so much as breathed a word of dissatisfaction about whatever she had done, she simply retreated into one of her own pursuits.

By the tender age of twelve, Patricia had resolved that, although she thought she might eventually enjoy having a daughter, she never intended to marry and subject herself to the plight endured by her mother and so many of the other women she overheard lamenting their lot in the small city of Dauphin. Soon, Patricia Rose became solely focused on studying and finding the means to attend university to become a schoolteacher.

✳

Over the years, when her mother and, later, her and her sisters needed to buy groceries, clothing, or any other household items, they made the purchases on credit at the local stores and then presented the bills to their father. Naturally, as he dutifully doled out the required cash, he always complained about how easily the women in his family frittered away his hard-earned money. When she observed her father, Patricia noticed that he was much more intent upon grumbling than he was on the nature, or even the amount of, the bills, and the best time to ask him for payment was after he had consumed dinner.

One evening, after serving her father's favourite meal of roast chicken, mashed potatoes, and peas, she said, "Dad, I need thirty dollars to pay this registration fee. I'll graduate from grade twelve this year, and I've applied to Brandon College to become a teacher."

"It's high time you went out and got a job like your brother. Before you know it, you'll be married and then just expect some poor man to work his fingers to the bone to take care of you. It's a waste of my money to send you to school. Look at your mother. She sits here day in and day out doing nothing." Terence complained bitterly even as he reached into his pocket for his wallet and handed her three ten-dollar bills.

"Thank you, Dad." Patricia answered.

The following morning, she promptly went to the bank and obtained a money order to mail along with her application. Early in the process, Patricia realized it would be quite a different matter to expect Terence Rose to give her the $375 necessary for tuition and books, so she proceeded to determine her eligibility for any student funding.

Being an excellent pupil, Patricia had earned the highest average in Manitoba on the five departmental examinations and thus qualified for the annual provincial scholarship given to the top student. Ever a resourceful individual, especially when her future depended upon it, she made a trip to Brandon, and with the assistance of the dean of the Teachers' College, Patricia soon found a room-and-board situation, where her rent would be offset by babysitting the owners' two young toddlers during the evenings and on the weekends.

Then, returning to Dauphin, she quickly found employment for the summer months as a waitress at the Husky restaurant on the highway, saving every penny she earned for her pocket money. Before the beginning of the semester, Patricia quietly packed her few belongings, garnered a ride from her neighbour, whose son was also attending Brandon College, and was gone, seemingly without the rest of her family even aware of her flight.

✷

The year at Teachers' College passed all too quickly. Patricia excelled in the academic requirements and was sorely tempted to stay in Brandon and find work for the summer months. Her professors encouraged her to continue toward her degree in education, and she was determined to earn the money, until she noticed a posting on the bulletin board. The district school in Hartney was looking for a new teacher for the elementary grades for the beginning of the autumn school term. Realizing there were seldom openings in small public schools in the country, where Patricia was convinced she preferred to teach, she immediately applied for the position and glowed inwardly with pride when she was the successful candidate.

Now nearing thirty years as one of the longest-serving teachers in the history of the school, Pat had been contemplating an early retirement to fulfill her dream of travelling beyond the borders of Manitoba, when Francine had fortuitously joined her grade two class. Within months of Francine's arrival, Patricia had readily determined that she would continue her career, at least until Francine had graduated from beyond her educational domain and up the stairs to Mrs. Devonshire's instructional realm. Not once during those delightful early days of teaching Francine did it ever occur to Patricia that she would find the love of her life and simultaneously become the mother of the only girl she could envision as her daughter.

For Daniel McGregor, their romance had begun on the first day of school, when he had set eyes upon the woman Francine had glowingly talked about after meeting her at Bible camp. From the very beginning, the gentle sheep farmer had agreed with his beloved niece that Patricia Rose was as lovely as her name, with her beautiful auburn hair coiled about her petite head and her sparkling violet eyes.

Having precious little experience in the fine art of courting, Daniel agonized about how he could possibly interest a pretty member of the fairer sex in an aging man when it occurred to him that the way to her heart might be through her stomach. After subtly observing Miss Rose over a period of several days, he decided that she was much too thin. Although he knew people who lived to eat, it was quickly obvious to him that Miss Rose was not one of them; more likely, she only consumed sufficient food to have enough energy for the necessities of living.

Subsequently, on the Friday of the first month of Francine's initial year at the school, when Daniel arrived to pick her up, he waited until Miss Rose had finished with her last student.

"Hello, Miss Rose. I baked fresh cinnamon buns this morning, and I was wondering if you might like to take some home for your breakfast tomorrow."

"Well, thank you, Mr. McGregor. I seldom have time to spend in my small kitchen, not that I've ever had much interest in developing my culinary skills."

On the following Monday morning, when Miss Rose complimented Daniel on the sweetness and flavour of his baking, he knew that at the end of every week, he would bake delectable pastries to bring to her. When Patricia consistently affirmed her delight with his tasty treats, Daniel's confidence grew, until at the beginning of December, he tentatively asked, "Miss Rose, if you don't already have plans, might you consider coming to our humble home to share our Christmas dinner?"

"I would be honoured to come for dinner and to finally meet your twin brother. Francine has told me so much about both of you, and I would especially like to see the exquisite bedroom her favourite uncles had constructed to welcome her to their home. But only on the condition that you call me Patricia, at least when we're beyond the schoolyard."

"You must then promise to stop addressing me as Mr. McGregor. And, since Darrin and I are Francine's only uncles, it is easy to see why she's so partial to us." Daniel smiled, overjoyed that Patricia had accepted his invitation and already beginning to plan his menu.

✳

Over the next two years, Patricia and Daniel became aware that their platonic friendship was blossoming into something much deeper, but since neither had any previous experience with the opposite sex, both were hesitant about chancing any expression of intimacy. In addition, they were always in the presence of Francine, either at school or in the McGregor home, where Darrin was also very much in attendance.

Finally, during one Sunday dinner, to which Patricia was now regularly invited, Francine took matters into her own hands. "Uncle Daniel, why don't you just ask Miss Rose to marry you, and then she can always eat with us?"

The three adults stared at each other during an awkward silence that was eventually broken by Daniel inquiring, "Patricia, after we've finished eating, would you care to take a walk with me?"

Later, after leaving Francine to help Darrin with the dishes, strolling under the starlit sky, Daniel said, "My dear Patricia, I realize I'm getting up in years, but Francine's question has actually been on my mind for some time now. I don't know if I would have had the confidence to ask you, but since my niece has brought it up, would you consider marrying me?"

"You're the first man I've ever had the slightest interest in marrying," she replied. "Although I'm going to say yes, Daniel, I hope you'll understand that I would prefer to wait until Francine has graduated from my classroom."

✳

The years passed quickly enough for Daniel and Patricia, and they planned their wedding for the Thanksgiving weekend of Francine's first year of high school. For Francine though, the time had snailed along, as she eagerly waited for her beloved teacher to become her new mother.

Francine was soon going to be twelve, and when Miss Rose asked if she would be her maid of honour, she was delighted. The very thought of being a flower girl when she was a high school student was more than she would ever be able to live down with her peers. Of course, the entire student body and their parents, many of whom had also been in Miss Rose's classroom, were invited to her unexpected nuptials. When the majority of the farmers in the district indicated their intention to attend out of respect for the McGregor twins, the venue was changed from the small Hartney parish to the much larger church and community hall in Souris.

✳

Miss Rose invited Francine to spend the Victoria Day long weekend in Brandon. The school term was nearing its end, and Patricia decided that the two of them needed to go on a shopping spree and have some time to familiarize themselves with their impending changed roles from teacher and student to mother and daughter. Once Patricia was betrothed to Daniel, she spent increasing periods of time at the McGregor farm, but Daniel was always close at hand. Patricia knew it was one thing to be Francine's teacher and quite another to become a first-time mother at the age of fifty; she was eager to begin the adjustment with her prized student. They motored the short distance in Patricia's new automobile to the local bed and breakfast she had booked on the outskirts of the city.

Before retiring on Saturday, following dinner and a movie, Patricia said, "Francine, I have some good news for you. Prior to leaving this morning, I arranged with Mrs. Webster for us to spend tomorrow with Cassandra and her parents at their cottage on Clear Lake."

"Oh, Miss Rose, you are full of surprises. I'm so excited, I don't know if I'll be able to go to sleep. May I please ask you to brush my hair? One of my best memories of my mummy is how we would sit and chat as she got the tangles out of my hair, especially if I couldn't fall asleep."

"And then if you like, you can help me comb out my long tresses," Patricia replied. "I'm looking forward to when you won't need to refer to me as Miss Rose any longer. Only six more weeks."

"I've thought a lot about that, but what will I call you?"

"I'm glad you brought it up. I wouldn't dream of trying to replace your mummy, and since she was obviously 'Mummy' to you, it might be nice if you just called me Mother Pat. I never considered I would ever hear someone address me by that wonderful word."

Suddenly turning around on the bed, Francine threw her arms

around Patricia's neck. "Oh, cool, Mother Pat. I've been telling my sheep all about you and that soon you'll be coming to live with us, but I always hoped I wouldn't have to call you Auntie Patricia."

The weekend was everything and more than Patricia or Francine would have dreamed, and by the time they drove into the yard on Monday evening, they were as compatible as two best friends determined to forever please one another. With great excitement, Francine showed her uncles the lovely maid-of-honour gown, which Mother Pat had insisted on purchasing for her, along with a matching pair of blue satin quarter-inch heels. Had it not been for the lateness of the hour, Francine would have rushed up to her room to change and model her new attire, but she decided to listen to Uncle Daniel when he announced it was time for her to prepare for bed. She was just as happy to savour the memories of her wonderful weekend as she succumbed to the delights of sleep.

Indian summer arrived the dawn of Thanksgiving morning. Everyone viewed the glorious day as a portent of the union between Patricia Rose and Daniel McGregor. Francine had been wide awake for hours before she could reasonably climb out of bed and had lost herself in the copy of *Pride and Prejudice* that Mother Pat had given her as an end-of-the-school-year gift.

The clock had not struck seven when Malcolm and Alice Webster were knocking at the door of the McGregor home, before anyone had risen to begin the chores. "Is anyone going to get out of bed on this splendid day? Malcolm, while you help Darrin outside, Francine and I will set the table for breakfast."

Alice proceeded to unpack the heavily laden basket of bread, cheese, and fruit she had prepared before sunrise. The church ceremony was still hours away, but she rivalled Francine in her excitement. She recalled with fondness that Sunday evening when Patricia had accompanied the McGregor twins and Francine to her home for dinner. They were enjoying Alice's famous chocolate cake when Daniel had hesitantly announced that Miss Rose had consented to marry him. Their longtime friend had looked first to her and then toward Malcolm as if seeking their approval. No one in the district could have been more pleased by the news, and if Alice could have had one wish, it had been that Patricia Rose have a sister who might become a suitable mate for Darrin.

As pleased as she had been for Daniel, Alice was thrilled for Francine. After years of listening to Francine enthuse about the virtues of her beloved teacher, Alice considered that having Miss Rose become her mother could not occur at a more opportune time. Francine was approaching the trying years of adolescence, and although Cassandra came often to visit, Alice knew Francine was a lonely child. Over the years, she had not formed a lasting friendship with any of the girls in school, and then something had happened just the previous week.

Francine had been unusually withdrawn when Alice unexpectedly arrived with a pineapple upside-down cake for their dinner. At first, Alice thought Francine's mood was due merely to another insult, to which Francine was regularly subjected, the entire school referring to her adopted granddaughter as "teacher's pet." Then, noticing Francine's tear-streaked cheeks, she sat down with her. "Would you like to tell Grandma why you're looking so sad just days before becoming the most beautiful maid of honour the district has ever seen?"

"Oh, Grandma, it's not important. Besides, I don't want those two rotten teenagers to ruin my excitement about the wedding."

"Which two might you be referring to, and are you sure that they're not just jealous?"

"Why would anyone ever be jealous of me? Except when they want me to play games, because I can run fast, most of the time hardly any of the kids in school even know I exist."

"Actually, Francine, I think the other students are only too aware that not only can you beat them in races but that you also outdistance them in learning all of the subjects taught in the classroom. I hazard a guess that many are quite envious of you."

"Let's not talk about school anymore. I already feel better, and I should change my clothes to go check on my lambs."

Driving home that Friday afternoon, Alice remembered thinking that Francine might be too perceptive for her own good, and she was heartened that soon she would have a mother to whom she could confide her innermost thoughts and feelings.

Francine bounding down from her loft quickly brought Alice out of her reverie. "Good morning, Grandma. You can't believe how happy I am to see you. I was beginning to wonder if those two sleepyheads were ever going to rise and shine. I don't know if I can eat anything. When can I start getting dressed?"

"Well, my darling, I'm going to make sure you have a good breakfast, and then we're driving into Souris to meet Mother Pat for our hair appointments."

✳

The church was packed long before the blushing bride walked down the aisle and Daniel and Francine turned and gazed lovingly upon her. For the first time, the majority of the congregants beheld Miss Patricia Rose with her long auburn tresses flowing down over her shoulders instead of pulled back into a bun, which made her face look severe. Was this the stern teacher whose classroom many of them had dreaded entering after making rude remarks behind her back? Several of the other bachelors from the district wondered how they had missed such an eligible woman to bring into their hearth and home.

Daniel beamed with pride when the minister pronounced them

husband and wife. Daniel proceeded to kiss Patricia firmly on the lips in full view of the parishioners. When he released her, the newlyweds enveloped Francine in an enormous hug. Even Darrin overcame his self-consciousness and joined in the family embrace. Unable to refrain from expressing their hurrahs, the members of the close-knit community burst forth with a collective cheer as they readied the bags of confetti they had promised to wait and throw outside the church. No sooner had Patricia and Daniel reached the front door than they were pelted with the traditional symbol of festivity, along with the occasional handful of rice.

The sun was just beginning its slow descent below the horizon when the couple was greeted with cameras clicking until they were all but blinded by the constantly flashing bulbs. The hired photographer, Cameron Brown, appealed to the guests to allow him to do his job, but his supplication fell on deaf ears as every friend and neighbour wanted their own snapshots to remind them of the day. When Mother Pat and Uncle Daniel requested Francine join them for the pictures, she turned to Cassandra, and together, the two girls pulled Darrin, who was resistant, into the limelight.

Soon, the chilly air of the autumnal twilight chased the wedding party and their guests to the waiting cars to travel the short distance to the warmth and enticing scents emanating from the community hall. Cassandra grabbed Francine's arm. "Hey, you can come with us, and let those two lovebirds have a couple of minutes alone? Besides, with all your duties as the maid of honour, I'm hardly going to get a chance to talk to you all night."

✳

Later, seated at the head table between Mother Pat and Grandma Webster, Francine felt as if she was the belle of the ball. Earlier, when she arrived, Cassandra saw her outside the church and was overflowing with praise. "Wow, Francine, you look terrific. Did you see the look on Susan Smith and Carole Martin's faces? You sure showed your two critics that you're not only the smartest but also the prettiest girl in the whole school!" Then, during the picture taking, when Francine overheard several people talking about how attractive she looked in her powder-blue dress with matching gloves and shoes, she enjoyed basking in the glow of admiration of being near centre stage.

Still, Francine's delight about being the maid of honour was marred by the possibility that she might be expected to stand up in front of all the guests and express a few words. From the moment Alice arrived one evening with a prepared speech for Darrin, Francine became anxious. "Grandma, do I have to say something about Mother Pat? I could never talk with a crowd of people listening to me. My teeth would be chattering, and my knees would be knocking so hard that no one would be able to hear me!"

"Just how do you think I feel?" Darrin said. "The last thing in the world I ever thought I would have to do is speak in public. Daniel, why can't you elope with Patricia?" he asked, glancing at the sheets of paper Alice had handed him.

"Come now, Darrin. Everyone says that public speaking is just a skill like any other, and the way to become proficient is to practice until you feel perfectly comfortable with what you're saying. I'm not all that thrilled about talking in front of a group either, but we can't have Patricia and Daniel getting married without us extending our well wishes. Francine can be your audience and tell you how you're doing, and I suspect she'll be a little kinder in her comments than Malcolm will be with me." Alice chuckled and turned to Francine, "But don't you worry, my girl. That's one responsibility I shall willingly relieve you of as your soon-to-be Mother Pat's maid of honour. Now, is anyone going to put on the kettle and make a cup of tea?"

After the guests had feasted on roast turkey with all the trimmings, when Darrin was called upon to talk about his twin brother, he surprised everyone, including himself, with his rhetoric. Once he overcame his initial nervousness, he no longer referred to his notes and spoke from his heart. "I could not be happier for you, Daniel and Patricia, on your special day. After all these years, who could have imagined that we would have such a wonderful woman become part of our family? In fact, since we have been blessed with Francine's arrival, our lives just seem to get better and better, and now two lonely old men will enjoy the company of not one but two of the fairest maidens in the land."

*

Francine's nightmares began five days after Uncle Daniel and Mother Pat's return from their one-week honeymoon to Winnipeg. The family was becoming accustomed to the bliss of their evenings with Patricia now firmly ensconced within their home. While Daniel helped Pat wash and dry the supper dishes, Francine sat at the kitchen table hurrying to finish her homework in time to join in the Scrabble game set up in the dining room. Usually, she played until nine o'clock, when it was time for her to prepare for bed, but since they had been late in starting, the adults decided to let her stay up longer on a Thursday evening to engage in one of her favourite pastimes.

It was after ten when Francine said goodnight and wearily climbed the stairs to her loft. Shortly afterward, Mother Pat and Uncle Daniel tapped on her door to tuck her in, a custom they had started since they had arrived home. When they did not receive a response, they entered quietly and were surprised to observe that Francine was already sleeping. Slipping out of her bedroom, Patricia said, "She must have fallen asleep as soon as her head hit the pillow. Poor girl, I didn't realize she was that tired."

Hours later, Patricia awoke with a start. Had she heard something? Listening intently with all her senses on alert, she strained in the darkness to pick up the slightest sound. When silence reigned, she turned over on her side, and repose claimed her once again. How long had she been sleeping when a scream pierced the still night? Patricia sat straight up and reached over to shake Daniel. Then she leaped out of bed and grabbed her housecoat from the chair. "Hurry, Daniel, Francine must be having a bad dream."

Following a cursory tap on the door, they rushed in to find Francine silhouetted by the moonlight streaming through her open window. "Are you okay, Francine? I'm certain I heard you cry out," Patricia said, wrapping her arms around Francine's shoulders. "Why, my child, you're trembling. What's wrong?"

"I'm sorry I woke both of you up. I was just having a strange dream, but I didn't realize I called for you."

Not wanting to alarm Francine by telling her that she had actually let out a loud shriek, Patricia gently held her for a few moments. "You're shivering from the cold, my darling. Come back to bed, and I'll stay with you until you fall asleep."

✳

The next morning, Francine was as right as rain as she bounded down the stairs and ate a hearty breakfast. "I'm so sorry I disturbed your sleep last night. Now I can't even remember what I was dreaming about. Hopefully, it won't happen again. Before school though, I'd like to tell you something in private, if I may, Mother Pat."

Seated beside each other on the double swing on the front porch, as they waited for the school bus to arrive, Francine confided, "I think I might have started my monthly cycle that you were telling me about. I noticed some spotting on my panties this morning, so I'm using one of the pads we bought that day we went shopping for feminine hygiene.

But otherwise, I'm feeling perfectly fine."

"Thank you for sharing your news with me, Francine. Just as I said, most girls don't have any noticeable discomfort when they start their menstrual cycle, and I'm glad it seems to be that way for you. It's such a natural part of growing up and becoming a woman. Perhaps I'll pick you up after school, and we'll drive to Souris for a soda at the drugstore as a celebration of your coming of age."

✳

Weeks passed before a second incident occurred. It was a wintry Thursday evening, and the McGregor family had retired earlier than usual. It could not have been much past midnight when, once again, Patricia bolted upright in bed to the sound of a shrill cry. Following the same routine, she and Daniel arrived in time to hear Francine yell out, "Go away! Just go away!" She was twisting about on her bed with the sheets wrapped around her body as her arms flailed above her head. Her duvet had been tossed on the floor.

Sitting down on the bed, Patricia gently caressed Francine's left side. "Francine, can you hear me?" she said quietly. "It's Mother Pat. You're having another bad dream."

After several minutes, Francine calmed down and opened her eyes. "Am I back in Cavendish? Is that you, Auntie Margaret?" Then, rubbing her eyes, she said, "Oh, it's you, Mother Pat and Uncle Daniel. I'm sorry."

"You must have been dreaming about your home before you came to live with us here in Manitoba. Was that what was upsetting you?" Daniel asked, stroking Francine's hair.

"No, I wasn't," Francine snapped, "And, stop bothering me about it." She pulled away clasping her arms to her chest.

Patricia noticed the hurt look on Daniel's face and realized that, quite possibly, Francine had never before spoken so sharply to her uncle. She was equally surprised when she suddenly recalled that she had never heard such a harsh tone in Francine's voice. On the spot, Patricia resolved that she would make some special time for Francine the next day and attempt to get to the bottom of what was happening to her.

On Friday afternoon, Patricia drove to Hartney School, arriving just before the noon break, and surprised Francine by taking her into Souris for a quick lunch at the Chinese restaurant. When they had finished their wonton soup and were waiting for the chicken with cashews, beef, and greens along with the shanghai noodles to be served, Patricia asked, "How have Carole Martin and Susan Smith been treating you lately?"

"I don't have anything to do with either one of them anymore. I just pretend they don't exist. Why do you ask?"

"I don't think you remember, Francine, but last night when you were crying out, you kept saying, 'Go away, just go away.' I recalled that incident with Carole and Susan and wondered if they were still bothering you."

At that moment, a young Chinese girl about Francine's age arrived at their table with a heaping plate of delicious looking green vegetables and seared beef. "Hi there, do you work here instead of going to school?" Francine asked politely.

"Oh, no, I've finished eating my lunch, and I often help my parents, especially if they're really busy in the restaurant before I go back to class in the afternoon. My name is Jessica Yang. What's yours? I don't remember seeing you at the Souris Junior High School."

"I'm Francine Stonehenge. I go to school in Hartney. It's nice to meet you. Do you get to eat this yummy food every day?"

"That's the problem, it tastes good to you, because you only have it once in a while, but I have to eat it all the time. Even if I ask my dad to make me a Denver sandwich, he thinks he has to put bean sprouts in it."

Francine burst out laughing. "I never thought about that. My Uncle Daniel is a terrific cook, and he's teaching both Mother Pat and me. How old are you anyway? Maybe you could come to my house for supper one night. Would that be all right, Mother Pat?"

"Hello, Jessica. I'm Francine's stepmother, Pat. If it's okay with your parents, you would be very welcome to join us for dinner. What if Francine and I bring her twin uncles to the restaurant tomorrow night, and when your parents are no longer busy with customers, we can meet them?"

"That sounds like fun," Jessica said. "And by the way, I just turned thirteen, so I'm in grade seven."

"Well, we're in the same grade," Francine replied. "I'll be thirteen this month."

After Patricia dropped Francine back at school, she drove straight home to find Daniel and Darrin still seated at the kitchen table enjoying a cup of tea.

"Yes, please, I'll have some regular tea. Up to now, I haven't developed a taste for green tea, although it could be on the horizon. I think I might have helped Francine find a new friend, which I believe she needs desperately. As it happens, the couple that owns the Lingnan Restaurant in Souris has a daughter the same age as Francine, and they seem to have hit it off."

※

Deciding it might give them a better chance of spending some time with Jessica's parents, the McGregor family arrived at the Lingnan after the supper rush. Sure enough, only two couples were in the restaurant, and they looked like they were nearing the end of their meals.

Greeting them at the door, Mrs. Yang showed them to a table by the window. "You must be Francine and Mother Pat. Jessica told me all about you and how excited she was to make a new friend."

By the time the McGregor family had consumed their egg drop soup, the other customers had vacated the restaurant. However, it was not until their entire dinner had been served that even Jessica took the empty seat beside Francine at the large table. She had to coax her parents, Sebio and Trin Yang, to join them. Then they sat quietly eating their meal, their chopsticks clicking against their bowls of rice.

Suddenly, Darrin broke the silence. "That was delicious. I haven't eaten much Chinese food in my life, but I loved the tasty sauces and how you mix all the different vegetables with meat."

"Thank you, Mr. McGregor. I'm so glad you enjoyed the special dishes we made for you. Several of the ones Mr. Yang prepared are not on our regular menu, because most people don't like the way we prefer to eat our food, so we often just make it to suit their expected tastes. Actually, I'm quite surprised you ate most of that last piscine dish that Jessica brought to your table."

"Please, call me Darrin. I had no idea what I was eating, but it was so tasty and tender, I couldn't stop. Not that I can say I know what it is even after you've told me."

Trin chuckled softly. "Well, I hope you don't change your mind when I tell you that what you were enjoying what we consider a real delicacy. It was the cheeks of fresh pickerel, and it's the best part of the entire fish."

It was Darrin's turn to laugh. "Probably if you had told me ahead of time, I never would have tried it, but you're quite right." Hearing his endorsement, Sebio picked up the dish and passed it to him. "Then you must finish the last serving rather than let it go to waste."

The ice was clearly broken, and as the adults continued to drink green tea, Jessica took Francine upstairs to her prettily decorated garret. Although small, it had room for a three-quarter bed, a chest of drawers, and in the bay window, a beautiful rolltop desk. "Oh, I love this!" Francine said. "Wherever did you find it?"

"It's my favourite too. It was practically buried behind a bunch of boxes down in the basement when my parents bought this place to open the restaurant. My dad took it out to the garage, stripped off the paint someone had so thoughtlessly smeared over it, and found it was completely constructed of cedar. He sanded it all down before sealing it with a natural stain, and then he gave it to me after fixing up the attic to make this bedroom for me."

"Already we seem to have a lot in common. Before I came to live with them, my uncles had Grandma and Grandpa Webster fix up the most beautiful bedroom loft, and they bought me a four-poster bed."

"Oh, I can hardly wait to see it. When do you think I can come to your place?"

"Do your parents ever close the restaurant and take an evening off?"

"Sure! We're not open on Mondays. You don't suppose we could visit you at the farm then, do you?"

"Well, there's no harm in asking. Let's go check with everyone right now!"

Dashing down the stairs with arms entwined, the girls soon discovered that little persuasion was necessary to convince any of the adults to continue their budding acquaintance on Monday evening at the McGregor farm.

"I think that's a marvellous idea, Francine," Mother Pat said. "I've wanted Daniel to teach me how to roast a turkey and prepare all the trimmings, just like he served the first evening I was invited for Sunday dinner. In the morning, I'll ring up Alice and invite Malcolm and her to join us. What do you think, Daniel? Are you willing to show me how to stuff that bird you took out of the freezer yesterday? Sebio and Trin, are you available? That's if you're okay with being my guinea pigs!"

"That would be lovely, except Jessica, weren't you planning on having Hope come for the evening with us?" Trin asked. "She would be so disappointed if you reneged on your usual invitation with her."

"Why not bring her along? If she's a friend of yours, then she's a friend of mine. Tell us about her. I think Hope is such a pretty name," Francine replied with more confidence than her family had seen for some time.

"Mrs. McGregor, would that be all right?" Jessica asked. "Three years ago, we were just becoming friends, when Hope's mother was diagnosed with a brain tumour. It didn't take long before she died, and although Hope had a horrible time, Mr. Harding doesn't seem to have recovered from losing his wife. He scarcely notices Hope when she's at home, except when she's practicing her violin lessons. She comes home from school with me every Monday."

"Of course, you must invite Hope to come as soon as school lets out, and if Mr. Harding has finished work, please ask him also," Mother Pat said. "We have a large dining room, and we can always add more chairs."

"Oh, Mr. Harding does some kind of work from his house and barely leaves except for every Monday morning, when he takes the bus to Brandon and comes back on Tuesdays. That's why Hope comes for supper and stays overnight with us."

✳

Realizing that Francine and Hope already had much in common, both sharing the tragedy of parental loss, Pat was hopeful that her stepdaughter would warm to Jessica's friend as quickly as she had to Jessica. Being an elementary school teacher for years had taught Pat that a trio could develop a positive relationship just as readily as the negative situation, in which one person was invariably excluded at the expense of the other two friends.

Neither Pat nor Alice had ever been able to convince Francine to tell them what had happened at the beginning of October, but the more Pat thought about it, the more she was certain that Carole Martin and Susan Smith were the reasons for Francine often waking at night yelling, "Go away!"

Pat wished for nothing quite as much as for her new stepdaughter to find two new friends with whom she could share her interests, hopes, and dreams. Even before meeting Hope, she suspected, from Jessica's comments, that she, too, was a solitary child, and Pat was determined to get the three girls together at every available opportunity until the seeds of their friendship could flower into a deep and everlasting love.

With her characteristic forward thinking, if all went as Mother Pat anticipated, long before the end of the current school term, she would convince Daniel and Darrin of the necessity of switching Francine from the school in Hartney to Souris. She would be only too happy to drive Francine every day if it meant she would have congenial classmates.

Francine could barely wait for the school bell to ring at the end of the day on Monday. The minute Mother Pat asked Jessica to include Hope in their dinner invitation Saturday evening, Jessica had taken Francine back upstairs to her bedroom, eager to tell her everything about her one true friend.

Hope was as slender as a willow with blond hair so yellow it sometimes appeared as if it was a sunbeam and eyes as blue as the sky in the light of midday. They often teased each other that they were complete opposites, since Jessica's jet-black hair and deep brown eyes were in sharp contrast to Hope's fair colouring.

On that first day of school three years earlier during recess, Jessica had spotted the new girl sitting on a tree stump at the end of the playground. Mrs. Tudor, the teacher who taught the combined class of grades three and four, had introduced Hope to the rest of the students, but other than briefly raising her head to glance around, she had stared at her feet.

Jessica had been born and raised in Souris and knew every student in the five-room elementary schoolhouse who, at one time or another, had eaten in her parents' restaurant. However, knowing them did not for one minute mean any of them had befriended the only Chinese girl in the small town. Jessica was acutely aware of how lonely she felt even when surrounded by the eighty other boys and girls attending the school, and she quickly decided to talk to Hope.

After observing Hope for most of the morning, Jessica knew that she had to be very shy, so she decided to quietly approach her. At first, she did not speak, choosing to simply sit on the ground beside Hope. After a few moments, she said, "Hi, my name is Jessica, and I'd like to welcome you to Souris Elementary School. I had Mrs. Tudor as my teacher last year in grade three, and she will try her hardest to get the other girls in the class to like you."

"And will they?" Hope's reply was so soft that Jessica had to strain to hear it.

Breaking into a smile at her unexpected question, Jessica replied, "Well, it hasn't worked for me, but it could for you."

"What makes you think they'll like me any more than you?"

"Are you always so full of questions? At least, that answer should be obvious to you. I'm the only Chinese kid in this little town, and although they all love to come and eat in my parents' restaurant, I'm not good enough to be their friend."

"So, what does that have to do with it? At my music academy in Brandon, many of the better students are the Chinese boys and girls. I just wish I could play my violin half as well as any of them."

"You play the violin? I've always wanted to learn how to play a musical instrument, but we're so busy in the restaurant, there's never been time."

As the bell rang, Hope jumped off the tree stump and, much to Jessica's surprise said, "Come home with me after school, and I'll play for you."

✳

Stopping quickly at the restaurant to tell her mother that she was going to her friend's house, before Mrs. Yang could recover from her astonishment, Jessica was gone. When the girls reached the small green two-bedroom bungalow at the edge of town, Hope burst through the door with more energy and enthusiasm than Jessica could ever have believed possible after her retiring manner all day. "Mummy," Hope said. "I made a friend at school today. This is Jessica Yang, and she wants to hear me play my violin."

"That's wonderful. Remember how I kept telling you there had to be at least one student in the school who would still like you even though you have to practice every day."

After a snack of milk and brownies, Hope sat down on a straight-back chair in the living room with a beautiful violin. If Jessica had been surprised by how Hope sprang to life when she had arrived home, her startling dynamism paled by what happened next. The moment the taciturn child brought the bow to the strings and began to play, she underwent a metamorphosis as natural as the pupae of a furry caterpillar transforming into a delicate butterfly.

The sound, which filled the tiny room, was so exquisite that Jessica sat mesmerized, unable to move a muscle and scarcely able to breathe. It was not until much later that Jessica learned Hope had just introduced her to Max Bruch's exquisitely beautiful "Scottish Fantasy for Violin and Orchestra in E- flat major, Op. 46." In fact, she was practicing hours every day for her upcoming recital with the Brandon Music Academy, where Hope was already becoming known as a young virtuoso.

It seemed like only minutes, although the wall clock indicated well over an hour had passed, when Hope stopped playing and, rising from the chair, gently placed the violin back into its case. Still spellbound, Jessica could not bring her hands together to applaud, although in her heart, she felt she had just received an incomparable gift.

*

When she heard Mother Pat calling to her that it was time to go home, Francine could hardly bring herself to leave. She wanted to discover much more about Hope. "Where would she have ever learned to play a violin like that? I thought you said she's our age!"

"Oh, she's a month younger than you. Mrs. Harding was an accomplished violinist, and before Hope was three years old, as soon as her mother started to play, she would reach for her violin. Mrs. Harding started to give Hope music lessons when she could hold her prized musical instrument and then enrolled her in the music academy in Brandon by the time she was six. Hope and I soon became inseparable, and before her mother was diagnosed with the brain tumour, she invited me to her house every day to hear her play. Now, since her mother's death, her grandma and grandpa take her to Brandon three evenings of the week and every Saturday to continue her lessons. Hope practices at least four hours every day."

The more Jessica told Francine about Hope, the stronger the sinking feeling in the pit of Francine's stomach became. "Hope and you sound like the very best of friends," she blurted finally. "Why would you ever want to share her with me?"

"Why not? We'll become the three musketeers of Souris!"

*

"How much longer before they get here, Mother Pat?" Francine asked as she raced back and forth to look out the window after every trip she made to the dining room to place another plate on the festive looking table.

"They should be along any minute now, and we aren't nearly ready for them. My goodness, if you were this impatient all day in school, I wonder if you were able to learn anything!"

"After what Jessica told me the other night about Hope, I can hardly wait to meet her. And, Jessica said she would ask her to bring her violin, so when we've finished eating, Hope might play for us. Just imagine being that gifted! Still, when you were my teacher, you were always telling me I had a flair for writing stories."

"And from the writing you've already done this year in school, I'm even more convinced that one day you'll become a famous author. Your stories are so real that I can see everything you write; you paint beautiful pictures with your words."

"Oh, thank you, Mother Pat. That might be one of the nicest things anyone has ever said to me. But do you really think I have enough talent to become a writer one day?"

"Absolutely. After you finish high school, we'll send you to either Brandon College or the University of Manitoba in Winnipeg, where you can enrol in an Honours English program. While you're studying, you'll learn about writing styles and techniques, which will enhance your natural capabilities."

"That sounds wonderful. But we'll have to convince Uncle Daniel and Uncle Darrin, won't we?"

"Leave that to me. You don't need to worry your pretty little head anymore about your future, now that I'm here for you."

"Can I quickly ask you a question before our guests arrive?"

Tousling Francine's soft brunette hair, Pat said, "You already have!"

"Mother Pat, you're always telling me that! What I want to ask is, do you think Hope will like me? I'm worried that since she and Jessica are already such good friends, the same thing will happen as with Carole and Adele when I first came to your school, and now this year with Susan Smith and Carole Martin."

Although it was on the tip of her tongue to inquire about what had transpired, Pat realized she would only be confusing the issue that was clearly very important to Francine. "I can't see any reason why three young sensitive girls won't become the best of friends."

"Funny, that's exactly what Jessica said. I sure hope both of you are right."

✳

Before the cold winds of winter began to blow and the caretaker started to flood the mowed grass to make the ice for the skating rink, every day without fail during recess, and right after quickly swallowing their lunch, Carole and Susan returned to their sheltered corner.

Even Mrs. Devonshire, the principal and teacher of the higher grades in the school, could hardly contain her curiosity about what the two young women talked about so earnestly every spare moment. During those prolonged Indian summer days of late autumn, Margaret often wished she could be a fly on the wall like the lazy bluebottles that lingered long after most of the other insects had disappeared for the coming winter months. Lately, the intensity of their discussions seemed to have heightened. More often than not, they were tardy in returning to the classroom after the bell rang.

Finally, as she donned her light jacket one Friday, Mrs. Devonshire asked Francine, clearly the most proficient reader in the school, to begin the afternoon class with an interpretation of Macbeth,

Slipping down the stairs, Margaret Devonshire wondered yet again what had happened that Friday before the Thanksgiving weekend. During the initial month of the fall term, Francine had invariably tagged along with the two older girls, but now she avoided them at all costs. Not that Susan or Carole acknowledged anyone, only speaking to Mrs. Devonshire whenever she made a direct inquiry, trying to encourage their participation in any subject.

Walking toward their secluded haven, it occurred to Margaret that perhaps she needed to be more proactive about addressing the fact with Carole and Susan that their exclusionary behaviour was unacceptable. They could occasionally interact with the other pupils to at least give the illusion that they were part of the student body and had a modicum of interest in maintaining school spirit.

As she rounded the corner of the rink, Margaret slowed her pace as she overheard Susan lament, "They'll never understand! We love each other more than life itself. We've known that we were soul mates from the moment we set eyes on each other. Robert and I must be together; what can it possibly matter that he's a mere fifteen years older than me?"

Not understanding that her question was rhetorical, Carole started to reply. "Maybe, you—" But she stopped when Susan glared at her with a look of condescension usually saved for the less-fortunate pupils who dared to speak to her.

"Well, we're not going to listen to them. Next Friday, he's coming to get me. I plan to pack as many of my personal belongings in my school bag every morning of the week and store them in my locker. You don't suppose you could bring a small suitcase from home and keep it for me in yours, could you?"

Realizing this time she could answer, although she still did not grasp Susan's intention, Carole said, "Why, yes, I have a lovely bag my grandma gave me last Christmas. So, you want me to bring it to school and keep it in my locker?"

"Exactly! When Robert picks me up in his beautiful red convertible on Friday, we're running away and eloping," Susan enthused with sheer delight.

Carole was on the verge of inquiring how she was to get her suitcase back when she glanced up, and saw Mrs. Devonshire descending upon them.

"Do you young ladies plan to return to class, or are you just going to while away the afternoon engaged in your never-ending tête-à-têtes?"

✳

Marching behind her two errant students, Margaret wondered how much truth there was in Susan's disclosure to her young counterpart. Bert and June Smith were longtime friends of her and her husband, James. The thought flashed through her mind that perhaps she should alert them to their daughter's proposed elopement.

Over the summer months, June had confided that Susan had been going for evening rides with Robert Wharton in his shiny red Cadillac convertible, and although she initially didn't have any qualms about their new neighbour coming to take her for a drive, Bert began to question his intentions. What possible interest could the older man have in his only daughter, who had just turned seventeen in the spring?

"Oh, he's probably just showing off his car. You know how you boys are with your toys!" June was quick to rejoin, not wanting Bert to get carried away with another one of his tangents about their adolescent daughter's recently insolent behaviour.

However, when school began, and Robert continued to arrive every evening right after supper to whisk Susan away from the kitchen table, where she had just begun her homework, June started to change her tune. Although Robert never got out of his car to come to the door, Susan seemed to know immediately that he'd arrived and quickly made her exit before June could protest her daughter's departure.

To make matters worse, by the time Bert and June retired after watching the late-evening news on their new black-and-white television, Susan still had not returned. Then she must have quietly slipped in the back door and made her way to her bedroom, because neither could recall hearing her come in. The next morning, she would appear for breakfast, looking as fresh as ever.

On the last Monday morning of October, June decided to take action. "Susan, since you've become a young adult, your dad and I have been reasonable about allowing you to make your own choices in terms of selecting your friends and deciding what you want to do. But, we're becoming concerned about why you're spending so much time with Robert Wharton, who is considerably older than you, and with the fact that you're out every school evening. As it is, we suspect that it's later and later when you are getting home. It might be one thing for him to be out until all hours of the night, but it's quite another for a high school student."

"Oh, Mum, you're exaggerating. We're not out until the wee hours of the morning. Just because Dad and you go to bed with the chickens, please don't think that Robert brings me home late. I'm always in shortly after eleven. In fact, aren't I up and in the kitchen making breakfast with you every morning?"

"Yes, you are, but what are you and Robert doing until after eleven? Besides, what possible interest could Robert have in a seventeen-year-old girl?"

"Since these late-autumn evenings are still so pleasant, we like to go for drives around the countryside. Robert always has the top down, and it's exhilarating to feel the wind breezing through my hair and caressing my face. There's a wonderful sense of freedom, as if I could do anything," Susan answered dreamily gazing off in the distance as if she was well beyond the confines of her parents' stifling mundane kitchen.

It was something about the look in her daughter's eyes rather than in what she said that suddenly cast a chill over June's body. Could she take what Susan was saying at face value? Surely, she could not be infatuated with a man so much older than her? Especially not Robert

Wharton, whose light-brown hair looked like it was thinning and who was developing the paunch so characteristic of today's young men from spending too much time in the beer parlour. No, Susan had to be enamoured with his flashy red convertible and being seen by her classmates as she was driven around town in style. After all, she'd always been a sensible girl, frequently declaring that she intended to do much more with her life than sit at home on a boring farm raising children and chickens.

Still, June decided it was time to lay down some rules about her daughter's evening escapades. "Well, my dearest, starting today, you will not be allowed to go out on school nights. If Robert wants to escort you around in his fancy car, he'll need to confine his joyrides to Friday and Saturday evenings, and then you better plan to be in this house by eleven."

"Whatever you say, Mum, if it will make you happy."

*

Once Susan left for school, June poured herself another cup of coffee. Sitting down at the table, it occurred to her that it had been far too easy. It was the first time in months that Susan had acquiesced to any of her requests, whether it was to clean her bedroom or help with her other household chores.

Maybe Susan had not heard her, or, more likely, she had not taken her mother seriously. Was June just overreacting to the situation, forgetting how she, as an adolescent girl, had tested her parents' limits? Well, that evening would soon tell the tale. For the moment, if she did not carry on with her usual fall cleaning, her house would never be ready for the family Christmas dinner she and Bert always hosted.

To June's surprise and relief, Susan did heed her supplication; as soon as the supper dishes were cleared, she returned to the kitchen table and brought out her schoolbooks. Fully expecting Susan to leap up at any minute and go flying through the door to flee with Robert, June eventually began to relax when first a half hour and then an hour passed with her daughter still seated at her post. All evening, Susan worked away as if she was attempting to catch up on the homework she had neglected from the beginning of the school year.

The entire week followed the same pattern. Susan was congenial and helpful, until June began to feel herself slipping into an uneasy return to their previously affectionate mother/daughter relationship. June had been delighted when she had given birth to her only child and had doted on Susan with loving reciprocation until a few years ago, with the tumultuous beginning of adolescence.

The first time Susan spoke harshly to June, telling her to stop coddling her like a baby, June quickly turned away to conceal the tears that flooded her eyes. Before long though, June began to tread more carefully around her daughter, because she often vacillated between being winsome and irascible, with June never knowing when Susan might sound off again. In short order, mother and daughter shifted to a love-hate relationship that June could not remember experiencing so intensely when she was going through the same difficult stage of life.

Still, in retrospect, other than that Friday evening during early spring when Susan had stormed out the door, declaring that she was leaving home, and spent the weekend with Carole Martin, there had been little in their family dynamics to alert June and Bert to the calamity that was about to befall them.

✳

Their guests arrived just as Daniel was carrying the golden-brown turkey to the head of the beautifully decorated dining room table. Suddenly, having nearly driven Pat to distraction as she was preparing for her first dinner party, Francine became as quiet as a clam. She stood at the entrance of the hallway and stared at the slight girl with the canary-yellow hair and striking blue eyes until Jessica teased her, "Has the cat got your tongue, Francine? This is Hope Harding, my friend. On the way here, I told her you could hardly wait to meet her, and now you can't even say hello?"

"I'm sorry. It's just that I've never met anyone with such lovely eyes. Please. come in, Hope, and welcome to our home. Mother Pat, do I have a couple of minutes to show the girls my room before we're ready to sit down and eat?"

"As soon as you help carry our guests' coats to my bedroom, you certainly may take Jessica and Hope to your loft. It looks like Hope has brought her violin, so please place it carefully on the cedar chest, and close the door to prevent your proverbial cat from wreaking havoc." Pat winked at Jessica before she asked Trin and Sebio to join Darrin in the comfortable chairs placed cozily in front of a warming fire in the living room.

*

To her delight, Pat's roast turkey with all the trimmings was a huge success. From the moment Trin and Sebio were seated at the table, they clearly enjoyed the rare treat of being a guest instead of having to prepare and serve meals for others. Jessica could not seem to satiate her hunger for truly Canadian food until her mother started to glance at her with a look akin to embarrassment. Only the fact that Hope also asked for the meat platter to be passed to her a second time saved Jessica from her mother's chagrin.

"Of course, Hope, please help yourself," Pat said. "I'm so pleased that you young ladies are enjoying the first dinner I've really prepared for company. Actually, you can thank Daniel for teaching me his culinary skills and for helping with most of this meal. Before I married him, I could scarcely boil water. But you might want to save room for the pumpkin pie and whipped cream that I can't take any credit for.

Besides, there will be plenty of leftovers, and I'll prepare a plate for each of you and another to take home to your father, Hope, before you leave."

The crowning glory of the evening commenced the moment Hope sat down on a straight-back chair, which Darrin had carried into the living room, at her request. With her deceased mother's treasured violin nestled under her small chin, Hope played the second piece she was practicing for the recital, in the event she was asked for an encore, Mozart's "Violin Concerto No. 2 in D major, K. 211."

A hush descended upon the old farmhouse as, for the first time in its history, the walls resounded with such an exquisite melody. Patricia had listened to classical music from the time she had finished teachers' college, and she was very familiar with Mozart's haunting concerto. But she had never been treated to a live performance played so convincingly by so youthful an artist. In a matter of minutes, Patricia recognized that Hope was a gifted musician.

At approximately the same time, her stepdaughter was overwhelmed with a surge of love for her new friend that Francine instantly understood would last her entire lifetime. At the end of Hope's stunning performance, everyone rose in a standing ovation. Jessica turned to Francine. "See! I told you that Hope was really special, didn't I?"

Glancing out the kitchen window and seeing Margaret's car turn into the laneway, June suddenly felt an unexpected premonition. Her friend often dropped by for a cup of tea after school hours on a Friday afternoon, but today, she seemed unusually early. Checking the wall clock confirmed June's fleeting foreboding—it was only three o'clock.

Quickly removing her rubber gloves and pulling off the apron she wore when washing walls, June hurried out the door to greet Margaret, just as she was climbing out of her vehicle. "How nice of you to come at this time. I'm desperately in need of a break."

"I'm not here for tea. Is Bert at home? If not, leave him a note, and tell him to telephone James to let him know I'm with you before grabbing your coat and purse. I think they likely headed towards the highway, and maybe we can catch them before they reach Winnipeg. I can't imagine they would stop in Brandon."

"Whatever are you going on about? Who is 'they?' I've never seen you so distraught, Margaret!"

"I'll tell you in the car. There's no time to waste. Now hurry and get your things."

✳

Speeding away the second June closed the passenger door, Margaret remained as silent as a stone as they turned off the gravel road and race along the pavement of Highway 1. Finally, June blurted, "For heaven's sake, can you stop driving like a woman possessed and tell me what's happening?"

Peering down at the speedometer and seeing that she was approaching seventy miles an hour, Margaret eased her foot off the accelerator. "Oh, God, I'm so sorry, June. I should have told you what those two were plotting last week, and none of this would have happened. I really did think about letting you know on Sunday, when you came for supper, but I didn't think she seriously wanted to run away with him."

Becoming increasingly frustrated, June said, "If you don't stop talking in riddles, I'm never going to find out what's distressing you, Margaret."

"At this very hour, Susan is eloping with Robert Wharton. I can hardly believe it myself. It occurred so quickly that she was down the stairs and opening the door of his car before I could even react. Susan had been fidgety all morning, and at lunchtime, she and Carole Martin were clearly up to something. Instead of dashing off to the skating rink, they stayed in the classroom until all the other students left. I would have waited, but Miss Swanson has a dreadful cold, and I told her I would supervise the students outside."

"Oh, I'm sure they're not eloping. They're probably just driving around showing off Robert's flashy red convertible, because it's such a warm afternoon. They've been doing that ever since he moved into the district."

"No, June, this time it's different. It was only after the fact that I started to piece together Susan's strange behaviour this entire week. Last Friday, when she packed most of her books into that large school-bag of hers, I thought she might actually be trying to catch up on some of her homework. But each morning when she returned to school, she stashed the bag away in her locker and looked over Samuel's shoulder whenever she needed to refer to a textbook. At the end of the day, she carried her backpack home, but it always looked empty."

"Susan did spend every evening this week working at the kitchen table, and when she left in the morning, her schoolbag was invariably full. As a matter of fact, she's been the picture of domesticity from Monday through Thursday, even making sure she did her laundry."

"No doubt because she wanted her favourite clothes clean, so she could pack them in her bag and also into a large soft valise she toted with her when she took flight. I had no idea she had a suitcase at school or how she stuffed everything into her locker. I suppose she manipulated Carole into taking part in her escapade, because that girl would do any of her bidding."

"How did she get out the door without you at least being suspicious? Did you not have time to stop her in her tracks?"

"That's just it! I was equally curious about the sound of the constantly blaring horn, and I was the first to go look out the window, followed by the entire class. While we were all bunched up against the wall, Susan made an easy exit. When I saw her emerge from the school carrying the two bags and then realized that she was running away with Robert, I was trapped."

"Oh, dear God, I often considered that she was infatuated by him, but quite frankly, I never thought she could possibly be in love with him. Without sounding smug, as soon as Susan started to mature, I realized she was going to be stunningly beautiful. Next year, when she planned to attend Brandon College, I fully expected she could have her pick of handsome, eligible, young men. But certainly not now if she marries Robert Wharton. Or, worse yet, perhaps he has enticed her to go away with him without any intention of matrimony."

*

Twilight was descending as the two women neared the outskirts of Winnipeg. Although they had travelled without stopping at a steady speed of sixty-five miles an hour, they never spotted Robert Wharton's fire-engine-red Cadillac convertible on the road or stopped in any of the little towns along the way.

"I think we're going to have to find a motel for the night," Margaret said. "I don't know about you, but I'm exhausted and starving. Also, we better telephone our menfolk and ease their minds about our whereabouts."

"As I recall, there are a number of motels along Portage Avenue, so surely we can find a reasonably inexpensive place to sleep and get a bite to eat."

"Don't you worry about the cost. This mad trip all the way to Winnipeg—in fact, the whole sorry mess—is my fault, so I'm going to pay your way."

"Margaret, I won't allow you to blame yourself for what my fool-hardy daughter has done. Nor, will you cover my expenses just because you feel guilty. Bert and I are the ones to blame. We should have been more responsible as parents and not allowed Susan to spend every evening with him. I can't imagine what we were thinking! Why would we believe they were only driving around during all those evenings they were keeping company?"

❋

Once they were settled in a small family lodge with quaint cabins, Margaret decided to telephone James first to give June some time to consider how she was possibly going to inform Bert about their daughter's bizarre flight. "What did you happen to say to Bert on the note you left him?"

"Not much, since I didn't have the slightest idea what was taking place. I just wrote that you and I were going for a drive and would probably end up spending some time shopping."

"Well, that's innocent enough. Let me call James and see if he's heard from Bert."

The telephone was seized on the initial ring, with James anxiously inquiring, "Margaret is that you? Where the hell are you? Bert and I have been sitting here for the last two hours worrying about what has happened to our neglectful wives."

"Calm down. The two of you have most likely been drinking beer and chin-wagging without so much as a second thought about June and me. At any rate, I'm glad you're together, because we have a bit of a tale to tell you, but maybe you should put Bert on the line."

With considerable hesitation, June took the proffered telephone. How could she possibly tell her husband that Susan was gone? That she had run away with Robert Wharton, who might at that moment, have already become her husband?

"June, is that you? For God's sake, say something."

Suddenly she was tongue-tied, remembering how, right from the beginning, Bert had his suspicions about Robert's designs on their lovely young daughter. Then, at the sound of Bert's beseeching voice, she burst into tears. The tension and fear of the past three hours let loose, and she sobbed uncontrollably.

"What's happened? It's Susan, isn't it? Pull yourself together, and tell me what's wrong!"

Bert's demands only made June wail harder, until he completely lost his patience. "For God's sake, woman, stop crying. You know damn well I can't stand it when you blubber your head off!"

Eventually, June apprised Bert of all that had transpired within the past four hours, which felt like an eternity. They had waited so long to finally be blessed with a child, and then the years just seemed to fly by, with their baby girl growing up much too soon. Susan had always been a delight: loving and considerate of her doting parents until they no longer cared that they did not conceive any more offspring. Bert and June had taken Susan everywhere with them and had even managed two major family vacations. On their first trip, they had driven to Vancouver, all of them equally awed by the majesty of the Rocky Mountains and of the vastness of the Pacific Ocean.

Still, they had not been prepared for the wonderment of their journey three years ago to Quebec. The history, the architecture, and the quaintness of the lifestyle in Montreal and Quebec City with their open markets and colourful street carnivals had enthralled them until they vowed to return to Eastern Canada again. They had excitedly been planning their trip to the Maritimes as soon as Susan had graduated from school the next summer, before she enrolled at Brandon College for grade twelve and her further studies. Now, in a flash, she was gone. A married woman by the age of seventeen. Their childless home and future lives would once again be lonely and barren.

✳

The following Monday morning, Hartney School was abuzz with the news of Susan's elopement with Robert Wharton. The older boys were convinced that the only reason the most attractive girl in school had run away with the aging farmer was because of his snazzy car. The girls were all aghast that she would waste her life on a man so much older than her.

Francine was the only student who had not the slightest interest in Susan's latest antic. For the first night for as long as she could remember, instead of her recurring nightmare, she dreamt about Hope. Her new friend was playing her violin in a beautiful concert hall just for her, and she awoke with the soft, sweet music still sounding in her ears.

✳

By the end of November, the pattern of rotating twice-weekly suppers between the McGregor and Yang families, which invariably included Hope, had become entrenched. Initially, Francine was hesitant around Hope, incredulous that the talented girl could possibly have anything in common with someone as plain and ungainly as her. In her presence, Francine felt as clumsy as one of her new lambs let loose in the kitchen. Then she worried that neither Jessica nor Hope could appreciate she was edging her way into their established friendship, especially since Hope was always so retiring, even when the three girls were sequestered in Francine's loft or Jessica's cozy bedroom.

At last, it began to dawn on Francine that perhaps Hope's reservation had nothing to do with her. She was quick to realize that between her two new friends, Jessica was definitely the more outgoing, and Hope just acquiesced to whatever she was saying or doing. Subsequently, when they were together, Francine soon found she also let Jessica do most of the talking, while she chose to detach and observe Hope. Francine told herself that she only wanted to get to know her, but the truth was she was captivated by Hope and her remarkable talent. Every evening right after supper, Hope graciously performed for the two admiring families, focusing so intently as she played her violin that she seemed to transcend the realm of her audience's existence. During her recitals, Hope became vibrant, her behaviour strikingly contrasted to all the other times when she was in the presence of adults or around her peers.

Before long, Francine's fascination with Hope began to permeate her waking moments, until she became convinced that Hope must be a musical prodigy. She asked Mother Pat to take her to the library in Souris, but after a thorough search, she could not find any books that contained specific documentation describing Hope's rare abilities. At the beginning of December, when Mother Pat took Francine to Brandon for a visit with Cassandra, Francine prevailed on her long-standing friend to help her scour the considerably larger public library in the city.

Francine was certain there was written information that depicted individuals with Hope's precocious virtuosity, and when Cassandra heartily agreed, the two young students of human behaviour spent several enlightening hours on a stormy winter afternoon engrossed in an array of psychology books. Although they did not succeed in their quest, they did formulate a plan, which would introduce Cassandra to Francine's new friends. At the same time, Cassandra's foray into the scientific study of the human mind and its functions would prove to be beneficial in her future career choice.

When Mother Pat returned to the library to retrieve the girls for supper at Cassandra's home, she was bombarded with their request to host Christmas dinner, including the entire Webster family. "Won't it be great for Cassandra to meet Jessica and Hope? Once I've shared my pal with them, instead of being the 'three musketeers,' we'll become a foursome of best friends."

"Of course, my darling girls, and what a bevy of beautiful young women you will make. Why, I can't recall how many times after our family dinners I have commented to Daniel that we must bring

Cassandra, with her lovely auburn hair and green eyes, into your new clique of friends to round out the full complement of hair and eye colouring!"

✳

When the reality hit that Susan had actually followed through with her constant chatter about running off with Robert, Carole was devastated. During their endless tête-à-têtes, she had never really believed that Susan could seriously be interested in the older bachelor, thinking Susan was content to be seen in his flashy red convertible.

Carole could barely bring herself to stay in the classroom, so aggrieved was she by Susan's clandestine behaviour, especially what must have transpired between the two fugitives over the course of the weekend. Quite naturally, the young women's topic of choice had often centred on the sexual relations between a man and a woman, but at least in Carole's mind, she invariably visualized herself ensconced in the loving embrace of a tall, dark, handsome male, not an aging man.

Oh, how could Susan have been so stupid and blind? She's thrown her life away, and to make matters worse, now that she's gone, I'm totally isolated in this boring school with these infantile classmates, Carole kept thinking to herself all morning, until Mrs. Devonshire insisted on adding to her embarrassment.

"Miss Martin, when you're ready to be present in mind as well as in body, perhaps you could read the next passage from Macbeth that I have now thrice requested. The other students and I are most anxious to hear your articulation."

Carole's frame of mind did not improve when the bell rang, signalling the morning recess. She was prepared to remain at her desk until, once again, her interfering teacher decided to oust her from the classroom. Hesitantly descending the stairs, Carole wondered what she was to do now that her only friend had deserted her. At first, she considered looking for Adele, but when she glimpsed her standing in the shadows on the far side of the school raptly listening to that acne-faced Cyril Cole, she quickly changed her mind.

Just then Carole spotted Francine strolling along the grove of trees encircling the back of the schoolyard. Remembering how eager Francine had always been about having Carole as her friend, she hurried to overtake the younger girl. Suddenly, it crossed her mind that Francine had not spoken to her since that one day at the beginning of October. What was it that she had said to her? Something to the effect of leaving her and Susan alone. Oh, yes, that was it. Well, Francine was certainly adept at following orders, but now she would be overjoyed that Carole had chosen to befriend her again.

"Wait up, Francine. I'll join you in your walk, and we can catch up on what's been happening to each other these past weeks."

"I prefer to be by myself. As a matter of fact, I'm not the slightest bit interested in talking to you, and definitely not this morning, just because your bosom buddy has run off and left you."

"You little snot! Just who do you think you are? You haven't got a friend in the world, and you have the nerve to rebuff me, you of all people?"

"You don't know what you're talking about. I have many more friends than you, which is hardly surprising, since you're such a fair-weather chum."

"Oh, sure there's that Cassandra something or another from Brandon who feels sorry for you and sees you whenever she's visiting her grandmother, but the reason you're always alone is because nobody in the school will have anything to do with you,"

"That's where you're totally wrong again. The reality is that I have two new talented friends, and there isn't anyone here who could hold a candle to either of them."

Suddenly, Francine remembered how the older girl used to pressure her to provide every little detail about her home and past life, and Francine realized that she had probably said too much to her nemesis.

Sure enough, over the next several weeks, Francine came to understand that she had made a serious mistake. Carole did not believe for one minute that Francine had a single new friend; however if, in fact, there was one iota of truth in her boast, Carole was going to drag it out of her and soon set those other girls straight. Maybe Carole could even find a new confidante amongst them, since Susan had abandoned her in the midst of another insufferably tedious school year.

✳

As Bert went about his chores waiting for June to return from Winnipeg, he could not decide with which of the two women in his life he was more furious. How in God's name did June think she was going to find their daughter in the city? Why had she not had the common sense to contact the Brandon police and stay at home, where she could at least cook his meals and keep the house?

Still, his irritation toward June paled in comparison to the frustration and anger he was being assailed with in waves as he thought about his daughter. How could she have been so foolish to run away with a man for a few days' excursion, particularly with one she hardly knew? For God's sake, Robert Wharton had to be almost fifteen years older than Susan.

Tossing forkfuls of hay to the waiting cows, Bert understood that he was more hurt than infuriated with Susan. From the day of her birth, Bert had been attentive and loving, to the extent of changing her diapers and feeding her the bottle, when many men of his day would never be seen engaging in what they considered strictly a woman's domain. Then, when Susan was old enough to tag along, he had taken her everywhere with him, often to her mother's dismay. From an early age, Susan had preferred to be outdoors around the farm animals than spend time in the kitchen or garden with June.

The more Bert deliberated on the bond between his only child and himself, the more he was confident that he had been a good father throughout Susan's life. How then could she need a father figure, because that had to be the only reason she would go away for a weekend trip with Robert. Not for one minute did he believe his precious girl could love Robert and have eloped, as her mother kept insisting on the phone. Well, wait until Susan returned home. That would be the last of her dalliances with their neighbour, who clearly had been coveting his lovely daughter all this time.

When days passed, and soon a week had come and gone with still no sign of Susan, Bert began to fear there might be an element of truth in June's supposition. It did not help that Margaret Devonshire supported his wife in her outlandish belief, although neither woman ever acknowledged the conversation that Margaret had overheard in the schoolyard. Long before they returned to the farm, Margaret had pressed June into promising that she must never breathe a word to either of their respective husbands about the fact she might have uncovered Susan's plan to elope prior to its occurrence.

Every morning since June's dramatic telephone call, Bert drove over to the Wharton farm but always found it as still as a graveyard. When Robert had purchased old man Johnson's land, he had promptly sold all the livestock, and since his first winter in the neighbourhood, as soon as the harvesting was done, he locked up his house and departed, presumably for warmer climes.

Day after day, climbing out of the car and peering into all the downstairs windows, Bert was certain that he would unearth some indication that his neighbour was about to return home. Feeling like a peeping Tom, on the first morning, he had taken comfort in the fact that none of the furniture in the parlour was covered with white sheets, and in the kitchen was a box of wood beside the stove in readiness to start a fire.

A week later, when the scene remained unchanged, Bert began to have serious questions. What had become of them? Had Susan really run away to marry Robert Wharton? Why did they not have the decency to at least telephone and let them know their whereabouts? Or had that lecherous old bastard kidnapped her? Maybe she was being held hostage in some godforsaken place. After all, Susan was underage, since she would not turn eighteen until the spring.

Countless times, Bert was on the verge of reporting that his daughter had been missing for days to the Brandon police. He was on an emotional roller coaster, vacillating between fear and fury. If he was not worrying about Susan, he was fuming at June. He could not understand how she could be so unreasonably calm about their only child's disappearance. Did she know something she was not telling him? How could she stand the thought of what that lewd old man was doing to Susan? Every time Bert picked up the telephone to press charges of abduction against his neighbour, he was overcome with shame, because he saw all too clearly in his mind Robert Wharton fornicating with his little girl.

✳

By the second week after her unsolved escapade, Carole surmised that Susan had arrived safely in Hawaii with her new husband. She knew from the increasing rumours, which had spread quickly throughout the community, that the young lovers had not been discovered before they reached the Winnipeg airport to catch their flight. When speculation about what had happened to them continued to heighten, it dawned on Carole that she was the only person who knew that Mr. and Mrs. Robert Wharton were happily vacationing in Honolulu.

If Carole had any awareness of the angst that Susan's parents might be feeling, it did not deter her in the least from keeping her promise to her friend. She had agreed with Susan that parents thought it their God-given right to make all of their children's choices, regardless of their age or own wishes. Carole was in no hurry to deliver Susan's letter to June and Bert Smith.

Of much more concern to Carole now was how she was going to lure Adele Perkins back into her confidence. She needed a friend, especially one she could manipulate, so the two of them could work on getting Francine to disclose the names of her supposedly new acquaintances. They obviously did not attend Hartney School; therefore, where had she met them, if indeed they did exist?

On Monday as soon as the noon bell rang, Carole was the first out the door and racing down the stairs. She reached the first floor just as Miss Swanson's class was lining up to go to the lunchroom in the basement.

"Hey, Adele, I was wondering if you wanted to sit with me. My mum made rhubarb cake for supper last night, and remembering how much you like it, I brought a piece for you."

Try as she might, Adele knew that her transparent face would reveal her surprise, so she decided to pretend she had not heard Carole. Although it did not work, she gained some time to think about her response before the older girl retorted, "Oh, come on, Adele. Don't bother being coy with me."

"Are you talking to me? Wait, let me pinch myself to make sure this is really happening!"

"Okay, I deserve that. I'm sorry I've been so inattentive since school started. But I didn't forget that your favourite dessert is my mother's brown sugar and rhubarb cake, did I?"

Overhearing the exchange, Francine lingered behind the two, wondering if Adele could actually be cajoled into eating lunch with Carole for a piece of cake. Although hesitant, Adele did succumb to the bribe, and, with disdain, Francine hastened to the last table in the corner with *Sense and Sensibility* tucked under her arm.

Every day for the rest of the week, Carole brought one dessert or another to share with Adele, knowing that the younger girl's mother never bothered to bake for her seven children. By Friday, Carole and Adele were once again bosom buddies, as if forgetting they had scarcely spoken a word to each other during the first two months of the school term, and Susan Smith had not existed.

✳

Initially, as Francine observed the renewed relationship between Carole and Adele, she felt a sense of relief. She had worried that Carole might try to harass her into disclosing Jessica and Hope's names, and much more, but she didn't have the slightest intention of sharing anything further about them. Even alluding to the fact that she had made new friends had triggered her overactive imagination, and for the last several nights, Francine had dreamt they no longer wanted to see her.

The older Francine became, the more she tried to understand why relatively minor daytime occurrences seemed to prey on her mind and then to haunt her in the middle of the night with all-too-often upsetting dreams. She knew she frequently disturbed Uncle Daniel and Mother Pat's sleep with her nighttime antics, but when they suggested she visit a doctor, she had adamantly refused. Before the age of twelve, Francine suspected that at least her recurrent terrifying nightmares revolved around the loss of her parents and her subsequent guilt from feeling responsible. But why she was so prone to reliving her ordinary daytime experiences and emotions in vivid dreams night after night was beyond her comprehension.

However, Francine's reprieve was short-lived. By Monday of the following week, it became apparent why Carole had teamed up with Adele. Francine had no sooner settled into her usual chair and opened her latest Jane Austen book, *Persuasion,* when Carole and Adele crowded in on her, one on each side.

"We've decided it's time you realized there are other people in this school besides you," Carole said in her customary derisive voice.

"Yeah, little Miss Stuck-up!" Adele chimed in.

Keeping her head lowered, reading her novel, Francine knew she was boxed in the corner, and her best approach was to ignore them, hoping they would soon tire of their little game. When Carole grabbed the book out of her hands, Francine stood up and reached for it, but Adele held her back.

"What's the matter with you two? Why can't you let me have my lunch in peace? I'm not bothering you."

"Sure, we'll leave you alone, just as soon as you tell us about your new friends. We just want to know who they are, and where you met them," Carole said so sweetly that honey could have been dripping from her mouth.

"If that's what this is about, you can forget it. I don't intend to tell you anything, so you may as well give me my book and be on your way."

"Not a chance. We won't give in that easily, so why don't you save us all time and trouble?"

The two girls continued to badger Francine until the bell announced the resumption of class. Then, tossing the book at her feet, Carole and Adele sauntered away, laughing.

The next day, Francine expected they would pull the same stunt, so she approached the elementary teacher. "Miss Swanson, would it be all right if I sit with the younger students from your classroom?"

"That's an unusual request, Francine, especially when I see you reading at the corner table every day. Why do you ask?"

Hardly about to reveal that she did not want to provide Carole and Adele with another opportunity to interfere with her lunch, Francine chose instead to say, "The heat from the furnace doesn't reach that far, and I get cold."

"Then I think it would be more appropriate for you to bring an extra sweater to wear during the breaks rather than join my pupils. Mrs. Devonshire has firm rules about me permitting interaction between my students and those from her classroom."

*

As each day passed, Carole and Adele persisted with their antics, trying to provoke Francine into talking about her new friends, until she did not have a moment's peace during the scheduled breaks from class. Adele began to believe that Carole truly was sorry for ignoring her since they had returned to school after the summer holidays, and soon there was little she would not do to please her.

The minute the bell rang, Carole sprang out of her desk and attached herself to Francine like an insect caught in flypaper. Then Carole steered her down the stairs, where Adele awaited them to take her position on her other side, so Francine was wedged between them. The only time her manipulators were not stuck like glue was when Francine pleaded with them to let her use the washroom.

Still, Carole and Adele did not stray far from the door, and if Francine was taking too long, according to their estimation, they taunted her about what she was doing. Certainly, they were clever enough to use muted tones, so they did not attract attention, specifically from either of the teachers. If Francine had initially been embarrassed, she soon began to feel smothered by the way she was being treated, but she was determined not to give in to her tormentors.

When Carole realized that verbal appeals were not going to be effective, she encouraged Adele to intensify their bullying by physical means. "Tomorrow when we're eating, I want you to knock Francine's lunch box onto the floor."

"Oh, I don't know if I want to do that. What would she do for lunch?" Adele said.

"That's precisely the point. We'll offer to share ours with her, just as soon as she tells us everything we want to know about her friends."

"I don't know about you, but I never bring enough food to give any away. Besides, that seems really mean."

"Well, too bad. I thought you said you would help me get Francine to open up, and now when the going gets a little tough, you're ready to quit!" Carole snorted and started to walk away.

"No, wait. I'll do what you ask. I'll sneak some extra food into my lunch kit tomorrow when my mother isn't looking."

For the rest of the week, Adele managed one way or another to make sure that Francine's lunch ended up on the basement floor and then to accidentally push Francine with her chair when she reached down to retrieve its scattered contents. Each time when either Mrs. Devonshire or Miss Swanson arrived on the scene and inquired if there was a problem, Francine quickly covered up by saying everything was fine.

Both women were aware that an unpleasant situation was developing amongst the three oldest girls in the school, but neither could ever catch the perpetrators in the act. They had little doubt that Carole was the instigator, and Adele was simply doing her bidding, although both were surprised by how clever and mean-spirited the elder student was becoming.

Margaret had known both of them since they were born, and she expected that Adele would follow along with whatever Carole prompted her to do, but she could not recall that the eldest Martin offspring had such a nasty bent to her character.

✳

The winter of 1963 could not have been more dismal for Bert and June Smith. Every morning, from the moment they woke up until they went to bed at night, they waited. At any minute, they expected Susan would telephone or walk through the door and announce in her singsong voice, "Hi, Mum and Dad. I'm home!"

Christmas came and went, and although they were invited to spend the day with Margaret and James, it was quite possibly more forlorn than if they had remained at home and chose to forget that it was a day of celebration. Margaret still had not forgiven herself for her culpability with Susan's flight and could scarcely buoy up her own despondent spirit, never mind that of her best friends. After several unsatisfying hands of their customarily lively bridge game, they decided to forego it and turned on the television to watch the queen's Christmas message. Even the roast duck was not as tender and tasty as in previous years, and shortly after the dishes were washed, June and Bert made an early exit.

Once they got home, June could no longer stand Bert's oppressive silence. "Oh, Bert, I'm so sorry I accepted Margaret's dinner invitation. It would have been easier if we had stayed here, and I'd cooked a chicken for the two of us. Nothing is right anymore, so what could we possibly celebrate?"

"There's no point in apologizing. You're only trying to make Christmas a little happier. We've been struggling through the motions of daily living in quiet despair. I can't understand how we could have raised a daughter who would not realize how hurtful she's being. Does it never occur to her that we can't get on with our lives until we know she's okay?"

"Although we spend every waking moment worrying about her, I believe she's too busy to waste any time or energy thinking about us. Perhaps that's the way young people are, only we have forgotten."

"I don't ever remember being that inconsiderate when I was her age. Even as a seventeen-year-old, if I had pulled a stunt like this, my father would have tanned my hide, so I wouldn't have been able to sit down for a week. Maybe that's the problem. We always allowed Susan to get away with everything instead of holding her accountable for her actions."

June was on the verge of reminding him that every time she tried to discipline their only child, he had been quick to encourage "Daddy's little girl" to escape from her mother's clutches and come outside with him. Realizing that laying blame now would not make either of them feel any better, she chose to bite her tongue.

✳

At the beginning of November, Francine's nightmares suddenly intensified, occurring two or three times before the crack of dawn. On the morning of the third sleepless night, Pat arose from her bed, determined to get to the bottom of Francine's troublesome nocturnal activities. Sitting down at the table with her coffee, Pat said, "Could you please tell me what's happening in school, Francine?"

"Much the same as usual, Mother Pat. Did you bake this bread yesterday? It's really good."

"Listen, my darling, this time you're not going to distract me. I need you to tell me everything, so we can come up with a solution. Soon this entire family will become walking zombies. I even overheard your Uncle Darrin asking Daniel this morning why you have such restless sleeps."

Francine was becoming equally frustrated with her nightly interruptions, finding she was often tired and had difficulty concentrating after lunch. She decided it was time to take Mother Pat into her confidence, although she chose to omit the incident near the beginning of the school year.

"After Susan made her dramatic exit from school, I made the mistake of flaunting my new friends to Carole, and now she has teamed up with Adele to find out who they are." Once she had begun, Francine blurted out every detail, relieved that at last she could make a clean breast of her angst.

Long before her stepdaughter finished, Pat had made up her mind, and the minute Francine was on the school bus, she was on the telephone to the superintendent of the Souris School Division. Preparing a cold plate for Daniel and Darrin, she left a note on the kitchen table, telling them their dinner was in the fridge, and then she departed for her early afternoon appointment with Mr. Munroe.

By the time Patricia was driving home, her last remaining decision was when she would tell Francine that, at the beginning of January, she would be transferred to Souris Junior High School. She knew she would have to tell Daniel about her unilateral undertaking, but she realized he would be easily convinced once she apprised him of the reason for Francine's nightmares. Still, he would not be happy when he heard that June would have to transport her daily, because the Souris bus would not travel to the farm to pick up a student when there was a school in the district.

"Ah, I do have a good sense of timing. I hear the kettle singing. I would love a cup of tea," Patricia said coming into the kitchen and giving her husband a kiss on the lips.

"I figured you would make sure you were back before Francine arrived home from school. But, my darling, other than telling us about where to find our dinner, you said precious little about the purpose for your sudden trip to town."

Daniel poured the tea and set a plate of freshly baked gingersnaps on the table. He held out a chair and waited until Pat was seated. "I can see the excitement on your face, so please enlighten me."

As he often did whenever he looked into Patricia's eyes, Daniel had to avoid pinching himself that this lovely woman was his wife and to pay attention to what she was saying. "I'm very happy you've finally got Francine to tell you why she has such a terrible time getting a decent night's sleep," he said when she was finished. "I know she'll be delighted to be switched to the same school as Jessica and Hope, but driving her twice a day during our harsh winter weather, even with Darrin running the snow plow for the district, will be onerous."

"I knew you would agree with me, and since there are three of us, we'll share the driving. Now, when do you think we should tell Francine? Shall we tell her tonight, or perhaps we should wait until Sunday when everyone comes for dinner."

Knowing that if Patricia asked him to fly to the moon he would not be able to consent fast enough, Daniel said, "Why don't you decide, although it might be nice for us to let her know ahead of time. Then, when her friends arrive, they can have their cozy tête-à-tête in her loft, and Francine can share her exciting news."

✳

For the next two nights, it was not disturbing dreams that kept Francine awake but rather excitement that, in two weeks, she would never have to set foot in Hartney School or see Carole Martin or Adele Perkins again. By the end of the week, Francine was running on adrenaline, but she knew she must try her best to get a proper sleep the night before Cassandra arrived for the holidays. Christmas was already shaping up to be a happier one than she could recall, and the best was yet to come.

One evening during their regular tête-à-tête at bedtime, with only a little persuasion, Francine convinced Mother Pat to display her flourishing culinary skills by inviting the Webster family to their planned festive dinner. Little did she know that by early November, Patricia and Alice had already been scheming a combined celebration, along with Hope and the Yang family, to at last bring Cassandra into the fold with the three budding soul sisters.

Since the McGregor farmhouse had a much larger dining room,

Alice had offered to prepare the salads and desserts while Patricia, with Daniel's capable assistance, would cook the turkey, complete with all the expected trimmings. Between the two households, there were enough card tables and folding chairs to extend the octagon antique oak table to accommodate all four families. The McGregor twins could hardly believe the walls of their not-so-long-ago lonely home would soon reverberate with the delightful sounds of a host of adults and youth enjoying the season of Christ's birth.

✻

On Friday morning as Francine was finishing her breakfast, Patricia arrived in the kitchen dressed in her winter coat and hat. "I'll drive you to school, my girl because I want to apprise Mrs. Devonshire that you are leaving Hartney and also obtain a copy of all your school records. I know you have kept all your report cards, but often the principal has her own notations about each student."

"Thank you, Mother Pat. I wondered if I was supposed to tell her. What reason will you give for me going to Souris?"

"I've a good mind to let her know about the bullying tactics of Carole and Adele, although I suspect she's already only too aware of what they've been up to this entire term, before and after Susan' sudden departure. From my experience, few people are able to pull the wool over Margaret Devonshire's eyes, least of all those two cowards."

✻

Patricia was ushered into the principal's office as soon as assembly was over, and Margaret had requested Francine to finish reading the last chapters of *The Catcher in the Rye* to the grade seven to eleven classes. "What a delightful surprise. We haven't had much time to spend together since the beginning of the year. Fortunately, I have a large thermos of coffee this morning."

Listening as Patricia narrated the purpose of her unexpected visit, Margaret wondered if the woman with the longest teaching history in the district would have changed her mind if she had been a fly on the wall at the board meeting at the beginning of December. Margaret had been ecstatic about the news that, the following September, she was being moved to the newly opened Hartney Consolidated High School as principal. Still, Margaret realized that once Pat had made up her mind, there was little, if anything, she could do to dissuade her from withdrawing her prized pupil.

"Both Miss Swanson and I knew what was transpiring amongst the girls, but Francine, to her credit, consistently maintained that she didn't want us involved. I'll certainly miss her capable assistance in the classroom. Speaking of which, I better return to rescue her from the majority of students, who are less than interested in the literature of J.D. Salinger."

✳

Francine had scarcely finished attending to her sheep when Grandpa Webster's ancient pickup truck pulled into the yard and stopped in front of the house. Racing to the passenger side, she nearly intercepted the opening door as Cassandra flung herself into the waiting arms of her best friend.

"This is a week of the most delightful surprises. I thought you couldn't come until the afternoon of Christmas day."

"My parents aren't able to, because Dad is on call until eleven o'clock in the morning, but Grandma and Grandpa were waiting for me when I got out of school. After we dropped Grandma off at home with enough groceries to feed an army, they said I could come and stay the night with you. That is, if it's okay with Mother Pat and Uncle Daniel."

The friends dashed into the house and disappeared into Francine's loft without stopping to ask, knowing that Cassandra's presence in the McGregor home was as natural as the sun rising in the east. "I'm so glad you've arrived early because I want to spend some time with you before you meet Jessica and Hope. And, I want you to be the first to know that at the start of school in January, I'm going to be joining them in Mr. Griffin's classroom. Can you believe it?"

"I don't know what you're talking about so how can I believe you? Slow down, start from the beginning, and then tell me everything again about Hope and Jessica. Are you sure they're going to like me?"

✳

The evening was a blur. The girls ate quickly and sat at the table only sufficiently long enough for it to be polite to ask if they could be excused. "Mother Pat, please call when you want us to help with the dishes," Francine said as they hastened out the dining room to the seclusion of her loft.

Darrin was the first to offer, followed promptly by Daniel, to take care of cleaning up the kitchen, so the friends could have a chance to catch up on their respective news.

It was well after ten when Patricia tapped lightly on Francine's bedroom door. "May I please come in? We have a myriad of tasks tomorrow with which I'll need your assistance, so I'm going to ask you to prepare for bed. I don't know about you, Cassandra, but I can't recall when last Francine has had a good night's sleep, and we hardly want her to become ill during Christmas."

Patricia had adequate experience with the characteristics of youth to recognize that the girls would continue to chat after the lights were turned out, but if they were at least tucked into Francine's cozy bed, there was a better probability that soon one, if not both, would be claimed by the quiescence of sweet repose.

✳

Francine told Cassandra everything she had learned and ever conjectured about Jessica and Hope until Cassandra felt she knew them before they walked in the door late Sunday afternoon. Similarly, Francine must have enlightened her two new chums about Cassandra, because they wrapped their arms around Cassandra as if she was a long-lost friend. As the celebratory day embraced the joys of budding camaraderie, the four girls felt as if they had known each other from the moment of their earliest recollections.

"Mummy Pat, we'll be up in my loft until you need our help again. Please call, and we promise to come running," Francine said, ushering her pals to her beloved haven. Fortunately, the adults were only too happy to undertake the tasks necessary for a large festive dinner, as it was unlikely that Patricia's voice would have had any chance of being heard above the laughter and excited conversations floating down from the upper echelon of the McGregor home.

Darrin stopped midway through carving the golden bird as Francine's deep chortle suddenly sounded above the giggling of the other girls. "Daniel, in your wildest dreams, did you imagine that two old bachelors would ever come to know such delight after spending so many lonely days and nights in this dilapidated farmhouse?"

"Not a chance, Darrin. I know neither of us will ever forget how devastated we were when we received word that Catherine was dead, but I firmly believe that when God closes one door, He opens another. Are you nearly finished with the turkey? I'll venture upstairs to invite our young guests to the table."

Overhearing the twins, Trin said, "I wonder if much later this evening you may come to regret your decision to have a sleepover for four young ladies, although I dare say it might do Hope a world of good. I haven't seen her in such high spirits since before her mother's untimely death. When Jessica first extended your invitation to her,

Hope was so despondent that she wouldn't be able to stay, because she always feels dreadfully responsible about being at home for her father."

"I'm very pleased that Hope can join the other girls," Patricia said. "What changed her mind?" she asked as she placed a delectable-looking jellied salad on the already overloaded table.

"Well, that's the remarkable thing. All the while we thought Mr. Harding was away on business, he was apparently enjoying the company of a woman in Winnipeg. In fact, he's with her now, although Hope simply refused to spend the holidays in a strange city with a family she has never met. To think that poor child has spent so much time and energy fretting about her father, and he was off having a good time. When her grandparents were invited to go to Hawaii for three weeks over Christmas, we were only too happy to have her with us."

"Both girls are welcome to stay here for as long as you're able to spare Jessica in the restaurant."

"Then they can come along to us when Patricia needs a breather," Alice said. "I know Cassandra and Francine are planning to alternate where they are, and what better way for the four of them to bond than to spend a whole week together. During these past few months, I have had my qualms about what might happen within a group of three. Invariably, one could feel left out, and as far as I'm concerned, there's nothing better when forming lifelong friendships than having an even number to offset the growing pains and differences that will naturally occur."

"I couldn't agree more, and after a couple of days with you, Patricia and Alice, I'll gladly take my turn, and put all four girls to work in the Lingnan."

After a sumptuous dinner and the gaiety of opening gifts, the girls hastily returned to the privacy of Francine's bedroom. While the four friends were relating experiences, sharing confidences, and disclosing secrets, hopes, and dreams, downstairs in the comfort of the parlour,

Patricia, Alice, and Trin were conspiring about how and where their children would spend the entire week of the school break between Christmas and the New Year. They proposed a plethora of pleasurable activities, including tobogganing, board games, and a shopping trip to maintain the youngsters' excitement and strengthen the ties of their unfolding relationships. Cassandra's mother sat and enjoyed their assiduous planning, knowing that when her only daughter arrived at her ancestral farm, she seldom had any say in what she would be doing.

During the eventful week when Francine, Cassandra, Jessica, and Hope coalesced the bond of friendship that would last a lifetime, each of them was convinced they had been the aspiring gardeners who had sown the seeds. None of the young women ever came to learn that loving mothers and a grandmother had played a discerning role in orchestrating the vacation, which all four would reflect back upon fondly as one of the best time of their lives.

Francine shot a cursory glance at Hartney School as Mother Pat drove by on the first Monday morning of the New Year. She had told no one that she would not be returning, and although Mrs. Devonshire would no doubt make an announcement in the classroom, she felt a smug sense of satisfaction at outwitting her nemeses. Neither Carole nor Adele would consider for a second that Francine was capable of such an adroit manoeuvre, and even though convinced that the former Miss Rose had perpetuated the coup, they would be furious their prey had escaped their clutches without revealing her coveted information.

From the moment Francine entered the grade seven classroom and was hailed by Jessica and Hope to join them in the vacant seat near the front, she experienced a welcoming sense of belonging. Then, when Mr. Griffin walked through the door, Francine felt her first flutter of infatuation. He was every bit as handsome as her friends had been telling her, and she could not take her eyes off him. He had dark wavy hair and the deepest brown eyes she had ever seen. Francine did not dare look at either Hope or Jessica, knowing that her flushed face and neck would give her away, yet she considered she was staring and finally averted her gaze to the floor.

After being introduced as the new student, Francine settled in, knowing that her new friends would hold their titters until the privacy of recess. They were the antithesis of her two classmates at Hartney, and as much as they would enjoy chiding her, they would not dream of embarrassing her in the presence of the other pupils. During a week of spending every waking minute together and learning that familiarity fosters intimacy, the girls had vowed that they would always be sensitive to each other's feelings.

"Hey, we saw you staring at our hunk of a teacher!" Jessica said as soon as the bell rang and the three were hurrying to the gymnasium, where pockets of students gathered during the inclement weather of a typical Canadian winter.

"You guys said he was good looking. You didn't warn me that he's gorgeous! How do you manage to listen to what he's teaching when your heart is beating so fast you can't hear a word he's saying?"

"And I thought I fell hard at the start of the school year." Hope laughed as she hugged Francine. "Don't worry, you'll soon get over him once you see some of the football team."

"Well, you're surprising me, Hope Harding. I was sure that you were too focused on becoming one of the greatest violinists the world has ever known to pay any attention to the opposite sex."

✳

Patricia arrived early and was waiting in the car when the "three musketeers of Souris" bounded out the front door of the school. If she had had any misgivings about how Francine was going to adjust, they were quickly erased when her beaming stepdaughter opened the door.

"Oh, hi, Mummy Pat. Have you been waiting long? Mr. Griffin asked me to stay for a few minutes after class to give me copies of the three English texts that we weren't required to read at Hartney. He told me that if I started them this week, it wouldn't take me too long to catch up with the rest of the class. I didn't have the heart to tell him that I've read *The Return of the Native*, *Great Expectations*, and *Pride and Prejudice* already."

"I'm sure Mr. Griffin will quickly come to learn what a consummate reader you are. Are you behind in any of the other subjects?"

"No, I'm pretty much at the same place in math, history, and geography as the Souris students. Mr. Griffin said he liked to choose a variety of English books for his class to read, and they just happened to be different from the ones Mrs. Devonshire assigned us at the beginning of the year. You should see him, Mother Pat. He's the handsomest man I've ever met."

"Well, well, it sounds like you're not only starting in a new school with close friends, but you already have a crush on your teacher. You can tell me all about him on the way home."

✶

June was dozing in her La-Z-Boy chair in the living room. The late-afternoon sun was streaming through the large bay window with an intensity portending an early spring. When Bert was eating dinner and said he was going to drive to Souris, she begged off, opting to stay home and finish the latest Agatha Christie novel she had started some time ago. But she had no sooner begun than her eyelids became heavy with sleep.

She was certain she was in the midst of a dream when she heard Susan say, "Hi, Mum. We're home." June remained in her slumber, reluctant to relinquish the resonance of her daughter's voice, a sound for which she had been pining for too long. "Mum, wake up. It's Susan, and I've brought Robert with me."

Slowly raising her drooping head and opening her eyes, June gazed at Susan, unable to utter a word. "Yes, Mum, it's really me. We arrived in Winnipeg last evening and left this morning. We ran into a snowstorm on the other side of Brandon, so we decided to have an early lunch and wait until it passed. Aren't you happy to see us?"

June continued to stare at her daughter, knowing she could not begin to isolate a single feeling, much less one of happiness. She was shocked, delighted, angry, and worried, all at the same time. The one and only clear thought coursing through her mind was that Robert Wharton could not be present in Bert's home when he returned from Souris.

Suddenly mobilized by the image of her irate husband confronting the man who had abducted their daughter, June rose from her chair. "Susan, you have to leave before your father comes home. Of course, I'm glad you're back from wherever you've been, but I need time to prepare him."

"What do you mean? I gave Carole a letter to deliver to you the day after we left explaining everything. I wrote you and Dad that we were eloping and spending three months in Hawaii. Surely you received it."

June shook her head before quickly narrating what had occurred during the protracted time of Susan's disappearance. "So, please go, before your dad gets back."

Too late June heard the footfall at the door and the turning of the knob. How had she missed the chugging sound of Bert's old pickup? Had she been paying closer attention, as soon as he had driven into the yard, she could have ushered Susan and Robert out the front door. Certainly, there was no mistaking the red Cadillac, but at least they would have been gone before Bert made it into the house.

Even June was unprepared for the vehemence of her husband's

reaction as he stormed through the back door and into the living room. "Get out! Right now! Before I do something I regret."

Robert did not expect to be warmly received by Bert, but not for one moment did Susan imagine that her father meant what he was saying. "Hi, Daddy, it's so nice to see you. I've really missed you and Mum."

"Leave my house this minute, and don't ever come back. I never want to see either of you again."

"Come on, Susan. It seems your mother knew what she was talking about when she said she needed to get your father into the right frame of mind," Robert said. "It's pretty clear he's not ready to accept me as your husband. Let's go, and they can come over later."

As the newlyweds made a hasty retreat, even June couldn't believe Bert's utterance. From the long experience of thirty-seven years of marriage, she was certain that once she had calmed him down, she could bring him around to forgiving his only daughter. She would prepare his favourite supper, and perhaps following an intimate evening, convince him to drive over to the adjoining farm the subsequent morning.

✳

A quick glance at Bert as he came into the kitchen for breakfast told June he was not nearly ready to forget the anguish Susan had caused, and definitely not to forgive her. She had believed for years that the way to her husband's heart was through his stomach, so she promptly set about making him a full morning meal of bacon and scrambled eggs.

Waiting until he had consumed his third piece of hot buttered toast slathered with her homemade rhubarb and strawberry jam, Bert said, "Don't think I'm not aware of what you're scheming, June. You're not the only one in this family to have many years ago figured out your mate. I must say though, I did enjoy a proper breakfast for a change instead of that gruel you're always feeding me, because it's supposed to be good for my heart. But I'm not about to change my mind about our daughter, whose name I never want to hear again in this house."

On the verge of retorting, June recognized the folly of further antagonizing Bert. What had happened to the man these past three months? She had never considered him to be a spiteful individual, yet here he was denouncing his only child. Surely Bert's fury had just been rekindled by the sight of Robert Wharton standing in his house with his arm around his daughter, and once he began to accept Susan's right to make her own decisions, he would come to his senses.

*

Within a month of being a student at Souris Junior High, Francine felt that she fit in better than in all the years at Hartney. Before long, she was confidently contributing to class discussions. Mr. Griffin encouraged a participatory style rather than the force-feeding approach so many of his colleagues perpetually practiced.

One day during their noon break at the Lingnan, where the three girls invariably ate their lunch, Hope expressed her surprise at Francine's academic performance. "I didn't realize you were such a good student, Francine. You ask questions in every subject almost as soon as Mr. Griffin starts to teach us anything new. How do you understand so readily?"

"Oh, I don't know, although my uncles are always telling me I have a very inquisitive mind. You don't think I ask too many questions, do you?"

"Well, you're so quick that the rest of us never seem to get a chance. By the time I've figured out what I want to ask, you've already said it."

"You sound upset. Are you telling me I shouldn't talk so much in class?" Francine asked, glancing at Hope with a look of wonderment. Surely someone with Hope's prodigious talent could hardly be bothered by Francine's questionable ability to spontaneously formulate inquiries on a variety of subjects. If she were even one-tenth as gifted as Hope was as a violinist, Francine knew she would never worry about competing with anyone about anything.

"Hey, you two, what's going on? Are you having a tiff?" Jessica said, bringing three fortune cookies to their table to chew on before returning to school. "Actually, when you think about it, in all this time, I can't remember any of us having had a disagreement. I suppose it was due to happen!"

Both Francine and Hope were quick to disclaim that they were in the midst of a dispute. Still, when the three friends walked the two blocks to school, Jessica was the only one with anything to say. She had not been entirely satisfied with their denial, and she was trying to pressure either one or both to expound on the reason for their altercation. Jessica did not think for a minute that what had occurred was serious, although she was surprised when neither would disclose its nature.

✳

For the first afternoon in several weeks, Francine did not say a word when Mr. Griffin initiated a class discussion. She kept looking at Hope, waiting for her to make an inquiry, but she too was silent. None of their other classmates volunteered any information or asked a question, and it was not long before Mr. Griffin began to glance searchingly at his most participatory student. "Has the cat got your tongue, Francine? It's very uncharacteristic for you not to be brimming with queries."

When Francine maintained her silence, Mr. Griffin, tiring of the futile endeavour, asked the class to continue reading *Great Expectations*. Sitting at his desk in the front of the room, he wondered what had happened. Over the past three weeks, he had been delighted that he finally had a bright, analytical student with the confidence to risk speaking in class. He was frustrated with the majority of his pupils, with the exception of Hope and Jessica, who trudged to their desks like drones, scribbled only God knew what in their notebooks, and kept checking the clock, waiting for the bell to ring.

Still, neither Hope nor Jessica was all that comfortable with self-expression, at least not in a group setting, although he hoped that, in time, they would soon follow suit with their new classmate, whom they obviously knew and were friends with. At the beginning of the school year, it had not taken him long to determine that Jessica and Hope were his best students. They had quickly surpassed everyone in all the subjects, but both were diffident around their classmates.

✳

At Thanksgiving, it had come as a total surprise to Michael Griffin when he happened upon an evening recital of Edvard Grieg's "First Violin Concerto" at Wesley United Church in Brandon. He had perused the name of the soloist on the poster affixed to the exterior door panel, but it obviously had not registered, because when he discovered that the performer was none other than Hope Harding, he was astounded. His reticent student had only just begun the difficult violin composition when he recognized that she was exceptionally gifted.

In his youth, Michael's mother had taught him piano for years, but he eventually gave up, believing he was not meant to master the subtle intricacies of a musical instrument. The irony that Hope, by the tender age of twelve, was already a virtuoso making her violin weep with the profound beauty of Grieg's brilliant creation was not lost on him, and he had sat mesmerized throughout the concert. His inability to play a far less challenging piece of music was what had caused him to throw his hands up in despair, never again to sit with his mother at her beautiful piano.

Following three encores, the audience gave Hope a standing

ovation before everyone was invited to stay for coffee and enjoy the opportunity of meeting the up-and-coming violinist. When he rose from the uncomfortable pew, instead of joining the throng descending the stairs, Michael, somewhat to his surprise, turned in the opposite direction and made a hasty exit from the church.

To this day, Michael did not understand why he had not offered Hope his congratulations or, for that matter, acknowledge that he had been at her recital. He was equally fascinated by the fact that now, halfway through the school year, not even the music teacher at the junior high was aware they had a prodigy in their midst. Ever since the evening of Hope's stunning performance, he had suspected the only ones who knew were Hope's friends, Jessica Francine. But, at least for Michael, the mystery surrounding his three star students was solved, and he diligently followed the arts scene in the *Brandon Sun,* waiting for another of Hope's appearances.

✻

When the second day passed with Bert still as immutable as the afternoon he had returned to discover that his daughter was back in the district, June was beside herself with concern. What would Susan think when her parents did not even have the grace to welcome her home? She did not dare to express her anxiety to her resolute husband, who had become as silent as a stone on the subject of their child.

On the third morning, tired of preparing a large meal with none of the anticipated return, June threw a bowl of cold cereal on the table before retiring to the bedroom. She searched for a pair of long johns, found a heavy sweater, and the minute Bert was out the door to attend to the chores, she pulled on her toque, winter coat, and boots and headed down the gravel road to the Wharton farm.

Susan answered the door. "Hi, Mum. I was beginning to wonder if you and Dad were ever coming to see us. Now that I think about it,

I didn't hear your old truck. Surely you can't have walked the three miles here?"

"It's just a little over two, my darling."

"Welcome to our humble home, June," Robert said, coming into the kitchen. "Please, take your coat off, and join us for a cup of coffee. Ah, I see from your multiple layers, you did come on your own. I suppose Susan's father isn't ready to acknowledge that his little girl is now an old married woman."

Sitting in the comfort of the large old farmhouse, June looked around and realized that her new son-in-law had a flair for decorating. He must have refurbished the entire kitchen, as it was adorned with all the current appliances, a solid-oak round table, and four cushioned swivel chairs. The ceiling and walls were freshly painted, the walnut cupboards were beautifully constructed, and the tile flooring was the latest fashion. The fabric of the chairs matched the pastel drapes on the recessed window, giving the spacious room the coordinated appearance of a professionally designed kitchenette June had seen recently in *Better Homes and Gardens*.

She wondered if Robert had finished renovating all of the rooms in the well-built two-storey home. Thinking about it, she realized she had not been in the house since Shirley and Hector Johnson had sold the farm to Robert. Shortly after the stranger had arrived in the close-knit community, the neighbouring farmers with their wives and children had, in turn, made the customary visit to welcome him. Rumour had it though that the young man had met each of them at the door and, following a cursory greeting, had wished them all a good day.

If there could have been a more definitive way to get off on the wrong foot in the Hartney district, none of his neighbours would have been able to identify it. It was, after all, common courtesy for newcomers to invite his visitors in, to provide refreshments, and allow them to ply him for information. June had always considered the practice questionable, having been subjected to it herself years earlier when Bert had surprised everyone by arriving home from one of his frequent trips to Winnipeg with her as his bride. In her mind, the element of curiosity had been far more apparent than that of a sincere welcome, and she suspected that Robert had recognized their overture for what it truly was.

At any rate, over the past few years, neither June nor any of the neighbours, according to the district rumour mill, had set foot inside the old Johnson home. Speculation was that the new owner had shipped off all the livestock and become one of those rare breeds known as a pure grain farmer. Still, he must have turned a tidy profit, given the fact that on the sporadic occasions when he was seen in Hartney or in Souris, he was always seen making large purchases.

Over time, Robert had maintained such a low profile in the farming community that the majority of his neighbours lost interest in him. As soon as the harvest was completed, he disappeared for parts unknown, not returning until spring to prepare his land for seeding. Then, a year ago, there had been a sudden parade of delivery trucks and workmen, presumably from Brandon, since they too were strangers, and conjecture had begun anew.

Once again, his closest neighbours had ventured along to his dwellings on the premise of providing their capable assistance, because it was now patently obvious that a restoration of the one-hundred-year-old Johnson farmhouse was underway. Bert had been one of the first to offer his services, since he was often called upon from as far away as Virden for his carpentry skills. But, as before, Robert met everyone, including Bert, and turned them away at the front door.

Sipping her freshly brewed coffee, June suddenly pondered whether her husband's resentment toward Robert was rooted in that rejection. Bert was very proud of his woodworking expertise, having a particular aptitude for designing kitchen cabinets, and he had felt understandably rebuffed. It was little wonder that he disliked Robert, although even she was quick to concede that the man was a conundrum.

✳

Francine was relieved that it was Uncle Darrin who had arrived to pick her up from school. If it had been Mummy Pat, she would have instantly detected that something was wrong and would have been full of questions. In the presence of her quiet uncle, Francine could be as brooding as she wanted, because neither of them ever experienced any feeling of discomfort during their lengthy silences.

She was still irritated with Hope for not saying a single word during Mr. Griffin's interactive session. Why had she not asked any questions after chastising her for monopolizing the discussions? Francine felt like a traitor sitting there, mute as a fencepost, especially when Mr. Griffin kept giving her that quizzical look. She was so frustrated with Hope that for the first day since coming to Souris, she had charged out of school without saying goodbye to either Hope or Jessica.

By the time they reached the farmyard, Francine had recovered enough to appear natural with Pat and Daniel, although she ate her snack quicker than usual before excusing herself to change out of her school clothes. She knew she needed to be outside with her sheep and to walk about in nature to try and sort out what she was feeling. Was it just because she and Hope had not had words before, and she had naively thought they were such good friends they never would?

What if Hope had not said anything, because she was still angry with Francine and wanted to show her up in front of their classmates? Then by leaving abruptly, Francine had likely increased Hope's annoyance with her, and she probably would not even talk to her tomorrow. Even in her analysis, Francine began to suspect that she could be making a mountain out of a molehill. She did not understand why she was so often filled with doubt and uncertainty about Hope's affection for her. Francine did not experience any qualms when it came to Jessica, tacitly accepting that they were close friends. However, for whatever reason, and never in her presence, only later after the girls had parted company, Francine could not bring herself to believe and trust that Hope actually cared about her. How could someone as accomplished as Hope Harding love her, Francine, who was so ordinary with no discernible attributes?

✳

During supper, as Francine pecked at her food instead of eating with her usual hearty appetite, Pat made a mental note to arrange a tête-à-tête with her stepdaughter. It was obvious that something was weighing heavily on Francine's mind, and she wanted to encourage her to get it out in the open before retiring. Over the past several weeks, they had all benefitted from a restful night's sleep, uninterrupted by Francine's recurring nightmares.

"Let's have our tea and dessert in your loft, Francine. I wonder, Daniel, if you'll excuse me from helping you with the clean-up."

As soon as they were seated on the alcove sofa, which doubled as a bed when Francine's friends were sleeping over, Pat said, "You've been very pensive since you returned from school. Are you ready to tell me what happened today?"

"I don't think I'll ever be able to fool you, will I, Mummy Pat? Most of the time, I'm just as glad. I'm not so sure that it's really anything, other than I seem to be more sensitive these days. I love my new school, and I couldn't be happier about being in the same class with Jessica and Hope. Did I tell you Mrs. Yang lets us all come to the Lingnan to have our lunch, and she always makes sure we have a little treat? Today, we had fortune cookies, and yesterday, she gave each of us a bowl of sweet-and-sour soup."

Pat squeezed Francine's arm but remained silent, waiting patiently for her stepdaughter to formulate her thoughts. She had come to learn that Francine was neither comfortable about expressing her feelings, nor was she, for the most part, able to identify her specific emotions. She subsequently often tried to gloss over them by changing the subject, and Pat knew that by being quiet, Francine would eventually have to attempt to verbalize her sentiments.

At the peak of Francine's recurrent nightmares, Pat had finally sought the guidance of her trusted family practitioner. When she disclosed her stepdaughter's history of how she had tragically lost both parents, Dr. Stoughton explained that the resultant trauma and stress would have had a major impact upon a young child's developing personality. If Francine had not received any psychological counselling to encourage her to cope with her emotions, it was possible that she could have suppressed or repressed her feelings of sorrow, dejection, and, more notably, guilt.

Dr. Stoughton had adamantly recommended that since Francine would not consent to seeing a psychologist, he would be prepared to meet with her, and perhaps, over time, he could encourage her to accept professional therapy. But Francine had stubbornly refused to meet with Dr. Stoughton, telling Pat that she only wanted to share what she was feeling with her. Patricia realized beyond a shadow of a doubt that of all she would gladly do for her beloved stepdaughter over the years, by far the most important would be to help her learn to get in touch with her emotions.

*

"I think it might have been easier when I had no one to talk to but my sheep," Francine said. "Then I could wander aimlessly in the pasture feeling sorry for myself. I never wanted to bother Uncle Daniel or Uncle Darrin, and I think I enjoyed running away, like a rabbit to its warren. But you won't let me crawl into a hole in the ground and hide what I'm feeling anymore, will you Mummy Pat? Well, he

Francine began with Hope's comment at lunch and then everything, including what she had been mulling over before supper. "I guess I felt guilty, since I thought I was responsible for Hope not having a chance to ask any of her questions."

"Since you don't decide whether Hope speaks or not, your sense of guilt is a kind of self-indulgence. What I mean is that it's just another way for you to feel self-pity. Besides, when you take responsibility for someone else's choice, you're trying to gain control over the consequence."

"Oh, Mummy Pat, you've lost me completely."

"Can you can make Hope talk? What did you learn this afternoon? Did it matter that you didn't ask questions? Hope still chose not to say anything. You had nothing to do with what she decided; therefore, you can't be responsible."

"Okay, tell me again why I would want to be responsible for what someone else chooses to do."

"I don't know if I understand it myself, but I think it was from my mother I first learned that one of our biggest mistakes about how we interact with each other might be our tendency to try and assume responsibility for another person's actions. My father was very critical, especially toward my mother, my two sisters, and me. Instead of standing up to him and trying to get him to own as well as to change his behaviour, Mum always let him off the hook by blaming herself. Since it was her fault, she thought she was in control, but most of the time, she wallowed in self-pity until, in the end, she became so dependent on him that she could hardly function as a person. Growing up, I found it very confusing, but it did teach me that I could only be responsible for my own choices and actions. Yes, it's complicated, but no one ever said that dealing with our emotions, so we can live compatibly with each other, was easy."

"No kidding! But if I don't soon get at my homework, I know I'll be in trouble with Mr. Griffin tomorrow."

"And we certainly aren't going to resolve all the subtleties of human relationships this evening, my darling. Call me when you're ready to be tucked into bed."

Later that evening, Patricia returned to Tolstoy's *Anna Karenina* but found it impossible to concentrate. She kept thinking about how impressionable Francine could be at times, but perhaps even more disconcerting was her level of self-absorption. She recognized it was a characteristic attributable to most prepubescent girls, but she suspected that with Francine, it likely stemmed from having spent so much time alone. Patricia vividly recalled how isolated she had been during her years at Hartney School and how, when she had married Daniel, one of Francine's first disclosures to her was that, with the exception of Margaret, her long-ago friend in Cavendish, she felt she had never fit in with any girls her own age.

Patricia was glad she had taken the time to prepare Francine for the physical and emotional changes she would soon experience with the onset of her menstrual cycle. As it happened, Francine had little awareness of what to expect, and Patricia was pleased by how their bond of love and trust had been strengthened during their candid discussion. As her teacher, and even long before she had married her uncle, Patricia had fostered a healthy relationship with Francine, but still, what did she really know about mothering her?

Suddenly, Patricia was back in her parents' home, a twelve-year-old child without a friend, and the only time and place she really felt she belonged was when engrossed in the world of books or communing with nature in the outdoors. Even by then she had known that she would need to depend on herself, because no one else would take responsibility for her. However, as the years passed, Patricia had come to realize that the real danger of being so self-sufficient, relying so completely on her own resources, was that she had never learned how she was perceived by or her impact on others.

Now going up the stairs to get ready for bed, Patricia questioned whether Francine was any more focused on inner pursuits than she had been in her youth. But, come what may, she was determined to assist her soon-to-be teenage stepdaughter to avoid a similar serious limitation in her relationships with others by making sure she maintained her friendships with Hope, Jessica, and Cassandra.

✳

The man might have been a mystery, but he was an excellent host— that is, when his callers managed to get beyond his front doorstep. The coffee and freshly baked blueberry muffins were delicious, and before June had a chance to empty her mug, Robert was refilling it. Susan had disappeared into the bedroom, returning with three full albums of photos they had taken in Hawaii. The morning passed in compatible bliss, and when June glanced at the striking pewter wall clock, she was amazed it was going on to noon.

"Oh, is that the correct time? Your father has no idea where I've gone, since I stormed out of the house after he left. He'll be ranting around the kitchen fretting about his dinner, so I better be on my way."

"Surely, if you're not at home, he can get himself something to eat," Robert said. "From what Susan has told me, you customarily prepare large meals, so presumably there must be leftovers in the fridge. I was about to ask you to join us for the meatloaf I've just put in the oven."

"Thank you, Robert. That's very kind of you, but I would be well-advised not to add any more fuel to the fire. Bert has still not relented about welcoming Susan and you back to the neighbourhood, much less into the house, even though I've slaved over the hot stove preparing his favourite meals the past two days. I do wonder though if one of you would give me a ride to the end of our lane, so I get home before the witching hour."

✳

Bursting in the door, June said, "Sorry, Bert. I went for a brisk walk and ended up going much further than I intended. Luckily, we have that baked ham I made yesterday, and I'll quickly fry up some of the leftover scalloped potatoes to go with it. Just give me a minute to get some of these warm clothes off, and you'll be eating in a jiffy."

In their bedroom, as she removed the long johns and sweater she had put on to avoid arousing Bert's suspicion regarding her whereabouts, June debated why she had told him a white lie. In all the years they had been married, she seldom felt the need to distort the truth, so what had prompted her now? Even while pondering her motive, she had an uncanny sense that Bert had seen right through her ruse. Well, too bad. If he had not decided to be so stubborn, she would not have had to sneak off to visit her only child.

Dinner was a quiet affair. June had spoken more over the course of the morning than she had all week and was not inclined to engage Bert in conversation. As for Bert, he was thinking about his strange behaviour the past three days. For months, he had yearned more than anything in the world to cast his eyes upon his beautiful daughter, and now that she was three miles away, he could not bring himself to go see her.

Bert had happened to glance toward the house when he was herding the cows into the barn and had been surprised to notice June disappearing down the lane. It had only taken seconds to realize where she was headed. He had been on the verge of yelling at her to get back into the house when an image of his father flashed through his mind, and he had curbed his tongue. From the day Bert was old enough to understand that old man Smith had ruled the roost with an iron fist, he had vowed that it was going to be different in his home with his wife, and children.

Bert had been true to his word. He could still remember that morning years ago when he had decided to have breakfast at the Salisbury House. It was a sultry morning in June, already oppressive under the unrelenting prairie sun, when Bert opened the door and stopped dead in his tracks. Behind the counter serving all the patrons was the most exquisite creature he had ever seen. She had flaming red hair, hazel eyes with green flecks, and a slim body like the models he had looked at in the magazines in the hospital while waiting for his mother to wake up or to return from her endless treatments.

Although a booth was available, Bert waited until one of the customers rose from a counter stool, and then he dashed to secure it before anyone could steal the front-row seat. When the beautiful waitress handed him a menu, Bert introduced himself. "Good morning, Miss. My name is Bert Smith, and I wonder if you would be so kind to tell me yours."

"Well, hello to you, Bert Smith. I'm June McDowell, and what can I get you to eat this bright sunny day?"

Bert was as enchanted by her accent as he was by her appearance, and he knew it was more than a coincidence that they should meet in the month of the year that shared her name. He had been coming to Winnipeg for almost a decade to visit his mother, and never once had he frequented the restaurant with the little red peaked roof. It had been entirely on a whim that he had stopped for breakfast, and he was convinced it was meant to be. Rather than return home that morning, when he asked for his bill, Bert invited June to join him for supper, and she accepted.

Following a whirlwind courtship, on one of his journeys into Winnipeg, which had become increasingly frequent, they had visited the justice of the peace, and much to the surprise of all his neighbours, Bert returned to the Hartney district with a beautiful young Irish lass as his wife. At first, he worried whether June would fit into the close-knit farming community, but she was so personable and eager to please, no one could resist her engaging demeanour for long.

They had been happy, and when June presented Bert with a daughter who was the spitting image of her, he could not have asked for more. His friends had always said that a man needed a son, but Bert was completely wrapped up in his little girl. On rare occasions, he regretted that they were not fortunate enough to have birthed other children, but he never lacked for companionship, with Susan traipsing along at his side throughout her growing years.

Then she had run away with Robert Wharton, and it had all but destroyed his spirit. Naturally, Bert had realized that one day his little princess would find her prince charming and would become his blushing bride in an elegant ceremony. Never before or after would such a beautiful young woman dressed in her exquisite finery grace the historic Hartney church, and as Bert envisioned walking her down the aisle, he knew no man would ever be prouder.

The last thought to enter his mind was that, prior to turning eighteen, Susan would elope with a man much older than her. For reasons he never understood, Bert disliked the stranger from the beginning, and when it became apparent he was wealthy, he began to resent him. No one in their serene community had money, and when the newcomer began to entice his impressionable young daughter to go riding about in his Cadillac, before eventually flying her away to some foreign land with hula dancers, Bert was filled with umbrage. Regardless of how rich Robert Wharton might be, what would happen the day that Susan awoke, and realized that she was encumbered for life with an aging husband approaching infirmity?

It was dread for Susan's impending doom that accounted for Bert's unusual behaviour, or so he kept telling himself. He could not stand by and wait for his precious daughter to carry such a heavy burden.

Still, in the farthest reaches of his heart and soul, Bert knew it was not for Susan that he was becoming overwhelmed with trepidation. During his infrequent moments of enlightenment, he understood that it was concern for his own being, his sanity, and his very survival that filled him with fear.

When it finally became clear that Susan was gone, his grief had vanquished him to the living dead. During the three months of her absence, Bert struggled to rouse himself from bed every morning and to pretend there was a reason for him to exist. It was not that he no longer loved June; they had just grown apart, and caring for each other had become more a habit than a feeling.

Besides, it was June's fault. If she had not insisted that Robert's interest was purely platonic, Bert would never have allowed Susan to go joyriding around the countryside with him. Then June had taken off with Margaret Devonshire instead of coming for him. If only he had been called as soon as Robert had made his daring escape with his daughter, Bert would have tracked them down long before they ever reached the airport.

Soon, Bert's shock turned to anger. He started to experience rage of such intensity that he had never known before in his life, and when it came upon him, he had to get outdoors, so he was not totally consumed by it. It scared the hell out of him. Suddenly, he could hear and see his father yelling and striking his mother. He knew he had to get a grip on his emotions, but there were countless days when he walked in the frigid cold for hours until the flame of his fury would subside.

It had only been after Christmas when Bert realized how devastated Margaret and June were by their ill-fated futile attempt to stop the runaway lovers that he understood it was unfair and fruitless to blame either of them. At last, just when he was reconciling himself to the loss of his daughter, she returned to the district as if it was as commonplace as the sun setting in the west. No, Susan could not come back into his heart, mind, and soul like she had never deserted him, because Bert knew he would not survive grieving for her again.

✳

The next morning at school, Hope behaved as if nothing had happened. As soon as Francine saw her, she apologized for dashing away, but Hope stared at her with a blank gaze. "Oh, I just thought you were in a rush to get home."

"You mean you didn't even know I was upset with you yesterday?"

Now it was Hope's turn to look dazed. "I had no idea. What did I do that bothered you?"

"Come on, you really don't know? Surely, you realized I kept quiet all afternoon, so you could ask your questions, after what you said to me at lunchtime."

Struggling to remember, Hope was relieved when the bell saved her. "It looks like we'll have to talk about this later, Francine. I have to get my assignment from my locker. I'll see you in class."

Hurrying down the corridor, it was all Hope could do not to shake her head. For the life of her, she could not recall what they had been talking about or why Francine had taken umbrage to some offhand comment she must have made. Jessica had told her that Francine could be very sensitive, but this was ridiculous. With another recital looming, Hope scarcely had time to keep up with her schoolwork while trying to fit in four to five hours of practice a day to worry about what she was saying to one of her friends. Perhaps she could slip Jessica a note during the morning class to ask her about the offending conversation before recess, because she knew Francine would persist like a dog searching for a bone.

How could Hope not have known how disquieting her behaviour had been? Mr. Griffin had practically glared at Francine while waiting for her, and Hope was too indifferent to have been aware. To make matters worse, now Francine would not feel comfortable asking questions until after she had allowed Hope an opportunity to make her inquiries.

Fortunately, the morning passed with Mr. Griffin introducing the class to the concepts of algebra. As soon as Francine grasped that this branch of mathematics used letters and general symbols to represent numbers and quantities in formulae and equations, she forgot all about Hope. From the time she had learned to count, numbers had intrigued her, and she soon discovered that she had a photographic memory for numbers. Now to be able to combine her love for linguistic symbols with algebraic equations, Francine was captivated for the balance of the day.

It was not until Mother Pat picked her up that Francine remembered her frustration with Hope. In response to Patricia's expected question about the happenings of her day, Francine decided to share her concerns with her. Since the three girls had become bosom buddies, she had not been as forthcoming with her disclosures, choosing instead to withhold the majority of her friends' shared confidences. Still, old patterns die hard, and Francine suddenly felt the urge to entrust her stepmother with her lingering doubts.

"I don't think Hope really loves me, at least not nearly as much as I love her."

"Perhaps you had better start at the beginning, and tell me what this is all about, because that's a pretty dramatic statement to make about your close friend," Pat said, immediately perceiving the depth of Francine's distress.

"I'll never forget the day I met Hope. I remember telling you that I loved her right from the first moment I heard her play her violin. But I often wonder if she cares about me." As Francine launched into the narrative of the current incident, Pat began to glimpse Francine's uncertainty. Still, she waited until Francine finished before she queried,

"Do you think that maybe Hope was preoccupied with something else, and that's why she didn't know you were upset?"

"I guess that could be it. I did overhear her telling Mr. Griffin that she has two more recitals coming up, and one of them is going to be at the Brandon College Conservatory of Music."

"Ah, now I'm starting to get the picture. It's quite an honour to be invited to the college for a solo recital, especially for a twelve-year-old. Hope is probably practicing every spare minute she has and doesn't have time to think about anyone or anything."

"Well, maybe that's part of the problem. I spend a lot of my time thinking about her and worrying what she thinks and says about me, but she always seems so self-absorbed."

"My darling Francine, you might be on the verge of learning one of the great lessons of life. While we spend our time and energy worrying about what others are thinking and saying about us, the reality often is that they aren't thinking about us at all!"

"That's hardly fair. I do concern myself about you, my uncles, and my friends every day. Don't you wonder about the people who are important to you?"

"Yes, Francine, both you and I spend considerable time in solitary pursuits and are given to analysis, to thinking about what has or will happen, but we're not all the same, particularly if a person is occupied with concentrated matters. Certainly, Hope's lengthy practices are reclusive in nature, but she has to focus intently on following the musical notes, so her mind can't wander aimlessly, like when you and I are looking after the sheep or working in the garden."

Following several moments of reflection, Francine replied, "Thank you, Mummy Pat. That makes perfect sense and gives me a better understanding of what it must be like for Hope."

"Life is full of lessons, my dear child, and when we have learned one, we go on to the next. To allow for individual differences and to accept each person for who she or he is might take us our lifetime to learn, but it is the only way we can truly love one another."

Patricia and Francine had been sitting in the car in the driveway for quite some time. Daniel had noticed when they arrived and put on the kettle for tea, but he waited patiently for the loves of his life to finish what appeared to be a serious mother/daughter conversation.

"I see Uncle Daniel peering out the window," Francine said, "but before we go in, I want to tell you how glad I am that I decided to share with you how I've been feeling. Lately, I've been really resentful towards Hope, and my ill feelings were beginning to affect our friendship."

Reaching over to hug Francine, Patricia said, "I always remember something I once heard the American comedian Buddy Hackett say, 'While you're holding a grudge, the person you are holding it against is out dancing!'"

✳

A month came and went, and still Bert adamantly refused to see Susan. Although June did not really fault her husband, she was surprised by his tenacity. On the other hand, she was hardly going to let it interfere with her visits. Soon on her morning strolls, she arrived at the Wharton residence, and Robert's consistently warm welcome began to endear him to her. He persisted in extending an invitation for her to stay for dinner, and finally, on one occasion before she departed the house, she prepared Bert's meal, placed it in the fridge, and left him an explanatory note.

That day after dinner, when Susan asked her mother to accompany her to Souris, June felt little compunction about accepting. Mother and daughter were no sooner alone in the car than Susan said, "Okay, Mum, now that we're out of Robert's presence, would you please tell me what's going on with Daddy? When will he get over his little huff and come with you to see us, or should I stop in with you this afternoon when I take you home?"

"That might be a better idea. But Susan, I want to alert you to the fact that your father is not experiencing some 'little huff,' as you call it. During the more than three months that you were gone, he was devastated to the point that I constantly worried that he would do something drastic."

"What do you mean? What might he have done?"

"It was all he could do to get out of bed in the morning, and if it had not been for the livestock, I don't think he would have bothered. Instead, he would have hunkered down between the sheets and stayed there until he succumbed. Please understand, Susan, that when you abruptly left, and we didn't hear a word from you, your father grieved you as if you were dead. Each day I witnessed him becoming a changed man, a man whose heart and soul were being torn in two with sorrow because of the loss of his only child. Then he became furious with me, since he was convinced it was all my fault." "Oh, my God, I had no idea that it was so dire for you and Daddy."

"Just what the hell did you think, Susan? We've doted on you from the moment you were born, and then you abandoned us in the dead of winter without a word. We spent the next three months dreading the worst-possible consequence while you were basking in the sun on a beach in Hawaii. And don't think for one second that it was any easier for me!"

"That stupid Carole Martin. She was supposed to deliver my letter the day after we left. I can't understand why she never gave it to you."

"No, Susan, I absolutely will not allow you to lay the blame on her. It's high time you took responsibility for your actions. Now, you better turn this car around and take me home."

The ensuing silence became ominous. Susan was baffled by her mother's sudden change of attitude, especially when she had been anticipating having some time alone with her. It had been months since they had engaged in one of their tête-à-têtes, and she had so many feelings and experiences she had been dying to share with her mother. Instead, they had only been together for minutes when she became as stiff as a board, staring out the windshield as if her life depended on being able to see the road ahead of them in the midst of a whiteout.

True, Susan had spent little time these past exciting months thinking about her parents or the shock her disappearance created for them. Still, she was home safe and sound now with a loving husband, so what was their problem? Pondering the situation as she found a gravel road to turn around to honour her mother's request, Susan began to grasp an inkling of the distress she must have caused her parents, particularly because they had been so completely in the dark. Then and there, Susan determined that, later in the afternoon when she dropped her mother off, she was going to visit Carole.

It was when June had sounded off in response to Susan blaming an innocent classmate that the full impact of her daughter's flagrant insensitivity and lack of responsibility hit her squarely between the eyes. The final realization that her daughter had considered her behaviour acceptable, because she had presumably told her parents about it in a letter, infuriated June. For three months, Susan had been so busy that she could not have sent a postcard or dropped a note to let them know where she was and how she was doing?

June felt like a traitor. Most of the time, she had been as despondent as Bert and had only forced herself to get up each morning for the sake of her husband. But when at last their prodigal daughter returned home, she had rushed to her, seeking her attention and maybe even her forgiveness for what only God knew. How could Bert not feel alienated, first from Susan and then, more importantly, from his wife? The minute the car came to a stop, June was out the door without so much as a backward glance, determined to make up for her blatant disloyalty to her husband during the past month.

✳

Michael had been annoyed when the principal sent him out to supervise recess for three consecutive days just because Marilyn Stravinsky, the grade eight teacher, complained about her recurrent sore knee. More and more, Michael was becoming convinced that Anthony Billanski had taken a dislike to him, with his primary supposition for their increasing antipathy being that he did not share the principal's cultural heritage.

Desperate for a cigarette, Michael figured that if he crouched down on the park bench almost hidden by the encircling grove of huge conifers near the back of the schoolyard, he would be far enough away that Tony could not see him indulging in the disgusting habit, which he had forbidden the teachers to engage in while on outdoor supervision. At the same time, his vantage point would facilitate an adequate overview of the clusters of students on the grounds.

He had no sooner struck the match to appease his nicotine addiction than he heard voices coming from the other side of his place of refuge. It took him several minutes to realize that, from the way their conversation resonated with a muffled sound, the girls must be sitting beneath the heavy overhanging boughs of the evergreen trees. Listening intently, Michael tried to determine which pupils were all but concealed by the protective branches when he heard Hope Harding say, "I still can't believe I've been invited to play at the Brandon College Conservatory of Music. It's like a dream come true."

"I'm not surprised at all. It won't be long before you have a host of music lovers imploring you to perform your magic, as your violin enraptures them with the sweetest sounds they will ever hear," Jessica responded.

"Nor am I. Before you know it, Hope, you'll be playing in all the great music halls of the world—New York, London, Rome, and Paris, just to mention a few," Francine said.

"You two are so full of optimism," Hope said, "but regardless of whatever happens, you'll always be my greatest fans. The conservatory deliberately chose the third Sunday evening in May, since it's the Victoria Day long weekend, and if people come from a distance, they can stay in the city and return home on Monday. Do you think you'll try to come?"

"What a ridiculous question! If our folks can't get away, we can always stay with Cassandra," Francine replied. "When Mummy Pat comes to pick me up this afternoon, I'll ask her if we can go visit with Grandma Webster. By this time tomorrow, I'm confident that all our arrangements will be made."

Careful not to make a sound, Michael was disappointed when the bell rang before Hope had a chance to mention the time of her recital. Nevertheless, that detail could be easily gleaned by stopping at his alma mater that coming weekend when he purchased his ticket to the event. He knew he should have left the bench immediately to get to the school ahead of the students, but he waited until he saw the three girls dash toward the front door.

Although Michael never had the slightest intention of becoming a peeping Tom, at some level of his consciousness, even at this early stage in his fascination with the budding musician, he recognized the merit of not revealing his hiding spot.

As he scurried back to open his classroom, Michael turned to take a cursory look at the large trees, realizing that for his entire time at the school, he had scarcely been aware of their presence. Yet, it was a magnificent stand of evergreens in an otherwise barren yard, and it did not surprise him that the three musketeers of Souris, as they referred to themselves, had discovered their potential for seclusion.

That afternoon when the bell at last tolled, heralding the end of another dreary day of trying to pour information into the heads of a class of primarily disinterested pupils, Michael returned to the trees. As a boy, he had loved to run through the grove of willow trees on his father's acreage in the blue hills of Brandon, but in the heat of the day, it was under the towering cedars where he sought relief from the scorching sun in the shade of their overhanging boughs.

Now, Michael swept aside the lower branches, and crawled under the welcoming cover of the conifers to find that the girls had created a comfortable haven. They had cleared out most of the pine needles and covered the hard-packed earth with a large braided mat. Since most of their classmates only paid attention to them when they wanted to aggravate them, they could seek refuge there at will. They had taken considerable precautions to protect their reclusive spot by concealing the opening with overlapping branches.

Michael was on the verge of striking a match to his cigarette when he stopped himself. He suddenly experienced an eerie sensation of Hope's presence beneath the trees. It was so palpable that he glanced from side to side, expecting to catch a glimpse of her, as he quickly returned the cigarette to it package. Long before Michael had any indication of what he would come to feel for the youthful aspiring musician, he knew he could not contaminate the air she would breathe or desecrate the sanctity of her secret hideaway. Before he departed, he carefully placed the branches in the exact position he had found them, knowing he would return time and time again to that hallowed place.

*

With disbelief, Susan watched her mother's retreating back as she all but ran to the house. *God, what is the matter with people over fifty? They have to make such a big deal about every little thing!* Susan thought. Then her mind quickly switched to what she was going to say to Carole the minute she saw her.

Backing the car out of the driveway, Susan debated what to do. Her mother's obvious necessity to get as far away from her daughter as possible had intensified Susan's wrath with her former classmate, and she hardly felt like driving home to sit and wait until the end of the school day. Checking her watch, she realized that it would soon be recess, and with firm resolution, she turned her vehicle toward Hartney School.

There was no way to be inconspicuous in the red Cadillac, and since she had no intention of reminding everyone and setting tongues wagging again about her dramatic escape in Robert Wharton's beautiful automobile, Susan parked behind a grove of trees a block away from the school. Once she had walked within visual distance, she hid and waited for the bell to ring, ready to call to Carole as soon as she came out the front door.

As luck would have it, Carole was the first pupil to come bounding down the stairs, Adele Perkins hard on her heels. Susan had not bargained that Carole would have resumed her friendship with Adele, but as she thought about it, the only other girl she might have anything to do with would have been Francine. Still, Susan speculated that once Carole heard her voice, she would come running; then she would readily dispense with Adele, and they would be on their way.

∗

Not ten minutes later, Carole was seated in the convertible being driven down the highway with the wind tousling her hair, just as she always imagined every time she daydreamed about Susan coming back and taking her for joyrides. She was confident that when her friend returned, they would be bosom buddies again. Months earlier, when Susan escaped her parents' clutches, Carole worried briefly that Susan might be cross when she discovered her letter had not been delivered according to plan, but soon she forgot all about their agreement.

At first, Carole had the best of intentions of doing precisely what her hero had asked of her, but then the evening before she was to deliver it, for reasons she still did not want to acknowledge, she opened the letter. She did not pay much attention to the contents but rather proceeded straight to the closing words: "Love, Susan." As soon as she saw them, Carole began to imagine that the epistle was really meant for her. After all, she had longed for Susan to tell her that she loved her in response to the many times Carole expressed her feelings for her.

Although Susan did accede that they were friends, she never once said the words Carole had yearned to hear, and now here they were, written and much more lasting. Similar to all the other girls in Hartney School, Carole had invariably admired Susan Smith from a distance, until the previous fall, when she was asked to spend every recess and lunch hour in the older student's revered presence. Before long, from Carole's perspective, their coveted association had taken on surreal proportions. Within weeks, Carole knew that she worshipped the ground Susan walked on and would do anything for her.

Besides, once she had opened the letter and handled it over and over again, how could she possibly take it to the Smiths? On the Saturday morning following Susan's departure, during the family's customary trip to Souris, Carole had searched in the drugstore until she found just the right card for "A Special Friend." When she returned home, she addressed it to herself, cut off the bottom page of the letter with the two precious words, and pasted them on before hiding it with all her other treasures.

Now cruising along the with Susan, Carole wondered if perhaps Susan's parents had never found out that they were to have been the recipients of a letter from their daughter, and subsequently, there might not be any recriminations. After all, so soon after returning to the neighbourhood, Susan was seeking her out with an invitation to go for coffee. Quite likely, she had missed their tête-à-têtes as much as Carole had, and now they would simply pick up where they had left off.

They had only gone a few miles before Susan pulled the car onto a roadside turnout. "Okay, you moronic punk! You better fess up about my letter right this minute."

Carole was taken completely by surprise but still had the presence of mind to know that she could never tell the truth. "Wh-what do you mean? I did exactly what you told me to do. Why have you stopped here? You told me that you wanted to take me to Souris, so we could catch up on everything."

"Look, you stupid idiot. Don't think you're going to weasel out by changing the subject. I plan to get to the bottom of this right now, because you wouldn't begin to believe the trouble you've caused between my folks and me. What the hell did you do with my letter?"

"I-I did exactly what you told me to. On that Monday after school, I walked across the fields and put it between the screen door and the wooden one. I didn't hang around, because it was cold and getting dark."

"You're lying through your teeth! If you'd done what you promised, none of this would have happened." Susan glared at Carole with so much contempt that Carole instinctively moved closer to the door.

"Yes, get out of my car this instant. I never want to have anything to do with you again. Now get out!"

"You can't leave me here in the middle of nowhere. By the time I get back to school, the bus will be gone. How am I supposed to get home?"

"Go tell someone who cares!" Susan leaned toward Carole and pushed her on the shoulder until the younger girl felt compelled to open the door and make her unwilling exit.

Standing on the side of the road, Carole stared in disbelief as Susan turned the car around and sped off toward Hartney. Glancing first to the right and then to the left, and with no vehicles in sight, Carole began to get a sense of her predicament. She had no idea how many miles they had travelled once they turned on to the main highway, but she was reasonably confident there was not the slightest possibility of her covering the distance in time to catch the school bus.

Her only option was to start walking. Her cheeks still flaming red from the embarrassment of her altercation with Susan, Carole appreciated the brisk air as she set off. She was used to running for sports activities at school, carrying water from the outside well to the house, and other chores on the farm, but she had never taken much interest in strolling about purely for the sake of pleasure. Now as she trudged along, she wondered how long it would take her to reach her farm. Was it possible that when her siblings arrived home, her father might decide to go looking for her?

But where was he to begin? No one, certainly neither of her younger sisters nor her brother, had seen her leave the schoolyard, much less what direction she had gone. How could Susan just abandon her alone miles away and with night approaching? Then Carole started to think about Susan's treatment of her, all because of one stupid little letter. Surely she could not have meant that she never wanted to see her again. Susan knew that Carole worshipped her; she must have said that out of spite, because she was so angry with her. Yet, as Carole plodded down the lonely highway, which stretched off into the darkening horizon, her deepening fear that she had lost Susan forever was confirmed by the sinking feeling in the pit of her stomach.

Twilight was reaching dusk when Mr. Perkins pulled up beside her in his half-ton truck, but Carole was so devastated that she could not have cared less. She scarcely heard her neighbour's inquiries about her current situation. He had to tell her at least three times to get into the vehicle, and he would take her home. When he delivered Carole into her front yard, and she stepped out of his truck without a single word of gratitude, Owen Perkins could only shake his head, and mutter,

"What's the younger generation coming to?"

✳

For the fourth consecutive Sunday, Hope was unable to partake in the family dinner, this week hosted by Jessica's parents at the Lingnan. Lately, every Friday her grandparents arrived at the school just before lunch hour to transport her to Brandon for additional lessons to prepare for her upcoming recitals. Then she would scurry into school on Monday mornings, often barely catching assembly.

Francine was seated on Jessica's bed when she blurted, "I'm really starting to miss Hope. We scarcely see her anymore, other than at recess and lunchtime. She never has any time to do anything with us after school, always running home to practice for hours, or taking off for Brandon."

"I know what you mean," Jessica replied, "but I think we're going to have to get used to only having limited time with Hope. You know that recital at the college she was telling us about. Well, it's actually some big musical competition, and if she takes first place, which everyone expects, she'll be offered a scholarship to study there this September."

"What are you saying? Hope's the same age as we are and will only be going into grade eight. She's not old enough to go to college!"

"Oh, yes, that's right! You weren't here the evening Hope came rushing into the Lingnan after supper to show me the letter she had received from Dr. Burton, the dean of music at Brandon College. Did you know that one of the professors is now her violin teacher?"

"Jessica, stop jumping from one topic to another. What was in the letter?"

"Dr. Burton indicated that Hope is a gifted musician, like he was telling her something we didn't already know! I've always said she's a prodigy. At any rate, if she's the recipient of some big scholarship, I can't remember the actual name of it, the college would make provisions for her to continue with her other school subjects while studying at the School of Music."

"You mean Hope will move to Brandon, and we won't be the three musketeers of Souris any longer? Don't tell me that. I don't know how I'll ever come to school day after day if Hope isn't here!"

"Hey, thanks a lot. I'll still be with you every day. Besides, Hope's father is moving to Winnipeg, and one way or another, she would have had to leave Souris. If she's in Brandon, at least we can stay with Cassandra and still see her. What would our chances be if Hope was as far away as Winnipeg?"

"When was that decided? How come I'm always the last to hear all the news, whether it's good or bad?" Francine lamented as she jumped off the bed and began to pace around Jessica's bedroom. "Not that I like any of what you're telling me. I know I should be happy for Hope, but I thought we would have her with us until we finished high school. Oh, I just can't believe it!"

"I'm sorry, Francine. I was every bit as devastated as you are when Hope told me, but I guess, because I've had some time, I've started to adjust to the likelihood of this being our last year of going to school with Hope."

"When was she going to tell me? Sometimes Hope makes me angry. It's like she never thinks about what anyone else is feeling; she's always so involved in what's happening to her."

"I know it often seems like Hope is self-absorbed, but the more I think about her, the more I realize she has to be so focused on her music."

"Why? You and I have lots of things we're interested in, and yet we're still concerned about other people."

"I know that, but Hope is a very special person. Even though she's young, she already has so many fans. I just can't figure it out, but everyone seems to love Hope as soon as they meet her."

"That's true, and when Hope does pay attention to me, she's so sweet. Before long, she makes me feel that I'm as precious as she is. But then she gets back into her music, and it's like I don't exist."

"Oh, Francine, we're very different from Hope. I think about her much of the time, and I believe she has been blessed with an incredible gift from God, so she is fated to be on a singular path. You and I will grow up and decide what we want to do with our lives, but it will not matter what she might prefer to do; Hope really has no choice. I think that we are very lucky we met her when she is young and before she embarks upon her career. I was convinced from the moment I heard her play that she was going to become a famous violinist, and I was so grateful we became friends. Deep in my heart and soul, I feel that our little pal, Hope Harding, is going to become a renowned concert violinist travelling to all the world's great music halls. She will be surrounded by a cast of thousands and be loved by many, but Hope is loyal and will always remember her two school chums regardless of how celebrated she becomes as she fulfills her destiny."

*

On Monday, Francine was anxious for recess, although she had decided she would wait to see if Hope was going to share her news. She had had a restless night, not falling asleep until the early hours of the morning, but she still leapt out of bed as soon as Mother Pat called up to her loft. If only Francine could believe and trust what Jessica had said about Hope always loving them. Why did she not have the same confidence?

No sooner had the three girls sequestered to their hideaway than Hope exclaimed, "Oh, Francine, I've been dying all weekend to tell you what I might be doing next year." After beginning to narrate about the Max Bruch Violin Competition, Hope stopped suddenly. "What was that? Did you hear it? It sounded like someone gasped."

The three friends listened intently for several minutes, holding their breath. When she was satisfied she was not being overheard, Hope continued with her exciting plans. "I really want to win the competition, although I'll be so sad that we won't be together for school next year. But my dad was going to make sure of that anyway. It was only after a huge fight with my grandparents that he finally agreed to let me have a trial year of living with them in Brandon. He's not convinced that I should spend so much time on my music, since he's certain I'll neglect my other school subjects. If I don't maintain my grades, he'll have me forfeit the scholarship—that is, should I be the recipient—and move me to Winnipeg to live with him and his new family. You don't know how lucky you are, Francine, with Mother Pat. My soon-to-be stepmother is already causing me grief."

Hope was about to expound on the nature of their constrained relationship when the bell rang. "It's probably just as well we have to go back to class. Once I get started talking about that woman, I become more and more churlish in what I say."

Michael sat immobilized in his crouched position on the park bench. He had been so stunned when he heard that Hope could be leaving Souris that he had nearly given himself away. He waited until Jessica, Francine, and finally Hope, but only after glancing back in the direction of the trees, had entered the school. Why had she paused? Was she still wondering if someone had been eavesdropping? There and then, Michael decided he could not return to his coveted hideout.

The afternoon dragged more than usual. Michael even found himself becoming impatient with Francine's endless questions during science class, until he ended it abruptly, and asked the students to begin reading Jack London's novel, *The Call of the Wild*. Michael's mind was still racing about Hope's announcement, and he desperately needed to determine why it should have had such an impact upon him. What was happening to him? Surely he was not becoming enamoured with a thirteen-year-old schoolgirl.

✳

"Oh, he's so cute!"

"What a gorgeous child with those dark curls and lovely brown eyes!"

From the time of his earliest memories, Michael could recall every possible expression of pulchritude voiced to his mother with reference to her beautiful son. He had heard the exclamations so often whenever his parents took him to church or shopping in Brandon that, eventually, the words had become meaningless to him.

It was not until he was enrolled in school, and the kids began to call him "Pretty Boy" and "Sissy," that it occurred to Michael that attractiveness could have its drawbacks. Being an only child with no one to whom he was compared, he seldom gave much thought to his appearance. He was much more concerned with the beauty of the trees that his parents had planted years earlier. When his parents had built their two-storey log cabin, they had decided to surround their new home with rows of their favourite tree. Jonathon Griffin had seeded conifers alongside his wife's grove of willows.

As soon as Michael was old enough to walk, he had been drawn to the treed area, and then when his parents presented him with a golden retriever for his fifth birthday, he and Cooper were lost for hours within the welcoming confines of their own forest. Michael soon came to consider every tree in the copse as his friend, and throughout his growing years in his tranquil woods, he seldom experienced a moment of loneliness or isolation. However, from the time he started school, and persisting into adulthood, often in the presence of others he felt totally alone.

He had been so excited the autumn he entered the one-room Blue Hills School. At last, he would have real playmates to run around with whom he could play baseball and soccer. Instead, Michael soon began to bear the brunt of the school bullies, the older boys more interested in coercion than learning. When the name-calling escalated to threats and then physical force, his parents, Marika and Jonathon, promptly transferred their son to Souris Elementary School.

During his four years there, Michael had tried to fit in and develop friendships. Although he had fared better in the schoolyard, he invariably was frustrated with the tedium of the classroom instruction. His mother had begun to teach him to read before he had reached his third birthday. Recognizing that her precocious son was bored to tears in an educational system that seemingly valued mediocrity, Marika initiated a campaign to homeschool Michael. It had been an arduous struggle, and she was required to argue her case all the way to the minister of education for the Province of Manitoba.

Marika won the right to educate her son at home when Michael was ten years of age. Then she surreptitiously obtained the books and syllabus for every subject of the required curriculum for two years at a time from the teachers at the Souris Elementary School. Michael arrived at the school for every scheduled written test, and after racing through those for his age level, sat the exams for the subsequent grade. Michael received notification that he had excelled in the provincial departmental examinations for his senior matriculation the day after he turned sixteen years old.

Long before he had reached the age of taking any interest in the opposite sex, he realized that being attractive also had its advantages. He noticed that most people prefer to be surrounded by individuals with a comely appearance, and at least in this regard, he was no different. Where Michael suspected he diverged from most of his peers was his proclivity for solitary pursuits.

By the time he enrolled in the Faculty of Education at Brandon College, he was aware that he was an object of appeal to a host of female students, and he was never at a loss for a date for any of the expected social functions. Similarly, the men on campus regularly invited him to join their fraternities and sports clubs, which, for the most part, he declined. In truth, Michael had little inclination to become close to anyone, preferring his own company to that of others.

Jonathon and Marika were both reclusive by nature, content with each other, and since Michael had never given them any cause for concern, they appreciated that he shared their desire for seclusion. They neither questioned nor asked whether he would like to entertain friends throughout his growing years. Once his home schooling was begun, he returned to the protective circle of the Griffin family, and tranquility was restored.

During his graduation year from Brandon College, Michael was finally convinced to join the football team, and it was at the practices and games that he was introduced to Samantha Ryan, by far the most alluring of the twelve buxom cheerleaders. For the first time in his life, Michael was smitten. Over the course of the year, their relationship developed, until nuptials were planned for the end of June, when they had finished their respective bachelor of education degrees.

Parents on both sides had been duly introduced, Michael had secured a full-time teaching position at Brandon Collegiate Junior High School, and Samantha had been hired by an elementary school in the same district. All was in accord until, less than a month before the scheduled date Michael, for reasons he had yet to ascertain, got cold feet, and called the wedding off. He telephoned Samantha, knowing how cowardly he was being, to tell his tearful fiancé that he could not go through with their proposed marriage, pleading that, at not yet twenty years of age, he was far too young to have a wife. He also notified the Brandon School Board about rejecting his contract and then retreated to the family farm.

His parents accepted his explanation with little discussion, and when a position at Souris Collegiate High School unexpectedly became available, Michael leapt at the offer. It was perfect; he could live on the family acreage and drive his father's truck to and from school every weekday. Nearing the completion of his second year, he was once again entrenched within the hearth of his boyhood home without the slightest intention of leaving, until he heard Hope's news that she was moving to Brandon. His first thought was to follow her. If the Brandon College School of Music decided to hire a private tutor, he wanted to be first in line to apply.

Michael spent the balance of the day after classes had been dismissed rationalizing that his interest in Hope stemmed exclusively from his love of classical music. For as long as he could remember, his mother had tuned the radio to the symphonies and operas of the great classical composers throughout the day. During the evenings, when the family relaxed in the living room, mesmerized by the flickering flames in the grate of the rose-marble fireplace, they listened to their constantly replenished recordings of Mahler, Schubert, Beethoven, and Mozart. Michael recognized Hope's potential to become a famous musician, and he intended to be associated with her from the onset.

✳

The tension between Susan and her parents increased with each passing day. June no longer walked over to visit Susan and Robert because of her sense of loyalty to Bert. Her anger with her daughter had soon fizzled, and now she missed them both. June had found her son-in-law to be an affable man, and she was convinced that if only Bert would give him half a chance, he too could begin to appreciate Robert's attributes.

June was sitting forlornly looking out the kitchen window on a Thursday morning when she noticed Susan walk into the yard. Bert was in the south pasture catching up on some fencing, but it was not long until dinner. Jumping up from her chair, she planned to intercept Susan before she made it into the house when the telephone rang.

"Hello, June. It's Robert. I just wanted to give you the heads-up that Susan is walking over."

"Yes, thanks, Robert. I've seen her, and I must go. I want to stop her before she comes in the house."

"That's exactly why she's—" June hung up and rushed to the veranda to prevent Susan from entering the home of her youth, but Susan was already striding through the doorway into the kitchen.

"Susan, if we're going to talk, we'll have to leave the house before your father comes in. He has vowed that you are never to set foot in our home again."

"Well, that's just ridiculous, Mother. What has come over that man? It's high time to let bygones be bygones and for all of us to move on with our lives. One of the reasons I'm here is because I want to deliver this invitation. Robert and I have concluded that part of Dad's resentment stems from the fact that we cheated you out of a traditional wedding. So, we've decided to have a church service and all the festive activities you would have planned had we not eloped. Daddy will be able to walk his 'precious daughter' down the aisle just like he always intended."

"Oh, my God, Susan, you can't do that! It'll only make matters worse, because it will confirm everyone's belief that you and Robert have been living in sin all this time. Your father will be overcome with shame. No, no, take your invitation, and leave right now."

"You're getting as bad as he is, Mum. Both of you are spending too much time in this house. You need to get out more and have a life. Besides, I don't care what other people think or say, and neither does Robert. We want to have a proper day, so you and Dad can celebrate our marriage, and we can start being a family again."

Neither woman had heard the back door open. "June, tell her to get out this minute," Bert said in a frigid voice. "You were told not to let her in."

"Dad, I'm not 'her.' Please don't refer to me as if you don't know my name. Can we not just sit down at the table and talk this all out? I know how deeply I've hurt you and that you had reconciled yourself to my death. But I'm not dead. I'm very much alive. I'm here now, and I want you to consider me your daughter again. I accept I made a mistake by not writing you from Hawaii, but I can't change that now. Daddy, please, can you forgive me?"

Time stood still as Bert gazed longingly into his beautiful daughter's eyes. He wanted nothing more than to rush over to her and envelope her in his arms, as he had done so often in her youth. His precious Susan was begging for his absolution, and every fibre in his body urged him to act. His heart and soul yearned for the joy they would both experience. But his mind resisted with all the force of his being.

He was rooted to the floor as pertinaciously as if he had turned into his tyrannical father. How could he have changed so much? Why was he behaving as he had vowed he never would toward the only two women in his life? With one last long look at Susan, Bert charged out the front door, brushing her arm in his haste to get away from her and his wife.

Hours passed before Bert returned to the darkening kitchen. June was seated at the table oblivious to the approaching twilight and her husband's entrance. Susan had stayed for dinner, and mother and daughter had talked, cried, hugged, and reminisced, as they spent the afternoon trying to understand what was happening to their beloved husband and father.

Finally, Susan had said, "I better be getting home, Mum. The last thing we need is for Robert to become concerned about me and run into Dad when he comes looking for me. Thank you for listening and for understanding about Robert and me. I'm so glad you and I have reconciled. I've missed you terribly, and I couldn't stand it when I was estranged from you and Daddy."

✳

Flicking on the light switch, the first thing Bert noticed when the kitchen illuminated was the white envelope propped up on the telephone table in the corner. Without a word, he picked it up and tore it open. "What the hell is this?" Even he was surprised by the vehemence of his reaction. He had spent the entire time since he had stormed out of the kitchen berating himself for his abhorrent behaviour, and no sooner had he come inside than he started all over again. God, how he needed help. Tomorrow morning he would drive to Brandon and check into the hospital for mental diseases.

Nonetheless, the second Bert glanced at the wedding invitation, his rage returned with a vengeance. "I knew it. Damn him to hell. That bastard has never bothered to marry my little girl. He has been using her like a whore all these months. Well, that does it. I'm getting my rifle, and I'll show that rich son of a bitch he isn't going to get away with treating my daughter as if she was his personal prostitute."

June leapt from her chair like a coiled spring, not believing that Susan had forgotten to take the invitation with her. "Don't be ridiculous, Bert. A justice of the peace in Winnipeg married them before they flew to Hawaii. Susan just wanted to have a traditional wedding ceremony for our sake."

"Get out of my way, woman. I'll never listen to you again!" Bert yelled, as he pushed June with all the zeal implicit in the self-righteous.

June glimpsed a brilliance of light accompanied by the rapturous "Allegro assai" of Ludwig van Beethoven's "Symphony No. 9 in D minor, Choral" and was suffused with feelings of overwhelming joy as her head cracked on the corner of the cast-iron stove in her homey kitchen.

✳

Unprepared to leave anything to chance, Michael was on his way to Brandon at the crack of dawn on Saturday. Failing to reach Dr. Elliot by telephone on Friday evening, Michael knew that his former ally would be in his office early in the morning.

Years earlier, when Michael's parents had petitioned Brandon College to allow him to challenge the entrance examinations, and he had scored in the highest percentile, it was Bryan Elliot's decisive vote that had permitted Michael to begin his university education at sixteen years of age.

Michael's educational history made him the perfect candidate to tutor Hope. He was fully cognizant of the discipline, self-direction, and dedication required to be a solitary student. During his four years at Brandon College, he had come to recognize how challenging it had been to continually be without peers to bounce ideas off, and even just to have classmates with whom to commiserate about the unrealistic learning expectations or the explicit shortcomings of a perfunctory teacher. Still, Michael was close enough to Hope's age that he knew he could be compassionate when she felt lonely and isolated.

From his two years of teaching Hope, Michael was aware of how focused she was about excelling with her music. She gave every impression of being intrinsically motivated; she was already an accomplished violinist, and there was no doubt in his mind that she was on a mission. He was prepared to predict that Hope's commitment would also extend to all facets of learning. Michael was already planning to employ all the strategies and techniques his mother had implemented during his home schooling to ensure that her educational experience was enjoyable and enlightening.

In addition, Michael recognized the advantages for him to be located on campus during the day and evening; he could continue with the graduate classes he had commenced during his bachelor of education program and pursue his master's degree. How difficult would it be to arrange Hope's tutorials around his schedule and her music classes?

When he was ready to start his mother's car, Michael checked the time on his watch. He wanted to determine precisely how long it would take him to drive from his doorstep to the school of music at Brandon College. Even during inclement weather of the prolonged Manitoba winter, he guesstimated that he could cover the twenty-nine miles between the farm and Brandon within thirty to forty-five minutes.

By the end of June, Michael planned to have enough money saved for a substantial down payment on the new 1963 Ford Mustang he'd had his eyes on for several weeks at Brandon Motors. Right after he met with Dr. Elliot, Michael intended to visit the owner to initiate the sale and begin the financial arrangements for a car loan. As much as he was eager to become Hope's tutor, Michael was not prepared to live in Brandon again and leave the sanctity of his parents' home.

∗

"I'm sorry, June. I didn't mean to push you so hard. I don't understand this rage that comes over me," Bert uttered as he hastily bent down to where his wife was lying in a crumpled heap on the floor. "Here, let me check your head. It sounded like you gave it quite a whack."

Kneeling beside June, Bert suddenly noticed that her open eyes had an eerie appearance of being vacant. "June, talk to me. Tell me that you can hear me, that you're all right. For God's sake, stop staring at me like you can't see me. It's Bert. I'm going to help you get up, and then I'll fix your head."

When a shudder ripped through his body, Bert turned ice cold as if he had been immersed into a tub of frigid water. "Oh, dear God, please don't let anything be wrong with my precious June." Gently lifting her head, he was surprised that there was no noticeable blood or gash. Maybe she had just knocked herself out when her head hit the stove. He would hold her until she came around, and then he would vehemently promise never to do it again.

Pins and needles were prickling through his bent legs, and still June had not moved a muscle. He had to do something. He had to put her down and call the doctor—or the ambulance, so they could get her to the hospital. Someone had to come and help him with his beloved June, his little Irish lass.

It was when Bert straightened up and could not see any rhythmic heaving of June's chest that the cruel grip of reality began to seize him as if his head was being squeezed in the vise on his workbench. Frantically, he lowered his face close to her mouth and nose to ascertain if she was breathing and then remembered seeing a doctor on television place his fingers on a person's neck to check for pulsation. Nothing. Bert could not feel anything. He could not see anything. Good God, had he killed his wife? Was life that fragile? Could a second of fury steal the breath and existence of another human being?

＊

Michael was about to rap on the office door that Dr. Elliot always kept open when he heard, "Come in, Michael. I was waiting for you to visit me, but even I couldn't have predicted how quickly you would appear. News must travel like lightning in your neck of the woods. As you know, the coffee is on, and it's fresh."

Bryan stood and was around his Mahoney desk before Michael could enter the large corner office overlooking the immaculately kept grounds of the campus. "As always, it's a pleasure to see you. Life in the country clearly agrees with you."

"It's all the fresh air and physical labour on my parent's acreage. Since I've moved back home, they expect me to resume all my chores, and I had no idea how much I'd missed the satisfaction of hard work.

You must come for a weekend; you would enjoy the scenery and nature hikes on their beautiful property."

"I'll take you up on that offer once I've finished with my grad students. Incidentally, now that you'll be returning to campus, I anticipate you will become one of them."

"That sounds very definitive. I'm here to put forward my application to become Hope Harding's tutor in the event she wins your prestigious music award and is the recipient of the proposed scholarship. I've heard Miss Harding play at several recitals, and I can't imagine that there is another contender within this entire province to give her the slightest competition."

"You're quite right, my young friend, nor do I think there is anyone else who could qualify as a suitable candidate to be her tutor. I have my recommendation ready to present to Dr. Burton, and I believe it will simply come down to all the concerned parties signing on the dotted line."

Lying down on the linoleum, Bert slipped his arms around June and cradled her as if he could force life back into her body. He fervently wished he could will himself to die right where he lay, and together they would enter the afterlife they both had believed would be their ultimate fate. What did he have to live for now?

As the house darkened with approaching night, Bert succumbed to a fitful sleep. When he stirred in the wee hours of the morning, every muscle was taut and numb from staying in the same position. As he resisted becoming awake, reality pressed him into consciousness. No, he was not having a nightmare. It had happened. June's body was now stiff in his aching arms, and she was as cold as the floor upon which they were recumbent. Gently releasing her as he slowly raised himself to a sitting position, Bert uttered, "Oh, my darling June, forgive me for what I have done."

In a daze, Bert left the house and made his way to the barn. The four cows were clustered around the pasture gate with their udders swollen and milk leaking from their teats. From the time he had been a boy, and during his fifty years of farming, Bert had never neglected his animals. He had to care for them now before he planned to be forever with his cherished wife.

After he had milked the cows, Bert released them back into the large pasture and opened the gate to the calves' smaller yard. He had only recently weaned the young animals, and once back with their mothers, they would soon return to suckle. Then he carried the milk to the pigs, which were hungrily rooting about in their pen. As if he was a sleepwalker he trudged back to the house in search of scraps of food, peelings, and garbage to mix as slop to supplement the pigs' liquid diet. Bert grabbed every available piece of food from the refrigerator—fruit, vegetables, meat, and chees—and threw it all into plastic bags before delivering the savoury mixture to the ever-hungry hogs. Even in his stupor, he had the presence of mind to remember pigs will eat anything, and he made a mental note that when he entered his home for the last time, he would make sure he firmly closed and locked both doors.

After years of watching his father shoot rabbits, deer, and moose, the day after his father was buried on the south quarter of his farmland, Bert had disposed of his entire gun collection, with the exception of a .22-calibre rifle. Bert had always been repulsed by what his father referred to as "the sport of hunting." How he could ever consider killing defenceless wild animals with high-powered rifles anything resembling sport had bothered Bert from the time he was young and had come to an understanding of the permanence of death.

Still, Bert, like the majority of farmers, was a meat-and-potatoes man, and he slaughtered his own pigs every autumn. He had retained the .22 to humanely kill the domestic animals before they were lowered into troughs of boiling water to facilitate hair removal and butchered. The balance of the time, he kept the gun locked in a cabinet in the garage, the key hidden in a safe in his shed.

Satisfied that his animals had been duly tended to, in the event that no one came to the farm for a matter of days, Bert, now intent upon his mission, strode to the aluminum storage structure. Not once did he question what he was about to do. June and he had planned to grow old together, to spoil their grandchildren, which they prayed would number more than their own offspring, and to travel to exotic parts of the world. Now, because of his senseless action, neither had a future.

Dawn was breaking on a hazy Manitoba morning, heralding the beginning of another scorching summer day, when Bert bolted both doors of his cozy family bungalow. As if fearful that someone might observe what he was planning, he methodically went around and drew the curtains of every window.

For neither rhyme nor reason, Bert went to the master bedroom and returned with June's pillow and the light quilt they always used on their bed during the heat of summer. As if he could make her comfortable, he gently placed her head on the pillow and covered her with half the blanket, leaving enough for him.

Now he had to prepare himself. He could hardly go to meet his Maker smelling of his barnyard animals, although he stopped for a second, recalling that Jesus had been born in a stable. Suddenly, he remembered his mother always telling him that "cleanliness is next to godliness," and he stripped in the kitchen before tossing his clothing into the porch. Then he made his way into the bathroom and had a scalding shower, shampoo, and shave.

Later, when Bert returned to the kitchen wearing his Sunday suit and tie, it occurred to him that he had not groomed June and dressed her in her finery. But Susan would have a better idea of what clothing and jewellery her mother would prefer to be buried in, and he was starting to experience a feeling of urgency about concluding his task. The last thing he wanted was to be interrupted by a neighbour coming to call or, heaven forbid, his daughter and son-in-law deciding to check up on them.

A breeze parted the calico curtains, and a ray of profuse sunshine poured into the kitchen at the moment Bert Smith lay down beside his wife for the last time. Remembering the blissful morning he had heard June McDowell's lilting Irish accent and seen her flaming red hair, Bert raised the rifle until it was positioned on his forehead and pulled the trigger.

*

Margaret telephoned June on Friday afternoon to beg off their end-of-the-week get-together because of a lingering migraine. She was relieved her friend did not answer the phone. Chances were that June was in her garden or out in the yard watching for her to arrive. She would lie down for a short rest and try her again later.

To her surprise, Margaret awoke as James was hovering over her and about to give her a shake. "Since you can't be feeling well, do you want me to make myself a sandwich and some soup for supper?"

"What time is it? I was only going to have a few minutes of peace and quiet before I tried to call June again. It must be the approaching summer holiday, because it's getting harder and harder to keep the students under control. I thought the day would never end."

"It's after six. I was on my way to Bert and June's until I went into the garage and saw your car. I hope you're not starting another of those painful headaches, Margaret. You really ought to see a specialist about them."

"Actually, the throbbing seems to have abated. A sleep was just what I needed. And now I'm hungry, so why don't you open a can of soup while I telephone June to let her know why I stood her up."

Coming into the kitchen after she had brushed her hair, Margaret lifted the telephone receiver from the wall and tried to reach the Smith residence for the second time that day. "They must be out for the evening. I'll contact June first thing in the morning."

✻

As she was enjoying her second cup of coffee, Margaret rang the Smiths' number again. "That's a little unusual. When you saw Bert in town on Tuesday, did he say anything about them going away for the weekend? I wonder if perhaps they have finally made amends with Susan and her new husband, and they all decided to make a trip to the city."

"Bert was more out of sorts than ever when I met him in Souris, so we didn't even bother going for a beer. I hope he soon comes to terms with Susan marrying that Wharton fellow, because he's starting to remind me more of his old man with each passing day. No doubt we'll see them tomorrow, and in the event that Bert's in a reasonable mood, maybe we can have them back after church for a barbeque. That is, if you're feeling up to it. Any sign of that headache?"

Coming around the table and draping her arms around her husband, Margaret rested her head on his shoulder. "I feel terrific this morning, thanks, James. There isn't anything like a good night's sleep to set me up for your spontaneous loving. It was just what the doctor ordered!"

✻

How strange, Margaret thought when she did not see June and Bert drive into the churchyard. She and James had started a pattern years earlier of waiting in their car until their friends had arrived, so they could enter together. The Devonshires had become grain farmers, so they could escape to warmer climes during Margaret's Christmas and

Easter school breaks, and in the absence of morning chores, they were always the first to reach Hartney's small St. Andrew's Anglican Church.

"Well, it doesn't look like they're coming today, and if we want to get our customary pew, I think we better go in. We'll keep their seats," James said with one last look down the long lane. On a clear morning on the flat prairie, one could see forever, and there was no sign of any approaching vehicles on the horizon.

With an increasing sense of dread, Margaret could not pay attention to the minister. She kept turning her head and checking the door.

The moment Reverend Walmseley said the benediction of the interminable service, Margaret uttered to James, "Something's wrong. We have to get over to June and Bert's right now. I have a sinking feeling in the pit of my stomach that June is in a terrible situation. It started when Reverend Walmseley was going on about that section in the matrimony vow for women 'to love, honour, and obey' in his sermon. It was the only thing I heard him say all morning. Good God, why was he talking about marriage, anyway?"

✳

They had scarcely rounded the circular drive of evergreens into the Smith's yard when Margaret exclaimed, "Look, all the curtains are drawn. June never closes her drapes even during the winter to help keep out the elements. Quick, stop the car. I need to get into the house to see June now."

"No, wait, Margaret. You stay in the car. I'll go in first and call you. If anything untoward has happened, I don't want you to be the one to discover it." By then, Margaret's apprehension had seized James, and he was dreading the worst. Bert had not been in his right mind for the last several months, and suddenly James was remembering all the times his boyhood friend had run to his home to seek the protection of James' family.

When he arrived in the kitchen and saw the small bloody hole in Bert's head, James turned to make a hasty retreat to the bathroom to vomit when he ran smack into Margaret. Reverend Walmseley's edict for wives "to obey" flashed through his mind. "I thought I asked you to wait!"

✳

The news spread like a grass fire raging across the wide-open prairie on a scorching Manitoba summer afternoon. And, just as an inferno gains impetus and speed when it sears across an expansive landscape, so too did the information gather momentum and magnification as the senseless tragedy was passed from the lips of one person to another. Before long, every family, friend, and neighbour in the Hartney District and acquaintances as far away as Souris and Brandon were conversing about the calamity in the tranquil farmhouse in the heart of the province.

The party line of the Manitoba Telephone System greatly facilitated the pervasion of Bert and June Smith's catastrophic demise. Margaret had rushed toward June when James stopped her from tampering with the crime scene. Eventually, they collected themselves enough to determine how they should proceed, with James insisting that the most immediate method of contacting the RCMP detachment in Souris was to telephone. Margaret was opposed, knowing exactly the frenzy of rumours it would initiate. However, James gave her no choice but to comply as he picked up the receiver.

"Have it your way, but give me the keys to your truck. I must get over to the Whartons and warn Susan about what has happened. I could never forgive myself if she found out by listening to everyone gossiping about her mother and father over the telephone. And worse yet, come rushing over here."

"I'm not sure the Mounties would approve of you getting involved, so maybe you ought to wait until they arrive and give you their approval. No, come to think of it, I can't let you leave with the truck."

"Then, I'll walk across the fields, James. Since you're making the call to broadcast this horrible news, I absolutely will try to break it to Susan with as much compassion as is humanly possible. Not for one second will I allow some immature, disinterested policeman to convey what has occurred with June and Bert."

"That's just it, you don't know what took place here," James said, but Margaret was gone.

✳

With sirens blaring and blue and red lights flashing, two black police vehicles screeched to a stop in front of the Smith residence. None of the current members of the Mounties stationed in Souris had any recollection of ever having been called to this particular farmhouse, but had they searched in the annals of the detachment, they would have readily discovered that the previous generations had repeatedly been summoned to the site for reports of domestic violence.

Although they had arrived in record time, the number of vehicles parked helter-skelter around the grove of conifers and the size of the gathering crowd surprised the three RCMP officers. The corporal immediately ordered the two constables to clear the area of the unwelcome spectators. "Send all these people home, and as soon as the coroner gets here, set up a roadblock at the beginning of the lane. Then one of you will remain at the front of the house and the other by the back door just in case some well-intentioned neighbour decides to come in and offer his assistance."

By and large, the farmers in the Hartney district were congenial and respectful of each other and of their adjoining properties. Aside from the occasional dispute over an unreturned piece of farm equipment or domestic animals breaking out of the pasture and grazing in a neighbouring wheat field, in recent years, the RCMP had rarely been called to any home in the community. Perhaps it was little wonder that people had been drawn with the force of a magnetic pull to the scene of such a macabre crime.

Corporal Dan Milnes had seen his share of violent crimes during his extensive years of policing in the northern towns of Manitoba and Saskatchewan, but when he had been sent to the peaceful county of Souris as his last posting before a well-earned retirement, he never expected to be summoned to a possible murder/suicide. At least, given the information provided by Mr. James Devonshire, that's what he gathered he was about to encounter once he entered the Smith's farmhouse.

*

Striding along at a steady pace, Margaret was becoming increasingly alarmed by the number of vehicles racing toward the Smith farm site. She knew what it meant. The multiple subscribers of the shared telephone lines had done their job, precisely as she had predicted, and soon the entire neighbourhood would be buzzing with speculation and prying bystanders. Margaret broke into a run over the summer-fallowed field, intent on reaching Susan ahead of any of the Nosey Parkers.

Once the newly renovated two-storey home came into view, Margaret slowed to her usual walking gait. She did not want to arrive flustered, and she began contemplating how she could approach Susan with any semblance of calmness. She had encountered many family crises in her extensive teaching career, but never had she been required to elucidate a tragedy of such magnitude.

In all the years Susan had been a pupil in her classroom, Margaret had never shown any favouritism toward her godchild. Of course, as the principal, she had engaged in parent/teacher discussions and the usual interactions expected as her teacher, but Susan always kept her distance. She performed adequately and applied herself, but she had the capability of being an excellent student.

Margaret had thought that even from an early age, Susan was self-absorbed and, more often than not, considered herself superior to others, whether it was her peers or the teaching staff. As their only child, June and Bert had flagrantly spoiled her, succumbing to her every whim. During the frequent social interactions between Susan's parents and the Devonshires, Susan seldom expressed anything other than the expected polite salutations at the beginning of the evening, and as she matured, was rarely around by the end. From what little Margaret knew about her best friend's daughter, she suspected that Susan had neither depth of character nor any sustainable belief in a Higher Being.

How in heaven's name was Margaret going to broach her life-shattering communication? Once she decided that her only options were to be honest and supportive, she rang the doorbell. Following several seconds without a response, she tried again and again. By the third attempt, Margaret was beginning to experience a feeling of relief. Perhaps she would not have to be the bearer of such horrific tidings.

Then she remembered all the talk the previous summer when Robert Wharton was refurbishing the farmhouse, about the addition of a pretentious veranda at the rear of his home overlooking a scenic ravine. It was a lovely summer day, and what if Susan and her husband had decided to have a romantic dinner on their newly constructed deck? Margaret could not leave in all good conscience if she did not at least go around to the back and check. Maybe that's why they had not heard or seen the traffic on the gravel road adjoining the end of their lane. Besides, she might find it easier to break the news to Susan in the outdoors surrounded by fresh invigorating air and the beauty of their secluded haven.

"Hello, are you there, Susan? It's Margaret Devonshire. I don't want to startle you. I must talk to you."

"Really, Mrs. Devonshire! You're the last person in the world I would ever expect to see coming around my rose bushes. This is my husband, Robert. We're just about to have our dessert and coffee. Since you're our first visitor, other than my mother, why don't you sit down and join us?"

"It's nice to meet you, Robert. Thank you, Susan. I welcome your offer of a chair, but I'll pass on dessert." Truthfully, Margaret could not have swallowed a morsel of food or drink if someone had forced it down her throat. The scene in the Smith kitchen was indelibly etched in her memory, and it was not until she had started to run across the fields that her waves of nausea had begun to subside. "But, please you and Robert go ahead. I want to sit for a minute to catch my breath."

"I don't understand why you would be short of breath. Didn't you drive here? I was sure I heard the sound of a vehicle. In fact, when I went into the house to bring the coffee, traffic on the road allowance seemed unusually heavy," Robert said, providing Margaret with a cushioned lawn chair.

Glancing toward the flourishing grove of trees in the gully, Margaret suddenly wished she were one of the yellow finches flitting from branch to branch near the top of the saplings.

"What a good idea it was, Robert, to build this veranda. I never realized that this house backed out over such a beautiful setting, and now you can enjoy nature morning, noon, and night." Lapsing into silence, Margaret continued to sit as if she were a million miles away.

"Mrs. Devonshire, are you all right? I've never seen you act so strangely," Susan said with a surprising tone of civility.

"No, Susan. I'm not all right, and I never will be again. I've just lost two of my dearest friends. And now I have to tell you that it was your parents. James and I found them this morning, both dead in the kitchen. God, I'm sorry. I am so sorry. I was going to break this to you gently, and instead, in my sorrow, I've just blurted it all out. Please, forgive me!"

"What are you talking about? I was over on Friday, and they were fine. In fact, Mum and I had a lovely day together and finally came to terms about many of our differences. Are you on some kind of medication, Mrs. Devonshire? Do you want us to call Mrs. Webster's son-in-law? When I picked up the receiver of the telephone on Thursday, I inadvertently heard that Dr. and Mrs. Jamison were bringing Cassandra to visit her grandparents for the weekend."

"Yes, please, Susan. No, no Robert, can you do it, and right now? Call Dr. Jamison, and ask him to get here as fast as possible. The phone will be busy, but just interrupt. And first go and lock your front door and draw the drapes. Thank God, your car is in the garage. Then come back immediately."

Rising from her chair, Margaret walked over and knelt beside Susan, where she remained until Robert had returned. "My dear child, I was out of breath, because I ran across the fields to be the first to reach you. In minutes, your driveway and yard will be teeming with all the morbidly curious of our neighbourhood. As much as it pains me beyond measure, I must tell you that your mother and father are both dead and gone."

Looking at her former teacher and principal as if she had sprouted two heads, Susan still did not give her information the slightest credibility. "Why don't you come into the house and lie down until Dr. Jamison arrives? You did speak with him, Robert?"

"I did. I had to tell some people to open the line, but I reached him. He'll be here any minute now."

Not before I heard what they were saying, Robert thought. Dear God, it was true. June and Bert Smith were dead. Had Bert killed her, and then shot himself? It was when Mrs. Pickard was broadcasting that there was blood everywhere in the kitchen that Robert had yelled at her to shut up and get off the line.

By the time George Jamison could inch his way through the cars and trucks lining the Wharton driveway, Susan was well into the throes of hysteria. She had observed the apprehensive glance Robert had given Mrs. Devonshire and was instantly suspicious. He was hiding something. When she turned and looked directly at him, there was no mistaking the trepidation in his eyes. Suddenly, Susan was seized with blinding fear. As she tried to stand, she was trembling so hard that she collapsed into Robert's open arms.

✳

They all came together for the joint funeral. The rift did not begin to appear until sometime later. It took Dr. Glasgow more than a week before he released the bodies to the mortician, which suited the mourners just fine. They needed time to accept that Bert and June Smith were dead. To the amazement of the entire community, the coroner had sent June's body to Winnipeg for a more extensive examination. None of them understood why. What possible difference could it make whether her death was accidental or homicide? Their beloved neighbour with the bright eyes that sparkled with green flecks and who spoke with a lovely Irish accent was gone.

Benjamin Glasgow was not acquainted with the family. Still, he wanted the truth written; he wanted it known that Bert Smith had not murdered his wife. Dr. Glasgow had three teenage children, and he understood how devastated they would be if, God forbid, their mother had met with a suspicious death. Above all else, it was Benjamin's fervent desire to prove to Bert and June's daughter, Susan Wharton, that there had not been any signs of ill treatment on her mother's body and that she had struck her head with such force that she had died instantly. Then, in his despair, her father had chosen to commit suicide.

As soon as he received the report from the medical examiner in

Winnipeg, which verified his identified cause of death, Dr. Glasgow requested that the RCMP sergeant from the Souris detachment accompany him to the Wharton farm. He would not accept that Susan was still so heavily sedated she could not comprehend the results of his investigation. Dr. Glasgow was determined to personally deliver the written documentation, so it would be available to her whenever she could understand the facts. The benevolent doctor would never come to know that it was of no consolation to Susan that her mother's death had been an accident; nonetheless, there was nothing that pleased him more than that the information spread like wildfire throughout the district.

The legal implications of Bert Smith committing suicide were far more serious. The act of voluntary and intentional self-destruction was considered a crime in Canada. Dr. Glasgow had no idea whether Bert and June had prepared a will, and he feared even if they had, it would be in probate court for a very long time.

*

The last place on earth where Francine wanted to be was at the funeral for Susan's parents. For once though, Mother Pat put her foot down. "My darling, I appreciate that you don't much care about Susan, but out of respect for Mr. and Mrs. Smith, I insist you come with me and your uncles. In all my years of teaching Susan, her mother and father were always willing to help with school activities, and they never missed a parent/teacher interview."

In addition, Patricia had enjoyed June's company on those frequent occurrences when Margaret Devonshire had invited her along for Friday afternoon tea. On three or four occasions, she had even accompanied the two friends to Brandon for a day of shopping and had found June to be a vibrant and amiable individual. Now Patricia was finding it very difficult to believe that June's life had come to such an abrupt and premature end.

Still, in the far reaches of her mind, Patricia had an ill-fated notion that the reason Francine continued to be haunted by her own parents' death was because she had never had any closure. From what little she could gather during discussions with Daniel, Francine had not been allowed to attend their memorial service. Perhaps if she could be present at a funeral, she might come to an appreciation that the intended purpose for the ceremony was to celebrate an individual's life.

"I'll only come for you, Mother Pat, but I'm not going to the cemetery, even if I have to walk all the way home."

"Fair enough. I've never been keen on being present for the interment either, so we'll walk back together."

It was not until they were in the church, and the minister had asked the congregation to rise, that Francine caught a glimpse of Susan. Even then she had to look twice to confirm it was really Susan. She seemed more like an apparition dressed in black than the arrogant and beautiful schoolgirl who had triumphantly taken flight less than eight months earlier in Robert Wharton's bright red Cadillac convertible.

Susan was so heavily supported by her husband on her right side and James Devonshire on her left that she appeared to be floating down the aisle. Quite likely, had they allowed her feet to touch the floor, she would have collapsed into a heap. Until that moment, Francine had not had the slightest empathy for her previous nemesis, but even she was filled with overwhelming sympathy. An audible shudder gripped the congregation, and it was several minutes after Susan was positioned in the pew before the minister could begin the service.

It was debatable whether many, if any, heard the scripture readings or the prayers. Although the organist dutifully played the hymns that someone had selected, other than the minister and the choir, there was no vocal accompaniment from the pews, other than the sound of weeping. When Reverend Walmseley was about to begin his sermon, he looked down at his parishioners and decided that preaching to his flock was an exercise in futility. What could he say to ease their anguish? How could he possibly praise the earthly lives of June and Bert Smith without feeling like a hypocrite, when all he kept thinking about was how they had come to their demise?

If any individual in the church was aware that Reverend Walmseley had made the choice of foregoing his message and the closing hymns instead going directly to the benediction, no one ever said. It was equally doubtful that anyone in the community—and everyone had come until the church was crammed—when remembering their friends and neighbours, gave much consideration to the celebration of Bert or June's life.

Long before the abbreviated service ended, Patricia was painfully aware of her mistake. The sight of Susan's desolation only confirmed why Francine, at age five, had been prohibited from attending her parents' commemoration service. What had she done? Rather than facilitate Francine coming to terms with the loss of her mother and father, had she opened old wounds, which might prompt the return of her nightmares that, as of late, had become more episodic?

Within weeks, Patricia's foreboding proved accurate. What she would never come to learn though was that the sense of loss, which precipitated Francine's recurring nightmares, had little, if anything, to do with her attendance at the Smiths' funeral or bereavement over the deaths of her own parents.

On the Monday morning following the obsequies, Francine hurried to catch Hope and Jessica as they were going into school. During their Sunday evening telephone conversation, her father had apprised Hope that he could not make it from Winnipeg to attend her competition at Brandon College on the upcoming Saturday evening, and now she had two extra tickets. Her grandfather offered to attempt to purchase one more, and then all three of her friends could have front-row seats for her musical milestone of the year. Instantly, they started to plan for Francine and Jessica to stay with Cassandra's folks for the weekend.

Francine was careful to display the expected outward signs of excitement and enthusiasm that Jessica so openly expressed, although lately, whenever she was tending to her sheep, her prayers invariably culminated on Hope not winning the competition. Francine reasoned that if Hope did not receive the scholarship, life would continue along its anticipated course, and the three musketeers would graduate from high school together in Souris.

Francine had not dared to disclose her unwonted supplications even to Mother Pat. When Patricia had become her stepmother, what Francine liked best was that she could share her innermost thoughts and feelings with her. She was hesitant though to confide that she did not want Hope to succeed, believing Mother Pat would think her selfish and possessive. In her heart, Francine knew it was the truth.

When all three arrived somewhere at the same time, Francine was confident with her two new friends, but she was jealous if she came upon Jessica and Hope with their heads together talking and snickering about something she had not heard. She automatically thought they were laughing about her, and then would feel inadequate in their presence. Too often she wished that Jessica would leave, because she wanted Hope all to herself.

It was so confusing. When Francine was alone with Hope, she knew that Hope genuinely cared about her, but as soon as she left, Francine's doubts would rear their ugly head. She did not know whether it was Hope she could not trust or if it was herself. Her feelings of melancholy and guilt would drive Francine outdoors to be with her sheep until she regained her equanimity. Still, when she saw Hope nearly every day, she could believe she loved her too, but how could she ever survive from one day to the next if she had to go for weeks without her affirmations?

✳

Hope played a stunning performance of Max Bruch's "Concerto No.1 for Violin and Orchestra in G minor, Op.26." With the final wave of the conductor's baton, the audience rose to their feet in a thunderous ovation with shouts of "Brava!" resounding from every corner of the recital hall.

She was by far the youngest of the three finalists in the competition, and the adjudicators had decided to place her first on the program. The lights had been lowered when a petite angelic figure in an iridescent gown floated across the stage carrying her gleaming violin. A hush settled over the audience. She was only a child; how could she possibly be vying for the prestigious provincial music scholarship?

From the moment Hope lifted her instrument to her shoulder, rested it comfortably beneath her chin, and started to play the "Allegro moderato," the Brandon Chamber Orchestra sensed the prodigious talent of the youthful virtuoso. Hope had never before been accompanied by such a large number of instrumentalists, and instantly she appreciated how much better she would sound with full orchestral support.

By the time Hope was performing the "Adagio," the more knowledgeable of the music lovers recognized they were in the presence of greatness. The strings of Hope's violin emitted the sweetest sounds they could ever recall hearing as a profound silence permeated the auditorium. No one moved a muscle, neither a cough nor a sneeze escaped from a single person; the entire audience sat mesmerized, oblivious of the space-time continuum.

Hope loved the finale and had practiced it so often she knew every note from memory. She closed her eyes, raised the bow to her cherished violin, and surging to the far reaches of her heart and soul, gave the performance of her young life. She felt as if she had taken wing and was soaring beyond the upper echelons of the concert hall when the orchestra arrived at the resounding crescendo.

Everyone, likely including the other two finalists, knew the name of the winner without having to wait for the adjudicators to make their announcement. It was questionable whether many of the audience, still lost in the glow of their brilliant predecessor, heard much of either Marjorie Burke or Thomas Brown's performances.

When Hope returned to the stage to receive the award, she was still holding her violin. At last, the applause lessened, and following her acceptance of the scholarship, Hope approached the conductor. After a brief consultation, she resumed her position on the soloist's chair. When they realized they were going to be graced with an encore, a state of breathless expectancy seized all those in attendance.

Seven minutes later, when she finished playing Massenet's "Meditation' from Thaïs," they knew beyond a shadow of a doubt that they had been blessed with a glimpse of heaven, and from that evening onward, the citizens of Brandon, Manitoba, would always claim Hope Harding as their own.

✳

Everyone's life was going to change. In five short weeks, Hope would be gone forever from Souris. Summer vacation would begin, and the three musketeers would come to an untimely end. If she was lucky, when she visited Cassandra, Francine might still see Hope, but it would never again be the same. *Why do we have to grow up?* ran through Francine's head over and over as she tossed and turned on her side of Cassandra's four-poster bed.

It was after three in the morning before the four girls finally settled for the night. When at last they had been able to leave the concert hall, Cassandra's parents had surprised their daughter and her guests by taking them out to the new pizza restaurant in the city. They chatted, laughed, and celebrated until the witching hour was fast approaching. Then, once they had returned to Cassandra's bedroom, the friends continued to be so wound up that sleep was beyond the realm of possibility.

Hope was still incredulous that she had won, Cassandra and Jessica were equally ecstatic for her, and all three kept talking at the same time. None of them seemed to notice that Francine had become unusually quiet from the moment of the adjudicators' decision. Though trying with all her might, Francine could not bring herself to share in Hope's success. She knew that her fear of losing Hope was about to become reality, and she was the last of them to finally fall into a restless sleep.

Returning to school on Tuesday morning, tired and dispirited, Francine was stunned by Mr. Griffin's announcement at the beginning of the day. After effusively congratulating Hope for the incredible performance, which resulted in her winning the Max Bruch Musical Scholarship, he conveyed the news of his own success.

At first, Francine could not believe her ears, and then she refused to accept what her mind was registering. Surely, Mr. Griffin could not be leaving Souris High School. It was too much to fathom that she was going to lose her best friend and her favourite teacher at the same time. It was not until the end of the day, one of the worst of her young life, when she was relating the information to Mother Pat on their way home that Francine began to assimilate the fact that Mr. Griffin was going to become Hope's private tutor.

Francine loved Michael Griffin, and it was not just a schoolgirl crush, a short-term infatuation because he was her teacher, or that he was the most handsome person she had ever met. She loved him with all her heart and soul. Being only thirteen, Francine knew that their age difference was prohibitive, but eight years from now, when she was an adult, it would not matter at all. Her father had been twelve years older than her mother, and they had loved each other until the day the ocean took them.

Life was so unfair. The two people, other than her family, whom she loved most in the whole world, would be together, and once again, she would be left alone. In the early hours of the next morning, Francine's nightmares returned with a vengeance.

✳

Several weeks passed before the McGregor family heard about the appalling episode at the cemetery. When Patricia explained to Daniel that Francine refused to go to the interment, all four of them slipped away from the church and drove home. Since Mother Pat or one of her uncles had started transporting Francine to school in Souris, they seldom went into Hartney. Now, with their rotating Sunday dinners with the Yang and Webster families, their interaction with most of the other members in their immediate community had become increasingly limited.

One Saturday afternoon, Patricia realized she had forgotten the horseradish to serve with her prime rib dinner the next day and decided to dash into Hartney while the men and Francine roamed about the hills tending to their sheep. Coming out of the grocery store, she ran headlong into Margaret.

Patricia was taken aback by her appearance. Her former colleague had always been meticulous about her hair and attire, and it took a few moments for Patricia to assimilate that the dishevelled, discernibly aged woman was the same person.

"Oh, thank God it's you, Pat. I just had to get away from the house and lose myself. I didn't even bother to comb my hair, and I'm not sure I washed my face. Would you have time for a cup of coffee? You have no idea how much I miss our conversations, and now that James and I rarely speak, I'm desperate for someone who will listen to me."

Taking Margaret by the arm, Patricia quietly led her to the small café on the corner of Main Street. Fortunately, it was a beautiful afternoon, and there was a secluded table under the shade of the overhanging maple tree. Once Margaret was seated facing away from the street, Patricia hurried into the restaurant to bring their coffee to the table, appreciating that the last thing Margaret wanted was to draw any attention to herself, even from the chatty waitress.

"You have no idea how lucky you are to be removed from the school and the district," Margaret said. "Our close-knit community is unravelling quicker than a woollen scarf caught on a barbed-wire fence."

"I know we've kept our distance since Francine left, and with new friends in Souris, we're usually busy with them. Then, to be perfectly honest, it became easier to stay away after June and Bert's deaths. Still, Margaret, I have been remiss not calling you." With a flash of awareness, Patricia remembered how much time the Devonshire and Smith couples had spent together and the subsequent feelings of loss and devastation Margaret must be experiencing.

Nonetheless, nothing could have prepared Patricia for the deluge when the dam of Margaret's emotions burst forth. "My God, my God, I'm so responsible. It's on my head that both June and Bert are dead. If only I'd gone to them the minute I heard those two girls plotting, none of this would have happened. I remember telling James about Susan's scheme, but I stupidly decided not to mention it, not even to June. And now, ever since that horrible scene at the gravesite, James is convinced I'm culpable. I just can't deal with the guilt anymore, and my husband doesn't help at all, because on the rare occasion when he still looks at me, his eyes are overflowing with blame."

"Margaret, you can't possibly hold yourself responsible for whatever happened in the Smiths' kitchen. No one in his or her right mind could think that! Good heavens, what's going on in James's head?"

"He and Bert grew up together, spent every day playing. They were like brothers. James misses him terribly, and you know how we humans are. We always have to find someone to blame, and I'm it!"

"It's hard not to fault others when life turns tragic, Margaret, but please, don't be so unfair and unkind to yourself. You have always given your best to all the students under your tutelage. The day of their funeral, Francine only came to the church service on the condition we did not insist she go to the interment, so we stealthily left right after Reverend Walmseley's abbreviated service. Tell me, what took place at the cemetery?"

Patricia waited and waited. It was as if Margaret had succumbed. Not a word escaped her lips, and not a muscle moved. Was she still breathing? Finally Patricia rose from her chair, quietly walked over to Margaret, and gently placed her arm around her shoulders. "I think you should come home with me. You need a peaceful environment to rest and to put some of the past events into perspective."

For a woman who invariably chided her students, particularly the females, to walk straight and tall with shoulders back and face the world with confidence, Margaret's stooped posture when she eventually stood was alarming. What had transpired over the last several weeks to have all but broken the spirit of one of the most respected members of their small farming community?

✳

They were not even on the outskirts of town when Margaret's head lolled back on the headrest that Daniel had attached to the passenger seat for their long driving tours, and she was sound asleep. There were still a couple of hours before Patricia would be expected to have supper on the table, so she decided to drive to a secluded spot on the east side of Victoria Park overlooking the swinging bridge across the

Souris River.

Once they arrived, she opened the windows of the car, turned off the engine, and relaxed to commune with the scenery of the rare prairie oasis in the heart of Souris. If Patricia had not been so concerned about Margaret, she would have left her sleeping in the vehicle and walked along the nature trails to sit below the infamous Old Oak Tree and perhaps to encounter some of the town's mascots, the beautiful peacocks.

Since Patricia had married Daniel, one of their favourite activities was to stroll along the walking trails until they reached the lookout tower located at the top of the sand hills. They always climbed the tall wooden structure for the panoramic view of the town, river, lush forests, and agricultural lands of the district. Invariably, they would conclude their hike by walking back and forth across the Souris Swinging Bridge, Canada's longest historical suspension bridge. They had soon learned, however, not to plan their outing on a Sunday, when the park was flooded with people, and since they had begun driving Francine to the high school, they were frequent visitors during the week.

Pat was anxious to learn what had happened at the gravesite and its subsequent ramifications, and as the warm breeze flowed through the open windows, she strived to contemplate its nature. But soon her reverie turned to the occurrences in her own family over the past week. She had been awakened for the past five nights by the almost-forgotten shriek of "Go away! Just go away!" It had been years since Francine had been afflicted with her terrifying nightmares. Patricia and the twins had considered that, thankfully, they had been laid to rest. What could have precipitated their recurrence?

Suddenly, she realized how tired she was. Reaching into the backseat for the blanket they always carried in the event that she and Daniel chose to have a picnic on one of their excursions, Patricia opened it to fold first over Margaret's shoulders and then her own. If the McGregor family did not soon have a full night's sleep, each of them might just come undone as surely as the other members of their community.

The next thing Patricia became aware of was Margaret gently shaking her shoulder. "What a pair of sleepyheads we are!"

"Oh dear, did I drift off too? You looked so comfortable. I thought I'd just rest my eyes for a few moments. What time is it? So, do you feel up to telling me what's going on?"

"I must have really needed that nap. I'm not nearly as dispirited now. But first, I could use another cup of coffee. Do you have time to return to our table at the restaurant before your family sends out a search party?"

✷

"The sombre proceeding was unfolding as expected, until Carole Martin stepped forward to toss her handful of dirt on June and Bert's coffins. Suddenly, Susan surfaced from her catatonic state, lunged at the poor girl, and would have flung her into the double grave had her father not had such quick reflexes," Margaret explained after the waitress had filled their coffee cups and departed.

"Dear God! That must have been upsetting to everyone."

"Not nearly as unnerving as Susan's shrieks that Carole deserved to be buried with them, since she was the reason they were both dead. It made no sense to anyone, except vaguely to me, when Robert shouted, 'You little bitch. What did you do with the letter Susan wrote telling her parents that we were flying to Hawaii and when we were returning home? If you had given it to them like you had been instructed, they would both be alive today.' Once again, if Fred Martin had not acted quickly and pulled Carole away through the mourners, I think Robert would have helped Susan throw her on top of the coffins. He seemed to be as unbalanced as Susan, who continued to screech at the top of her lungs."

"It must have been horrible! But what did you mean by 'vaguely'? Were you aware that Susan had written an explanatory note to her parents?"

"Since that day, I've racked my mind, and there are times when I can almost swear that I heard Susan say something about a letter she was going to give Carole, but I must have blocked it from my memory. I didn't have the slightest recall until Robert hurled his accusation at Carole. But how could I have not remembered and, more importantly, not followed up on it? I'm as responsible as Carole is and, presumably, I'll have to come forward at the inquest."

When a sudden premonition seized her, Patricia glanced furtively at her long-time colleague and friend. "At the funeral, I felt everyone was united in their grief over losing two of their stalwart members. Are you now suggesting that the community has become divided, all because of a supposed letter?"

"Yes, I think it has. From the moment news of the tragedy spread throughout the district, everyone blamed Robert Wharton, the rich outsider, with his flashy car and proclivity for exotic trips. Even Susan was faulted, but now with the possibility of an explanatory letter, many of them are only too ready to accuse Carole. Poor girl! I can't imagine that the last few weeks have been pleasant for her, from some of the talk I've overheard in school. Of course, all the while she and her parents unequivocally deny the existence of any kind of written epistle."

"So, the only other person in the district who might have the slightest inkling that Susan had communicated her plans to her parents is you?"

"From all the gossip going around, I believe that might be true. No one else appears to know anything about a letter. That does seem like an unusual question though, Patricia."

"I'm not quite sure how to say this to you, Margaret, but I have a strong conviction that you should just let it go. After all, you're uncertain whether you actually knew there was a letter, and unless you come forward, the coroner could only conclude that it was Susan's word against Carole's."

"Pat, I don't believe I'm hearing you correctly. Why would you, of all people, make such a request?"

"Think about it. What good can come out of you acknowledging a possible letter? You've already told me that James can hardly look at you, much less talk to you. Good God, woman, what might he do if you were to publicly announce you considered it conceivable Susan did leave information for June and Bert saying that she was eloping with Robert Wharton? It would doom your marriage and cause another broken relationship in our community when more than ever, we need to try and heal. Susan, Robert, and Carole are young and have their whole lives ahead of them, but we're all getting up in years, and we should scarcely be expected to take on their hardships. Oh my, look at the time. If I don't get home, I'll be in trouble with my own husband."

As Patricia drove away, Margaret was still trying to overcome her surprise at her friend's advice. In all the years the two women had taught together, it would never have occurred to her to question Pat's integrity, and yet, in the face of the crisis in their district, she was asking Margaret to withhold evidence. Or was she? Could Margaret place her hand on the Bible and swear that she knew beyond a reasonable doubt that Susan had given a letter to Carole? Even if she could, what positive purpose could it serve now?

✳

Patricia was tremendously relieved when Alice mentioned that Cassandra and her parents were coming for the weekend. She was at the end of her tether with Francine's nightmares and was finally going to ask Dr. Jamison for a referral to a psychologist. Patricia realized her stepdaughter would resist, but for her sake, and for the rest of the family, she needed help.

On the Saturday of the appointment, Patricia served a light breakfast of toast and juice. "Your uncles have offered to tend to your sheep this morning, Francine, so you and I can have a long overdue mother/daughter day in the city. I thought we would leave for Brandon in time to enjoy some shopping before we have lunch at that new pizza restaurant." Patricia, Daniel, and Darrin had agreed that the only way to get Francine to see Dr. Eleanor Donahue was to maintain the element of surprise until the last possible moment.

✳

It was not until they were seated under the spiral staircase at a discreet table covered with a red-and-white checked plastic cloth that Francine said, "So, Mother Pat, are you finally going to tell me the real reason for our unexpected trip?"

"Ah, I see I've underestimated you again, Francine. The truth is, your uncles and I are sorely in need of a full night's sleep, and since we have not been able to help you come to terms with your nightmares, we decided it was time to seek professional assistance." Steeling herself for one of Francine's outbursts that had suddenly emerged along with the physical changes of adolescence, Patricia waited, thankful for their secluded spot.

To her surprise, after a few moments of reflection, Francine said, "It might not be such a bad idea. I know that I'm disturbing all of you, and besides, I'm finding I can hardly stay awake in school after lunch." Over the years, Francine had become insightful enough to suspect that her nightmares were related to feelings of grief. Certainly, this time she knew it was because at the beginning of summer not only was she going to lose Hope, more importantly her chances of seeing Michael Griffin again were seriously compromised. Still, she could barely confide her feelings of love for him to Mother Pat without risking her dismissing them as nothing more than a schoolgirl crush. Maybe talking to a stranger might be the answer.

✳

Once Francine was seated in a comfortable chair in the homey office with pastel-blue walls and white fluffy scatter rugs arranged at random, she began to breathe a little easier. It had been one thing to feel confident in the reception area with Mother Pat sitting at her side, but it was quite another to venture forth on her own. When Dr. Donahue stood, walked around her desk, and took the easy chair opposite her, speaking in a soft, lilting voice, Francine felt the tension in her body begin to ebb.

Francine was not sure what she expected when Mother Pat told her Dr. Jamison had recommended a psychologist, but it was not this tall, young, gorgeous woman with lovely dark hair. She scarcely looked older than a high school graduate, although Francine appreciated that she would have had to study for many years at university to become qualified.

From as early as she could remember, Francine had been attracted to beauty, whether it appeared in scenery, animals, or people. It had started with her pretty little friend, Margaret Dwyer. Then, when she moved to Manitoba and set eyes on the elegant Susan Smith, she began to dwell on how plain she must appear to others, with her unruly brunette hair. As the years passed, however, Francine came to realize that she had been gifted with a creative mind, and she eventually rationalized that she preferred to be intelligent to being beautiful. Now, gazing at Dr. Donahue, Francine began to appreciate that one of these attributes did not necessarily preclude the other.

If she was going to share her deepest thoughts with anyone, it would be to someone as lovely as this woman, and Francine soon began to express her feelings. Before the hour was over, she had confided what was upsetting her and even how she suspected that her nightmares recurred whenever she experienced a loss.

"That's very insightful, Francine. It sounds to me as if you have given considerable thought to your disturbing dreams. Do you recall how old you were when you first began to experience them?"

For the first time in their conversation, Francine hesitated. As much as she felt at ease with Dr. Donahue, she would never disclose that her nightmares had actually started soon after her mother and father's disappearance. It was one thing to share what was happening to her now, but Francine did not have the slightest intention of talking about the death of her parents. Shuddering at how abandoned she had felt, and the terrifying dreams she had lived through then, she could not possibly dredge them up years later.

"I only started to have nightmares about a year ago, when I went into grade seven at Hartney School."

Eleanor Donahue sensed her young client had suddenly stopped being forthcoming. She persisted. "Do you recollect your parents ever telling you about having night terrors as a young child?"

"I just told you they started last autumn. Is there anything I can do to stop them, so I don't disrupt my family's sleep every night?"

"I wish I had a quick solution, but I don't. The best suggestion I can offer until we meet again next Saturday is for you to try some physical and mental relaxation exercises before you go to bed. Then I believe we will need time to explore your feelings of loss and to discover ways for you to cope with them."

Closing her office door after asking her receptionist to set up a return appointment, Dr. Donahue was pleased with the progress they had made during their initial hour, particularly since George Jamison had prepared her for Francine's reticence.

The subsequent Saturday, Francine awoke eager to return to Dr. Donahue's office. Francine had taken the psychologist's advice and found that having a hot bath and then relaxing with a light read before retiring had lessened the intensity, if not the frequency, of her nightmares. During the past week, she had managed to wake herself up soon after their onset, so she did not always bring Mother Pat running up the stairs to her loft.

All week she had not breathed a word to Hope or Jessica that she was seeking counselling, and in some strange way, Francine felt that she had placed herself above their usual teenage conversations. Whether she was experiencing a feeling of detachment or a sense of superiority, she had not been so drawn into all of Hope's exciting future plans, which invariably dominated their discussions.

To Patricia's surprise, Francine had chosen to be tight-lipped about her session with the psychologist, and it was not until their return trip into Souris that she commented. "Well, my dearest, whatever Dr. Donahue recommended for you to do last Saturday seems to have worked. This past week, your nightmares haven't been nearly as bothersome, because your uncles and I have enjoyed fewer interrupted nights."

Francine knew that Mother Pat was expecting her to confide, as she had always done, but for reasons she did not understand, Francine could not bring herself to share anything about her discussions with Dr. Donahue, not even with her stepmother. Perhaps once she had come to terms with her growing dependency on Hope and her nagging doubts about whether her accomplished friend really did love her, she would share with Mother Pat. Nonetheless, Francine knew that how she felt about Michael Griffin would remain her secret, at least until she was old enough for them to start planning their future.

They all came streaming through the doors the minute they were opened, the citizens of the district of Hartney instantly affirming their rift when they filed into the opposite sides of the Brandon Courthouse. When Judge Samuel Franklin entered on the last syllable of the court clerk's announcement of "Please rise," he was surprised by the public interest in what he viewed as a routine inquest. As tragic as the deaths of June and Bertram Smith were, from what he had garnered following his perusal of the coroner's report, the causes could be concluded a straightforward accident and a subsequent suicide.

Even the eleventh-hour subpoena from the daughter and son-in-law's lawyer summoning a schoolgirl by the name of Carole Martin to appear in court had not sparked Sam's prodigious skepticism. He had tried to discourage their lawyer from the inevitable prolonging of the inquiry on the basis of a purported letter, but Derek Barclay would not be deterred. Although his wife was in no condition to be put on the stand, Robert Wharton was adamant about testifying that the professed epistle could have saved Susan's parents' lives.

Now glancing around his court, Judge Franklin began to wonder if exploring the possible existence of an explanatory letter might reveal a vestige of truth. The glaring looks darting back and forth among the individuals on opposing sides of the room gave frank testimony to the fact that something was seriously amiss. What could have planted such seeds of dissension within a customarily close-knit farming community?

＊

A cloak of stillness descended upon the courtroom the moment Carole Martin was summoned to the stand. The rumours had been rampant during the past months. Had Susan entrusted Carole with a letter? If so, what had she done with it? Why would Carole not have delivered it? Had anyone actually seen it? Why had Susan not confronted Carole when she returned home instead of nobody hearing about the letter's existence until after the tragedy? Would it have made a difference to the outcome? Was Susan simply using Carole as a scapegoat to appease her guilt for her parents' deaths?

Although Fred and Betty Martin had somehow managed to scrape money from their limited resources to hire a lawyer, during the preliminary investigation, Peter James had failed to quell Robert Wharton's accusations. Then the subpoena had arrived, and the die was cast.

The evening before Carole was summoned to be in court, Betty and Fred sat their eldest daughter down at the kitchen table. "Enough already, Carole. You have to be honest with us. This is no longer just another situation when you string us a line to save your neck. Did Susan give you a letter to deliver to June and Bert Smith? If you lost it, just say so. Surely, you understand that tomorrow, you must tell the truth, because, according to Mr. James, if you don't, you could be charged with perjury."

What was Carole going to do? She had been surprised that her parents were even aware of how, more and more, she tended to lie and manipulate to get what she wanted. Turning on her reading flashlight and checking her watch, Carole saw that it was two in the morning. She had gone to bed after midnight, knowing she would have a difficult time falling asleep, and had been tossing and turning ever since. Her parents had tried as hard as they could, asking her over and over again, but Carole had persisted with her denial. Finally, in exasperation, they had stopped and told her to get on with her chores and homework.

From an early age, Carole had discovered that when she was in trouble, she could get out of taking responsibility by making up a falsehood. She soon realized that by looking her accuser straight in the eye and maintaining an innocent facial expression, she could be pretty convincing. As the years passed, she had perfected her skills, until she became increasingly adept at telling untruths.

Why not persevere with her proven pattern of behaviour tomorrow? So what if she had to swear on the Bible? She no longer believed in God anyway. It was purely a matter of her word against Susan's, who seemed to be in a stupor most of the time. Carole knew for a fact that she was the only person in the world to have ever seen or known about the letter. She had never breathed a word to anyone, and she had always rigorously checked to make sure her mother or nosey sisters were nowhere in sight before reading it.

From the moment Susan had stranded her on the highway, Carole realized that Susan had never cared about her, and no one could blame her for wanting some revenge. What a fool she had been, treasuring Susan's letter and reading it four or five times every day, because it was the only keepsake she had of her beloved friend. So, now how could she possibly face a courtroom full of people and tell them that, when she had come to her senses, she had torn Susan's letter into a thousand pieces, before throwing it down the toilet hole of the family outhouse?

✳

When her name was called in the hushed courtroom, Carole felt the excitement of being the centre of attention. As she walked to the front, all eyes were on her. Instead of becoming nervous, she experienced a surge of power and knew exactly what she would say. During her lawyer's preliminary questions, he appeared flustered as Carole responded in a clear confident voice.

Derek Barclay watched the youthful defendant with interest. She was certainly poised, as if she had been in court before, yet he knew that she had had no previous entanglements with the law. Nonetheless, he was confident he would quickly alter her composure once he began his cross-examination. Derek had believed his client's claim that Susan had given Carole an explanatory letter, and before the session was over, he intended to get to the bottom of what she had done with it.

Approaching the stand, Derek began gently, asking innocuous questions to establish rapport with the young woman. He was a handsome man with dark black hair, deep brown eyes, and a muscular build. He was aware of his appeal to the fairer sex, and he had never been above using his charm to extract the information he was seeking. Derek had noticed the provocative look in Carole's eyes as she kept gazing around the courtroom before finally turning to look at him.

"I understand there are less than forty students in the two-room schoolhouse you attend in Hartney. Do I remember what that was like, especially by the time I reached secondary school, and the number of my classmates continued to dwindle. By grade nine, my only chum was a fellow two years ahead of me, who, for some unlikely reason, took pity on me. I still recollect how happy I was that he had even noticed me. You must have felt very special when a beautiful senior like Susan Smith befriended you, didn't you, Miss Martin?"

"Why, yes, I did. Everyone had always said Susan was so stuck up, but she wasn't like that at all. She even told me how glad she was that I had the courage to be her friend, because she was lonely. Susan and I spent all our free time during the school day together. We became bosom buddies, and there wasn't anything she didn't tell me."

Derek was pleased with the ease he had initiated a feeling of trust with the respondent by projecting a similar school background and experience. It would only be a matter of time before he brought Carole to the point of confessing.

"I see, so you soon become Susan's confidante. Did she share her love for Robert and swear you to secrecy?"

Without allowing Carole to answer, sensing his set-up of the unsuspecting girl was ripe, Derek pounced. "She even entrusted you with a letter of her plan to elope, didn't she, Miss Martin?"

Carole quickly realized what game was afoot and, smiling inwardly, thought that the smooth Mr. Barclay would have to get up much earlier in the morning to trap her at one of her favourite pastimes.

"Susan did confide in me that she was planning to run away with Mr. Wharton, but I never really took her seriously. Look at him; he's practically old enough to be her father. Why would my attractive and intelligent friend want to elope with him?"

"Answer the question, Miss Martin. Did Susan give you a letter to deliver to June and Bert Smith?"

Without a second of hesitation, and without wavering in her direct eye contact with the plaintiff's lawyer, Carole responded clearly. "No."

"I'm going to ask you again, Miss Martin, and I remind you that you are under oath. Did Susan Smith give you a letter to take to her parents? What did you do with it?"

"I've already answered your question. She never gave me a letter, so how could I have delivered it to them?" Carole's eyes did not move from Derek's face, which, by walking right up to her, he had placed very close to hers. Aware that the judge was also peering at her, Carole continued to look straight ahead at the lawyer while at the same time maintaining a demeanour of utter innocence.

"Look, young lady, why else did you think a woman as sophisticated and beautiful as Susan would have bothered to form a friendship with you, a lowly junior, other than to have an ally to carry out her bidding? Now, I've had enough of your lying. Just what did you do with Susan's letter?"

Before Carole had a chance to answer, Peter James was on his feet. "Objection. The defence is badgering the witness."

"Objection overruled, Mr. James." The judge steadied his gaze upon the defendant. "Miss Martin, before you reply again, do you understand what perjury is and that you can be charged for lying under oath?"

"Oh sure, I do, your honour, and that's why I would never lie," Carole said immediately, switching her intense scrutiny from Mr. Barclay to Judge Franklin. Staring hard at the adolescent in the witness stand, Judge Franklin fully expected it would only be a matter of moments before Mr. Barclay broke her equanimity. She was but a schoolgirl and could hardly be a practiced manipulator by the age of fourteen or fifteen years.

The large clock on the side wall ticked for a full five minutes without either of the adversaries blinked. Realizing that he might give in because of the strain of his recent ophthalmic surgery, Judge Franklin ended the impasse. "Once again, Miss Martin, did Susan Wharton, née Smith, give you a letter for her parents?"

Rather than respond instantly, Carole carefully measured her time, perusing the entire courtroom before turning back to the judge and fixing her gaze on his stern face. "No!"

"She's lying through her teeth!" Susan said, leaping up from her wooden seat. "What's the matter with you people? Are you stupid as well as blind?" Then she glared at Carole. "You manipulative little bitch! You killed my parents!"

The succeeding stunned silence gave way first to murmurs of disbelief, and then to words of condemnation that rippled through the courtroom, gaining volume. "Order, order in the court!" Judge Franklin brought down his gavel on his polished oak hardwood bench. Then it was his turn to look upon the incredulous faces of the people of Hartney, most of whom had known Carole all of her life. Had she openly defied the judge? Was the girl lying? Had the truth at last pulled Susan out of her apathy?

✻

Patricia awoke on the morning of the inquest with a sense of foreboding. She did not have the slightest intention of driving to Brandon to attend, and she planned to return straight home after transporting

Francine to school. As she prepared breakfast, she had a niggling feeling that she should telephone Margaret. Still, she knew her friend would be busily getting ready to open Hartney School, so she chose not to follow her instinct.

But, after delivering Francine to school, her premonition heightened. When she reached Highway 10, instead of turning left to return home, she signalled right and was soon speeding toward Brandon. As fortune would have it, Patricia pulled into the courthouse parking lot as Margaret was getting out of her vehicle.

"Good morning, Margaret," Patricia said as she rolled won her window. "I must say I'm surprised to see you here. Who's taking your class and running the school?"

"Actually, the school board called an emergency meeting and decided to close Hartney today, because so many of the students and their parents were planning to come to the inquest. News has spread in the district like wildfire that Carole had to appear as the defendant. However, what brings you to Brandon? You and your family take little interest in what's going on in Hartney anymore."

"Just let me find a parking space, and we'll go in together." Patricia was not about to share that she had come to save Margaret from doing anything foolish because of her misguided sense of responsibility. She glanced around for an available spot, quietly praying that her friend would heed her request. Patricia had determined to be seated right beside Margaret once they were in the courtroom.

During Carole's testimony, Patricia kept glancing nervously toward Margaret, seeing her friend was becoming fidgety. Her concern grew when, after restoring order in his courtroom, Judge Franklin announced, "Mr. Barclay and Mr. James, please approach the bench."

Following a few moments of discussion with the two barristers, the judge addressed the courtroom. "I want every one of you present this morning to take some time to think about whether you ever heard or saw any evidence of a letter written to Mr. and Mrs. Bertram Smith. Even the most inconsequential indication is of utmost importance, and I decree that it is your civic duty to bring forth that information in this court of law."

As an ominous silence descended, Patricia placed her right hand on Margaret's knee and reached with her left arm across her midsection. If Margaret had the slightest inclination of speaking up, Patricia's steadying deportment acted as a deterrent, and she continued to stare straight ahead.

Following an interval of at least ten salient minutes, when no one came forward, Judge Franklin turned his attention back to Carole. "You may step down, Miss Martin. I warn you that if anyone or anything ever brings it to my cognizance that you have lied in my courtroom today, you will face charges and be sentenced for perjury."

✳

As the end of June approached, Dr. Donahue's recommendations were no longer curtailing her nightmares, and Francine was once again disturbing the McGregor family's nocturnal peace. Patricia began to wonder why they were continuing to pay for counselling and was on the verge of cancelling the regular Saturday sessions. This latest Sunday morning, after being awakened three times, Patricia lingered in bed debating whether she would have enough energy to prepare dinner for the Yang family.

Glancing across the queen-sized bed, Patricia noticed that Daniel was already up and was probably in the kitchen starting breakfast. Turning over so the sun streaming through the window was not in her face, she thought she would allow herself a few more minutes of repose.

The next thing she knew, Daniel was sitting beside her and gently shaking her shoulder. "Pat, I have breakfast ready, and if we're going to make it to church, we'll have to eat soon. Are you feeling all right? Maybe we should forget about going this morning."

"That sounds like a good idea, my dear. I want to fry chickens and make a potato salad for dinner tonight, and after my interrupted sleep, I'm not sure I'll have the energy to get everything ready if we go. How come you don't hear Francine in the middle of the night lately?"

"As you know, if I'm sleeping on my good ear, I can't hear her. Although I must confess that sometimes as soon as I do, I turn over on my pillow, so I'm not lying on my deaf ear and just let you go to her. I don't understand why Dr. Donahue can't seem to help Francine."

"I agree, and perhaps this coming week we should make an appointment with her, just the two of us, and determine what, if anything, can be done. But, let's have breakfast, and then I'll start my potatoes. After I have them on the stove to boil, we'll go to the garden to pick lettuce. I think there's enough now to make my salad with cream that Trin and Sebio enjoy so much."

✳

As it happened, Jessica came to Patricia and Daniel's aid that afternoon when the Yang family arrived early. While the adults went for a walk over the rolling hills of the sheep pasture, the girls retired to Francine's loft for their customary chit-chat.

"Are you planning to spend time with me in town during the summer again, Francine? We can ride our bikes to the swimming pool in the afternoon and then help in the restaurant during the supper rush. Who knows? There might even be a decent movie at the theatre."

"I'm not sure I'll come to Souris this summer. It'll be too lonely without Hope to join us."

"Well, thanks a lot. What about being with me? Is that why you've been so distant and dreary lately? You hardly ever talk when the three of us are together, and I was hoping that when Hope permanently left for Brandon, you might remember that you and I are still friends. When Hope first went to live with her grandparents, I missed her too, but we have to move on and enjoy those who remain behind. Surely you don't plan to pine away the entire summer holiday. What a waste!"

"It's more than just losing Hope. Don't you get it, Jessica? Mr. Griffin is also leaving, and they'll be together every day. How can that not bother you?"

"I don't understand why it would bother me or you. I sometimes think that you dwell on other people and their lives too much instead of focusing on what's best for you. You're young, smart, and have a loving family with your whole life ahead of you. Sure, we'll miss Hope, but we can plan trips to stay with Cassandra and spent time with both of them."

"I wish I could be as lighthearted as you are, Jessica. Then maybe I could stop going to counselling, especially since Dr. Donahue can't seem to do anything about stopping my nightmares."

"What? What are you talking about? Who is Dr. Donahue, and how long has this been going on? Aren't you the sneaky one? Is that why you've seemed so secretive lately? Come on now, you have to tell me all about it."

As Francine apprised her friend about her sessions with Dr. Donahue, Jessica sat quietly. "So, now," Francine concluded, "I have to talk to Mother Pat and my uncles about her latest suggestion, that she try hypnosis."

"Well, if nothing else works, maybe it's the answer. Besides, it might be kind of cool, and she could learn all manner of things about you. There has to be some reason why you're so dependent on Hope but can't seem to trust that she's your friend. Look, Francine, I know that Hope is totally absorbed in her music, but she's still loyal and will always love us. The truth is, I feel sorry for Hope, because I think her life will be controlled by the gift God gave her. Instead of you being so needy of her, I believe that Hope will come to rely on you and me to keep a measure of balance in her life."

"Oh, Jessica you always seem so wise. But I haven't been completely honest with Dr. Donahue. I've only told her that my nightmares started last fall. I can't bear to tell her how they began when my parents died and how devastating my feelings of loss and abandonment were then."

"Good heavens, Francine, that's probably the reason you can no longer trust anyone, and you haven't even told her! Then it's a good thing she wants to hypnotize you and get to the real root of your problem. But you have to promise me that you'll talk to her about losing your parents before she tries hypnosis. Otherwise she'll know you weren't truthful with her."

"Perhaps, you should think about becoming a psychologist when we go to university."

"I've already decided that I'm going to study medicine. Eventually, I want to become an oncologist and find the cure for cancer. I think her mother's death is why our beautiful musical friend has let playing her violin take over her mind and soul."

✳

Seated at the secluded table in the restaurant she frequented every Saturday with Francine, Patricia ordered her usual mushroom-and-pepperoni pizza. After Margaret requested the same, the two women, who had been friends for decades, lapsed into an uncomfortable silence. For her part, Pat did not have the slightest intention of referring to what had transpired in the courtroom, but she knew Margaret would not let it pass.

At last, without looking Patricia in the eye, Margaret said, "To be honest, you were the last person I expected to see drive into that parking lot this morning. I know it was more than a coincidence that brought you to Brandon. And I fear that because of your presence, I may have made a grave mistake today that will come back to haunt me over and over again."

"I realized you would know perfectly well why I arrived, but I had to save you from yourself, Margaret, from trying to be responsible for Carole's actions. I don't believe for a minute that the presence of an explanatory letter would have prevented June and Bert's tragic deaths, although I suspect you do. When Judge Franklin issued his directive to the spectators, because that's what we were, all of us, you would have jumped up and said you might have heard the girls talking about a letter."

"But, that's just it. The more I think about it, and I can't get it out of my mind, I believe I could have. Maybe it wouldn't have changed the outcome, because although James and I visited often, even we had little idea of what went on in the Smith's home after Susan's disappearance. Still, look at the power it has now given Carole, because whatever happened, she got away with it. Good God, Patricia, she manipulated that situation in the courtroom and lied to the judge in front of everyone. Then, before she stepped down, did you see the look of victory in her eyes as she stared at the rest of us, as if we were lowly cattle?"

"You know, Margaret, I think you're making too much out of the level of success Carole might have experienced. Besides, even if you'd testified that you might have heard about a letter, Carole's lawyer would have argued that it was hearsay, nothing more than sheer speculation. Did you see the letter? Did you read it? So, if you feel honour bound to denounce yourself, could you please think of it as conjecture rather than as withholding evidence?"

"More like a sin of omission. You clearly have been away from teaching too long, my dear friend. You neither know nor have seen how manipulative Carole has become since Susan left the school, and she is now the oldest female student. I suspect after this debacle I shall have little control over her in the classroom and certainly none beyond its walls in the schoolyard. I wonder how Betty and Fred are handling their oldest daughter at home, because even at school, she lords it over her younger sisters and brother. Furthermore, I'm also concerned about the possible far-reaching effects for a conniver like Carole, since she has increased her sphere of success."

"I have to admit that Carole didn't seem to be such a manipulator when I had her in my classroom. Actually, it wasn't until she started to bully Francine last fall that I became aware of her controlling behaviour."

"I think that's when it started, when she became friends with Susan, and it went to her head. Little does she know that probably the only reason Susan befriended her was to have someone she could complain to about her parents not liking Robert Wharton. Once Susan was gone, Carole smartly stepped into Susan's shoes and began patronizing everyone."

"Well, what becomes of scheming Carole Martin is of little concern to me. I just know that your testimony would have caused serious recriminations between you and James, and it was strictly for you that I changed my plans this morning. Oh, Margaret, I'm so sorry. Since we enrolled Francine in the Souris high school, we've become more and more involved with the Yang family and their daughter Jessica's talented chum, Hope Harding. Finally, Francine has pals who appreciate her, and we seem to have forgotten our friends in our own community. I'd like to make amends and invite you and James for supper on Saturday."

"Thank you, Pat. I'm sure it would cheer James up to get out for an evening. He's always enjoyed teasing the McGregor twins, especially about their refusal to eat lamb. Can I bring an apple pie for dessert?"

*

It had been one thing to be confident about telling Dr. Donahue the truth when Jessica was offering her words of support, but it was quite another after Francine departed for home after Sunday dinner. How could she turn around now after nearly two months of counselling, and tell her pretty therapist that her nightmares had started years earlier? Why would she believe her? If she finally told her what had actually happened, how could she ever convince her that any other word she said was not a lie?

After brushing her teeth, Francine climbed into her cozy bed. Although she was tired, sleep was beyond her. Even the thought of disclosing that her night terrors had begun when her parents died sent Francine right back in time to that horrific morning when Auntie Helen and Uncle Scott, who she heard from less and less often, had sat her down to tell her that her mummy and daddy had been lost in the ocean.

For years, Francine had blocked everything from her mind, because it was the only way she could cope, and if she were to talk about it again, her feelings of desolation and abandonment would surely resurface. As she tossed and turned, she was already feeling overwhelmed. All the terror, all the pain, and all the hopelessness were returning along with her consuming sense of responsibility and guilt. How could she not blame herself? If only she had stayed at home instead of going to Margaret's to play, Mummy and Daddy would never have gone out in the boat. If only . . ..

In the midst of her anguish, Francine sat bolt upright as she experienced a flash of insight as bright as if someone had shone a flashlight in her face. That's what she had done when she came to live with her uncles. She had come to think of herself as a different individual who moved to Manitoba than the Francine Stonehenge who had been born and raised for the first six years of her life in Cavendish, Prince Edward Island. She had denied her past and had willed herself to become a separate, totally new person.

It had been the waiting, the terrible waiting. After Auntie Helen had explained, Francine had sat long hours at the window watching for her parents to come walking up the driveway to the Dwyer home. Even when the searchers found Jake's fishing boat, Francine did not believe that her mother and father had drowned. As day after day passed, and their bodies were not recovered from the briny depths of the Atlantic Ocean, she was certain they had disappeared.

As a five-year-old, Francine had told herself that her mummy and daddy had gone away and left her. They had abandoned her, because she had been naughty and did not clean up her bedroom before running off to play with her best friend. No amount of convincing by Helen and Scott, her teacher, the minister, or anyone within her sphere of friends would ever change her mind.

With the resiliency of small children, Francine eventually came to terms with living in her friend's home and had never returned to her own house. Helen deemed that it would be too painful for Francine to go home, and between her and Scott, they had retrieved Francine's clothing, toys, and pictures before closing the door on the Stonehenge cottage. When photos of her parents upset Francine so that she screeched every time she looked at them, Helen had carefully wrapped them in tissue paper for safekeeping before putting them out of sight.

During the day Francine appeared to be recovering. It was once she went to sleep that her torment resumed its revenge. Waking night after night to blood-curdling screams, Helen and Scott were beside themselves with trying to cope with Francine's recurrent night terrors. More often than not, they succumbed to giving her the sedative Dr. Brewster had prescribed.

When she came to live in Manitoba, Francine had thought that the silence of the prairie, devoid of the relentless sounds of the ocean, had healed her. Now with blinding clarity, she understood that she had detached the childish Francine so completely from whom she currently was that she debated whether she had recovered at all. Long years would pass before Francine would come to comprehend that she had to reconcile the two divergent components of her being if she were to reclaim her life.

✳

The next morning, Patricia awoke early, realizing she'd had an uninterrupted rest. As she started breakfast, she was pleased that Francine had slept well for a change. However, one look at her daughter's bleary eyes and slouching posture when she came into the kitchen, and she knew her assumption was wrong.

"Francine, you look exhausted. When I didn't hear you last night, I thought for sure you mustn't have had a nightmare. I seldom sleep so soundly that even when I don't come dashing to your bedroom, I still always know when you're having one."

"I didn't sleep at all last night, Mummy Pat. That's why I didn't wake you up with my nightmares. I don't know if I'll be able to stay awake in school today. Do you think I could stay home and just go back to bed?"

"That might be a good idea, but first tell me why you couldn't fall asleep," Pat said, pulling up the chair to sit down beside her stepdaughter.

"I told Jessica about my sessions with Dr. Donahue and how, although I really like her, she doesn't seem to be helping me. I confided to her that Dr. Donahue wants to try hypnotizing me to determine if she can dig deeper into the origin of my nightmares. She also explained that when she has me under hypnosis, she will suggest ways for me to stop one of my night terrors just as it's starting. Then I couldn't get things out of my mind, and I tossed and turned until I heard the rooster crow."

"What a relief it would be if you could nip your nightmares in the bud. Actually, just the other day, your uncles and I were discussing the likelihood of stopping your sessions, because they seem so ineffective. On the other hand, if Dr. Donahue believes hypnosis might work, would you be willing to try it?"

"I'll try anything right now, so I can have a full night's sleep. I'll telephone her office later and let her know that she can go ahead this coming Saturday. Now, can I please go back to bed?"

"I'll come tuck you in for the morning, and after lunch, I'll drive you to school for the afternoon classes."

Francine wrestled all week with whether she would at last confide the truth to Dr. Donahue. When Saturday morning arrived, she had decided it was easier to say she was sorry and to ask for forgiveness if she revealed the death of her parents during hypnosis.

It did not take Dr. Donahue long to put Francine into a trance, and Francine was surprised when she awoke and glanced at the wall clock that forty minutes had passed. "How do you feel, Francine?"

Stretching and then taking a deep breath before gazing intently into Dr. Donahue's eyes, Francine said, "I can't believe how rested I feel, like I've been in bed for hours. What did you do? Did I say anything surprising to you when I was under?"

With a chuckle, Dr. Donahue assured her young client that she had only induced a light state of hypnosis, and while Francine was in the dreamlike condition, Dr. Donahue had proposed that, on cue, Francine would awaken feeling relaxed and refreshed. Then, as she deepened the trance, Dr. Donahue had suggested that the next time Francine was starting to have a nightmare, she would come fully awake and move mentally beyond the dream before it caused her to experience any strong emotional response.

"That's all we'll do in this session. During our next three or four weeks together, when I hypnotize you, I plan to bring you to the point where you are able to effectively use self-hypnosis. I'll teach you steps to take you past your dream by reaching a heightened state of focused concentration. You can practice them before you go to sleep every night and again after you have awoken yourself at the beginning of your nightmare. Do you think you'd be receptive to this approach, Francine?"

"It sounds kind of cool. You mean I'll be able to put myself into a trance?"

"Yes, that's precisely what I'm saying. More and more psychologists are considering self-hypnosis as an effective method for helping their clients make positive changes in their lives and to feel relaxed and refreshed while practicing the technique. I've taught it before to several other clients, although not to anyone as young as you. Still, I suspect you're a quick learner, and I'm confident it can help you take control of your nightmares. By the way, I was so pleased to receive your message early in the week that you were willing to try hypnosis."

"Oh, you're welcome. Now I'm really glad I decided to consider it. Wow, once I become really good at self-hypnosis, I could practice it throughout my life, especially when I'm encountering negative or upsetting experiences, couldn't I?"

"Well done! You've already grasped the potential purposes for this self-induced technique. Now, before we wrap up, let's go back to your query about whether you made any unexpected disclosures during your trance."

"I'm not sure why I asked you such an unusual question. I have no idea what I meant. Thanks very much for allowing me to be your youngest client to become proficient with self-hypnosis. I'll see you next week," Francine said as she bounded out of her office before Dr. Donahue could stop her.

During their customary lunch at the pizza parlour and all the way home, Patricia was amazed by how enthusiastic Francine was about her initial session of hypnosis. This was the first time in her months of therapy that she had opened up to Patricia about her discussions with Dr. Donahue. Even though Pat had been saddened by Francine's obvious resolve not to include her, she had come to appreciate why an adolescent girl might want to withhold some of her private reflections and concerns from her stepmother.

Furthermore, it had occurred to Patricia that Francine was becoming very fond of Dr. Donahue. The day she remembered learning about the phenomenon called transference, she had dug out her old university textbooks. If Francine was redirecting some of her intense feelings for Hope to her therapist, Pat recognized that it could prove to be healthy, at least in the interim.

In three short weeks, Hope would be gone, and if Patricia was any judge of Hope's capability, she recognized that Francine's young musician friend was fated for greatness. Before long, her prodigious talent for playing violin would take her well beyond the confines of Brandon College and eventually to the great concert halls of North America and possibly even to Europe. As delighted as she was for Hope, Patricia understood that the promising virtuoso would have little time for others as she strived to master her destiny.

*

By the beginning of June, Trin and Sebio had posted notices that the Lingnan would be closed on Saturday, June 21, for a private function. It was after the Victoria Day weekend that Jessica had approached her parents with their proposal that Francine, Cassandra, and she would like to plan a surprise farewell party for Hope and for Mr. Griffin, since he was also leaving Souris at the end of the school year.

There was little chance that Hope would see any of the signs, nor would it be difficult to keep the pending festivity a secret, because Hope was only in Souris on weekdays. Her grandparents dropped her off in the mornings as the bell was ringing and were often back at the school before classes ended to whisk her back to Brandon for yet another lesson or rehearsal. Fortunately, Patricia had had the foresight to recommend that the young friends contact Hope's grandparents well in advance to confirm they were available for the upcoming event.

✳

Hope was surprised when her beloved grandparents suggested they drive to Souris after her late lesson on Saturday afternoon to have dinner at the Lingnan. She had hoped to begin studying for final exams, but she could appreciate that her grandparents had never had an opportunity to eat in the Yang family restaurant, and she was the one who was always telling them that the Yangs prepared the best Chinese food she had ever eaten.

It occurred to Hope that since it was a Saturday evening, they were unlikely to encounter Francine and her family. She realized she was being uncharitable, especially after all the fun times and delicious meals she had enjoyed in the hospitable McGregor home. Mother Pat had even asked Hope to address her in the same manner as Francine did, and Francine's identical twin uncles were so gentle and kind to the four friends, regardless of what havoc they might cause around the sheep or the farm.

Francine had become a problem that Hope was trying to avoid having to come to terms with, as her approaching departure grew nearer. During the past several months, Francine had become increasingly needy, and following Hope's success for the musical scholarship, she had been so morose and distant that she was a mere shadow of the vivacious person she had been when Jessica had introduced them.

Then, when Mr. Griffin announced he was leaving to become Hope's tutor, she thought Francine would unravel. It was as if Francine loved their popular teacher, perhaps even more than she doted on Hope, which was almost to the point of obsession.

Hope had lost track of how many times she had affirmed to Francine that she loved her, and yes, equally as much as she cared for Jessica and Cassandra. Still, it never seemed to appease her, and eventually Hope had become impatient with Francine's interminable need for affirmation. Why did she have to be so exasperating? Why couldn't Francine just believe and trust that, regardless of where her violin was fated to take her, Hope would always be loyal to her childhood friends, cherishing the memories of all their wonderful adventures together?

Gazing out the window as her grandfather drove into the parking lot adjacent to the Lingnan, Hope thought it strange that there were hardly any vehicles about for a Saturday. Almost every evening, the restaurant was filled to overflowing, and serious patrons knew to make a reservation. When Hope looked through the windows, she also found it unusual that the colourful Chinese lanterns, which were lit during the bright summer days as well as the early dark nights of winter, were not glowing.

"You know, Grandma and Grandpa, the Lingnan doesn't look like it's open. Do you want to wait in the car while I run and check?"

"No, it's okay my darling. Just let your grandfather park the car, and we'll come with you."

When the trio walked around to the front of the building, her grandparents held back while Hope went up the four short stairs to try the door. Much to her surprise, it opened, although the Lingnan was the quietest she could ever recall. Pausing until her grandparents joined her on the wide landing, Hope became aware of a peculiar silence.

A quick glance back at her grandparents' beaming faces gave Hope a hint of what was to come. Nonetheless, when she entered the restaurant, she jumped several inches into the air at the resounding cry of, "Surprise!"

The evening was an unequivocal success. Hope knew instantly that her three best friends had orchestrated the memorable event and had enlisted their parents to carry out the details. What astonished her though was that the restaurant was bursting at the seams with people she never considered would be in attendance.

To Hope's delight, her father and his new family had arrived from Winnipeg. Cassandra and her parents had come from Brandon, accompanied by her grandparents. Mr. Griffin and his parents, whom she met during the course of the evening, many of the professors from the school of music, and, most exciting of all, Dr. Burton, were present to enjoy the festivities.

Still, when Hope learned that she was invited for a sleepover at the McGregor farm with Francine, Jessica, and Cassandra, she knew that the most memorable hours of the party would be the private time with her friends. True to form, the foursome chatted, laughed, and shared secrets until the wee hours of the morning before finally succumbing to the sweet delights of sleep. With confidence, Francine practiced self-hypnosis and did not disturb anyone's repose.

On Sunday, following an early supper prepared by Mother Pat and Alice Webster, Hope said goodbye to Francine and Jessica before returning to Brandon with Cassandra and her parents. The four friends stood draped in each other's arms while George Jamison took pictures and promised to send each of them a photo. Sitting in the backseat with Cassandra, Hope was lost in thought, contemplating how lively Francine had been all weekend. At last, she seemed to have accepted that Hope was leaving but that their friendship would endure.

✳

After the inquest, if the dissension between the citizens of the

Hartney community had lessened, the Martin family had not been informed. In fact, Betty and Fred soon started to notice that those who had supported them were now giving them a wide berth. When they went into town, it was not uncommon for their friends to pass them quickly on the street with a terse salutation, and when they entered a restaurant, it was interesting how all conversation ceased.

On the way home one Wednesday afternoon, Betty turned to Fred. "Let's stop at the Perkins' and see what Ethel and Owen have to say about how we're being snubbed by the good people of Hartney. Can you believe it? We're one of the original families in the district, and suddenly, everyone's treating us as if we have leprosy."

"I'm not sure we should just drop in on Ethel and Owen. What if they've joined the ranks of those who believe Carole lied in that court-room and, to make matters worse, is now gloating about it everywhere? I'm convinced that's why no one will look us in the eye anymore."

"Good God, do you really think that's why all our neighbours have turned against us? If it's because of Carole, there'll be hell to pay. As soon as the bus drops her off today, I intend to drill her about what she thinks she's doing."

"Hmm . . . lately the more I've considered calling Carole to task, the more I'm beginning to realize she might be way beyond our discipline. Didn't you see how she stared down that judge? I could never have done that in a hundred years. I wonder where she learned to be so defiant and manipulative."

"Actually, I have to say that I've been aware of her insolence for quite some time. Of course, you haven't seen it, because you've invariably been blind when it comes to Carole. The other kids and I have always known she's your favourite."

"So, now you think you can hang Carole's lying and manipulation on me? Well, no damn way. I saw all the times you believed her stories and let her get away with mischief the younger children would never have even thought of trying."

"Listen to us! What is it about daughters that can cause so much strife between their parents? Because I believe Bert and June were likely having an argument about that wayward Susan when the so-called accident happened."

"What are you getting at, Betty? The judge ruled that June's death was accidental, and then, in his despair, Bert committed suicide."

"Didn't you even consider that they could have been fighting, and Bert pushed her? I've heard that June's head was split wide open and her neck broken. Seems a bit extreme for slipping and falling, don't you think? My bet is that in the midst of an almighty quarrel, Bert struck her, and she landed on the corner of the stove."

"Where do you hear rumours like that? For heavens' sake, don't you start distorting the truth, just like your daughter."

"Interesting how all of a sudden Carole is mine, but when you're bragging to your old cronies about how clever she is, she's 'your' daughter. Besides you have to admit that Bert had changed for the worse after Susan eloped. Even James Devonshire, his longstanding friend, no longer had anything to do with him."

"Thank God, we're home. I can't stand to listen to any more of your nonsense. You women must have too much time on your hands if you can think up tales like that!"

The minute the car rolled to a stop, Betty was out the door, slamming it with more force than necessary. Stomping into the house, all she could think was, *Men! They never have a clue about what really goes on in a home.* After she had put on the kettle for a soothing cup of tea, Betty reached for the telephone and dialled the Perkins' number.

It rang four or five times before Ethel finally answered. Following her salutation, Betty came right to the point. "I'm roasting one of my hens for dinner tomorrow night, and I want to invite you to join us."

Without a second of hesitation, Ethel said, "We have plans for

Thursday, and then on Friday we're leaving for the weekend to visit Owen's parents in Winnipeg. I'll give you a call when we get back."

If she did not know better, Betty would have thought she had just been given a brush-off. Pouring her tea, she sat down on her favourite chair in the living room. Surely Ethel had not spurned her invitation; the two women had been friends since grade school, and it was not uncommon for the two families to share a meal every one or two weeks.

What was going on? Was there any truth to the rumour that Carole was always bragging about how she had outwitted a judge and that no one could ever prove if Susan had given her the letter that might have saved her parents' lives? What everyone did know was Susan was in such a dreadful state that Robert had finally taken her to see a psychiatrist. Could Carole be so malicious that she was enjoying what was happening to a girl not much older than her, a young woman with whom she had been enthralled just last autumn when they became friends?

*

Midway through her telephone conversation with Margaret Devonshire the following Monday morning, Betty developed a sinking feeling in the pit of her stomach. Her mind played with what the principal of Hartney School was telling her. If Carole was such a clever student, what was motivating Margaret to make such an unusual request?

"I'm sorry, Margaret, but I don't follow you. Are you asking Fred and me to make arrangements for Carole to attend a different school in the fall? I've never heard of other capable pupils being removed from Hartney in all my years in this district. Of course, I know that a few troublemakers have been expelled, but you've just said Carole is a good student. So, why would we even consider it, since Fred's grandfather was instrumental in having that school built?"

Reluctant to delve any deeper into the issues she was having with Carole over the telephone, Margaret queried, "I know I haven't given you any notice, but would it be possible for you and Fred to meet with me at the school sometime this week?"

"I'll check when my husband has time and call you back."

Betty did not know whether to be angry or embarrassed when she replaced the receiver in the cradle. Regardless, her feelings came nowhere near the range of emotions that she knew Fred would experience and then would vent when he found out Carole was being kicked out of the school her great-grandfather had constructed.

Pouring herself another cup of coffee, Betty debated how she could bring up the subject. Fred had been strangely distant since their argument last Wednesday, so she had chosen not to say anything about Ethel's snub. And she had not dared approach Carole about what she was boasting about to her classmates. When Carole had come home that day, she had given her mother such a ferocious look that Betty turned back to the pudding she was stirring on the stove without saying a word. She'd had enough acrimony from Fred; she hardly needed to initiate a quarrel with an adolescent reminiscent of a pit bull itching for a fight.

By the time she had downed her third mug of strong coffee, and her hands were starting to shake, Betty knew she could never tell Fred. Suddenly, she rose from the table, went to the fridge to see if there were any leftovers for her husband's dinner, and when she decided that the beef stew and dumplings would be sufficient, scribbled a note telling Fred she had gone shopping.

Glancing at the wall clock, Betty figured she could arrive at the school just about the time Margaret was going into her office for her lunch break. She was not going to call and risk having the eavesdroppers on the party line hear any more about an appointment between the Martins and the school principal.

When she drove into Hartney, Betty decided to park across the street and use the back door. She quietly made her way up the rear stairway of the building and came around the corner just as the noon bell rang. She had little choice but to push open the principal's office door and step inside before the throng of students emerged from the adjacent classroom. Feeling like an errant student, she chose a chair in the corner and waited for Margaret to come.

*

"Oh, you frightened me, Betty. I seldom have a visitor to my office that I haven't sent, and I didn't expect to see you this soon. Is Fred planning to join us?"

"No. I've decided that if I want any peace in my family, you and I better get to the bottom of what's going on with Carole. You can't begin to believe how upset Fred would be if he knew I was here, or if he'd heard any of our conversation this morning. Good heavens, Margaret, surely you remember who built this school!"

When she was considering her options about what to do in relation to Carole, Margaret anticipated that she would hear all about the family link. One would have thought the Martin ancestors had mortared every single brick of the two-storey building. Still, she could hardly wait for the end of June, until Carole was out of her classroom, much less contemplate the daunting prospect of teaching her for another two years. The mere thought of Carole's increasingly spiteful behaviour toward the other pupils and even with Miss Swanson and herself gave her a persistent headache. Now sitting at her desk facing Betty, the pain in her frontal lobes threatened to reappear.

"I'm sorry, Betty, but this is my lunch hour, and I need to eat if I'm to have any energy for my afternoon classes. I was hoping to arrange a meeting with you and Fred on a Saturday morning or after school."

"You go ahead and have your meal. This is it for our meeting. You and I will work this out here and now, and not one word will ever be breathed about our discussion beyond the walls of your office."

Margaret was opening the bottom drawer of her desk when it flashed through her mind that Carole came by her obstreperous behaviour quite naturally. "Have you eaten, Betty? Would you like to share my ham-and-cheese sandwich?"

"The last thing I want to do is eat when you have implied that my eldest daughter is no longer welcome in your school. I don't expect for a moment that I'm going to change your mind, because, like everyone else in this community, I'm well aware of your stubborn streak. So, what you and I are going to do, Margaret Devonshire, is make damn sure we get our story straight."

Almost choking on her lunch, Margaret peered over her spectacles at the usually genial woman. It had to be a case of a mother lion defending her cub, since she had never before seen Betty so spirited. "Just what do you have in mind, Betty?"

"You are going to tell everyone that Carole is so smart that she needs to attend a school that can offer her the level of teaching and courses that will challenge her. In other words, that she is wasting her time and abilities in this two-room schoolhouse, where mediocrity is the rule. You cannot provide the instruction she requires, because you are teaching students in grades ranging from seven to eleven in your classroom. Her report card will reflect her high marks, and you will make a written recommendation to the school board that Carole should be transferred to the Souris high school."

"Now just a minute, Betty. I will not jeopardize my integrity, so if you expect Carole to score high marks on her report card, you need to advise her to get studying today for the final examinations. I'll write the recommendation that she needs to be moved to a larger school, but under no circumstance will I inflate her grades."

The two women glared at each other. The pain in Margaret's head had become a full-blown migraine, and she could not begin to fathom how she would return to her classroom in a few minutes. She did know that she needed time to compose herself, so she stood up. "You better leave. How you explain Carole's grades to anyone who asks will be up to you, but her report card will be based on her performance in every subject. You'll have a copy of my recommendation to the school board by the end of the week."

✳

The end of the school year could not come soon enough for Hope. She was so ready to leave Souris far behind. Following her stunning recital in Convocation Hall at United College in Winnipeg at the beginning of June, her grandparents had treated her to a weekend at the iconic Fort Garry Hotel. Then, after her brilliant debut, she had been fêted to a delectable dinner in the Palm Room. Much later, as Hope stretched her long legs between the luxurious silken sheets in the queen-sized bed, she vowed that regardless of wherever her violin might transport her, she would always travel first class.

At Hope's request, Michael Griffin had sought an arrangement with the school principal that, once she had written the five departmental examinations in the middle of June, she could be excused from further attendance. On Friday morning after the final exam, when Mr. Griffin had confirmed her early dismissal and that he could deliver her report card, Hope had taken Francine and Jessica into her confidence about not returning to Souris High School.

At first, she was concerned that Francine might burst into tears, but with effort, she had managed to maintain her composure. Jessica, as usual, was Hope's stalwart supporter and had eased the tension by placing one arm around each of her two friends as they strolled to their secret hideaway for their last lunch together.

"Since we have to become accustomed to being the 'two musketeers' anyway, we might as well get started early, right Francine? As much as we'll miss you, Hope, you can rest assured that no one will ever take your place in our little clique. Besides, remember we're all getting together for the July long weekend at Cassandra's."

Seeing the look of expectancy on Francine's face, Hope did not have the heart to explain that she would have to bow out of their much-anticipated weekend at the Jamisons' beautiful cottage on Clear Lake. The four friends had been planning the adventure from the moment Cassandra's parents had invited the other three girls to join their family in celebration of Hope's scholarship triumph.

Now as she sat eating her chicken-salad sandwich, Hope decided that once she was on the airplane, she would write each of her friends a letter explaining why she could not join them. She knew she was being cowardly, but if she mailed the letters as soon as she arrived in Montreal, they would be delivered in plenty of time for all of them, including Francine, to adjust to Hope's unexpected absence.

Since her stunning victory, Dr. Burton had been pressing her to practice longer and longer hours. Hope did not have the slightest notion that she had been commissioned for an orchestral solo to perform Mozart's "Violin Concerto No. 1" with the Orchestre Symphonique de Montreal on Dominion Day. When Dr. Burton had surprised her with the incredible news a week earlier, there had been no question about where Hope would be on the first of July.

Hope felt as if her life was becoming a whirlwind, and she could hardly sleep, much less try to study, after Dr. Burton's tidings. She had never travelled beyond the Manitoba border, and to be invited to perform in Montreal was a dream come true. She had imagined playing her violin in some of the larger Canadian cities, but to journey to historic Quebec made her head spin. With great restraint, she had not told anyone, not even Mr. Griffin, when her grandparents had arranged their flight for that Friday evening as soon as she completed her final exam.

From the edge of the evergreens' protective branches, Hope saw her grandparents' car turning into the driveway in front of the school. The minute she arose from their pine-covered cushion, Francine and Jessica were also on their feet.

"You're not leaving until the end of the day, are you?" Francine asked. "I thought we'd at least have all of lunch hour and the afternoon recess to visit with you."

"I'm sorry, but we have to leave for Winnipeg right away." Turning first to Jessica, Hope gazed into her deep brown eyes as if she was photographing a permanent image into her mind, before she enveloped her in an enormous hug. Then she grasped Francine by both shoulders, looked intently into her beautiful hazel eyes, and embraced her as if she never wanted to let her go. Before either of her friends could see her brimming tears, Hope uttered, "You two are the best! I love you both," and then she was gone.

In what seemed like a lifetime later, when they finally arrived at the Auberge de la Place Royale in the heart of old Montreal, Hope was still feeling a sense of abandonment almost as profound as when her mother died. She loved Francine and Jessica more than she had cared for anyone, other than her father during the past several years. In the depths of her heart and soul, she knew that she would never again have the chance to be so close to them again. Hope had had but a glimmer of what her life could become if she pursued her dream of a career as a concert violinist, but she was already aware it would be accompanied by more sacrifices than she would ever be able to count.

✳

Fortunately, Margaret was blessed with foresight. She had written her letter of recommendation to the school board, but before anyone would have the opportunity to read it, she was going to prepare

Patricia. When she arrived home on Wednesday afternoon, she telephoned her. "I have a matter of rather an urgent nature I need to discuss with you tomorrow. What time do you generally return from picking up Francine?"

"My, you do sound formal, Margaret. Is it something we can discuss while you help me prepare supper for you and James? Daniel is so besotted with the new barbecue he purchased a couple of weeks ago that he'll be delighted to cook hamburgers, while we make the salads."

"Thank you. That would be lovely. What if I bring dessert?"

Being invited out for supper, especially on a weeknight, was always a treat for Margaret. Her mother had been quite insightful when she had invariably advised her to pursue a teaching career because her cooking skills would never endear her to a man and their growing family. James was remarkably tolerant about some of her culinary disasters and took over the reins in the kitchen on weekends. On the other hand, Margaret was a whiz at baking, and as luck would have it, James had a very sweet tooth. As much as they had wanted children, perhaps it was a blessing when none arrived, since they might soon have tired of eating cookies and cakes.

As she gathered the ingredients for a double chocolate-layered torte, Margaret recalled the day Patricia rescued her from her doldrums in Hartney. Her friend had been true to her word and had James and her over for several meals since she had saved her from risking their relationship by coming forward at the inquest. Once James began to reconnect with the McGregor twins and returned to meet with his friends at the Hartney Pub, he started to shed his cloak of grief. Still, if he had ever had the slightest notion that Margaret might have professed to have knowledge of Susan's letter, their future would have unfolded very differently. And she knew that Carole would have manipulated the situation to make it look like it was Margaret who was lying.

By the time Margaret and James arrived, Pat had put the finishing touches on a delicious-looking potato salad and was tossing a variety of greens with tomatoes, red onions, and celery. Setting the torte on the kitchen counter, Margaret said, "Well, it doesn't look like you left much for me to do, and are those your famous beans I smell baking in the oven?"

"I know how tiring it is to try and keep the reins on the students this close to the end of the year. I've just steeped a fresh pot of tea, and I thought we'd sit on the patio while we discuss your exigent matter. Francine is out in the pasture with her uncles, so why don't you send James to look for them? Then we can talk without any interruptions."

Margaret summarized the current situation with Carole before handing the letter of recommendation to Pat for her perusal.

"This is an unusual decision for you, Margaret. In all your years as principal, I don't recall you ever expelling a student, much less advising that one voluntarily leave the school. But you certainly don't need my permission. I can just imagine how difficult Carole has been since her triumph in that courtroom."

"I'm not seeking your sanction, Pat. I want to warn you that Betty Martin will expect you to drive Carole back and forth to Souris. And in her typical fashion, to heighten the drama, she'll wait until the last minute to spring her request on you. I'm aware of the antipathy Francine feels for Carole, and I don't want to subject either of you to the strain of beginning and ending every school day in her company. You need to come up with a good reason why you can't transport Carole, so you're ready for Betty. I'm starting to realize that the apple doesn't fall far from the tree when it comes to manipulation."

"Good heavens, you're a planner, but what possible justification would I have to refuse?"

"I've given some thought to that too. I don't know if you're aware that the Town of Souris is trying to start a centre for seniors, and they're looking for a coordinator to run it from ten in the morning until four in the afternoon. When I heard about it, I immediately considered Alice Webster to be an excellent candidate. So many times over the years whenever we we've talked, Alice remarks that she wished she had pursued a career other than just being a mother and grandmother. She has much to offer, the hours are perfect, and I think that, with your suggestion and support, she might apply for the position. And there's your reason. Since you've offered to drive Alice, there's no room in the cab of your new truck for Carole."

Following a delicious dinner and enjoyable evening, Pat was getting ready for bed when it crossed her mind that perhaps not only Betty and Carole were adept at manipulation, although when it came to her friend, Pat preferred to believe Margaret was well versed in the fine art of gentle persuasion.

The summer holiday passed far too quickly, as every student was wont to complain, although not many parents agreed. But for young and old alike, it was one that could not be on its way soon enough. Before the end of June, the temperature had soared, and one scorching day followed another, until even the adults were joining their children at Hartney's outdoor pool to seek relief from the blistering heat. Farmers got at their haying, fencing, and gardening during the early hours of the day and later in the evenings, so they could have respite from the afternoon sun's relentless rays.

The invitation to spend the first three weeks of July at the Jamisons' cottage could not have been better timed, and it came about quite by accident. When Jessica and Francine received their letters from Hope, they decided to telephone Cassandra from the Lingnan to check if she had received the distressing epistle too.

"Mine came in the mail yesterday, and I was so upset I burst into tears. I couldn't believe that Hope would do this to us. All we've talked about for the last six weeks was what we were going to do on the Dominion Day weekend. But guess what? When Mummy heard how upset I was, she made a wonderful suggestion. I was just about to telephone to ask you two about it."

"Well, what is it?'" Jessica asked as Francine drew even closer, trying to hear Cassandra.

"Mum has invited both of you to stay the first three weeks of July with me and her at the cottage, rather than just the long weekend. Daddy has to go back to his office, but he can fend for himself while we have a girls' getaway."

"Wow, that's terrific! We'll let you know as soon as Francine and I clear it with our parents. It's a perfect summer to be at the lake."

✳

The first thought to flash through Francine's mind was how fortunate it was that she had scheduled her last counselling session for that coming Saturday. At the beginning of June, knowing that Hope's departure from Souris was imminent, Dr. Donahue had asked if Francine wanted to continue through July and August. Initially, Francine wondered if she could still control her nightmares with self-hypnosis once Hope was permanently gone, but then she decided that the summer might be the best time to test her skills.

The timing was perfect. Now she could spend three blissful weeks with two of her best friends at a cottage on one of Manitoba's most beautiful lakes. Francine had gone on trips with her uncles and step-mother during the past several summers, but this would be her first vacation without their supervision. Although she wished Hope could be with their foursome, she knew that any disappointment she would experience would quickly dissipate as she frolicked in the shimmering waves of Clear Lake with Cassandra and Jessica.

✻

Never had a summer vacation been so eventful. The invitations to perform at summer festivals across the country began to pour in following Hope's momentous week in Montreal. Naturally, her grandparents had expected to accompany her, but their plans suddenly went awry when her grandfather suffered a mild heart attack. Following an overnight stay at the Brandon General Hospital and an extensive battery of tests, Dr. Jamison discharged him home on the condition that he would not venture out of the city, especially with the oppressive heat.

When the telephone rang early on Sunday morning, Michael was surprised to recognize Dr. Burton's voice. "Oh, thank God you're home. How soon can you be ready to travel to Regina? Hope's grandparents have been confined to Brandon, and we're leaving right after the morning service at the chapel for an evening recital on the grounds of the legislative building."

Two hours later, relaxing on the plush cushions in the backseat of Dr. Burton's luxurious air-conditioned Mercedes Benz, Michael could not believe his good fortune. Not for one second had he ever harboured any ill will toward Hope's grandparents, but right from the beginning, he had known she would be touring throughout the summer with them. After moving into a small one-bedroom apartment at the end of June, he had already begun to envision a long boring vacation preparing the lesson plans for Hope's tutorials come September.

Now he was riding in style to the first performance on Hope's tour throughout Saskatchewan and Alberta. Dr. Burton had arrived within the hour to pick him up before driving to the college's chapel to meet Hope and her grandparents for an early lunch. When Michael opened the door to climb into the front seat, Dr. Burton said, "Thanks for your spontaneity, but you may as well get used to the back. Hope is prone to motion sickness, so she always rides up front with the driver."

On the outskirts of Brandon, Dr. Burton pushed the accelerator to the floor, knowing that they had lost valuable time when Hope had experienced a little meltdown in front of her grandparents after lunch. She had suddenly decided she didn't want to leave if they couldn't come with her, and it was only Michael's gentle persuasion that had overcome the crisis. Then when he had offered to ride in the back-seat, so she could enjoy the scenery, Hope consented and tearfully said goodbye.

As far as Ian Burton was concerned, Hope had a tendency to become emotional too quickly. Still, as he spent more and more time instructing her, he appreciated that her sensitivity was crucial to her impassioned violin performances. He did not want to interfere with the ardour with which his young virtuoso played, so he accepted that he was the one who would have to compromise and find ways to cope with her outbursts.

Michael's approach to Hope's little episode was not lost on Dr. Burton. He had suggested that she ride in the front seat, as if the thought had just occurred to him, before opening the door for her. Then, striding around the car, Michael had positioned himself behind the driver's seat, so he could easily maintain eye contact with her as they conversed during the nearly five-hour drive across the prairie.

And chat they did, until Ian began to feel as if he was but the chauf-feur. Michael had begun by asking Hope to tell him what she had enjoyed most during her trip to Montreal. She soon became animated and talked at length about her recital and then all the eventful excur-sions her grandparents and she had taken over the six days they spent in the beautiful city.

When Hope reached the end of her chronicle, Michael began to regale both of them with stories about his boyhood and being an only child growing up on the acreage with his parents. By the time he was describing how their rustic two-storey log home came to be surrounded by a circular grove of willows, his mother's favourite tree, and one of conifers because his father was partial to them, Hope was laughing so hard she was on the verge of tears.

Ian not only found Michael's narrative entertaining, he also began to get a sense that this young man had potential for assisting him with Hope's career well beyond being her tutor. Although Dr. Burton guesstimated an age difference of maybe eight or nine years, he became aware of the rapport between them. Whether it was that Michael appeared young for his age or that Hope was in many ways more mature for hers was of little consequence.

Touring together throughout the summer gave credence to Dr. Burton's supposition, and prior to classes starting in September, he requested that Michael join him for lunch on the last Friday of August.

"To begin, young man, I want to thank you for giving up your entire summer vacation to tour across western Canada with Hope and me. I've enjoyed your company, and I know Hope did as well, not to mention the calming effect you had on her. I realize we didn't give you much time to prepare your tutorials, although I have a strong hunch that you will not allow that to compromise Hope's instruction."

"No, sir, I would never permit anything to interfere with Hope's education. Actually, while you were teaching Hope, and when she was practicing for what I timed to be at least four hours on the days that we were not on the road, I studied the curriculum and developed a plan for each of the prerequisite subjects."

"Ah, during your interview, I had an inkling of your defined sense of responsibility, and I assure you, it was the deciding factor in hiring you. Now, after seeing how well you and Hope relate to each other, once she has completed her basic educational requirements, I believe there is another way for you to continue working with her. I would like to recommend that you enrol in business-management courses with the view of eventually becoming her musical agent. When Hope excels beyond the limited confines of Brandon College, she'll need a capable director to promote her career by booking concerts, negotiating contracts, and managing her finances. Even if it were my forte, which it isn't, I wouldn't leave my position with the college to do it."

"Thank you, Dr. Burton, for your vote of confidence and your recommendation. From the first time I happened to hear Hope play at a recital here in Convocation Hall, I believed she could become an acclaimed concert violinist. I'd like nothing better than to assist her in achieving her potential."

"Excellent, Michael. Since our timing is a little late, I'll arrange with Dr. Linton for your registration in Business Administration 101. Once you have your class times, please let me know, and we'll schedule Hope's tutorials and practices accordingly. Now, are you going to have a chance to see your parents before the beginning of the semester?"

"I'm driving home right after our lunch. In fact, I'd like to invite you to come with me for the Thanksgiving weekend, if you don't have other plans. After your obvious enjoyment of my stories about them, I believe you would enjoy meeting Jonathon and Marika. My mother loves to cook, and with this much notice, her table will be laden with her most delectable fare."

"Thank you. I'll take you up on your offer. I love autumn, and a trip to the country would be most welcome. Could you please confirm the invitation with your parents?"

✳

When Lindsay picked up the clamouring telephone, she was pleasantly surprised to hear Hope's voice. Her delight increased when her daughter's friend apologized. "Mrs. Jamison, I'm so sorry about not coming to Clear Lake for the Dominion Day weekend. To make matters worse, I've been on tour for most of the summer, and I've not had a chance to visit with any of my friends. I hope that Cassandra, Jessica, and Francine had an enjoyable time without me."

Any number of replies flashed through Lindsay's mind, not the least of which was that the three friends probably had had a better holiday because Hope was not in attendance. As anyone who had ever heard Hope play her violin was aware, she was a gifted young woman with prodigious talent. She was also more mercurial than the majority of girls her age, and during previous weekends when the Jamisons had hosted the foursome, there was always a level of tension, which had not surfaced throughout the entire three-week vacation at the beginning of July.

In retrospect, Lindsay had been the most pleased with how Francine had come out of her shell, believing that her behaviour might have been quite different in Hope's presence. Prior to Francine's arrival, Patricia had given Lindsay an update about her sessions with Dr. Donahue, sharing how she had taught her stepdaughter self-hypnosis as a means of coping with her nightmares. It was only rarely now that the family were awakened by her screams, and should they occur during her stay, Pat had counselled Lindsay about reminding Francine to practice her centring and relaxation techniques.

Neither Lindsay nor her mother, Alice, could comprehend what had caused Francine's nightmares to resurface. When the McGregor twins had initially brought their young niece to Manitoba from the Maritimes, their occurrence had been understandable, even expected, given the tremendous upheavals in her life. But why, after she had adjusted to her new home with a stepmother she clearly adored, friends who accepted her, and a different school, where she fit in, had they returned?

Perhaps the root of Francine's recurring nightmares was much deeper than they could possibly know. Perhaps she was being unfair, but Lindsay had an inescapable feeling that there was a correlation between their reoccurrence and Francine's friendship with Hope. For reasons Patricia, Alice, and Lindsay could not decipher, Francine had allowed Hope to overshadow her while at the same time becoming increasingly dependent upon her. At any rate, never once during the three weeks at Clear Lake were Francine or the other girls troubled by any disruptions of their sleep.

"Mrs. Jamison, are you there?" Waiting anxiously for Cassandra's mother to respond, Hope realized she had not asked her a question. But if her prolonged silence was any indication of her reception, how could she possibly make the request that had prompted her to place the call in the first place?

"Oh, I'm sorry, dear, I was lost in thought. In fact, I was remembering the delightful time I had with the girls. We sent Dr. Jamison home after the weekend, and Francine and Jessica stayed with Cassandra and me for the first three weeks of July. Now, what were you phoning about?"

Almost losing her nerve, but at the same time not wanting to feel silly for telephoning, Hope's words came in a rush. "I'm not sure I have the right to ask, but I feel so sorry I missed being with my friends at the beginning of summer, I wondered if we could all come for the Labour Day weekend."

Lindsay heard Hope's sigh of relief and realized how much courage it had taken for her to make her inquiry. "Cassandra and I were just talking this morning and wondered if you would be available to join your friends. You've been away so much that a relaxing time on the beach might be just what the doctor ordered. Since you can come, I'll ask Cassandra to confirm with Francine and Jessica. I know Daniel and Pat will want to drive Francine, so Jessica and you are welcome to make the trip with us. It'll be lovely to see you."

As she returned the receiver to its cradle, Lindsay became pensive again. Perhaps she had been unnecessarily harsh in her judgement of

Hope. How many other people overestimated her age because of her growing list of musical accomplishments? In all fairness, Hope was younger than Cassandra, yet she'd had precious little opportunity to engage in the usual adolescent activities of trying on make-up, changing her hairstyle, or giggling about boys. Instead, she was travelling from coast to coast giving violin recitals, entertaining enthralled audiences, performing on stages with a level of poise and passion that were well beyond her years.

✻

Listening to Betty's explanation about Carole being transferred to Souris High School and subsequently needing a ride brought a smile to Patricia's face. Margaret's prediction had been so accurate that, on the Thursday morning before the Labour Day weekend when the telephone had rung, she almost answered it by saying, "Hello, Betty, I was wondering when you were going to call."

Continuing to search for the elusive piece of the landscape jigsaw puzzle she always kept on the table beside the phone, Pat only half heard Betty going on and on about how Carole had to be presented with more challenges, so she could maintain her interest in school. If her neighbour had any thoughts that she would blindside Patricia with a commitment to transport her every day, she was about to be proven wrong. Her words, "So, Fred and I both really appreciate you picking up Carole on Tuesday morning," were scarcely off her lips when Pat interrupted her.

"That won't be possible. I've promised Alice Webster that she can ride back and forth with Francine and me from Monday to Friday. I guess you haven't heard that Alice was hired as the full-time coordinator for the new senior's centre in Souris."

"Of course, I know Alice got the job. I just can't imagine why she would want to start working for someone else at this stage in her life.

Doesn't she have enough to do on the farm and looking after Malcolm? Anyway, you have plenty of room in the backseat of your car."

"As it happens, I haven't been driving my car for quite some time. Daniel doesn't think it's very roadworthy anymore, so he put it up on blocks in one of the old sheds. And you know how men are! He still hasn't got around to fixing it, since I'm perfectly comfortable motoring about in our new truck."

"Well, surely Carole can squeeze into the truck cab with you. Neither she nor Francine need that much room for such a short distance."

"I'm sorry, Betty, but am I hearing you correctly? You're expecting me not only to jeopardize our safety, but also to break the law? I'll do neither, so as harsh as it might sound, I guess either you or Fred will be driving Carole."

"Come on, Pat, don't you think you're being just a bit dramatic? I can't believe you wouldn't help out your neighbour. My God, you've known Carole since she was a baby, and what's more, you taught her until she graduated to Margaret's class."

"I really don't have an option here, Betty. I will not squash four people into the cab of the truck."

"Don't tell me you're getting to be just like everyone else in this godforsaken district. I thought you would be above all that."

"I have no idea what you're talking about, and I'd better run. I was just getting my bread dough ready to put in the oven."

"You know perfectly well what I'm referring to, and you better not hang up on me like everyone else has been doing since that bloody inquest. What the hell has happened in this neighbourhood? Just who do you people think you are? If it hadn't been for Fred's family, the district of Hartney wouldn't even exist, and now the whole damn lot of you are treating us as if we've suddenly developed leprosy!"

"Look, Betty, I'm not interested in becoming embroiled in a debate with you. I have to get my bread baked in time for us to leave this afternoon."

"Oh, don't start using your fancy words on me, because you think I can't understand what you're saying. I'm not stupid, you know!"

"I hope you have a nice day, Betty. Goodbye."

As Pat kneaded the dough to fold into the three greased bread pans, she could not help but wonder what Betty might be thinking. No doubt she had added Patricia to the increasing list of neighbours who were spurning her and her family, even though Patricia had not intended to alienate her.

Or had she? Maybe that's exactly what she wanted, and would it not be sweet revenge for the way Carole had tormented Francine day and night for the first four months at the start of the school year? At some point, rot had set in within the confines of the Martin household, and Patricia knew it would be hard to stop as long as Carole was still living at home.

Cassandra could not believe her eyes when she interrupted her conversation with Jessica and glanced out through the back window. Lindsay had asked the girls to wait in the car while she went in to give her regards to Hope's grandparents before they left for the lake. It was the first time she had ever seen Hope go anywhere without her violin case in hand.

When her mother had apprised her of Hope's request for the foursome to spend the last weekend before the return to school at their cottage, Cassandra had been ambivalent. Although she had not discussed it with her mother or her friends, Cassandra had been happy that Hope had not spent the first three weeks of the summer with them. In the depths of her heart, Cassandra had always felt that everyone made too much ado over Hope. Cassandra had never particularly liked classical music, far preferring jazz, and lately, rock and roll, especially the more she listened to Elvis Presley. In short order, Cassandra had become fixated on the King of Rock 'n' Roll, and for the most part, her instrument of choice was the guitar, not a screechy violin.

Still, in all fairness, the moment she thought about Hope, Cassandra knew that her friend could make the strings of her violin soar. Whenever she performed what was becoming her signature piece, Massenet's "Meditation' from Thaïs," she would bring her listeners to the verge of weeping. Even Cassandra had to admit she often had tears in her eyes when Hope was playing yet another beautiful piece.

*

Jessica was delighted to see Hope and jumped out to give her a welcoming hug. Cassandra stayed rooted to her seat, still miffed that she could not ride up front with her mother. Had anyone ever witnessed Hope's feigned motion sickness, or was it just another means of her getting her own way? Chiding herself that she might be considered petulant, Cassandra flashed Hope a beautiful smile, saying she was saving her embrace until they arrived at their destination.

Once again, Cassandra could hear her father's words, that she was a natural-born lawyer. Regardless of how hard she tried, she could not curb her tendency to question and analyze every single circumstance of her life, even when spending the weekend with her three best friends at the lake. Nonetheless, she considered her cherished father's assessment to be valid, and she knew she would follow in her uncle's footsteps. Cassandra was already reading Uncle Robert's law books, aspiring to his seat on the Manitoba Court of Queen's Bench in Winnipeg.

While Jessica and Hope launched into enthusiastic chatter, Cassandra lapsed into thought. She could see her mother continuing to glance back at her through the rear-view mirror, so she closed her eyes and pretended to be asleep. She was tired, since Jessica's parents had stayed late after coming for supper to deliver Jessica to Brandon the previous night, so Lindsay and the girls could be off to an early start in the morning. Naturally, she and Jessica had been awake until the wee hours chatting and laughing, finally bringing Lindsay to the door of the bedroom to settle them.

As she had so many times before, Cassandra marvelled at the increasing depth of the foursome's friendship. Since she had been introduced to Jessica and Hope over two years ago, she had become as fond of them as she had always been of Francine. Although Cassandra had her fair share of school chums, a remarkable bond had readily been forged among the four girls. She often wondered if it was because each of them was a single child that they had so quickly come to love one another as profoundly and as permanently as any birth sisters. Even though she suspected her occasional resentment stemmed from the "green-eyed monster," Cassandra was as enamoured with Hope as was anyone who had been blessed with the good fortune to make her acquaintance.

✳

As it happened, Francine was not the only one to question why, on Thursday, they had driven all the way to Dauphin to visit Terence Rose. When Mother Pat had proposed the journey, Francine had been resistant, because she wanted to be at Clear Lake as early as her friends. But how could she not appreciate why her stepmother would want to see her father, when she explained she had not been home for more years than she could remember? Especially when she had promised that they would leave at the crack of dawn on Friday to be waiting at the cottage door before the rest of their party arrived.

Patricia had hesitated to tell Francine much about her own parents, although eventually, she had disclosed to Daniel that first her and then her mother had simply walked away from the three-bedroom bungalow, never to return. Years earlier, when her brother had telephoned demanding that Pat send their mother home, she could not believe her ears. She was dumbfounded that her mother had come out of her catatonic dependency and had mustered the courage to leave, even though neither Patricia nor, as far as she knew, any of the family had ever heard from her again.

Finally, Pat decided that she must make the trip back to her ancestral home. After all, Terence was her father, and he was well into his eighties. If she did not go to see him before he died, she would regret that she had not at least attempted to make peace with the man who, even though it had been rather surreptitious, had facilitated her teaching career.

Still, it was with considerable trepidation that she, after requesting that Daniel and Francine wait in the truck until she motioned to them, walked up the decaying steps to ring the doorbell. Suddenly, she remembered that her father hated the sound of the chimes and had disconnected them when she was a young girl. He had not been much better with a knock on the door, but she certainly was not going to just step into the dilapidated house.

Following three loud raps on the paint-stripped wooden door, Patricia pounded with more force. She saw a faint light coming from the kitchen, and the noise of a radio or television convinced her that someone was inside. Then, as she leaned closer to the door, her nostrils were suddenly assailed by the most unbelievable stench. What could cause such a foul smell? As she was debating whether to make a hasty departure, she heard a voice.

"Who's there? What do you want?"

Taken aback by the gruffness of the voice, she gulped before answering with as much bravado as she could summon. "It's me, Patricia, your oldest daughter."

As the minutes passed, Patricia began to wonder why she was

feeling as if she was once again twelve years old.

"You don't have to tell me that Patricia was my eldest daughter," he replied finally. "I might be old, but I'm not daft. And if my memory serves me right, I considered that you were dead and buried alongside your mother after the two of you abandoned me and the rest of the family."

"I'm very much alive, and I want to come in." With more confidence than she felt, Pat pushed open the door just as Terence lumbered down the hallway to the foyer. He walked with the aid of a cane, his hair was long and wild, and he looked like he had not shaved or washed for years, but his eyes were bright and piercing.

"Well, well so it is you. Just what the hell do you want?"

With great effort, Patricia controlled her urge to retch from the fetid smells emanating from the man and the house. How could a human being live in such filth? Now what was she going to do? She realized instantly there was no way she could bring Daniel and Francine into the dregs of her father's existence.

Without another word, Patricia turned on her heel, bolted to the truck, opened the door, and climbed into the cab. "Drive away, Daniel. I want to get out of here now, please."

Daniel would have driven Patricia across Canada without inquiry, and he immediately responded to her unusual request. He headed back to Highway 10, and when she lapsed into a pensive silence, he continued to travel the approximate forty miles through Riding Mountain National Park until they reached Wasagaming. Francine had never seen Mother Pat so distracted, and taking her lead from her uncle, she chose not to question her. Entering the town, Daniel spied the rustic Clear Lake Lodge and noticed that they still had a vacancy. "What do my two favourite ladies think about spending the night in this quaint country inn?"

When Lindsay drove into the driveway on Friday morning, she was surprised that Daniel's new bright-red Ford truck was parked by the grove of caragana trees on the left side of the cottage. With a closer look, she determined that the vehicle was vacated and assumed that the McGregor family had chosen to take an early morning walk along one of the many hiking trails surrounding their picturesque property.

The girls had bailed out of the car, and as Cassandra was giving Hope her promised hug, over her shoulder she spied Francine and then Aunt Pat and Uncle Daniel emerging from the copse of conifers.

Francine burst into a run and was headed straight for Hope when she recalled one of Dr. Donahue's suggestions. Instead, she turned toward Cassandra and hugged her. "It's great to see you. Thanks for organizing this weekend."

"Hey, I'm always the first one you hug, Francine," Hope said. "What's happened to you?"

"Remember how you've changed, and just be you," Cassandra whispered into Francine's ear.

Francine turned to Hope and gave her a warm embrace. "It's terrific you could join us this time. The four of us are going to have an awesome visit. There are so many exciting things to do at the lake. Hey, Mummy Pat and Uncle Daniel, come and see who's here."

After everyone had extended their greetings, Patricia and Daniel offered to help carry the innumerable bags of groceries, suitcases, pillows, and blankets into the cottage. "The young ladies can be responsible for all their personal effects, but I could sure use a hand with all the food," Lindsay said. "I think Cassandra asked me to bring enough to feed an army."

"I can certainly understand why. There's something about being outdoors in the fresh air, especially when you're splashing about in the water that stimulates the appetite. This is a beautiful location close to the lake yet surrounded by trees to give you some privacy." Pat replied.

"Once we've trucked everything in, I'll give you the grand tour. George's father built the cabin years ago, and we love spending time here so much that we're always fixing up one thing or another around the property. You're welcome to stay and have a bite to eat with the girls and me."

"Thanks for your gracious offer, but we'll be on our way. We're planning to return home this evening, but there's something I need to do before we leave. What time do you want us to pick up Francine and Jessica on Monday?" Patricia asked.

"Oh, that won't be necessary. George is coming up on Sunday morning as soon as he finishes his rounds at the hospital, and with the two vehicles, we can drive everyone home."

✻

Walking back to the truck, Daniel slipped his arm around Patricia's waist. He waited until he had driven around the circular road in front of the rustic two-storey cottage before he said, "So, my darling, have you decided what you want to do about your father?"

The previous evening, Patricia had held her peace as they checked into the lodge, found a restaurant, Francine had gone into the adjoining bedroom, and still Daniel had waited. Finally, when they were seated on the small balcony off the master bedroom, Pat shared the reason for their abrupt departure from her father's house on the outskirts of Dauphin. "I just couldn't have either Francine or you see my father in his dreadful condition. It was all I could do not to vomit with the stench."

Reaching for her hand, Daniel remained silent, knowing that when Pat was ready, she would continue. "What am I going to do, Daniel? Now that I know how he's living, I can't just leave him in that appalling state until he succumbs. He's absolutely right. I did abandon him and my siblings. Once I found my teaching position, I never bothered to return. Oh, I sent Christmas cards every year, and when I didn't hear back, I suppose I just assumed they had all scattered like me and my mother. To be honest, it was only recently that I even thought about my father getting old. In my mind, he was still the same age as the day I'd made my long-awaited departure."

"I wonder if most of us don't have a tendency to consider that a person remains the same once we no longer see them. We get busy in our own lives and seldom think about what's happening for those we've left behind."

"Yes, I suppose that's true, but now I have an obligation to help him. Can we please drive back to Dauphin and see what we can do to get him out of that horrible environment?"

Daniel's brow creased with concern even as he exited Wasagaming and turned right onto Highway 10. He had no idea where his wife was suggesting they would take Terence, but he suspected the butterflies in his stomach were more for Patricia than for him. How likely was a man in his eighties, who was content to live in his own pigsty, to want help from a daughter he had not seen for decades? Could they even persuade him to bathe, shave, and make himself presentable? Even if they could convince him to leave, where would he go?

"You've become very quiet, Daniel. I can tell from the pensive look on your face that you're trying to figure out how to say something crucial to me."

"You know me so well, my dearest. As it happens, I'm trying to decide how best to caution you that your father is probably going to resist all your best intentions. I recollect reading an enlightening statement in a magazine once that went something like this: 'Help is defined by the person who needs it, not by those who want to give it.' At the time, I didn't really understand what it meant, but since you've described your father's situation, I think I might have an idea what it was conveying."

"You never cease to amaze me, my darling husband. You give full meaning to the notion that 'still waters run deep.'"

Daniel chuckled. "It's all my years of roaming about in the pasture with the bleating of my sheep the only sound I would hear for hours at a time. Such profound silence gives a man plenty of time to think and to find peace in his life."

Sliding closer to Daniel, Patricia rested her hand on her husband's leg. "I never considered for a second that my father might not want me to rescue him. I was just going to rush in and save him from his feculence. Thank you for sharing your perspective about such a possibility."

"No, I thank you every day for coming into my life. Before I met you, I seldom expressed any of my deepest thoughts or feelings to anyone. Yes, to my sheep but never with another human being, especially not one as beautiful as you."

✳

By Friday afternoon, Betty still had not mentioned to Fred that they would be driving Carole to Souris every day. She realized that as long as the weather was decent, she would be expected to make the trips, but as soon as the snow flew, her husband would be required to take on the interminable task, because she would not feel confident about being on the road. She was sitting at the kitchen table pondering the situation when Carole burst into the house.

"Hi, Mum. Here's the last of the raspberries. There's hardly any left on the vines. Besides, it's getting really hot in the garden. The other kids wanted to stay outside to play hide-and-seek, but I've decided to come in and read. What are you looking so glum about?"

"Don't be glib with me, young lady. You're the reason I'm going to have another fight with your father. As it turns out, you can't get a ride with Francine, so your dad or I will need to drive you twice a day, and I'm trying to think of a way to tell him. Although he doesn't let on to you, he doesn't really understand why you can't just stay at Hartney School."

"Well, I wouldn't want to ride with that snot-nosed little punk anyway. Ever since she made a couple of friends at that two-bit school in Souris, she walks around with a swelled head."

"Watch your mouth. That's exactly why Margaret Devonshire doesn't want you back in the fall. Do you have any idea what it's going to cost us in time and money to drive back and forth to Souris all the time?"

"I have the solution that will save your precious time and cut the expense in half. I could get my licence and drive myself in the station wagon or even the truck."

"I don't need your quick fixes for every problem. I thought you came in the house to read, so get about your own business."

Pouring another cup of tea, Betty considered that Carole might have a point. She was old enough to get her driver's licence, and she'd been operating the small John Deere tractor in the fields for years. Surely Carole could pass the test, and if she could get a hold of Mr. Gibbs to arrange an appointment for tomorrow, she would be ready to drive herself to school. Then, rather than say anything to Fred and ruin their weekend, she could present the resolution as a fait accompli on Tuesday morning.

"Carole, get your butt out here this minute. I need to talk to you, and grab the telephone book from the front desk."

"Could you please make up your mind, Mother? One minute you're sending me to my room, and the next you're yelling at me to come to the kitchen."

Hearing her tone resounding in her daughter's strident voice, Betty had a sudden flash of insight. Perhaps it was true what so many of their family and friends said, that of her four children, Carole most closely resembled her. Certainly, Carole was a fast thinker, as was Betty, and maybe what Margaret and her cohorts considered to be manipulative behaviour was Carole and Betty's propensity to comprehend situations quicker than others.

*

Pulling into the Esso station on the northern edge of Dauphin, Daniel turned off the engine. "Let's have coffee and a bite to eat before we go to your father's. From what you've described to me, we would hardly want to eat or drink anything in his house."

"Even given the little I saw, I can't imagine how he could or, for that matter, what he would possibly have to consume. Maybe after lunch, we should stop at the store and pick up groceries to take with us."

As they lingered over a second cup of coffee, Daniel made a silent vow that regardless of how disgusting a scene they might encounter at Terence's house, he would curb his tendency to overreact. He had always been the more meticulous of the McGregor twins, and over the years, in his chosen role as the housekeeper, he had become increasingly fastidious about the cleanliness of their farmhouse. Since Daniel no longer did much of the cooking, with Patricia delighting in her newly acquired culinary skills, he paid even more attention to maintaining a scrupulously tidy and spotlessly clean environment.

Although Darrin had willingly installed a shower in an add-on attached to the back door and had agreed that it was an ideal solution for keeping the barnyard smells out of the house, he frequently forgot to make use of it. For years, he had come in the front door, removed his boots, and gone upstairs to the bathroom to clean up, and all too often, he reverted to his usual pattern. On those occasions, Daniel was careful to provide gentle reminders, because he did not want his twin to feel any more left out than he already did since Patricia had become his wife.

Even as Daniel stood outside hammering away to gain entrance, a foul odour assaulted his nostrils and made him retch. Patricia had decided to linger behind on the cracked sidewalk overgrown with weeds, remembering that her father had always been more hospitable to men.

"Who are you, and want do you want?" a voice bellowed from within, accompanied by the sound of several bolts being released. "When the hell are you meddling people from town going to leave me alone?

No amount of resolve could have prevented Daniel from uttering, "Dear God in heaven!" when the door was finally opened.

Hearing the stranger's exclamation, Terence's response was immediate. "Let's hope so, because He sure as hell is not here. Don't tell me that my useless daughter has come back and brought you along to get into my home. I don't know why she's suddenly so anxious to come back after all these years, but I don't want a damn thing to do with her."

It was instantly obvious to Daniel that Terence had no trouble with his vision or his mental faculties, despite his predilection to live in abject filth. As Daniel was deliberating on how necessary the cane was to the old man's mobility, Terence raised the roughly carved stick and shook it dangerously close to Daniel's head. "Now just a minute here, Mr. Rose. Lower your cane. We have not come to harm you."

Patricia was beside Daniel in a flash. "Look, Dad, we've brought you some groceries, and we just want to come in to help you put them away."

"I don't need your bloody charity. I can pay for my own food, and the last thing I want is another do-gooder trying to help me."

When Patricia advanced up the decrepit front steps, Daniel, against his better judgement, slipped behind Terence into the house. Even with his handkerchief pressed firmly to his nose, the fetid air was suffocating, and he felt as if the walls were encroaching on him. Stumbling to retreat, he ran straight into the heavy end of Terence's cane.

"Just where the hell do you think you're going? You're damn well trespassing, and you better get your ass out of here before I beat you to a pulp."

Raising his arms to deflect the surprisingly strong blows, Daniel made a hasty exit. Grasping Patricia's arm, they raced back to the truck.

"I'm glad you were spared from seeing how your father is living. I had a full view of the kitchen, living room, and bathroom, and I've never seen such an almighty mess in all my days. Yet, he appears to be of sound mind and body, the way he was swinging that cane about, so it would seem he's choosing to live in that environment. I've never been in a barn or a pigpen that smelled that bad, and it's so cluttered I'm surprised he can still walk around. It's obvious he doesn't want help from anyone, not just from you. I just don't know what we could do."

As they drove away, both became lost in thought. It occurred to Patricia that if she was incapable of helping her father, she could contact the Dauphin Public Health Department and arrange for a nurse and an inspector to do an assessment of his situation. What did she have to lose? He could not be any more furious with her. Whatever had compelled her to become involved with him after so many years?

Daniel, on the other hand, was convinced that the place was nothing but a foul-smelling tinderbox, and the only possible solution was to burn the house and everything inside to the ground. How could one of God's creatures choose to exist like that? It was a rhetorical question he would never ask, nor would he ever articulate his true feelings to his wife.

*

The first hour had yet to pass, and each girl sensed their four days together were going to be even more special than Hope's surprise fare-well party at the end of June. The moment they said their goodbyes to Patricia and Daniel, they gathered their belongings and dashed to the large den at the rear of the cottage. Not for the first time, Lindsay congratulated herself for having had the foresight to redecorate the spacious area and turn it into a bedroom complete with two bunk beds.

Within twenty minutes, the foursome reappeared resplendent in colourful bikinis and sun hats, beach towels draped over their shoulders. Lindsay was on the verge of preparing lunch. "Well, my lovelies, you all look exquisitely beautiful, but aren't you going to eat before you beguile every unsuspecting young man on the sandy shores of Clear Lake?"

"Thanks, Mum, but we decided we would just grab a burger or something at the corner confectionery later. None of us is really hungry, since we all had a big breakfast."

Watching the four friends stroll toward the beach with arms linked, Lindsay realized that the girls were maturing into comely young women. At that moment, she spotted the weather vane in her peripheral vision, and it occurred to her that the foursome could represent the four points of a compass, since each one of them exhibited discernible characteristics of a specific direction of the horizon.

Lindsay returned to the cottage, made a sandwich from the leftover chicken she had roasted for dinner the previous evening and a glass of iced tea before, then grabbed her latest novel to read while sitting on the deck. Suddenly, she was pleased that Hope had mustered the courage to call her and arrange the weekend. As enjoyable as Francine, Jessica, and Cassandra's summer retreat had been, their circle of friendship was incomplete without Hope.

Instead of opening her book, Lindsay returned to her dawning analysis that each of the girls could signify one of the four corners of the earth. Beyond a doubt, Francine represented north, with Hope clearly being south. One never knew what a north wind would blow in or what to expect from the south. Although polar opposites, both were temperamental and changeable, perhaps because each had experienced tremendous loss at a very early age.

On the other hand, Jessica and Cassandra were balanced and as predictable as the sun rising in the east and setting in the west, which respectively denoted their position on the compass.

As she continued to explore the comparison of each girl to a compass point, Lindsay realized with a start that she was long overdue in returning to her chosen profession. She had just completed all the course work for her master's in psychology when her physician had confirmed, after she had been trying for years, that she was pregnant. She had barely started the research for her thesis when she began to experience morning sickness, which persisted throughout most of the day. Then, instead of abating by the end of the first trimester, her nausea and frequent vomiting continued until her obstetrician had recommended that she postpone writing her thesis until after the baby had arrived.

However, once Cassandra was placed in her expectant arms, Lindsay forgot all about research or writing. She had decided to breastfeed their beautiful daughter and soon became so wrapped up in mothering that the rest of the world could pass by without her noticing. Besides, George was so busy in his burgeoning practice that if she resumed her thesis, a stranger would care for their long-awaited infant.

Lindsay did seek out her adviser at Brandon College once Cassandra began grade one, but too much time had elapsed, and she would be required to take additional coursework before she could obtain approval to proceed with the subject she had chosen for her thesis. It seemed too complicated at the time, and since she enjoyed being a full-time housewife and mother, she put the completion of her graduate degree on the back burner.

Earlier that afternoon, when the four girls strolled down to the beach, Lindsay had understood that until George arrived, and probably even then, she would don her usual cap of chief cook and bottle washer for the entire weekend. Her brief psychoanalysis of the foursome had triggered in her mind that the time had come for her to get on with her own career. As she disappeared into the kitchen to begin preparations for dinner, Lindsay resolved that Hope would not be the only one of their current company entering the hallowed halls of learning when classes began at Brandon College in mid-September.

*

From that first morning, when Carole roared her father's half-ton truck into the parking lot of Souris High School, she had intended to make a statement. If anyone in that two-bit town thought for one minute that she could be treated like a country bumpkin, she would soon set them straight. She had bested a judge and would not be averse to taking on any student, teacher, or, for that matter, the principal. After all, she had driven Margaret Devonshire to distraction, until she had been forced out of her hick school in the middle of nowhere.

Climbing down from the truck, Carole looked around with disdain at the pupils assembled in pockets in the schoolyard and clustered by the front door waiting for the bell to ring. And who should be standing first in the line but her old nemesis, Francine Stonehenge. However, unlike her days at Hartney, was she actually conversing with someone? On closer observation, Carole saw that the other girl had slanted eyes, dark hair, and dark skin. Good God, could the friend Francine had gone on and on about been that "chink" Carole had seen at the Lingnan Restaurant in town?

Carole pushed her way through the gathering horde and burst up to the door. "Well, well, so I do know someone in this school. If it isn't my old pal, Francine, who I haven't seen in ages. And where are your manners? Aren't you going to introduce your chum, although now that I think of it, I'm sure she has waited on me many times in the Chinese café, haven't you?"

The school bell began to toll, and Francine gently urged Jessica to go through the door ahead of her. Then she turned to Carole. "Nice to see you again," she replied in her most casual voice. "I'm sure we'll have a chance to catch up later."

Instantly, Francine realized her mistake in not having taken Jessica into her confidence on the weekend. Mother Pat had told her that Carole had transferred to Souris High School, and although she refused to transport her every day, she had warned Francine to be on the alert once she arrived at school. Mother Pat had specifically asked Francine to warn Jessica regarding Carole's tendency to be manipulative and controlling, so she did not become engulfed in her obnoxious behaviours.

But the foursome was having such a terrific time that the last thing Francine had wanted to do was introduce the subject of Carole Martin. Then, even though Jessica and Francine had ridden home with Dr. Jamison, both had climbed into the backseat, and lapsed into a subdued silence, each savouring the memories of their bonding weekend. Francine could not bear to mention Carole's name, much less recall the torment she had suffered at her hands.

Now as they were putting their belongings in the adjoining lockers, Jessica was intent on finding out Carole's identity. "Who was that? I don't like the way she looked at me, nor did I appreciate the reference to me serving her. She mentioned it in such a derogatory way, as if she was superior to me."

"Shh . . . don't let her know we're talking about her. She likes nothing better. We'll both stay in the classroom at recess, and then I'll walk home with you at lunch to fill you in. Why don't we hurry now and claim two desks at the front close to the teacher's desk? From what

I remember, Carole will sit in the back row, where she can cast her malicious eyes over everyone in class."

✳

Carole had used the word "chink" one when her father had been within hearing distance, and he had become furious, telling her to never let him hear her use it again. If there was one person whom she respected enough to curb her tongue, it was Fred Martin. Still, he could not control what she thought or what she said in his absence, and already she knew precisely how she would harass Francine and her precious friend.

From the moment her mother had shared that Patricia McGregor had refused to drive her back and forth to Souris, Carole had begun to plan her vendetta. She had always been convinced that the prevailing ill will in the community toward her family stemmed more from the rampant rumours circulated regarding Francine's abrupt departure from Hartney School than from the possible existence of Susan's letter. Carole could imagine how the neighbours' tongues would wag once it became common knowledge that she could not even garner a ride from her former elementary schoolmarm.

Although the rest of her family was distressed by how they were being alienated in their community, more and more, Carole was enjoying the notoriety. Steadfastly, she was learning that unfavourable attention was preferable to none at all, and with her heightened awareness in the district, her feelings of personal power were beginning to escalate. Carole was becoming tenacious about advancing her reputation as being a "nasty piece of work," because she believed she could exercise control over those around her if she was known and feared.

✳

When Patricia contacted the Dauphin Public Health Unit, she was initially perplexed by the vague responses she received. Then, recognizing that she was most likely conversing with a receptionist, she asked to speak with one of the nurses.

"The only one in this morning is Miss Wilson, and she seldom goes out on calls, so she wouldn't know Mr. Rose."

"In that event, may I please speak to the head nurse or whoever is in charge?"

"We don't have a head nurse. Miss Wilson is the senior nurse of the health unit, but I already mentioned that she's not familiar with Terence Rose."

"Given that you know Mr. Rose's Christian name, surely the nurse in charge is aware of him. Now, if you don't mind, could you please put me through to Miss Wilson?"

After a lapse of several minutes, a brisk voice came on the line. "I'm the nurse in charge. Who wants to know about Mr. Terence Rose?"

"As I told the receptionist, I'm Patricia McGregor, and Terence is my father."

"I've been the senior nurse in the Dauphin Health Unit for nigh on to twenty years, and this is the first I've heard that he has a daughter. I know he has a son, but I haven't spoken to him for a long time."

Without delving into the past with too many of the vital details, Patricia eventually convinced Miss Wilson that she was Terence Rose's prodigal daughter. Miss Wilson's retort confirmed Patricia's suspicion that whatever had propelled the senior nurse to her administrative position, it was certainly not her sensitivity or her impeccable communicative skills.

"And just what brings you back now?"

Instead of responding to her abrupt question, Patricia chose to express the purpose of her call. "Would it be possible for you to arrange for one of your unit nurses and the health inspector to make a home visit? My husband and I stopped to see him on the weekend, and we were appalled by his living conditions."

"For your information, Mrs. McGregor, we at the Dauphin District Health Unit, and the entire town, are only too aware of the incredibly gross environment in which Terence Rose elects to live. He is, in fact, a public health and, most definitely, a fire hazard. Some time ago, when he still had distant neighbours, and they registered a complaint, I sent in my most experienced nurse with our male health inspector, and they were both run out of the house at knifepoint. When our medical director, accompanied by the inspector and two officers from the local RCMP detachment, arrived, they were greeted at the door and told to get the hell off his property. Finally, our town council voted that since your father's house and property are not within the town's jurisdiction, he can decide how he chooses to live, regardless that his circumstances are a disaster waiting to happen. I would never again expect any one of my nurses to set foot anywhere near that despicable old man, and if you don't agree with my position, I'll hand you over to Dr. French."

Patricia was still seated at the table by the telephone when Daniel and Darrin came in for dinner. It took Daniel mere seconds to realize why Patricia was paralyzed in the chair. On several occasions, he had gently tried to persuade her there was little doubt that both the public health and fire departments in Dauphin would be aware of the state of her father's house, but she was adamant about her obligation to persist in rectifying it.

After he had changed his clothes and washed, Daniel opened the refrigerator and brought out the leftover baked ham before starting to prepare a salad. By the time Darrin had the table set, Patricia had mustered the energy to join the brothers in the kitchen. They ate lunch in relative silence, their conversation limited to the sheep and which pasture to move them to for the month of September.

When Darrin excused himself from the table and retired to his bedroom for his usual twenty-minute nap, Daniel refilled Patricia's and his teacup. "Are you ready to tell me what you've learned, my dearest?"

After she recapped Miss Wilson's information regarding her father's disastrous history with the health unit, as well as disclosing her rude manner, it was Daniel's turn to sit immobilized. He could certainly appreciate the nurse's reluctance to go anywhere near Terence Rose, but clearly Patricia was distraught by her lack of recourse. Could there be any help for a man so set in his ways? And why was Patricia suddenly so determined about assisting her father after all these years?

Once again, with her unnerving tendency to read his mind, Patricia eventually said, "I'm beginning to believe you've been right all along. When I think about my father, I realize that neither my mother nor my sisters and I were ever able to live up to his expectations. My brother was the only one my father thought could do anything right, but from what Miss Wilson implied, he too must have fallen out of favour. I wonder if, because I'm getting older, I wasn't just struck by an ill-defined sense of accountability for him, even though I've always accepted that we make our own beds and, therefore, have to live with the responsibility of our decisions. Thanks for your understanding, my darling Daniel. Now I realize I have no option but to let matters lie."

Suddenly, the atmosphere was charged with an unusual tension, and Samantha Robertson turned from the blackboard to observe a young woman haughtily striding into her classroom. She had written her name and was just starting her favourite quotation—the last two lines from Alfred, Lord Tennyson's noble poem "Ulysses." She knew instantly whom it was, thanks to the detailed file Margaret Devonshire had sent to her during the summer. As she resumed, Samantha made a mental note to express her gratefulness to the principal of Hartney

School at their next teachers' convention.

It was immediately apparent to Samantha that she would need to establish her authority right from the beginning with this group of students, although it had always been far from her preferred approach. Over the past decade in her career as a high school teacher, she had learned that most young adults respond favourably to a democratic style based on mutual respect for each other's position and expectations. But Margaret had been resolute in her warning that if she gave Carole Martin an inch, she would take a mile, and once engaged in a power struggle, her defiance knew no bounds.

When the second bell rang to signal the commencement of instruction, Samantha placed her chalk on the ledge before facing her new class. With a quick perusal, she noted that all her other students had been at Souris High School the previous year. Subsequently, instead of her customary interactive start of requesting each to provide a brief introduction, she expressed some general welcoming remarks before asking them to open their copy of *Pride and Prejudice*.

"We'll commence our grade nine literature course with Jane Austen's most notable piece of work. If anyone has already had the pleasure of reading this remarkable novel, please read it again, or go to the library and sign out *Sense and Sensibility*. Are there any questions before you begin?"

"Miss Robertson, my name is Carole Martin, and since I'm new to this school, I would like to meet my fellow students. Why can't we at least have some introductions?"

"I believe you have just told us your name, and I'm aware, as are the other pupils, that you're the only new student in my class. I doubt that if I asked everyone to say who she or he is, you would remember all twenty-nine classmates. I'm confident that, over the course of the day and week, you will eventually come to learn their names."

Maintaining direct eye contact with Carole, Samantha remained silent until the girl grudgingly resumed her seat. Then she walked behind her desk and sat down, even as she struggled with her feelings of discomfort. Her only hope was that since the students had been in her grade eight English class, they would recall that she was not customarily so autocratic and abrupt. On the other hand, if Carole had expected any kind of a platform on her first day, Samantha had effectively nipped her intention in the bud.

✳

Initially, Francine and Jessica were confident they could deal with Carole's blatant attempts to divide and conquer. From that first moment, when Carole had stood and boldly proclaimed her name to the class, Jessica had a glimmer of what they might be subjected to by a girl who, although she was new to the school, was unbelievably audacious. In the event no one other than Jessica had understood why Miss Robertson was being so uncharacteristically brusque, Francine could have enlightened them within a fraction of a minute's notice.

Jessica was quick to realize they would need to minimize their contact with Carole, and by recess, she had begun to think of strategies, including taking Francine to the restaurant every day at lunchtime. The mere mention of Carole's name had revived Jessica's vivid memories of the stories of how she had tormented Francine, and Jessica was not about to let Carole control her friend on Jessica's own turf. But what she never considered was that this time she would be the object of Carole's bullying, nor the devastating form her abuse would take.

✳

Being tutored in a small dedicated classroom by Mr. Griffin was everything and more than Hope could have anticipated, and she was quick to share whenever anyone asked her. She became the envy of the other girls in the student residence as soon as they became aware that, instead of sitting in a dreary classroom with some dowdy middle-aged professor droning on and on, Hope was receiving private lessons from possibly the most handsome man on campus.

Hope loved every aspect of college life. Initially, when her grandparents had resisted her living in residence, preferring that she continue to live with them, she had wondered if perhaps Dr. Burton was being unreasonable regarding the demands of her schedule. However, from the first day of the semester, there had been little doubt that her days and evenings would be heavily programmed.

Still, what she soon came to appreciate was her autonomy and the respect with which the other members of the music faculty, their colleagues, and Mr. Griffin treated her. Hope suddenly felt very mature, as if she was now truly launched upon her career, not knowing that her musical scholarship and studies with Dr. Burton would pale in comparison to the momentous event of the forthcoming year.

*

Will wonders never cease? Ian wondered he arrived at the music hall with ten minutes to spare, time he could utilize to review Hope's lesson for the afternoon. Gently opening the heavy cedar door, he was halted in his tracks by the most sensitive performance of the "Andante con moto" of Beethoven's "Piano Concerto No.4 in G major, Op. 58" that he had ever heard. Standing mesmerized, it dawned on him that this astonishing pianist would be the perfect accompanist for his violin prodigy.

At the completion of the second movement, the playing stopped. Slipping through the doorway, Ian was about to request a continuation with the "Rondo" when, to his amazement, he saw Hope's young tutor seated on the piano bench checking his pocket watch. "I had no idea you're such a gifted pianist, Michael! Why have you never said?"

"I suppose the glib answer is that you've never asked, Dr. Burton."

"Good heavens, surely you have heard me agonizing over finding the right person to play with Hope. Could you please complete the concerto?"

"Don't you need the hall for Hope's lesson? I'm only here to return her essay, which I've finished marking."

"I want her to hear you. Please, carry on!"

Michael was midway through the piece when Hope arrived, and, as had her professor, she stood spellbound, caught up in the masterly performance. Glancing about, she spotted Dr. Burton, who placed his finger to his lips. Hope was equally surprised when she realized that Mr. Griffin was the pianist, but it was Dr. Burton who spoke as soon as Michael rose from the piano seat. "Well, well, aren't you a boy wonder? Where did you learn to play with such finesse? More succinctly, what prompted you to graduate with an education degree rather than joining our music department? What do you think, Hope? Shall we play Brahms' "Piano and Violin Sonata G Major, Op. 78 2 Adagio," and verify if Mr. Griffin has the ideal touch to be your accompanist?"

✳

What could cause a person to become so rude and arrogant, especially when her parents and siblings were reasonably nice people? By the end of the first week of school, neither Francine nor Jessica could believe how intent Carole was on resuming her obnoxious behaviour, now toward both of them. The two friends had hoped that since Carole was a new student, she might be interested in becoming accepted into the popular group, to no avail.

While Jessica saved them from Carole's lunchtime antics by spiriting Francine away to her home, they had limited options during the morning and afternoon recesses. If they hurried to be the first out of the classroom, Carole invariably found them, and when they lingered within the safety of the school, she would be waiting for them at the door.

Still, neither of the girls was eager to report Carole's intrepid stalking to either their teacher or their parents, even when their initial annoyance began vacillating between frustration and anger. Surely, their nemesis had to realize that if she persisted in associating with them, she would be considered a nerd, the label Jessica and Francine had acquired the day they had entered the hallowed halls of learning at Souris High School.

Carole's name calling reached a new height one Thursday afternoon near the end of the first month. Jessica and Francine had been the first to dash out of class, and even though students were prohibited from leaving the schoolyard during recess, they had hurried toward Main Street to thwart Carole. Perhaps it was because the bell had rung before they could return, and Carole realized she would also be the recipient of detention that made her hiss, "Where the hell were you two going? Does your little chink friend have to run home twice a day to see her mummy and daddy?"

Francine had never heard Carole's latest term, but knowing that it had to be derogatory, she turned around to say, "So, when you've run out of disparaging words, you make them up?"

Urging her friend onward, Jessica whispered, "Just forget what she said, Francine. Let's hurry and get back to school."

As it happened, Miss Robertson was delayed in the principal's office, and all three tardy students had slipped into their seats before she returned to the classroom. The balance of the afternoon dragged on, until at last, the day was done. Francine was anxious to return home and bade Jessica a quick farewell before getting into the truck. Mother Pat and Grandma Alice were deep in conversation about some event at the seniors' centre, pausing only to greet Francine as she closed the door.

Only half listening to what they were saying, Francine was much more interested in the latest word that Carole had hurled at her friend. She was beginning to believe that the focus of Carole's tormenting was shifting to Jessica, and she had an unsettling feeling that it was more sinister than the antipathy she had displayed toward Francine. Although she suspected Carole had crossed a boundary in her abusive language, she wanted to talk it over with Mother Pat during their afternoon tea.

However, when they arrived at the Webster home, the two women were still engrossed in their discussion, and Alice invited them to come in for some leftover angel food cake. Francine could hardly urge Mother Pat to decline, especially when no one baked a fluffier angel food cake, and Grandma would probably serve it with fresh strawberries from her garden, topped with whipped cream.

Arriving home late, Francine quickly changed out of her school clothes before hurrying outside to check on her four frisky lambs. As so often happened, once she was outdoors and with her sheep, Francine forgot all about the cares and woes of being a teenager and communed with nature. As soon as she stepped into the pen, the playful animals searching for their customary baby carrot treats surrounded her. She could still hardly believe that during the past seven years since she had come to live with her uncles, she had acquired her own herd of over twenty sheep.

Every autumn, when the time came to sell her spring lambs, Francine pleaded with Uncle Darrin until he acquiesced and allowed her to keep them. Daniel invariably teased Darrin about being a soft touch, but the truth was, he could no more have convinced Francine to part with any of her sheep than could his twin brother. Throughout her adolescence, the brothers were fortunate their niece was generally observant of the house rules, because had it not been for Mother

Pat, on the rare occasion that Francine required being reined in, little discipline would have been forthcoming.

It was not until Mother Pat had knocked on her door before coming in to say goodnight that Francine remembered her inquiry. "Mummy Pat, have you ever heard the word 'chink'? I heard it for the first time today."

"Unfortunately, I have, and let me guess whose lips introduced you to this offensive term. Just how did Carole Martin use it?"

The tone of Pat's voice caused Francine to hesitate for a few moments, but she realized now that she had chosen to broach the subject, she would be expected to provide the context. She knew that her stepmother would be much more concerned about why she and Jessica had left the grounds than that it was against school regulations. So, what was causing her to feel as if she was betraying Jessica to confide in Mother Pat? Oh, why had she simply not taken the time to look the word up in her dictionary?

*

Was she ever going to recover? Did she even want to, or would she rather wallow in self-pity? Robert was just about at the end of his tether. He had been sympathetic, and from experience, he had recognized that Susan needed psychotherapy. He had subsequently driven her back and forth to Brandon three times a week, but it did not seem to help. Then there was the nagging feeling in the pit of his stomach that Susan still blamed him for her parents' death.

Following her brief outburst at the inquest, Susan had slipped back into a stupor, barely going through the motions of living. After preparing breakfast, Robert woke her to eat with him, but when he returned for lunch, she would often still be sitting at the table in the same position. At first, he had blamed all the sedatives the doctor had prescribed, but she was no longer on medication, and in his anguish,

Robert began to fear that his impetuous decision to marry her might soon resurrect his all too recently laid-to-rest demons.

He had thought that Susan's beauty, energy, and youth were going to keep them at bay, and he had whisked her off to Hawaii to become his wife. How could he have known that a parallel tragedy would befall her? What Robert did understand was that he had to stay detached from Susan's sorrow, or he would risk his own hard-earned precarious equanimity.

The afternoon his new tractor suddenly stopped working at the farthest perimeter of his section of land, forcing him to walk home in the scorching heat, was the final straw. He stormed into the house to find Susan fast asleep on the sofa, the remnants of lunch still spread all over the table and rotting as the sunshine poured through the window.

Robert strode across the room and grasped his wife by the shoulder, shaking her awake. "Enough already. It's bloody well time you got your act together and came back to the land of the living. It was your parents who died, not you, but if you don't stop carrying on like a zombie, you might as well join them."

Susan gingerly pulled herself to a sitting position and stared at Robert. "What did you say?"

"You heard me. Now get up off that couch, and start by clearing the table before you go to the freezer to see if you can find something you can possibly cook for supper. I have to go into town to arrange for a mechanic to come look at the tractor."

Whether it was Robert's tone of voice or the way he stood glowering at her, a spark was finally ignited within Susan. She rose to her feet, and standing at her full height, which was three inches taller than her husband, she glared down at him. "You're not my lord and master, so don't think you're going to order me around in my own house."

"I'll have you know that this is my home, and until you're ready to start acting like my wife, instead of a spoiled brat, I'll do whatever I want. By the time I come back, you better have this mess cleaned up, and dinner on the table, or I'll show you just what kind of lord and master I can be."

*

For nearly a month, Patricia honoured her promise to Francine not to address Carole's racial slurs to Miss Robertson or the principal. Even though her stepdaughter no longer pierced the silence of the night with bloodcurdling screams, when Patricia awoke in the mornings, she knew when Francine had been struggling to cope with her nightmares. After a week of hearing her roaming around in her loft and her subsequent tiredness, Patricia realized she had to act.

On the last Friday of October, Patricia prepared Francine's favourite breakfast of waffles slathered with strawberries and poured herself a fresh cup of coffee before sitting down at the table. "Okay, precious, we need to talk about what's happening in school, and there's no point in denying that Carole Martin is destroying your equanimity once again."

"No matter how hard I try not to disturb your sleep, you always know when I'm awake in the night. Oh, Mummy Pat, what makes a person so mean? She doesn't like us in the slightest, but she won't leave us alone or even try to make friends with any of the other students. What's more, Carole isn't interested in picking on me any longer. Now all she seems to care about is calling Jessica 'chink' and other nasty names the minute no teachers are within earshot. Jessica is becoming more and more upset, but, of course, she denies that it bothers her."

"Carole's racism has to be addressed. Neither Jessica nor you can continue to pretend that the best way to deal with Carole is to avoid her or ignore her. It's obviously not working, and it's having a negative impact on both of you, while Carole's increasing her control over you. Has Jessica said anything to her mother and father? If so, what are they prepared to do about it?"

"No, Jessica has sworn me to secrecy. We never breathe a word about Carole when we go to the restaurant to eat our lunch. She told me that her parents would be so upset they might take her out of school."

"When I return from driving you to school, I'm going to sit down with your uncles to brainstorm how we can convince Trin and Sebio to bring Carole's blatant discrimination to the attention of the school authorities. Then, after we have supper here on Sunday, we'll share our support and suggestions with the Yang family. Thank God, it's Friday, but Francine, it will be up to you to apprise Jessica about our intentions. You might want to ask her not to tell her parents until we are all together."

Instead of driving straight home after taking Alice to the seniors' centre, Patricia decided to head to Victoria Park, hoping a stroll on a beautiful misty Manitoba morning would clear her head. She could not get Carole out of her thoughts, and regardless of how deeply she delved into her memory, she was unable to recall any behaviour during all the years she had taught her that might have indicated how manipulative and controlling Carole would become. Had she not paid enough attention to her to notice such undesirable characteristics?

Was it when Carole had come under Susan Smith's influence that Margaret had started to become aware of her true nature? Thinking of Margaret, Patricia glanced at her wristwatch and realized that if she left right away, she could be outside her classroom as the recess bell was ringing.

Sure enough, bounding up the flight of stairs, she reached the office just as Margaret opened the door of her classroom. "What a pleasant surprise. Come in and join me for a cup of coffee."

Once the women were seated, each with a steaming cup from her thermos, Margaret said, "So, James wins our wager. He bet you would be here about Carole before the end of October, whereas I gave you until November, although we were both close. Now, in fifteen minutes, tell me what's happening."

Even before she began, Patricia knew that it would be impossible to obtain the advice she was seeking from her trusted friend and colleague in a few short moments. "You're absolutely right that I'm here about Carole Martin, who has now resorted to racial discrimination toward Jessica Yang. Can you meet for lunch tomorrow? I need your recommendations before Sunday evening about how to deal with this troublesome young woman."

*

Never could he have anticipated that he would come to know such joy. Michael had surpassed Dr. Burton's expectations as Hope's piano accompanist and was now tutoring her during the weekdays and often performing with her in the evenings and on weekends. Before the first two months of the semester had passed, Michael was convinced that the spark of his infatuation with Hope was flickering into full-blown love. She was so gifted and so beautiful, but so young.

Still, whenever Michael found their age difference daunting, he reminded himself of the deep abiding love his parents shared, even though his mother was almost ten years older than his father. There was little more than eight years between Hope and him, which was only significant, because she had just celebrated her fifteenth birthday at the beginning of October. Once she turned twenty-one and reached the age of consent, he would propose marriage, and they could tour together as husband and wife.

Before long, Michael was appreciating that the next six years could be challenging indeed. Hope was so captivating, and they spent so much time together in close proximity that he constantly had to curb any show of affection toward her, afraid he might lose control of his emotions. Fortunately, his restraint was aided by the fact Michael held Hope in such high esteem that it almost bordered on reverence.

Usually, Hope was so focused on pursuing her passion for music that she was innocent of how she affected other people and of what was occurring about her. When Michael was not accompanying her on the piano and was but another member of the audience, wherever he glanced around, he observed a sea of adoring faces. Hope was such an accomplished violinist by age fifteen that Michael could hardly imagine what the next six years would bring. He did know, however, that if he were to hold his urges at bay, he would be required to keep Hope firmly affixed on her pedestal.

✳

At times, Hope reached the height of frustration. Dr. Burton, and her grandparents, her friends, and even Michael seemed to have exceedingly high expectations of her. Most of the time, they handled her with kid gloves, as if she was only defined by her musical talent and was as fragile as her violin. Lately, even Michael had become distant, and Hope missed the camaraderie they had enjoyed during the summer, when he had been like a chauffeur for her and Dr. Burton.

If it had not been for Cassandra and her mother, Hope did not know how she could have endured her increasing feelings of isolation. When she was on stage, she lost herself in her music and transcended any need for human connection. But by the next morning, following the afterglow she invariably experienced from knowing she had performed well, combined with the applause and outpouring of praise from her steady stream of admirers, she felt an overwhelming feeling of loneliness.

✳

Every moment of the long weekend in September at the Jamison's cottage on the shore of Clear Lake had been wonderful. Being together with the only true friends she had ever known, Hope had relished the excitement and gaiety of just being a teenager, not a prodigy: sunbathing on the sandy beach, painting her toenails, giggling, and sharing stories into the wee hours of the morning. For the first time in as long as she could remember, she had not travelled with her prized violin, and she soon forgot all the expectations, trials, and tribulations of being consumed by the passion of her music.

Perhaps even more salient was the deeper understanding Hope had begun to develop with Mrs. Jamison. She had always been reserved around Cassandra's mother, believing the older woman was critical of her, because of the supposed tension between Francine and her. But now that Francine was much more confident and not nearly as dependent on Hope whenever the foursome was together, even Jessica had noticed that they were all more relaxed in each other's company.

Then, when Cassandra's family were returning Hope to the student residence, Mrs. Jamison had disclosed that she was going to be joining her at the college. "I'll be on campus on Thursday morning. Do you have any time in your busy schedule to have coffee and refresh my memory about resuming the life of a student?" From that day onward, she and Lindsay had met at least once a week, sometimes for lunch but more often for an afternoon coffee when Cassandra could catch the bus after school to join them.

＊

Dr. Burton had been invited to spend the Thanksgiving weekend with Michael's parents, and subsequently, Hope was free from any scheduled recitals. She arrived at her grandparents' late Friday afternoon, and had a lovely celebratory dinner with them on Saturday. She was looking forward to another Thanksgiving feast on Sunday when she had been invited to accompany the Jamisons to the Webster farm for a gathering with the McGregor and Yang families. But most of all, Hope was anticipating a recurrence of the fun the foursome had enjoyed the last long weekend they had all been together.

As it happened, Hope and Cassandra were both sadly disappointed by the reception they encountered from the moment they arrived. They were amazed by how subdued and quiet Francine and especially Jessica were throughout the day. It was as if they had a big black cloud overshadowing them, but when Cassandra or Hope attempted to discover what was bothering them, their entreaties were met with a stony silence. What could possibly be troubling their friends?

On the way home, the girls shared their concerns with Lindsay. "I have to agree with you," Lindsay replied. "Jessica and Francine were both unusually taciturn, and I thought that even Pat seemed out of sorts. I know she's worried about her father, but I sense there are much deeper undercurrents feeding the stream of tension our friends are experiencing. I tried different approaches with Pat to encourage her to disclose her concerns, to no avail. Did you have any success with either of the girls?"

"No, both were so tight-lipped it was next to impossible to get a single word out of either of them. There have been many times when I've found Francine to be reticent, but in all the years Jessica and I have been friends, I can't recall once when she was uncommunicative. What could have taken place within six weeks? Even worse, why wouldn't they tell us?" Hope asked.

"I suppose we'll have to be patient and wait until they're ready to confide in us. But it must have been a letdown for both of you, but particularly you, Hope, since you have precious few weekends when you're not performing and can unwind and enjoy the company of your peers. Why don't we check with your grandparents about you spending the night with us, and I'll treat my lovelies to a fancy lunch tomorrow and then that new movie everyone is raving about?"

Lindsay knew how to show her daughter and her many friends an enjoyable time. When they arrived home, she let them share confidences until midnight, and then she knocked lightly on the door. "Okay, ladies, if we're going to have a terrific date tomorrow, I need you rested and full of energy, so it's time to settle down."

The young women were tired, convinced their fatigue had been increased by the strain of spending the entire day trying to cope with their friends' inexplicable stress. Both were soon ensconced in the serenity of sweet repose and awoke rejuvenated, ready to begin their day. After a quick cup of coffee and showers, the trio was on their way. They savoured a delectable brunch at the elegant dining room in the recently opened Royal Oak Inn before becoming enchanted by *The Sound of Music*.

By the time Lindsay and Cassandra returned Hope to her grandparents' home, the young women's spirits had been restored. Lindsay made a mental note to involve the two of them in similar pleasurable outings whenever Hope had time free from the compelling responsibilities of her musical endeavours. Although another two months were to pass before they would learn the root of their friends' distress, that weekend, Lindsay became acutely aware of a reality that the youthful prodigy would not fully comprehend for years to come: that she would always be torn between pursuing her dream and leading a normal life.

*

Robert's outburst shook Susan out of her lethargy. When he returned, the kitchen had been cleaned, and she was at the stove preparing an omelette with pork sausage for supper. The problem with the tractor had been minor, and seeing his wife up and about improved his mood immeasurably. When they conversed during the meal and, later, as they washed the dishes, Robert became hopeful that Susan might be starting the long road to recovery.

Gradually, over the course of the next several weeks, Susan began to feel like she was returning to the land of the living. She had been so overwhelmed by her grief, compounded by the heavy sedation the doctor had prescribed, that as she came out of her torpidity, she was astonished to learn that more than four months had passed since her parents' demise. Where had she been? How could she not have any memory of all those days? Perhaps it was little wonder that Robert had lost his patience with her.

Nonetheless, as days, weeks, and months passed, and Susan experienced a return of her youthful vigour, she began to question what she had done when she had impetuously eloped with Robert Wharton at the tender age of seventeen. Now, instead of living at home and being pampered by her mother, she was saddled with all the household responsibilities of a wife. And if the tedium of the never-ending chores was not distressing enough, there was the return of the almost nightly conjugal duties.

As tragic as her parents' premature deaths were, Susan began to contemplate a fate far more dreadful. What if she became pregnant, which was a likely possibility given Robert's appetite for sexual relations? Good heavens, she was still a teenager; she wanted to go to parties and dances like the other girls her age, not prepare meals and keep the house clean enough to measure up to her husband's expectations. But if she became a mother, Susan realized she would be trapped.

To the best of her knowledge, Robert had never taken any precautions to prevent conception, even when she had been hardly able to care for herself, much less a baby. More importantly, what did she know about looking after a completely dependent human being? She had seldom been around babies. What was the matter with her husband's head?

That evening at the supper table, Susan said, "Can we go to Brandon tomorrow? I need to see my doctor about a woman's matter."

"Certainly, my darling. If it's because you think we might become parents, I couldn't be more excited. I'm not getting any younger, and I want a large family." Robert rose from his chair at the head of the table and came to place his arms around Susan's shoulders.

Susan was relieved that he was standing beside her and could not see her mouth drop open. She had no idea he wanted a houseful of squalling brats, but what did she really know about Robert Wharton? Her only interests had been to ride around the countryside in his flashy red convertible and to become the talk of the town. When he had shown her the pictures of the beautiful sandy beaches in Hawaii, before pleading with her to elope with him, all she had thought about was his obvious wealth.

When Robert resumed his seat at the table, Susan took a long look at him, as if seeing him for the first time. No wonder her parents had been upset when she started spending every evening with him. This man sitting across from her, grinning like a Cheshire cat, had thinning hair, was developing a paunch, and was fifteen years older than her, but now the law bound her to him for life. Oh, God, why had her parents not put their foot down and forbidden her from going anywhere with him? Her mother and father would be alive, and she would still be in her home sleeping in her own bed.

It was as if Susan was waking from a prolonged nightmare. She had not reached the age of consent, was married to a man she did not love, and was on her own without the support of her loving parents. Furthermore, she had left school without graduating, had never held a job, and had precious few skills that would lead to gainful employment. As the reality of her situation dawned on her, Susan knew she had to find the means to improve her lot, and quickly, without revealing any of her intentions to her husband.

Her first scheme was to travel to the city and arrange for a doctor to prescribe the pill, the one that she and Carole had spent so much time secretly chatting about at school. Her reasons last year for considering contraception were so far removed from her current circumstances that it flashed through her mind she might have been well-advised to have remained in her stupor. Still, if there was one contingency Susan knew beyond a doubt, it was that Robert must never have the slightest notion about what she was planning to do.

*

The autumn of 1966 was spectacular. The scorching heat of summer gave way to cool mornings and blissfully warm afternoons. Indian summer had arrived, and it stayed for weeks, with still no indication that a bitterly cold Manitoba winter was peering around the corner. On the Friday that Mother Pat had asked Francine to tell Jessica about the pending meeting with her parents, she could not break her promise to her friend and had not breathed a word.

Francine had every intention of confessing her omission to Mother Pat the next morning, but she slept through breakfast, and when she came to the kitchen, her uncle was seated alone at the table drinking a cup of coffee. "Good morning, Uncle Daniel. Don't tell me Mummy Pat is also a sleepyhead. I need to talk to her about something."

"You must have been very tired, my girl. It's almost eleven, and she had to leave for a luncheon date with Mrs. Devonshire in Brandon. But she'll be home this afternoon, and you can tell her then, unless I can lend you my good ear."

"Oh, thank you, Uncle Daniel. I'll wait though until she comes back. I wonder why she's seeing Mrs. Devonshire."

"We older people like to get together with our friends now and then just as much as you young people do." After a poignant pause he asked, "Did you and Jessica have a good visit with Hope and Cassandra at her grandparents' place on Thanksgiving?"

Glancing abruptly at her uncle, Francine thought his question unusual. Mother Pat could have passed on her observations about how quiet she and Jessica had been that day. Or, on the other hand, her astute uncle might have noticed the lack of chatter and spontaneous gaiety among the four friends.

Neither of them had been able to confide their distress regarding Carole to Hope and Cassandra, but later, Francine and Jessica both realized how strange their behaviour must have seemed to their friends. Nonetheless, they knew they could not risk any of the adults overhearing their disclosure. But the following evening, Mr. and Mrs. Yang would hear the truth, and Francine feared the outcome.

As soon as she had eaten, Francine went outdoors to absorb the warmth and peace of yet another beautiful late-autumn day. She had to be alone, to consider how she would be able to carry on at Souris High School without Jessica, since likely she would soon be the only recipient of Carole Martin's venom.

Francine found herself thinking about how, over the course of the past two months, she and Jessica had become remarkably close, whether because of Carole's unrelenting oppression or rather, as Mother Pat often expressed, "We love the ones we're near." Francine seldom thought about Hope anymore as she became increasingly aware of Jessica's attributes. She knew Jessica could not bear to tell her parents about Carole's racial slurs, because they would be mortally wounded to learn their family was being discriminated against in the town they had called home for their entire lives.

One of Jessica's most endearing qualities was her consideration for the needs of others, whereas Hope was so self-absorbed that she frequently did not seem aware of anyone else's feelings. Then Francine remembered how solicitous Hope had been during their weekend at Clear Lake. For the first time since they met, she had not been expected to perform. Hope was just one of them, and she had revealed that she could be as much fun as the rest of the adolescents.

And to be fair, having been in attendance at several of Hope's recitals, Francine had come to appreciate why Hope had to be so dedicated to practicing hour upon hour each day. How else could she possibly develop the confidence to be alone or, depending on what she was performing, to have Mr. Griffin as her accompanist on stages across the country, the centre of attention with all those expectant eyes glued to her?

Strolling through the pasture's browning grasses, Francine reflected upon how each of the foursome's personality was suited to her career aspirations. Jessica was determined to become an oncologist and treat the increasing numbers of people being diagnosed with cancer, which would require utmost devotion to her patients' needs. Cassandra, with her inquiring mind and capability for quick rebuttals, would make an excellent lawyer, and there was no doubt that Hope was on her way to becoming a renowned concert violinist.

And what about Francine? She knew that before long, she would become a student at Brandon College, enrolling in the Arts faculty to begin her bachelor's degree. Of course, her major would be English, and although she had not confided to anyone, other than Mother Pat, that she intended to study until she had completed her doctorate, and then she planned to become a university professor. Still, at the back of her mind, she remembered how, when she was in elementary school, her stepmother, who had been her teacher, had convinced her that she was a gifted storyteller and could pursue a literary career.

However, once she had climbed the stairs to start grade seven at Hartney High School, for reasons Francine had never determined, she had stopped writing her tales. Was it because of Carole and, to a lesser extent, Susan? When their bullying began, and her nightmares resurfaced, Francine had lost her confidence. According to Dr. Donahue, she had become submissive to their torment and was suffering from a condition called oppression. The psychologist was quick to identify that she was in uncharted waters, that there was no listing for the mental distress Francine was experiencing in the recently released *Diagnostic and Statistical Manuel of Mental Disorders*. The DSM, which was published by the American Psychiatric Association was now used by all healthcare practitioners, classified several distinct types of depression, but there was no mention of a subtler disorder where an individual could be weighed down by anxiety and guilt to the point of self-mutilation because of prolonged harsh or cruel treatment and control. Yet, Dr. Donahue had counselled many patients whom she was convinced were not depressed but were unhappy and distressed because of their living environments, where they were continually subjected to oppressive situations. Nor did she consider their feelings of oppression, whether real or imagined, were merely a symptom of a more serious mental disorder.

✳

By the time Eleanor Donahue graduated with her bachelor of psychology summa cum laude from the University of Manitoba, she had embarked upon her quest to become recognized in her chosen field. When her dissertation for her doctorate was printed not only in the *Canadian Psychology* journal but also in the *American Journal of Psychology*, she was convinced that she was well on her way. But much to the surprise of many of her prospective employers, she elected to establish a clinical practice in the small city of Brandon, of all places.

None of her fellow students, nor any of her professors, had ever been taken into Eleanor's confidence, or they would have been astounded by what they learned. Once she had won the scholarship, which allowed her to escape from under the thumb of her father's coercion, she never returned to the family home in Thunder Bay. Even after all her outstanding accomplishments, Eleanor still struggled with feelings of submissiveness particularly at the end of the day when she was alone.

Following several sessions with Francine, Dr. Donahue was convinced that her young client shared her own symptoms of subservience, but she was at a loss to identify any controlling factors to account for her oppressive feelings of guilt. Francine was loved and even pampered by her uncles, and her stepmother was devoted to her. What was eroding her self-esteem, destroying her sense of trust, and dragging her down to a pit of despair, primarily, as Eleanor knew from her personal experience, when in the absence of others?

When Francine agreed to be hypnotized, Eleanor had been confident that her young client would disclose the suspected traumatizing events that must have occurred early in her childhood. But Francine had responded so favourably to her recommended relaxation exercises and her hypnotic suggestion to awaken herself at the start of a nightmare that Dr. Donahue had not taken her beyond a subconscious level in an attempt to unearth what might lay buried deeper in her unconscious personal experiences.

Never once was she inclined to diagnose Francine as suffering from any type of depression, nor was she tempted to simply prescribe an antidepressant medication. She knew too well from her own ineffectual results and from follow-up sessions with many of her patients that drugs all too often reduced a patient's cognitive awareness and thus only increased the potential for the oppressor to exert control. Were it to span her entire career, Dr. Donahue intended to prove the hypothesis of her doctoral dissertation, that oppression was a standalone mental disorder and, as such, needed to be included in the disease classifications of the *DSM*.

*

It was not until she happened to glance up from *The Catcher in the Rye* and spotted Mr. and Mrs. Devonshire driving into the yard late Sunday afternoon that Francine realized Mother Pat was guilty of a sin of omission. Now she understood why her stepmother had arranged a luncheon on the spur of the moment with the principal of Hartney School. After all, who could more capably attest to Carole's malicious behaviour?

For the first time since her nemesis had arrived at Souris High School, Francine began to feel hopeful. If only Carole would be expelled, which Francine considered the best possible resolution, although she realized that after only two months, it was highly unlikely. Still, the Souris School Board would probably take a dim view of such blatant racial discrimination and would most certainly impose definitive rules to restrain Carole's interactions with Jessica.

But then, Francine wondered if, once again, she would bear the brunt of the older girl's vitriolic actions. Oh, why could Carole Martin not "just go away," as she had hissed at Francine a few short years earlier?

*

Once Patricia had mastered the art of preparing light fluffy Yorkshire pudding, she loved to serve the traditional English roast beef dinner, and this Sunday she had outdone herself with her prime rib. As soon as her guests completed their meal, complete with rhubarb custard pie and coffee, Pat said, "Before anyone asks to be excused, I must bring up a subject that is causing our two youngsters a great deal of distress. Furthermore, I suspect, Trin, that you and Sebio are the only ones here who don't know what's happening. That's the reason for me acting as the spokesperson."

Trin's initial look of surprise turned to dismay as Patricia narrated what had been occurring since the beginning of the school year. Finally, Trin could not contain herself any longer. "Jessica, why have you kept all this from us? We've always encouraged you to tell your father and me when you had a problem. Who is this girl, and what does she have against you? Maybe you can bring her home, and by talking together, we can get to the bottom of the reason for her dislike of you."

"I appreciate that we've just met, Trin, but I feel I must warn you about inviting Carole into your home," Margaret said. "I know this young woman well. I've seen her in action too many times, and her behaviour toward Jessica and Francine reaches far beyond any mere objection to something either one of them might have said or done."

Seeing the look of disbelief on Trin and Sebio's transparent faces, Margaret realized she would have to be more specific if she were to convince Jessica's trusting and honourable parents. Margaret made a quick decision to summarize the long list of manipulative incidents, including those directly involving her, which had prompted her to write the letter to the Hartney Board recommending that Carole be removed from the school division. It was on the tip of Margaret's tongue to also disclose her belief Carole had committed perjury in a court of law, until she noticed the glances being shared back and forth between Jessica and Francine. Prior to the start of school, almost two years had passed since Francine had had her last encounter with Carole, and during that time, her previous tormentor would have been the least likely person about whom she would given any thought. Although Jessica had no prior knowledge of Carole, Francine could not possibly have known how much more spiteful she had become.

Not wanting to alarm the girls any further, Margaret said, "I'm quite prepared to accompany both sets of parents to meetings with the teacher, the school administrators, and the board. I have grave concerns about Carole, and I believe she needs professional counselling before she's beyond help."

Patricia glanced furtively at Margaret before turning to Trin and Sebio. "I'm so sorry to spring this on you during our Sunday family gathering, but Daniel and I would like to accept Margaret's offer. Do you concur that we need to arrange a meeting with the school as soon as possible?"

Patricia and Margaret were loath to disclose the conclusion they had reached during their luncheon that Carole was a seriously disturbed young woman and that she was already beyond reach. By mutual consent, they agreed they would do everything within their power to protect Jessica and Francine from becoming any further embroiled in Carole's malevolence, and nothing short of seeing her removed from the school division would suffice. Subsequently, the two women shared a collective sigh of relief when Trin and Sebio consented to their plan.

*

November was a month that Patricia was unlikely to forget. Within the week, she and Trin had arranged a meeting with Miss Robertson and Mr. Anthony Billanski to request a parents' conference, with Margaret Devonshire participating as their resource person.

Initially, Anthony was resistant, confident that overt racial discrimination could not possibly be occurring in the school where he had been the principal for almost two decades. However, when Patricia said that Jessica was repeatedly being called "chink" by one of his other students, a memory that he thought was completely buried reared its ugly head.

Suddenly, Anthony was back on the school grounds in the small predominantly English town of Bruce Mines located on the north shore of Lake Huron in Ontario. The majority of the families were miners, who had arrived from Cornwall, England, although his Ukrainian father was a fisherman, who had settled in the area long before the copper mine opened. Anthony could not remember when or who among his classmates had started referring to him with derogatory words, but even before he knew what they meant, he did not like the sound of them. When he asked his father, he told Anthony not to listen, because the boys' parents were only too eager to purchase every fish he could catch. Since there was not a single book in their rustic cabin on the edge of the lake, Anthony had found his answers in the small school library.

If only his father had taken the initiative to meet with his teacher and put an end to his being called "Ukie" or "bohunk," how differently his life might have been. Instead, it had not taken Anthony long to realize that the more lucrative his father's sales during the day, the more he drank in the evening. It was up to him to scrounge their meagre meals from the remnants of the filleted fish until he was sick of making soup or stew from the heads. Even before he made his escape, never to return, Anthony had determined that home was little more than a place of use and abuse, and he had no desire to have a family of his own.

Anthony had stayed only until he could complete his schooling, and when he left, he worked at menial jobs day and night in Sudbury to earn the money to put him through teachers' college. Now he had the opportunity to save a bright student like Jessica Yang from a similar fate of constantly being subjected to blatant prejudice, and Anthony would not rest until he had reached a resolution with the perpetrator.

One brief discussion was all it took to convince Anthony that there truly was an incident of discrimination and, furthermore, to confirm that Carole Martin had to be removed from his school. He had zero tolerance for racism and immediately called an emergency meeting of the Souris School Board for the following week, armed with signed notes from both sets of parents and each of the two students, Mrs. Devonshire's original letter of recommendation to the Hartney School Division, and documentation of their subsequent action.

However, as was so often the case in small communities, news of a special school board meeting was leaked, and on the preceding

Saturday morning, Patricia received an acrimonious telephone call from Betty Martin.

"Just what the hell is your problem? Why can't you leave Carole and my family alone? What did we ever do to you and that misplaced orphan from the Maritimes?"

"Good morning to you too, Betty. Could you please tell me what you're going on about, or at least allow me to answer one question at a time."

"Why do you always play dumb with me, like you don't know what I'm talking about? Or maybe you really are the fool that you take me for. I don't have the slightest doubt that, once again, you're the reason for another emergency board meeting to get Carole out of school. What's she supposed to have done now?"

"I don't appreciate your accusations. If you can't be civil, I'm going to terminate this tirade."

When Betty proceeded to rant and rave, Patricia quietly replaced the receiver back into its cradle. Then, on second thought, she disconnected the telephone from the wall plug. It was a beautiful sunny morning, and she did not need to have it ruined by her obstreperous neighbour, who would no doubt call again. As she poured a cup of coffee, she wondered how Betty seemed to have her finger on the pulse of the community and invariably knew what was occurring almost before it happened.

Patricia's decision to disable the telephone would come back to haunt her before the weekend was over, and she would always blame herself for being beyond her father's reach the one and only time he asked for her.

✳

By chance, Susan remembered the name and address of the physician her mother had attended a year earlier when she had been experiencing menopausal problems. Equally fortunate, the doctor's office was on the upper level of the Brandon mall, so after seeing the doctor, she could go to the drugstore. Recognizing it might take longer, because she did not have an appointment, Susan asked Robert to run his own errands during the morning.

Climbing up the stairs rather than wait for the elevator, which promised to be crowded, given the number of people standing in front of it, Susan was pleasantly surprised at the clip with which she reached the landing. Over the last several days, she had felt livelier, and now it dawned on her that she was coming out of her grief.

When she opened the door to the office, she was disheartened to observe that the waiting room was teeming with people. She would have to think of a reason for her unannounced arrival, knowing it needed to be of an urgent nature if she had any hope of seeing the doctor that morning.

Not only was Susan's energy returning, so was her ability to think quickly. As luck would have it, she had begun her monthly cycle the previous evening and was experiencing an unusually heavy flow. She rushed up to the desk.

"Oh, please, can you help me? I was doing some shopping when I felt a rush of vaginal bleeding, and I'm worried I might be having a miscarriage."

"Come with me, please. I'll take you in to see Dr. Walker immediately. Please, change into this gown before she arrives."

The moment the door closed behind the receptionist, Susan disposed of the sanitary pad she had been wearing, putting it in the garbage receptacle under the sink, and then slipped into the gown. She had scarcely climbed up onto the table when an attractive woman not much older than her with jet-black hair and deep-brown eyes entered.

"Hello, I'm Dr. Marlene Walker. Karen has advised me of your medical situation, and I'll examine you now. However, you'll be required to complete our admission forms before you leave, although you do look vaguely familiar. Have you attended my clinic before?"

"Not personally, but before my mother died, she was your patient, and I usually came with her."

At Susan's words, Marlene suddenly recalled the articles in the *Brandon Sun*, recognizing the young woman from one of the family pictures and remembered her parents' tragic deaths. However, as she proceeded with her examination, Dr. Walker became aware of a glaring incongruity.

"I'm uncertain what's happening with you, Miss Smith, but you most definitely have not had a miscarriage. You could not have been pregnant, since you're clearly in the midst of your menstrual cycle, and I question your intention to waste my time."

The brusqueness of the doctor's tone instantly reduced Susan to tearfully exclaim, "I'm actually not Miss Smith any longer, and my husband, who is much older than me, is eager to start a family, but it's too soon after my parents' deaths. He won't listen to a word about my choice to use contraception, even though my family doctor has told him that I'm mentally too fragile to care for a newborn. As well, this is my body, and I need you to write me a prescription for the birth control pill."

"As much as I don't appreciate your manipulative approach, I agree that it's your decision, although clearly you need to advise your husband. I'll prescribe the contraception, but I caution you about ever seeking my medical attention in such an underhanded manner again. Now, what is your married name, so I can write the prescription."

"My name is Susan Wharton. I'm so sorry for deceiving you, Dr. Walker, and I assure you it will never happen again. Thank you for understanding."

Later, as Susan exited the examination room, clutching the prescription form in her hand, Dr. Walker was ambivalent. She recalled

Susan's mother as a vibrant woman and remembered thinking at the time of the inquest how sad it was that her life had ended in her prime. Although Marlene was miffed by Susan's brazenness, she could only imagine how devastated Susan must be at the loss of both parents, and she understood her hesitation to begin a family so soon after the tragic event.

✳

The door of the office down the corridor opened precisely the moment Susan was hurrying by, and she all but collided with the man who stepped out. Derek Barclay was rushing to a meeting when he stopped in his tracks and stared at the stunning redhead with the emerald-green eyes. Who was she, and why did she look so familiar?

"I'm terribly sorry for nearly bowling you over. Have we met somewhere? I must be losing my touch if I can't put a name to your beautiful face." Even as she introduced herself, the mental image of the distraught plaintiff at June and Bert Smith's inquest surfaced in his mind. He was astonished by the transformation in her appearance. "Can you possibly be Susan Smith-Wharton?"

Grasping her gently by the arm, he turned around and headed through the door from whence he came. "Mrs. Thomas, please telephone my eleven o'clock appointment, and ask if we can reschedule at an alternate time that works for him."

Once Susan was seated in one of the comfortable chairs in the plush office, a cup of coffee in hand, Derek sat down behind his large walnut desk. "I'm Derek Barclay, and I've been your family's lawyer for a number of years. It is most fortuitous that we've encountered each other today, because I've been attempting to contact you for months, both by telephone and letter to arrange a reading of your parents' last will and testament. Although I have frequently spoken with your husband, you never returned my calls or responded to my letters.

You do realize, Mrs. Wharton, that you are the sole beneficiary of all their holdings, which are considerable. I must say I'm very surprised I haven't heard from you."

Wondering if Robert had a manipulative tendency of his own, Susan decided to give him the benefit of doubt. Furthermore, she was not about to reveal any of her husband's characteristics to this man, who claimed to be her lawyer, although she had no recollection of ever having made his acquaintance. He must have been at the inquest, but other than Carole, Susan's memory of who was present was a complete blank.

"I can't imagine why Robert didn't mention your calls, but since I'm here now, is it possible for you to show me my parents' will?"

"It certainly is, since you are the only person named. I'll ask Mrs. Thomas to forward the telephone to the answering service, and she can act as our witness. Would you like another coffee while I ring for her?"

Mr. Barclay assiduously read every word of the lengthy document until Susan became tired of the legalese. However, she abruptly focused her attention when the total sum of approximately $70,000 was mentioned as the estimated value of the Smith's property and livestock, combined with their chequing and savings accounts.

Susan did not have the slightest idea that her parents had that kind of money, especially the amount in their savings account. They always lived so conservatively, although she knew they had set aside more than sufficient funds for her to complete university. A vague memory of her father's wealthy aunt leaving him an inheritance suddenly surfaced, but Susan had never heard the amount. As she quickly reflected, it must have been substantial, and a pang of guilt assailed her that instead of using some of it for a return visit to Ireland, as her mother had so often dreamed, they had banked it for Susan's higher education. Now they were both dead and buried, she was a high school dropout with a husband and minimal prospects of ever attending university.

Finally, Derek's voice penetrated her dismal thoughts. "I'm sorry, Mrs. Wharton, but I don't think you have heard what I've been saying to you. The total amount of your parents' worth is based on an assessed value of their section of land and could change in the event you decide to put it up for sale, depending on the purchase price. Incidentally, what is happening on the property? Is someone farming it, and were the crops harvested this fall?"

As the silence continued, Susan peered at Mr. Barclay as if she was seeing a ghost. Why was he asking her all these questions as if she had any awareness of her previous home? She had not been near her parents' farm since their deaths, so how could she possibly know what had occurred in the interim? Suddenly, she burst into tears. "I don't even know what happened to my dad's dog. He followed him everywhere."

Mrs. Thomas rose hastily from her chair and wrapped her arm around Susan's shoulder. "There, there, my dear. This has all been such a shock to you. Perhaps a drop of the brandy that you keep for medicinal purposes would be helpful now, Mr. Barclay."

Reaching into a small cabinet adjacent to his desk, Derek handed a small crystal glass half-filled with the light-brown alcoholic spirit to Susan. At first, Susan shook her head, but then she decided that after the morning's events, she needed a drink stronger than the coffee, which had become cold. "Thank you, Mr. Barclay."

"Please, call me Derek. And I believe we have covered enough ground for today. Given the hour, I wonder if you would care to join me for a bite to eat."

"Oh, is that the time already? I'm to meet my husband in front of Woolworth's before noon. Thank you for your offer, but I must run."

It occurred to Derek that he was not prepared to let this beautiful woman slip out of his life without at least having the opportunity of treating her to lunch. "Ms. Wharton, I'll need you to determine if someone has been farming your parents' land and to advise me of your decision in terms of the property. Could you please give it some thought over the next two weeks and then return for a lunch meeting? Mrs. Thomas will make the appointment, and I'll make a reservation for the dining room at The Royal Oak Inn."

∗

This time, Betty was not going to wait and receive another letter from the school board announcing that Carole was being requested to leave the division. On the Monday morning of the week of the proposed meeting, when Carole was getting ready to leave for Souris, Betty told her that she would be driving the truck. However, when they reached the intersection, Betty bypassed the small town and continued on Highway 10.

"Your mind must be addled, Mum, because you just missed the turn for school."

"We're going to Brandon today to meet with the principal at one of the high schools. I'm sick of the way everyone blames you for anything that happens in these small country schools."

"Wow, driving to Souris is one thing in the winter, but I'm not so sure about going back and forth to Brandon every day."

"That's not the plan. Once I get you registered, we'll go visit Grandma. I'll ask Fred's mum to take you in during the week, and you can come home by bus when the weather permits."

"What's going on? When did you decide I didn't belong at the Souris High School, and why? I was actually enjoying some of the other students and getting along just fine."

"Oh, stop it, Carole. I'm not your father, and you don't fool me for one moment. I know you're causing trouble just like before with Francine Stonehenge and also with her friend, a Chinese girl."

Silence descended in the cab as Carole wondered what her mother had heard and how. No doubt it helped that their telephone was a party line, but still, her mother impressed with her ability to always know what was happening within her own family as well as with most of the other people in the community. It flashed through Carole's mind that she had come by her manipulative skills quite naturally, as well as to her ability to find a quick solution to any presenting problem.

✳

It was not until early Monday morning that Patricia realized she had neglected to plug in the phone. No sooner did she do so, and it rang. "Yes, this is Patricia Rose-McGregor. Who's calling, please?"

Fortunately, she was close to a chair, and as she listened, she sank heavily into its wooden frame. Following several minutes of intense silence, Patricia uttered, "Oh, my God. You have no idea how sorry I am that you couldn't reach me. Yes, I'll leave immediately and be there as quickly as I can."

By that time, her family were all in the kitchen anxious for her to complete the call and apprise them of what had happened. Even when she could no longer hear a voice on the other end of the line, Patricia continued to clutch the telephone as she sat immobilized, staring into nothingness. Francine looked at her uncles until Daniel quietly approached Patricia and gently removed the receiver from her clenched fist.

Once he led her back to the table, Francine refilled her cup. After taking several sips of Daniel's strong coffee, the colour returned to Patricia's face, and she began to recover. "That was the head nurse from the emergency department of the Dauphin hospital," she said. "Last evening, my father practically burnt himself to a crisp in that tinderbox he called his home. The firemen somehow managed to get him out, and shortly after the ambulance arrived at the hospital, he briefly regained consciousness. His last words were that he wanted to speak to me, and although they tried right up until the moment he died, they couldn't get through. But it was no wonder, since I'd unplugged the telephone on Saturday after my conversation with Betty Martin, and none of us gave it a moment's thought during the rest of our busy weekend."

Daniel was the first to speak. "Oh, my darling, I'm so sorry. Of course, I'll drive with you to Dauphin, and unless you really want to come, Francine, Darrin can drive you to school."

"I'm very sorry about your father, Mummy Pat, but I have a math exam this morning I don't want to miss. Will you think it awful if I don't go with you and Uncle Daniel?"

"No, my girl, I understand. There isn't anything we can do now, not that there was when he was still alive, as your uncle and I found out the hard way. I'm just shocked that he wanted to talk to me on his deathbed when he wouldn't let Daniel and me in when we tried to visit with him in September. Darrin, will you and Francine manage, since we'll be gone three or four days to arrange for his funeral? And don't forget to swing by and pick up Alice on your way to Souris. Shall we pack some clothes and get to Dauphin early enough to check into a motel?"

As Daniel climbed the stairs to their bedroom, he suddenly recalled his disparaging thought when he had seen the pigsty that was Terence Rose's home, that the only conceivable way to deal with it would be to burn the house and all its contents to the ground. He certainly had not envisioned that Patricia's father would be inside, although now he stopped in his tracks and wondered if the old man might have made that choice. His knowledge of Patricia's father was limited to her infrequent and brief comments about why she had never returned to visit him until two months earlier, but from his only unpleasant encounter, Daniel would not be wholly surprised if Terence's actions might have been deliberate to leave his daughter with a legacy of guilt.

Daniel drove in silence, knowing that Patricia would speak when she was ready. They had reached the outskirts of Dauphin when she said, "Daniel, before we go to the funeral home, could you please swing by my father's house?"

"Are you sure that's a good idea, my love? In fact, why don't we stop for a cup of coffee before we do anything?"

"I could use some coffee and even a bite to eat, but if you're trying to divert me, my dear husband, it won't work. I must see what's left of the home to help me make a decision."

Thirty minutes later, they arrived to see the smouldering ashes of what had been Patricia's ancestral home. "Could you please wait in the truck, Daniel? I want a few moments alone."

Softly closing the truck door, Patricia walked to where the front steps had been before she proceeded to amble around the remaining cement foundation and then further afar. When she disappeared into the surrounding woods, Daniel lost sight of her. After what seemed like an hour, he was on the verge of getting out of the vehicle. Then he stopped himself. He had always respected his wife's privacy, particularly because, from the beginning of their life together, Patricia had realized his need for solitude. They were both aware that many in the neighbourhood had considered their marriage doomed from the start, since each of them had been alone for so long. However, their love and regard for each other's needs had quieted the naysayers. Why would he allow an old man's death to change the way they interacted?

Just then, Patricia emerged and appeared to be headed back to the truck when she stopped to gaze off into the distance. Finally, as if she had come to terms with whatever she was weighing, she flashed Daniel a smile and returned to him.

✳

Exactly as Patricia had suspected when they arrived at the funeral home, the director waited alone. He had not heard from her mother or any of her siblings and was relieved that at least one member of the family had appeared to take responsibility for Terence Rose's remains. If Mr. Dostdowich considered Patricia's request to arrange his memorial service at twilight on Wednesday as out of the ordinary, he kept his long thin face expressionless. Daniel, on the other hand, viewed his wife's decision to bury her father's body on the acreage on the outskirts of Dauphin at the edge of darkness a fitting end to the man's life.

Had Daniel ever expressed his belief to Patricia that Terence's intention might well have been to incinerate himself, he would have been surprised by her agreement. Their only point of difference was Daniel's fear that she would experience an overwhelming feeling of guilt. As it was, Patricia had long ago exorcised her father's malignant influence and had only returned in September to give him an opportunity to seek her forgiveness. As she walked about in the trees surrounding her childhood home, Patricia had come to accept that, on his deathbed, her father had awakened for the sole purpose of asking for her absolution.

Following the interment on Terence Rose's land as the sun slipped below the horizon, Patricia found more peace in her father's death than she ever had during his life.

At Thanksgiving, it only took Ian Burton a matter of minutes to understand why Michael Griffin was such a fine young man. Driving around the treed circular drive and coming to a stop in front of the picturesque two-storey knotty pine home and adjacent replica cabin, the ambience engulfed him. When the beautiful golden retriever treated him as a long-lost friend, and then Jonathon shook his hand so heartily that he thought his arm might break, Ian began to appreciate the origin of Michael's affable nature and of his handsome appearance. He bore a striking resemblance to his father, who looked so youthful he might have been an older brother.

But from the moment Dr. Ian Burton set eyes upon Marika Griffin's exquisite face, he understood the meaning of love at first sight. Throughout his almost fifty years, he had been so focused on his musical career that he had never given much attention to the fairer sex, and now the reason why was instantly apparent. Welcoming him into her cozy home with the aroma of bread baking in the oven was the woman for whom he had unknowingly been searching the duration of his life. Nonetheless, it was equally obvious to him that the profound love Marika felt for her husband and son would never acknowledge the existence of any possible rival. Suddenly, Ian was transported back to his parents' home, where he had always experienced an overwhelming sense of loneliness. Cynthia and Alexander Burton had been so openly devoted to each other that until they sent him away to boarding school, Ian was convinced he was an intruder whom they had taken in out of pity.

Unlike Ian's mother, however, Marika graciously brought him into the intimate circle of her family with open arms. "Welcome, Dr. Burton. We're happy you're able to join us for the weekend. Michael has sung your praises for so long that I'm concerned my feelings of awe may be off-setting to you."

If only this gracious beauty with the flowing silvery-blond hair and refined facial features could have known that the mere touch of her dainty hand had set his heart racing, she would have pondered which one of them was wonderstruck. It took Ian several minutes before he murmured, "Please, call me Ian, Mrs. Griffin. I can't begin to thank you for inviting me to your lovely haven in the country and including me in your family's festivities."

"I assure you the honour is all ours, and please, my name is Marika. We seldom have company, and although Michael has repeatedly asked us to travel to Brandon to hear your young protégé perform, Jonathon and I have always been wrapped up with the myriad activities in our own little realm."

"Michael and I must combine forces to alter your tendency to sequester yourselves here in the country, although I don't have the slightest difficulty understanding why you have no desire to leave. I wonder, Marika, if you are aware that now Michael is not only Hope's tutor but also her accompanist. He's an accomplished pianist, and he credits you solely for his incredible skill and expertise."

Suddenly, Marika was completely lost to her guest. Unknown to him, Ian's words had carried her back to the great concert halls of Europe. By the outbreak of World War II, Marika had been firmly established as one of the most celebrated concert pianists across the Continent. She would never forget that evening's performance at Royal Albert Hall, when she had been signing autographs and happened to glance up into the adoring brown eyes of an incredibly handsome Royal Canadian Air Force officer. Approaching the age of thirty-two, Marika had given little thought to matrimony since her true love was her Grotrian-Steinweg grand piano, but a momentary thought flitted through her mind that perhaps her choice had been questionable.

When the young man asked in a gentle voice if he could wait at the end of the long line until she had finished, before escorting her to the nearby officers' mess for a nightcap, Marika surprised herself by responding in the affirmative. Prior to the pilot's request, she had never even entertained the notion of accepting one of her multiple invitations, yet suddenly, here she was, eager to dispense with her devoted fans, so she could accompany him.

*

Soon, Marika and Jonathon Griffin became inseparable, spending every free moment they could garner together. Within the first week, she had taken him to meet her aging parents in their small apartment overlooking the Thames. They were equally enamoured of the polite, dashing flyer from across the ocean.

Three weeks later, following a sold-out recital at the London Coliseum in St. Martin's Lane, Jonathon proposed to Marika, and she accepted. None of her friends could believe her precipitate decision, and they urged her to reconsider, convinced that she was simply infatuated with the young handsome man in uniform. Her parents were also surprised, but they encouraged her to follow her heart, and the next Sunday morning, with one of his fellow officers as his best man, Jonathon and Marika were married in St. Pancras Old Church in Somers Town, central London.

By the time Jonathon was the pilot selected for the inaugural flight of the Avro Lancaster Mk I on January 9, 1941, he was the proud father of a bouncing baby boy. When he began flying night bombing raids over Germany at the beginning of 1942, he vowed to Marika that regardless of how many assignments the Royal Air Force sent him on, he would always return to her and their son, Michael.

Return he did, mission after successful mission, and at the end of the hostilities, Jonathon proudly brought his wife and child home to Canada. Since he always kept his promises, as soon as possible, he had Marika's beloved piano shipped across the Atlantic Ocean, and it still occupied a dominant position in the high-ceilinged open living room of the log house they had constructed. During all the years they had been together, Marika had no regrets about leaving her career as a concert pianist, although she was deeply saddened when Michael suddenly chose to stop taking her lessons.

✳

"I'm terribly sorry, Dr. Burton . . . Ian. Your words triggered my memories of a time long before our son was born. Did you say Michael is Hope's accompanist? Years ago, he decided, quite out of the blue, to discontinue our lessons, and to my surprise he has never mentioned that he was playing the piano again."

"I assure you that Michael is not only playing but with each performance, his innate talent is increasingly obvious. He is a natural-born pianist. I can't begin to imagine why he ever became a teacher. You and Jonathon absolutely must attend Hope's upcoming recital in December, which will feature a very special guest, Dr. Charles Farrington, the concertmaster of the CBC Halifax Orchestra and the Atlantic Symphony Orchestra. He is a famed violinist, and if we can entice him to join the Brandon School of Music, we're anticipating he'll accept Hope as his protégé."

✳

Within the week, the atmosphere in Souris High School was totally altered. By the end of the day on Monday, Miss Robertson had alerted Mr. Billanski that Carole had not arrived for school. In truth, everyone was aware of the fact when the roar of her truck had not disrupted the morning's peace.

The harmony that had prevailed throughout the day was palpable to the teaching staff, to Jessica and Francine, and to the majority of the student body. When Tuesday came and went and then Wednesday with no sign of Carole, Mr. Billanski was on the verge of cancelling the emergency board meeting. Miss Robertson, however, was adamant that they proceed as planned, confident that Carole's absence could be but another of her manipulative ploys. Should the administration not take definitive action, she could just as precipitately return, and they would look like fools for believing she had opted to leave of her own volition.

On Thursday evening, although Patricia and Daniel were still in Dauphin wrapping up Terence Rose's affairs, Trin and Sebio presented a convincing case for having Carole expelled from the school division. In all their years of living in and running a successful business in Souris, they had never heard anyone refer to their family as "chinks," and they were not about to permit the discriminatory slur be applied to their only child.

Within a matter of days, the rumour circulating in the Hartney community was that Betty had been in agreement with her daughter about having to attend school with a member of an "inferior race," and it soon reached the good people of Souris. There was not one person in Souris or for miles surrounding who had not eaten in the Lingnan and come to enjoy the gentle, friendly nature of the Chinese owners. There was subsequently little interest in allowing racism to invade their hospitable town, and the consensus was that if Betty shared her daughter's prejudice, they could both leave.

*

When Fred Martin returned from Hartney late that Monday afternoon to find his three youngest children sitting at the kitchen table eating ice cream, he quickly learned that was precisely what his wife had done.

"Why are you three alone in the dark? Where's your mother, and what else did you have for supper?" Fred asked as he flipped on the light switch.

His son, Randy, was the first to reply. "This morning, when we were getting on the school bus, Mum told us she was driving Carole into Brandon to see Grandma. We haven't been able to find her since we got home, although we searched through the garden, the barn, and everywhere else we thought she might be."

"After we had bread and peanut butter, we decided to have ice cream for dessert," Wendy chimed in, glancing up at her father. Fred tousled his youngest child's hair and then reached for the telephone.

Betty answered at his mother's house on the first ring. "Hello, Fred. I've been waiting for your call, although I thought one of the kids might have tried to reach me."

"How the hell could they have phoned you, when you didn't say a thing about where you would be?"

"I told them I was taking Carole to Brandon. They know where to look for Grandma's number."

"Oh, they looked all right—all over the farm for you. Why would they even consider that you would still be in Brandon instead of here to make their supper when they came home from school?"

"Since you're always telling me how easy it is to run the house and look after the kids when they're away all day, you can find out for yourself. I'm staying with your mother for a few days until I can get Carole settled into a new school. There's lots of food in the house, and they're old enough to help you."

"What do you mean, 'new school'? That girl just started at Souris High two months ago. Don't tell me that she's causing problems there."

"I have to run, Fred. Something's burning in the oven, and Carole has gone with her grandmother to take her new puppy for a short walk. I'll call you in a couple of days."

"No damn way! You get on the road first thing tomorrow morning—" Fred suddenly realized he was yelling into the receiver of a disconnected telephone line.

＊

The morning following her return from Brandon, Susan waited until Robert had departed for his daily trip into Hartney, and then she walked across the field to her parents' home. Fortunately, Indian summer had persisted until the end of October, and although the weather had turned colder, they only had a skiff of snow.

In the months since her parents' tragic demise, Susan had given little thought to what had happened to the house and farm, let alone go anywhere near her childhood home. She tried to imagine what she would feel when she pushed open the front door into the chilly abandoned farmhouse. Would she be flooded with memories? To the best of her recall, she had rarely entered the foyer without her nostrils being enticed by the aromas emanating from the kitchen accompanied by her mother's cheery voice.

Susan did have enough sense to fortify herself for the assailing emotions she might initially experience upon her arrival. She had consumed a healthy breakfast, had a second cup of strong coffee, and had dressed in several layers of warm clothing. Also, the brisk two-mile walk would help strengthen her resolve to determine what had occurred to her family's property, so she could report back to her lawyer during their luncheon meeting in two weeks' time.

As she had anticipated, the front door was firmly locked, but the key remained hidden under the flowerpot still standing forlornly by the entrance to the garage. After a moment of hesitation, Susan climbed the four cement stairs, but she stopped before gingerly inserting the key to spring open the door and enter.

Immobilized in the foyer, Susan was struck by the silence and stillness. It was so quiet. She forgot to breathe until, at last, she found herself taking deep gulps of the stale air. Suddenly, she felt lightheaded and a little dizzy, and she turned back to the open door to fill her lungs with fresh air before going into the kitchen and marginally opening one of the windows. Her mother's multiple houseplants were all gone, but everything else seemed to be in the same place, just as she remembered.

It was then that she noticed the white envelope on the table. Who could have left it there, and why? Then it occurred to her that someone must have cleaned the floor, because suddenly, Susan had a vivid mental picture of the policeman's comment that she recalled hearing at the inquest. There had been a small puddle of blood where her father had lain down beside her mother. They could have been sleeping, except for the tiny hole in the middle of his forehead.

Shaken, Susan pulled out a chair and sank down just in time to avoid falling on the floor. Oh, God, what had she done? In all these months, she had never felt accountable for what had taken place in that kitchen, but now the magnitude of her responsibility struck her to the core of her being. She was the undeniable reason this tragedy had occurred. Had she not run away with Robert, or if she had at least telephoned her parents to tell them what they were doing and where they were going, they would most likely still be alive today. The onerous burden of her mother and father's death sat squarely on her shoulders, just as surely as if she had pulled the trigger that killed her father.

Susan had no idea how much time had lapsed before she finally reached for the envelope, which strangely, was addressed to her, and slowly opened it. She recognized Mrs. Devonshire's flowing handwriting from her years of providing comments on her report card.

March 17, 1966

Dear Susan,

Perhaps, you will think me a sentimental old fool, but I decided to date this note for St. Patrick's Day, because I miss your mother, my lovely Irish friend, so much.

As soon as we were able to muster the courage, and the RCMP had given us permission, James and I let ourselves into the house and cleaned up every sign of what had taken place in your mother's immaculate, bright kitchen. I felt a sense of relief when we finished, because I knew June would not rest in peace until it was done. Your loving mother would never have wanted you to see any indication of the calamity that had befallen her and your father in the home they'd had constructed in preparation for your long-awaited arrival.

Aside from rescuing your mother's plants, which she nurtured with such care, we have not removed anything from inside the house. The truck is in the garage, and when you want to drive it, the keys are hanging in the usual spot beside the back door. Quite naturally, James herded the livestock to our farm, but he had them all tagged, so they will readily be identified when you decide what to do with them.

James and I will care for your parents' home and farm until you're ready to make a decision about what to do with the property, because, of course, all that belonged to them will now rightfully be yours. Also, we will be available to assist you in any conceivable manner that we can whenever you choose to take the necessary action.

Your godmother,
Margaret Devonshire

With the letter clasped in her hands, Susan brought her head down on the familiar tabletop. She was unaware of the passage of time until her stomach began to growl. Glancing up, she was surprised that her mother's prized electric wall clock encased in a beautiful coloured ceramic peacock continued to tick away. Susan stared at the clock and thought how ironic that the only indication of life left in her childhood home was an object measuring the unrelenting march of time.

Expending more effort than she could have imagined necessary,

Susan heaved herself to an upright position. She needed to leave and get dinner on the table before Robert came home. Still, she stood motionless as she took a cursory look down the hallway leading to the bedrooms. Even if she had the time, she certainly did not have the energy to peer into the intimate domain of her parents' room.

As Susan inched toward the door, she considered seeing if the truck would start, so she could drive home. But then it occurred to her that she was not ready for Robert to know where she had been. She realized she must return tomorrow, and day after day until she eventually came to terms with how she would dispose of her parents' farm, their house, and, most difficult of all, their personal possessions. And the last person she needed to have urging her to make any decision was Robert.

Before the events of that morning, in what seemed like another lifetime, Susan would have also thought it was Robert's fault that the past months had unfolded with such tragic consequences, but over the last three hours, she had aged more than during the first eighteen years of her life. She resolved to walk home along the road, just in case Robert had already returned and might be suspicious of why she was traipsing across her father's field.

✳

The next morning, Susan was on her way the moment she saw the exhaust from Robert's truck dissipate into the crisp early November air. She was energetic enough while walking to what she still considered her home, but the minute she was in the house, she became rooted to the kitchen floor. Every time she tried to lift one foot in front of the other to proceed down the hallway, even to her own bedroom, her courage failed her.

What was she going to do? Then she caught sight of the telephone sitting on the desk and wondered if it was still connected. Suddenly, it occurred to her that the house was warm, and when she flicked the switch, the kitchen was flooded in glowing light. The Devonshires must have been paying for the utility bills all these months. Since it was Saturday, she wondered if she dared telephone Margaret, whom she'd forgotten was her godmother, to take her up on her offer.

*

Neither one could believe it. They were not being ignored or ridiculed. The week passed with first their classmates and then more of the students in the school exchanging greetings with them. It was not until Sunday dinner when Trin was telling the McGregors about the board meeting that Jessica and Francine shared a sudden glance of understanding across the table.

Within two short months, the other pupils must have realized the pernicious impact that Carole Martin had been exerting and had subsequently decided that the last two musketeers were responsible for having her ousted from Souris High School. For the most part, although none of them had ever come to their assistance, they had not joined in Carole's discriminatory tactics against Jessica and her inseparable chum.

When Francine had registered in the school, she was instantly accepted in the clique with Jessica and Hope, but the term most often used to describe them had been "the three musketeers." Before long the girls were vying with each other to be the top student in every subject, with the distance between them and their fellow classmates eventually being so insurmountable that the only other label they had earned was "nerds."

Still, they had been left alone, with many of the other students admiring them, albeit unacknowledged, from a distance. Each of the three friends was so self-assured and mutually exclusive of anyone else in the school. Yet, when Jessica served her schoolmates in the Lingnan, she was always affable and outgoing, to the point that many of the youths, male and female, might have liked to spend time with her.

✳

Marilyn Stravinsky sat bolt upright in bed. She had been troubled all week about the emergency board meeting, and since Monday morning, the conspicuous absence of the new student in school. Now, on Friday night, she could not succumb to sleep, because in her mind, the situation with Carole Martin had resurrected a subtle dilemma regarding the two remaining musketeers' interaction.

As far as Marilyn was concerned, by the very nature of their exclusion of the rest of the students, they were being equally segregating toward them. Was their self-enforced isolation not a reverse form of discrimination? Obviously, Carole did not like being ostracized by Jessica and, in particular, by Francine, a girl she had known for years, and who, according to rumours, had caused negative feelings toward the Martin family in the community her forefathers had settled. Everyone knew that Fred's father had spearheaded the construction of Hartney School, and then, in a strange twist of fate, Carole had been expelled from the school her grandfather had built.

Maybe Carole had directed racial slurs against Jessica to retaliate for Francine's gossip about her family, but now it appeared that she had also been expelled from Souris High, although Anthony Billanski downplayed his morning announcement by simply stating that she had left the school. Marilyn had never liked cliques, but as she tossed and turned until the wee hours, she realized her feelings extended well beyond empathy for Carole Martin.

✳

During her first few years at Souris High School, the speculation by many of the townsfolk was that because of their shared heritage,

Marilyn and Anthony would become an item. Little could any of them know, Marilyn did not have the slightest intention of considering a relationship with a man who, in short order, had reminded her of her traditional Ukrainian father. The final straw came when Michael Griffin, by far the most innovative teacher in the school, resigned, because Anthony had been persistent in his criticism of him.

Elmer Stravinsky had cost her the love of her life, and although Marilyn returned to the farm near Vegreville once or twice a year for Christmas and her mother's birthday, she scarcely said more than two words to him. She had completed her elementary grades in a small parochial school south of Vegreville, where every student was of Ukrainian descent. Finally, Marilyn had graduated to Vegreville High School and could barely wait for classes to start that fall, when she would encounter a broader selection of peers. She was especially eager to meet the offspring of the two new families rumoured to have recently arrived in their town in east-central Alberta from England.

The five new students, two sisters in one family and two in the other, along with their brother, kept pretty much to themselves, although right from the beginning, Marilyn had noticed Colin Armstrong. He was so unlike any of the rough and tough, large-boned, broad-shouldered farm boys she had known all her life. Instead, Colin was of slight stature, tall, and willowy with a soft-spoken voice and impeccable manners.

Before the end of the first week of school, the other boys had singled out Colin, with Marilyn's older brother, Maurice, being the ringleader. The most dominant label that was soon tossed about the school ground was "fairy," with "Limey" added now and then to give spice to their name-calling. The girls fared much better, with the four of them sticking together like glue in the classroom and every moment they were outdoors, until they were safely behind the closed doors of their respective homes.

At first, Marilyn was prepared to think they did not venture beyond their group, because they fully expected that the dominant contingent of female Ukrainian students would be equally derogatory toward them. Some of the other girls did start to make disparaging comments about them being stuck-up and arrogant, but Marilyn soon put an end to the insults. She was a lanky, raw-boned youth, not afraid of standing up for her deep-seated belief that everyone is created equal. Besides, regardless of how the siblings might disagree, Maurice could always be counted on to back up his sister.

In truth, she was fascinated by the English students' accents and loved listening to them speak. Marilyn wanted nothing more than to become their friend, and she eagerly tried to welcome them to the school and the community. Nonetheless, every attempt she made to involve if not the group at least one of them in conversation or in any activity resulted in her being ignored. Marilyn had never felt so invisible in her life; she could not understand why they would not interact with her, especially when she could likely persuade Maurice to stop harassing Colin.

One day during the lunch hour, it all became crystal clear. The four girls were strolling around the schoolyard, as was their custom, before stopping to cluster by the evergreen grove. Unknown to them, Marilyn had decided to eat her lunch alone seated under the overlapping branches. She was on the other side concealed from their view and was on the verge of speaking when she heard, "At last we've discovered a secluded spot where we won't encounter that bothersome Marilyn Stravinsky, or whatever her name is. Why can't she get the message that we don't want anything to do with her? The other students have figured it out, but for some reason, she seems to think we would actually consider bringing her into our circle. Good heavens, what could we possibly have in common with such an uncomely Ukrainian farm girl?"

Marilyn held her breath and sat as silent as a stone, hoping that they would soon move along. She could hardly believe her ears. All the while, she had been feeling sorry for them, because she thought the other students in the predominantly Ukrainian school looked down on the English strangers in their midst. Instead, it was the other way around. They were the ones who were being condescending, to the point of excluding the rest of the pupils, all of whom had been born and raised in the community.

Finally, they left. Marilyn was about to stand up when she heard, "I'm sorry you had to listen to my snooty sisters and their friends. I like the fact that you've gone out of your way to befriend them, but they have snubbed you at every turn. As you probably know, I'm Colin, and this is my favourite place in the entire schoolyard."

Thus began Marilyn and Colin's endearing friendship, which, by the time they were both in grade twelve, had developed into a budding romance. When Marilyn asked Maurice to stop the other boys from tormenting Colin, threatening to squeal to their folks about his smoking habit, he had reluctantly agreed. Then she and Colin spent every minute in each other's company during the scheduled breaks throughout their years of secondary schooling, and invariably arranged to meet for all the extracurricular activities.

Neither had been introduced to the other's parents, both being wary about how their respective families might view their relationship. Still, in a few weeks, they would be graduating, and Colin was intent on formally asking Mr. Stravinsky's permission to accompany Marilyn to the prom. As it happened, their vigilance was well founded. Elmer chased Colin off his property with his shotgun aimed just marginally above his head, accompanied by the threat that it would be lowered if he ever came near his daughter again. Bravery was not one of Colin's strong points, and from that day onward, he stayed as far away from Marilyn as if she had suddenly contracted leprosy.

Initially, Marilyn blamed Colin for being so spineless, but in the end, she placed the fault squarely upon her father's shoulders. She had expected he might be upset she had a boyfriend, but she was not prepared for the violence of his reaction. It made no sense, and the only conclusion she could reach was that he had judged her suitor solely on the basis of his accent. True, her family had always gathered with people who shared their heritage, but until that day, Marilyn had no idea her father was so prejudiced.

In grade elven, she completed a paper on the history of Vegreville and was amazed to discover as many as thirty different ethnic groups were living in their area. Marilyn was also surprised to learn that one of the most frequent commentaries about the small town was the harmony with which so many people from different cultures had lived and worked together. The four largest groups were English, Ukrainian, French, and German.

So, what was her father's problem, and was Maurice nothing more than a chip off the old block? Had he discriminated against Colin because of his effeminate characteristics, as Marilyn originally thought, or was Maurice equally prejudiced against people of different nationalities? But had the newly immigrated English students been any more tolerant? By excluding every other pupil in the school, had they also been bigoted?

Now, ten years later, Marilyn was teaching in a school where another small clique had been formed and allowed to continue, even though she had addressed the issue about segregation on numerous occasions. The teaching staff had been divided on the topic, claiming that students would always gravitate toward those who shared similar interests. What harm could come of it? Marilyn had been surprised that Michael was in favour of the three musketeers, and she considered his overt support the one flaw in his progressive teaching approaches.

His replacement, Miss Robertson, had also sanctioned Jessica and

Francine's coterie, and now Carole Martin bore the brunt of the discriminatory actions in the schoolyard. Finally, drifting off to sleep, Marilyn had the good sense to realize that she could do little, if anything, to rectify what had happened to Carole and nothing at all to change the fact that humans often have an inherent need to lord it over their fellow beings.

*

It was exhilarating being back on campus. On the first morning, after driving around for thirty minutes trying to find a parking spot, and subsequently being late for her initial class, Lindsay elected to ride the bus. She soon realized the advantages of having free hands and a mind uncluttered by the requirements of driving; she could review the previous day's notes and peruse the syllabus in preparation for her upcoming classes.

Lindsay was by far the oldest student registered in the post-graduate psychology program, and although she lacked only three courses to complete the requirements before beginning her thesis, she was uncertain about her transition back to formal study. Prior to her precipitate departure from Brandon College, when she had nearly miscarried Cassandra, Lindsay had always been at the head of her class.

Long before the mid-term examinations, however, Lindsay's classmates had recognized that her age and attendant life experiences had conferred upon her a heightened awareness of the intricate workings of the human mind, and perhaps more significantly, the elusive attribute of wisdom. Soon, Lindsay became the centre of attention, with many of the female students and an ever-increasing number of the young men intrigued by the mature and still very beautiful woman in their midst.

During the sixteen years she had spent mothering Cassandra, Lindsay had never thought she was bored or unfulfilled in her role as a housewife. Most of her friends were also stay-at-home mothers, and they had always planned activities to bring their families together. When the children reached school age, her circle extended the hours of their luncheons, tennis games, and the time spent with whatever charitable group for which they happened to be volunteering.

George worked long hours in his medical practice, and when he came home, he enjoyed being greeted by his wife and daughter. Every possible opportunity, when he was not on call and did not have a woman in imminent labour, they made a hasty retreat to the cottage at Clear Lake. Cassandra was the light of their lives, and in addition to sharing her with Lindsay's parents in Hartney, they were a close-knit family throughout her growing years. Now in her sophomore year at high school, their daughter had an equally loving relationship with her parents and had never given them a moment of grief.

One of the highlights of Lindsay's week was when Cassandra joined her and Hope on campus for their regular Friday afternoon coffee break. From the beginning of the semester, it had been common for Lindsay and Hope to eat lunch together, since neither of them knew many of the other students, and Lindsay was eager for her daughter to have an equal opportunity to pursue her relationship with Hope. The more she interacted with Hope, the more Lindsay recognized what a remarkable young woman she was, but she also realized that in the incredible years that almost certainly lay ahead, Hope would require the stabilizing influence of a surrogate mother and family.

Then, when Lindsay was informed that Dr. Eleanor Donahue had been selected as her graduate adviser, she felt as if all the stars were lining up for her success. She had met Dr. Donahue at several social functions she and George had attended, and she was her husband's psychologist of choice whenever he needed to make a referral for one of his patients. In addition, to her clinical practice, she was recognized as one of the more forward-thinking professors in the Faculty of Psychology.

As the weeks passed, Lindsay became aware that her friends telephoned less and less. At first, she wrestled with pangs of guilt. Only one or two had expressed any sentiment of support, with most of them wondering, and probably whispering behind her back, if she was going through a mid-life crisis, or worse, she and George were having marital problems. Still others openly questioned what could possibly motivate her to become a student at her age.

Whether it was because she was surrounded by young people, or perhaps due to the necessity of having to use her grey matter for more than making household decisions, suddenly, Lindsay felt more stimulated and invigorated than she had in years. She arose early, reviewed her notes as she prepared breakfast, and had the kitchen in order before she ran out the door to catch the bus. If George and Cassandra noticed or commented on any changes in their lifestyle, it was that she had become even more organized and capable in the management of their home.

Still, if the truth was known, both her husband and daughter would have jumped hurdles to do anything Lindsay might request to assist in her transition from housewife to grad student. They had been so excited by her decision to continue with her master's degree, appreciating that it was time for her to return to the profession she had begun to pursue in her youth. George was enjoying his wife's newly discovered passion for life and in their bedroom, while Cassandra was delighted to be drawn into the aspirations and realities of her mother's journey.

*

Answering the telephone on the third ring, it took Margaret several minutes to determine the identity of the caller. "Hello, I'm sorry. Could you please speak up? I can barely hear you. Yes, this is Margaret Devonshire. Who is this, please? I'm having difficulty placing your voice."

When at last Margaret deciphered that it was Susan Wharton, she was more than a little surprised. Still, she did not want to discourage her from expressing the reason for her call, and she chose her words carefully. "I'm glad to hear from you, Susan. Please, forgive me for taking so long to figure out it was you."

The gentle tone of her former teacher's voice heightened Susan's resolve to make her request, and she haltingly said, "I'm at the house, and I was wondering if you would please come over. I know you're probably very busy on your day off from school, but even if you could come for a short time, I would be grateful."

"Yes, for sure. I've just been sitting here with the newspaper. I'll throw on something decent and be along within half an hour. Stay at the house, and I'll bring us a flask of coffee and some muffins."

Thankful that she had just made a fresh pot of coffee, Margaret poured it into her large thermos and gathered up the blueberry muffins she had set out for breakfast. She quickly scribbled a note to James, telling him where she was going but not to follow unless she called him and to make himself toast when he came in from tending to the chores. Margaret believed Susan was reaching out to her, and haste was of the essence. She was dressed and was out the door before fifteen minutes had passed.

Margaret drove slowly into the Smith's driveway, noting the absence of any vehicle, and hoped it was confirmation that Susan had walked across the field. What she planned to disclose to Susan had to be expressed to her and alone. She would not offer the slightest advice to June and Bert's daughter in the presence of Robert Wharton, and she might never have another opportunity.

Walking on the grass to avoid the sound of the crunching gravel, she let herself into the house, and called softly from the foyer. "It's me, Susan. Don't be alarmed. I didn't want the chime of the doorbell to unsettle you, so I've used my key."

When Margaret reached the kitchen, she found Susan still seated in the chair by the telephone desk. She suspected that Susan had already expended considerable energy walking to her parents' farm and then mustering the courage to call her. After Margaret set the refreshments on the table, she calmly approached the subdued young woman and knelt beside her. "Susan, I'm so sorry about your mum and dad."

It was too much. Susan would never have expected such solicitude from Mrs. Devonshire, and the dam burst. All the tears Susan had welled up when she had finally awoken from her drug-induced comatose state to the reality that her cherished parents were gone came gushing to the surface. Margaret gently brought her down from the chair to the floor, took her into her arms, pressing her to her bosom, and allowed Susan's suppressed deluge of sorrow to flow.

Between her heartrending sobs, Susan kept trying to articulate something that Margaret could not comprehend. She could only soothe her by stroking her hair, saying, "Hush, my dear, hush. You can tell me later."

Unknown time elapsed before Susan regained a modicum of calm and coherence. Margaret was stiff, and once up off the floor, needed to stretch and work the kinks out of her tired muscles. Then, offering her hands to Susan, she helped bring her to an upright position before guiding her to one of the kitchen chairs.

The two women drank the steaming coffee from the mugs Margaret had brought and ate a muffin in silence. Finally, Susan took a deep breath, and in a voice that came from the depth of her soul, said, "I'm to blame. It's all my fault my parents are dead."

Not wanting her face to reveal her astonishment, Margaret lowered her head as questions coursed through her brain. Could Susan at last be growing up? Was she actually taking responsibility for the tragic events that had occurred in the kitchen where they were now seated?

Even as she was having these thoughts, Margaret's own culpability rushed to the forefront. "No, Susan, you're not alone. As God is my witness, I can't allow you to carry the entire burden of guilt."

It was Susan's turn to be surprised, and raising her head, she looked directly at Margaret. "What are you talking about?"

"Oh, Susan, if only I'd listened to my instincts. Several times I followed you and Carole to your secret hideaway by the rink, and although I could not hear you clearly, I pieced together that you were planning something with Robert. I should have told your mother, but I didn't think for a minute that you meant anything you were saying."

Suddenly, Susan was alert. "If you were there, did you ever hear me telling Carole about giving her a letter to deliver to Mum and Dad the day after we left? Tell me!"

"I might have, but I had no proof. I wanted to speak at the inquest, but it was all hearsay. Besides, I knew Carole's lawyer would have eaten me up and spit me out if I'd come forward. Even when the judge made his final appeal, I might have said something, if I hadn't been held back in my seat. But, it wasn't the letter that was so important. Your mother and I made our mistake as soon as I picked her up, and we decided to try and find you. Dear God, to this day, I don't know why we didn't telephone the police."

"What do you think the police could have done? At the very least, Mum and Dad would have known where I was if Carole had delivered the letter."

"You would never have left the country. All we needed to do was get in touch with the Brandon police and have them request their counterparts in Winnipeg monitor the international airport. You were under age. Robert could have been detained for kidnapping."

At first, the changes in their relationship were subtle. Even during the initial week of Carole's departure, Jessica did not seem as enthused about seeing Francine when Pat dropped her off at the Lingnan, so the two of them could walk together to school. On Friday morning, Jessica waited until they were on their way before she said, "Thanks, Francine, but now that Carole's gone, I'll be fine on my own. On Monday, Mother Pat can just drive you right to the school."

Francine was a little taken aback. She had enjoyed starting every morning with Jessica, but she decided not to say anything. However, by the next week, she noticed that Jessica was hesitant about being with her at recess, and then she was no longer needed to walk to the Lingnan at lunchtime. For the first two months of the semester, Francine had spent every minute of every recess and lunch hour with Jessica, but now her friend was drawing away from her. Sometimes, Jessica hardly managed a cursory greeting and goodbye at the end of the day.

By the beginning of the third week, Francine was becoming concerned, but she tried to make light of the situation by tossing out comments such as, "I did have my shower and brushed my teeth, although I know Uncle Daniel likes to overuse garlic!" Jessica had the grace to laugh, but then she would walk away to chat with one or another of their classmates.

Still, every Sunday when the families gathered for dinner, Jessica was as friendly as always, full of gaiety, confidences, and plans, especially when Cassandra, and on those rare occasions, as she had for the Remembrance Day long weekend, Hope were able to join them. When they were all together, Francine felt that their foursome was alive and well and would endure for the rest of their lives. However, Jessica's behaviour at school was incongruous, and one of Francine's greatest stumbling blocks in her relationships with others was inconsistency.

Was she just being oversensitive? Should she have a tête-à-tête with Mother Pat and share how Jessica was acting at school? But what could she really tell her when Francine did not know herself what, if anything, was happening. Whenever Jessica did interact with her, she was always polite and considerate. So, why did Francine feel that her one true friend at Souris High was becoming increasingly elusive?

On the other hand, Francine did not want to let her anxiety build until she experienced a recurrence of her nightmares. During her sessions with Dr. Donahue, they had concluded that a feeling of loss precipitated her terrifying dreams, and if Jessica were in fact excluding her, the deprivation of her friendship would be profound.

When, on the next Sunday at the Lingnan, Jessica had been affectionate and once again full of hijinks, Francine decided to wait another week and see if her overactive imagination was the culprit. But then on Monday morning, Francine expressed her salutation three times before Jessica even acknowledged her presence. This was real. Before the bell rang, Jessica apologized, saying she had not heard her, but Francine would have had to be a fool not to know she was being ignored.

Pat placed two mugs of steaming hot chocolate on the table. Francine had sat mute, looking out the side window all the way home, and Pat had pre-empted her retreat to the sanctity of her loft with the offer of a hot drink. No sooner had they sat down than Francine asked if she had a few minutes before beginning supper and then blurted out her frustrations with Jessica.

Taking a sip, Pat said, "I was wondering when you were going to confide what has been eating away at you for weeks now. I'd expected that with Carole unequivocally out of your life, you would be overjoyed. But, as this month has progressed, you've become more and more sullen. So, let's get to the bottom of it. What do you think about me checking with Trin Friday morning, and then, if her mother can spare her, you invite Jessica for a sleepover on the weekend?"

"That sounds okay, but I'm not sure it will work. When there's just the two of us, Jessica still treats me like I'm her bosom friend. It's only at school since Carole has gone that she acts like she wishes I would also disappear."

"It sounds like you have good reason to be upset with Jessica, my darling girl, but it'll be up to you to share with her how you're feeling and to encourage her to tell you what's motivating the discrepancy in her behaviour when you two are in the presence of others. We could role play, if you like, how you might approach the situation."

✳

The ensuing silence was deafening. It would never have occurred to Susan that her parents had the option of sending the police after her and arresting Robert. At the time, if anything, such drastic action would only have heightened her resolve to elope with him, while intensifying her resentment toward them. But now, in the aftermath, Susan fervently wished that she and Robert had been intercepted at the airport.

As soon as the words were out of her mouth, Margaret was convinced she had alienated Susan, the last thing she wanted to do. She needed her to be responsive, not to turn against her or, worse, to withdraw into the near-catatonic state she had occupied for months. Why had she dug up the past? Still, Margaret could no longer deny her responsibility in the deaths of her best friends and allow their only child to believe that she was wholly culpable.

When Susan broke the uneasy stillness, which had descended upon a house that felt as if it was a mausoleum, Margaret could scarcely believe her ears. "If only I could turn back the passage of time, I would tell the police to take him."

"What are you saying, Susan? Surely, you and Robert can't be having marital problems already?"

"I've made a terrible mistake. What in God's name was I thinking? How could I ever have considered I was in love with a man so much older than me? Now when it's too late, I realize I was only infatuated by his worldliness, his money, and his flashy car. I was bored and wanted some excitement in my life. Then, when we were in Hawaii, he treated me like a princess, and even for a while when we returned. But he bitterly resented my father's reaction to him. After their deaths, he was considerate for a time, but eventually his patience ran thin, and he expected me to be his wife, in the kitchen and in the bedroom. Oh, what a bloody mess I've made of my life!"

Susan's confession infuriated Margaret. She felt like standing up and shaking the living daylights out of the stupid impulsive girl who had caused her parents such torment before they both paid with their lives. It had not mattered to her that June's death was ruled accidental; she and Bert would never have been fighting about anything other than their pampered daughter. And now, within months, Susan had reached the same conclusion they had tried in vain to tell her from the beginning.

Margaret took several deep breaths to calm herself. There was no going back now; what was done was done. However, as God was her witness, she would do everything in her power to make certain that Robert Wharton never got his hands on one penny of June and Bert's legacy. Nevertheless, it was not going to be easy, with the law stating that each partner in a marriage was entitled to half of all the assets. Margaret had no idea of Robert's actual worth, but she knew full well that with the Smiths' property and Bert's inheritance from his wealthy aunt that the amount bequeathed to Susan would be substantial.

Suddenly Margaret sat upright as if she had been struck by a thunderbolt. "Susan, take your time, and think very carefully. Then tell me everything about your wedding in Hawaii."

"Well, what I really liked about getting married on that island was how causal it was, without all the usual fuss and bother. On the first evening after our arrival, we went to a performance of hula dancers on the beach, and during a break, Robert spoke to their leader. At his request, the elder came forward to marry us, and after a toast to the bride and groom, they resumed the dance, with everyone joining in our celebration until dawn. I've never had so much fun in my life."

"And then when did you and Robert sign the papers, and who were your witnesses?"

"What papers? That was it. To be honest, we both proceeded to get very drunk, but I don't remember ever signing anything, and we certainly didn't know anyone who was there. Come to think of it, we only told the elder our first names, and when he pronounced us man and wife, he just said Susan and Robert. Why, what are you getting at, Mrs. Devonshire?"

"Oh, for heaven's sake, call me Margaret already. I wonder how legitimate your little beach ceremony actually was. Did you go to a justice of the peace or a church any other time you were in Hawaii to legalize your marriage? You might not be Mrs. Robert Wharton at all!"

"What? I really am stupid! Now I know why Robert suggested we get married here. I thought he was trying to make my parents happy, because they missed putting on a big wedding for me. Dear God, it was only days after I delivered the invitation to Mum that they were both found dead in this kitchen."

Sensing that Susan was on the verge of slipping once again into the oppressive pit of self-condemnation, Margaret said, "Stay with me, Susan. There's no point now in either one of us wallowing in guilt. From what you expressed earlier, I gather you are neither in love with Robert nor do you have any desire to be married to him. But the first thing we must do is get in touch with your parents' lawyer and have him contact the authorities in Hawaii to verify if there is any legal record of your marriage."

"I'm seeing him in ten days. I ran into him earlier this week in the hallway of his office, and that's why I came over here. He asked me to find out what's been happening to my parents' property, and he's going to read me their will again. I have his telephone number in my purse."

"Where's Robert right now? Can you walk home and call me at my house with Mr. Barclay's number? I'll telephone him first thing on Monday morning. Over the next couple of days, I expect you to think very seriously regarding what you want to do about your situation, and don't breathe a word to Robert. If indeed you aren't married, and you want to be free from this man, who might have duped you into believing you're his wife, we're going to act quickly and legally.

＊

When Trin opened the side door of the Lingnan leading into the family's adjoining residence, she was not surprised to see Patricia. Aside from no longer having their morning coffee breaks, Trin missed having Francine join them at the restaurant for lunch every day.

"Come in, Pat. Sebio has gone to open up. I think you and I need to have a chat about what's happening with our girls."

"It sounds like you've noticed the changes too, Trin. I'm glad, because I'd like them to sort out their differences and resume their friendship. Has Jessica said anything to you?"

"Actually, what alerted me is not what Jessica has said. It's whom she rarely ever talks about anymore. Suddenly, I'm hearing the names of many new friends and what she's doing with them, but Francine is seldom mentioned. So, during our last two Sunday dinners, when the girls were within earshot, I listened and watched them carefully but was not able to notice anything that indicated dissension."

After Patricia narrated Francine's concerns as she had expressed them to her, she said, "Francine and I would like to invite Jessica to spend Saturday afternoon and evening at the farm. We could have lunch at the Lingnan, and if you agree, then she would come home with us."

"Better yet, Pat, come for supper on Friday, and Jessica can spend the weekend with you. Sebio and I can manage for one day without her."

At first when her mother delivered the invitation, Jessica was resistant. Several of her new chums at school had been talking about going to a movie at the theatre, but then she thought about how much she enjoyed spending time on the McGregor farm. It had been unseasonably mild, and if the prediction for the weekend was accurate, more pleasant weather was in store, which meant leisurely hikes and tending to Francine's sheep.

By the time the bell tolled the end of the school week, Jessica was excited about the next two days. As she waited for Francine to gather her belongings from her locker, she realized that the two of them had not spoken since Monday. No wonder Francine was in no hurry to walk to the Lingnan with her.

Suddenly, Jessica thought it odd that, after Jessica avoided her all week, Francine had asked her for a sleepover. Whose idea was it, and what was the real purpose? Was she going to be drilled about why she was becoming friendly with many of their other classmates? If that was what Francine had up her sleeve, it might not be much fun after all, and she certainly was not going to put up with a petulant Francine Stonehenge for two long days.

Even as these unkind thoughts were flitting through her mind, Jessica recognized how unfair she was being. Why had she started to find fault with practically everything Francine said or did as if she had become her arch-enemy instead of her closest friend? Francine had been Jessica's only supporter during those first months of the year, but after Carole departed, Jessica had turned on her.

In the depths of her heart, Jessica did not believe what some of her new friends were telling her. Regardless of what she felt, she could never blame Francine for being the reason Carole had singled her out with her racial slurs. Even if the reason Carole resented Francine was because of what had happened at Hartney School, she could hardly be held responsible for how Carole chose to behave years later. Nor was Francine likely to have any awareness of what Miss Stravinsky had taught in a special class on reverse discrimination.

✳

The grade twelve students were still talking about the afternoon their history teacher came into the classroom and told them to put away their books. "Today, instead of learning about prejudice in other parts of the country and throughout the world, I'm going to introduce you to its possible existence right here, albeit in a much subtler form."

Then Miss Stravinsky delved into a detailed definition of the concept of discrimination, explaining how it can work both ways, like a double-edged sword. At first, the pupils were at a loss, many of them glancing at each other and then back again. It was not until she started to talk about cliques that a collective murmur of understanding crept into the corners of the room.

As their teacher continued, heads slowly began to lower in comprehension, and for some of the more astute, in acknowledgement. Who in the classroom had not, at one time or another, snubbed and excluded a fellow student? Which one of them was not guilty of judging someone because of individual differences, whether in terms of size, gender, or appearance? But then, surely it was not possible to like everyone.

When Miss Stravinsky was commencing to expound on the importance of acceptance and tolerance, true to form, Jacqueline Benson blurted, "You mean like those two girls who never talk to anyone else, Jessica, and Francine, oh, what's her last name? They were always with Hope Harding, before she left school, calling themselves 'the three musketeers.' Are you saying that they've actually been discriminating against the rest of us?"

"I'll not single out any student in the school, because I know each of you has your own circle of friends. Of course, it's perfectly natural for any of us to associate with those who share similar interests, but when we deliberately exclude someone all the time, it can become a type of segregation. Often, it is so subtle that the individuals who are isolating themselves from others are unaware of the impact of their behaviour, as are those who are being left out. But since they are consistently excluded, those people could claim what I view as reverse discrimination."

Again, it was Jacqueline who risked questioning Miss Stravinsky. "Well, what are we supposed to do if we feel like this is happening?"

"That's exactly why tolerance and acceptance of individual differences are so important, Jacqueline. It's when we interact with everyone that our school, our community, and our country can be said to be integrated, that we are all being treated like equals."

That day on their way home from school, Jacqueline and several of her classmates decided to have tea at the Lingnan. When Jessica was approaching their table to take their order, Rebecca whispered to Jacqueline, "Don't say anything about what Miss Stravinsky taught this afternoon."

"Why not? You know, I think Jessica is smart, but I bet she doesn't realize she's segregating us. I've always thought she seemed really nice, and I, for one, would like to get to know her better. Maybe if we explain what she's doing, she'll understand and be more likely to talk to lots of other kids in school. She's always friendly with us at her parents' restaurant, and I'm sure it not just because we're customers."

✳

The restaurant was overflowing with hungry patrons on Friday, so rather than sit down with Mother Pat and her uncles to eat, Francine helped Jessica bus the tables. They had not worked together in the Lingnan for a long time, and after frequent brief exchanges by the swinging door into the kitchen, their camaraderie was restored.

It was after eight before the rush was over, and then the friends collapsed at the table, ravenous. As they devoured hot-and-sour soup, barbecued pork, chicken balls, and shrimp-fried rice, served by Mother Pat, Jessica and Francine chatted and laughed as they always had before their archenemy, Carole Martin, had arrived at Souris High.

The stage was set for the weekend, and by the time they were comfortably settled in Francine's cozy loft, both girls realized how much they had missed each other's company. Even though they had been constantly together, they had underestimated the stress they were under during the first two months of school. Their estrangement over the past several weeks had heightened the strain upon the friendship that they had forged more than four years earlier.

It was well after ten before Patricia heard the girls stirring and began to prepare a second breakfast for the morning. If they had stayed up late, they must have been unusually quiet, because they had not disturbed the rest of the household, as they had been known to do on so many other occasions. On the other hand, Pat wondered if they might have slept late because of the tiredness that often accompanies what she suspected had been a mutual catharsis.

The sun had been casting its wintry rays through the kitchen window from the beginning of daybreak with convincing warmth. As soon as Francine and Jessica had consumed the bacon-and-cheese omelette, Patricia said, "Since it's such a beautiful day, your Uncle Daniel and I were talking about going for an afternoon hike in Victoria Park. Do you want to come with us, or would you rather stay here to tend to your sheep, which, I might add, you've been neglecting lately?"

After a quick glance at Jessica, Francine replied, "Thanks, Mother Pat, but we've already decided to go for a walk over the hills later. We realized that it's been so long since just the two of us have roamed around to all our favourite haunts, and it looks like the perfect day. And you're quite right about me needing to spend time with my sheep."

"Whatever you prefer, my lovelies. There's pop, salads, and cold chicken in the fridge when you return. We don't intend to hurry home, since I've made a picnic lunch for us."

∗

Smiling inwardly, Patricia was pleased that the plan was unfolding as she and Trin had hoped. It was also the kind of day Pat had been waiting for since the death of her father. Although she had felt a sense of peace after burying him on his land, she recognized that she could benefit from a strenuous communing walk with Mother Nature to resolve some issues in her own life.

When they arrived home the afternoon after the burial, Patricia had promptly sat down and penned letters to her two younger sisters to mail to the addresses where she had sent them occasional Christmas cards. She had little compunction about reconnecting with her brother, Matthew, but during those few days in Dauphin, memories of the happier times she had experienced with her sisters had been resurrected, and they tugged at her heart.

Knowing she had been responsible for the estrangement heightened Patricia's feelings of remorse and guilt. When she walked out the door of the family home, she had never looked back. She had become so immersed in getting on with her life that she seldom gave any thought to Martha and Bella. How had they fared with their father and brother controlling them? How long before they had taken flight after her abandonment, and how had they survived?

On the way to Souris, Daniel said, "You're very pensive, my dear, and whatever you have on your mind, I suspect it's the reason for our stroll around Victoria Park. Do you want to tell me now or wait until you've sorted things out?"

"First, I want a good brisk walk to straighten out my head. In fact, I'd like you to park by the swinging bridge, and we can take the path to the mystical old oak tree. If ever I needed the reputed 'aura of spiritual peace and knowledge' of that five hundred-year-old oak, it's now."

They walked in silence for close to an hour and a half, taking turns carrying the small basket with the lunch that Patricia had packed. The sun's rays were surprisingly warm, and in the shelter of the oak's boughs, she was certain it would be pleasant enough to enjoy their picnic. The temperature was well above zero, and long before they reached their destination, both had opened the zippers of their light winter apparel.

The tuna salad and cucumber sandwiches never tasted so good, and it was not until she opened the small thermos of hot sweet tea that Patricia finally spoke. "Thank you for your patience. I'm sure you must be wondering what's bothering me."

"You haven't really been yourself, my love, since your father's death, which is perfectly understandable. I've always considered grieving a private matter, and I knew that when you were ready to enlighten me, you would."

"As strange as it may sound, my grieving is not for my father but rather for my younger sisters. Yes, I found it sad that we were the only mourners at his service. However, I have always believed that we reap what we sow. But the entire time we were in Dauphin, I kept hoping I would have a chance to see Martha and Bella."

To Daniel's surprise, Patricia began to cry softly. As he took her into his comforting arms, she explained what she had been feeling and her subsequent disappointment that she had received no response to her letters. When her sobs began to subside, Daniel said, "I'm at a loss for what to say, Patricia, other than perhaps one day they'll choose to search for you. On the other hand, you may never see either one of them again. But you had to leave, my darling, to pursue your dream. Had you stayed, your destiny would have been thwarted, and then we would never have met. All I know is that whatever happens, everyone has to follow their own path in life, and none of us can be responsible for any other person's choices."

"Thank you for sharing your sage perspective, Daniel. Oh, how I would have missed loving you, my precious husband, and Francine, Darrin, and all our friends. Well, it sure didn't take you long to become the fount of wisdom under the branches of this ancient tree, did it? Now, let's go home and see what our girls are up to before we make pizza for supper."

✳

As soon as they had washed their dishes, Francine and Jessica were off to the sheep pen. They had barely rounded the corner when the spring lambs came bleating to see them. Over the years, Francine's herd had been steadily increasing, and now there were over thirty animals in her enclosure. Still, her uncles never pressed her to sell the young or the old, simply adding to the size of the fence year after year.

"Wow, Francine, I didn't realize you owned so many sheep. What are you going to do with them when you go off to Brandon College?"

"I really haven't wanted to think about that. Sometimes, I can't believe how quickly we're growing up and that, before long, our entire lives will be changed. Of course, I want to get my arts degree, and pursue a literary career, but it'll be hard to leave my parents and the farm."

"It just occurred to me that if you learned how to drive, you could almost travel back and forth every day for classes, except maybe during the worst months of the winter."

"That's a great idea! We could travel together and share the driving. Tomorrow let's ask one of my uncles to start teaching us how to drive the truck. After all, it can't be much different from driving a tractor, and I've been all over the farm on the little John Deere."

Francine was distracted at that moment by one of her lambs rushing up to her for a pat on the head, and Jessica used the brief lapse as an opportunity to change the subject. She had a number of serious topics she wanted to discuss with Francine, and she knew that her friend would receive them much better when they were strolling about on the prairie hills that had always been so calming for her.

They sauntered along in silence enjoying the tranquility of the undulating landscape still sparse with snowfall, although it was the last day of November. Jessica had thought assiduously about how she would approach Francine, being acutely aware of how sensitive she could be, especially if she viewed a comment as a criticism, and decided to wait until they took a breather. When they crested the knoll surrounded by the grove of Colorado blue spruce, Jessica led the way to the opening of the branches where, years earlier, they had constructed their imaginary house amongst the conifers.

"What a glorious day! I can't believe how warm it is here under the shelter of our trees, or how hungry I am after exercising in the fresh air. Great idea grabbing snacks and pop on our way out of the house." Munching on a Mars bar, Jessica continued. "I absolutely love our haven on the hillside of your farm, Francine. You know, I think our foursome should make this our retreat, at least once or twice every year, where we gather, regardless of how old we become or how far our respective paths may take us."

"You seem even more philosophical than usual, Jessica, and you still haven't answered my question about travelling back and forth to

Brandon together. Just what are you planning to tell me, while trying so hard to avoid upsetting me?"

"God, I'd forgotten how perceptive you are. Sometimes it's downright eerie how you seem to read my mind. You're going to be a terrific writer with your proclivity for getting into other people's heads. Okay, here goes, first of all, I want to apologize for the way I've been treating you these past few weeks in school. I've been churlish and unfair, especially after you stuck by me all the time that witch was harassing me."

Francine's mouth dropped open, and it was only her quick reflexes that enabled her to stop in time so the Coke she was about to drink did not dribble down her chin. She started to accept Jessica's apology, but the words would not come. She turned away as she felt tears stinging and overflowing her eyelids. It had hurt so much, and now she realized she was having a problem accepting Jessica's sincerity.

As Jessica waited for a response, it occurred to her that she had betrayed Francine's trust, and it was little wonder that now she would not look at her. "Oh, Francine, I'm so sorry. I have given little consideration to how my behaviour has been affecting you. Please tell me that you forgive me, and that I haven't damaged our friendship beyond repair."

Several more moments elapsed before Francine diffidently said, "I want to believe you, Jessica, but I'm afraid you will be the same when we return to school on Monday."

"Please look at me, Francine. I know there's no excuse for my behaviour, but I want to try and explain what made me act the way I did."

Francine glanced at her and then sat perfectly still as Jessica reiterated what she had heard from the older students about Miss Stravinsky's lecture on reverse discrimination. "I really liked her comments about how most of us choose to have two or three close friends, but we shouldn't exclude others. We have to allow for individual differences, but I haven't been accepting of the fact that you and I have very distinct preferences when it comes to friendships. I'm gregarious and outgoing, whereas you are serious and reclusive."

Jessica bit her tongue, because she was on the verge of adding possessive and, at times, needy, as Hope had so often shared with her in private. Although she had come to realize that was exactly how she had been feeling about Francine, she knew that to express those words would only cause her friend to retreat further within herself. "It goes without saying, Francine, that we'll always be the best of friends, but at the end of every day, you return to the serenity of your farm, and in town I often see other kids. So, it's awkward to socialize with them in the evening and then ignore them the next day at school."

Thinking that lately Jessica had no trouble ignoring her during school, Francine had more than sufficient insight to know that she would only ever need one or two close friends, rather than a group, as Jessica was now saying she preferred. Even though she had been so protective of her when not one of her new friends had come to her aid the entire time that Carole had been calling her a chink, Francine did not own Jessica.

Francine had made her choice unconditionally, and if Jessica had suddenly developed a short memory, she was free to do so. It briefly crossed Francine's mind to wonder if this tendency to readily forget was a characteristic of the human condition, but she had the sense to keep that thought to herself. "You still haven't answered my question about driving to college together."

Not wanting to cause any more distress for her oft-dependent friend, Jessica decided to forego telling Francine about her recent plan to apply to the Faculty of Medicine at the University of Manitoba rather than begin her post-secondary education at Brandon College. "Oh, what a glorious sunset, but shouldn't we start back before the sun drops below the horizon? Francine, come what may, always remember you will be in my heart forever." Jessica stopped short of adding, "If only you could ever believe that we all love you."

✳

Two weeks later, when she walked into the dining room of the Royal Oak Inn in Brandon, Susan was no longer Susan Wharton. As it turned out, she had never been married to Robert, and she felt as free as a bird soaring into the heavens.

Margaret, her godmother, had also become her best ally, and in short order, the two women had restored Susan's youth and her life. Over the days they had spent in each other's company, they cried together, commiserating with one another, perhaps as much in an attempt to assuage their mutual feelings of guilt as in grieving for June and Bert. They began to realize that although they were powerless to change the past, they could move forward and reclaim their future.

On the Monday morning following Susan's timorous appeal for Margaret to come to the Smith farm, she had contacted Derek Barclay at the onset of the business day. The lawyer was as intent upon probating his client's will, as was Margaret. Furthermore, when she requested that he determine the validity of Susan's marriage, for reasons of his own, which he certainly did not disclose, he assured her that he would begin proceedings immediately.

Within the week, Derek had confirmation from the authorities in Hawaii that there was no legally binding document to authenticate that a marriage between Robert Wharton and Susan Smith had occurred. The ceremony on the beach conducted by the leader of a group of hula dancers was nothing but a sham, and Derek wondered if the man who had passed himself off as her loving husband at the inquest was only too aware of the fact.

Derek was incensed. The Smith family had been clients of the

Barclay & Barclay law firm from the day his grandfather had opened the doors of the practice, and over the years, Bert's grandfather, his father, and then Bert himself had become valued clients. To think that Bert's life had been cut short because of the duplicity of a man with designs upon his only daughter was almost more than Derek could bear.

Before he telephoned Margaret with his findings, Derek wrestled with the notion of bringing charges against Robert. He knew he could argue that the farmer had abducted Susan, since at the time of the supposed elopement, she was under age eighteen. His stomach churned at the thought of the unmitigated pleasures that Robert had reaped from her beautiful, supple body. But what positive purpose would it serve now if he were to dredge up the past? If Susan were finally on the arduous road to recovery, would a trial, with all its attendant publicity, throw Susan back into the depths of her guilt and despair?

At that moment, an image of the gorgeous red-headed woman flashed before his eyes, and he knew then that the last place he wanted Susan Smith to retreat was the pit that had engulfed her for months after her parents' death. Upon further reflection, he knew there were more effective ways to deal with the likes of Robert Wharton, not the least of which would be a substantial settlement out of court, while at the same time avoiding the degrading disclosure of Susan's exploitation to the world beyond. Suddenly, Derek became impatient for the next week to pass, so he could be seated across the table from her, although his own yearnings were still buried so deep he had yet to grasp them.

※

Hope had chosen Beethoven's daunting "Violin Sonata No. 9 in A major Op. 47, Kreutzer." At the beginning of November, Dr. Burton had heard the rumour that the famed Dr. Charles Farrington from the

University of Halifax was contemplating a move to Brandon. What would motivate a man of his prodigious talent to relocate to a small college on the Canadian prairie was beyond Ian's comprehension, but he was elated with the endless possibilities for Hope and the music program at Brandon College.

He would never forget the morning that Dr. Elliot had called him into an unexpected meeting to announce that Dr. Farrington was planning to attend Hope's Christmas recital. Not for one moment was Ian audacious enough to consider that the brilliant virtuoso had ever heard of Hope Harding, and months would pass before he discovered that Dr. Farrington had been in the audience to listen to Hope's performance on July 1 with the Montreal Orchestre Symphonique.

At first, when Hope decided on the "Kreutzer," Ian was overwhelmed with misgivings. He was certain she would have little difficulty with the meditative second movement or the joyous third. But could she handle the fury and intensity of the first movement of a sonata legendary for its demands, unusual length, and emotional scope? Although, if she could master it, what an exuberant way to end a recital for the renowned maestro.

"I caution you, Hope, that if you persist with your choice, you must be prepared to give up everything for the next six weeks. I've performed the "Kreutzer" once in my career, and following five to seven hours of practice every day for weeks, I vowed never again. And what about you, Michael? How do you feel about not having any time to pursue your own interests?"

"As you well know, Dr. Burton, I'm here to assist in whatever Hope requires of me." Michael's eyes shone with a brilliance that comes only from deep within the inner reaches of a man, and for the first and only time, Ian wondered if Michael could be in love with their protégé. He refused to accept it, since he often had to suppress his own feelings of ardour toward her, but Ian assumed both of them were too old for the beautiful young woman.

Then Ian recalled the age difference between Jonathon and Marika Griffin. He had considered it unusual when Michael had said his mother was several years older than his father, but throughout history, men have often taken women much younger as their wives. A sudden wave of empathy for Michael flooded over Ian. In that moment of insight, he understood that Hope had but a singular passion in life, and no one would ever deter her from her course.

"In that case, let's begin right now. This is an opportunity of a lifetime, and if we succeed in convincing Dr. Farrington to come to Brandon and accept you as his student, Hope, your career as a celebrated violinist will be assured."

✳

Margaret received Derek's telephone call on Thursday morning just as she was about to leave for school. She glanced at the clock and knew instantly that she had missed Patricia. She said a silent prayer that this would be one of the days she returned from Souris shortly after she had delivered Francine. Thanking the lawyer for his illuminating news, she decided to risk calling Susan. If Robert answered the telephone, she would simply hang up and try later. Fortunately, Susan picked up on the third ring.

"Good morning, are you alone in the house?"

"Yes, he's just left to drive into Brandon for one reason or another. Why?"

"Terrific! It's appropriate you didn't refer to him as your husband, because Mr. Barclay has just confirmed that you were never legally married. I'm leaving for school now, but by recess I hope to have reached Patricia and arranged for her to take over my class until the afternoon break. In the meantime, I want you to pack everything that belongs to you, and as soon as I can, I'll pick you up. You will be residing with me and James until this mess is sorted out and you've decided what you want to do."

"I can't believe he had me convinced that I was his wife."

"It may be possible that he really does think you're married. But now I must go."

"Thank you, Margaret. I've already been secretly gathering my personal belongings these last few days whenever he's been out. I can hardly wait to be free."

Lady Luck was on Margaret's side. Patricia had just walked in the door and still had her coat on when she answered the telephone. "Why, yes I could be at the school within fifteen minutes, but are you going to tell me what this is about?"

"I'll be back at school in time for you to leave for Souris. Once you drop off Alice and Francine this afternoon, come along to my place, and I'll bring you up to date."

*

Susan was in the Devonshires' spare bedroom unpacking when Patricia arrived in record time after delivering Francine and Alice to their respective homes. Patricia's curiosity had been piqued all day, but there had been no time to satisfy it as she and Margaret had exchanged places at Hartney School. In all her years as principal, Margaret had never made such a strange request, and Patricia was anxious to hear what could be motivating her unusual behaviour.

Over a cup of tea that Margaret had scarcely steeped when she saw Patricia walking up the driveway, she said, "Let's sit in the living room. It's more private than the kitchen, and I don't want Susan to surprise us in the midst of our discussion."

After Margaret had narrated the occurrences of the past week, Patricia sat in silence. At last, in an anguished voice, she said, "Please pardon my language, but June and Bert are dead because of that bastard! And he had the nerve to return to our community pretending he had married her. I don't believe for one minute that Susan was totally innocent, probably more naïve than she would like any of us to think, but he's a man of experience. But why in God's name are you supporting Susan now? Bert and James were lifelong friends."

"That's just it, Patricia. I think Susan got carried away with his attention, his fancy car, and his worldly ways. I'm sure she thought of his proposal as a grand adventure without the slightest regard for the consequences, and let's face it, would any one of us in this neighbourhood ever have considered the ultimate outcome? James is not pleased that I'm helping her, but on the other hand, he would never allow that seducer to touch one cent of Susan's inheritance."

"Surely, she'll sell the farm. I hardly think she would want to live in the house where her parents died. Would James consider buying the land?"

"We've talked about it, but after finishing the seeding this spring and then taking the crop off in the fall, he was exhausted. James is finally realizing that he's getting up in years, and he can't farm another section, even if Susan chooses to stay and asks him to rent her land."

"We better pray that Susan's lawyer has his facts straight and knows what he's doing. The only farmer in the district presumably with the money to purchase more land is Robert Wharton, and he'll be opposed to buying it when he thinks that because of his trumped-up marriage, half of it already belongs to him."

"James and I have always dealt with Barclay & Barclay. Derek might be the most skilled lawyer from that family yet. I could hear the anger in his voice. I suspect he's highly motivated to make that cradle robber pay for his duplicity."

❋

Derek was the initial customer to arrive, and he sat in the chair at their reserved table fronting the door of the dining room. He was eager to observe Susan's entrance, and he was rewarded when she glided into the restaurant. His heart skipped a beat, and he had to remind himself that she was a client, and a very young one at that. By the time he rose from his chair to greet her, Derek was convinced that his surge of feeling was because he was about to right a tragic wrong that had been perpetrated against one of the firm's longstanding clients.

Nonetheless, he was aware of every aspect of Susan's appearance as she gracefully accepted the chair he was holding out for her, and once again he had difficulty believing she was the same woman he had represented at the Smiths' inquest. Susan was wearing an emerald-green silk dress that matched her eyes, and her glowing red hair was piled atop her head, fastened with a lime-coloured hair clip. Her elegance belied her age, and not for the first time, Derek questioned how that unattractive grain farmer could have led her astray.

The dining room was beginning to fill with the usual crowd of businessmen, who had begun to frequent the new posh restaurant, and not one of them could resist casting more than a cursory glance at the exquisite stranger in their midst. Nonetheless, Susan took it in stride, as if she was quite accustomed to being the centre of attention.

*

Carole had been standing by the door of the kitchen memorizing the day's special menu when she glanced up to observe Susan's grand entrance. It had taken Carole a few minutes to recognize her former school friend, but when Susan stood momentarily and perused the room, there was no mistaking that luxurious head of red hair. She could hardly believe her eyes. When she had last seen Susan at the inquest, she had been as limp as a rag doll.

Carole watched in fascination as every man who walked into the restaurant could not keep his greedy eyes off Susan, and suddenly

Carole understood how she could transfer their scrutiny to her. With menus and two glasses of ice water in hand, she waltzed over to the table, swinging her hips in tune to the easy listening music playing in the background.

"Good afternoon, Mr. Barclay. It's always my pleasure to serve you, and yet another young lady you have accompanied to our restaurant. Why, if I'm not mistaken, I know your current conquest. I believe it's Susan Wharton, a previous acquaintance who makes it a habit to run away with older men."

Derek turned his admiring gaze from Susan's beautiful countenance to glare at the waitress. He vaguely remembered her from prior visits, although he had only ever given her cursory glances. Aside from being overly friendly, she had always been appropriate in her manner. But today, she was clearly on a personal quest, and he intended to nip it in the bud before she could detract him from his enjoyment of his dinner guest.

"Please leave the menus, and return when they are closed to confirm we are ready to give you our selections."

Ignoring his request, Carole switched her focus, speaking in an even brassier tone. "Well, well, Mrs. Wharton, you have certainly become a woman of means as the sole inheritor of all your dead parents' property, in addition to being married to the wealthiest farmer in Hartney. You must be due for another vacation abroad, although I wonder who will be found deceased upon your return."

Struck by a sudden flash of memory, Derek grasped why the waitress had always been so familiar to him. Her hair was a different colour, her face was covered in makeup, and she had filled out in all the right places, and although Miss Martin had been very self-assured in the courtroom, she had been dressed in attire appropriate to an innocent high school student. Now she wore a blouse that revealed her generous cleavage and a skirt so short that Derek could well imagine the exposure, should she bend over ever so slightly.

She certainly had the floor now, as every eye, including those of the manager, became riveted on her. With three long strides, Mr. Afton, the maître d', was beside Derek's table and without a single word, he clasped Carole's arm and whisked her out of the dining room.

Never one to depart silently, Carole shouted, "Don't worry, my old school chum, we'll meet again, and the next time you won't have a sleazy lawyer to come to your aid. And, you, Mr. Afton, can take your crummy job and shove it up your derrière."

The silence ensued until Mr. Afton reappeared with a bottle of white wine in one hand and red wine in the other. He proceeded from table to table, offering his patrons a glass on the house, and then returned to take their orders. Harold worked as quickly as possible in the nearly full dining room, but had it not been for the patience and cooperation of his guests, he might well have lost any number of them. Instead, many of the businessmen were impressed with his approach of rolling up his sleeves and taking over the reins from the unruly departed waitress.

When the maître d' arrived at their table first, Derek asked, "Susan, are you in any particular rush? I've cleared my appointments until later this afternoon, and if you're not in a hurry, perhaps we can wait to place our order after those gentlemen, who may be dashing back to their offices."

"My time is my own, and I'd be perfectly content to enjoy this refreshing wine before we have something to eat. In fact, why don't we discuss our business first?"

Three hours later, as Derek escorted Susan to her car in the parking lot, he realized he was suddenly eager to relinquish their client relationship as expediently as possible. He had thoroughly enjoyed being with her. Once the will was probated, and the legality of the sale of her property was completed, he did not anticipate any reason why his new associate could not take over all exigent matters of business. Regardless of how tempted he was, Derek would not initiate any kind of personal involvement until that time, but then he would invite Susan out for an evening on the town.

✳

Time was running out. The beginning of December was fast approaching, and Hope was not ready. She kept vacillating between performing below her capability and bordering on brilliance. She had perfected the second and third movements, but even Michael was secretly starting to become concerned about whether, in such a short period, she could master the formidable first movement.

Finally, in exasperation on the last Friday in November, Dr. Burton said, "I think we all need a break. Let's disperse off campus, away from each other's company, and do something totally different tomorrow. If you start to think about the "Kreutzer" block it from your mind, and enjoy yourself. We'll resume at our usual hour on Sunday morning."

Hope was delighted. If she hurried, she might still catch Lindsay and Cassandra for their customary Friday afternoon coffee break. She had missed their regular get-togethers for the entire month, and she desperately needed to commiserate with someone other than the two men in her life, with their constant expectations of perfection.

As she entered the cafeteria, she spotted Lindsay sitting alone at their usual table in the far corner. She was preparing to depart by the time Hope reached her, and breathlessly said, "I'm sorry I'm so late. Could you please stay for a few minutes longer, Mrs. Jamison, and I'll treat you to another coffee? Has Cassandra already left?"

"Hello, my dear. We thought you weren't going to be able to join us, so Cassandra dashed off to do some shopping before she meets her dad at his office. But I don't need to leave right away, and it's been weeks since we've had a chance to chat. Tell me what you'd like, and

I'll order it while you get comfortable."

Lindsay sensed Hope's anxiety and thought perhaps it was fortuitous that Cassandra had other plans. Hope's grandparents and all her friends were thrilled about the potential impact on her career if Dr. Farrington chose to relocate to Brandon and accept her as his protégé. Lindsay might have been the only one, aside from Dr. Burton, to fully grasp the implications of such an onerous prospect. Like the dean of music, Lindsay understood the compelling force of Hope's talent, but she was convinced not even he realized the extent, without balancing influences in her life, to which Hope could be consumed by her passion.

Setting two cappuccinos on the table, Lindsay sat back down in her chair. "Would you like to talk about it now or wait until I drive you back to campus later? Whether or not the good Dr. Burton knows it, you need an evening off. You can telephone him and then your grandparents to let them know that I'm taking you home for supper."

Feeling her melancholic mood begin to lift, Hope smiled. "You're going to make a terrific psychologist, Mrs. Jamison. The only reason I made it here is because Dr. Burton told Michael and me to leave and then locked the music hall until seven on Sunday morning."

"Thank you, my lovely. As it happens, Dr. Donahue concurs with you. Now, please call me Lindsay, and pour out your heart. Another attribute I have in abundance is great listening skills."

An hour later, on the way to her grandparents to gather a few items for an overnight bag, Hope was starting to feel like a human being again. As she had practiced hour after hour over the past month, she had become more and more like an automaton, whose existence was controlled by the strings on her violin. Although she knew she was as capable of perfecting the first movement, as she had the last two, something was holding her back.

It was when Lindsay had questioned if Dr. Burton was pushing her too hard that Hope began to grasp where the budding psychologist was guiding her. After more astute queries about how she felt when playing, a light finally went on in her head, and she began to understand that when her teacher persisted in pressuring her to perform at his tempo, she would lose her own rhythm. Even this early in her musical career, Hope was beginning to comprehend that to attain her peak performance, she needed to feel her passion to empower the release of her inner dynamism.

✳

At almost nineteen years of age, she scarcely needed godparents. Nonetheless, when Margaret had moved Susan from the Wharton farm, she felt as if she was honouring a longstanding commitment. She still remembered how happy she had been on the morning of Susan's baptism, when she and James had been named as her sponsors, especially in light of the devastating news several years earlier that Margaret would not be able to conceive a child of her own.

Now, after two weeks of residing with them, not only Margaret but also James had begun to notice the marked improvements in Susan. She had started paying attention to her personal appearance and was communicating more than she had in months. When she returned from her visit to the lawyer in Brandon with boxes of new clothes, Margaret was confident that she was well on her way to recovery. Even James, who had assisted he carry her purchases into her bedroom, mumbled good-naturedly under his breath that, at this rate, it would not take Susan long to spend the money her parents had bequeathed to her.

As soon as Susan closed the door, Margaret quieted her husband by querying if he preferred her to be as lifeless as a ragdoll under the thumb of an older man who had only pretended to be her husband. Each passing day had confirmed for Margaret that Susan was still an adolescent, albeit one who had been forced to grow up quickly, and she knew she had made the right choice to bring her to their hearth and home. Deep in her heart, Margaret hoped that if she could play any role in guiding Susan into becoming a productive adult, she would assuage her guilt and, furthermore, June might forgive her when they met again in the hereafter.

Although they still never said a word about Bert and June to each other, James was becoming less reproachful toward her, until Margaret began to believe they might be able to salvage their marriage. During those few months after their friends' deaths, had she not been able to get away from her husband five days of the week to go to her job and on Sunday mornings for church, she would have left him.

In all their years of marriage, James had treated her with respect, so to suddenly be held accountable for such a tragedy was almost more than Margaret could bear. She had also lost her closest friend, and instead of being censorious of her, she had expected they would console and support one another. Initially, James's criticism had been so hurtful that Margaret had begun to query who her husband loved more, his childhood friend or her.

Fortunately, Margaret had the good sense not to draw such a pejorative comparison, and she chose to keep her distance, to the extent of moving into the guest bedroom. But when she rescued Susan from Robert's clutches, she returned to their conjugal bed. At first, James waited until she retired before he came anywhere near the master bedroom. When he finally slipped into bed, he lay so close to the edge, she feared he would fall off.

It was following an evening with Patricia and her family that, at last, James reached for her. Neither said a word as they resumed their marital relations, but the next morning at the breakfast table, they actually engaged in a conversation. Margaret had no idea what they talked about, and she did not care. The mere fact that James was finally speaking to her again was enough to lift her spirits for the entire day.

Once he rediscovered his vocal chords, James began to engage in their usual morning chatter when Margaret joined him at the counter for breakfast before she departed for school. By the end of a week, she stopped crossing her fingers and began to believe that his thaw was going to persist. And now, with Susan seated across the dinner table from them every evening, Margaret and James were enjoying the lively dialogue that accrues when a young person is in the midst.

✳

By eight o'clock Sunday morning, it was impossible to determine which of the two men was more astounded. Hope was the first to arrive at the music hall, and when Michael and then Dr. Burton joined her, she scarcely acknowledged either of them. It was as if she was in a trance, and the moment the door was opened, she headed straight to the cabinet in which her violin was locked.

Michael was on the verge of conversing with Hope when Dr. Burton cautioned him with a barely perceptible shake of his head. Instead, he motioned him to the piano, and as soon as he was ready, Hope began the first movement of the "Kreutzer." Ian was on the verge of resuming his position to turn the music sheets when he noticed that Hope was playing with her eyes closed. He had not realized that she had committed the entire sonata to memory, and he instantly perceived that this latest accomplishment, although he had no idea when it had been achieved, boded well.

Her performance was exquisite. By the time Hope launched into the second movement, still with her eyelids quivering to the rhythm of the music, Ian and Michael grasped that now her mastery was complete. The minute they heard her play the last exuberant strains, both were on their feet with boisterous applause.

Dr. Burton was the first to speak. "If all you needed was a break from practice, Hope, I wish you would have let us know sooner. Or perhaps it was because you were tired of looking at Michael and me? At any rate, whatever you did yesterday, please remember to do it again before the evening of your recital, and the hallowed walls of Brandon's concert hall will resonate with 'Brava.' And Dr. Farrington will have little choice about accepting you. Now, shall we go for coffee and then repeat your feat once more?"

Later that afternoon when they had returned to the small classroom where Michael had just finished quizzing Hope about some algebra equations, he said, "If you don't mind me asking, where did you disappear yesterday? I looked for you on campus and thought I might suggest we go for a bite to eat, but you were nowhere to be found. Finally, I figured you must have gone to visit your grandparents."

"Actually, I met Mrs. Jamison for coffee and then had a sleepover with Cassandra. After a longer lie-in than I've had in ages, the three of us went cross-country skiing in the Blue Hills. Although we had a terrific day, it was what Mrs. Jamison helped me to understand on Friday that enabled me to play the way I did this morning. Bet you were worried that my first performance was a fluke, weren't you?"

It was heavenly to share a lighter moment with Hope. The entire semester had been gruelling for both of them and Michael laughed good-naturedly before saying, "I was hoping not because I worry about all the demands placed on you. Most of the time, Dr. Burton is an exacting taskmaster, and you do have final exams looming as well. But now, surely we can practice the sonata once or twice a day, and then you'll be free to study."

They were seated so close that it was all Michael could do not to gather her into his arms and smother her petite mouth with his ardent kisses. Was she not yet sixteen? How was he ever going to spend another five years working together with such intensity, always so near to her, before he could give vent to his feelings? His love grew with each passing hour, and yet most of the time, Hope seemed oblivious of him.

Glimpsing a flicker of sadness in her tutor's eyes, Hope said, "Why don't we work for another hour and then go to Grandma and Grandpa's for dinner? They are expecting me, and they're always delighted when you can join us. The reality is that I'm just as demanding of you as Dr. Burton is of me, since we practically do everything together. I know you haven't even had a chance to go home since Thanksgiving. In fact, let's wrap up right now and go for a walk while there's still daylight before we leave for my grandparents. We don't want all work and no play to make us dull and boring."

Surprised and touched by Hope's offer, Michael was quick to agree. Perhaps there was a possibility that every now and then Hope did actually see him as a person, not only as a means to achieve her aspiration of becoming a concert violinist. A plan began to take shape in Michael's prolific mind. His mother had always dreamed about opening a bed and breakfast, and Jonathon had humoured her by turning the gable of his most recently constructed log cabin into a cozy suite. At long last, Michael would bring his parents into Brandon to attend Hope's performance, and after her stunning recital, he would take her home to be the first guest in the new loft.

✳

Finally, on the drive to Brandon for Hope's concert, Jessica decided to share her university plans with Francine. Patricia and Daniel had picked up the girls from school that Friday afternoon, and now, companionably settled in the backseat, she thought it was as sound a time as any to disclose that she had applied for pre-medicine at the University of Manitoba.

They were on their way to spend the evening with Cassandra and her parents. Jessica accepted that, of the other three musketeers,

Francine was the most comfortable with Cassandra, likely because they had known each other for the longest duration. If she became distressed by her news, Jessica expected that either Mrs. Jamison or her daughter could bring Francine out of her sulk, should she slip into one of her increasingly morose moods.

She was doing it again. When had Jessica become so intent upon judging Francine at the slightest turn of events? True, she had been friendlier with the other students at school, although most often she was still seen as being aloof, either reading or walking alone during the classroom breaks. However, Francine had been quick to point out that if Jessica expected her to accept her gregariousness, she had to allow Francine the right to be reclusive.

After offering Francine a chocolate mint, Jessica took a deep breath before launching into an update about her future. "I'd intended to tell you much sooner about my decision to apply to the University of Manitoba, but we don't seem to have the same time for each other anymore. At any rate, last summer when I started to check into the entrance requirements for medical school, it soon began to make much more sense for me to go directly to Winnipeg rather than take my bachelor of science at Brandon College. In fact, if my grades are high enough after the first two years, I can apply to pre-med without having to finish my degree. And yesterday I received a preliminary letter of acceptance, depending on my marks in the departmental exams."

"Wow that is big news! But, you certainly were tight-lipped about it, or am I just the last one to find out?" When Jessica hesitated, it occurred to Francine that she had hit the nail on the head and, as she had so many times in the last month, she wondered when the rot had set in. Still, she was not about to allow Jessica's announcement to deter her enjoyment of the weekend. "I'm so pleased for you, Jessica. Congratulations! You're going to make a terrific doctor, and one day you'll probably find the cure for cancer."

It was all Jessica could do not to pinch herself. Had Francine just taken her changed plans in stride without so much as a single lament about the foursome all being together again come the fall? Or maybe she had quickly determined that, with Jessica out of the way, she would have Hope all to herself. No doubt, Cassandra would have many of her high school classmates to interact with at college, and then, as she had before, Francine could resume her dependency on Hope. Very likely, she did not have the slightest notion that Hope was so wrapped up in her music, from what she had overheard her mother telling Patricia, that she had precious little time for anyone.

When Francine fell silent and continued to gaze demurely out the window at the city lights as they entered Brandon, Jessica suddenly realized that she was more than a little miffed with Francine's nonchalance. Francine could have at least registered a modicum of protest about the imminent unravelling of the four musketeers or was Jessica just being impossible to please? As she studied Francine's reflection in the glass, Jessica had her first glimpse into one of her friend's characteristics, which would take her years to fully comprehend. Francine was so engrossed by the internal world of all those whom she loved that the external realm of their lives often remained a mystery to her.

Charles Farrington was the first to arrive. Not wanting to be recognized, he had cautiously walked down the street, but just as he had speculated, the members of the press were already beginning to gather at the front entrance of the concert hall. Turning off the sidewalk, he slipped through the grove of barren maple trees surrounding the ornate old structure and approached the back door, where he rapped three times to signal Wyatt Lowe.

That first morning, when Charles had arrived on campus, even before he met with Dr. Burton, his first endeavour had been to familiarize himself with the music building, specifically to make the acquaintance of the caretaker. It had taken some time for the man to open the door and even longer to convince him of his purpose, until Charles finally asked him to ring for campus security.

Fortunately, Mr. Lowe was quicker to understand what Charles wanted to arrange for the evening of the recital. He was in charge of security for the upcoming Saturday performance and had been apprised that a celebrity from the east was going to be in attendance. Later that day, when he was telling his wife about meeting "the great man," he acknowledged his surprise that Dr. Farrington did not want to be the centre of attention. In fact, he was intent on gaining early access to the hall, remaining out of sight of the reporters and blending in with the audience as filed in for Miss Harding's recital. And then Charles wanted the seat in the middle of the auditorium, directly in line with the spot where Hope would stand to play her violin.

As head of security on campus, Wyatt had been in attendance for the majority of Hope's concerts, and he was delighted that the size of her audiences and her popularity were ever on the upswing. He had never enjoyed the scratchy sound of a violin, which he had always viewed as an irritating instrument, until the first time he heard the youthful virtuoso perform. Wyatt had no idea what piece of music she had been playing, but it was so plaintive that, without realizing it, tears were streaming down his cheeks.

From that moment onward, Wyatt had become one of her most devoted fans and would never assign any of his staff to safeguard her during her recitals. Several months later, he had even convinced his wife to attend one of her concerts, and now they shared their enthusiasm for this prodigious talent in their midst. So, when Dr. Farrington expressed his request, Wyatt was only too eager to assist him. From the beginning of Charles's tenure at Brandon College, Mr. Lowe would become much more understanding and far less disenchanted than would Ian.

✳

On the Thursday morning he had been scheduled to meet Dr. Charles Farrington, it seemed Ian had been pacing the parquet floor of his office for hours waiting for the famed maestro to arrive. Where was the man? Had his flight from Halifax even arrived the previous evening? Ian had barely been able to keep the disappointment from his voice when Dr. Farrington had declined his offer of a ride from the airport.

"Thank you for your gracious offer, Dr. Burton, but I prefer to take a taxi. Then I won't risk holding you up from other evening activities in the event my airplane is late."

"On the contrary, Dr. Farrington, meeting with you is the only event on my evening agenda. I just need to know your flight number and the time of arrival, so I can confirm your press conference with the Brandon Sun."

"Dr. Burton, could you please cancel the press? By the time my airplane touches down for the final time on Wednesday, the last activity I'll have any energy for, not to mention patience, will be to talk to reporters."

Reluctantly, Ian agreed, but there would be no putting off the media from the noon conference hosted by the Royal Oak Inn. After all, the college and the city had arranged extensive publicity well in advance of having such a renowned musician come to Brandon for the much-anticipated Christmas recital, and surely he had to comprehend the significance of making himself available for interviews.

Glancing out his large office window, Ian observed a middle-aged man sauntering along the pathway headed in his direction. Upon closer inspection, he noticed that the man's overcoat looked threadbare, and since it was only partially closed, he could see his informal apparel of an open-necked shirt and loosely fitting cardigan. Ian returned to his pacing, convinced that whoever the stranger was, it certainly was not the distinguished gentleman he was eagerly anticipating.

Moments later, when Mrs. Stanley opened his door in her usual genteel manner to announce that his expected guest had arrived, Ian struggled to maintain his composure. Dr. Farrington must have forgotten about the formal luncheon with the mayor and city council that Ian had apprised him of before ending their previous evening's telephone conversation. Catching himself checking his wristwatch, not wanting to be obvious, Ian peeked at the wall clock and quickly determined there was insufficient time for Charles to don more appropriate attire.

Taking a deep breath and pretending to be oblivious of what he considered the man's unkempt appearance, Ian said, "At last we meet, Dr. Farrington, and I assure you the pleasure is all mine. As much I would like to show you our concert hall, we must leave immediately to arrive in time for our luncheon. Please, come with me. My Mercedes is parked in the driveway."

"Thank you, Dr. Burton. However, I have been given a complete tour of the auditorium, and all that remains is for me to assess the acoustics of your beautiful theatre. Perhaps, following lunch I could listen to some of the music students practicing, although I have no desire to hear Ms. Harding until the moment of her recital."

"I'm sorry, Dr. Farrington, I was not informed that you were acquainted with our music hall. It had to be before I joined the music faculty many years ago."

"Why, no, this is my initial trip to Brandon. I've just come from being shown the facility by Mr. Lowe."

If Ian had not been stopped for a red light, he might have slammed on the brakes at the mention of Wyatt Lowe's name. He was outraged. Who did that security guard think he was? Just because he insisted on being on hand for all of Hope's recitals, more in the role of an usher than in any protective capacity, as he seemed to believe, how could he possibly have presumed he had the right to conduct the tour for their illustrious visitor?

Ian made a mental note to address the man's inappropriate behaviour the minute he was back in his office. He was still seething when he inched his way into the busy circular driveway in front of the inn and waited for the valet to park his vehicle. At the moment, a more pressing concern was how he could bestow his guest with sufficient propriety to introduce him to the city dignitaries and the members of the media.

Long before the end of the luncheon it was abundantly clear to all those fortunate enough to have been invited that Dr. Charles Farrington did not subscribe to the notion that "the clothes make the man." Within minutes of their arrival in the foyer of Brandon's newest country inn, Charles, with his impromptu demeanour, had calmed even the most boisterous of reporters and enamoured them with his pithy responses. The musician from the east equally captivated their usually decorous mayor, and it appeared that the only person in attendance aware of his unbecoming appearance and casual behaviour was Ian. But then it would take him months to accept that Dr. Farrington was all about his music and, to a far greater extent, about his brilliant protégé, than he ever had been or would be about being recognized as the celebrated Canadian master of the violin.

＊

Brandon College's exquisite concert hall was filled to capacity, with scarcely enough space in the vestibule for the standing-room-only crowd to meet fire-safety standards. But where was he? Ian was still reeling from his dismay when Charles declined his Saturday dinner invitation prior to the concert, and now he could not even locate him, with the sold-out audience milling around as they searched for their seats.

The two men had met in Ian's office on Friday morning before walking over to the music hall. The students were either in the midst of examinations or had gone home for the break, and subsequently, Dr. Burton performed on both piano and violin to facilitate Dr. Farrington's evaluation of the acoustics. After he expressed his satisfaction, they had strolled across campus to the faculty club for a late luncheon.

They had chatted amicably over French onion soup and chicken pot pie, sharing their intense love of music, but Ian was more than a little disgruntled when Charles made it clear that they would not meet again until after Hope's recital. On Thursday following the formal lunch, Ian had expected that Charles would likely want the evening to recover from his lengthy flight, but he had certainly expected to spend Friday and most of Saturday together developing their relationship.

Ian could not fathom why his guest was being so aloof, especially when Ian was so eager to show him Brandon's many attributes to further entice his relocation to the prairie city. In fact, Charles treated Wyatt Lowe with more affability when they encountered the security guard on their way to lunch than he had yet to display toward Ian. As soon as he returned to his office, Ian requested Mrs. Stanley to page the man who had had the audacity to pre-empt him as Dr. Farrington's tour guide of the music faculty, chiding himself for not having addressed the issue in the morning, as he had planned.

On Saturday, Ian ate little of the prime rib roast and Yorkshire pudding his housekeeper had taken considerable effort to prepare for him and his honoured guest, only raising her eyebrows in the late afternoon when he indicated that he would be dining alone. As the grandfather clock in the hallway struck six, he retired to his bedroom, showered, and then dressed with great care. Once he had donned his tuxedo and the scarlet red cummerbund, he was about to put on his top hat, when suddenly he was assailed with the image of Dr. Farrington's attire for the Thursday luncheon.

Oh, dear God. Surely the man would know to wear formal dress for the evening gala. Since Ian had expected they would be spending most of the weekend together, he had intended on reviewing the program with Charles long before they arrived at the auditorium. He had been so surprised when Charles had literally dismissed him the previous day that it only now occurred to him that he had not explained that prior to Hope commencing her recital, he would ask Dr. Farrington to join him on stage for an official introduction.

At the last moment, Ian chose to forego the top hat, on the premise it might be perceived as pretentious, and, pulling on his overcoat, he left his home for the short three-block walk to campus.

*

After his reprimand by the dean of music, Wyatt realized he could not risk being seen showing Dr. Farrington to his designated seat in the hall. Subsequently, when he opened the back door to Charles, who was still wearing his frayed overcoat, although he was now dressed in a stylish suit, Wyatt explained that he would take him to their pre-arranged hiding spot behind the most distal stage curtain but that he had asked one of the ushers to lead him down the aisle when the lights were dimmed during the five-minute notice before the start of the performance. Furthermore, because the auditorium was filling so quickly, Wyatt had requested one of his staff to occupy Charles's seat until he signalled he was coming to claim it.

Shortly afterwards, Wyatt noticed Dr. Burton enter the theatre and then observed, with more than a little glee, his near-frantic search for the maestro. As time marched on, and the concert was about to begin, Dr. Burton finally proceeded to his front-row seat, following one last despairing perusal of the audience.

For a full minute, the music hall was in total darkness, with the exception of the dim floor lights. Slowly, the spotlight surfaced above the stage to illuminate a man and a woman gracefully crossing to its centre. She was exquisitely attired in a long sky-blue gown that brought out the colour of her eyes. Wisps of her shoulder-length light-blond hair caressed her beautiful countenance as she cradled her violin to her heart as if she was holding a babe in arms.

Her male accompanist was dressed in a black tuxedo, and everyone was drawn instantly to his cummerbund, which matched the colour and fabric of the violinist's apparel. The tall man was dashingly handsome, his dark hair a stunning contrast to the fair young female. When they glanced at each other before taking their respective places, a surge of enchantment permeated the Brandon Concert Hall, and the performance had yet to begin.

Charles Farrington was mesmerized once again. When he happened to be in the audience the past summer to listen to an unknown woman from the west perform with Montreal's symphony orchestra, he had been overwhelmed by the impossibility of what he had heard. How could a person so young with such an obvious dearth of experience and maturity have already discovered her one true passion? During his misspent youth, Charles had many passions, but by the time he decided on becoming a concert violinist, his performance anxiety had spiralled beyond his control.

On Dominion Day during his vacation in Montreal, he had been sauntering along Ste-Catherine Street following a delicious dinner when he chanced upon an evening concert at the Place des Arts. Noticing that the guest performer was a violinist, Charles had purchased his ticket with minutes to spare and had been shown to his seat as the concert was about to start. He had no time to study the program in the dim lighting and subsequently decided to sit back and enjoy.

The introductory selection was mediocre, and he was slipping into a comfortable snooze when the guest performer came on stage and began to play Mozart's melodious "Violin Concerto No.1." Suddenly, Charles was wide awake. He thought he was aware of every promising violin prodigy in Canada, but he had no recollection of having been apprised of Hope Harding from some small city in Manitoba. How could he have missed her?

He sat on the edge of his seat, enthralled as much by her poise as by her unbelievable talent. She was positioned in front of the spell-bound audience with her closed eyelids fluttering to the euphonious resonances emanating from her violin and wafting beyond the still auditorium. Along with every other concert-goer, Dr. Farrington was standing and applauding as "Brava!" rang throughout the new music centre, even as the violinist was bringing her masterful performance to its spirited finale.

Following three curtain calls, the moment the lights came on at the end of the concert, Charles was all but scrambling over those in front of him to reach the aisle. He had anticipated navigating backstage to meet the maestro and his incredible virtuoso before they could slip away. He had seldom been so impromptu in his life, but Charles knew beyond a doubt that Hope was the musical genius he had been search-ing for throughout his career, and he was disheartened when he lost her to a beguiling Montreal evening.

Now here she was, six months later, still believing she had to give the performance of her young life if she could have any expectation of being accepted as his protégé. On the other hand, Dr. Farrington suspected that even if Hope had known he had decided to relocate to Brandon long before her recital, she would have changed nothing.

She floated across the stage knowing she would play the "Kreutzer" with as much intensity and passion as anyone. With grace and aplomb, and eyes closed, Hope began the demanding first movement, dominating the hall with her dynamism, gathering the audience to her until her ardour embraced them all into one complete whole. Nobody moved, they scarcely breathed, and once again, they were on their feet in a standing ovation as she finished playing the jubilant third movement.

For the first time in years, Dr. Farrington's paralyzing stage fright vanished when Dr. Burton asked for the famed maestro to come forward and shake Brandon's esteemed musician's hand. Still buoyed by their virtuoso's vitality, Charles waited until the applause died down before speaking.

"My congratulations to you, Miss Harding. Your interpretation of the "Kreutzer" was the most remarkable I've ever had the honour to hear. I'm thrilled to announce that I'll be moving to your fair city at the beginning of the New Year. Furthermore, I was so confident of accepting you as my current student that I had already taken the liberty of enrolling you in the Meadowmount School of Music in Westport, Upstate New York, this coming summer."

✳

By the time the guest of honour arrived, the faculty club was teeming with her well-wishers. As soon as she spotted her grandparents, Hope rushed to their side and enveloped them in an enormous hug. All their years of encouragement and sacrifice had reached a pinnacle at the moment of Dr. Farrington's announcement. They had become increasingly confident that their granddaughter was a prodigy, and during years of research had read marvellous reviews about the celebrated music school in the Adirondack Mountains. Now they knew that Hope was irrevocably on her way to achieving her potential.

The crush of people was overwhelming, and when at last Michael found Hope chatting with Mrs. Jamison, he slipped his arm around her waist and whispered, "Congrats, Hope! You're on your way to fame and glory. But now my parents want to escape this crowd, and I must leave you to your throng of admirers. Unless, you would also like to flee and come home with me."

Michael had tossed his invitation out like unfurling a kite on a calm day, never expecting for a moment that Hope would accept it. She gave him a fleeting glance that, had she been anyone else, he might have considered a look of longing before she turned back to Lindsay. "Forgive me, Lindsay, but I'm going to renege on your kind offer to spend the rest of the weekend with you. Could you please extend my apologies to the others and explain that I'll see them before Christmas?"

Asking his parents to meet him at the car, Michael and Hope snuck toward the door, stealing away like children who had been caught with their hands in the cookie jar. Soon, they were back at the concert hall. Hope hurried to her dressing room, where she had left her small overnight bag, coat, and boots, while Michael raced to the music office to gather his winter apparel. He could not believe that Hope had consented, and he was not about to give her time to change her mind.

*

Jonathon had the car started, and when he saw Michael running with a guest, he motioned them to the backseat, where, for once, Hope willingly went. Gliding through the door, they were as giddy as school chums, and following brief introductions, they returned to their chatter, intermingled with laughter. They talked the entire distance to the acreage outside of Souris, yet neither would ever remember what they had said.

When the car was safely inside the warm garage, Marika said, "Michael, you can have the honour of showing Hope to the guest loft. It's late, and your father and I will be far livelier in the morning over breakfast. Then we can talk in detail about this incredible evening, but for now, congratulations to both of you. And Michael, thanks so much for convincing us to be in attendance."

When Michael realized his mother was entrusting him to extend the warm hospitality with which she would welcome all the guests to her Country Garden Bed and Breakfast, he became serious. He was surprised that she had chosen not to take her inaugural visitor to the long-awaited loft herself; she had been anticipating the first guest since his father had completed it several weeks earlier. The excitement of the evening must have been tiring, or his mother was beginning to age, a concept that had never before crossed Michael's mind.

He turned on the outside lights and, carrying her small suitcase, went ahead before he asked Hope to follow him up the stairs. The crystal chandelier illuminated a spacious well-designed suite that ran the length of the log cabin, a comfortable queen-sized bed located at the head of the far wall. He helped Hope take off her coat before hanging it in the front closet and then placed her boots on the rubber mat.

Once Michael had carried her suitcase to the collapsible rack beside the bed, he explained that he would place the orange juice, coffee, and cream that his father was going to leave at the bottom of the outside step in the kitchen refrigerator before leaving. Completing his last task, he was almost at the door when Hope said, "Before you go, would you mind coming back here for a moment?"

Michael returned to the bed, and it was not until he was standing beside her that he realized Hope had changed into a silk negligee, much the same colour as her evening gown. He was even more astonished when she slipped her arms around his neck, luring him to her. As she was about to kiss him, the negligee's belt dropped away, revealing her gorgeous lithe body.

Michael was dazed. This could not be happening. He had to stop it before they went too far; they had years to wait. He would not allow anything to interfere with Hope's career. But Hope's kisses were becoming more and more passionate, and when she started to unbutton his shirt, Michael felt himself harden, driving all thought from his head. He moaned as she thrust her tongue deeper and deeper into his mouth and her fingers inched down to his groin. His hands found her soft perky breasts, and by the time she started to unzip his trousers, Michael was a ready accomplice.

Then Hope stopped and said, "Let me look at you. I want to know your body completely. I want to caress all of you before you to come to me."

When Michael was reaching the peak of his passion, she opened her long exquisite legs, wrapping them around his supple body, and drew him into her depths. As one, they soared, transcending far beyond the exuberance of the "Kreutzer."

It was the Friday afternoon before Christmas when Lindsay suddenly realized that Hope was no longer a young maiden but rather a woman loved. Oh, dear God, she would have to act quickly, before the young lovers could orchestrate another tryst that very weekend. She had to catch George before he left his office and request that he try to reach Marlene Walker. Should he be unsuccessful, Lindsay could only hope that her husband might still have some samples at his disposal.

As always, Lindsay had been the first to arrive and was seated at the table wondering if either of her companions was going to show, when Hope came gliding into the cafeteria. Her eyes were aglow, her face was flushed, and she was as effervescent as a child catching Santa Claus coming down the chimney. But once Hope was gracefully settled on the chair, it was the aura of contentment visibly surrounding her body that affirmed Lindsay's conjecture.

"Hello, my darling. You look exquisite. What would you like to drink? Oh, and do you mind if I give George a quick call before I grab it for you?"

"I can pick up my coffee while you telephone. Would you like a refill, Lindsay?"

✳

Within the hour, Lindsay and Hope were climbing the stairs to the upper level of the Brandon mall, but not without undue protest. Lindsay had breathed a sigh of relief when George picked up on the private line in his office, and when he had asked her to allow at least twenty minutes before calling back, she had returned to the table in the cafeteria.

She hesitated as she was about to resume her seat, noticing that Hope was as serene and still as if she was in a trance. Lindsay could not recall ever seeing her so tranquil, and she knew that if she did not address her suspicion instantly, she might be tempted not to bother. After all, what right did she have to proceed with the action she had sought from her husband? Certainly, Hope was underage, but the legal implications were the least of her concerns. How could Lindsay possibly approach Hope's grandparents? On the other hand, she was only too aware they were equally intent on ensuring that nothing interfere with their granddaughter's ultimate success.

Quietly moving her chair so it was adjacent to Hope's, Lindsay placed her arm gently around the youth's shoulder. "We need to talk about the most recent exciting development in your life, and I'm not referring to Dr. Farrington's announcement. I gather Michael and you were intimate last weekend, and I consider it my responsibility as your mature friend to make sure you take appropriate precautions."

Startled, Hope peered at Lindsay. "Were you reading my mind? We never told a soul. How could you possibly have known? Wow, what an incredible psychologist you are going to be if you can perceive what your patients are thinking!"

"I suspect I'm not the only one. I hazard a guess that Marika Griffin also realized sometime during the course of your visit. I'm not judging you, my dear girl, but I must ensure that the next time Michael and you make love, you are protected from the natural consequences."

"I promise it's not going to happen again. We just got carried away with the excitement of the evening."

"Your life is going to be one enthralling evening after another, and Michael Griffin will always be there with you. Now, drink your coffee; we have places to go before everyone starts their weekend."

Lindsay was accurate in her prediction about the frequency of memorable milestones throughout the duration of Hope' eventful life and about Michael's constancy. Nonetheless, she had no way of knowing that each of Hope's momentous accomplishments were to culminate in the joy she would experience in her lover's arms.

✳

Had he been dreaming? When Michael observed Hope flitting down the outdoor stairway on Sunday, he was so spellbound that all he could do was stare. Was she a vision? The sound of her lyrical voice wishing him a good morning flooded his senses, but still he stood as entranced as a schoolboy.

When he had awakened sometime during the early hours, with Hope's arm draped across his chest, his entire body still tingled with ecstasy. But when the realization of what he had done began to invade his thoughts, Michael was assailed with shame and guilt. How could he have allowed it to happen? He was her protector, her tutor, her friend, and he had taken advantage of her in his moment of weakness.

Gently removing her arm, Michael crept away from the bed, gathered his clothes, and, once dressed, slunk out of the safe haven that his mother was so confident she had created for her honoured guests. Although he quietly climbed the stairs to his bedroom on the second floor of his parents' log home and lay down on his bed, the welcome oblivion of sleep would not claim him for the remaining hours of the long winter night. How could he face any of them—Hope, his mother, his father—at the dawn of a new day?

Yet there she was, as blissful and exquisite as the Mona Lisa. For hours in the breakfast nook, Hope had chatted and laughed with Marika and Jonathon as if she had been their most frequent house-guest and had known them for years. If she was upset with him, she gave not the slightest indication, engaging Michael in the conversation and often glancing at him with an enigmatic smile spreading across her beatific face.

By midafternoon, when Michael was driving Hope back to Brandon before returning to his parents for the Christmas break, much of his guilt had abated, replaced with desire. He had never seen Hope so relaxed and exuberant, and the longer he spent in her presence, the more he wanted her. But aside from checking into a motel on the outskirts of Brandon, where could they go? He could not risk Hope being seen going into his small apartment near campus, and now she was too well-known in the city for them to register in one of the repu-table hotels.

Furthermore, no doubt her grandparents would be waiting for Hope to arrive home, since he had so unceremoniously snatched her away following the evening's performance. For the sake of discretion, they would likely have to wait until the end of the festive season, unless he could entice Hope to join him again sometime during the holiday on his parents' acreage. As much as he realized she would be welcomed though, Michael suspected it would not take his mother long to appreciate the changed nature of their relationship.

As they were approaching the city, Michael found himself perus-ing the motels along Highway 10. After the pristine beauty of the Griffin property, they all looked rundown or sleazy, hardly the type of establishment he would ever expect Hope to enter. Still, his longing to make Hope his again was consuming his thoughts, when her voice brought him back to reality.

"Why are you driving so slowly, Michael? I promised Grandma and Grandpa I would be home today by five o'clock to join them for dinner at the Royal Oak Inn. After all, I did run out on everyone last evening."

Glancing toward her, Michael was surprised by the discernible difference in Hope's tone of voice and in her demeanour, as if her earlier effusiveness had been brushed aside by her usual reticence as soon as they reached the city. Surely, Hope could no longer be so dispassionate with him now that they had become lovers. Of course, Michael expected they would always maintain their professional detachment in the presence of others, but not when they were alone.

On his journey home, Michael found his ardour for Hope momentarily dampened by his astonishment of how quickly she had reverted to her cool and distant behaviour. When he had lightly kissed her under the mistletoe above her grandparent's front entrance, he had whispered for her to telephone him, and he would bring her back to the Country Garden Bed and Breakfast. Although his passion was not curtailed for long, the entire Christmas season came and went without a word from her. Three months passed before they were intimate again, but it took Michael much longer to realize that Hope's need for him would only surface after one of her ebullient violin performances.

Francine felt honoured, and more than a little in awe, to be seated in the third row of the concert hall as one of Hope's special guests. Long before Hope's performance was over, Francine had reached two definitive conclusions. She was fortunate to have such an accomplished, beautiful friend, and secondly, the love of her life, Michael Griffin, would never have eyes for anyone other than Hope Harding.

Lately, whenever Francine was in attendance at one of Hope's frequent recitals, she found her excitement mounting about studying at Brandon College by autumn of the following year. Following that weekend, when Jessica had explained why she was interacting with so many of the other students in school, Francine had also tried to become more involved with their classmates.

When the bell rang releasing them from the classroom, Francine initially approached some of the other girls, and after listening to their conversations, she would share her own plans and interests. When her comments seemed to fall on deaf ears, she began to launch into the discussions as soon as they gathered outside. Still, try as she might, she could not fit into any of the cliques, and when her fellow pupils persisted in looking at her as if she had two heads, Francine had resumed her customary solitary activities during all the scheduled breaks.

During conversations initially with Mother Pat and later in sessions with Dr. Donahue, Francine became convinced that once she was on campus she would find more compatible friends. No doubt, her English classes would be filled with students who could understand what her stepmother was always maintaining, that with her poetic sensitivity, she perceived the world from a different perspective. And they would realize that her literary pursuits required her to be reclusive.

When Francine came to live with her uncles, as long as she could be outdoors, she had little need for any companions. She had been content to look after her lambs and to wander about, climbing, and even naming the many trees on their sheep farm as she communed with nature. After enduring the heartbreak of leaving Margaret Dwyer far behind in Prince Edward Island, Francine had vowed to never again have such a close friend. But when she had been taken under Cassandra's wing, Francine had begun to rediscover the joys of having an affectionate playmate.

Then, when Uncle Daniel married Patricia Rose, her heart had slowly reopened with all the love she had been suppressing or denying since the tragic deaths of her doting parents. With the passage of time, her surrogate mother had erased much of her pain, so Francine could even appreciate Mother Pat's jesting about the misfortunate that her best friends, aside from her trees and her lambs, were literary and dead—L. M. Montgomery, Jane Austen, Charles Dickens, and Leo Tolstoy.

Eventually, Dr. Donahue helped Francine come to terms with her tremendous losses and also, to a lesser extent, with the oppressive feelings of guilt she had experienced by believing she had been responsible for their accident. When Dr. Donahue taught her relaxation and centring techniques, Francine was successful at managing her nightmares and, much more significantly, overcoming much of her mental distress precipitated by her feeling of being subservient to others.

Nonetheless, while still in her adolescence, Francine recognized that she would never allow herself to completely love another person. When Dr. Donahue first suggested that she might be using guilt as an indulgence, specifically as a self-serving means, so she did not have to get to know others and risk becoming too close to them, Francine objected strenuously. She argued her problem was that she was always so concerned about the needs of others that she could not acknowledge her own.

Now, sitting in the audience listening to Hope's evocative violin performance, Francine began to wonder if Hope was not as self-absorbed as she had always considered her to be. Was it because of this commonality that Francine had been so drawn to Hope, and so quickly? Did their respective grief and guilt cause them both to be emotionally crippled, to be as afflicted by and set apart from others as surely as if they were lepers?

During the exhilarating finale of Beethoven's "Kreutzer Sonata," it dawned on Francine that neither young woman would ever fully trust again. Throughout her life, Hope would lose herself as totally in her music as Francine already had in nature, and one day soon, she hoped to do in her writing.

✳

Dare he hope? Early in the morning, when they were about to leave for Winnipeg, Michael had dashed around to the driver's side of Dr. Burton's Mercedes, so he could be positioned in the backseat diagonally across from Hope in the passenger seat. Then he could observe her during the two-hour journey while he conversed with Dr. Farrington.

In three short months, the famed musician had endeared himself to Michael in ways that Dr. Burton had never been able to achieve. Still, he would always appreciate all that Ian had done for him—hiring him as Hope's tutor and facilitating his impromptu enrolment in the Master of Business Administration Program for the express purpose of eventually becoming her financial advisor and agent.

In addition, Michael would all but revere Dr. Burton for his unexpected recommendation that he become Hope's piano accompanist. His days as her tutor were numbered, it was much too early in her career for him to provide any business services, and before long, she would have two professors equally intent on arranging her ever-increasing recitals. Were it not that Michael was required to partner with Hope during her practices and performances, he would soon need to find alternate employment.

But after another night of wrestling with his bed sheets, of yearning for Hope and of awakening alone, Michael was beginning to wish he did not spend every day by her side. It was agony being so close to her and not being able to gather her into his arms, carry her away, and make passionate love to her. More and more, his burning need for Hope and his bitter resentment that she could act as if nothing had happened between them were tearing him apart.

The only one who seemed to be aware of his torment was Dr.

Farrington. From the first time they met, Michael was drawn to the kindly gentleman from eastern Canada. When he had been content to remain in the background and allow Dr. Burton to continue with the prevailing decisions about Hope's musical tutelage, Michael was on the verge of expressing his surprise. Then he started to observe Dr. Farrington, and he realized what he was doing.

In many ways, the two men were the antithesis of each other. Whereas Ian was always so formal in his approach, attire, and demeanour, Charles was relaxed and casual, seemingly about everything. But he was clever. He knew full well that he was the new kid on the block, and the last thing he was interested in doing was alienating Dr. Burton or Hope by rushing headlong into a new program midway through the year. Charles could wait in light of Dr. Elliot's unprecedented announcement, at the beginning of January, that he had been offered a tenured position with Brandon College.

At the end of their practices, Charles, as he insisted Michael address him, began inviting him to go for coffee or lunch in the cafeteria. Michael did not realize that Charles was still living in the students' residence and regularly eating on campus, but he was pleased to join him. Before long, Michael began to sense that although he had not breathed a word about his involvement with Hope, Charles appeared to understand his anguish. Wondering if he was that transparent, more times than he could believe, Michael had been on the verge of pouring his heart out to him.

As Charles and Michael drew closer, it occurred to him that the one commonality between the two aging maestros might be that both men had exclusively expended their passion on music. From what Michael could glean, neither had ever married or raised a family, devoting their lives instead to the pursuit of their destiny. As much as he wanted to be successful in all of his endeavours, Michael would never dedicate his life solely to his work. He could scarcely wait until the month that Hope turned eighteen, when he planned to ask her to become his wife. Michael did worry that she might not want to interrupt her career to birth their children, but he would cross that bridge when the time came.

✳

When Hope opened the invitation requesting her to play Mendelssohn's "Violin Concerto in E Minor, Op. 64" in accompaniment with the Winnipeg Symphony for the inaugural performance of the Centennial Concert Hall in March 1968, she could scarcely believe her eyes. Years earlier, her mother had read an article to her about the proposal for a new concert hall in the capital city, as part of the Manitoba Centennial Centre, to be built as a Canadian Centennial project. It was to become the home of the Royal Winnipeg Ballet, the Manitoba Opera, and the Winnipeg Symphony Orchestra.

Construction of the arts centre had started in 1960 on Main Street in Winnipeg. At that time, Hope was not yet ten years old and had barely embarked upon her quest to become a violinist. Although she had dreamt of playing in concert halls throughout the country, she would never have imagined that she would be seated in the orchestra pit with the Winnipeg Symphony for the opening of their beautiful facility.

Naturally, Michael provided her accompaniment during practices, but since she would be performing with the full orchestra, Dr. Burton suggested he would not be required to travel with them to Winnipeg. But Hope would have none of his proposal. "Wherever I go, I'll always have Michael accompany me for my encores, rather than performing my selections with the orchestra. And since my audiences seem eager for more, I've decided to add specific sonata and concerto movements to my repertoire. Michael, would you be prepared to take on extra practices?"

"Of course, Hope, you know I will. Are you planning to change your signature piece that you always play at the end of your recitals?"

"No, I just want to have more pieces on my fingertips, although I'll never complete any performance by not playing Massenet's "Meditation' from Thaïs." It was my mother's favourite."

Even as she was replying, Michael was rejoicing that not only had Hope insisted he journey with her but also that Mendelssohn's concerto also had an exuberant finale. And for the night of the performance, they would be staying at the beautiful Hotel Fort Garry, hopefully on the same floor, and maybe even in adjacent rooms.

Michael would have been surprised by how closely Charles was reading his thoughts and, furthermore, that he had decide to look after the Fort Garry booking to facilitate that exact arrangement. He had immediately discerned Michael's distress when Ian made his recommendation and secretly applauded Hope for her instant rebuttal. Whereas Charles already recognized that Michael would fly to the moon if Hope were to ask him, Dr. Burton was oblivious to the fact that he had created any tension in the music hall.

At the last minute, Michael remembered the prophylaxis, but as he began to inch off the bed to dash to the bathroom in his adjoining room on the seventh floor of Winnipeg's grand railway hotel, Hope groaned, "You can't leave now."

The concert had been a stunning success. By the time Hope and her entourage had arrived for the reception in the ballroom of the historic Fort Garry Hotel, their limousine was the last in a row that extended completely around the circular driveway. Every dignitary from the province and the city was in attendance. As much as they had been aglow with the exquisite design, the artistic décor, and the unbelievable acoustics of Manitoba's premier performing arts facility, they had been enthralled with the guest violinist.

When the wisp of a girl walked across the stage to stand beside the concertmaster, a gasp of surprise went through the full house. A handful had heard or read about the prodigy from Brandon, and even fewer of the 2,305 patrons had experienced the thrill of being in attendance during one of her performances. With the distinctive aspect of the almost immediate entrance of the violin in Mendelssohn's famed concerto, an instant hush fell upon the audience.

But the half an hour in which the three movements were melodically and harmonically played was not nearly long enough. They wanted more. Before the break for the intermission, Michael joined Hope on stage for the first movement of Vivaldi's "Concerto in G minor." Still, the usually sedate audience clamoured for another encore, and the young virtuoso responded with the "Allegro" from Mozart's "Violin Concerto No. 3 in G major, K. 216."

Then, at the end of the concert, when Hope was brought back on stage for several curtain calls, Michael joined her at the piano. Her closing performance of Thaïs was so poignant that the boisterous crowd was silenced—but not for long. Their enchantment was quick to resurface and then to swell in the ballroom, with everyone desiring to make her acquaintance, the receiving line going on forever, and the hour well past midnight when Hope, at last, requested Michael to escort her to her bedroom.

*

The door had hardly closed when Hope was all over Michael. He would have been profoundly dishonest if, right from the beginning of their journey to Winnipeg, he had not been consumed by his desire for her. During the last three months of hell, Michael had vacillated between throes of passion and of despair. Night after night when he had lain awake for hours on end, he had hoped, fantasized, and queried if they would ever be lovers again. And, if they were, might it be after another scintillating performance?

When they arrived early on Monday afternoon, Dr. Burton pulled up in front of the Radisson Hotel on Portage Avenue. It was all Michael could do to conceal his disappointment that Hope was registered on the top floor, and his room was on the second. What were their chances of being together? His only consolation was that when they left the Radisson after the week of rehearsals and switched to the Fort Garry on the morning of the concert, they might not be so far apart.

Finally, his prayers had been answered. Michael evanesced so completely within Hope's ardour that he was hardly aware they were both naked and in her bed when, with agony, he remembered that this time he had to take precautions. Aside from the fact that Hope was underage, it was even more important that they not risk an unwanted pregnancy. His every instinct urged him to stay, but he could not be that irresponsible. As he struggled to leave, with more strength than he would ever have thought she could muster, Hope pulled him back on the bed, drew him between her majestic legs, and took possession of his body, his mind, and soul.

He was in paradise. He had no idea how many times he climaxed, but still she demanded more. At last, totally spent, Michael lay immobilized beside her. He was just fading away into exhaustion when once again Hope began showering his body with her ardent kisses. She wanted to devour him, but now, after waiting an eternity, Michael had passed the point of being able to respond.

*

At the end of August, after Francine had returned from her homecoming to the east, the original two decided to go ahead with their long-weekend plans at the Jamison's cottage. Neither had been very optimistic about the likelihood of Hope returning from the Adirondack Mountains in time. In fact, if either had been asked, both would have expressed with confidence that they expected Hope would be available for very few of their foursome activities in the years to come.

But Cassandra and Francine had every reason to believe that Jessica would join them, especially since, last September, as they were leaving Clear Lake, she was the one who had made them all promise to come back for an annual retreat before the beginning of university. And this was without consulting their hosts to confirm if that was a possibility. Nonetheless, Cassandra would never have predicted that Jessica would become as elusive as Hope, although Francine had certainly wondered after their last semester of high school.

Although Cassandra had never chanced to ask, she suspected there continued to be discord between Francine and Jessica. She had felt the undercurrent of tension that went beyond Hope not spending that Saturday evening of her Christmas recital and the following Sunday with them. The other three girls were becoming accustomed to Hope bailing on them at the last minute, so whatever was causing the current disagreement, Cassandra had concluded it could not be blamed on their illustrious friend.

Whether because of Hope's sudden absence or the strain between Jessica and Francine, Cassandra felt let down for the rest of the Christmas vacation. The next day, when she shared her feelings with her mother, Lindsay speculated that perhaps her sadness stemmed from the reality that the four young women were growing up and apart as they prepared to forge ahead with their lives.

Still, Jessica had been so adamant about planning this last foursome long weekend at Clear Lake precisely because of that fact. It was to be the send-off for each of them before they went their separate ways, and then at the last moment, she had decided not to come.

✳

The weather had fully cooperated—cool, crisp mornings, balmy afternoons, gorgeous sunsets, and beautiful moonlit evenings. On their last evening after sitting on some large rocks watching the fiery sun disappear below the horizon, Cassandra and Francine decided to walk along the north shore of the tranquil waters. "I'm glad the other two didn't make it. You've been so outgoing and relaxed since your trip, and I was just thinking that, after we became a foursome, you and I have not spent one single weekend together. Although it's always great fun being around Hope and Jessica, I enjoy having you all to myself again."

"Thank you for saying that, Cassandra. It certainly is more peaceful when we're alone. I've often thought that everything is so supercharged around Hope, and Jessica seems to encourage her frenetic pace."

"Oh, I agree, although when we first met them, for reasons I've never understood, you seemed to let both of them overshadow you. I'm so happy you're no longer awestruck, especially of Hope, but tell me, what has happened between Jessica and you?"

Francine shot Cassandra a sideways glance and was suddenly overcome with memories. It had been more than ten years since her cherished friend had seized her by the hand and escorted her to the loft in her uncles' home. She had been so frightened and lonely until Cassandra took her under her wing and proceeded to instill a feeling of hope about her new life. And not once had she wavered in her unabashed love and friendship.

A pang of guilt gripped her, and, as Dr. Donahue had instructed, she took several deep breaths to restore her calm. During that flash of insight, Francine recollected that when she became friends with Jessica and later with Hope, she had all but forgotten about how important Cassandra was to her. She was right that they no longer spent any holidays journeying back and forth between the Webster and McGregor farms, as they had done for years, because Francine always insisted on including her two new friends in every one of their plans.

"Oh, Cassandra, it doesn't matter what's going on with Jessica and me. You've just made me realize that not only did I allow them to overshadow me, I also let them usurp your place in my heart. I was obsessed with Hope and how she could play her violin. Yet there were times when I got a sense they, or at least Jessica, felt superior to me, maybe because she had deigned to introduce me to her talented friend. But Hope and Jessica became all-important to me, and to make matters worse, I often projected my own feelings of condescension onto you. I'm sorry, Cassandra."

When Cassandra became as silent as a tomb, Francine began to grasp just how deeply she had wounded her longtime friend. She turned and slipped her arm around her waist. "I am so sorry, Cassandra." Noticing tears trickling down Cassandra's cheeks, Francine gathered her into her arms. "Please forgive me for taking you for granted. You are the best friend I've ever had, Cassandra, and you always will be."

Feeling foolish for letting her emotions get the better of her, Cassandra was on the verge of claiming that it had not mattered to her when she blurted, "I was so sure you had forgotten your promise when you first came to Manitoba, that I would be your one true friend for life. It really hurt when suddenly Hope, especially, seemed to be the only person you cared about, when most of the time she's so wrapped up in her music she scarcely knows we exist. Did you know that even the one time Hope did come was because she had telephoned my mum and asked her to arrange the weekend for the foursome? Whereas I assure you, Francine, I have and always will be here for you."

Now it was Francine's turn to remain quiet. During the stillness of those few moments, she was suddenly wrenched by an ominous feeling of betrayal and overwhelming loss. No, it was not Cassandra, so who was it? A vague image kept floating before her eyes, and although she tried as hard as she might, Francine could not grasp the person's face. But it was then that she understood their friendship would endure and that Cassandra would be with her at the time of her greatest need.

*

Sitting alone in her tiny room in the University of Manitoba student residence, Jessica still could not comprehend why she had chosen not to go to Clear Lake for the weekend. Her mother had driven her to Winnipeg on Monday to help her get settled on campus but had to leave the city on Friday morning to help her father at the Lingnan that evening. And because Lindsay and Cassandra were registering for their fall courses at Brandon College, there would be no one at their cottage until late Saturday morning.

Although it was a two-hour bus ride to Dauphin, Jessica knew that all she had to do was ask, and one of the Jamisons, most likely Cassandra, driven by Francine in her new Mustang would have been more than happy to pick her up at the bus depot. Her parents had offered to pay for the ticket, and she had gone so far as to telephone and determine the cost, but on Thursday evening, she declined, saying she did not want to return late on Monday evening. She wanted to be alert for her first class at eight o'clock Tuesday morning.

Both Trin and Jessica knew it was an excuse. One of Jessica's attributes was her ability to be bright and fresh after relatively few hours of sleep, a strength that would hold her in good stead throughout her lengthy medical training and subsequent distinguished career. Since it could have little to do with Hope, who, as usual, was not likely to arrive, Trin could only conclude that it had to be related to the negative feelings between Jessica and Francine, which had surfaced and remained unexplained long ago. But she certainly was not going to argue with Jessica. It was hard enough having to abandon her baby alone in the big city without leaving on acrimonious terms.

*

The mothers had finally agreed that their respective daughters would have to work out their differences. Their faint glimmer of hope following that weekend in November had soon faded, and although they continued to discuss ad nauseam what the issue might be, they chose to act as if they were unaware of its existence.

The McGregor and Yang families still enjoyed their rotating Sunday dinners, which often included Malcolm and Alice Webster, and when they came to visit, the Jamison trio. Although, the adults really only had an opportunity to interact with the two or, as the case may be, three young women during the sit-down meal, with the exception of Pat and Trin, they were convinced of the deep abiding friendships among their beloved children.

On occasion, Francine and Jessica noticed Lindsay observing them, and both wondered if she suspected there was strife between them. Now though, since the two girls seldom engaged in a discussion of any depth, neither shared their awareness of the budding psychologist's scrutiny with the other. At any rate, Jessica knew that no one, not even her own mother, would believe her possible personal inclination that had inadvertently been revealed by her new friends.

*

How could he ever have created such a dilemma? Even from that chance encounter outside his office door, Derek had been surprised by how his heartbeat had quickened. Then, when it happened again as Susan entered the dining room of the Royal Oak Inn, he should have heeded his well-honed precautionary sign.

Long before he had been admitted to the bar and ushered into the corner office of the prestigious Barclay & Barclay law firm, Derek had vowed he would uphold its founder's standards. Cornelius Barclay had begun his criminal law practice with a deep sense of justice, a profound ethical commitment, and an oath to search for the truth for every individual who sought his legal services. His grandfather had always been his mentor, and Derek was determined to model his professional conduct.

When his father tainted the company's reputation by being suspended by the Manitoba Law Society for violating client confidentiality, Derek was even more convinced to rigorously follow his grandfather's footsteps. Years later, he discovered his father had engaged in indiscriminate affairs with an unknown number of beautiful female clients and that Barclay &Barclay had survived only because of Cornelius.

Whether it could be considered an attribute or a shortcoming, the Barclay men were all dashingly handsome, and the fairer sex were drawn to them like magnets. From that first day when Cornelius had welcomed Derek to the office previously occupied by his father, he had resolved that if ever his heart should skip a beat at the sight of a stunning female client, he would erect a wall around it to rival a mountain cliff.

His first mistake occurred when Derek had invited Susan to lunch. And to prolong a business meeting for over three hours with a ravishing beauty in a restaurant had been unconscionable, particularly after the adversarial encounter with that waitress. Had Derek been thinking with his head rather than with other parts of his anatomy, he would have proposed that Susan and he make a hasty exit and return to the propriety of his law office.

It was not until hours later, when Derek had returned alone to his office, that he began to comprehend the extent of his folly. How could he not have recognized that the waitress who had served him on several occasions at the Royal Oak Inn was the defendant at the inquest into Susan's parents' death? Even though, up until the moment of his recollection, Derek had already decided he was going to turn the probate of Bert and June Smith's will over to the new associate they had recently brought into the firm, it was the last restaurant in

Brandon that he should have escorted Susan, knowing there was a risk of bringing the two women together.

Derek had already convinced himself that since Susan was not going to be his client, he could consider a possible personal relationship with her. But not now, not with Judge Franklin's summation suddenly haunting him. During the inquest, both men were tacitly confident that Carole Martin had been guilty of perjury, and following the episode in the restaurant, Derek was even more certain. This young woman was dangerous, and in the pit of his stomach, he knew she would offend again and again with increasing regularity and severity.

What had really happened preceding that tragic day on the Smith farm? Could Susan also be culpable in what had culminated in the untimely demise of her parents? She was young, beautiful, and intelligent, and now the beneficiary of a sizeable estate. Was there any possibility that the two women had contrived together and only maintained an adversarial front? Good heavens, Derek was being terribly unfair to Susan. He had witnessed firsthand how devastated she had been by her parents' death. Still, how could he be considering any kind of relationship with her when he knew that he had a legal commitment to delve much deeper before the Smiths' will was probated?

✳

It was the third Thursday of January, since business was invariably slow at the beginning of the New Year, that Trin had agreed Jessica could have the evening off from the Lingnan to meet her new friends. The other five girls had already arrived at the most likely spot in town, if not the café, where young people gathered, the soda fountain at the back of the pharmacy, when Jessica walked down the aisle loaded with hair products.

"Wow, you actually made it! I would have bet a month's allowance that you were never going to join us," said Rebecca, who liked to consider herself the ringleader of the group and was always ready with a sarcastic comment. "Well, grab yourself a Coke, and take the vacant chair at the head of the table for our guest of honour."

"Why don't you cool it, Becky? Or Jessica will hardly want to come again," Stephanie retorted.

As soon as Jessica claimed the last seat, Rebecca resumed her supposed dominance of the group. "I guess we can thank Miss S. for her surprise class on reverse discrimination for finally having the pleasure of your company. Until then, I wondered if you were too stuck-up to associate with your lowly classmates."

"I thought it was the other way around, especially after I acquired the label 'chink' from Carole Martin," Jessica said as she took a sip from her glass.

"Yeah, she was really something, wasn't she? She made no bones about discriminating against you, but I must say, I didn't have the slightest idea that you and your friend were also segregating the rest of us. It's amazing what you can learn when you pay attention in class. And, by the way, what's with you and the strange Francine Stonehenge? You two were so inseparable that I often wondered if you had a thing for each other."

"I don't know what you mean. Francine and I have been friends for years, even before she came to school in Souris."

"Oh, come on. Give me a break. A bright student like you understands only too well what I'm talking about. In fact, I always considered that the Martin chick was unfair just labelling you when she could have used 'queer' and nailed both of you. You know the old saying—kill two birds with one stone," Rebecca said with a smirk.

"Shut up, Becky. What's the matter with you? We invited Jessica to come out with us to have fun, not for you to pick on her." Stephanie glared at Rebecca and then continued. "And wipe that smug look off your face, or we'll all just get up and leave."

"No, wait, Stephanie," Jessica said. "I want to hear what Rebecca honestly thinks about me."

By this time, the three girls who had not had a chance to contribute much other than their salutations were looking very uncomfortable. Suddenly, Amy stood up. "I'm out of here!" Emma and Marlene joined her. In a matter of minutes, they had donned their hats and coats, and were out the door. It only took Stephanie another moment to gulp the rest of her Coke and to follow suit. With the hasty exit of all the other girls, Jessica had a quick change of mind about listening to any more of Rebecca's caustic remarks, and without so much as a word, she rose and left her most recent nemesis seated alone at the table.

*

Fortunately, when Jessica came in the door, her mother was serving a guest in the restaurant, so Jessica went straight to her bedroom. The minute she closed the door, she reached for her favourite book, the *Merriam-Webster Dictionary*. She had heard the word "queer" bantered around enough in the school ground to have a pretty good idea what it meant. But until then, Jessica had never considered that it could have any application to her.

Staring out her frosted window at the darkness of the midwinter evening, Jessica was suddenly transported back to that stormy night the September long weekend at the Jamison's cottage. The foursome had finally settled down, and Jessica had fallen into a deep sleep, when she was awakened by Hope, saying, "I'm so cold, Jessica. Can I crawl into your bunk with you?"

Without waiting for Jessica to answer, Hope had snuggled up to her under the feather quilt and was promptly sound asleep. Jessica was surprised by the electrifying sensation that had coursed through her entire being when Hope started to cuddle her and was instantly wide awake. She had never felt so excited, and realizing how good she felt to have Hope lying so close to her body, she was too aroused to go back to sleep.

The next morning, Jessica was still tingly all over, and she spent most of the day in a trance. Even when she started waking up in the middle of the night, dreaming about being in bed with Hope, Jessica never gave it much thought. She had loved Hope for years, and as her best friend had admired her for following her mother's dream. When Hope's mum succumbed to breast cancer, Jessica had decided that she was going to become an oncologist and search for a cure to save Hope from the same fate.

During the fall, Jessica often found herself resenting how driven Hope was in the pursuit of her music and had been devastated when she had disappeared after her Christmas recital. Jessica had been secretly longing to be alone with Hope and to once again experience the joy of her nearness. Would she have the same feeling of pleasure she had experienced when they were together the last time?

Then, when the foursome spent a day on the McGregor farm during the Christmas holiday, Hope seemed so different. She was aloof and gave the impression that she was much more mature than the other three, as if she had somehow crossed the realm into adulthood, leaving the rest of them far behind. Jessica had scarcely had any time alone with Hope, and during the few moments she did, strangely, she found that she was tongue-tied.

Now Jessica began to question just what it was she did feel for Hope. Was her love for her only that of a close friend, or was it much deeper? Had her feelings heightened since Hope left to live in Brandon, and was that why she had suddenly become critical of Francine? Was Jessica jealous of Francine because. from the moment she had met Hope, she had been possessive of her? The more she considered her friendship with Hope, the more Jessica realized she had never been attracted to anyone of the opposite sex. Not a single male she had ever encountered had made her feel the way she did when she was with Hope Harding.

Over the course of the next several weeks, Jessica had gone to the public library, not wanting to be seen searching for books about sexuality in the small confines of the school, and then, if finding any books marginally related, hiding them in the bottom of one of her drawers as soon as she arrived home. However, the information was severely limited, and she certainly was not going to ask the librarian to assist in her research. As a result, Jessica might have ended up with many more questions than answers.

Soon the only discernible consequence of Jessica's reading had been the frequency of her dreams about either anticipating or actually being in bed with Hope. When months passed before she saw Hope again, Jessica began to believe that she was being spared from revealing her true feelings. During the day when she was in school, and in the evenings in the restaurant, she made a concerted effort to engage in conversations with any male adolescent who crossed her path. Nonetheless, Jessica's nighttime longing for Hope persisted with increasing regularity, until she concluded that Rebecca had not been wrong about her sexual orientation. Her only error had been the object of Jessica's desire.

*

Sitting in the backseat of Dr. Burton's Mercedes on their return journey to Brandon, all Michael had been able to think about was that he needed to search for a new apartment away from the campus as soon as he had a free moment. Once when he had glanced in the rear-view mirror, he noticed that he was still grinning like a Cheshire cat, and he cautioned himself. He could not convey to either of Hope's professors the slightest indication of what was transpiring between him and their protégé.

Still, Michael had wondered how he came to be registered in the suite adjacent to Hope's, which conveniently had a door opening between the two rooms. Was it just a stroke of good fortune, or had Dr. Farrington surreptitiously played a hand in the ideal arrangement? Although they had only known each other for a short time, he could have confided his innermost thoughts to Charles. There were times when Michael was conversing with him that he felt as if the cordial maestro from the east was peering into his soul.

It had been a godsend the next morning that he had been able to access his bedroom through the inner door. Michael's last thought before he succumbed to oblivion was that he could never have believed his body was capable of such ecstasy and such fatigue. When sunlight pouring through the high narrow windowpane awakened him, he was still in the same position, lying flat on his back, as when he had descended into the depths of repose.

Realizing that Hope was still asleep, Michael carefully stretched his muscles, but he was in no hurry to get out of bed. It was heavenly lying beside her, gazing upon her beautiful face and hoping that, when she did awaken, they might have a repetition of the previous evening's activity. Michael felt rejuvenated, and the mere thought of making love to Hope again was all he had needed to arouse his desire.

So lost in anticipation, Michael nearly leapt off the queen-sized bed when Hope sleepily said, "Good morning. Are you awake? I wonder what time it is. Wait, I turned the clock toward the wall, but I'll check it now."

"Never mind the time, my darling. I'm ready now to resume where I had to leave off last night, and luckily, I had the foresight to place the 'Do Not Disturb' signs on both our doors."

"Wow, it's after ten, and we have a luncheon before our tour of the legislative building. You have to go right now, Michael, so I can get ready."

Feeling like a culprit caught in the act, Michael dejectedly rose from the bed and slunk away to his own room. He had not been able to believe Hope's tone of voice and apparent detachment from him. How could she be so cold and distant toward him within hours of all but swallowing him in his entirety?

After a shower and a shave, Michael felt restored. He decided to slip down to the restaurant alone for coffee and a full breakfast. He was famished and not about to wait for lunch at some fancy café, which would probably serve delicate sandwiches and tea. Of course, he would attend and be Hope's congenial companion, but at the same time, he intended to show her that he could be equally aloof.

When he was satiated and lingering over a second cup of coffee, Michael remembered Hope telling him that she was taking the birth-control pill. Following their initial coupling, for the second time that evening, he had been about to return to his bedroom to retrieve the condoms he had purchased several months earlier when Hope had enlightened him. The perceptive Lindsay Jamison had coaxed her husband to arrange for Hope to see the gynecologist to whom he primarily referred his patients, and she had subsequently been on contraceptive medication since shortly after their first tryst.

Seated in the posh dining room, Michael had vacillated between amazement and anger. If Hope was protected, why had she waited until after her next recital before they made love again? If she had been concerned about where they could meet, Michael would gladly have taken her to his parents' place. Maybe Hope felt she would be imposing, especially if Marika was intent on having paying guests in the loft of her bed and breakfast.

The thought flashed through Michael's mind that he would even have been prepared to pay his mother her going rate for Hope to be a guest, but he instantly realized she would never consider charging his friend. It made much more sense for Michael to rent a different apartment, when it dawned on him that he had no idea what he would be doing for the summer, even less in the fall.

As much as Michael did not want to think about it, the chance of him going with Hope to Westport for seven weeks of summer school was remote. Furthermore, if he were to finish his master's degree during the subsequent academic year and also travel with Hope for her recitals, he would need to obtain employment while she was away. His best option would be to work with his father in his busy construction company, so he could hardly lease an apartment in Brandon when soon he would complete Hope's grade twelve tutoring and return to live with his parents.

By the time Dr. Burton was pulling onto the campus of Brandon College, the smile had been wiped off Michael's handsome countenance. He realized his life was about to undergo dramatic changes over the next few months, and he would have precious little control regarding most of the decisions. Not only would he not see Hope for the entire summer, come September, they would only be together when they were practicing for upcoming recitals. How could he stand being separated from her after having spent most of their waking moments in each other's presence for years? Michael's feelings of desolation were heightened by his inkling that she really only needed him to vent her intense passion after her effusive violin performances. He was beginning to fear that Hope was so compelled by her destiny that her one and only true love would ever be music.

✳

Although Cassandra had become familiar with the college, she appreciated her mother taking her, Francine, and Mother Pat for a guided tour the day before classes commenced for the freshmen. They had returned late on the Monday morning of the September long weekend, and, following a delicious lunch with Patricia, who had driven in to meet them, the four women had trooped all over the campus of Brandon College. It was a gorgeous afternoon, and the majestic red maple, elm, and oak trees were resplendent in their brightly clad autumn colours.

Francine would have been just as happy to linger outside soaking up the ambience of the old buildings and the serene beauty of the exquisitely manicured grounds. She had little need to check out the lecture halls, which she was certain she could find without assistance the next day. After the remarkable events of the past summer, Francine's confidence had grown by leaps and bounds, and she was ready for any new challenge.

*

When, out of the blue in late February, a letter postmarked from Cavendish, Prince Edward Island, had arrived for Francine, the timing could not have been better. During her final semester of high school, she had been feeling even more lonely and isolated than she had subsequent to Jessica's choice to enlarge her circle of friends. Francine did not have the slightest idea what had happened, but at the end of January, Jessica had stopped talking to her new female friends as well as to Francine. She came to class, was responsive to their teachers, spoke to any of the boys who would listen, and then left the minute the bell tolled to end the morning and afternoon classes.

What really hurt though was that Jessica had stopped accompanying her folks to the McGregor farm for their rotating Sunday dinners. The first time she did not come, Francine considered that she would repay Jessica in kind, but at the last minute on the following Sunday, she changed her mind and went to Souris. Why would she forego time with her family and with Mr. and Mrs. Yang just because Jessica had decided to close herself off from practically every other human being on earth? Besides, Francine loved the delicious Chinese food at the Lingnan.

"Oh, look at this, Mother Pat. It's a letter from my friend Margaret and her parents inviting me and anyone else in our family who wants to come to visit during the summer months. Wouldn't that be wonderful? I haven't seen Margaret for ten years, and other than our Christmas cards, we stopped writing to each other long ago."

"It would be a lovely way to spend part of this summer. I well imagine that either Daniel or Darrin or perhaps both of your uncles would be eager to return to PEI with you."

"But what about you? Whenever we've talked about the Maritimes, you've always said it was your dream to one day journey to the east coast."

"I would feel like I was imposing on your friend's parents if I decided to tag along. How long is she suggesting you plan to stay with them? Then again, perhaps you would rather travel on your own when you return for your homecoming."

"Auntie Helen is recommending that we think about coming for at least a month, given the cost of the train fare and the distance. But I'd much rather go with you, Mummy Pat, than go all that way by myself. I would really like you to meet Margaret and her parents. They were my family after my mummy and daddy drowned in the ocean."

"Let's chat about it with your uncles over dinner, before you answer Margaret's letter."

Patricia had immediately discerned the subtle change in the inflection of Francine's voice. She realized it would be emotionally challenging for her stepdaughter to revisit the home of her birth and to pick up the threads of her former life. Even the mere sound of the incessant sea might be enough to take her back into the depths of despair. A journey that had the potential of a long-overdue catharsis could turn out poorly if Francine did not have a blending of support from her current family as well as from all those who had loved her in the past.

Especially now when she was at a crossroads in her life.

There would have been little to consider if only Patricia had not plotted with Daniel and Darrin to purchase a new Ford Mustang for Francine as her graduation gift. The three of them had lengthy discussions about where she would live when she started college. Then, the day Lindsay had confirmed that Francine would always be welcome to stay with them whenever the weather was inclement, they had agreed she would be perfectly capable of driving the short distance from their home to the city and put a substantial down payment on the automobile.

As soon as they reached their decision, each of the adults took turns teaching Francine how to drive around the farm and the back roads of the countryside. They became more diligent when the snow started to fly, because they wanted her to be proficient during the winter months. As it happened, Francine readily acquired the essential skills, since her Uncle Darrin had been allowing her to drive the old truck to town whenever the two of them were off on yet another excursion.

Naturally, the car was to be a surprise, and even if the dealership would agree to cancel the order and return the money, there would still be the practical issue of how Francine would travel back and forth every day for her classes. Would they be able to come up with the finances to cover the cost of a trip to Cavendish over and above the price of the vehicle? Patricia was not about to disclose the dilemma to Francine and decided to take her own advice about waiting to discuss it with the McGregor twins.

*

Susan could not understand why Derek Barclay did not call her. When she had returned in the afternoon after her relaxing lunch with him, she felt confident it would only be a matter of weeks, maybe a month or two at best, before she would be able to access her inheritance.

She had actually debated driving back to Brandon the subsequent day to begin searching for her own apartment, even though Margaret had repeatedly assured her that she was welcome to live with James and her for as long as she wanted.

As it happened, time had a way of playing tricks on Susan. More years than she knew had come and gone, and she had minimal recollection of anything that had occurred. It was not until she came to stay with the Devonshires and was ensconced in Margaret's solicitude that, at long last, she had begun the lengthy process of restoring her mental state. But then one night weeks after she had seen the lawyer, Robert came pounding on their door. He was drunk; in fact, he was still waving a bottle of whiskey around demanding his wife return to his home and marital bed. While James forcibly escorted him back to his farm, Margaret tried to calm Susan. Unfortunately, the episode set her off once again, and for another four months, she vacillated between turmoil and stupor.

✳

As the weeks passed, even Margaret began to wonder why Susan had not received any definitive news back from Barclay & Barclay. She had been so enthusiastic following her luncheon with Mr. Barclay, and for the first time since that ill-fated day when she had eloped, Susan had shown a remnant of her youthful energy.

Margaret was having difficulty comprehending that, almost three years later, Susan was still so vulnerable that the slightest incident could throw her back into despair. She began to think that Susan must have an underlying psychological condition, and it might be wise to at least consult with a psychiatrist. From her own experience, Margaret fully recognized that it could take a lifetime to recover from such a devastating personal tragedy, but Susan was a young woman with years ahead of her.

Deep in her heart, Margaret knew that she and James ought to have taken action to help their godchild much sooner. At first, she rationalized that she had been so overcome with grief and guilt that she could barely exercise control over the daily requirements of her own life, much less be of assistance to anyone else. But now it was all too clear to Margaret that she had not reached out to Susan long before, because she had held her responsible for June and Bert's death. Finally realizing how unfair she had been, Margaret was ready to do whatever she could to ensure that Susan regained some semblance of a life.

Late one summer day when Susan was having a nap, Margaret telephoned the law firm and requested to speak with Derek Barclay. After waiting nearly ten minutes for the lawyer to come on the line, she was surprised by his very different tone with her, compared to their previous calls. She was astounded when he said the Smith will was being prepared for surrogate court, and it was essential to allow for the due process of law.

Margaret was still staring at the telephone, which she had eventually returned to its cradle, when James came into the house for his afternoon tea. After quietly apprising her husband of the current legal situation, she said, "I have no idea what's going on with June and Bert's will, but I do know it's high time you and I take more accountability for our godchild and determine how we can encourage her to move beyond her fluctuating periods of desolation and normalcy. Tomorrow morning, I'm going to arrange an appointment with either a psychiatrist or a psychologist and hopefully set her on the road to recovery."

"I couldn't agree with you more, Margaret. It's heartrending to watch Susan bounce up and down like a yo-yo. Well, that is strange about the Smiths' will! Nonetheless, there's something we're going to arrange immediately, and that is a restraining order against that bloody Robert Wharton, so he can't come around here upsetting Susan again."

Attending the prom had never been on her lengthy list of aspirations, and Francine had expected that her high school graduation would come and go without much fanfare. Furthermore, when the invitation from the Dwyer family in Prince Edward Island had arrived in February, and her uncles had insisted that Mother Pat and Francine take the train to visit them during the month of August, she thought she had received the best graduation present anyone could possibly imagine.

Apparently, the formal dance at the beginning of June was an unprecedented success, although neither Francine nor Jessica had participated in any of the planned festivities. Presumably, as their vying top scores for the province of Manitoba would eventually attest, both had been far too busy studying to spend time on frivolities.

All the pupils had eagerly anticipated the morning of Friday, June 28, 1968, but most especially the graduating class. The grade twelve students had finished writing the five final departmental examinations on Thursday afternoon and were required to complete their year by returning at nine o'clock to pick up their report cards.

During supper the previous evening, Darrin had said, "Francine, since tomorrow's your last day, I'll look after your sheep, so you can have a little lie-in before you and Pat leave for school."

"Oh, thank you, Uncle Darrin. I really do appreciate that after getting up so early all month to review for my exams. I'll be back on the job on Saturday."

Little did Francine know that the three adults had been plotting for some time about when they would present her with her graduation gift. Patricia had taken the telephone call from the Ford dealership the past Saturday morning advising them that their purchase had arrived. Daniel and Patricia had driven to Brandon with Malcolm and Alice Webster on Monday to finalize the arrangements. On the way, they decided not to give Francine her new black Mustang until the last day of school. Subsequently, Pat had had the honour of driving it to their neighbour's farm to be locked in their garage until the end of the week.

On Friday, while Francine was sleeping, Patricia and Daniel took the truck to pick up the vehicle, and upon returning, parked the shiny new automobile in front of the house. When they went into the kitchen to prepare breakfast, neither had much interest in eating. The anticipation and planning over the past months for Francine's surprise was reaching a peak, and they could barely wait to see the look on her face.

What made the gift even more special was the fact that it was Francine who had actually provided the solution to their cash dilemma. Without disclosing any details to her, the three McGregor adults had quickly concluded that there might not be enough money in the chequing account to pay for a trip to the east, purchase a car, and cover the tuition for the fall semester at college. To contemplate such extensive expenditures in one year would require selling a substantial number of their herd of sheep.

One Saturday after supper, when they were seated on the veranda enjoying the balmy spring evening, Francine shocked them all by poignantly proposing to do just that. "I've spent the entire day thinking about this summer and fall. I know it would be unrealistic to expect you to pay for my ticket to Cavendish over and above the cost of my books and tuition. I really want to visit with my eastern family and introduce them to you, Mummy Pat. Also, it will be hard for me to take proper care of my sheep when I'm at university, so, although it might break my heart, Uncle Darrin and Daniel, I want you to get the best price you can for all my sheep."

In the ensuing silence, it seemed as if even the birds stopped trilling, the crickets ceased chirping, and the wind stopped blowing. None of her family had ever expected Francine to agree to sell her beloved sheep, much less to be the one to broach such a preposterous notion. Had she overheard their discussions? When had she become so mature that she was ready to make such a tough choice?

Patricia was the first to recover her voice. "Thank you, Francine, for your generous offer. But before we do anything quite so rash, we need to consider our options. A very viable one, which I've not had a chance to tell you, is that I have consented to Mrs. Devonshire's request to return as a substitute teacher at Hartney for the spring and possibly into the fall while Miss Swanson takes time off to look after her dying mother."

"Do you really want to go back teaching? I thought you liked not having to go to work every day."

"To be truthful, my dearest, I'm worried about what I'll do with my time once you go away to university. I need daily routines, and I won't even see Alice every morning, because she has decided to resign as the coordinator at the seniors' centre by the end of June. Then, of course, I'll also miss my morning coffee with Trin. At any rate, apparently Mrs. Swanson has cancer, and her doctors are not confident about her prognosis, so my foray back into the academic world may well be short-lived."

✳

While Francine sat down at the table for breakfast, Patricia and Daniel remained standing close to the door. When Uncle Darrin made an unexpected entrance, since he was always out herding the sheep at that time of the day, she looked at the three adults in her life with more than a cursory glance. What was going on? As Francine thought about it, it occurred to her that they had been acting strangely for the past week.

Still, Francine did not have the slightest suspicion of what was about to unfold. She was drowsy from her unusually long sleep, and once she had a cup of coffee and something to eat, she would be more than ready to put Souris High behind her forever. She had already prepared Mother Pat to wait for her at the Lingnan after dropping her off at school, because the students had been advised that they would be released for their summer vacation within the hour.

At twenty minutes past eight, Francine rose from the table, peered again at her family, who had remained immobile while she was finishing breakfast, and said, "Okay, are all three of you taking me to school, or do you have some news that was too dreadful to convey to me on an empty stomach?" Even as she was expressing her question, Francine had a sudden pang of fear and wished that she had not been so glib.

Her equanimity was restored when Pat calmly said, "Shall we do this, guys?" As if on cue, the identical twins sprang into action and raced ahead to open the door. Francine had scarcely reached the landing when, with one foot suspended in mid-air, she froze. Her mouth opened, but no words came as she stared at the sleek object conspicuously occupying the driveway.

At that juncture, Pat held up a set of keys, and in unison, they sang out, "Surprise!"

When Francine finally found her tongue all she could say was, "Oh, my gosh, my gosh! Is this for me?"

It was Daniel who at last spurred her to take the proffered keys and to get behind the steering wheel. "The one condition, young lady, is that at all times you observe the speed limit. Now you better leave for school, so you won't have any reason to drive too fast."

*

Her timing was impeccable. The first bell had rung, and the students were beginning to gather by the door just as Francine glided into the schoolyard with the smoothness of silk. She turned off the motor that purred like a kitten, gently closed the door, and strode up the stairs for the last time, while most of them stood and stared long after the second toll.

Neither before nor after the abbreviated class did Francine respond to a single comment, question, or innuendo about her beautiful new Mustang. She accepted her outstanding report card and Mr. Billanski's well wishes with the same nonchalance that had enabled her to complete the final year of her secondary education as perhaps the most ostracized student in the history of Souris High. Upon her departure, Francine was suddenly the most sought-after student in the school. The irony that her instant popularity sprang solely from the persuasion of a material possession was not lost on her.

For all intents and purposes, the foursome had ceased to be. Although three were presently on the campus of Brandon College, only the original two friends continued getting together on a regular basis. Aside from a brief encounter on the first day of classes, Cassandra and Francine could go for days, soon to become weeks and even months, without crossing paths with Hope. If Hope were to interact with anyone, chances were that it would be Lindsay rather than her daughter. And not a single word was heard from Jessica Yang.

After the initial week of welcoming activities, the freshmen began to settle into the expected requirements of college life. Francine loved every aspect, from having been able to select her program of study to choosing the time of attendance and, most of all, to meeting new classmates in practically all her courses. It was an entirely new start, and she had quickly grasped that what she did with this wonderful opportunity was primarily up to her.

Driving to and from class every day, Francine still could hardly believe that the Mustang was really and truly hers. Several times during the month of July, she had visited Cassandra and had allowed her to get behind the steering wheel on many occasions. The two friends even journeyed to Clear Lake and spent a week at the Jamison's cottage before Francine left on her trip to Prince Edward Island.

Returning to her place of birth and being enveloped in the embrace of the Dwyer family and so many others in the community had an incredible effect on Francine. As soon as she heard the incessant waves crashing to the shore, she was flooded with memories of her parents, which she had blocked from her mind. At last, she acknowledged how much they had loved and doted on her until her feelings of abandonment began to be exorcised from her heart, mind, and soul. Before long, her journey had become a catharsis; she was set free from guilt and oppression, and her true spirit started to rise like the phoenix. As each day passed, Francine regained confidence, vigour, and the bright clear vision of youth.

Reminiscing on a misty Manitoba morning on her way to Brandon, Francine recalled how, when she had pulled into the driveway of the Jamison cottage for the September long weekend, Cassandra was astounded by the obvious changes in her, especially by her uncharacteristic optimism. "Wow, you look terrific! You and Aunt Pat must have had an awesome time. Let's grab our swimsuits and towels; it's already warm enough to lie on the beach, and you can tell me all about it."

After sharing all the exciting details, Francine said, "You know, Cassandra, I finally feel like the person I was meant to be. Although everyone, especially Dr. Donahue, kept telling me that there was no reason for me to feel guilty or responsible, I always felt that I owed someone—I don't know who, God maybe—a huge debt, because I was alive, and Mummy and Daddy were dead. Dr. Donahue has always maintained that I suffer from oppression rather than depression, because I was weighed down by worry and a profound sense of obligation. When I returned to Cavendish, at last I realized what she had been talking about during our sessions."

With a start, Cassandra suddenly grasped the magnitude of what it must have been like for Francine to lose both parents at once. She tried to remember what she had told her over the years about the death of her parents, and now, on quick reflection, she realized that Francine had said very little. Cassandra's grandparents had expressed to her only meagre details. She went cold all over, as she comprehended how she would feel if, even as an adult, something happened to either one or both of her beloved parents.

"Oh, Francine, I honestly never considered how devastating it had to have been for you, and when you were so little. Please forgive me. But what a relief that revisiting your past has healed you. Now you can move forward in your life and be who you truly are, while all of us who love you, can enjoy the real you. Sorry, I've been spending too much time around my mother this summer. I'm starting to sound like a psychologist, and guess what? She's going to be at college with us because she has decided to study for her PhD."

"Wow, that's cool. And, there's nothing to forgive. You've been my best friend from the time my Uncles Darrin and Daniel bought me to Manitoba."

"Changing the subject, and not to sound glib, it just occurred to me that you might want to find a parking spot close by, rather than right on campus. After what you told me about your experience on the last day of school, I don't think you want anyone to know that you own a flashy new sports car. We both realize what a magnet it could be, and I know that you hardly want to attract new friends who are only interested in your material possessions."

Pulling into Mrs. Stevenson's secluded driveway, Francine realized that never before had she possessed anything that would have been the envy of anyone. She'd had little interest in things, always caring much more about the people and pets in her life, but she did have to acknowledge that she liked cruising around in her new Mustang. As she recalled Cassandra's comment, she realized that being the owner of an expensive car might say more about her than about the potential friends to whom it appealed. Still, deep in the recesses of her mind, Francine knew she had no desire to be defined by materialism. She was determined to value individuals for their personal worth rather than for what they had or did, and once again, she reflected with joy that she and Cassandra had reaffirmed their enduring friendship over the September long weekend.

✳

At last, the weekend was over. Even though it had been her decision, Jessica had never felt so alone. Several times before her mother left, Jessica had been on the verge of confiding in her, but envisioning the look of repulsion that would have invariably appeared on her demure face was enough to stop Jessica in her tracks. How could she tell her loving mother, who already longed for grandchildren, that she might be a lesbian?

Instead, Jessica had suffered through the three seemingly endless days by going for long walks around the beautiful campus and beyond, until she had reached the banks of the Red River. The trees were beginning their autumnal transition, and the warmth of the sun pouring through the colourful leaves lightened her mood. The more she thought about what she would do, the more certain she became that she would never disclose her sexual orientation to anyone.

It did occur to her that she could likely feign an interest in the opposite sex. She could even marry eventually and have children, but how fair would that be to the poor man, who might actually be in love with her? Still, she really did want a family. In fact, as a little girl, she had always longed for siblings and had vowed to have at least four children. Now Jessica could barely stop wallowing in self-pity, believing that because of a strange twist of fate, she was destined to be solitary for the balance of her life.

Classes could not begin soon enough. She had slept very little during Monday night and was possibly the first student in the cafeteria searching for a cup of coffee. In the early hours of the morning, Jessica had resolved that she would not only survive but also thrive by pouring herself into her studies. She would deny her sociable nature and curtail interaction with all of her classmates. She had always been an adept student, and by burying herself in her books, she would eventually succeed in becoming a highly-skilled medical practitioner.

As far as the foursome was concerned, Jessica was determined to allocate her three former friends to the realm of a fond memory. She would only return home once a year to be with her parents during the Christmas season, and she vowed not to get in touch with any of the others. Francine was the only one she would likely encounter if their families decided to gather for dinner, but Jessica suspected that it would take considerable time before she was forgiven for all her previous exclusion. That was fine with Jessica. Regardless of how much she might long for her, none of them must ever find out about her ardour for Hope, especially Hope herself.

During the summer, Michael had nearly worked Hope out of his heart and mind. He had returned home to work with his father for July and August, and by toiling from dawn to dusk, he dropped into bed so exhausted that he did not have the energy to yearn for her. Other than short notes from Dr. Farrington about Hope's acclaim at the renowned music school, Michael neither anticipated nor received any news from the woman he loved beyond measure.

On the Sunday of the September long weekend, Michael returned to the furnished studio apartment in Brandon that he had put a deposit on at the end of June. After the comfort of his parents' spacious home, he found it cramped and wondered why he had not just rented a room in the dorm on campus. He did not even know when Hope was expected to return, not that it would likely have any significance for him, unless his services were required to accompany her for a violin recital.

Michael had long suspected that Charles was very aware of his feelings for his protégé, and now he hoped that the maestro would schedule an impromptu concert to welcome her home. The moment Michael drove into the city, all of his arduous summer labour to quell his sexual desires evaporated like the dew on a hazy Manitoba morning. Other than rigorously sublimating his urges into the pursuit of his master's degree, Michael had no idea how he would survive the coming semester.

Furthermore, if Michael had been apprised that another person on another campus in another city was similarly yearning for Hope, it would have come with little surprise. He had long ago anticipated that, throughout her life, Hope would be pursued by a host of individuals, all wanting to be near her, to touch her, to be one with her, to be drawn into her greatness.

On Monday morning, no longer able to stand the confines of his small flat, Michael ventured out for a walk. He had been oblivious of his whereabouts when, suddenly, he heard his name echoing on the wind. "Michael, Michael, wait for me."

Glancing up, he realized he had wandered onto the college grounds. But he had to be dreaming. It sounded so much like Hope's voice that he dared not turn around and look. Not once during their past years on campus had she ever called out for him, and he had barely stopped to change direction when she flew into his arms.

"Didn't you hear me? I've been trying to get your attention since you passed Dr. Burton's office. I was beginning to think you were deliberately ignoring me, when all the while I was certain that you would be happy to see me."

Almost overwhelmed by Hope's spontaneous embrace, Michael gingerly released her before he found his voice. "I guess I was lost in thought, and I didn't know that you were back in Brandon. So, I guess, welcome home. I don't suppose you have time to go for a coffee and maybe tell me about your summer?"

"My, aren't you the standoffish one? I'm getting the impression you didn't miss me at all, if you even realized I was away."

How could she talk like that? Did she still not have the slightest idea of her impact on him? It was all Michael could do not to gather her back into his muscular arms and crush her to his body as he covered her petite mouth with his ardent kisses. If they had been on any other spot on the campus instead of in full view of the Dean of Music's large office window, he would have thrown caution to the wind. But Michael knew that if Dr. Burton had any inkling of his true feelings for his virtuoso, he would be terminated as her pianist so fast his head would not stop spinning for a week.

"Actually, Dr. Burton was just telling me that you found an apartment not far from the college. Why don't we go there, and you can show me your new lodgings? Do you have anything to drink, or should we pick something up on the way?"

Although his mind raced, Michael could not think of a word to say. Was it possible that Hope had actually missed him during the summer? Could she be propositioning him, asking him to take her to his home and perhaps to his bed? Then, realizing he was reading far too much into her simple request, he knew he had better get a grip on himself before she began to consider that he was becoming like one of her love-struck fans. "Fortunately, I went grocery shopping this morning and can offer you a coffee, along with some of the muffins Marika sent with me yesterday."

"Well, let's go. I'm dying for a cup of coffee and, now that you've told me, for one of your mother's yummy muffins," Hope replied, linking her arm into Michael's. She was desperate to be alone with him. She had needed him so much that now she could barely stand being in his presence without caressing his strong body and crushing him to her.

✳

More than two hours later, Michael came out of the shower dressed in his bathrobe to brew the promised pot of coffee. If Hope had not been seated on the sofa wearing only the shirt she had all but ripped off him, Michael would have thought he was sleepwalking. And the interim had been the most glorious dream he had ever had.

"I love your cozy studio, Michael. Whenever did you find it? I was sure you planned to rent a single room at the men's residence, although right now, I couldn't be happier that you didn't."

Turning to gaze at her, Michael smiled, thinking that she looked like an exotic Persian cat that had just swallowed the elusive canary.

"Why don't you stop staring as if I'm going to disappear before your very eyes?" Hope said. "Come sit beside me, and I'll tell you about my summer before you regale me with all your adventures while I was away."

Could this be the same person who had only seemed to need him as a release after one of her scintillating performances? In two short months, had she changed from a girl obsessed with playing her violin into a mature woman who was capable of loving beyond the realm of her music? Or was he the one who had been unfair, forgetting that she was his junior by more than eight years? Like almost everyone who would ever meet Hope Harding, had he expected so much more of her because of her prodigious talent? Carrying a plate of buttered warm muffins to the coffee table, for the first time in their relationship, Michael felt a sudden ray of hope. Would their love be strong enough to endure the daunting responsibilities of Hope's career?

"That smells like freshly brewed coffee." Francine said coming down the stairs to join Mother Pat in the kitchen. "I could use a break from studying for my finals."

"I was hoping I could entice you to join me. You've been at those books for most of the day now."

"There's so much to learn in such a short time. I don't know where this semester has gone. In some of my courses, I've barely kept up with the required readings, even though I've been diligent every evening and most weekends. I can't believe how every professor seems to think that you're only taking his or her course and stacks on the homework. But I'm sure you remember from your college days."

"I suspect that my course load was not nearly as heavy as yours, and I wonder if driving back and forth each day might be interfering with your study time, my dearest."

"It does take longer now that winter has arrived, but like coming home every night. Even so, I hardly feel I know what's happening with you and my uncles. Tell me what's going on with you guys, and in the neighbourhood."

"Oh, just our usual activities. We've started to play canasta again every Wednesday and Friday afternoon with Malcolm and Alice, who's thrilled to call her time her own. She admits that working away from home was not all it's cracked up to be, and we're also curling twice a week. And you won't believe who Margaret and James have added to their team this winter."

"Is it someone I know? How can I possibly guess when I haven't made it to the rink once this season to watch you?"

"You're right, Francine. It's unfair to ask you to speculate when everyone was stunned."

"Now you have me intrigued, Mummy Pat. Who is it?"

"Well, we found out one evening when Margaret and James invited us over for supper. As you know, we usually have them here, because Margaret's always so busy, and I daresay she has never had any illusions about her culinary skills. To our incredulity, who should be helping her but Susan Smith, and together, they'd made the most delicious Irish stew. Unbeknownst to anyone, Susan has been living with them in secrecy, because of all the acrimony in the district."

"What! You better fill me in, because I'm totally amazed by this turn of events."

After refilling their coffee mugs, Patricia brought Francine up to speed with Susan's current situation. "You're not alone! Apparently, when Susan walked out on Robert, Margaret and James opened their home to their godchild. However, following one debilitating episode after another, they realized Susan needed additional psychological counselling and sought the assistance of Dr. Donahue. Subsequently, the Devonshires have taken Susan under their wing and are starting to involve her in their activities. Margaret's even tutoring her at home, so that eventually she might be ready to sit her grade twelve departmental examinations."

"Wow! I thought, and probably so did everybody, that Susan had left when the Wharton farm was sold. Good for Mr. and Mrs. Devonshire. Who would believe I'm now further along in my schooling than at least one of my nemeses?"

"If the truth is told, you long ago surpassed both of the girls who took such delight in tormenting you. Did you know that Carole dropped out of school soon after moving to Brandon and works as a waitress? Her grandmother couldn't control her, and the rumour is that she spends her nights with any man who makes her an offer."

"You're a veritable fount of knowledge. We need to have coffee more often." Francine chuckled as she rose from the table to resume her studying. "Please call me when you need my help to make supper."

*

For reasons he would never understand, Derek could not get Susan out of his mind. Even when he had proposed to Tiffany Franklin, the woman their families had, since his childhood, been expecting him to marry, an image of Susan flashed before his eyes. It was more than the fact that the Smith family had been clients of Barclay & Barclay for decades. Even after his afternoon of meditation, when he decided to assign the probate of Bert and June's will to his associate, Derek knew it was much more. There was an undercurrent of intrigue about the red-headed beauty with the piercing emerald eyes that he had fantasized exploring.

More times than he dared to recall, Derek's hand had lingered over the telephone before he decided against placing a call to the beguiling young woman. He would suddenly become as nervous as a schoolboy and then chide himself about what he would say. "Oh hello, Susan. Just checking on how you're doing after I hastily passed you off to my associate and bowed out of your life. And by the way, I've become engaged, but I can't resist inviting you to join me for lunch, or preferably dinner, one more time to see how our evening might unfold . . .."

Before Derek had accidentally encountered Susan when he was coming out of his office, he had been hesitant about proposing to Tiffany. They had known each other since grade school, and by the time they were completing their secondary education, Derek had been thoroughly infatuated with her. With chagrin, he remembered the dozen red roses he had sent her every week for months before the prom to entice her to be his date. If Tiffany had accompanied him, Derek would have eloped with her before the evening was over.

At that time though, Tiffany only had eyes for Eric Page, the captain of the football team. It was not that Eric was any taller, handsomer, or more proficient at sports than Derek, but rather that he preferred playing tennis, which challenged his individual skills. Although regarded by some as more of a gentleman's game, tennis was not nearly as popular as any of the team sports at Brandon Collegiate. Then, when Eric arrived at the dance already inebriated and holding Tiffany in a manner similar to how he had hoisted the football trophy, Derek had been disgusted.

If only he had stayed instead of barging out of the school auditorium like a wounded animal and returning home to sulk in his bedroom. At the very least, he should have remained at the dance, and if he could not have wrestled Eric's car keys away from him, he could have insisted on driving the rest of his friends home. Although he was acquainted with Tiffany's father, Derek was not quite audacious enough to telephone Judge Franklin and alert him to the fact that his daughter was under the influence of alcohol.

The next morning, his clock radio alarm blared with the news of the tragic accident. Derek leapt out of bed and raced to the kitchen to rescue the *Brandon Sun* from his father before he escaped to his office with it under his arms. The front page of the daily newspaper was covered with the wreckage of an automobile heading toward the city that had smashed into the railway underpass west of the small community of Kemnay around 1:30 a.m. The vehicle was so badly demolished that it was all but impossible to determine the make, although there was no mistaking its fire-engine-red colour. Furthermore, the journalist at the scene had included a photograph of the dual headlights of the second-generation Ford Thunderbird, the only segment of the car that was still recognizable.

The heading of the article identified that three adolescents were pronounced dead at the scene. Fearing that it was Eric's prize automobile, Derek had quickly scanned the rest of the article. He read that, as if by some miraculous act of God, the passenger in the front seat had been flung from the speeding car onto the grassy embankment, just as it failed to negotiate the sharp curve and careened into the cement foundation of the underpass. The sole survivor had been rushed by ambulance to Brandon General Hospital.

Praying that Tiffany had been in the front with her date, Derek was devastated when he read that the names of the victims and the survivor were being withheld, pending notification of next of kin.

"What's the matter, son? You look like you've seen a ghost!" his mother, Ethel, remarked as she came into the kitchen and poured her first coffee of the day.

"Oh, don't say that, Mum. I'm leaving for the hospital while you read all about it."

✳

It had taken Derek the better part of the morning to confirm that it was Tiffany who was alive. She was in the intensive care unit, and although her vital signs had stabilized, she was still unconscious. Only her immediate family were being allowed to see her. Regardless of how much Derek appealed to the nursing staff, he was advised to return home and wait.

"Go home? I can't leave until I've seen her, or at least found out what's wrong with her. We were planning to get married as soon as we graduated."

One of the nursing students, who was not much older than Derek, noticed that the well-dressed young man was on the verge of tears. She caught up with him at the door. "If you hurry, I just saw the patient's father take the elevator to the cafeteria. Perhaps he'll give you some information about how she's doing."

✳

Within the week, Tiffany had been discharged from the hospital relatively unscathed physically. At first, her family expected her to be weepy and to grieve for her boyfriend and classmates, but months later, even Derek was ready to concede that Tiffany must actually have been in love with Eric. She cried the minute anyone called to see her, refused to eat, scarcely slept, and did not return to school to write the departmental examinations.

Every day when he stopped by the Franklin home, Tiffany's mother was encouraging. "Just give her some time, Derek. Before long, Tiffany will appreciate your concern, and it helps her dad and me to know that her friends are supporting her."

Summer came and went, and Tiffany seemed to become more anxious and withdrawn with each passing day. She started going to Dr. Matthews' office on practically a daily basis with an ever-increasing number of ailments, until her family physician became more than a little skeptical. Initially, he ordered all the appropriate laboratory tests to rule out a physical basis for her numerous complaints, but when every result came back negative, he began to question his medical approach.

Since she did not appear to have any particular illness, it did occur to Dr. Matthews that Tiffany could be seeking attention. But why would she be spending her days in his office when she had far preferable ways to interact with people her own age? He realized she seemed to have little interest in her family, friends, activities, and even in the usual pursuits of daily living, and yet, David Matthews was hesitant to diagnose his young patient as being depressed. Her symptoms were different. It was almost as if she continued to be traumatized long after the time of the motor vehicle accident. Was she overwrought with guilt because she had lived and her friends had died?

David nearly dropped his keys as he was locking up his office when he remembered a lecture he had attended well over a year earlier. The chief psychiatrist of the Brandon Hospital for Mental Diseases had given the presentation about an unusual diagnosis called gross stress reaction. The majority of the participants were surprised that the condition had appeared in the official nomenclature when *DSM–I* was published in 1952.

The major drawback of having a mental institution on the outskirts of the city was that no provisions had been made in the construction of the Brandon General Hospital for an acute psychiatric ward. David was confident that he could refer Tiffany to the chief psychiatrist at the Hospital for Mental Diseases as an outpatient, but he had grave concerns about Judge Franklin's reaction when he discovered where his family doctor was recommending sending his daughter. Would Dr. Mathias Werner consider providing a preliminary assessment and perhaps even counselling within the confines of David's professional setting?

✳

"Hey, would it be all right if we joined you? I'm Jill, and this is Sandra and her new boyfriend, Edward Wong. We're all in the same Anatomy and Physiology class with you."

"Hi there, we've noticed that you always sit alone." Sandra said, "And Edward is not my boyfriend!"

"Sure, have a seat. I'm Jessica Yang. It's nice to meet you. Doesn't that professor remind you of a sergeant major?"

"Well, you always seem to know the answer when you're the one she decides to pick on. I'm terrified that one day she's going to put me on the spot, and I won't be able to say a word, even if I do know the answer," Jill said, setting her tray on the table and pulling out the chair across from Jessica.

"That's exactly what she wants to do. Didn't you hear her say that she expects more than half of us to fail her course? She thinks her job is to save the medical profession from 'a bunch of duds,'" Jessica answered, glancing at Edward, who had claimed the seat beside her.

"I'm impressed that you're never stumped by Professor Kulberg's questions," Edward said, peering into Jessica's deep-brown eyes. "Do you spend all your time studying? When I think about it, I don't recall ever seeing you at any of the freshman activities."

"My parents have worked hard to give me this opportunity to study medicine. I don't intend to disappoint them. In fact, I aim to be the top student of our class."

"I don't think so, because I plan to follow in my father's footsteps and graduate magna cum laude from the university's faculty of medicine."

"Perhaps you will, but I'm aspiring to graduate with the highest distinction of summa cum laude and then study to become an oncologist. What specialty did your father select?"

"Dr. Alexander Wong is the head of internal medicine here on campus, and if you're lucky, eventually, you might be invited to attend some of his lectures."

"Well, these two seem to be vying for the top honours already, Jill. Shall we leave them to figure out which one will succeed six years from now?"

When Sandra and Jill departed, Edward laughed. "Do you get the impression our classmates deliberately decided to get us together? I wouldn't put it past my mother to have secretly arranged for them to introduce us, since she's always suggesting I look for a nice Chinese girl in my classes. But now that we've met, would you consider accompanying me to the Christmas ball on Saturday?"

Jessica thought for several moments before she agreed. After all, it was just a dance, and Edward was correct in his observation that she had not participated in any of the events to welcome the freshmen to the university. Besides, Jessica was tired of being alone all the time. Sandra had made it clear from the beginning that she did not have any amorous intentions with Edward, but then neither did Jessica. So, what harm could there be in having a platonic relationship with a handsome guy whose family was well established in the medical faculty? And presumably, her new friends, Jill and Sandra, would attend with their dates, and Jessica would be part of a group for the evening.

✳

If ever she considered that Dr. Burton had high standards, Hope was becoming increasingly challenged by Dr. Farrington's expectations. Following her successful debut the past summer, he enrolled her in the seven-week intensive program at the Meadowmount School of Music for the following year. He was also preparing her for an audition for the Juilliard School later that fall, anticipating that she would become an undergraduate eligible for the bachelor of music degree.

For the first time since her journey to become a concert violinist had begun, Hope was having doubts. Although the pressure had been intense during the summer at the school in Westport, she had been so focused that she often exceeded the required five hours of daily practice. And she thoroughly delighted in the opportunity for weekly concerts. When she was not practicing or performing, Hope enjoyed the camaraderie of her fellow students and her frequent strolls in the nearby Adirondack Mountains of upstate New York.

Still, was she beginning to falter in her quest to follow her dream because of Michael? Hope had never been given to long solitary walks until she had left to study in the United States. At first, she was convinced she was just lonely, but once she became friends with a number of the other students, she realized it was much more. Whenever she was alone, and especially at night, when she was tossing and turning yet again, her yearning to be in Michael's loving arms was almost more than she could bear.

How could she have ever allowed herself to fall in love with him? Hope knew that her one great love was music, and from the moment of her mother's death, nobody and nothing would interfere with the pursuit of her destiny. In fact, she had always thought that the only reason she made love to Michael was because she had been on an incredible high following her exhilarating performances. She had been confident that she could maintain her detachment and walk away from him at will.

But since that day when Hope had encountered Michael outside of Dr. Burton's office, they soon were apart only for their respective practices and classes. When each day reached its painfully slow end, they raced to Michael's cozy apartment, and the moment the door slid closed behind them, they were all over each other. They could not get enough; they were so ready to devour one another that sometimes they made it to the bed, sometimes they managed to undress, and sometimes they came together wherever their passion peaked.

✳

Soon Hope was returning to her grandparents' only once or twice a week for a brief visit and to do laundry. She explained that because of her rigorous schedule, Dr. Farrington had arranged for her to have a room in the student's dormitory, and it never occurred to either of them to question her. Although they missed her, they accepted that Hope would always have to make sacrifices for her music.

One Friday afternoon, Hope arrived early for the customary coffee klatch. She had only attended once during the entire semester but remembered that Lindsay was invariably the first to find her way to the cafeteria. She missed her, and Hope would dearly love to thank her for her perspicacity almost a year earlier, but what would she say?

Lindsay's lilting voice roused Hope from her reverie. "What a lovely surprise! I've been wondering when you would remember those of us who knew you before you became famous. Would you like your usual?"

"Oh, Lindsay, it's so nice to see you. Today's my treat, and could we please wait until Cassandra and Francine get here? I've been so remiss with our friendships that I'm hoping to buy back everyone's favour."

"Don't be silly, my darling girl. We all know your career choice is very demanding, and I, for one, at least suspect your dedicated accompanist has certain expectations of his own."

Hope looked sheepishly at her esteemed friend. "You know, don't you? You're going to be one astute psychologist, Dr. Lindsay Jamison. Before your arrival, I was sitting here trying to figure out how to thank you, because I've realized what a risk your husband and Dr. Walker had to take to prescribe contraception to me when I was still a minor. Not to mention what could have happened to Michael if anyone had taken issue with our relationship."

"Don't you worry your pretty head about either doctor's choice. You're a mature young woman expected to cope with a myriad of adult responsibilities, and besides, I firmly believe that the Government of Canada has no business in the bedrooms of the nation. I hazard a guess that Dr. Charles is aware, although I suspect if Ian Burton knew, he would be less than supportive. But, of course, your secret is forever safe with me."

"Thank you, Lindsay. I'm so glad we had this chance for a chat before the other two come. Oh, here they are now."

✳

Cassandra and Francine were deep in a discussion as they entered the cafeteria, and initially had not located the table, where they knew Lindsay would be waiting for them. Then, without thinking, Cassandra blurted, "Well, well . . . look who has deigned to grace us with her presence."

"Now, my dearest, sarcasm does not become you," Lindsay replied quickly. "Please, have a seat, and tell us what you fancy. Hello, Francine, you are looking as gorgeous as always."

"Hi there, you two. It's great to see you." As Hope spoke, she glanced first at Cassandra, and then her gaze came to rest on Francine.

"Wow, I really like what you've done with your hair, Francine. That stylish pageboy accentuates your pretty face, and your eyes sparkle more than ever."

"You don't look so shabby yourself when we finally get to see you up close and personal instead of from the elevation of a stage." Soon the three youthful friends were engaged in spirited teasing, while Lindsay made her way to the cashier for coffee and chocolate chip cookies. Upon her return, she placed a cup and plate in front of each girl before resuming her seat, delighted to sit tranquilly and savour the gaiety and energy exuded by the young.

✳

Nearly two hours later in the car on the way home, Cassandra said, "Oh, Mummy, I've just realized that you never had a chance to say a word with the three of us chattering non-stop. I'm sorry, we were very rude."

"I enjoyed every minute of your conversations. It's been far too long since you gals have had a good chinwag, and my only regret was that Jessica wasn't there to join you. Have any of you heard from her? Knowing Jessica, I can well imagine that she's studying furiously to be the best student in pre-med, but I hope she remembers that 'all work and no play makes Jessica a dull girl.' I still can't believe she didn't come to the cottage for the Labour Day weekend."

"I don't want to gossip, but from some of the things Francine has shared about the way Jessica treated her during the last semester of grade twelve, I wonder what's happening to her. You know how Francine can be so closed-lipped; I practically had to drag comments from her piecemeal, and the only conclusion I could reach was that Jessica must have been practicing for a Dr. Jekyll and Mr. Hyde persona!"

Lindsay burst out laughing. "Cassandra, with your overactive imagination and flair for the dramatic, you could become an accomplished author, never mind spending your time studying to be a criminal lawyer. Oh, I agree with what your father says about your incessant questioning and insatiable curiosity, but both are also very advantageous attributes to the art of writing. Now, are you going to leave me in suspense, or can you share without breaking your confidence to Francine?"

"Writing is Francine's forte. She loves her English literature courses and has determined that, one day, she will become a published author."

Cassandra lapsed into silence. As she tried to decide what to tell her mother, she realized she could make little sense of what Francine had hesitantly expressed about Jessica's unusual behaviour. What Cassandra was emphatic about was that Francine's return to Prince Edward Island was the best undertaking she had embarked upon since she had moved to Manitoba.

When she noticed that Hope was joining them for coffee, Cassandra wondered if Francine would slip back into her shadow and then had been pleased by her confidence around their famed friend. For the first time since they had become chums, Cassandra and Francine were interacting on a daily basis, and the more they were together, the closer they became. For reasons she could not comprehend, Cassandra was becoming increasingly protective of Francine, as if she was anticipating another calamity to befall her oft-beleaguered friend.

✳

In time, with Dr. Werner's solicitous intervention, Tiffany recovered. Deciding that a change of scene would also be beneficial, she chose to venture to eastern Canada and study in Montreal. Nearly seven years later at Judge Franklin's annual Christmas gathering, Derek had once again been entranced when he caught sight of her in the midst of an admiring crowd. She was more beautiful than ever, with her flowing blonde tresses and a chic black gown accentuating her tall slender body.

He had been about to join the circle of young people when Brenda Franklin accosted him. "Good evening, Derek, thank you for coming. Samuel and I always look forward to seeing you for the festive season." Then turning to her daughter, she said, "Tiffany, could you please come here for a moment? It's been so long that I wonder if you two recognize each other."

As Tiffany turned, her eyes locked into Derek's intense gaze, and a smile flitted across her attractive face. "How could I ever forget a beau who presented me with a dozen red roses every week?" Sashaying across her parents' elegant living room, Tiffany embraced Derek in a casual hug, much to his surprise and delight.

They spent the balance of the evening in each other's company, and before his departure, Derek had invited Tiffany to dinner for the upcoming Saturday evening. During their first date, he was thrilled to learn that, over the course of her years in Montreal, Tiffany had qualified as a chartered accountant and had recently returned to join the Brandon branch of Clarkson & Gordon. By the time Christmas arrived, the two former high school classmates were sharing the season's festivities with their respective parents.

*

Within months, the city's society circle was claiming that Derek Barclay and Tiffany Franklin had become an item. They could be heard prophesying that, before long, subscribers of the *Brandon Sun* would be reading about their imminent nuptials. Both were aware of the rumours circulating about their relationship, but neither Derek nor Tiffany seemed upset by them.

In fact, the more time they were together, the more they discovered how well suited they were for one another. Soon, they were spending every available hour afforded by their demanding careers in each other's presence. Most evenings ended at one or the other's apartment, and even though their courtship was becoming increasingly intense, Derek always stopped at the height of their passion.

He desired her as much as Tiffany wanted him, but almost a year later, he still could not consummate their love. Oh, God, how could he possibly reveal that, at the ripe age of twenty-six, he was a virgin? Furthermore, he was aware that she had been expecting him to propose for some time, but although weeks and months had passed, he had not asked her to become his wife. His schoolboy infatuation had deepened into love, and yet for some reason, he had difficulty visualizing her as his lifelong partner. What was holding him back? Even Derek realized that he needed to get his head examined. Tiffany was gorgeous, bright, successful, and, no doubt, she would be most utilitarian in helping him achieve his aspiration of succeeding Judge Franklin and becoming the first Barclay to be appointed to the bench.

Derek's reluctance came to an abrupt end following his lengthy lunch with Susan at the Royal Oak Inn. After several hours of contemplation, he gave his head a shake. Then, just as he was about to leave his office, he happened to notice an announcement in the *Brandon Sun*, and suddenly Derek knew the time was right. When he arrived home, he called Tiffany.

"Hello, my darling. I'm delighted you're in, and though I realize this is well in advance, I've just stopped by the box office to purchase tickets for the Winnipeg Symphony for their New Year's Eve concert. I hope I wasn't being presumptive, but I've just read that Brandon's own virtuoso is performing, and Hope Harding's concerts sell out almost the minute she's booked."

"Thank you, my love. That sounds delightful. Shall we be returning from Winnipeg that evening?"

"If you can manage to escape your usual Saturday morning office commitment, I'd like to suggest that we meet for brunch and then be on our way. Are you all right with me making a reservation at the Hotel Fort Garry for dinner before the performance and also with arranging our accommodations?"

"What a wonderful surprise. I may be compelled to treat myself to a shopping spree. I believe a new gown would be in order."

Thinking that exquisite lingerie might be more desirable, given Tiffany seemed to be attired in one elegant outfit after another every time they went out, Derek chose to keep his own counsel. He had already made an appointment with Henry James at Ben Moss Jewellers as his first stop the following morning, since he had no other pressing commitments. Upon consultation with Mr. James, he had confirmed that the Franklins were regular patrons, and yes, he had Tiffany's ring size on record. Furthermore, he had just brought in a marquise cut diamond solitaire 18 carat gold engagement ring that would suit Tiffany beautifully.

∗

Every time she turned around, Edward was by her side. Jessica was surprised by how much fun she had at the Christmas dance, but since she left soon after to be with her parents over the break, she had given him little further thought. Now that classes had resumed, he seemed to consider that they were dating.

By the end of the first week, Jessica agreed to have coffee with Edward. He seemed like a nice guy, and after the onslaught of Trin and Sebio's questioning during the holiday about whether she had a beau, she began to appreciate the value of having a male friend. Still, Jessica wanted to be careful about presuming Edward's intentions, and she resolved that her best approach was to be candid.

After meeting Jill and Sandra and then seeing the foursome over Christmas, Jessica realized how lonely she had been since she had arrived in Winnipeg. She decided to accompany her parents to the

McGregors for dinner and was surprised by how warm and open Francine had been with her. Although she was the first one of the foursome she had seen, Jessica wondered why she had so totally cut herself off from her friends.

The young women readily resumed their camaraderie, and following Pat's delicious dinner, they bundled up and walked to their haven of Colorado blue spruce on the knoll cresting the farm. When they were snuggled under the protecting boughs of the conifers, Francine said, "So, we have a chance for the retreat that you proposed last year."

"Once again, it's only you and me. And perhaps that's the way it will always be, although I'm surprised that Cassandra and her parents didn't come to visit the Websters."

"Lindsay decided to give Grandma Alice a break for a change and prepared Christmas dinner. Actually, we're invited to visit them whenever we want this upcoming week. How long are you at home? Would you like to drive to Brandon with me for a couple of days?"

"Terrific! I was so sorry that I missed going to the cottage for the September weekend, and I'd love to see Cassandra. How's she doing?"

"Well, since you were the one who was so adamant about us all being together before we went our separate ways, we couldn't believe you didn't come. As it happens, we're having the time of our lives on campus. Cassandra and I both love our classes, the freedom, and the independence, and if we get out of rein or experience any difficulty, her mum is there for us. We have coffee every Friday afternoon to catch up on all the latest before I drive home for the weekend."

"Does Hope ever join you?" Jessica asked as she glanced away and stared down the hill.

"On rare occasions, but she's incredibly busy, and besides, we think she's having a fling with Michael Griffin. The rumour we heard was that he was taking her to his parents' exquisite log home for most of the holiday."

"What about you and Cassandra? Do either of you have a special fellow, or are you playing the field for now?"

"You could pretty much say that for both of us. We tend to gather as a group rather than worry about pairing up for most of the social functions. Hope doesn't ever get involved in any of the usual extra-curricular activities that Cassandra and I attend, nor do I expect that she would."

"You don't sound like you miss Hope much at all. In fact, you're so confident and poised that, during dinner, I could hardly believe you're the same person who graduated from Souris High just six months ago. And by the way, thanks for suggesting that we come here, because before we talk about anything else, I want to apologize for how horrible I was toward you not only for the last semester but also for most of grade twelve. I've done a lot of soul-searching since the end of June, and I make no excuse for my behaviour. Can you forgive me for the way I treated you? You must have felt so isolated."

"I accept your apology, Jessica, and yes, I forgive you. During the summer when Mother Pat and I returned to Cavendish, I laid many of my ghosts to rest, most importantly, holding myself responsible for my mummy and daddy's drowning. I no longer feel haunted, because at last, I'm free from the guilt and oppression of their deaths. Dr. Donahue is convinced that now I'll become the person I was truly meant to be, and she has discontinued my counselling. Instead of clinging to anyone else, I can depend on me."

"Oh, I'm so happy for you, Francine. When I think about how we just expected you to get on with your life, neither Hope nor I or even Cassandra really understood how traumatic it was for you. I couldn't believe how much I missed my mum and dad during these past short months, and I can't imagine how devastated I would be if I were to lose one of them even now."

"Dr. Donahue often told me that my remarkable resilience was because I've always been surrounded by people who love me. The moment when I saw my friend, Margaret, in Prince Edward Island, I remembered how her mum and dad became my instant surrogate parents, and then I was blessed a third time with my uncles and Mummy Pat. Some children can go a lifetime without knowing the love of a parent, and, in essence, I have had seven adults care for me as their own. So, once I let go of my guilt, I started to heal, and now even my nightmares have stopped. But since it's getting dark, we should think about going home."

The two friends began their descent down the gentle slope as the sun slipped below the horizon. Both had fallen silent. While Francine was lost in reverie recalling her joy of being reunited with her childhood chum and Margaret's parents, Jessica was coming to the realization of how foolish she had been in deciding to cut herself off from her closest friends. She could not deny that she loved Hope or that she longed to be alone with her.

Coming to terms with her sexual orientation would never be easy, but Jessica recognized that her resolution to limit her interactions with others was not the answer. As soon as she returned to university, she decided to pursue new friendships, including with Edward. Somewhat to her surprise, Jessica was relieved to hear that Hope was in a relationship with Michael. At least she would be spared the agony of being an outcast.

✳

The holiday was heavenly. They arrived at Michael's parents' midafternoon on Christmas Eve and disappeared into the loft. When they emerged some two hours later, Marika and Jonathon had not yet returned from their shopping excursion to the city. Michael's golden retriever was overjoyed to see him, and they decided to go for a leisurely stroll around the sparsely snow-covered pasture.

"It's so beautiful and peaceful. What a great place to grow up, but it must be hard for you to leave," Hope said, skipping ahead of Michael through the row of willows. "I can imagine all the fun you had as a boy."

"That's why I've never ventured very far. I'm so grounded here that on the rare occasions I have not returned for a couple of weeks, I start to feel anxious and unsettled. I could never be a world traveller."

Michael had no sooner made his declaration than an image flashed into Hope's mind of being on stage after stage of the renowned musical halls in Europe. Throughout the past semester, Dr. Farrington had been explicit about his expectation that, with her prodigious talent, she aspire to become an international concert violinist. If Michael were to continue as her pianist, agent, and lover how would he fare during one of the lengthy tours to which the maestro had alluded? Hope would not deny that their loft would always be a haven, to which they could return, but already she sensed that confinement to any specific house and property was not in her destiny. But she was getting ahead of herself. Although she had promised to practice every day for her New Year's Eve recital in Winnipeg, she had taken this time off to come and have some fun.

A world beyond the peace and joy of their Christmas in the country did not surface until the afternoon of Boxing Day. It was the first time Michael had ever brought a female friend home to celebrate the season, and when Marika and Jonathon returned, they welcomed the young people to their hearth and home.

They were in the midst of a gripping game of Monopoly in front of the fireplace when the telephone rang. Since Hope had been sent to jail and had to miss her turn, she chose to answer the jarring instrument and then surprised when Cassandra was on the line. Once both recovered, and exchanged the usual Christmas greetings, Cassandra came to the gist of her call. "I know this is spur of the moment, but can you join the rest of us for an evening of gaiety on Thursday at my parents'?"

"You mean the foursome could all be together? I would love to come, and not to be bossy, but could we possibly make it Wednesday? I have to be back in Brandon to have dinner with my grandparents on Thursday before leaving for Winnipeg on Friday morning. If Wednesday could work for you, Francine, and Jessica, I wouldn't miss it for the world."

"It's six and two threes for me, but I'll check with the others and get right back to you. By the way, Francine is driving her Mustang to the city with Jessica and will pick you up at Michael's. When I phone you back to confirm the changed date, I'll give you the McGregors' number, and you can telephone Francine with the directions to the Griffins. Then I'm sure she'd take you to your grandparents in time for dinner on Thursday."

"Oh, terrific! Thanks for your flexibility. It seems like I'm always the one to throw a monkey wrench into the foursome's plans."

"Not this time, Hope. All of us have the week off, and we really want to see you. In fact, our only concern was that we would be taking you away from Michael for the evening, but we decided there could be no harm in asking."

✳

"Are you feeling all right, Jessica? You're unusually quiet. I thought you would be excited about a foursome get-together, since we haven't had one in ages, and you were always the planner."

"I'm just admiring how adept you are at driving this sports car. After I suggested that you acquire the skill, I asked my dad to teach me. I have my license, but I sure don't have my own wheels. You're a lucky girl!"

"Oh, don't I know that. And I really appreciate being able to come home, although if there's something going on, I spend the night at Cassandra's. Like Dr. Donahue often said, I'm surrounded by the love of many families. I think we're getting close, so can you watch for the sign to the Griffins' acreage? It's supposed to be on the left."

Jessica welcomed the opportunity to focus on a task rather than make conversation, seeing as she was trying to still her conflicting emotions of excitement and anxiety. Nonetheless, Francine had scarcely brought the car to a full stop before she opened the door and dashed up the short flight of stairs. She was about to ring the bell when the oak door opened, and Hope stood in the entranceway resplendent with a full-length green leather coat draped over her shoulders.

"Oh, Jessica, I've missed you. I can't remember how long it has been since we've seen each other." At first, Jessica was hesitant, but when Hope enveloped her in an enormous hug, she soon reciprocated. As much as Jessica had vowed to be detached, promising to only enjoy Hope from a distance, she felt as if every fibre in her body was electrified by her touch. She had spent the past year longing to be in her arms, and even though Hope was only holding her as a trusted friend, it was enough for now.

After greeting Michael and meeting his parents, they decided to be on their way. When Michael was ardently kissing Hope goodbye, Jessica hurried out the door to give them privacy. Only she knew how many times she had daydreamed of caressing Hope with the same passion. Of course, it was perfectly natural for a woman and a man to be observed embracing, but never the overt act of two persons of the same sex. Even if Hope had shared her sexual preference, they would always have to hide that they were lovers. Jessica's envy soon turned to self-loathing, and for the interminable time hating her perversion, she wondered if she had been wise to come.

When Jessica reached Francine's Mustang, she chose to access the backseat through the driver's door. The other members of the foursome were well aware of Hope's tendency for motion sickness and always ushered her into the front seat. By the time Hope was getting into the car, Jessica had collected herself and, seated behind Francine, she anticipated her unimpeded view of Hope for the duration of the trip. When she was dashing to the car, Jessica resolved that this excursion would be her final farewell with Hope, and she wanted to absorb every aspect of her beauty.

Shortly after they arrived at the Jamisons', Cassandra suggested they bundle up and embark upon a hike in the blue hills just north of her parents' home. The wind was brisk, but once they were encircled within the trees, the sun's wintry rays would keep them warm. Soon, the four friends were frolicking in the snow and enjoying their outdoor activities on an uncharacteristically balmy winter afternoon across the Canadian prairies.

"Thank you, Cassandra, for getting us all together," Jessica said when she happened to be next to her. "I was so sorry that I didn't come to the lake in September."

"I can't take the credit. Francine telephoned me on Boxing Day morning to ask if I wanted to host a gathering or whether she should arrange it on the farm. We quickly concurred that our chance of involving Hope was probably better in Brandon, since we had no idea of her schedule over the holidays. We both thought that you would be especially happy to see Hope, but you seem distant with her."

With a quick glance at Cassandra, Jessica nearly blurted out that she did not think she had been that obvious. Then she remembered that little escaped her perceptive friend, and not for the first time, she considered that Cassandra would become an astute lawyer. So many times, Jessica longed to disclose the truth about her feelings for Hope to one of her closest friends, and even though she realized Cassandra would be much more likely than Francine to maintain her confidentiality, she could not take the risk. Being in the frosty outdoors was restoring Jessica's composure, and she became increasingly convinced that she was better advised to keep her secret from the other three for the duration of her lifetime.

✳

It was not until night fell, and Cassandra was getting ready to share her bedroom with Francine, while Hope and Jessica were to sleep in the double bed in the spare room, that Jessica began to unravel. When she had decided to come, how could she have forgotten that she always slept with Hope whenever they had sleepovers? To make any kind of bother now would be suspicious.

As soon as they were in the bedroom, Jessica gathered her pyjamas and toothbrush before heading to the adjoining bathroom. If she stayed as long as possible, with a little luck, Hope might have changed into her nightwear in the interim. Twenty minutes later, when Jessica emerged, Hope greeted her. "Finally! I was beginning to wonder if you'd taken your book with you."

"I'm sorry, I should have been more considerate. It won't happen again, I promise."

Glancing about the room, she noticed that Hope had turned on her small bedside lamp. When Jessica walked by, she flicked off the switch of the overhead light and slipped into bed. Her friends had always teased her about sleeping on the edge and that one night she was going to fall out of bed. Facing toward the wall and clinging so close to her side of the mattress that even she wondered if she might, Jessica pretended to be sleeping when Hope returned.

Still, she dared not fall asleep until she heard Hope's gentle snoring. Then Jessica kept herself awake for the mere pleasure of listening to the soft sounds of the one she loved lying in bed beside her. Knowing she would not return for another foursome sleepover, she wanted to savour the feeling of sharing the same bed one final time. Jessica remembered turning over to gaze at Hope's beautiful features illuminated by the rays of the moon streaming through the skylight before sweet repose claimed her.

Jessica was aroused from a deep sleep by the most sensual feelings she had ever experienced. Every cell in her body was on fire, tingling with the anticipation of her passion, at last, being fulfilled. Easing into consciousness, she was certain she must have been dreaming until she became aware that they were lying side by side, and Hope was caressing her neck. At first, her heart soared with the expectation of gratification, until she heard Hope murmuring in her sleep, "Oh, Michael, love me now." Even though Jessica knew she should gently slip out of her embrace, she became perfectly still. Scarcely breathing, Jessica remained locked in Hope's arms, cognizant that this one encounter would be the closest she would ever come to loving Hope. She wanted to indelibly etch every sensation in her mind and in each cell of her body, so she could relive it over and over again throughout her life.

✳

Waking to the sun shining through his bedroom window, Derek perceived the bright rays as a positive omen. He had taken a long time to fall asleep, fretting about his decision and wondering if he was getting cold feet. It had been an unseasonably mild winter, and springing out of bed, he was soon anticipating the drive to Winnipeg under a clear blue sky while travelling on pavement dried by the warmth of the winter sun.

All his anxiety had dissipated by the time he stepped into the shower and began to vigorously cleanse his body. Not for the first time, Derek pondered how his worries could become so magnified in the wee hours of the morning, when sleep would not come only to disappear in the light of day. Anyone who knew Derek would almost find it laughable that he was often overwhelmed by a sense of diffidence that came close to immobilizing him. He tried not to place the blame on his father, but perhaps if the man were not such an arrogant philanderer, Derek would not have been compelled to embark upon the onerous responsibility of restoring the honour of the Barclay name and the integrity of the family firm.

With his grandfather's admonitions, Derek had painstakingly guarded his reputation by observing almost perfectionist standards of conduct from the time he graduated from high school. When it became apparent that he could not rescue Tiffany from her presumed grief of losing Eric Page and capture her heart, he had thrown himself into his studies. During his years of university, Derek found there were precious few women to entice him from his celibate path.

The years came and went, and although his classmates tried everything to lure him into the bedroom of one vixen or another, Derek resisted, until they left him alone. Then, as more time passed, he became embarrassed that he was still a virgin. Derek was surprised by how aroused he had been on both encounters with Susan, although, fortunately, he had recognized the virtue of not pursuing one of his clients. He even began to believe that he had been saving himself for Tiffany, so why his hesitation and doubts? Contrary to what several of his peers had speculated, Derek was not attracted to other men. Damn his father for being such a womanizer. Derek feared that once he had tasted the fruits of the flesh, he would follow in his old man's footsteps.

At first, Tiffany thought the problem was her. She would hardly consider herself an experienced lover, since, after losing her virginity to Eric in her adolescence, she had only been with two other partners over the years. Still, her past sexual activity could not be inhibiting Derek, given the fact he had yet to come close enough to make that discovery. Whatever was going on, Tiffany was becoming increasingly frustrated, often lying awake at night after their aborted lovemaking.

If his concern was an unwanted pregnancy, why had he not broached the subject of contraception? Tiffany hardly wanted to be obvious and disclose that she had resumed taking the pill since they began their courtship. She had been on the verge of apprising him that they were protected when she wondered if Derek had issues with commitment. Then a thought flashed through her mind. Could he possibly be chaste, given how flustered he became whenever she was eager to receive him?

Even though her father never came home with tales out of court, Tiffany, like the majority of people marginally associated with Brandon's legal community and beyond, had heard the rumours abounding in relation to Lawrence Barclay's sexual exploits. By high school, the girls had begun speculating that the acorn likely did not fall far from the tree. However, other than his fruitless pursuit of Tiffany, Derek never had the slightest interest in any of them, not without their considerable disappointment.

The more Tiffany considered the pattern of their flirtations, and as inconceivable as it had initially seemed, the more she began to believe that she had uncovered the truth. So, when Derek telephoned about the plans for New Year's Eve, she decided she was going to change her approach. Although he had not been specific about their overnight accommodations, she did not think for one minute that he would book two rooms. Subsequently, until they were within the confines of the hotel, whenever they were together, instead of making out at one of their apartments, it would be a cursory kiss goodnight at the door. If Derek was indeed as pure as the driven snow, Tiffany planned to curtail their amorous caressing in the hope of frustrating him sufficiently that he might be ready to achieve the pinnacle of his ardour.

*

The last notes of the finale, "Allegro vivacissimo," of Tchaikovsky's technically difficult "Violin Concerto in D major, Op. 35" were scarcely performed before the audience were on their feet in a standing ovation. Shouts of "Brava!" could be heard throughout the Winnipeg Concert Hall. For her third encore, Hope mesmerized her adoring fans with her signature piece, and even though they continued their avid applause, anyone who had been in attendance when she was the guest soloist knew that her recital was over.

If Tiffany had not pulled Derek up, he would have remained seated, still in the trance into which he had been absorbed since early afternoon. Throughout most of the drive to Winnipeg, he had been quiet, with the question of when he would propose being uppermost on his mind. When he opened the door to the suite at the Hotel Fort Garry, both of them had been surprised by the grandeur of the newly renovated rooms.

"I must say you do travel in style, my darling." After turning to check that the door was locked, Tiffany wrapped her arms around Derek and kissed him with more passion than she had in weeks. At that moment, the sexual impulses that Derek had sublimated and suppressed for years coursed through his virile body like a bolt of lightning. He swept Tiffany in his arms and carried her to the bed.

Every fibre of his being was more alive than he had ever experienced. Reaching his first orgasm with another person, his ecstasy exceeded any of his imaginable expectations. He felt as if he was soaring off the peak of the highest mountain, riding a tidal wave off Australia's Gold Coast. Much later, after climaxing again, Derek finally grasped the force that drove his philandering father.

Lying spent in Tiffany's arms, Derek roused enough to say, "Thank you, dearest Tiffany. I'd planned quite a different scenario for us, starting with me proposing to you. Instead, you've presented me with a most incredible gift. Please, give me a few minutes, and I think I'll be able to muster the energy to get up and find yours."

"Be still, and stay as you are. The day is ours, and we have hours before dinner, so, let's seize these moments to savour our love. As it is, your loss of innocence has been far too long in coming. I've often thought you spend a disproportionate amount of time in deliberation and not nearly enough in implementation. It must be a carry-over of your profession, since my father displays a similar characteristic. We'll wait for your gift until just before we're leaving for the dining room, shall we? That one can shine in the sparkle of the chandeliers," Tiffany suggested, caressing his inner thigh.

At that point, Derek would have leapt any number of tall buildings had it occurred to Tiffany to ask. His transcendence was so complete that he remained enraptured throughout the day and evening. Dinner in the elegant dining room and the exquisite concert were but a prelude to what was yet to transpire, and it was almost enough to make Derek believe he could fly without wings, like Peter Pan. The only thought that prevailed once his feet finally touched the ground was that they must invite Hope to grace their impending wedding with one of her daunting performances.

✳

Three years in this godforsaken district were three too many. A year earlier, when Robert had decided to put his farm up for sale, the only interested purchaser was Fred Martin, and Robert would be damned before he would sell to him. As soon as he finished the spring seeding, Robert left Hartney and returned to Winnipeg, staying in the family home until the fall, when it was time to harvest his crops. The day after he arrived, he listed the half section of land in the *Winnipeg Free Press* and was determined to find a buyer before the beginning of the following year.

It had been a mistake. It had all been a terrible mistake. Whatever had made him think he could run away from the tragedy of his parents and younger sister's deaths? Only weeks before they booked the flight to England, Robert had been scheduled to accompany them on their second family holiday to Cornwall, his father's place of birth. However, the position of chief aeronautical engineer at Bristol Aerospace was an offer he could not refuse, and Robert had declined joining his family.

Two weeks into the vacation, Robert had been devastated when he received the telephone call from his grandmother, a woman he had met once on their previous trip across the ocean. Returning from an evening visit with one of his father's oldest childhood friends, their automobile had been involved in a head-on hit-and-run collision with a large lorry, and all three had perished at the scene. It was only later that Robert was apprised that the truck driver was so drunk that it was not until the following morning when the police arrived at his door that he learned what he had done.

Almost a year had passed in a haze. Robert journeyed to England and, with his bereaved grandparents, arranged a memorial service in their small community before sending the bodies back to Winnipeg for burial in the family plot. After spending a month with his grandparents, he promised to stay in touch and return to visit them as often as he could.

He found a measure of peace in the brilliantly green countryside of his grandparents' village of Tregenna, but once he arrived back in Winnipeg and resumed living in his childhood home, Robert could not pick up the threads of his life. He went back to work but could scarcely concentrate, thinking constantly that if he had not accepted the job, he would have likely been killed with the rest of his family.

Robert was not surprised when, at last, his boss, David Standish, called him into his office. "Please, take a chair, Robert. May I offer you a cup of coffee?"

Glancing into David's deep-brown eyes, Robert felt a flash of empathy for the older man, knowing full well his was not an easy task.

"No, thanks, Dr. Standish. Please, just say what you have to, and spare us both."

"I'm sorry, Robert. Sorry for the tragedy that befell your family and sorry for how it has affected you. When I hired you, I was convinced you were the man for the position, and had things been different, you would most likely have had a promising career with us. Still, I believe you can appreciate that the responsibilities of our chief engineer in this industry are huge, and the safety of our products are tantamount. Perhaps if you were prepared to take an extended bereavement leave and to seek professional assistance, we could consider reinstating you at a later date. As it stands, I've lost confidence that you can perform your job."

"Thank you, Dr. Standish. I'll apply for that leave as soon as I return to my office." Closing the door quietly behind him, Robert walked down the hall, past his office, and continued right out the front door of the building until he reached the parking lot.

∗

Days came and went, with Robert barely able to function. At some level, he accepted that Dr. Standish was right about him needing help, and he recognized that his immobility only emphasized his depressive state. Whether Frank Rusk, one of his former colleagues, arrived at his door on his own volition or at his boss' instigation a week later would remain a mystery to Robert, but his intervention changed his life.

After Frank insisted that Robert shower and attend to his personal appearance, he took him to a nearby restaurant for a proper meal. When Frank returned the following morning to accompany Robert to the office of a psychiatrist, Robert put up little resistance. Within weeks of starting on an anti-depressive medication, he began to feel that there might just be light at the end of the tunnel of darkness, to which he had become accustomed.

During one of his counselling sessions, Robert disclosed that the only peace he had experienced since his family's demise was when visiting his grandparents' home. It was this realization that may have triggered his notion of moving to the country. Maybe he could escape. Make a fresh start. He began visiting real estate offices, and as chance would have it, he saw a listing for a scenic farm surrounded by the natural beauty of the Souris River for sale near the town of Hartney, within the Municipality of Cameron.

Then, when Robert purchased the land and moved into the district, for reasons he could never understand, he chose to present himself as a sophisticated city dweller come to live among the country folks. He had no illusions that it was his new flashy red convertible that attracted Susan's attention in the first place, but it was of little importance to him. His real mistake had not been falling in love with his neighbour's beautiful but underage daughter. Neither, as far as he was concerned, had it been in eloping with her a little more than a year later nor in even relying on Susan's friend, Carole, to convey the message to her parents. Robert's fatal flaw had been in withholding all information about his previous life from everyone in the community, most notably from Susan and her parents. If only he had been honest with June and Bert, over time, they might have developed a modicum of acceptance for him and come to appreciate the depth of his love for their daughter. Had he been prepared to wait until Susan turned eighteen the next year, their elopement might not have even been necessary. But Robert had persisted with the image the district quickly came to attribute to him as a wealthy interloper and flying off to Hawaii with a young, attractive woman had been the height of consolation for a man who had recently found himself alone in the world.

In all innocence, Robert had considered that the Hawaiian wedding ceremony was as authentic as Susan's professed love for him. His experience with women had been limited to casual dating, usually along with a group of his buddies from high school and university. Although skeptical at first, he had come to believe that their budding love was mutual, and since his father had been seven years older than his mother, he did not view their age difference as much of a concern.

Their romance had begun one Saturday afternoon when Robert was driving along the road allowance and came across Susan walking about in her father's pasture. He stopped to introduce himself, and before long, she accepted his offer for a ride in his Cadillac. It had been Susan's idea that they drive to Souris for a drink at the soda fountain in the centre of town. Robert had been equally surprised when they returned to their adjoining farms when she suggested they arrange to meet again on Sunday afternoon at the same location.

Soon, they were meeting every afternoon on the weekends, until on a balmy summer evening, Robert arrived at her home to meet her parents. When they appeared surprised, it crossed Robert's mind to wonder if Susan had apprised them of their excursions, but since they consented to her joining him for a drive, he did not inquire. However, when Robert kept returning evening after evening, he began to sense that, if not June, at least Bert was questioning his intentions.

Since his sister had been eight years younger than him, Robert had minimal awareness of the tensions that could exist between a mother and her adolescent daughter; otherwise, he might have appreciated that Susan could have been using him as a means to establish her independence or, worse yet, to rebel against her parents. But he was so blinded by his increasing love for the vivacious, beautiful Susan that all he could think about was making her his wife.

Still, when Susan returned to high school that autumn, Robert was quite prepared to wait until she graduated. He was blown away at the beginning of October when she started to plead with him for them to run away and elope. Robert could not have been more amenable, and it had been his idea to escape the dreaded Manitoba winter by sojourning in Hawaii for three months, never for one moment contemplating the disastrous outcome.

How could one man be so cursed? It was inconceivable that two complete strangers could meet, fall in love, and ultimately lose both their parents simultaneously, albeit under different but equally catastrophic circumstances. Yet, once Susan moved out of his home to live with Margaret and James Devonshire, and his pleas for her return went unheeded until the local RCMP had to serve him with a restraining order, Robert was finally forced to accept he had lost her forever. Subsequently, in the spring of 1968, when a realtor was showing his farm to a young couple from Saskatchewan, Robert interceded with a substantially lower price and a latchkey agreement to facilitate a quick sale. The morning the papers were signed, he drove his red Cadillac convertible out of Hartney, vowing to never return.

Classes were into the second day of the fall semester of her sophomore year, when Francine stopped mid-sentence. She and Cassandra had been dashing to the bookstore to begin the task of acquiring the required textbooks when she spotted her. "Oh, my gosh, my eyes must be deceiving me. If I didn't know better, I would argue that one of my old nemeses is headed our way!"

Cassandra gave the approaching female a quick glance to rule out her own skepticism and then had to readily confirm that her friend was not seeing a ghost. Of all the students on the Brandon College campus, the last person she would have expected to see was Susan Smith. It had been years since either Cassandra or, very likely, Francine had given a single thought to the woman who had played such havoc with Francine's peace of mind at the start of high school.

"Keep walking as if you haven't seen her," Cassandra whispered to Francine as they abruptly turned the corner. "We'll go to the cafeteria and return later for our supplies." Heeding her friend's advice, Francine began to wonder whether seeing Susan or Cassandra's reaction was more surprising. To her delight, she had not experienced the slightest qualm about coming face to face with her archenemy, who had given her such nightmares when she was younger. On the other hand, Francine knew that if it were Carole they had been on the verge of encountering, it would have been quite a different story.

*

When the friends were seated at a table in the far corner, Francine said, "Thank you, Cass. You are ever my protector, but somewhat to my surprise, I never felt any tension when I realized who was coming toward us. Now, if Carole had been accompanying Susan, I would've run, not walked, in the opposite direction. And thanks for the Coke. Next time, it's my turn."

"Well, that's curious. I'm so glad Susan no longer makes you feel apprehensive, but why does Carole?"

"Actually, one day after Mr. and Mrs. Smith were found dead in their home, I mentioned to Mother Pat how sorry I was about them, but as far as I was concerned, Susan had received what she deserved. Now you're looking at me exactly the way she did when I said it!"

"Sorry, Francine but your comment does seem cruel—" Cassandra stopped herself just in time. She had been on the verge of saying, "Especially for someone who experienced so much sorrow and desolation when a similar fate had happened to her own parents."

"Wait, let me finish, before you judge me. Mother Pat and I had many long talks about precisely what you're thinking. At first, I couldn't accept that it was the same for Susan as it had been for me because I never had anything to do with my parents' accident. Like many people in our community, I believed that Susan was to blame for her parents' deaths. If she hadn't run away with Robert, they would likely still be alive today."

"From what I heard from my father, that was hardly the widespread feeling at the inquest. Rather, he felt that Susan's lawyer, Derek Barclay, came just short of convincing Judge Franklin that Carole was culpable."

"You're already starting to sound like a lawyer. Mother Pat happened to agree with your dad, and she said the judge made an impassioned plea to everyone in the courtroom that if anyone had ever seen or heard of Susan's letter to her parents, to come forward, even at a later date. But back to what I was telling you. Following our in-depth discussions, at last I came to realize that it didn't matter how June and Bert died. The consequences would have been equally devastating for Susan. Once I accepted that she was feeling as much grief as I had, I was overcome with empathy for her. And then, as time passed, I began to feel liberated from any influence she might have had over me, along with a sense of forgiveness."

"Why do you continue to fear Carole? I've heard that she hasn't returned to Hartney for years, so she should scarcely have any impact on you." Even as Cassandra voiced her question, she experienced a sudden dread in the pit of her stomach, recalling the deep foreboding she had always felt about Carole and her cherished friend. Occasional nightmares had precipitated discussions with her mother, and perhaps in an attempt to alleviate her daughter's ominous concern, Lindsay, the perpetual psychologist, had teased her that she had named her appropriately, since she appeared to possess the Cassandra syndrome. More often than she cared to admit, certainly never to her mother, once she had understood the metaphor and seen the paintings of the beautiful auburn-haired, green-eyed woman, Cassandra wondered what could have motivated her mother to choose her name.

"Cass, are you all right? You've become as white as a ghost. If it has anything to do with Carole, you can stop worrying. I never give her a moment's thought, other than to relish yet another rumour that's circulated weekly about the district."

"Tell me what you've heard."

"It's pretty banal stuff, like how, once she moved to Brandon, she quit school. When her grandmother called her on it, Carole found her own apartment, and now she's making her living as a waitress. Not much of the sinister nature you seem to be reading into it, so let's change the subject."

Although she was taken aback by Francine's perspicacity, Cassandra was quick to follow her suggestion. She had no desire to share with her the snippet she had read in the *Brandon Sun* about a Carole Martin, who was arrested for drug possession. There had been no follow-up, and she did not have the slightest idea of the outcome, nor did she want to know. It was trying enough that she continued to be haunted by a premonition that Carole was going to resurface much later in Francine's life, possibly with dire consequences. Furthermore, Cassandra realized that there was little purpose in attempting to warn Francine, knowing she was as likely of convincing her as she was of altering the event. Perhaps she really had been born with the Cassandra curse.

＊

Jessica could neither believe how much she had missed Edward over the summer break nor that she was eagerly anticipating seeing him again. Last Christmas after she returned to campus, and he became her steadfast shadow, to her surprise, she began to enjoy his unwavering presence. Edward was charismatic as well as highly intelligent, and every time he invited her for Sunday dinner with his family, she felt very much at home.

In fact, the fonder she grew of Edward, the more she began to question her decision to limit her involvement with him. That evening with the foursome at the Jamison's home during the week between

Christmas and New Year's had been a real eye-opener for Jessica. It had not taken her long to become aware of how much Hope had changed since she had seen her. With Francine and Cassandra, she had simply picked up where they had left off at their last parting, but she had not been able to come anywhere close to reconnecting with Hope.

Initially, Jessica had been prepared to accept all the blame, since, in the interim, she had realized her love for Hope extended far beyond that of a friend. During dinner, it dawned on Jessica that Hope seemed so much more grown-up than the others, Jessica included, making them seem like high school girls. At first, Jessica had attributed Hope's maturity to the extensive experiences that Hope was no doubt encountering because of her fame as a burgeoning virtuoso. But it was more.

From the moment she met her at the Griffins' door, Jessica discerned that Hope was perceptibly different, and she had become intent on ascertaining what was happening to her. She was so elusive, so sophisticated, and so desirable that, as the hours passed, Jessica's need for her became more and more insistent. She could not look at Hope without blushing, yet every chance she could, she feasted her eyes on her, as if she wanted to devour her. Jessica could hardly speak to her long-time friend without stammering, as if she was a lovesick teenager, but Hope did not appear to notice. Most of the time she lounged, listening to Cassandra and Francine with an air of detachment to which neither of them paid the slightest attention while they chatted and laughed, reminiscing about old times. Similarly, neither of them was affected by the fact that Jessica had become quieter and quieter as the shadows of the evening lengthened.

✳

In the middle of that fateful night, when the reality that Hope was very much in the throes of loving Michael, Jessica had irrefutably known she must find some way to get over her. Even though her entire body would retain the tingling sensations of what she would always store in her mind as a conjured tryst, albeit with a totally unaware lover, Jessica realized that Hope was never going to belong to her. From that time onward, she began to re-evaluate her sexuality.

Throughout the spring semester, during the rare times when she was not pouring herself into her books and competing with Edward to achieve the highest grade, Jessica had been full of questions about her supposed preference. Was she really lesbian, or had she just been so captivated by Hope, her inseparable friend, who was so accomplished and so beautiful, that she wanted to be like her, to possess her until her love crossed a psychological boundary into a sexual realm? True, she had never been attracted to any of the boys in Souris, but when she thought about it, what were her options?

Staring out the window as she rode the train back to Winnipeg following four months of separation from Edward, Jessica became increasingly convinced that she might have been a fool for keeping such an appealing prospect at a distance. Over the course of the summer, she realized how much she missed their animated conversations, their energizing walks through Winnipeg's plethora of beautiful parks, and those casual moments of touching, when they had accidently found themselves in very close proximity.

The golden wheat fields flowed by as Jessica continued her vigil of the expansive prairie countryside. It was a beautiful autumn day, and she had the passenger car to herself. She had never taken the train to or from Winnipeg. When her mother had not driven her, she had always chosen to ride the bus. In fact, the only reason she had elected to journey by train this time was because of a conversation she'd had with Edward. He shared how his parents had taken him on a railway adventure through the Canadian Rockies when he was in his early teens, and it was the most memorable trip of his life.

Before she knew it, Jessica became mesmerized by the rhythmic clickety-clack of the train wheels moving over the tracks. She did not move, and in her stillness, a profound sense of peace permeated her soul. As realization dawned, she understood that her infatuation with Hope may have stemmed from her unidentified deep-seated longing to be Caucasian, like everyone in the town in which she had spent her entire life.

Although Jessica had initiated their friendship, she had always carefully concealed her envy of Hope. It was not fair. Not only had she been born with an incredible gift, she was also beautiful, with her fair skin, golden-blond hair, and sky-blue eyes. Hope would invariably stand out in a crowd, as Jessica did in Souris, but not because she was the only 'chink' in the district.

When she was growing up, her parents had treated her like a princess, and even when she became aware that she looked different from all the other students in school, she knew she was loved. It was not until she became friends with Hope that Jessica began to wish she was white. If there was any silver lining in the cloud of Hope moving to Brandon, it was that Hope had never heard Carole's racial slurs.

Going to university and living in a large city had insidiously changed Jessica's perspective. The campus had an inordinate share of Asian students, many of whom were also vying to gain access into the Faculty of Medicine. Jessica was no longer the only one with slanted eyes, and perhaps Jill and Sandra had been prudent to introduce her to Edward. They had a great deal more in common than the fact they were both Chinese, and Jessica was confident her parents would be as delighted with Edward as his parents obviously were with her. If Jessica's presumed preference had originated from her lack of self-acceptance, combined with an absence of any real experience, it was possible that a rendezvous with Edward might unveil an interesting revelation about her actual sexual orientation.

✳

Tiffany had arrived home in time for Sunday dinner with her parents, ushering Derek through the door when, Brenda glimpsed a flash of light reflected from the foyer chandelier sparkling off the finger of her daughter's left hand. Waiting for a more thorough perusal in much better light, her heartbeat was already quickening with anticipation for the event, which had been far too long in coming.

From the moment Tiffany announced she and Derek were attending Hope's New Year's Eve recital in Winnipeg, Brenda had kept her fingers crossed. She suspected Derek was the type of man who celebrated the momentous decisions in his life with significant events. She could never forget how he had tried to persuade Tiffany to attend the prom with him rather than with that football captain.

To this day, Brenda could not believe her daughter had not been swayed by Derek's approach. If a prospective beau had ever made such a romantic overture toward her, she would have caved, certainly by the time the second or third bouquet of roses had arrived. But then, if a gorgeous, tall specimen of the human species, as Brenda always deemed Derek, had ever courted her, she would never have chosen to date Eric Page.

Every parent with an student in the newly opened Vincent Massey High School was devastated by the horrible aftermath of its first graduation. Brenda thanked God every day since that fateful crash for sparing Tiffany. Although she had grieved with the parents of the three students who had been killed, she soon made it a point to limit ongoing interaction with any of them, whether out of gratitude or guilt, she was never able to decide.

It had been difficult enough persuading Samuel to allow David Matthews to refer Tiffany to the Chief of Psychiatry at the Brandon Hospital for Mental Diseases, never mind coping with Dr. Werner's eventual diagnosis. When they met with him in Dr. Matthews' office, upon his explanation that Tiffany was suffering from a strange ailment he called "gross stress reaction," she thought that if Samuel had a gavel with him, he would not have been able to refrain from rapping it on David's desk. It had not helped when the reputed psychiatrist identified that treatment consisted primarily of rest, counselling, and time.

When weeks became months, and Tiffany was exhibiting little improvement, Brenda was reaching the end of her tether. Finally, in exasperation, she suggested a mother/daughter vacation to eastern Canada, hoping a change of scene would provide the impetus for Tiffany to move forward in life. Little did Brenda know that her daughter would remain in Montreal for the subsequent seven years before returning to Brandon.

She was years past due every mother's dream of planning her daughter's wedding. Dare she hope that, in the not-too-distant future, she might even become a grandmother? Brenda had been on the verge of considering that happy dimension of her life was readily becoming little more than a pipe dream and had actually begun limiting her interactions with many of her friends. She was finding it increasingly challenging to feign interest in little Suzy's dance lessons or Bobby's hockey games when it seemed like she would never be blessed with the love and joy of her own grandchild.

Brenda had stopped wondering when Kevin would meet the right girl and settle down. By tacit agreement, she and Samuel rarely spoke about their son, who had left home fifteen years earlier. Although he was only living in Winnipeg, he might as well have been in Australia, given the number of times he came back to Brandon. Initially, Kevin returned for two or three days every Christmas, but once Tiffany remained in the east, they could wait for months to hear from him and much longer before one of his impromptu visits.

Following needless analysis of why both her children had little inclination to live in their hometown, Brenda concluded that it most likely was related to the fact that their father had been the honourable associate chief judge of the Provincial Court in Brandon for over a decade. Even Brenda still had to think about how she should respond when encountering a disgruntled family member of an offender whom her husband had incarcerated to consistently maintain the expected impeccable standards of conduct required of the judge's wife.

There was little doubt that, as adolescents, Kevin and Tiffany had experienced the scrutiny of living in a fishbowl. Of course, the *Brandon Sun* had dredged up every barely known, and presumably buried tidbit about Judge Franklin's family for weeks after his daughter was the sole survivor in the tragic vehicular accident in Kemnay. Then, to make matters worse, the reporters became aware of Tiffany's lingering illness, and frequent mention by the press had done little to hasten her recovery.

Still, Brenda sensed that Kevin's absence from his family stemmed from a much more deep-seated reason than trying to avoid Judge Franklin's judicial limelight. Although she would never dare mention her suspicions to Samuel, she often would awaken in the early hours of the morning wondering if their son was such an enigma because of the dark secret he was intent on concealing.

At any rate, perhaps Brenda was finally about to receive happy tidings. Her initial action would be to ascertain the date, so she could arrange the booking at First Presbyterian Church, where her father had been the inaugural minister when it was officially established on October 7, 1925. Henry Sterling was instrumental in the plans for the construction of the beautiful Tudor-Gothic structure, the church in which she and Samuel were married. As its long-standing secretary, Brenda could hardly wait to print the Saturday program for the upcoming nuptials of Ms. Tiffany Franklin and Mr. Derek Barclay and to send invitations to the broadening circle of Brandon's finest society.

Welcoming her daughter home, Brenda said, "Come in, my darlings, and reveal whence that sparkle is originating."

※

It made perfect sense since she was driving back and forth from Monday to Friday. Nonetheless, it never crossed Francine's mind until she arrived home at the end of the first week of the fall semester. Margaret had usually departed following Mother Pat's standing invitation for coffee by the time she returned home, but not so this Friday, and she wondered if something was afoot.

"Hello, Mrs. Devonshire. I guess the beginning of the academic year at Hartney High is well under way. You probably started the week before we did at college."

"For heaven's sake, Francine, please, call me Margaret, and yes, we did. I won't tarry long, because I know this is your special time with Pat, but we've just been discussing a practical solution to the dilemma of Susan's transportation. Although James has driven her to Brandon and brought her home this past week, to my mind, it makes no sense for him to continue. Would it be too great an imposition for you to pick up Susan in the mornings and return her at the end of the day? We would be more than prepared to contribute for your gas and even for the wear and tear on your Mustang."

Her request was spoken. Margaret had worried for three days about how to approach Francine, and Margaret knew her well enough not to sugar-coat her appeal. She had taken to the forlorn little girl from the moment she entered Miss Rose's classroom at Hartney School and had come to care about her, as had so many others in their district. Margaret also appreciated why there was no love lost between Francine and her goddaughter, but now Susan was a very changed person.

Following years of tragedy, turmoil, and debilitating depression, Susan was beginning to piece her life back together. Margaret had managed to spark her interest in completing her grade twelve through correspondence courses, coupled with her private tutoring, and was pleased by her steady progress. Nonetheless, the real impetus had been the sale of Robert Wharton's farm and his permanent departure from the community. At last, Susan was free from the fear of his perpetual harassment and her devastating memories.

When Susan approached Margaret at the end of her second day on campus about the possibility of travelling to and fro with Francine, she had almost dropped the teapot she was carrying it to the kitchen table. In all the years since Susan had lived with them, she had declined accompanying Margaret and James to the McGregor farm, and when the two families gathered at the Devonshires, she quickly became invisible.

"Well, that would make good sound sense, wouldn't it? She lives so close, and it would save James an incredible amount of time. Did you have a chance to chat to Francine?"

Glancing away to prevent Margaret from seeing her diffidence, Susan said, "Oh, no. I just caught a glimpse of her at school today. But I know how busy James is with both farms, and I wondered if maybe you could ask her." Susan was only too aware of how dependent she still was on Margaret, but she had trembled at the thought of speaking to Francine. She had no idea how she would ever be able to sit in Francine's car day after day, even though she knew she had to become more self-reliant.

A sudden stillness permeated the walls of the McGregor kitchen. Francine's first thought was an adolescent knee-jerk reaction. Could Mrs. D. actually be asking her to transport the condescending Susan Smith back and forth to college every day? Fortunately, she bit her tongue, and in the ensuing silence, Francine reflected upon her discussions with Mother Pat as well as her recent comments to Cassandra. Was she ready to prove her developing maturity and put her burgeoning empathy for a woman who shared the similar fate of simultaneously losing both her parents into practice?

"Okay, I'll drive Susan for the rest of this month," Francine finally replied, "and then I want a chance to reassess my decision. Also, I'm only going to drop her off and pick her up in the parking lot. For the rest of the time, she's on her own."

*

Against all odds, Francine began to like Susan. On the first Monday, Susan slipped into the car with a scarcely audible "Hi" and then sat like a stone, staring straight ahead all the way to campus. For the next two mornings, and also on Monday and Tuesday afternoons, Susan was rigorously consistent in her behaviour until, on the way home on Wednesday, Francine could not believe it any longer.

"Do you think we're ever going to exchange any more than two words a day?"

"Sorry, I understood that I wasn't to bother you with idle chatter while you were driving, not that we have much to say to each other."

Glancing in Susan's direction, Francine wondered if her former archenemy had recovered her sarcastic form. To her surprise, Susan seemed subdued as she peered at her feet. Could this be the same girl who had tormented her just a few years earlier? With sudden clarity, Francine knew she was being unfair. Aside from the occasional times when she had been patronizing toward her, Susan had never instigated any malefic actions. Such behaviour had been solely Carole's domain.

What insight had she really gained when she and Mother Pat talked about Susan's plight? Did she understand how her former classmate felt following the tragic circumstances of her parents' deaths, or was she just being self-righteous in thinking she was not judging her, as did so many others in the Hartney district? So, out of a misguided sense of pity, she thought she would drive Susan back and forth every day but treat her as if she barely existed.

"No, Susan. It's me who owes you an apology. I've been rude by hardly acknowledging your presence. If my motive was only to be a goody-goody, I would have been far more gracious by never consenting to Margaret's request."

Now it was Susan's turn to steal a furtive peek at Francine. To her consternation, tears began to trickle down her cheeks, and she quickly peered out the side window. Other than Margaret and James, Susan could not remember anyone being so kind to her. She had long ago given up trying to understand why that lawyer had pretended to like her and had even taken her to lunch. On the other hand, with the fledging resumption of her confidence, she'd had no trouble believing it when he dropped her as if she was a piece of burning coal.

All weekend, Susan had prepared herself to expect Francine to be distant with her. After all, they had not been friends at school, and she had decided to adopt Margaret's advice of letting Francine take the lead in their conversations. When it was obvious that Francine did not have anything to say to her, Susan had maintained her silence.

During her first week on campus, Susan was relieved that she did not know a single person in any of her classes. Not only was she pursuing her education, she also began to cling to the possibility that she might be able to make new friends with people who were not aware of her history. Until Margaret had managed to pique her interest in reading and then in resuming her schooling, Susan had viewed her future as a bleak abyss. Now she felt a ray of hope that, maybe in the hallowed halls of the college environment, she might escape the ghosts of her past.

"Oh no, thank you for agreeing. James would have continued driving to Brandon twice a day, but he's so busy now, since he farms my parents' land as well as his own. I would never have expected you to apologize to me," Susan said as she gazed briefly in Francine's direction.

On the outskirts of Souris, Francine realized they needed an icebreaker, so she turned into the Esso station on the premise of getting gas. When the attendant had serviced the car, she pulled into the parking lot. "Since we're here, why don't we have a coffee in the restaurant?"

Once she recovered from her disbelief, Susan opened her door and gingerly walked behind Francine. No sooner had they sat down than a grey-haired waitress came to their table with a steaming pot of coffee. Francine responded in the affirmative as Susan followed suit and turned over her cup. "Could I please also have a glass of ice water? I don't know about you, Susan, but I find the classrooms hot and dry. Are you studying for an arts or a science degree? What classes have you enrolled in for this semester?"

It seemed so natural. Francine was chatting with her as if she really was interested in knowing what she was doing. Although, for several minutes, Susan could not look directly at Francine, she began to respond to her questions. Before long, Susan even started to breathe normally, and when their server offered to refill their mugs, she was surprised that she had drank its contents. Then, just when Susan was on the verge of enjoying herself, she was haunted by an image of her luncheon with Derek. During that afternoon, she thought he had accepted her, only to never hear from him again. Was this to be another one-time exchange? Would Francine revert back to ignoring her, day after day?

"It's been fun getting to know you better, but I think we should start for home, or our surrogate mothers will be worried that we have come to harm," Francine said as she placed fifty cents on the table. "Say, Susan, every Friday afternoon around three o'clock, I meet my friend and her mother in the cafeteria for coffee, and I was wondering if you'd like to join us this week before we drive back."

*

Now was the perfect time, but once again, Michael could not muster the courage to ask. For several weeks following Hope's return from her second summer at Westport, she could not get enough of him, and he needed her every bit as much after almost four months of abstinence. She was thrilled with the much larger one-bedroom apartment he had moved into while she was away. Aside from the fact that it was in a new complex, it was close enough to campus that they could enjoy a spontaneous tryst between classes and practices.

After a summer of interminable yearning, questioning, and doubting, Michael had often regretted that he had not proposed the evening before Hope's departure for the Meadowmount School on the first of May. At least he would have known her answer and could have saved himself from what had seemed like a lifetime of agonizing.

He had everything planned to the precise moment when he would drop down on his right knee and request her hand in marriage. He had prepared for the anticipated event by purchasing an exquisite engagement ring with a heart-shaped half-carat diamond clustered by seven small diamonds as an early eighteenth birthday gift, and for months had been waiting to see the joy and love on Hope's face when he presented it to her. After driving to Winnipeg in the late afternoon, and checking into the Fort Garry Hotel, they had strolled the short distance to the Chef's Table for a lavish dinner.

When Hope fell asleep soon after they left Brandon, Michael vacillated between feelings of relief and resentment. For the past two weeks, they had both been so busy that they had scarcely seen one another. Whereas he was relieved that, with a nap, Hope would be more energetic that evening, he could not deny that he had been looking forward to conversing with her. He wanted to listen intently to every word she said and store each in his memory, to be savoured over the long summer ahead.

On the outskirts of Winnipeg, Hope roused from her slumber but seemed drowsy and preoccupied. Was she not feeling well, or was she just anxious about leaving him and her friends for another extended period of time? Following the summer's sojourn at the school, Hope was very reticent about sharing her experience, until Michael decided not to persist in acquiring the details. At any rate, he was in the height of rush-hour traffic, and he chose to let her have peace and quiet as she awakened.

If he were not confident about her feelings for him, Michael might have thought that Hope was trying to avoid him. As soon as they were checked into their spacious room, she said she planned to enjoy a hot relaxing bath and then disappeared into the bathroom. He was loath to knock on the door, but nearly an hour later, Michael was becoming concerned. "Hope, are you all right? We have to leave soon for our dinner reservation, and I also want to freshen up before we go."

✻

It was a beautiful warm evening with robins chirping in the tree-tops, the sweet scent of budding flowers, and a light breeze rustling through the opening poplar leaves. Even Hope's silence could not dampen Michael's spirits, and he clasped her arm through his as they sauntered along the boulevard. Spring was a close second as his favourite season, and he was a man very much in love with an incredible young woman with whom he was hoping to spend the rest of his life.

Upon entering the exquisite candlelit dining room, with Mozart resonating softly in the background, Hope gazed into Michael's eyes and flashed him one of her stunning smiles. "Oh, this is elegant. What an excellent choice for our last evening together. I didn't know if I wanted to celebrate after my demanding semester of classes, exams, practices, and concerts, but you have chosen the perfect place."

Once they were seated, Michael gestured to the maître d' to serve the chilled bottle of champagne. On impulse, he was tempted to deviate from his plan and propose during their toast, but then he reconsidered.

They were about to enjoy their second glass when Hope enthused, "I was going to wait until after we'd returned to the privacy of our hotel, but I can't keep my news to myself any longer. This morning before you arrived, Dr. Farrington told me that he believes I'll soon be ready, so in early February, he's going to complete an application for me to audition at the Juilliard School. My first round could occur in Toronto by the beginning of next May, and if I'm selected, I'll continue with a second round at the Lincoln Centre for the Performing Arts in June. Then, should everything go according to plan, I will actually transfer to one of the world's most prestigious music schools by the subsequent fall."

Michael sat dazed. The more Hope effervesced, the more distressed he became. How could she be so enthralled about going to New York City? What about him? What about them and their future together? Even though Michael realized they would never have a marriage anything like his parents, they would still be husband and wife.

Surely Hope loved him, if not as profoundly at least a modicum of how much he loved her. How could she possibly deny having amorous feelings for him in light of the frequency and intensity of their lovemaking? Lately though, every time they visited his parents, Michael was haunted by the questions and expectations reflected in their eyes, until he could scarcely look at them. Deep within his heart, he knew he would most likely never present his loving parents with what they longed for more than anything.

The more he thought, the more upset he became, until he hardly remembered eating the delicious meal they had ordered. Their waiter was serving their smoked salmon and capers when it occurred to Michael that if Hope moved to New York, he would be almost completely excluded from her life. The Juilliard School of Music would hardly condone an essentially self-taught pianist as Hope's accompanist, and it was far too early in her career to require his services as her musical agent.

A more pressing question suddenly loomed in his mind, so that he did not even taste the delectable pheasant under glass, which Hope consumed with obvious delight. In the spring, he had finished the course work for his master's in business administration and would complete his thesis during the upcoming fall semester. Aside from teaching graduate students, he could always count on Dr. Farrington to request that he accompany Hope for all her practicing and for a majority of her recitals. But how would he earn a living when she left Brandon College?

By the time the crème caramel, his favourite dessert, was served, Michael was more disheartened than he could ever recall. How could his well-planned proposal have gone awry? It was unthinkable for him to proceed now with Hope rhapsodizing about the enviable merits for her attending Juilliard, as one of its most successful graduates informally referred to the reputed school. She had discoursed about her musical aspirations throughout the meal, focusing little on Michael, apparently not noticing that he was silent to the point of sullenness all evening. When they were strolling back to the Hotel Fort Garry, Hope apologized for monopolizing the conversation, but had she not been so insistent, he would have foregone their lovemaking. Even in the afterglow of their shared intimacy, Michael's spirits did not revive enough to risk a future he could not imagine, and he decided to wait with his promissory ring.

*

They had become inseparable, and it was not only that Edward was her eager shadow. Jessica was every bit as desirous of being in his presence as he was in hers. During the winter semester, they had been enrolled in all the same courses, and before long, they were meeting before and after each class or lab to study together. Also, they were soon spending every Sunday afternoon at Edward's home, since his parents were adamant that Jessica join them for their family dinner.

Not once though had Edward initiated any amorous overtures toward Jessica. Therefore, he was very surprised one evening when they had been strolling in St. Vital Park before he returned her to the dormitory. They had passed out of the glow of the streetlight into the deepening shadows of the towering maples when Jessica pulled him to her supple body and kissed him passionately on his lips.

When at last she released him, Edward was more flustered than he had ever been in his life. "Wow!" he said, catching his breath. "I didn't have the slightest idea you felt that way about me. I was afraid you were only interested in me as a friend, even though, on the first day we met, I went home and told my mother that I'd been introduced to the girl I wanted to marry."

"Oh, you didn't! No wonder your parents are always so nice to me!"

"Well, I never let on that you didn't consider me a possible beau. Does this mean we're dating, and I can take you out for dinner, movies, and concerts, and we can escape together on exotic vacations?"

"But, of course, in all our spare time when we aren't cramming for exams, running to labs, and trying to impress the medical faculty that we're two of their best candidates!"

"On that note, if I don't get you back to your dorm before the witching hour, you will create a most unfavourable impression on the powers that be," Edward said, grasping her hand in his and all but skipping back to the car.

It was a dream come true. He had been smitten with Jessica long before two of their other classmates had, for an obvious reason, decided to introduce them. Edward had noticed Jessica the first morning on campus, but she was always so elusive that he would never have had the nerve to approach her. Initially, she had been distant with him, sending a clear message that they were competitors, not classmates sharing a common pursuit. To his surprise, following the Christmas break, she was much warmer toward him, and he began to have a glimmer of hope that they might become more than just friends. Now driving Jessica home along the treed circle of University Boulevard, Edward was flushed with excitement, knowing there could be no mistake about the nature of her kiss and its portent for their future.

✳

They were hurrying from the parking lot to their respective classes when Francine said, "Don't forget, Susan, if you're free around three this afternoon, come to the cafeteria for coffee with my friend and her mum."

Francine and Cassandra were seated at their usual table in the secluded spot at the rear of the cafeteria. Francine kept peering around the large rubber tree until Cassandra said, "I don't know why mum is late. This has to be the only time that she hasn't been the first to arrive."

"That's right, but actually, I've invited Susan to join us this afternoon, and I don't want to miss her."

"Really? What motivated you to invite your nemesis for coffee? Ah, perhaps we truly are becoming grown-ups and are learning to leave our childhood grievances behind. Oh, look, I think she's just come in. Maybe you should go and meet her, Francine."

Waiting until Susan had purchased a pot of tea, Francine guided her over to the table. "This is Cassandra," she said. "She's Alice and Malcolm Webster's granddaughter and has been my friend since I moved here from Prince Edward Island."

The trio were engrossed in small talk when Lindsay glided up to the table. "Sorry I'm late, my lovelies. And please, introduce me—" Lindsay stopped mid-sentence when she recognized Susan from one of her joint sessions with Dr. Donahue. Before giving her a chance to realize who she was, Lindsay continued. "The reason I'm not staying is that as I was rushing out the door, there was a telephone call for me from Dr. Mathias Werner, chief of psychiatry at the Brandon Hospital for Mental Diseases. He apparently had a cancellation and can meet with me at four o'clock to discuss possible research for my dissertation. Francine, could you please drop Cass at home? I'm uncertain how long I'll be, and her father has a golf game scheduled for five. I'll catch up with you later, Cassandra."

As fleetingly as she had appeared, she was gone. Susan was the first to speak, "I've seen that woman before, but I don't remember where. What's her name?"

"Lindsay Jamison, and I'm delighted to say that she's my mother. Perhaps you've noticed her on campus. She's a graduate student completing her doctorate with the Faculty of Psychology."

"I know that name, but I didn't realize she was your mother, since Francine only introduced you as Cassandra. Does she usually come for coffee?"

"This is the only time she has ever missed. Are you okay if she joins us? Just now, I've sensed some tension in you, Susan, possibly in relation to my mum."

"I think she sat in on some of my counselling sessions with Dr. Donahue, and I wonder if it's appropriate for us to meet socially."

Francine had been paying close attention to the conversation. She glanced at Susan and then at Cassandra. She had no idea that Susan was one of Dr. Donahue's patients, but she could recognize her dilemma. Francine was more surprised by how cognizant Susan was about the doctor/client association than she was that Susan had been in therapy. Given the traumatic nature of her parents' deaths, it was little wonder that Susan had been in sessions with a psychologist, and once again, Francine realized how astute Mother Pat had been about their shared similarities.

"That's an excellent question, Susan. Cass, perhaps you could check with Lindsay and let us know before next Friday."

When they arrived at the Devonshires' home, as she was getting out of the car, Susan said, "I really appreciate you asking your friend to confirm with her mother. It made me feel like you care."

*

They had been striving to revise the details of the topic for her dissertation for quite some time. At first, when Lindsay had approached her with the notion of researching and writing about a possible condition she would classify as oppressive personality disorder, Eleanor was incredulous. Over the years, she had noticed that many of her patients suffering from clinical depression did not typically fit the signs and symptoms as outlined by the first *DSM –1*, published in 1952. Eleanor had often speculated that they presented more as being weighed down with overwhelming guilt than with excessive melancholy.

Eleanor had even ventured so far as to modify her counselling for one of her young patients, Francine Stonehenge, considering that she was being controlled and oppressed by her onerous feelings of responsibility for her parents' death. She had debated continuing the premise of her dissertation regarding the subtle differences between depression and possibly a related but distinct condition, although she was so busy in her growing practice that she'd had little time for research and writing.

Now, to have a graduate student submit it as the subject matter for her thesis was close to serendipity. Lindsay Jamison was by far the most brilliant and perceptive individual Eleanor had ever chosen to advise in all her years on faculty, and she already had a penetrating grasp of the differentiation between the classified illness and her proposed syndrome. The two women had been deep in discussion when the receptionist interrupted them with the telephone call from Dr. Werner.

One of the advantages of visiting the Brandon Hospital for Mental Diseases late on a Friday afternoon was the availability of staff parking close to the administration building. Lindsay was intent on spending every possible moment with the chief of psychiatry. She had been following Dr. Werner's career even before she ventured back to the college as a grad student, and she was impressed by his prodigious capacity for work and research.

"Thank you so much for making time to see me, Dr. Werner."

"Oh, please, call me Mathias. I assure you the pleasure is mine, since research is the aspect of psychiatry that has always been closest to my heart. After my many years of counselling and providing treatment, I'm still not convinced that I've achieved any measure of effectiveness or success. May I offer you a cup of coffee? I find that I usually need a jolt of caffeine at this time of day, and I've just made a fresh pot."

Once they were comfortably seated, Lindsay elucidated for the elderly doctor the precise nature of her dissertation, clarifying that she was fascinated by the concept of oppression, both by internal and external forces. Although she believed that more study was critical regarding the impact on human beings by outward worldly influences, such as the tyrannical rule of a dictator, she was focusing only on the pressure from inner personal dynamics.

"The thesis I'm attempting to prove is that there are causes, signs, and symptoms of oppression that are elusive in their presentation and are divergent from those of depression," Lindsay said following a sip of the delicious coffee.

"Ah, interesting. I'll tell you what. I'm going to sit back, close my eyes, and give you my full attention as you expound on your theory. Don't think that I've fallen asleep. I have always concentrated best when I block out external stimuli."

"Okay, here goes! As debilitating as the altered mood, extreme dejection, and morbid melancholy of depression are for the patient, I think the symptoms are not as crushing to the human spirit as the weight of oppression. Whereas with depression, there is often a mood of hopelessness combined with feelings of inadequacy and a subsequent reduction in vitality and vigour, the illness does not present as profoundly as the powerlessness of being smothered, of being choked by oppressive guilt. My hypothesis is that, eventually, the overwhelming burdens of responsibility, obligation, and reprehensibility result in a heightened tendency to subservience, which, with the passage of time, becomes a deeply ingrained pattern of behaviour. Individuals lose, or never gain the ability to identify and to express emotions, because they allow others to become their lord and master. Soon, the only feeling that remains is guilt. It looms as a constant companion, always coercing until it becomes a self-serving indulgence, and the person comes to perceive herself as shunned by society as deeply as a person affected with Hansen's disease. Furthermore, I suspect it is equally challenging, even if a person does learn to overcome the guilt and get in touch with her emotions, to assess how others feel toward her."

Lindsay paused and glanced at the affable gentleman seated across from her. When he did not move, she continued. "I think the subtlety is in the different ways the respective patients interact with others. From all I've gleaned, those with depression often become alienated from family and friends, and even when they are around other people, they maintain their defining symptoms. Not so with the oppressed person. When she is in the presence of others, and guilt can be held at bay, all doubt disappears, and her true confident self emerges. Indeed, most people who know them would never believe that such a spirited individual was the host of burdensome demons when alone."

"How fascinating and astute, Ms. Jamison. There is not the slightest doubt in my mind that your thesis will earn you your doctorate. In fact, the only regret I have is the timing of your dissertation, because the *DSM-II* is scheduled to be published this month."

"Thank you, Dr. Werner, for your ringing endorsement. Now, of course, my challenge will be to identify sufficient research subjects."

"Actually, you have described my great-niece, Justine Cardinal, to the letter. She was a registered nursing student on affiliation to this hospital a little more than two years ago, and it was only happenstance that we met. My wife, Rebecca, and I were so sorry that we weren't able to attend her wedding to Fred Forrester not more than three weeks past, but I have her address in Winnipeg. If you like, I can telephone her to inquire if she would consider participating in your research. Justine graduated the top student in her class here, is as bright as a penny, engaging, and confident, but she carries a heavy legacy of oppressive guilt because of her abusive mother. I believe she would be most intrigued by your thesis and more than willing to become one of your case studies."

The wedding was everything and more than Brenda could have imagined. Tiffany had been very gracious about endorsing most of her mother's ideas and plans, inclusive of whom to include on the guest list. Given that the Franklin and Barclay families had not only resided in Brandon for generations but also had a high profile within the city's legal, business, and political sectors, Tiffany had anticipated that her parents would want to be assiduous in their selection.

Tiffany and Derek would have been just as happy to elope with a honeymoon escape to warmer climes within weeks of their wonderful weekend to start the New Year in Winnipeg. To Tiffany's delight, Derek was still in a trance the morning following the concert. Fearing he might think, in his state of ecstasy, that he could fly, as they were about to leave, she decided to drive them home to Brandon.

Derek had yet to allow even his father behind the wheel of his new Porsche 911, but at her request, he gladly handed Tiffany the keys. Once they were out of the city, and she was cruising along the highway, she fully understood the significance of her choice to drive. With the slightest pressure on the accelerator, the sporty automobile surged forward with the grace and speed of a greyhound lunging out of the starting gate at a racetrack.

It was not until they were nearing Brandon when Tiffany realized it was the first time she had driven on the highway since the accident. During the years in Montreal, she had never bothered with a car, and when she had returned home, she had only ventured to drive her mother's vehicle around the city. In a sudden flash of insight, Tiffany grasped that the weekend may have been a turning point for both of them. Derek had at long last lost his virginity, and she had had a catharsis of the anxiety that had pervaded her soul since high school.

Derek waited, standing tall and straight as an arrow, staring at the ornate altar at the front of the church, which Foster's Floral Fashions had beautifully decorated. He had managed to maintain his poise even when the "Jesu Joy of Man's Desiring" processional commenced until a collective expression of awe resonated throughout the congregation. Turning his head ever so slightly to glance at his bride, he was once again flooded with all those feelings of infatuation and wonder that he had experienced so long ago as an adolescent. Was this really happening? Was Tiffany Franklin about to become his wife?

Where had the years gone? It was as if he had been frozen in time, and it had taken Tiffany's passionate lovemaking to thaw him back to life. Sadly, it was not until after their rapturous weekend away that Derek had at last realized he had only been going through the motions of living, while his heart had still belonged to the first and only woman he would ever love.

As Tiffany advanced toward him on Judge Franklin's arm, he was riveted by her breathtaking image. After sharing with him about how she and her mother had searched through every bridal studio in Brandon before journeying to Winnipeg, Derek expected that she would be wearing an exquisite wedding gown. Tiffany had even minutely described her choice for him, not that it had made much sense until that moment, as an "A-line/princess scoop neck floor-length chiffon lace wedding dress with beading sequins." Still, Derek could not believe how stunning Tiffany looked as she glided down the aisle to take her place beside him. With her platinum-blonde hair coiffured in a stylish French knot enhanced by a sparkling diamond clip, she graced her elegant wedding apparel on her day of nuptial glory like a Greek goddess. He had not been in attendance at many marriage ceremonies, but his feelings of admiration were affirmed by the coveting look in every man's eyes. Within the hour, under the magical spell of Beethoven's "Ode to Joy," Tiffany would be Mrs. Derek Franklin Barclay, and the only thought coursing through Derek's handsome head was to thank God that he had waited and saved himself for her.

The reception in the splendid Convocation Hall at Brandon College was as auspicious as every perfectly organized detail of the event that would become known as the city's wedding of the year. Following a plethora of photos on the campus grounds, with the majestic maples dressed in their autumnal colours, and a lengthy receiving line, a succulent dinner of prime rib and Yorkshire pudding was served. The speeches were commenced with an address from Honourable Walter Weir, Premier of Manitoba, followed by several lighthearted toasts to the bride and groom from respective family and friends.

During a musical interlude the guests were mesmerized by Hope Harding's quintessential performance of classical wedding favourites, most notably Cesar Franck's "Panis Angelicus," and Gounod's "Ava Maria," and, of course, with the finale of her signature song. Michael provided the piano accompaniment with his own unique flair, and no one would ever have surmised that his heart was breaking. Throughout the day, he could not help feeling that his wedding would never become a reality. Every time he was on the verge of giving Hope the engagement ring, which had languished in the top drawer of his bedside table, an image of her refusal assailed his mind. If only he could have known that Derek had waited for ten interminable years for his memorable day, he would have been heartened about his prospects.

*

They decided to forego their usual Friday afternoon coffee, so they could enjoy an early start to the weekend. Francine made sure to apprise Susan, with Cassandra reminding her mother on their morning drive to the campus. Lindsay had assured Susan that as long as they confined their discussions to social matters, it would not represent any breach of client confidentiality. Since then, the four women, and on the rare occasions, five, when Hope chose to join them, had met every week.

When the three young women reached the parking lot, Cassandra said, "Let me climb in the backseat, Susan, since you'll be getting out before me."

"Yes, of course. That is, if you don't mind me sitting in the front when you're riding with Francine." Susan was well aware that, at first, the two longstanding friends had been surprised by the deference with which she addressed them, although by now they had surely come to appreciate her sincerity. If she had the confidence to be candid, Susan would have divulged that she was full of envy for the obvious fondness the two shared. In fact, over the past few months, Susan had often wished that it had been Francine whom she had befriended at Hartney School instead of that manipulative Carole Martin. During their hours of carpooling, she felt that the younger woman had come to accept her, but Susan knew in the depths of her heart that she would never enjoy the camaraderie and love that was so apparent between Cassandra and Francine.

The moment they reached the McGregor farm, the girls were off to see the lambs. Although her uncles had always planned to vend the yeanlings every fall, they could not bring themselves to sell until the following year, when they were fully grown. There was an ever-increasing market in the district and beyond for the meat of the young animals, but Darrin and Daniel could not begin to fathom how they could allow anyone to consume Francine's perennial pets.

Much later, the friends were lounging in Francine's cozy loft with instrumental music playing softly in the background, when Cassandra said, "I have a confession. Part of the reason for our weekend together is because the budding Dr. Lindsay asked me to act as her emissary."

"Oh, really! How intriguing, although you know very well that you don't need anyone's secret mission to spend two fun-filled days with me in my humble home."

"As it happens, it's more a special favour than any kind of a dark secret. Nonetheless, my mother's request is rather unusual, and she wants you to have time to contemplate the pros and cons before you give your consent. Of course, you know she's preparing to write her dissertation, although you could hardly be aware of what her faculty adviser has approved for her topic. To make a long story short, she's hoping to prove that there are subtle distinctions between depression and a related condition she proposes to call oppressive personality disorder. Naturally, there are an unlimited number of research subjects and volumes of documentation regarding depression, but even she recognizes the difficulty in finding sufficient case studies for an as-yet-unclassified syndrome."

"Your mother does have a proclivity for complicated projects, doesn't she? I'm curious though about how she plans to proceed if there has been little research."

"As a matter of fact, that's where you come in. I think I told you Dr. Donahue is her adviser, and she recommended that Mum conduct a thorough case history on you, if you're willing to participate in her study. Apparently, the reason Dr. Donahue opted for other therapies rather than to seek drug intervention for you was because she was never convinced that you suffered from depression. She had diagnosed that you carried an overwhelming burden of responsibility and guilt for your parents' deaths, but she recognized subtle discrepancies between your symptoms and those of her depressed clients. Dr. Donahue is fully supportive of Mum's proposition, since she'd actually researched a similar hypothesis for her dissertation."

"That's all well and good, but one person could hardly be considered a representative sample. Of course, I'll help your mum in any way I can, though I know she'll need to find many more individuals to support her research."

"Remember a couple of weeks ago when she couldn't stay for coffee, because she was rushing off to meet with Dr. Werner at the Brandon Hospital for Mental Diseases? Well, he was very excited about Mum's theory, particularly because he treats several patients who fit her criteria, not the least of whom is a great-niece he only recently met. Justine is about five years older than you. Lindsay has already contacted her in Winnipeg, and she has agreed to be one of her case studies. So, if you consent, my mum will have two eager candidates with whom she can conduct in-depth case histories, along with the extensive documentation from Dr. Werner's outpatients and many others who are hospitalized. It will all be strictly confidential, of course."

"I know, Cass. Since I already trust your dad with my life, I'm perfectly comfortable with another Dr. Jamison figuring out my psyche. It might be interesting though for your mum's two test cases to meet and determine if we've shared similar experiences. Now, if we're finished with our clandestine assignment, maybe we can get some sleep and be up to watch the sun rising over the blue hills in the morning."

✳

"It's becoming more than a little alarming to me how quickly the years are flying by," Pat said, as she replenished Margaret's teacup. More and more, the two longtime friends relished each other's company, with Margaret often lingering on Fridays until Francine arrived home from college. Furthermore, she knew Cassandra was coming for the weekend, and she wanted to thank both girls for the way they had taken Susan under their collective wings.

"Of course, the real reason is that soon our young will be leaving the nest and getting on with their lives. Before we were blessed with having Susan live with us, I must admit I only considered the perspective of my students graduating from school, but now I can appreciate how a mother feels when her children move away from the family home."

"Oh, how right you are. I thank the brothers every day for agreeing to purchase that car for Francine. At least, we'll have her with us for another two years before she transfers to the University of Manitoba for her master's degree in English literature. As it happens, the Jamisons may well be the most fortunate of the lot of us, because Cassandra plans to study law at Brandon College. On the other hand, we could have lost our offspring to the quest of higher learning straight out of high school. Trin is still missing Jessica so much, and now that she has a steady boyfriend, she has even less time to write or telephone."

"I'm not surprised that, at this time, Susan doesn't have any interest in men, but you have yet to mention whether Francine has brought a beau home for your approval," Margaret said, with a glint of mischief in her eyes.

"Cass and Francine are inseparable and go out together for most of the extracurricular activities with a group of other girls and boys. So far, neither seems that interested in pairing off with any one fellow in particular, and I must say, at this age, I think that it is a healthy way to establish relationships with the opposite sex."

"It's strange how life so often comes full circle. I remember how close Francine and Cassandra were for years prior to enlarging their clique to become the foursome with Hope and Jessica. Now, with Jessica in Winnipeg, and even though they're on the same campus, I suspect they don't see much of Hope anymore either," Margaret replied.

"Yes, I believe the foursome has become a remnant of the past," Pat mused. "Albeit, Hope does have an exceedingly busy schedule, especially now that Dr. Farrington is preparing her for a spring audition to the Juilliard School of Music in New York. Also, at the risk of becoming a gossip, she's apparently having a fling with her former teacher, Michael Griffin."

"Perhaps we should thank our lucky stars that our girls return home every evening. The rumours are rampant in the district about the nightmare Carole Martin has caused her family. At the parent/teacher meeting the other evening, the talk was about how her parents speculate that some time ago, she gained access to her grandmother's bank accounts and has all but cleaned her out. Betty and Fred have been forced to put her small bungalow up for sale and bring Sadie back to the farm to live."

"That young woman seems to be headed down the path to her own destruction, and I have a strong hunch that she'll do a lot of damage to others on her way." The instant Patricia said it, she was sorry, as she caught the look of guilt that crept into Margaret's eyes. She did not have the slightest interest in allowing her friend to slip back into that abyss, and when she heard a car turn into the driveway, she provided an immediate distraction. "Ah, here they are. Maybe we'll be able to entice them to have a spot of tea with us before they dash out to tend to the lambs."

Her deception had been so easy. Her grandmother did not like to stand in line at the bank, and Carole was sick of waiting on tables. One afternoon when she was returning from being fired by yet another restaurant, Carole had nearly knocked her grandmother over as she was coming out the door of her house. "Where are you off to, Granny?"

"I'm finally going to the bank to pay my bills before they cut off my utilities, although my legs are so sore, I don't know if I'll make it back. It's too bad you can't run these errands for me."

"Actually, why don't I come along with you, and you can make arrangements with the manager to give me signing authority to your account. Then, every month, I'll look after paying all your bills."

At first, Carole only withdrew money from her grandmother's savings account. Since she was no longer required to work, she had all kinds of time to indulge in her preferred pastimes of eating out and going to movies during the afternoons, while frequenting a variety of bars late into the evenings. Soon though, she found her expenditures were increasing. When the teller advised there were insufficient funds, Carole switched her withdrawals from the savings to the chequing account and thereafter did not bother to pay any of the bills.

Carole had seldom paid much heed to the consequences of her actions. After several months, when one by one the utilities in her house were turned off, her grandmother telephoned her son, Fred, and asked him to drive to Brandon to ascertain what was happening. Overhearing the conversation, Carole gathered her few precious belongings and made a hasty exit to her current boyfriend's dingy apartment. Stan was initially happy to welcome her, but since she made no effort to clean or cook during the hours he was at work, his pleasure quickly turned to resentment. It hardly mattered to Carole, because she only intended to stay long enough to ensure that her father had returned to his farm. Once he was gone, she would find a new address, while she searched for her next source of income.

With some of her remaining cash, Carole booked a room for a month at the YWCA on 11th Street. Several days later, when she was washing her long blond hair, an idea came to her. On the rare occasions when she had accompanied her grandmother to the Ladies Auxiliary with the Royal Canadian Legion on 13th Street, she had been surprised by how eager the elderly ladies were to spend time with her. What if she befriended some of those old gals, and earned their trust? She suspected it wouldn't take her long to gain access to a few more bank accounts.

Inasmuch as Carole did not take responsibility for her behaviour, she did have the sense to learn from her experiences. The flaw in her deletion of her grandmother's finances had been to take money out of her chequing account. If she limited her withdrawals to her benefactors' savings accounts, it was quite conceivable that considerable time could pass without the generous souls becoming aware of their dwindling assets, if they ever did. After all, if she were prepared to socialize with the lonely old women who fawned over her, with each trying to be more attentive than the next, they would surely reimburse her for her time.

From the beginning, Carole delved into her memory and focused only on the women who were widows amongst her grandmother's friends and acquaintances. She had no interest in raising the suspicions or the ire of some overbearing husband. Furthermore, she realized she was much wiser to maintain a residence separate from any of her sources of revenue, in the event that a similar situation, as had occurred with her grandmother, might arise.

Each time she accompanied one of the seniors to her respective financial institution to implement the signing arrangement, she had to provide her proper name, along with her personal identification. Fortunately, her address was still listed as her grandmother's home, and Carole congratulated herself for having the foresight to assume the alias of Karen Wood when she checked into the YWCA. She considered it unlikely that, in their dotage, any one of her ever-increasing number of elderly female friends would suspect that she was dipping into their monetary funds, but even if they did, it would be difficult to track her down.

Initially, Carole was surprised that her father had not come back to Brandon searching for her, and she wondered if her grandmother had been too embarrassed or perhaps too forgetful to tell him what had actually happened with her bank accounts. Did she even know? The more she thought about it, the more she realized that unless her father had requested a full-scale investigation, the chances of her deceit being discovered were remote. The bank would hardly be pre-pared to be forthcoming when a consensual agreement had been put into existence.

Would the same not be true with her new clients? It did not take Carole long before she recognized the potential of expanding her sphere of influence. What if she ingratiated herself to other groups of elderly women who had too much time and money on their respective hands? Many of them had already come to expect they would pay for a myriad of domestic and personal services, so why not, for a nominal fee, have additional assistance with the trifling details of handling their monthly bills?

Carole's transition to full-time grifter was remarkably smooth. She began establishing her credibility by paying the monthly bills from the chequing accounts with due diligence. Once her bona fide pattern was set, she made a small withdrawal from each of her six benefactors' savings accounts, ensuring that, at every financial institution, she was provided with the remaining balance in each fund.

It was when Carole arrived back to her room and studied the state-ments that she was amazed by the amount of money some of her new friends had accumulated, with three of them having substantial assets. Armed with this additional knowledge, and never having had the capacity for long-term commitments, she formulated a new plan. The following morning, she paid for her room, extending her stay at the YWCA for an additional three months, until the end of June. Her next stop was the hardware store, where she invested in a small but sturdy strongbox, which she stealthily carried back to her room and tucked under her bed.

On July 1, Carole intended to be on the bus to Winnipeg with the fruits of her labours. Until then, she was prepared to provide impeccable service to all her clients, and then, over the course of the last week of June, when she paid their monthly bills, she planned to withdraw a generous sum from each of the three most lucrative savings accounts. It never once occurred to her that she might be impeded in carrying out her scam, because no one had ever caught her at anything. Besides, all her dear old friends doted upon her, and by the time they became aware that their retirement savings were near depletion, she would be comfortably established in Winnipeg under the name of Julie Adams.

When Lindsay overheard Dr. Farrington telling Ian that Hope's audition for the Juilliard School of Music was confirmed for May 15 in Toronto, she knew she had to arrange a farewell party. The close-knit foursome had enjoyed too special a friendship for the group to disperse without a memorable celebration that each of them could savour in the years to come.

Recognizing that the date would be determined by Hope's busy schedule, she retraced her steps, and headed back into the music centre. Perhaps, Lady Luck would shine her countenance upon her, and she would find the virtuoso still in her domain. Then Lindsay would refuse to leave her in peace until they had judiciously studied her calendar and arrived at a definitive date.

As it happened, when Lindsay swung around, she nearly knocked Michael over as he was coming down the corridor. "Oh hi, Michael, so sorry! I really must pay more attention to how I tend to charge ahead as if I have sole occupancy of the hallways."

Actually, she had stopped in her tracks when she saw Hope's pianist. Lindsay had not seen Michael for quite some time, and she was surprised by how haggard and thin he looked. To the best of her recall, Lindsay had always considered Michael to be a robust, youthful man, and she wondered if he was recovering from a bout of illness. She knew he accompanied Hope on her demanding schedule of recitals and concerts, but to her trained eye, his appearance reflected more than even a protracted physical ailment. Then it occurred to her that if the rumours were true about the clandestine relationship between the college's prodigy and her accompanist, an element of Michael's conundrum was understandable.

If Hope was successful in Toronto en route to Juilliard, where did Michael fit into the picture? The famed school of music would hardly need a student to arrive with an accompanist, given the level of expertise that would exist within its walls. Also, it was much too premature in Hope's career to require a musical agent, which was presumably the prime motivator for Michael completing his master's in business administration. Furthermore, from what Lindsay knew about Hope and the single-minded quest of her musical aspirations, she suspected that if Michael entertained other expectations, he could be travelling down the road to frustration and disappointment. But she was not there to psychoanalyze Michael. In fact, if her plans came to fruition, she could become another interruption in his desire to have sequestered time with Hope.

Faintly hearing the strains of a violin, Lindsay bid Michael goodbye and carried on down the hall. When she reached the partially open door, she stood and waited, soon becoming lost in the plaintive sounds of the "Adagio" from Mozart's "Violin Concerto No.3 in G major, K. 216." In her transfixion, Lindsay remembered why Hope had to sacrifice her youth and eventually her life in the pursuit of her God-given gift. Once again, she realized what an exquisite rendition of one of her favourite pieces of music she was hearing, and in that moment, Lindsay could commiserate with Michael as she felt the profundity of his ineluctable loss of his one true love to the fulfillment of her destiny.

Still, she needed to entice Hope into returning to the Clear Lake cottage one last time, to capture some enduring memories for each of the foursome. Soon after she heard the last note of the "Rondeau: Allegro," and silence reigned supreme, Lindsay quietly pushed the door open. Hope was alone and was reverently placing the priceless Stradivarius, which had recently been loaned to her by the Winnipeg Symphony in preparation for her audition, into the padded violin case. Lindsay scarcely breathed, for fear she would interrupt Hope's utmost care of the precious instrument.

When Hope had completed her task and glanced up, Lindsay softly said, "As always, Hope, I was mesmerized by the sheer artistry of your playing. I'm convinced that soon you will become recognized as one of Canada's most talented violinists."

"Thank you, Lindsay. You have invariably been effusive with your praise, which I really appreciate. I didn't hear you come in; are you here to see me?"

"That I am, and I anticipate you have your calendar with you. I'd like you to check what day will work for you to spend an exclusive foursome excursion at the Jamison cottage before you leave for Toronto, and I won't accept a negative answer. I've not chatted with any of the others, but I've already confirmed that undergraduate exams are scheduled for completion by April thirtieth. And once it is organized, I promise it will just be the four of you; no meddlesome adults underfoot."

"Oh, that sounds like a wonderful send-off. But what about Jessica; will she be finished writing her finals?"

"I've also contacted the University of Manitoba, and their programming is simultaneous with ours; if I'm anything, I'm thorough. You select the date, my love, and I'll make all the arrangements, so my four favourite gals will have a fabulous celebration."

Hope studied her calendar for an inordinate period of time, with a faint crease of concern gracing her beautiful countenance, as if attempting to remember some commitment she had neglected to record, before identifying that Friday, May 1 was her preference.

"Terrific! Thank you, and I'll be in touch when all the pieces are in place. Francine will no doubt drive all of you in her sporty Mustang, with dire warnings to observe the speed limits."

*

The minute she arrived home, Lindsay set the wheels in motion. First, she telephoned Pat, and after a brief summary of her plan, asked for her assistance. As she expected, Francine's stepmother was on board within minutes, adding her ideas and suggestions to make the event unforgettable for the foursome.

"I'm seeing Trin this evening, and while we're at the Lingnan, I'll make sure she telephones Jessica to confirm the date. What if we gathered individual and group pictures of the girls and created a photo album for each of them as a keepsake of their close friendship? Remember to ask your mum, because I know she captured many of their moments, first of Cassandra and Francine but also of the four of them when they biked over to see your parents. Together, we'll provide them with enough food, pop, and juice to take care of an army, and may I suggest that Daniel and I drive to the lake on April thirtieth to deliver their supplies before they arrive? Oh, it just occurred to me, could you please contact Hope's grandparents for photos of her?"

With a burst of laughter, Lindsay said, "I knew I could count on you. By the time May first arrives, we'll have such a delightful festivity organized, our only regret will be that we promised not to crash their party. Thanks, Pat. Let me know what you hear from Trin. I must run and pick up Cassandra, who will likely have a plethora of her own inspirations of what they can do, no doubt extending their gathering over the course of the entire weekend."

If Lindsay had had any way of knowing, she might have considered, neither for the first nor the last, that she was nearly as accurate a prognosticator of future events as her aptly named daughter. Still, as a firm believer in the fundamental truths of the *Desiderata*, one line in particular, "And whether or not it is clear to you, no doubt the universe is unfolding as it should," it is debatable that she would have chosen an alternate course of action.

They were lying naked side by side in Michael's three-quarter bed, caressing one another's relaxed bodies after their passion was spent, when he said, "I can hardly wait for our weekend at the Fort Garry Hotel. I've booked us a suite with a king-sized bed, so for a change, we'll be more comfortable when we're making love. Who knows? With all that luxury, we might just order room service and never leave the confines of the hotel. We can check in by one o'clock, and I was wondering if we could be on our way after brunch on the morning of the first. That way we will have nearly two full days together before we have to check out on Sunday morning."

A perceptible quiver coursed through Hope's body, and for once it was not because of just having had exhilarating sex with Michael. She had done it again. For the second time in as many weeks, she had forgotten about their plans together and had double-booked another social activity. On the morning of May 1, Francine was picking her up at nine o'clock, so they could have all day to enjoy the unusually warm spring weather at Clear Lake. Hope knew she could not bail on the foursome yet again, or she would be taking the risk of being excluded from their group for as long as she lived.

But now what could she possibly say to Michael? It had been one thing to change their plans of spending Easter with his parents when, at the last minute, her grandparents had received the invitation to drive Hope to Winnipeg for a long-overdue visit with her father and his new family. Michael had consented reluctantly, although he had argued that Marika and Jonathon had treated her more like a daughter than her own father had, if not in her youth then at least for the past several years.

However, it was going to be an entirely different matter to apprise Michael that she had agreed to spend May 1 with her three female friends. As her mind raced, it occurred to her that she could suggest a compromise and ask Michael to pick her up at the lake on Saturday morning. Since neither of them had any firm commitments on the following Monday, they could simply postpone the date of their departure.

Abruptly, for reasons Hope would never comprehend, a feeling of intense anger toward Michael seized her, and she was no longer eager to reach any kind of mutual resolution. Ever since their trip to Winnipeg last September, Michael had become increasingly possessive, until lately, all too often she felt like she was being swallowed. They saw each other every day, usually for several hours, and then, unless she had a recital, they were together evening after evening, just the two of them. They never went out with any friends, and other than going for meals, they were always alone in his small apartment.

Perhaps if Hope had waited until her sudden inexplicable ire had subsided, she might have chosen her words with more diplomacy. "Actually, Michael, I can't leave with you on Friday. I've been invited to spend that day with the foursome at the Jamisons' cottage at Clear Lake, so you can pick me up there on our way into Winnipeg on Saturday."

"What are you saying? We've had our final weekend together planned for weeks now. When did you decide to go to Clear Lake? You can't just ditch me at the last minute because a group of your female friends wants you to come to the lake. Once you leave for Toronto, it could be months before we see each other again."

"Precisely why Lindsay Jamison has organized a farewell celebration for the four of us. As it happens, we have not all been together for over a year."

"Why did you have to pick our weekend?"

"Because there wasn't another date that would work. And it's not for the weekend. We're leaving Brandon on Friday morning, and I'll be ready to go with you by noon on Saturday. I don't think either of us has anything pressing on Monday, so we can return then. What's the big deal about postponing our trip for one day?"

"I don't exactly like being pre-empted by a bunch of women, especially when we have reservations at the priciest hotel in Winnipeg. At this late date, they'll probably charge me for Friday night, and I don't know if we can get the suite for Sunday."

"Well, there's just no way that I'm going to miss our foursome party, so work it out."

"Yes, of course, you wouldn't change any of your all-important plans for me. But then it has always been about you and only you, hasn't it?"

"That sounds more than a little petulant coming from you, Michael!"

"Oh, how dare I? Pardon me for momentarily forgetting that the great Hope Harding has the monopoly on querulous behaviour."

"I don't have to stay here and listen to this."

"You're absolutely right. You're free to leave whenever you want, and what's more, you don't have to bother coming back, as far as I care."

The quarrelling lovers rose hastily and put on their clothes, as if they were embarrassed by their preceding intimate dalliance. With Michael's last words, an eerie silence descended upon the room. As the stillness deepened, they stood staring at one another, each aware that what was said next could have far-reaching consequences.

Over the years, they'd had their share of disagreements but none that had ever been even remotely suggestive of bringing their relationship to a close. Yet, Michael's fear of rejection had, during the past six months, prevented him from proposing to Hope. If only he had given her his engagement ring, he might have felt more confident that they could weather this storm. Still, he was the one who had introduced the finality into their argument, and he knew beyond a doubt it was because of his steadily growing conviction that Hope would never love anyone or anything nearly as much as she loved her violin.

✻

The beginning of their marriage was more auspicious than either Derek or Tiffany would have anticipated. But then, if they had given any consideration to the possibility that the criteria for marital bliss might originate with perfection of the wedding celebrations and a honeymoon of two glorious weeks in the Cook Islands, they may have had an inkling of what to expect.

They had driven to Winnipeg the morning after the festivities to begin their long flight to Rarotonga, with the afternoon Air Canada departure to Toronto. Neither had flown very much, and both appreciated that the journey via Hawaii to New Zealand and then to their final destination would be long and arduous. Nonetheless, more than twenty-six hours later, when they checked into the Moana Sands Beachfront Villas, each had a sudden resurgence of energy.

Regardless of the level of exhaustion, they soon agreed that it would be impossible to arrive in paradise and not experience at least an ephemeral revival. Instead of crashing onto the inviting queen-sized canopy bed, they opened their luggage, changed into swimming apparel, and strolled along the white sandy shore of the South Pacific Ocean. The stunning scenery was a veritable feast for the eyes, with sunbeams shimmering off the ubiquitous aquamarine water, the landscape picturesque with verdant ferns, and a plethora of other yet-unknown species of lush vegetation, all surrounded by endless groves of palm trees.

Their idyllic fortnight came to an end sooner than either would have desired or imagined possible. To their delight, by the first day, they fell into a routine that suited them both, starting with coffee and breakfast on the deck overlooking a lagoon bluer than the sky. Their mornings were spent in an array of water activities—swimming, boating, snorkelling, and surfing—before retiring to the resort for a light lunch. In the afternoons, they were quite content to walk, read, rest, and converse before dressing for a delectable dinner at one of the many restaurants in the lavish resorts.

On their last evening, as they sat on the terrace of one of the elegant dining rooms watching a spectacular sunset, Derek raised his glass of champagne. "You have been worth the wait in every sense of the word, my darling Tiffany."

Neither had lived with another person for years, and without expressing it overtly, both had worried they were too set in their ways. When Tiffany sublet her small apartment several weeks prior to the wedding, she had moved back into her parent's home. It had never even occurred to her to have a trial run of living with Derek before they were married. They had decided they would reside in his town-house until they designed and built the large two-storey home, where they planned to raise their family. Having children as soon as possible had been uppermost on both of their list of priorities, with neither prepared to set a limit on the number.

Even after the so-called honeymoon period of three months, the newlyweds were still flourishing in their apparent compatibility.

During the last year of high school, if Tiffany had not thought that Derek was a geek before, she certainly did after he started sending her a dozen red roses every week. Why was he throwing his money away? What did they possibly share in common? Although grades were important to her, Tiffany would never that let on to anyone, much less date a guy who prided himself as always being at the head of the class. What a waste that he was one of the handsomest boys in school?

Still, if Eric had not noticed her, Tiffany would never have dreamed that she would become one of the popular students. Then when she refused to sleep with him, and he continued to take her out, she began to really care about him, regardless of his reputation for drinking. Had it not been for the accident, she probably would have accepted his proposal to marry him as soon as they graduated.

Now the longer she and Derek were together, the more Tiffany realized how similar they were in their choice of music, books, activities, and especially their desire to have a family. Subsequently, when her obstetrician confirmed her suspicions, Tiffany made an impromptu decision to prepare a celebratory dinner for the evening. She returned to the accounting office, postponed her three afternoon appointments until the following day, and drove to the grocery store.

✳

The minute she heard Derek drive into the garage adjoining the townhouse, Tiffany lit the two long slender candles in the crystal holders and turned off all the overhead lights. She had changed into the silk hostess gown Derek had given her for her birthday the previous month and freshened her make-up. Meeting him at the door as soon as the key was in the lock, Tiffany said, "Welcome home, darling. If you don't mind, I'd prefer you leave the lights off, so we can enjoy the ambience of our evening."

Taking her into his arms, Derek gave her a long passionate kiss before he replied. "Not at all, my dearest. What a wonderful way to be greeted after a hard day at the office. You look ravishing, and my only hope is that we have some time before whatever that delectable scent emanating from the kitchen is ready. To be on the safe side, shall I douse the candles until we're about to eat?"

Later, Derek re-lit the candles before coming into the kitchen to finish the preparation of the Greek salad, as Tiffany opened the oven to reveal two succulent racks of lamb, baked acorn squash, and scalloped potatoes.

"All my favourites. This is a feast fit for a king! How did you manage all this after work?"

"Actually, I took the afternoon off. Could you please uncork the champagne?"

"Oh, now I know I've forgotten an important anniversary. Sorry, could you please refresh my memory?"

Tiffany wrapped her arms around Derek's neck. "No apology required, my dearest. Everything's ready, so shall we eat before the lamb gets cold?"

It was not until they had savoured every mouthful of their dinner, including the crème brulee, that Tiffany suggested they retire to the drawing room with their coffee. Seated together on the love settee, she at last disclosed her obstetrician's findings, with an anticipated arrival date near the end of June. Derek was so overwhelmed that several moments slipped away before he responded by enfolding Tiffany into his arms and whispering, "Thank you," in her ear.

✳

Within the week, Michael had vacated Brandon. Ever the gentleman, he had driven Hope back to her grandparents' home the evening of their quarrel. The subsequent day, while she was communing with her violin in the music room, he had boxed all Hope's belongings and delivered them to the house with minimal explanation when her grandmother opened the door. He initially refused her offer for refreshments, although, on second thought, when he was halfway out the door, he changed his mind and accepted.

He had always enjoyed Mr. and Mrs. Harding's company, and he was grateful for the many times they had included him in their family Sunday dinners. Before she returned with a silver tea service, bone china teacups, and a floral plate laden with her delicious butter tarts, Michael realized that this might well be the last occasion he would see Hope's grandmother. Aside from saying farewell to Dr. Farrington, he was eager to leave at the earliest opportunity, and without any idea of what he would do once he returned to his parents' home, he knew he would not darken the streets of the city for a long time to come.

When Michael signed the lease on his apartment, he had the foresight to insist that he only wanted it until April 30, since it was the end of the academic year. Long before he was apprised of Hope's audition for Juilliard, he had planned to bring her to his parents' acreage for a week or two prior to her anticipated return to Meadowmount School. On the all-too-frequent occasions when he had dared to indulge in his wildest imaginings, Michael had even fantasized that they might be married in a quiet ceremony in the college's chapel prior to Hope's departure for the east coast.

Now, with all his hopes and dreams dashed, the best Michael could anticipate was a return to his teaching position at Souris High School at the start of the fall semester. As much as they might wonder when it became apparent that Michael had come home to dwell, neither Jonathon nor Marika would query him about his decision. They might ask if they could expect to attend his convocation later in the spring, but never would a word pass their lips regarding when they would see

Hope again.

Marika had always worried that the love between the two young people was not equally reciprocated, although she certainly grasped the conflicting emotions churning in Hope's heart. From personal experience, she understood that the young woman was facing that same difficult choice she had made at the height of her career. Marika had been following her dream; she had become the person she'd always wanted to be, mired in all the trappings of success, fame, and glory. It was not until she fell in love with Jonathon that she began to appreciate the interminable sacrifices she was making in the pursuit of her passion. Perhaps it had been easier for Marika, because she was older when Jonathon swept her off her feet. By then, she'd become aware that she desired more in life. She wanted love, family, and time to be her own person, not only to perform and to entertain others on the world stage.

Every time Michael brought Hope home, Marika saw the longing in his eyes but also the creeping despair as Hope spoke more and more about fulfilling her promise to her dead mother, while at the same time displaying her determination to achieve her destiny. There was little doubt in Marika's mind that Hope had the potential to become a renowned international violinist, but she feared for her son. She knew Michael was so rooted in his home and in his family that before long he would flounder and be set adrift if he were to travel the world with Hope without the opportunity to return on a regular basis to rejuvenate his soul. Marika had always been convinced that Michael had abruptly ended his piano lessons, because even by age thirteen, he had realized he could not bear to leave hearth and home for any prolonged period of time.

The morning Michael arrived in the circular driveway with his car loaded to capacity, his mother was toiling in one of her numerous flower beds. As she rose from her knees and watched her only child, her heart went out to him. His unusual slow faltering step, his hunched shoulders, and his obvious lack of awareness that she was observing him confirmed all her trepidations.

Last September, Michael had been so excited when showed her the engagement ring he had selected prior to giving it to Hope. However, on the rare occasions over the autumn and winter when Marika had been in Hope's presence, she had wondered about its glaring absence. Now, watching Michael carry his personal belongings back into their home, she realized he must have reached a definitive decision, and it appeared not to include the possibility of impending nuptials. All she could do was wait and then listen to him, if he chose to pour out his anguish.

✳

The foursome conversed around the dying bonfire until three or four in the morning. At last, one by one, they slipped into the cottage and retired to the communal bedroom. Hope was on the verge of falling asleep when she sat straight up in bed. It had just occurred to her that she had not spoken with Michael since the evening of their quarrel. Had he telephoned the Fort Garry Hotel to change the reservation? Was he still picking her up at noon that day? Did she want him to come?

It was so unlike Michael not to have called or to have sought her out on Thursday in the music hall to confirm their arrangements. Surely, he was not still holding a grudge regarding her spending one day with her girlfriends. If he was, he had better get over it, or she might decide to stay at the cabin with her friends for the balance of the weekend. The more Hope thought about the trip to Winnipeg, the more she considered that, given the weather forecast, her preference was to remain at Clear Lake and return to Brandon on Monday morning with the rest of the foursome.

They had been having a terrific visit, and the chance of all of them getting together again for a long time was remote. For the past year, Dr. Farrington had worked fervently to prepare Hope, and she had very positive feelings about her upcoming audition in Toronto. In fact, if her lucky stars lined up, she might well be in New York for several subsequent years. Suddenly, perhaps for the first time, she wondered what Michael would do in her absence.

With this disquieting realization, Hope rose from the bed and went outside to walk along the shore. She knew she was hardly likely to fall asleep now. Why had she given so little thought to Michael over the past few months? Ever since Dr. Farrington had apprised her of his plans for her to study at Juilliard by the autumn semester, Hope's entire focus had been consumed by her future. She had spent precious little time considering Michael, never mind the implications for their relationship. Could that be why Michael had become so needy, so dependent on her since last fall?

Hope had always suspected that Michael cared for her at a much deeper level than she did for him. Still, she had never been dishonest with him about her aspirations. For as long as she could remember, Hope had known that she was defined by accomplishments, certainly not by the expectations of others. From the moment she had devoured Alfred Lord Tennyson's famed poem "Ulysses," she had affirmed his oft-quoted line, "To strive, to seek, to find, and not to yield" as the fount of her inspiration on her quest to become a concert violinist.

Yet, much too often lately, she had sensed that Michael was anticipating something more from her, that she had some kind of obligation to him. There were times when she felt he wanted to possess her, to make her his own. Had she not been clear enough from the beginning that she could not belong to anyone, that music would always be her life? It dawned on her that, on two or three occasions, he had actually hinted they should get married. Surely Michael understood she had no interest in acquiring a husband or, heaven forbid, providing him with offspring.

A faint recollection flashed through her consciousness. What had Michael been alluding to on their drive to Winnipeg the previous May before she was to leave for the Adirondack Mountains? It was starting to come back. He'd mentioned that he had a special early gift for her eighteenth birthday, but now, as she struggled to retrieve the memory, she realized she had forgotten until that minute that he had not given her anything. How strange. Michael had referred to it with such emphasis, but when he had not presented it during their memorable dinner at the Chef's Table, it had never crossed her mind again.

God, could Michael have had an engagement ring? Could he be intending to propose that evening when they returned to Winnipeg, and was that why he had been so insistent that they spend the weekend together? Suddenly, Hope was overwhelmed with a feeling of dread. She knew she would have to refuse him. Although she had no desire to cause him any angst, she could never promise to become his wife, not now, and not ever.

She turned back toward the cottage as fatigue began to claim her. She had no idea how Michael would respond to her rejection, but it was clear she would need to get some sleep prior to his arrival. She taped a note beside the coffee pot requesting to be awakened by eleven o'clock. At the very least, she would need two cups of strong coffee to brace her for Michael's inevitable reaction. If only she had ever availed upon Marika Griffin to learn more about her history, she might have enlisted her assistance in helping Michael to understand the compelling nature of pursuing her destiny. Although Marika had married and had a child, she had been much older than Hope when she made her dramatic life-altering choice.

*

It was so unlike Margaret to be late for their Friday afternoon cup of tea. It was a balmy spring day, and when her friend had not arrived by four thirty, Patricia decided to carry her glass of iced tea, which she had made in lieu of the hot beverage, to the deck overlooking her greening garden and blossoming trees. The previous evening, she had started to reread *To Kill a Mockingbird*, but it remained unopened on her lap as she soaked in the warmth and beauty of her small corner of paradise.

Every year, Daniel had planted more caragana, lilac, ornamental crab apple, flowering dogwood, and honeysuckle shrubs, framing her small garden plot, so that by this time of the year, her backyard was emblazoned with yellow, pink, white, and purple hues that created a colourful circle all the way to Francine's now-vacant lamb pasture. When Patricia opened the sliding patio door, all her senses burst into life with the sights, sounds, and scents of being outside in nature when spring made its sublime return to the Canadian prairie.

She must have dozed for a short spell, because when she opened her eyes, Margaret was seated beside her on one of the padded lawn chairs.

"Why didn't you give me a nudge when you got here? Have I been snoozing very long?"

Chuckling after she swallowed her mouthful of iced tea, Margaret said, "I've only just arrived so it depends on when you tired of waiting for me and escaped to your serene haven. I'm sorry I was late. I lost track of time when I slipped back into my office after the bell rang to review my notes from last evening's school board meeting."

"Good gracious, what would prompt you to go into your office on a beautiful Friday afternoon? I would have thought you'd have been out of that mausoleum as soon as your charges had left the premises."

"Funny you should say that. After a very enlightening meeting, I might just have the means of escape at my fingertips." Taking another sip of the delicious lemon iced tea, Margaret became very pensive while she absorbed the picturesque scene surrounding her friend's garden.

"You can't become mute with me after a statement like that. I was being facetious, but I know that's the furthest thought from your mind."

"Sorry, Patricia, as it happens, Michael Griffin has applied to return to teaching at Souris High, but there will not be any available position come the fall term. Michael was always highly regarded at the school, and his value has increased substantially with his soon-to-be conferred master's degree in business administration. In addition, Hartney has recently adopted the slogan that it is "the little town with a lot of heart," and Michael's youth, energy, and musical talent precisely fits the bill for the school's projected high priority on extra-curricular sports, clubs, and bands. Not to mention, what a feather in their cap it would be if, in the year of the final stage of their amalgamation into the Souris Valley School Division, the Hartney Consolidated School Board could boast of hiring the most qualified principal to ever hold the position not only in the history of their school but also in the Souris division."

"I must still be half asleep. You've completely lost me. Do you mind taking me through that again?"

"To cut to the chase, last evening, the soon-to-be defunct Hartney School Board asked for my resignation as the principal of the school. They apparently have the unanimous approval of the Souris Board to offer me a full retirement package and facilitate Michael Griffin taking over my position come September. Does that make it clearer, my friend?"

"I believe this calls for something a little stronger than tea. Would you prefer a glass of Bristol Cream sherry?"

On her way into the kitchen, Patricia stopped in the hallway to place a telephone call. Luck was with her when James answered on the first ring, and he was perfectly amenable to jumping in his truck to join them for an impromptu barbeque. Although without any specific awareness of what was occurring for Margaret, when Patricia had awakened that morning, she had experienced a sense of foreboding regarding her dearest friend. She had subsequently prepared extra potato salad and taken more than the usual number of hamburger patties from the freezer in the event the Devonshires might be joining them for dinner.

When Patricia returned to the patio with a decanter and two sherry glasses, Margaret was staring straight ahead, deep in thought. Finally, she spoke. "In the pristine silence of your prairie sanctuary, I can all but hear the voice of God carried on the gentle breeze. As I listen and heed His message, the more I appreciate that I should be thanking the board instead of feeling as if I've been betrayed. What would possibly motivate me not to be grateful for an early retirement, complete with a generous incentive package and a full pension? I could be enjoying my life like you so obviously do, since you've left teaching, rather than dealing with disgruntled parents, marking interminable papers, and coping with the antics of adolescents ravished by their raging hormones."

"I can understand your sense of betrayal, Margaret. Why could they not have used a far more amenable approach, such as talking to you first regarding your thoughts and inclinations, before discussing it with the members of the Souris Board?"

"Yes, that would have been a more appropriate starting point considering my thirty-five years of service with the Hartney School Division, of which the last twenty-nine have been as the principal. To be perfectly truthful, what I found the most upsetting was they didn't even imply I had a choice in the matter. In their collective minds, it was a fait accompli, and I was present at the meeting simply to hear their decision and to sign the papers. And I'm hardly likely to get any sympathy from James. He has been pleading with me for years to give up the reins, so we can travel to warmer climates during our frigid winters. Oh, bother, on the subject of James, I better gulp this delightfully smooth sherry—what a waste—and be on my way home."

"James will be turning into the drive at any minute. He planned to have a quick shower and will join us for dinner. Francine's going to the lake with Cassandra again for the weekend, but she was taking Susan home before they left. I mentioned to James to ask her if she wanted to join a bunch of old fogeys. If not, I'm sure she'll find something in your fridge to eat. By the way, although it will not be of any consolation to you, I think your plight has unwittingly provided the missing piece to a puzzle Francine brought to my attention last week."

Patricia was on the verge of explaining when the twin brothers and James joined them on the deck, each carrying a bottle of Molson Canadian. Daniel was the first to speak. "Hello, ladies, what a pleasant way to end the week. Thanks for thinking of it, my darling, and I see the fridge is overflowing with delicious salads. Just let me know when you want me to start the barbeque."

Margaret liked nothing more than a mystery, although she had yet to solve why men always seemed to appear at that moment when women were about to share confidences with each other. Now she would be compelled to wait until they were alone again to hear what was intriguing Patricia. In her typical fashion, the former teacher had waited until she could gather the facts, rather than gossip and start yet another rumour. But what information could she have gleaned from Francine that would have had an impact on Margaret's forced retirement?

It seemed that lately, the Hartney district had become such a veritable hotbed of scandal regarding one family or another, such that those individuals who placed even a modicum of value on safeguarding their reputations chose their conversations with a great deal of precaution. Rumour-mongering was reaching a peak that precluded mentioning anything that could be misconstrued, especially over the party line telephone.

The last thing Margaret wanted to come full circle was that she had been fired as the longstanding principal of Hartney Consolidated School and replaced by a young man. It would come as no surprise to her that some would have cheered, and many more who would have been incensed by the injustice of such an outcome. Nonetheless, since she had had no control over the decision, Margaret intended to make an alacritous announcement to her family, friends, and her community that she was choosing to take early retirement, so she could travel with her husband.

It was such a pleasant spring evening that, after enjoying Patricia's delicious dinner, which was followed by angel food cake, seasonal strawberries, and fresh cream, everyone was too satiated to move. As anxious as Margaret was to hear more about Patricia's riddle, she was hesitant to interrupt the camaraderie they were all feeling as the sun began its colourful descent below the horizon. It did occur to her that it might be an opportune time to share her news with her husband, since she had not yet mustered the courage or energy, and their friends that she would be unemployed by the end of June. Still, Margaret wanted to hear what Patricia had to disclose, in the hope it might provide another perspective.

At last, Darrin rose from his comfortable lawn chair and started to gather up the dishes. James and Daniel were quick to follow suit. "Please just place the salads in the fridge in the bowls," Patricia said, "and I'll be in shortly to put them in plastic containers. Margaret and I are going to enjoy the scenic sunset. Thanks, guys."

As soon as the patio door was pulled closed, Margaret picked up the thread of Patricia's conversation precisely where they had left off when the men arrived. "At last, out with it. What tidbit of information did Francine share that completed the puzzle for you, and how could it possibly be related to my dismissal?"

"I thought at first it was just my overactive imagination leading me astray, as usual. It was based on something that Hope Harding had said about Michael Griffin. Apparently, he was to have picked her up at Clear Lake last Saturday afternoon for a final weekend trip to Winnipeg before she departs for Toronto, but he neither arrived nor contacted her in any way. Of course, you know they've been an item for years."

"Actually, I did hear that rumour during those preliminary meetings in Souris, when it was being proposed that Hartney become part of their school division, although I can't say I paid much attention. I know that Hope is one of Francine's friends, but I'm so pleased by how your stepdaughter and her friends have included Susan in their college activities that I didn't care who was seeing who. I must be thicker than I normally am though, because I'm still not following you."

"I'm not exactly making myself clear. As it happened, Hope was initially upset when Michael stood her up, but when she started to share her feelings with the other girls, she disclosed that she thought it might be for the best. Hope was convinced that Michael had planned their rendezvous, so he could propose to her, and she knew she would have to reject his offer of marriage. Furthermore, if she was accepted into Juilliard, she could not imagine what he would do or where he would go, although she was not above expressing a rather disparaging comment about "Michael running back home to stay this time." As is my wont, I speculated that Michael would almost certainly return to his parents' acreage, and he might very well want to resume his teaching position at Souris High. I kept my conjecture to myself, although now I wonder if you might have been forewarned had you known that Michael was returning to the district."

"Don't beat yourself up over that, Patricia. Even if you had told me, I would never have suspected it could make one iota of difference to me. Quite frankly, it didn't ever occur to me that my job could be in jeopardy after all these years. I guess you've gathered I haven't told James yet. I'm not sure what's holding me back, since it would have been perfectly natural to have told him this morning at breakfast."

"Perhaps you need to take your own advice and stop blaming yourself, Margaret. You persist in perceiving the situation as being fired instead of the more positive perspective of stepping aside to facilitate a younger candidate being given the opportunity to prove his merit. Early retirement, rather than opprobrium, could be a reward for all your valuable years of service, my dear friend. And if I were you, that is precisely the manner in which I would present it to James first thing tomorrow morning."

"Thank you, Patricia. You always did have a way of viewing life in a different light, and it is one of your most endearing traits. It could be quite edifying to travel beyond our national border. While we're on the subject, maybe you and I should consider planning a trip together." Presumably with her sense of humour restored, Margaret chuckled. "Who knows? We might even invite our men to join us on some of our excursions."

✳

Where had the years gone? It was early on Friday afternoon, and Patricia had ventured up the stairs to Francine's loft with a dust cloth in her hand. Spying her stepdaughter's cozy bed tucked under the sloping eaves, she decided to rest for a few moments before beginning her cleaning. She felt tired, and her head had scarcely touched the pillow before she dozed off. Perhaps twenty or thirty minutes later, Patricia aroused from her slumber, refreshed but nostalgic.

In all the time Patricia had been married to Daniel, she hardly ever napped during the day, and certainly never in Francine's bedroom. Still, since she had awakened this morning, she had been feeling melancholic, and as close as she could determine, it was because yet another weekend would pass without Francine bursting through the door full of energy and tales from college.

During the past three months since Francine had started her master's program at the University of Manitoba, she had only managed to make it home for the Thanksgiving weekend. For some reason, although they had not talked about it, Patricia had been confident that Francine would return every Friday evening and stay with them until late on Sunday. The weather had been cooperative, the roads were in excellent condition, and the trip could be accomplished in little more than two hours.

Patricia knew she dared not complain to Trin during their frequent get-togethers for morning coffee and family dinners. Her friend's heart had been broken when Jessica decided to depart right after high school for Winnipeg, although, over the past four years, Trin had learned to cope with her absence. But there was nothing that could have prepared Trin for where her daughter chose to study medicine that autumn.

When Patricia lamented to Margaret about how much she was missing Francine, her friend would duly commiserate, but Patricia was always left with the vague feeling that she was only half interested, presumably because she did not want to be reminded that Susan could make a similar choice when she graduated with her bachelor of science the following spring.

Strangely, neither woman had ever verbalized that since they had inadvertently come to be in a mothering role by virtue of acquiring daughters who had lost both their parents, they each harboured a profound secret fear that one day, their girls would not return to them. For years, the longtime friends had been content to teach the children of other women, never expecting to have their own. Although Patricia and Margaret had, on many occasions, shared with one another how blessed they felt that Francine and Susan were now part of their lives and spent hours chatting in great detail about their current activities, they assiduously veered away from any in-depth discussions about what the future held for their respective daughters.

When Francine arrived home for Thanksgiving, she had been aloof for the better part of Friday evening and then for most of Saturday morning. It was not until early afternoon when Patricia suggested that the two of them go for a stroll in the hills that Francine began to relax and resume her usual pleasant demeanour. They were standing side by side in the shelter of the blue spruce, and Patricia was on the verge of inquiring if Francine was having difficulties at university, when an obscure feeling pervaded her body.

She sensed that Francine was not alone. All but visibly giving her head a shake, Patricia chided herself for being ridiculous. Her step-daughter, a single figure, was right beside her, and yet Patricia's perception was so strong, it was eerie. It was as if Francine had become possessed, as if another living creature, parasitic in nature, was occupying her body, mind, and soul, to the point of exerting control over her. It was the most unusual sensation Patricia had ever experienced.

Not wanting to break the fragile camaraderie that mother and daughter had re-established, Patricia chose to remain silent. The women stood rooted, gazing over the autumnal landscape where only the willows down by the creek retained any of their colourful leaves, lost in thought. When it was clear that Francine was not about to be forthcoming, Patricia said, "Are you ready to make your way down the knoll and join me for a cup of tea?"

Since her uncles and Patricia had expected that Francine would also spend most of Monday with them, they were surprised when, right after their Sunday Thanksgiving dinner with Sebio and Trin, she rose from the table and announced she was leaving to drive back to Winnipeg. A glance from Patricia silenced Daniel, who was ready to protest her hasty departure. Then, as they were attending to the cleanup in the kitchen, Trin was about to express her opinion when, seeing the stern look on Patricia's countenance, she changed her mind.

From her edifying experience with Jessica when she initially became involved with Edward, Trin understood the reason for Francine's preoccupation, but Patricia's demeanour belied her awareness. How odd. To the best of Trin's knowledge, Francine shared everything with her stepmother from the time she had married Daniel, and she could not help but think the girl would have been bursting at the seams to disclose to Mother Pat that she was in love. What could be transpiring that Francine would choose not to bring her stepmother into her confidence?

*

There were too many days when Michael desired Hope so much that every fibre of his being called out for some measure of relief to quell his yearning. He had neither initiated nor received any communication from Hope since the night he had delivered her to her grandparents. He had not returned to Brandon for his convocation, and had it not been for her devoted music professor, he would never have learned that she had succeeded in her quest to be accepted at Juilliard.

Ian, this year accompanied by Charles, had accepted Michael's parents' customary invitation for Thanksgiving dinner. Dr. Burton was no sooner through the door than he was effusing about Hope's incredible audition during her week in Toronto. Apparently, the trio of adjudicators were stunned by her prodigious talent and could scarcely wait to welcome her to their prestigious school of music.

Marika was convinced that Ian was stealing Charles' thunder, but her son understood that the only reason Dr. Farrington chose to hold back was because of his sensitivity to Michael's feelings. In all the years Michael had worked with Dr. Burton, not only tutoring but also accompanying Hope, the maestro had never accepted that the young man was desperately in love with his protégé.

Later, after a sumptuous turkey dinner with all the trimmings, Charles surreptitiously invited Michael to tour him through the encircling groves of conifer and willow trees under the guise of wearing off some of the excess calories he had heartily consumed. When they were well out of earshot of the others, who had stepped out onto the sunny veranda, Charles said, "I'm sorry, Michael, that in his enthusiasm, Ian paid such little attention to what you might be experiencing in relation to Hope's triumph."

"Please, don't come to Dr. Burton's defence, Charles, nor would I expect an apology from him, because he always refused to be aware of my feelings for Hope. Between you and me, for such a brilliant man and musician, Ian Burton is remarkably obtuse about human emotions. I've been repeatedly amazed by the heights of passion to which he transcends with his music, and yet he's seemingly devoid of affection or pathos for his fellow beings."

"How very astute of you, Michael. It is that exact discrepancy that I ponder every day in my interactions with Ian. My only conclusion is that he chose detachment in order to achieve his potential in music, unlike me, as a means of survival."

They had reached the edge of one of Marika's exquisite floral gardens, where she had strategically placed another of Jonathon's hand-carved cedar benches to facilitate her guests' appreciation of the peace and beauty of her horticultural design. With the unseasonably warm autumn, some of the hardier flowering plants were still in bloom and offered a rich contrast of colour to the dark green leaves of the surrounding willows.

With apparent weariness, Charles sat down and disappeared into the serene landscape. Michael also took a seat, quickly deciding to wait and see if Charles would expound on his last comment. To his surprise, after several moments passed, Charles asked, "How are you doing, Michael? Have you been able to move on with your life?"

Michael had always appreciated Charles's acknowledgment of his relationship with Hope, although he had never made any reference to the reasons for his empathy. Just as he was wondering if the older man might be on the verge of some disclosure, Charles blurted, "I'm the one who left, and it took me years to regret what I'd lost." Then, as abruptly as he started, Charles stopped and gazed off into the distance.

Michael waited. The minutes ticked away, and yet only silence prevailed. He dared not move or speak for fear that anything could destroy the possibility of Charles continuing. Suddenly, he was intent on hearing about this amiable gentleman's life. At last, as if from a great distance in the past, Charles said, "We were so in love. When I received the telegram, we were only five weeks away from being married. Against all odds, I'd been selected to attend the great Juilliard School of Music. In a flash, my entire future was changed, and I was blinded by this unexpected opportunity. Gisele pleaded that we go to a justice of the peace, so she could come to New York with me, but quicker than I would ever have imagined, I became oblivious to her. I was so puffed up with my own importance that I impetuously believed there was no room for her in my life. I was not about to let anyone or anything stop me from fulfilling my destiny. You see, it was all about me, and as swiftly as my chance of studying at Juilliard surfaced, I threw away my love for my beautiful Gisele."

Sitting on the edge of the bench, Michael was fascinated by Charles' revelation, and he wondered if Hope might have been overwhelmed by similar feelings. Was that why she had been so unconcerned about him and their future together? But at the moment Michael did not want to think about them; rather, he was eager to learn more about Dr. Farrington's intriguing past. Perhaps he might even glean sufficient insight to help him cope with Hope's absence until she returned to his hearth and home.

However, when Charles lapsed into a much more impregnable

silence, Michael lost his patience. "You can't stop sharing your story now, Charles. You have to tell me what happened to Gisele."

Even before Michael asked, Charles realized the immensity of his error. Dear God, what had he been thinking? From the moment he arrived, he was aware of the anguish Michael must have endured during the past months. In fact, Charles had been taken back by how much Michael had aged, with tinges of grey on both sides of his dark-brown hair, which was longer than he had previously worn it. He still retained a summer tan from working outdoors alongside his father, but even with Marika's expert culinary skills, the young man was uncharacteristically gaunt. Furthermore, his ardency for hearing about Gisele might stem from a fervent expectation that it was only a matter of time before Hope would come to her senses and choose a life of love and family instead of fame and fortune. How in heaven's name could Charles reveal to Michael that, in her despair, Gisele had committed suicide?

Shuddering as if a shadow was crossing over his grave, Charles rose abruptly from the cedar bench. "Over the years, Gisele and I lost touch with each other," he said before making a hasty departure along the path through the grove of willows to reach the sanctity of the log home. For the balance of the weekend, Charles was as affable as ever, although he assiduously avoided being alone with Michael.

✳

After she caught herself speeding several times, Francine pulled over to a rest area on the outskirts of Portage La Prairie. If she did not calm down and get a grip on her raging emotions, she would not make it back into Alex's waiting arms. She had spent less than forty-eight hours in the home that had been her haven for years, and yet she had never been so anxious to make an exodus from anywhere in her life.

Francine had observed the bewilderment that initially surfaced on her family's faces, followed by annoyance, at least on Mother Pat's distressed countenance. Francine had never witnessed such hurt in her uncles' gentle eyes, but then, she had seldom been so blunt and indifferent to either of them. Nonetheless, her transitory pangs of guilt were erased the moment another image of Alexander Winston III flashed through her mind.

Walking through the browning grasses flowing along the side of the small park, Francine tried to grasp what had prevented her from sharing her exciting tidings with her family. She had met her true love, the man who vowed to marry her, and she had kept any news about him from them. When they were standing on the crest of the knoll overlooking the sheep pasture, Francine sensed Patricia had intuited that she was in love, and still she rejected the perfect opportunity for a mother/daughter revelation.

At first, she deluded herself into believing it was because of the fear that Mother Pat would judge her for being intimate before she had a wedding ring on her finger. Also, she would no doubt be anxious about the possible consequences of her liaison with Alex. Yet, as easy as it would have been to blame her decision to keep her news a secret on the basis of her stepmother's prudishness, and possibly her uncles' disapproval, even as she was returning to the Mustang, Francine knew with niggling certainty that she was not being honest. The root of her deceit went far deeper than finding fault with those who had loved and supported her in all her endeavours for nigh on to fifteen years.

Had it begun with her first invitation to 393 Wellington Crescent? Before Francine stepped into the foyer and observed the huge crystal chandeliers, lofty ceilings, and marble floors overlaid with handwoven brilliantly coloured Indian carpets, she had no idea that a single family home could contain so many commodious rooms, wide hallways, and spiral staircases. Then, on Alex's guided tour to encounter not one but two libraries with oak panelling encasing volumes of books from floor to ceiling, where the more aged tomes could only be reached with a wheeled platform ladder, was almost beyond Francine's most ecstatic imaginings.

Her introduction to the privileged lives of the affluent occurred within her second week of becoming a graduate student at the University of Manitoba. Francine did not have the slightest intention of attending the campus party to welcome new students until a class-mate urged her to accompany her. She did admit that, after one week of eating the unappetizing fare in the student cafeteria, the promise of savoury food had considerable appeal. Furthermore, it could prove to be a far preferable way to meet members of the opposite sex than in the classroom.

Prior to reaching the recreational hall, Francine decided to imple-ment her usual approach of hanging back and assessing the attendees with an air of detachment. However, as she entered the door, a young man accosted her with a tray full of drinks, which he proceeded to tip over the front of her blouse and blue jeans. Reeking like a brewery, with the offending liquid running into her scandals, Francine turned around, ready to make a precipitate exit.

"Oh, I'm so sorry. In my haste to rescue my beverages from that lout behind me, who was hell-bent to abscond with them, I didn't notice you, an oversight that, under normal circumstances would never have occurred. I'll drive you home this instant, so you can change and return to the party."

"That will hardly be necessary, since I live in the student resi-dence," Francine said as she glanced into his robin's egg blue eyes and boyishly handsome face, enhanced by blond hair and a muscular build that qualified him as the most strikingly attractive man she had ever encountered.

"My name is Alex Winston," he replied. "I'll walk you to your dor-mitory, so that when we arrive back, I'll be the first to escort the most beautiful woman on campus onto the dance floor."

To her amazement, Alex not only kept his word about twirling her around the dance floor once they returned, he monopolized her for the entire evening. When, at last, she excused herself to freshen up, Francine walked through the door of the lavatory and actually pinched her arm. No sooner had she done so than she was approached by a gorgeous brunette in a beautiful silk dress. "Who the hell are you? And just what do you think you're doing stealing my boyfriend?"

Months of being subjected to Carole Martin's torment had toughened Francine to the extent that she did not allow anyone to harass her anywhere or any time. "I was always told not to talk to strangers, so until you introduce yourself, I'll maintain my anonymity." At which point, she waltzed out of the bathroom, where Alex was waiting to lead her back onto the floor in a jive.

It occurred to her to ask Alex about the woman who had claimed him as hers, but when he continued to be so focused on her, Francine decided to adopt a literal translation of *carpe diem*. She had never received such undivided attention from any man in her life, never mind the most exquisite specimen she could ever hope to meet. The party was winding down, and when Alex asked her to accompany him to his home for a nightcap, Francine accepted.

The sleek black Porsche would have been an indication of his social circumstances, but by that time, after hours of being enamoured by Alex, Francine scarcely noticed what kind of vehicle he was driving. Furthermore, being a newcomer, she was unfamiliar with the city's subdivisions, although once they were cruising along a well-treed crescent, she began to observe the sizes of the houses and the adjoining property. Nonetheless, it was not until early the following afternoon that Francine learned that Alexander Winston lived in the wealthiest neighbourhood in Winnipeg and that his family's beautiful stately home occupied a major riverbank site, which tiered down in lawns and shrubs to the water's edge.

✳

Almost three years earlier, when Tiffany had presented Derek with healthy fraternal twins, one of each gender, he was convinced their family was complete. As her time drew near, he assiduously limited his court appearances, because he was bound and determined to be her coach during labour and delivery. Office appointments were much easier to delegate, and every morning, he ensured that one of the junior partners was available to step in at a moment's notice to facilitate his instant departure.

Still, as so often happens, the best-laid plans of mice and men go awry. On the morning that Brenda had to rush her daughter to Brandon General Hospital, Judge Franklin required Derek's attendance at a criminal proceeding. Mrs. Thomas, his receptionist was close to wearing a hole in the carpet as she paced back and forth outside the chamber's door. Finally, through the minuscule crack of the opening aperture, she uttered, "Mr. Barclay, your wife needs you at the hospital right now."

By the time Derek reached the case room, scrubbed and gowned, the baby's head was crowning. He clasped Tiffany's hand. "I'm so sorry my darling. Your father requested my presence during a particularly problematic hearing, and I've just been informed." It was doubtful whether Tiffany registered that Derek had arrived, as she gave a tremendous push, and their daughter made her entry into the world.

As her contractions continued, to the obstetrician's surprise, another infant head was presenting. Derek was beside himself with worry about what could be happening when, several moments later, Dr. Walker announced, "Now, subscribing to the notion of ladies first, your son has made his arrival, and I must admit I had no idea you were carrying twins, Tiffany. Allow me to be the first to congratulate the proud parents."

From the moment Marlene Walker had confirmed she was pregnant, Tiffany knew she would nurse her newborn, and she was not about to be deterred with the unexpected delivery of a second baby. Waiting for the placenta to be expelled, Tiffany asked to have one infant placed on each of her breasts. With some adroit manoeuvring by a skilled nurse, her daughter and son were soon attached and beginning to suckle.

Within days of leaving her obstetrician's office after that first visit, Tiffany joined the La Leche League group in her community. During her gestation, she had become fully informed and committed to the obvious benefits of breastfeeding. Even during those initial weeks and months of the twins' lives, when Tiffany felt that every day was a blur of nursing, she refused to waver, because she had accepted that the supply of breast milk she could produce would be determined by her babies' demand.

All four grandparents, including Derek's father, much to the surprise of the others, felt blessed with two grandchildren, especially one of each gender, and proved to be very supportive. As could be expected, every available pair of hands was required, and although the respective mothers had taken over the majority of the tasks for their household's management, the quotidian routines of life for Tiffany and Derek were challenging during their flourishing family's initial year.

Once Sara and Ryan reached their first birthday, their parents began to resume some semblance of normalcy in terms of their sleep patterns. Tiffany had quickly adopted the approach of resting whenever she was not caring for her babes, but Derek could not enjoy such flexibility. There were days, more than he cared to count, when he arrived at work with so little repose that he wondered how he would stay awake during the day.

It was not that Tiffany expected Derek to help during the night with the twins, who awakened every two to three hours to be fed, but rather that he had always been a light sleeper, and when his daughter and son needed attention, he could hardly loll about in bed. Regardless of how Tiffany urged him to stay between the covers, Derek followed her to the nursery, remaining until she was comfortably seated in the rocking chair with one baby positioned on each breast.

Over the past year, both grandfathers had delved into their respective families' ancestry to discover that, as far back as they could explore, neither had a previous history of twins. His adorable grandchildren captivated Samuel Franklin, and it was during their birthday party that the idea began to form in his head. When Sara was not reaching out her little arms toward Derek's father, Ryan was, and for the first time, Samuel was envious of Lawrence Barclay, especially of the fact that he had decided to retire the previous year, shortly after the twins' arrival.

That evening as they were preparing for bed, Samuel said, "Our twins are becoming more and more delightful, but during the festivities, I began to realize how much I'm missing with my long hours of work. My first action tomorrow morning will be to begin the process of resigning from the bench. Surely by Christmas, a new judge can be appointed, and I'll be able to retire."

If Brenda had known that grandchildren would spur her husband to seek retirement from the Queen's Bench, she might have spirited her daughter home from Montreal years earlier to find her way back into Derek's heart. She was not only worried about Samuel's hours of work but also by the demands and responsibilities required of the judge of one of the superior provincial courts of Manitoba. Although he never brought his work home with him, Brenda had conducted her own research to discover that his jurisdiction included hearing the most serious indictable offences and civil cases.

Since he had been appointed twelve years earlier, Brenda had witnessed, with increasing concern, the steady toll on Samuel's health and well-being. He no longer had much time or energy to get together with their friends, and more often than not, Brenda found herself spending most of the summer alone at their cottage on Clear Lake. She hated to go without him, but he had convinced her that it would only be until he had acquired a firm grasp of his new role. From the beginning, what Samuel had failed to comprehend was that every single case presented unique challenges, and more poignantly, that there would never be an end to the crimes humanity could perpetrate against its own race.

Brenda could not have been happier when Samuel arrived home late one Friday evening at the beginning of December and announced that, by the first day of April in the upcoming year, he would be relieved of his judgeship of the Brandon Court of Queen's Bench. After they imbibed a celebratory glass of champagne, he felt duty bound to enlighten his wife of forty-three years that their son-in-law was the new candidate to be appointed for the position. Not two days hence, Brenda wondered if their family might have jumped from the frying pan into the fire, when during Sunday dinner, Tiffany and Derek proudly proclaimed they were going to be parents once again. This time, their longstanding friend, Dr. Marlene Walker, knew that another set of twins was on their way.

*

Never in Francine's life had she ever dreamed she could feel so loved. It was as if every cell in her vibrant young body had been awakened by Alex's caresses. If any of her friends had ever had the audacity to suggest that she would tumble into bed with any man on their first date, Francine would have been incensed. Yet, after Alex gave her the grand tour of the mansion and then taken her to his private cottage near the river's edge, they could hardly wait to cast off their clothing before feasting on each other's bodies.

In the wee hours of the morning, spent from the rigours of their lovemaking, they slipped into a deep satisfying sleep, with neither stirring before midday. Francine awakened first. It took her several moments to realize where she was, even though as she was trying to make this determination, she became aware of how self-indulgent she felt. There could be little doubt that the silk sheets covering her lithe body enhanced her feelings of sensuality, but Francine was quick to recognize that the glow coming from deep within her stemmed from the exuberance of youth, vitality, and fulfillment.

"Well, my little country bumpkin, you're awake. I must say that you sure know how to give a man pleasure. So, do you fancy another tryst before I ring for the maid to bring us a hearty breakfast?"

Francine could not answer before Alex's mouth was all over her face, eyes, ears, throat, and breasts until he had covered her entire body with his hungry kisses. When she thought she could not bear his urgent caresses any longer, he entered her and, once again, they were both carried to the heights of passion. Later, when they were lying side by side, Francine remembered his offer for breakfast.

"Can you really arrange for someone to bring us something to eat? I'm starving, aren't you?"

"But of course. While you're having a shower and making yourself presentable, I'll ask Hazel to bring a full breakfast for two."

When Francine came out of the bathroom towelling her luxuriant brunette hair, Alex stared at her. "Wow, you shine up real well." The words were no sooner out of his mouth than it occurred to him that Francine could have come along at just the perfect time in his life and might prove to be the solution to his parents' recent unrelenting pressure. Alexander Winston III could not believe they were still persisting with the absurd notion that he honour his betrothal to Shannon Riley, the daughter of the Winstons' best friends and his father's lifelong business partner, which had been arranged during their childhood.

✳

Margaret glanced out her living room window at the precise moment a car pulled onto the driveway. She neither recognized the vehicle nor the young man who stepped out once he had turned off the engine. If Susan had not chosen to spend the weekend in Brandon with a girlfriend, she might have considered that a beau was coming to call. Margaret remained mesmerized until she heard the welcoming sound of her new doorbell.

As soon as she opened the door, she was greeted with, "Good afternoon. Is this the Devonshire residence?"

Standing before Margaret was a handsome, athletic, and well-groomed man who looked vaguely familiar, although she could not recall his name or the sound of his voice. "It is indeed. I'm Margaret, and with my husband, James Devonshire, I've lived in this home for nigh on to forty years. To whom might I be speaking?"

"It's nice to make your acquaintance, Mrs. Devonshire, and it would seem that I'm very much in your debt."

"In that case, you'd better come into the kitchen and join me for a cup of tea while you elucidate how you could possibly have any obligation to me."

Both lapsed into silence until Margaret had set the tea cozy along with two cups and a plate of her freshly baked gingersnaps on the table. Seated across from each other, on closer perusal, she realized that, at some time or another, she had indeed met this young man, when suddenly she remembered it was at one of Hope's recitals. Of course, then she knew precisely the identity of the usurper, who had yet to say his name or to look her directly in the eye.

Even though Margaret had poured their tea, her unexpected guest hesitated to partake in the refreshments. "Mrs. Devonshire, my name is Michael Griffin, and it is only recently that I've learned you were forced to vacate your position as principal of Hartney School so the division could hire me. On my way here, I couldn't decide whether it would be appropriate to apologize or to thank you, and your warm hospitality has heightened my incertitude. It never occurred to me that you would invite me into your home and then serve me my favourite cookies."

At that moment, with Michael looking very much like an errant boy who had been caught with his hand in the proverbial cookie jar. Margaret started to laugh. "Oh, my dear young man, for starters, please call me Margaret. Although I admit I didn't think so at the time, I'm the one who should be expressing my gratitude. I've enjoyed this past summer and autumn more than I have since I was a preschool child. During July, I relaxed and discovered hours of solace in my garden, before James and I toured the United Kingdom with our closest friends throughout the month of August. Aside from fulfilling one of my lifelong dreams, I take great delight in the irony that our trip was financed entirely by the Souris School Division. Since my return, I haven't experienced the slightest regret about not having to gear up to deal with administrative hassles and reluctant students come the first September in decades. So, for heaven sake, Michael, drink your tea, and enjoy my home-baked gingersnaps."

More than an hour later, when Michael was getting ready to leave, he could scarcely believe how comfortable he had become in Margaret's presence. She seemed like a longtime family friend rather than a woman who had been dismissed to facilitate his return to the school district. Her parting words of encouragement and offer of assistance at any time remained with Michael over the years to come and confirmed for him time and time again what an assiduous educator Margaret Devonshire must have been during her lengthy career.

*

On the spur of the moment, as Hazel was about to depart his suite, Alex said, "Could you please inform my parents that I'm bringing a guest for dinner tonight?" Hazel had been in service with the Winston family long before Alex was born, and although she knew he would never disclose to his mother whom to expect, she hesitated, hoping he might take her into his confidence, to no avail. There was always enough tension around the elegant oak table on a Sunday evening with select family members in attendance without a female stranger seated in the only vacant chair.

From the moment Hazel informed Mrs. Winston, Hazel was aware her fastidious employer was convinced that at last her wayward son had seen the light. Penelope's brusque comment only served to confirm her expectation. "Tell Cook she'd better make sure the Yorkshire is up to standard for a change."

It was more than an hour later before Hazel noticed the young master exiting his suite with his most recent conquest. The steady stream of beautiful women Alex had been bringing home since he had learned to drive the Porsche his father had lavished on him for his sixteenth birthday did not surprise her. Alexander Winston II had long given up hope of having a son and heir when, thirteen years after the arrival of his daughter, Penelope had delivered a healthy baby boy. Alexander's mother, sister, and all their friends had cocooned him from the time he was still in the cradle, and as the years passed, the crush of females attracted to the charismatic and exquisitely gorgeous youth had incrementally increased, albeit with different intentions.

The staff at 393 Wellington Crescent were all equally fond of the gallant Alex and, in turn, had covered for his indiscretions with the opposite sex. Although, over the years, Hazel and her counterparts— the cook and the gardener/chauffeur—had heard about the impending nuptials between the progeny of the two business partners. If ever any of the loyal personnel had doubts about the advisability of such a union, they kept their own counsel, while unknowingly sharing great empathy for the unsuspecting Shannon Riley.

On the dot of six, Alex brought the Porsche to a standstill behind his brother-in-law's Mercedes on the circular driveway. Stealing a glance to the front foyer as the great door opened, Hazel barely suppressed a gasp, when she recognized the woman to whom she had served a hearty breakfast less than five hours earlier rather than the elegant Ms. Riley. Stunned, the only thought that coursed through Hazel's mind was the hope that Cook had exceeded her usual culinary expertise with the Yorkshire pudding to accompany the standing rib roast; otherwise, dinner would be very strained indeed.

It was oft cited that Penelope Winston possessed impeccable manners, and thus she refrained from any display of impropriety when Alex introduced Francine Stonehenge to her family in the parlour, where they had gathered for a pre-dinner cocktail. Even while struck with horror, she thought, *Where could he possibly have met this waif? And what in God's name would have possessed him to bring her to dinner when he has never brought a female guest to our home, other than when they compelled him to invite Shannon?* She managed to smile in terse acknowledgement. If his intentions were motivated from spite, Penelope would never give her son the slightest satisfaction that he had succeeded.

Following cursory salutations from the other members of Alex's family, they resumed their conversations with no more interruption than when the shadow of a cloud briefly crosses the firmament on a brilliant sunny day. Francine might not have found it so overwhelming if Alex had remained by her side, but he promptly walked toward his brother-in-law to engage him in a discussion about his new automobile. Subsequently, she stood alone in the centre of the oversized room until Hazel approached her to inquire about what she would like to drink.

After what seemed like hours but may have been only fifteen or twenty minutes, by tacit agreement, the family gravitated into the even larger dining room and proceeded to be seated on designated chairs, leaving the lone one at the far end of the table beside Alex vacant. When he padded the velvety cushion of the ornate oak armchair, Francine sat down, remembering to maintain her best posture. She watched in fascination as Alexander Winston II carved the delectable-looking roast, placing succulent slices on each plate before having Hazel pass the first one to his wife, then his daughter, and her husband, and then to his son, while setting one aside.

When but one china plate remained, the lord of the manor moved the blade of the sharp knife to the butt end of the beef roast, slicing off an inordinately tiny dried portion of meat. Mesmerized by his actions, Francine was suddenly reminded of a scene in *Oliver Twist* and had to bite her tongue to stop from uttering, "Please, sir, I want some more." For her part, Hazel's only consolation, when she was required to serve Alex's friend, was she knew from what little remained that the slender girl must have eaten her share of a substantial breakfast not long ago.

*

For the better part of two weeks, Francine vowed that she wanted nothing further to do with Alexander Winston III. She had never felt so humiliated and inconsequential in her life. During her beginning years at Hartney School, and even after she had switched to Souris, there were times when she realized that she presented like a country bumpkin. But she had always been a quick study and soon found she could alter her behaviour by observing how the more gracious and affable students interacted with their peers and the teachers.

Quite simply though, Francine did not have a template for how to act in the company of the very affluent, especially in their domain, not that it had ever occurred to her that it should be different. At the very least, Alex could have prepared her for how she would be expected to dress, so she would not have arrived in blue jeans, albeit he was similarly attired. Still, Francine was aware that the family's superiority and disdain stemmed from factors far beyond the clothes she was wearing. It was apparent that she was being judged because of her lack of social position and respectable upbringing. Although in the brief time that she had known Alex, to his credit, he had not given the impression that he or his family were first-rate snobs.

When Francine did not return his telephone calls and refrained from all extracurricular functions where Alex might be in attendance, she thought she was well and truly done with him. In fact, she was surprised that he even persisted in calling her after that disastrous evening when, as soon as the cherries jubilee were served, she had whispered to him to take her back to her dorm. During the painfully silent drive, she had scarcely been able to wait until she could leap out the door and reclaim the sanctity of her humble residence.

Subsequently, on Wednesday afternoon, ten days hence, when she was returning to her room and spotted Alex coming toward her, she was too late to avoid encountering him. "Francine, wait, please. I've been trying to catch up with you for days now. You have no idea how sorry I am for my family's rude behaviour, and I owe you an apology."

"Other than not telling me how to dress and then deserting me the minute after I was introduced, you're not the one who needs to apologize."

"Rather than become a spectacle, could I please take you off campus for a cup of coffee? I promise I won't impose on you any longer than an hour."

For the balance of her life, Francine would ponder whatever made her consent. She had never reneged on an oath, especially not to herself, but something in Alex's demeanour convinced her that his humility was sincere. Was it his unusual stooped posture or the flash of pleading in his blue eyes? With a flippant wave of her hand, she said, "All right, I'll give you an hour of my time, starting this minute."

To Francine's surprise, from that moment onward, Alex was a perfect gentleman. Once they were seated in the café, he apologized for his error in judgement when he extended his spontaneous invitation. "Never before had I asked a girl to come home for dinner, and I wouldn't have believed how ostentatious and ill-mannered my family could be. It actually took me some time to realize how despicable they were being toward you. It wasn't until my father sliced a portion of roast smaller than what he reserves for his prized German shepherd and then asked Hazel to serve it to you that the truth struck me like a bolt of lightning. On too many occasions, I've witnessed him treat others badly, those people whom I suspect he considers beneath him, but nothing had ever compared to his blatant behaviour of you. I couldn't understand his reaction, because you seem like a really wholesome person. But then, Alexander Winston II has always been a formidable patriarch, and I've never had the courage to stand up to him, so I was just as happy as you were to make our escape."

Long after the hour had passed, they remained sitting in the booth, until Alex asked, "Would you like to look at the menu? I don't know about you, but I'm starving, and the rumbling of my stomach is starting to embarrass me."

✳

For the next three weeks, as soon as they were dismissed from their respective classes, they were inseparable, and yet other than a light peck on her cheek, Alex did not make the slightest advance. If Francine had not enjoyed their lovemaking so much, she might have wondered if she had fantasized the entire night. However, she was readily brought back to her senses by recalling the singed smell of roast beef assailing her nostrils.

When he finally invited her to return to his cottage with him, following a romantic dinner at Hy's Steakhouse and an exciting performance at the Centennial Concert Hall, Francine was tingling with anticipation. After that eventful evening, they made love whenever they were alone, with Francine scarcely ever returning to her dormitory, until she began to feel as if Alex was swallowing her. When she made her obligatory return to her uncles' sheep farm for Thanksgiving, only a shadow of Francine Stonehenge walked through the door.

✳

He had recognized her the moment she entered the front door of the Bristol Aerospace office on Berry Street. It had been years since Robert had seen her, but still, the fluttering of his heart was unmistakeable. Her red hair flamed in the autumnal rays of sun streaming through the windows. When she glanced at him, and he caught a gleam in her emerald eyes, he could barely speak. What could possibly bring Susan Smith into an aircraft firm in the heart of the city? And what were the odds that he would be manning the office during the lunch hour on the day she came?

When at last Robert recovered his voice, the rush of words that flowed astounded him. "I'm sorry. Our administrative assistant won't be back for at least twenty-five minutes. I'm sorry she's not here to help you, and I'm sorry for all the unspeakable grief I caused you years ago. I never ever said that to you until now, and I'm sorry it has taken me so long."

Once Susan realized who had leapt to his feet upon her entrance, she was stunned. It was more than the fact that his appearance was drastically changed. He looked younger and better dressed than she had ever seen him. As she took long moments struggling with her feelings, Susan began to understand that she had never expected to find herself in Robert Wharton's presence again. She had gone through years of anguish, turmoil, and anger before her slow, steady recovery had steeled her mind from his continued existence.

Breathe. Be calm. Take another deep breath, Dr. Donahue's reassuring voice resonated in her head.

In the painful ensuing silence, Robert could not stop himself from staring until he finally accepted that he was the one compelled to speak. Dear God, what could he possibly say to this woman who must still hate him? At last, he mustered the courage to hand Susan a piece of paper and a pen. "Please, write out why you came, along with your telephone number, and leave it on the desk. I'll wait outside and make sure Mrs. Andrews notices it when she returns from her lunch."

As he bolted out the door, he was surprised to hear, "Thanks." Robert froze with his hand on the doorknob. The sound of Susan's voice suddenly flooded his being with poignant memories. Contrary to what everyone, including Susan, seemed to have thought, he had truly loved her, and in his loneliest moments, he envisioned what his life might have been if only he'd been honest about his reasons for buying the Hartney farm in the first place.

Without realizing what he was doing, Robert sank down onto the park bench on a small grassy knoll at the side of the building. He had no idea how long he had been there, so deep was he in his reminiscing about those wonderful months in Hawaii. How they had loved and laughed and lived without a care in the world. He thought those blissful days would last forever, but at least now, he had finally found a measure of comfort and peace.

He was so far away that he had not heard her approach, and when Susan spoke, he nearly jumped out of his skin. "Did you really mean it when you said you were sorry?"

"Oh, yes. I would swear on the Bible that I have never uttered truer words in my entire life."

"Then why couldn't you have said them to me during all those days, weeks, months after my parents' deaths? If only you had expressed some sorrow, shown the slightest bit of sympathy, I might not have felt so isolated, so alone, so totally abandoned. You became self-absorbed, as if you'd turned into a stone, not at all caring that I was destroyed by grief."

"I couldn't cope. I couldn't go through that kind of desolation again. If I had opened myself up to your devastation, I would have come undone again and been right back in that shrink's office and on those mind-numbing pills. I hated myself for being so weak and cowardly, but I had to protect myself. I knew I could not relive my parents' accident again and survive."

Robert felt Susan's eyes boring holes into him until he dared to glance upwards. She was staring at him as if he had just stepped off a spaceship from Mars. "What in God's name are you talking about? I'm the one who lost my mother and father, not you."

"But that's just it! I was trying to recover when I saw that farm for sale in a real estate office and purchased it as a chance to start all over. I was running away from the vehicular homicide that killed my parents and my younger sister in England more than a year before I came to Hartney."

The silence became so heavy it was crushing. Susan felt her knees giving out, and if Robert had not risen suddenly to steady her until she was sitting on the bench, she would have collapsed in a heap on the ground. As he grasped her shoulders, Robert was stirred by feelings he had not experienced for years; emotions he'd struggled to suppress after the police had arrived with the restraining order signed by his wife. Once Susan was seated, her eyes rooted to the grass, Robert stood frozen in front of her.

When she was returning from lunch, Mrs. Andrews happened to notice the chief engineer in her peripheral vision. What was he doing? Who was that with him? Should she just proceed into the office? The air was eerily still, both of them as motionless as if they were sculptured from fired clay. Something drastic had to be wrong.

Dana Andrews had always liked the quiet-spoken young man who had readily ascended the corporate ladder at Bristol Aerospace to become the chief aeronautical engineer. His future had been assured until the horrible tragedy that took his entire family. At the time, she'd thought that Robert had not allowed enough time to recover and returned to work too early to escape his despair. Dana could feel his agony and suspected right from the beginning that he was sinking deeper into a depression. She was subsequently not surprised the day he strode past her without a word and then disappeared for years.

Upon his return, he never breathed a word about where he had been or what he had been doing. She was relieved Dr. Standish had reinstated him and delighted when, months later, Robert had proven that he was capable of resuming the role of the chief engineer of the mechanical division. Dana became quite protective of Robert, often inviting him to join her and her husband for weekend barbeques. Now seeing him standing like a statue in front of a stranger, her rescuing instinct prompted her to act.

Within minutes, Dana returned carrying two cups of coffee on a tray. "Sorry, I don't mean to intrude, but you both look like you could use some refreshment."

Glancing up, Robert did not even begin to disguise the relief in his eyes. "Thank you, Mrs. Andrews. This young woman is Susan Smith, and she's actually here to see you. Could you please take her back into the building with you? I must run along to my office."

✳

She had not given it a second thought when she missed her period in mid-October, but when the middle of November arrived, and she still had not menstruated, Francine began to fret. Neither had ever brought up the subject of contraception, invariably because their passion consumed them from the moment they entered Alex's abode. Suddenly she was besieged with apprehension wondering if Alex did not use a condom, because he'd assumed she was on the pill.

What could she have been thinking? The truth was, whenever she was with Alex, her mind ceased to function, and she became overwhelmed by her emotions. And she loved how it felt. Francine had always lived her life in her head, spending so much time examining, debating, and planning until often she reached a state of analysis paralysis. But when she and Alex and were in the throes of passion, she was free, no longer subservient, and her soul soared.

However, an unplanned pregnancy would bring her spiralling back to earth. Mother Pat and her uncles would be so disappointed in her not waiting until she had finished her master's degree before getting married, although they might be thrilled with the prospect of a grandchild. One Sunday, the only evening now that Francine slept in her dormitory room, she was about to brush her teeth when an ominous sense of dread stopped her in her tracks.

How would Alex feel about becoming a father? Surely, he would marry her and give their baby his name. But what would his parents do when they discovered she was going to be their daughter-in-law? Since that appalling Sunday dinner, Francine had never set foot into the big house. Furthermore, she had blocked Alex's father and mother from her mind, as if they no longer existed. How could she have been so stupid? She was twenty-three years old, and she knew the likely consequence of engaging in sexual relations.

If Jessica had not married Edward and joined him to intern at the Toronto General Hospital, Francine could have sought her ready assistance for a pregnancy test in the university laboratory. She reached for the telephone when she realized Jessica probably still had friends on campus who would be more than willing to help. On the fifth ring, she was about to place the phone in the cradle when it was answered.

"Hello, this is Dr. Wong. What may I do for you?"

"Well, hi, Edward. This is Francine calling. How do you like the big city of Toronto? Of course, regardless of how many interns there are, I have no doubt you and Jessica are at the top of your class, as always."

"It's terrific! Very busy, but we're so glad we decided to have our wedding in the summer before we started our internships this fall. At least on occasional evenings, we get to spend some time together. Let me get Jessica; I know she'll want to talk to you."

The memory of Jessica and Edward's resplendent wedding on the second-last day of June surfaced in Francine's mind. She would always remember how stunning they had looked, Jessica in her traditional red dress and Edward contrasting handsomely in his ebony tuxedo and wide cummerbund designed from the same silken fabric and colour. Her three bridesmaids, the remaining members of the foursome, had been dressed in pristine white satin gowns. Now, as she waited, Francine wondered if that might have been the only time she would wear the virginal colour in a marriage ceremony.

"Oh, hello, Francine. Sorry it took me so long, but I was in the shower. How are you? It's serendipitous that you're phoning. Just at supper, I was telling Edward how much I was missing my four-some pals."

Perceiving the excitement in Jessica's voice nearly rendered Francine to tears. As she gulped for air, she could hear Jessica say, "Are you still there, Francine? Is something wrong?"

Finally, Francine collected herself enough to utter, "Just give me a minute, please. I'm so sorry. I hadn't expected the sound of your voice to make me sob about my predicament."

*

Within a week, Jessica's friend, Dr. Theresa Chow, confirmed that Francine was almost two months pregnant, with her due date somewhere between the end of May and mid-June. The irony dawned on Francine that she must have conceived on their first tryst, because for the next month, she and Alex had abstained from sexual intercourse. As much as she rued her fertility, she knew Alex could not fault her for the absence of contraception during their impetuous initial liaison.

Francine never slept a wink the night after she received the news. She so desperately wanted to telephone Mother Pat and cry on her shoulder, but she realized she was obligated to speak first to Alex. While waiting for the laboratory results, Francine had gone into denial and had not breathed a word to Alex, although they had slept together every night since her appeal to Jessica.

In her tossing and turning, Francine noticed that the time on the clock on the bedside table was shortly after six. She decided to have a shower before Alex arose from his slumber and used all the hot water. Walking out of the bathroom, she was towelling her hair when she heard Alex grumbling, "God, what time is it? Why the hell are you up so early? Can't a man get some sleep in the morning?"

Over the past month, Francine had learned that Alex was not civil until he had consumed at least two cups of coffee. Before returning to the bathroom to dress, she turned on the percolator. What had ever possessed her to wait until the morning to inform Alex that she was going to have his baby? If she had any sense, she would have told him before they started to make love the previous evening, but he was always so insistent about getting her into bed.

By the time Francine arrived back into the kitchenette, the coffee was ready, and after pouring a cup, she sat down at the small two-seater table.

Leaning on his elbow while lying in bed and watching her, Alex said, "My, aren't we taking a leisurely approach to the day!"

"Could you please join me? We need to talk."

"I'd rather screw!"

"Yes, and that's at least one half of the reason we are experiencing our current dilemma."

"Oh, my little English major, why so serious this morning? Come here, and it won't take me long to lighten your mood."

"I'm afraid Mother Nature has determined that it might be a very long time before either of us feels footloose and fancy-free again."

"I hate it when you talk in riddles. Could you just get to the point? And they always say it's men who don't know to communicate."

Francine rose from the table and refilled her cup before she poured a second one for Alex. "Could you please get out of bed? I need you to be fully awake and cognizant for what I must tell you."

"Okay, but hold your horses. I need to relieve myself first, because my back teeth are floating!"

After years of faltering about how to express herself, Francine had eventually learned from Mother Pat and Dr. Donahue that the best policy was to be honest and direct. She waited until Alex had consumed his coffee, in practically one gulp, before she said, "We're going to have a baby in about seven months' time."

＊

After relocating to Winnipeg, Carole had used so many aliases that she started a list to avoid confusing which name she went by at each of the eight new Winnipeg Senior Citizen's Day Centres established by the Age and Opportunity Bureau, which had opened its doors at 368 Colony Street on May 8, 1957. The centres had readily become the hub of educational, counselling, social, and recreational services for older adults. Carole was quick to determine it was essentially women who participated and began to speculate there might be some lonely widows with too much money and not enough to do.

When she first arrived, Carole frequented some of the upscale functions held by the city's educational, hospital, and philanthropic foundations, but she was quick to discern that she would be beyond her depth. The majority of the individuals in attendance were much more sophisticated than those she had previously encountered, with many being married couples. It was not that she doubted her ability to charm the men, but experience had taught her they were not only the breadwinners but also that they managed the family finances. From the onset, Carole recognized that her target audience was women who had never handled money until after their husband's passing.

Before beginning her research, Carole rented a room at the YWCA in the heart of the city. Eventually, when she learned that some of the members at the two most recent centres were women from the prosperous neighbourhoods of South and Old Tuxedo, as well as some from Wellington Crescent, Carole began to divide her days as a volunteer between the two facilities. Consistent with her belief that she was wise to keep her names short and simple, at the Crestwood, she introduced herself as Sandra James, and at the Charleswood Senior Centre, she used the name Kate Stone.

It did not take Carole long to realize there was enough money shining in the shadows of the two centres that, if she played her cards right, she could be rich beyond her dreams. Subsequently, she decided to forego her pursuit of other retirement centres and endear herself to these wealthy widows of Winnipeg.

Arising from her days at the Royal Canadian Legion, Carole found it enjoyable to interact with women of social standing. She had learned to emulate the graces of the upper class during her short tenure at the Royal Oak Inn in Brandon. In fact, her time had proven to be the training ground for her edification, much to her surprise, by means of the process of elimination. When she served condescending customers, she did not like how they responded or how they spoke to her. On the other hand, she soon realized that the patrons of higher breeding had no need for any airs of superiority. They were courteous and gracious, displayed impeccable manners, and even, at times, what Carole perceived as a sense of humility.

At first, Carole could not believe how politely she was being treated and how good it made her feel, until she realized that she preferred positive attention so much more than what she always initiated with her acrimonious approach. Then, when reality reared its ugly head with her untimely encounter with Susan and her lawyer, Carole decided to change her behaviour, and it aided in her lucrative scam of the unsuspecting women of the Brandon Legion's Ladies Auxiliary.

Nonetheless, Carole's instincts tingled with the awareness that these moneyed women from the two most affluent residential areas in Winnipeg were going to be considerably more difficult to deceive. She understood that she would be well-advised to select only two quarries, one at each centre, one from each community, and to allow a substantial period of time to establish relationships of respect and trust. Fortunately, she had sufficient funds in her bank account, with her living and transportation costs low enough to avail her of the opportunity to pursue these essential requirements. In the interim, Carole planned to perfect the details of her fraudulent scheme.

Carole was quick to ascertain that Mrs. Riley was by far the richest widow from either of the programs or communities, not to mention she had the sweetest demeanour of any elderly woman she had ever met. Still, it was her lilting Irish accent that initially drew Carole to her. When she returned to her room downtown the evening following their introduction, she recalled how much she had always enjoyed listening to June Smith. Aside from a subtle difference in her inflection, when Mrs. Riley spoke, she sounded just like her ex-friend's dead mother. It was exactly the sort of omen that Carole would rely on to affirm her decision.

The attraction was mutual. The lovely young woman who was always eager to be her partner at bridge, accompany her to the swimming pool, and provide a gentle massage after her aerobic exercise routine readily charmed Aileen Riley. What delighted her even more was that "Sandra" seemed to dote on her much like her only granddaughter, Shannon, had when she was a child. At first, Aileen was suspicious that the girl might be a gold digger, but Sandra was so earnest and beguiling that, before long, she came to trust her implicitly.

In fact, Aileen soon began to be frustrated that Sandra only came to the Crestwood Centre on Mondays, Wednesdays, and Fridays. "My darling girl, why am I not able to enjoy your company every day of the week?"

"Oh, Mrs. Riley, I also miss you, but I'm committed to the Charleswood Senior Centre on Tuesdays and Thursdays."

"What must I do to entice you to be with me all the time? I so enjoy your companionship, and my very busy family, who have no time for me other than for Sunday dinners, have noticed a spring in my step. Even though I live in the beautifully renovated cottage on their Wellington Crescent property, my precious granddaughter can seldom make the effort to walk across the garden to visit me, and then only when she wants something."

As tempted as she was to only focus her designs on Mrs. Riley, Carole recognized the potential pitfalls. She wondered if the elderly lady might be quite possessive, and she could hardly afford to have someone who would become jealous or clinging. Besides, Carole was keen on getting to know more about Elise Hathaway at the Charleswood Centre. For some time, Kate had been uncertain whether she was the most desirable candidate, until Mrs. Hathaway happened to mention that she still lived in the stately family home in Old Tuxedo.

By nature, Elise presented as the antithesis of Mrs. Riley. She was unpleasant, abrupt, and became condescending when any of the other members gave her unsolicited advice, whether it was a particular move in a card game or the way she was performing an exercise. It was this air of haughtiness that caused Carole to suspect rather than being told what to do, Mrs. Hathaway was the one accustomed to giving the orders, most likely to a maid, a gardener, or both.

Once Carole had selected her two pawns, she realized if she wanted to become intimate with their financial affairs, she needed to spend time with them beyond the confines of the day centres. Not that she thought it would be very difficult. Both women seemed lonely, with a dearth of social engagements, one since her family was otherwise engaged and the other, because she appeared not to have any relatives. Subsequently, when both seniors were comfortable with her, Carole acknowledged that, since she was new to Winnipeg, she would enjoy spending time with them for an evening outing or during a weekend.

Within a week, Aileen Riley had invited her young companion to join her for dinner at the Fort Garry before attending an opera at the concert hall. Concerned that Sandra may not own the appropriate attire for the evening, three days before they were to go, Aileen orchestrated a shopping spree to the best shops in the city. In addition, she arranged an appointment with her hairdresser and aesthetician for both of them right after her morning swim on the day of the event.

When they were leaving the shop, Mrs. Riley handed Sandra a twenty-dollar bill. "Now, dear, I want you to hire a taxicab, so you can go home and dress. When you are ready, please hail another one, and come to my address at 514 Wellington Crescent. Remember to tell the cabbie to go beyond the circular drive and come to my cottage at the waterfront. I'll be watching for you, and then we shall go together to dinner."

Carole was eagerly anticipating her evening out. Her gown, coat, shoes, and matching pieces of costume jewellery must have cost Mrs.

Riley a pretty penny, and Carole had to admit that, along with her new coiffure, she did look smashing. Besides, she had neither eaten in a posh dining room nor attended an opera, so it could prove to be an eventful evening. The stare that the cab driver who picked her up in front of the YWCA gave her when she told him where she wanted to go was priceless.

As they neared the crescent in the gathering twilight, he drove slowly. As unbelievable as the houses and the properties were, Carole was more astounded when, unmistakably, she saw Francine Stonehenge coming out of the brightly lit side entrance of one of the mansions and getting into a black Porsche.

✳

Summer had passed in a flash illuminated by her anticipation of attending Juilliard. Since Hope had no particular reason to return to Brandon, she invited her grandparents to travel to New York prior to the beginning of her first semester. When her grandfather resisted flying to the United States, Hope's grandmother boarded the airplane without him, and the two women proceeded to have a fabulous week in the city fondly known as the "Big Apple." During the days, if they were not engaged in shopping sprees to the major department stores, they were touring the museums, before dressing for an evening of fine dining and taking in yet another performance on Broadway in Manhattan's Theatre District.

Although her grandfather chose not to come, he insisted that his wife and granddaughter spend their vacation in style, and they had subsequently booked into a luxurious room at the Drake Hotel on Park Avenue and 56th Street in midtown Manhattan. The location was superb in terms of their preferred activities, and when the attraction for the day, or the hour, was not within walking distance, they accessed the subway. The week flew by, and on their last evening, they celebrated by dining in and ordering one of the Drake Room's most famous dishes, Steak Nino. Later, when her grandmother suggested they check out the music and dancing in the most notable and successful discotheque in Manhattan, the Shepheard, Hope was only too happy to consent.

The following morning, on the way to the airport, Hope could not shake the encroaching melancholy that threatened to engulf her as soon as her beloved grandmother boarded the plane. She would be entirely alone once more in a huge metropolis that constantly teemed with people. Since the premature death of her mother, Hope had grown accustomed to loneliness, and she hazarded a guess that had she not become intimate with Michael, she might never have known what it was to feel bereft again. But now, especially at night, she would awaken and still long for his caressing arms to gather her to his supple body.

Nonetheless, Hope knew there was no going back. At Clear Lake, when Michael had stood her up, she recognized their relationship was over, and in the long run, it was the only resolution that could work for both of them. Neither was prepared to compromise on what they wanted in life. It was far healthier for Michael to find someone who would love him for all his attributes and fulfill his dream of a wife and family. Regardless of how forlorn she might feel, Hope understood that music would always be her lover and her performances the pinnacle of her aspirations.

During the subsequent taxi ride to the Juilliard School in Lincoln Centre on the Upper West Side of Manhattan, Hope was relieved that freshmen were required to live in the university residence. She had enjoyed the camaraderie in the student dormitory over the past two summers at the Meadowmount School, and it never occurred to her that her classmates would not share the same trust and sociability at the New York school.

When Hope was notified that she was not only accepted at Juilliard but that she had won a full scholarship, she was too thrilled to consider any possible implications of being the recipient of such an auspicious award. Certainly, Dr. Farrington had prepared her that the music program at the famed school was fiercely competitive, but it was not until the end of the first month of the initial semester that she realized her achievement translated into being ostracized by her peers. If Hope thought she had experienced alienation before, she was about to learn the true meaning of the word.

*

"So, what the hell are we going to do now? My father will go ballistic, and beyond a doubt, my mother will have one of her histrionic fits. Are you sure? God, we've only been having it on for a couple of months. Maybe you've just missed a period, and we can wait and see what happens," Alex blurted, leaping out of the chair to pace back and forth in the small kitchen.

"That's exactly what I thought at first. I know only too well how hope springs eternal. But I realized that if I were pregnant, we would need to get married, and the sooner the better. Then, with a little luck, our families won't have too many queries about a baby that arrives a little prematurely. So, I contacted a friend of a friend, and she arranged the testing at the university lab. It has been confirmed."

The shock of Francine's proposal stopped Alex in his tracks. "What do you mean get married? There's no way that can happen. I've already told you that I'm betrothed to Shannon Riley. It's only a matter of time before the date of our wedding is set."

"Well, now that you're going to be a father, be prepared for your life to change. The embryo in my uterus is not the result of immaculate conception, and I've no intentions of being an unwed mother or a single parent."

"Isn't there something else we can do? You can't be that far along."

"Just what are you suggesting, Alex?"

"I'm sure my father has some physician friends who could make our problem disappear, no doubt for a hefty fee, but nonetheless, it would be gone."

"And you're so willing to kill your unborn son or daughter, to destroy his or her only opportunity for life?"

"Oh, my God. Don't say it like that. I don't know if I really want you to have an abortion, but you can be sure it's the first thing that will come out of my father's mouth."

"I suspect that, since fate is forcing our hands, we both have some serious growing up to do, and facing our respective parents is the first step. If you like, we can telephone, and I'll tell mine before we go to see yours."

"You would actually come with me? Remember how, after you met them, you avoided me for weeks? And now you're ready to hear my father tear a strip off us before ordering you to get rid of the baby?"

"Maybe what we need to do, Alex, is take control of our situation, so your parents can't dictate our actions. After all, I'm twenty-three, and you must be around the same age. We're hardly teenagers who haven't finished high school. Although I know Mother Pat and my uncles may initially be disappointed, they'll soon get over it and be happy that they're going to be grandparents."

"Sure, easy for you to say, but how am I going to support you and this kid? Unlike you, I haven't graduated with a degree yet. My parents keep me in spending money and allow me to live here at no cost."

Alex sank into the sofa. Was Francine right? Surely, it was high time for him to stand up to his father and stop depending on his folks. Suddenly, Alex became pensive as a design took shape in his mind, and he started to work out the essential details. If the baby were not due until sometime in June, there might still be time for him to get his life in order. He could buckle down for the upcoming exams and during his last semester, to make certain he graduated in May. Once he had his business degree, with all his father's connections in the city, how difficult would it be for him to obtain full-time employment? Alex had money in trust from his grandmother that was to be paid to him when he finished university, and they could use it as a down payment on a small house. For now, after a quiet wedding, they could manage by living in his cottage. If Francine and her family would go along with his plan, his only hurdle would be to convince his parents, a task as formidable as climbing Mount Everest.

Francine did not disturb the ensuing silence. He stole a furtive glance at her and wondered what she was thinking. However, she stayed at the table and waited. That was one of the many reasons Alex liked her. She was neither pushy, nor had she been full of demands and expectations. She could allow him to be. She was wholesome and unaffected, and best of all, at least from his perspective, she was not a social climber. And he liked her a lot. The problem was, he didn't love her; he knew that Francine would never make his heart soar with undying passion.

Still, Alex was certain the baby was his. She had been a virgin when he had enticed her into his bed. Inasmuch as he was hardly ready to become a father, he could not renege on his responsibilities to support the child. There was little doubt that Francine was fertile, but she was about as likely to have been promiscuous in the two weeks following their first tryst as was the Pope. Their most pressing problem was that, although he claimed to be a devout Catholic, Alexander Winston II would have no qualms about demanding Francine have an abortion, so that his only son could marry his best friend's daughter.

*

Carole would have given anything to find out how her old prey could possibly know someone who lived on Wellington Crescent.

She had not seen Francine for years, and now, to catch a glimpse of her in the most affluent neighbourhood in Winnipeg was near mind numbing. Regardless, Carole instantly understood that she must avoid being spotted by her at all costs.

When Aileen asked Carole to hire a taxi and then pick her up at her home, Carole chose to ignore the alarm bell sounding in her head. She had always recognized the danger of risking a chance meeting with any of her quarry's family members but having an opportunity to view the imposing properties situated on the most prosperous street in the city had piqued her curiosity. *Just this once,* she repeated to herself as the cab driver cruised along the picturesque crescent under the arch formed by the overlapping branches of the towering American elms.

After she recovered from the shock of seeing Francine, Carole broke into a cold sweat as she realized how close she might have been to revealing her true identity. Upon her arrival at Aileen's beautiful quaint cottage, the elderly woman said, "Don't you look lovely? Join me for a glass of sherry before we leave."

As much as she considered that a drink might calm her nerves, Carole quickly replied, "I've asked the taxi to wait. When I telephoned for a cab, it took him so long to come that I didn't want to jeopardize us being late for our dinner reservation."

"Good thinking, my dear, but then you're a sharp little cookie! I'll just have to invite you over another time when you can meet my granddaughter. You and Shannon would really hit it off, since you're about the same age."

"Sure, that sounds like a nice idea," Carole replied, cringing inwardly at the mere thought that she would benefit from meeting this snotty rich girl about as much as she needed a hole in her head. She hastened down the walk without a backward glance and climbed into the backseat through the door held open by the curious driver.

"I must say you're very anxious for us to be on our way. I was going to suggest that we proceed slowly around the crescent, so you can take a look at the grand homes, especially my granddaughter's fiancé's stately mansion."

"Could we please just begin our evening? I'm really looking forward to dinner, because I deliberately haven't eaten since breakfast. Also, it'll be so much more comfortable to visit in an elegant dining room."

✳

It was not until they were seated in the Palm Lounge at the Fort Garry Hotel that Carole began to relax. As a rule, she did not partake of alcohol when she was working, but at Aileen's insistence, she accepted a glass of champagne from the bottle she had ordered the minute they were seated. Carole had scarcely touched hers, when her companion accepted a refill from the young waiter. Always on the alert for clues that might define her patrons, Carole began to wonder if Aileen had a propensity for imbibing.

By the time their hors d'oeuvres were served, Aileen had finished half the bottle and asked for the wine list. "Do you prefer white or red wine with your dinner, my darling girl?"

"Thank you, Aileen, but I'll just stick with this glass of refreshing champagne. I don't usually like the taste of alcohol, and I want to be clear-headed to enjoy my first opera."

As the four-course dinner progressed, and Aileen consumed the better part of the bottle of wine, she divulged more and more about her family situation. Carole started to question if Aileen harboured resentment in regard to her personal finances and dared to delve into the details. "It sounds as if your deceased husband left you ample funds to enjoy the life to which you're accustomed."

The elderly woman became even more responsive. "Oh, yes, Joseph always knew that I like the finer things in this world and promised me that I would have all the money I desired until I joined him in heaven.

'And I did, until my interfering son decided he was going to protect his inheritance."

"But surely, since you are your husband's beneficiary, your son can't determine what you do with your money?"

"That's just it. My ever-thoughtful Joseph never had me 'bother my pretty head' with any financial matters, and he appointed Paddy as the executor of my estate. Shortly after his father died, he told me that I was spending too much and decided to put most of my money in a trust fund. Oh, he gives me a monthly allowance, can you imagine? But I can't take out any more without two signatures. Because he travels out of the country so much, he gave my negligent granddaughter signing authority."

"I'm beginning to understand your problem. Didn't you tell me that Shannon only comes to see you when she wants something?"

"You got that right. Never once has she accompanied me to my bank, even though I've asked her time and time again. Oh, she frustrates me so much. The mere mention of her rattles my nerves. Do you mind if I have a liqueur with our dessert?"

As far as Carole was concerned, she was quite content to remain in the exclusive restaurant. She had no interest in opera, and it was only on the way to dinner that she realized it was likely they would encounter some of Aileen's friends at the concert hall. She had not given enough thought to that probability, and she was annoyed with herself for making such a tactical error. Although she was using an alias and presented much differently from her day-to-day appearance, there was still a good possibility that one or more of Mrs. Riley's sharp-eyed cronies might pick her out of a lineup.

Besides, Carole was beginning to formulate a plan. What if she was able to convince Aileen that she could impersonate her granddaughter? Mrs. Riley must have Shannon's current signature on a birthday or Christmas card, and with due diligence, Carole could achieve an exact forgery, given her past successes. Moreover, she had no difficulty duplicating identification papers. Then, after confirming with Aileen that no one at her bank had ever met Shannon, she would be introduced as Shannon Riley. The longer the evening wore on, the more precise Carole became in the details of her proposal.

✳

They agreed to drive Francine's Mustang to her uncles' farm, because it was less conspicuous than Alex's sleek black Porsche. On the way, he rested his head on the back of the seat with his eyes closed. Not that he slept. His mind was churning with the thought he was just days away from being a married man, and all he had the nerve to tell his parents was that he would not be home for Christmas. Both had given him a skeptical look but refrained from making any comment.

Since that Sunday when he spontaneously invited Francine to dinner, Alex had made it a practice to be unavailable for the ritualistic family gathering. During the subsequent month, his mother made her feelings about his continued absence known, but as each week passed, and he did not arrive, she decided to let the matter rest. Every now and then, she caught glimpses of Francine going into her son's cottage, but when she mentioned it to her husband, his only comment was, "Let him have his last fling before we announce his nuptials to Shannon next spring."

When they telephoned Francine's family from the graduate students' library, Alex stood nervously by her side. The moment she heard Mother Pat's voice, all thought that she would keep her pregnancy a secret went out the window, as she blurted the reason for her call. He felt the intensity of the silence on the other end of the telephone and had to admire the patience with which Francine had waited. If it had been him, he would have felt compelled to offer all manner of justifications to accompany the undesirable information he was providing.

Alex leaned even closer to Francine so that when a response finally came, he was able to hear it. Much to his surprise, the woman he had yet to meet simply said, "What are you planning to do about it?"

Whether it was the relative calm that ensued, or the participants' aptitude for resolving challenging situations, a proposal was in place within the hour. Once mother and daughter re-established their communication, Francine introduced Pat to Alex.

"Hello, Mrs. McGregor," he said after hesitantly taking the receiver. "Francine has told me so many nice things about you that I can hardly wait until I make your acquaintance."

Handing the telephone back to Francine, he slid into the chair on the other side of the small table. Alex caught snippets of their conversation as he slipped into a daze. Was this really happening? Could Francine's mother simply accept her daughter's untimely pregnancy without an outburst or any kind of judgement and then proceed with wedding plans before the month was over? Was he ready to become a husband and father and possibly commit the deed behind his overbearing parents' backs?

When at last Francine hung up, Alex uttered, "Did you have to hammer out all the details of our marriage before I even had a chance to inform my father and mother?"

"As a matter of fact, we did. It's not as easy as you may think to arrange a wedding, especially during the Christmas season. Once the date for the church has been set, you can invite your parents and whomever you want to stand up with you."

"What if my folks want to host the ceremony at the country club in Winnipeg? God, since I'm getting married without their blessing, at least my father might have been able to save face by throwing a big party for all his friends and business associates."

"As it happens, it is neither your father's nor your decision, Alex. Weddings traditionally occur at the bride's place of residence. Now, do you want to hear what Mother Pat is going to try and organize on such short notice? I have a strong hunch that you'll need to be convincing when you break the news to your parents."

✳

Francine's wedding was a remarkable testimony to what can take place when the enterprising women of a close-knit group combine their best efforts. With little information other than it was to be a small family gathering, and with a great deal of speculation, the ladies set to work. As soon as Mother Pat convinced Reverend Walmseley to postpone his Christmas vacation by one day, so he could officiate at Francine's nuptials on December 27, she initiated her telephone campaign, possibly the only time she was grateful for the district's party line. Then, primarily with the assistance of Alice, Trin, Margaret, and Susan, who surprised them with her offer to help, Patricia organized a celebration that far exceeded Francine's expectations.

✳

Two hours after their departure on the Friday before Christmas, Francine slowed down and turned off the highway. Alex opened his eyes to see them approaching a large stone farmhouse. She had no sooner stopped than she was out the door and bounding up the front steps. He hung back, wondering what kind of reception he would receive. He could not believe Francine's family would welcome her with open arms, never mind the man who had managed to impregnate her within months of her leaving for Winnipeg.

He had his hand on the handle when the door was flung open. "Well, hello, you must be Alex, Francine's young man. I'm her Uncle Darrin. It's too cold to sit out here much longer, so you'd better come in."

Later, sitting in front of a roaring fire in a cozy living room, Alex could hardly refrain from shaking his head about the ease with which the formalities had been dispensed. Everything that Francine had said regarding the warmth and acceptance that her family would extend toward him seemed to be true. No arguments, accusations, or threats, all the reasons why he had chickened out time and again whenever he was on the verge of telling his parents and inviting them to his wedding.

Following a delicious meal of stewed chicken and dumplings, it occurred to Alex that he might be well-advised to stop worrying and enjoy the ten days in the homey environment. No wonder Francine was so open and wholesome. Mother Pat and her twin uncles were by far the friendliest adults he had ever met, devoid of pretensions, sarcasm, and comeuppances. Still, in the back of his mind, Alex could hear his mother and father's mockery of their soon-to-be countrified in-laws as surely as if they were sitting in the room beside him.

The evening slipped away, and as the witching hour was nearing, Mother Pat decided it was time they all get some repose before their early start the next day. Francine cautioned Alex that they would not share her loft until after they were married, but when he was ushered into Darrin's bedroom, no amount of protesting would deter the man from sleeping on the living room sofa. Much later, as Alex tossed and turned, he wondered if maybe he was the one who had been unfair. Would his folks have accepted his decision to marry Francine? Would they have chosen to come to their wedding? Was it possible they would be more upset by being excluded? Although his mother's expected hysterics put him off, it was his father's potential anger that scared him more. As the hours passed, Alex began to question if he even wanted to become a married man. Was that the reason Francine had insisted on driving her car, so he couldn't bolt?

*

When Alex stumbled into the kitchen looking for a cup of coffee, Pat was coming through from the dining room, which was a hubbub of activity. "Well, good morning, Alex. I thought we were making enough noise to wake the dead, but I know Darrin always keeps his window open, so our invigorating country air must have facilitated your sleep. I'm just brewing a fresh pot, so it'll be ready in a couple of minutes. What do you like to eat for breakfast?"

"Thanks, but I'll only have coffee for now. It sounds like you have an army of people in the next room."

"Friends arrived a while ago to decorate before we have the men set up tables to hold the food for the buffet. I'll introduce them after you've had a chance to wake up. Francine was awake early and has been outdoors with Darrin walking through the sheep pasture. She was in such a rush when she was last home at Thanksgiving that she hadn't checked on our animals. At least now we know why she was in a hurry to return to Winnipeg. You two have certainly had a whirl-wind romance."

Pat gave Alex a very thorough look and hesitated only a moment before she said, "You seem to be a likeable fellow, and we enjoyed meeting you last evening, Alex." She gathered two mugs from the drying rack by the sink and set them on the table, steaming with aromatic coffee. When they were seated, she said, "I'm going to get straight to the point, because this is likely the only time we'll have when there isn't someone else bustling around. Do you love Francine, or are you marrying her because of the baby?"

Alex almost choked on the sip of hot coffee he was swallowing. Had this woman been in his bedroom during the wee hours of the morning seeing his restlessness and reading his mind? With a cursory glance toward the door, he was relieved that no one had joined them. Unknown to him, Pat had advised everyone, specifically Daniel, that she wanted some time alone with her future son-in-law.

"Of course, I love your daughter, Mrs. McGregor, and she loves me. We're both adults who just got a bit ahead of ourselves," Alex blurted with as much conviction as he could muster in his sleep-deprived state. Fortunately, he was able to maintain Pat's direct gaze.

"We need to know that, Alex, because Francine and her child will never be judged or left destitute if your only commitment is a sense of obligation. I feel confident that Francine loves you, but on the other hand, she has had precious little experience with men. Now, I need you to tell me when your parents are arriving and what arrangements, if any, they have made for their accommodations. With a stroke of good fortune, we've all been invited to have Christmas dinner with our friends in Souris tomorrow, but there is still a great deal to be done."

Alex began to have an uncomfortable feeling that Francine's mother had seen through him from the moment they had met. Suddenly, he realized he needed to think and get his act together within the next three days. "Thanks for the coffee. That's one of the things I need to talk with Francine about, so I'm going to join her outdoors, where we'll have privacy," Alex said, grabbing his coat, and heading out the door.

It was an unseasonably warm day for December, with the sun momentarily blinding Alex when he stepped off the porch. Looking around, he had no idea what a sheep pasture was or where Francine might be. As he wandered past the driveway, the only thought coursing through his mind was how he had to confess to Francine that his parents did not know where he was or what he was about to do, so she and her family should not expect them to arrive for their wedding.

In his peripheral vision, Alex saw a red building, which he vaguely thought might be a barn, when he heard voices. Shading his eyes, he saw Francine and her Uncle Darrin coming around from behind the large structure. With relief, he called, "Francine, wait up. I've been searching all over for you."

"Well, good morning to you too, sleepyhead. I was wondering if you were ever going to roll out of bed."

Without acknowledging Darrin, Alex blurted, "Francine, we need to talk right now. Is there somewhere we can go?"

Thinking that Francine's well-bred young man had questionable manners, Darrin turned to his niece. "I'll catch up with you later and show you the new lamb pens we built this spring. Enjoy my niece, Alex."

"So, what's the big rush that justifies you being rude to my uncle? It couldn't wait until after a brief morning greeting?"

"Sorry!" Alex shouted to Darrin's retreating back. "Oh, God, Francine, I've made such a mess of everything, and we have to try and sort it out."

"*We* have to?" Francine stopped and turned toward Alex with a long searching look.

"All right, all right, I'm the culprit. At any rate, what I have to tell you is that my parents won't be coming, because I didn't let them know we're getting married."

"What? Why the hell didn't you? How do you think that makes me feel? Were you afraid they would stop the heir of the manor from throwing his life away on a country hick like me? I should have known the lord and master wouldn't want to have anything to do with the lowly wench once he had bedded her."

"Please stop it, Francine. I've told both you and your mother that I love you and want to marry you."

"My mum knows your folks aren't coming? You told her before you thought to mention it to me? And how many of your friends will be here? Who's going to be your best man? No wonder you were so quiet on the drive yesterday."

"Francine, please calm down, and listen to me. Until now, I haven't said a word to anyone about our wedding, but we can still make the ceremony work by asking if your bridesmaids' husbands would stand up for me. Sweetheart, I want us to have a beautiful day, and I know that if I invited them, my parents would ruin it for everyone. This way, it will be like we eloped, but we're still having a celebration for you, your family, and your friends. My father and mother would never feel deprived that they weren't at my wedding, but now that I've met your folks, I know they would. You wouldn't believe the preparations that are underway already this morning. But most importantly, Francine, you would always feel sad that you were cheated out of what's recognized as the most important day of a woman's life. So, why don't we go and help with the festive activities to get ready for our memorable day?"

✳

They all arrived, with the exception of Hope, whom no one expected could make it from New York on such short notice. Cassandra had driven to her grandparents' house on Saturday as soon as she finished her morning responsibilities at Barclay & Barclay, the law firm that had hired her after she completed her articles and was called to the bar. Even though she was the valedictorian of her graduating class, Cassandra could still hardly believe that the most prestigious law practice in Brandon had offered her a junior partner position. However, it was well known that the longstanding law practice was desperately in need of highly proficient personnel, since Derek, the last member of the Barclay family, had been appointed to the bench.

Less than a week earlier, when Francine telephoned out of the blue, Cassandra was rushing out the door on her way to the office. When, without preamble, Francine asked her to be her maid of honour, she was so astonished that the only thought to course through her head was that she had neither the time nor the money to buy a new outfit. She did think to inquire if it would be appropriate for her to wear the light-green suit she had purchased for her graduation ceremony. Then, conscious that she would be late for work, Cassandra was about to hastily ask about her impromptu wedding when Francine agreed and abruptly ended the call.

The two friends had not seen each other since the September long weekend at Clear Lake, and Cassandra had no idea that Francine was seeing anyone, much less planning to be married two days after Christmas. Later, when Cassandra had a minute to get in touch with Francine, she realized she did not have a current telephone number for her. A quick call to her mother proved fruitless, and when Cassandra reached her grandmother, she still was not much further ahead. The best Alice Webster could relate was that Pat had enlisted her help to organize Francine's wedding for December 27.

Ever resourceful, that evening, Cassandra telephoned Jessica's mother. "Hello, Trin. It's Cassandra. Do you have a minute to chat, or are you still busy in the restaurant? I'm curious if Jessica and Edward will be attending Francine's sudden wedding, since they're arriving home on Christmas Eve. Have you heard anything about who she's marrying?"

Trin chuckled. "You are ever the lawyer, my dear Cassandra, seeking information obliquely rather than going straight to the source. Although I don't share your inclination, I haven't been any more successful. If you ask me, I'm convinced that Pat doesn't know much more than the rest of us regarding the identity of Francine's suitor. And 'sudden' is most definitely the operative word."

Amused, Cassandra replied, "You would have been a very skilled lawyer, Mother Trin. Is Jessica going to be a bridesmaid, and has anyone heard from Hope?"

"Yes, Jessica will be standing up with Francine, although it was Pat who asked her. She also reached Hope by telephone, but our virtuoso has a Boxing Day recital and can't come. As it happens, that's about the extent of what any of us seem to know, which is rather sad. Our little Francine is getting married, and none of us will have a chance to anticipate and enjoy any of the preliminary events prior to her wedding. As your mother probably told you, Sebio and I are hosting Christmas dinner here in the restaurant for everyone invited to Francine's wedding, so we'll all have a chance to meet the groom, his family, and friends."

✳

When Pat telephoned on the afternoon of Christmas Eve to let Trin know that Francine's young man would not have anyone coming for dinner the next day, she said, "Presumably, his wedding party are planning to arrive then on Boxing Day. Where are they all staying?"

"Alex has just told us not to expect any of his family or friends to be in attendance on Tuesday."

"Really? How interesting! Everything about Francine's fiancé seems to be shrouded in mystery. Well, I guess the same sixteen of us will have dinner at your home following the light reception for the other guests in the church basement after the ceremony."

"I thought I counted seventeen. There are the four of you, five with the Websters, three of the Devonshires, and now with the confirmed five of us. Who have you not included, Trin?"

"Oh, sorry, I forgot to mention that Margaret telephoned the other day to say that Susan was planning to visit her new friend, a woman named Dana Andrews, in Winnipeg for the Christmas season. Even though she was so helpful with the preparations, it might be better if she didn't come. I know that Francine came to appreciate Susan during the three years she drove her to college, but, quite frankly, Jessica never could understand how they became friends. Actually, Margaret hinted when Susan drove to Winnipeg in August to check out Bristol Aerospace, she shared with her, without giving up a name, that she'd run into someone she had known several years ago, a mutual acquaintance of Dana's who she's seeing over the holidays. It all sounds very mysterious to me. Were you aware that when Susan finishes her science degree next year, she's considering applying to the University of Manitoba to study aeronautical engineering?"

"No, and it's funny that Margaret has never said anything about it. But, to be honest, she's still very circumspect in relation to disclosing much about Susan. It's almost as if Margaret won't allow herself to forget how June and Bert died, and she feels guilty that she has come to love Susan like her own daughter. Well, good for Susan! As it happens, over the years, I've also developed positive feelings for her, and I'm happy she's getting on with her life. I hope that eventually Susan meets another man. She's young and could start a family of her own. I think one of the lessons Francine learned during their drives to Brandon was that Susan deserves a second chance. Of course, Jessica never had that opportunity, and women can be so unforgiving of each other."

✳

Enlightenment did not occur until after the traditional Chinese Christmas dinner when Alex stood and asked if he could offer a toast to the gracious hosting family.

"Thank you, Mr. and Mrs. Yang, for this delicious meal. I admit that some of the foods you served I've never tasted before, and it was novel to share your customary dishes rather than having to chew through a dry old turkey dinner seated around a huge oak table in a stuffy dining room. But it was not only your delectable meal. I can unequivocally say that so many warm, fun, and appealing people have never surrounded me in my life, and I certainly can't recall when I've enjoyed Christmas Day so much. Now, without going into detail, I must announce that I haven't invited any guests to our wedding on Tuesday and, subsequently, I have several unusual requests."

Turning first to Darrin, he said, "Uncle Darrin, if I may address you in such a manner in light of my discourteous behaviour toward you this morning, I would like to ask if you would do me the honour of being my best man. Jessica and Edward, I'm very pleased to have met both of you, and I wonder, Edward, if you would consider pairing with your lovely wife in the bridal party to be my groomsman."

✳

The morning of the wedding dawned in the midst of a typical blustery Manitoba day. Francine had a restless sleep, not settling until well after midnight. A winter storm had blown in during the early hours, and strong winds were gusting, along with a heavy snowfall. When at last she rose from the warmth of her bed and peered out the window, she could scarcely see the front of the barn. The previous day's forecast had not predicted inclement weather, and instantly, Francine's mind reverted to the very thoughts that had kept her awake. Was the squall an omen?

Ever since Alex's glib explanation for not inviting his parents, Francine began to wonder about the wisdom of marrying him. She had not realized he was such a smooth talker, and she could still feel the sense of apprehension she had experienced even as he was placating her. Later, when he was conveying the news to her family, although Pat's face was impassive, Francine noticed the flicker of concern in her eyes. Reflecting that she knew so little about him, Francine started to question if she did, in fact, love Alex, or did she only want to legitimize her unborn child? How could she have been so stupid to get pregnant? By twenty-three, she ought to have known better.

A light knock on the door spared Francine from further self-abasement, at least for the moment. "I thought I heard you moving about. May I come in?" Pat asked, peering through a slight opening. "I hazarded a guess that you might appreciate coffee."

Seated at the table in front of the window and comforted by the steaming cup in her hands, Francine said, "What a good thing you arrived when you did. I was on the verge of returning to my bed, covering my head, and staying there for the rest of the day."

"Hmm . . . that doesn't sound like a ringing endorsement for marriage from the bride of the event!"

Francine glanced over the top of her mug to ascertain if Pat was jesting, but the serious look on her face refuted the slightest possibility of banter. How could she have thought otherwise? She had never succeeded in concealing her feelings from Mother Pat, and now, given the precipitate nature of her wedding, why had she considered that she could fool her? Trying to find the words to speak the truth with the least umbrage, Pat indulged her for the second time by saying, "Francine, we'll love your baby as unconditionally as we love you. Your uncles' and my only concern is that you're marrying Alex, because you two care for each other and want to raise your child together. If that's not the case, we'll always be here for you."

"Oh, Mother Pat, you understand me so completely. That's the exact question I've been wrestling with since I've come home. If only we had more time, but I want my son to be born to legally married parents."

"Since you seem convinced about your child's gender, perhaps you should be equally confident about your decision, my darling. Now, we must start getting ready for your big day."

The next five days had all the semblance of being heaven sent. By the time the bride and groom were dressed and in Uncle Darrin's new Chrysler to be driven to St. Andrew's Anglican Parish in Hartney, the weather had cleared. The sun had burst forth in a dazzling blue sky, and if the unexpected gale had been an omen, then Francine was prepared to accept the favourable portent of the ending of the storm.

Reverend Walmseley greeted the wedding party with gaiety, possibly more attributable to his pending vacation to visit his parents in Palm Springs than to uniting a young couple in holy matrimony. He had arranged for two of the deacons and their respective wives to manage the celebration in the church basement and the subsequent cleanup to facilitate his immediate departure for the Winnipeg airport.

Mirth permeated the air, and once the vows were exchanged, the guests adjourned to the lower level of the historic old English church, situated on the western edge of the picturesque town. Alex had immediately endeared himself to its curious citizens by effusing about the classic traditions of austere Anglican church architecture. By the time the wedding party were readying to leave for the McGregors' farm, Alex had charmed everyone in attendance.

He also continued to enchant Francine, her family, friends, and guests for the duration of his initial sojourn to the sheep farm in Manitoba. By Friday, the weather had warmed sufficiently for the newlyweds to don cross-country skis and venture as far as Francine's long-cherished knoll overlooking her uncles' land. Their days were as filled with adventure as their nights were consumed by passion. Alexander Winston III was so taken with the simplicity and ambience of Francine's home and the love of her family that both became confident they could weather the wrath of his parents when they were informed that their son and heir had married Francine Stonehenge in an Anglican church in a small town called Hartney rather than Shannon Riley in the Saint John XXIII Roman Catholic Church in Winnipeg.

The setup at the bank was easier than Carole predicted. She had expected she would encounter little difficulty adding another alias to the existing string of monikers she had used over the past years, and she was eager to experience the sensation of being addressed as Shannon Riley. However, in the aftermath of their aborted attempt to attend the opera on Saturday evening, Carole came close to shelving the entire idea.

Aileen had become so intoxicated that she was almost unmanageable.

Then she began insisting that Carole accompany her back to Wellington Crescent and spend the night. Carole was on the verge of walking out on her when the maître d'hôtel and a middle-aged woman came to her rescue. "Thank you for joining us for dinner, mademoiselle. Anna will now see to it that Mrs. Riley is comfortably settled in her suite. Enjoy the rest of your evening."

As Carole burst out the front doors of the Fort Garry Hotel, she could not believe her feelings of relief. The seven-minute walk down Broadway Avenue to the downtown branch of the YMCA on Vaughan Street was not nearly long enough. She needed to think. She knew she was hardly in a choice part of the city for an evening stroll, but she decided to stride along at a clip conveying the clear message that she was to be left alone.

Carole had no idea that Aileen Riley was such a drunk. She had seemed so classy at the centre. It had not occurred to Carole that one person could consume so much alcohol in one sitting and still be upright, but it was obvious it had happened before. As she strode along, her first resolution was that never again would she socialize with her. The potential pitfalls would be deep enough to bury her. And certainly that was the last time Carole would ever go anywhere near Wellington Crescent.

On Monday morning, she debated whether she would even go to the Crestwood, but in the end, she determined that she would see if she had to completely rule out her plan.

When she arrived at the centre, Aileen greeted her as if nothing had happened. Maybe she didn't remember what a fiasco their first and last evening out together had been. Carole decided to stay and let the week play out.

When Carole returned to the Charleswood Senior Centre on Tuesday morning, surprise news confirmed that she would need to focus on Aileen Riley as her only object of pursuit. It seemed Elise Hathaway had taken ill on Sunday, and when she was rushed to Winnipeg General Hospital, she was pronounced dead on arrival. Apparently, she had suffered from a weak heart for years, and her distant family were saddened that, this time, the medical team was unable to revive her. Making a quick departure, Carole realized she would now retire the "Kate Stone" alias and replace it with "Shannon Riley," albeit only in the limited circumstance of accompanying Aileen to the bank.

Even as she reached her decision, Carole recognized that the stratagem she was about to develop would be her most complex duplicity to date and would require the utmost intricacy to pull it off. No more foolish mistakes, such as accepting social invitations to see how the other half live or placing herself in any situation where Aileen had access to alcohol. Carole had imbibed to a state of drunkenness only once in her life. The hangover the next morning was bad enough, but the fact she could not remember her actions convinced her she would never drink to excess again. The total loss of control in whatever had happened still scared her to this day.

Realizing that her first requirement would be to practice forging Shannon's signature, before she left on Wednesday, Carole asked Aileen to search for a document to bring with her for Friday morning. True to her word, the older woman brought along a receipt that Shannon had signed for a delivery to the house. Thanking her, Carole quickly tucked it away in her purse. Although the writing on the duplicate was faint, she explained that, over the weekend, she would begin by tracing over it with a sharp pen until she had a clear impression. Then she would copy it time and time again until she had mastered Shannon's handwriting, to the extent that no one would be able to discern the difference.

Finally, the following Friday, when Carole caught up with Aileen at the centre, she led her to a secluded corner of the art studio. "Whenever you want to go to your bank, I'm ready," she whispered. "But before we set a date, are you absolutely certain that Shannon has never been to that branch with you and that no one there could identify her?"

"You must be kidding, my dear! Shannon has refused to be seen anywhere alone with me since she became a teenager, and that was ten years ago. So, you can lay your concerns to rest."

✳

During her week of preparation, Carole had focused on her plan from every possible angle. She debated if she might be well-advised to isolate an inexperienced teller, preferably a younger man, who might serve as an obsequious insider. Once she had earned his confidence with a heavy dose of flattery, he could be very helpful from the moment Aileen introduced Carole as her granddaughter and cosigner, Shannon Riley.

On the first Friday before they proceeded to the bank, Carole hailed a taxicab to take them to an obscure coffee shop she had previously sought out on Ness Avenue within a short walking distance of the Bank of Montreal. Once they were seated, she explained that they should not be driven to the front of the building every week, in case someone started to notice their established pattern. Of course, Carole had considered that, following two or three weeks of both of them tediously traipsing back and forth to the bank late on Friday afternoons, Aileen might elect to give her a signed cheque and just send her to collect the money.

By the time they had walked the three blocks to the bank, Aileen was winded. "Are you sure this is necessary? Who's going to care if we arrive by taxi every week?"

"Listen, Aileen, if you want me to help you withdraw your money, you'll follow along with my proposal. The last thing we want is for anyone to become suspicious about what we're doing."

"Okay, I hear you. I'm so glad though that Jimmy has it set up for me to do my banking in his cubicle, where I can sit in a comfortable chair rather than stand in line with the rest of the customers."

"Who's Jimmy? You never said a word about having any private arrangement, and didn't you say you couldn't take money out of your trust unless Shannon was with you? Won't he be surprised to meet me?"

With a sinking feeling, Carole realized she had been so busy formulating her strategy that she did not consider that even if Aileen was unable to access her trust fund, it was quite conceivable she could have a chequing account at the branch. In that event, she would be well known by practically everyone in the bank. Bloody hell, what was she getting herself into? How likely was she to be caught and subsequently sent to jail for years?

Carole emerged from her misgivings to the sound of Aileen's hearty laugh. "Don't look so despondent, my dear. Jimmy Reeves is the sweetest fellow you'll ever encounter, and he will do anything I ask. Just wait until he meets you; he'll fall head over heels in love with you. I believe you're underestimating me. Remember, I've been around the block more than a couple of times, and I assure you that I'm very much aware of the potential implications of our little subterfuge. In fact, I would hazard a guess that you and I are not as different as you might think. I suspect there is a touch of the con artist in both of us. So, why don't we work together, and I promise you'll be well rewarded for your little impersonation."

The truth was that Aileen was far too superior to entertain even the slightest notion that this young whipper-snapper from the country could ever outfox her. When Joseph Riley had arrived in the city as an immigrant, he did not have two pennies to rub together. By the sweat of his Irish brow, he had earned enough money to purchase and operate a small pub along Portage Avenue. Then, throughout his life, every time he had any extra cash, he invested in real estate, becoming a shrewd entrepreneur. Although she had never been expected to handle money, over her many years of serving and listening to her husband's corporate associates, Aileen had realized that the world can be full of trickery, and she recognized the necessity of exercising caution in her business affairs.

✳

When Robert fled toward his office, Dana sat down, handed a coffee to Susan, and took a sip from the second cup. Both of them had long since finished their beverage, and still Dana waited. Who was this woman, and why had she had such a profound impact on Robert? She had not seen him so agitated since the day he had vanished for three years. Since his return, Robert had re-established his equanimity, and Dana Andrews would be damned if she was going to allow this stranger to destroy it.

At last, Susan spoke. "May we please go to your office? I have some forms with me that I need your assistance to complete. Currently, I'm a third-year bachelor of science student at Brandon College, and I'm submitting my application to the University of Manitoba to pursue a degree in aeronautical engineering after I graduate."

"Well, you've certainly come to the right place. We have one of the best in western Canada in Mr. Wharton."

"That's a huge surprise. I had no idea Robert was an engineer. No wonder he wasn't very interested in farming," Susan said more to herself than to the middle-aged woman walking beside her.

"I'm sorry, what did you say? Why would farming have any appeal to Mr. Wharton? As I said, he is recognized as one of the brightest aviation minds in the industry."

"That's where we met, on the farm he purchased in the Hartney District, driving up in his bright red convertible as if he owned the world."

The women had reached the front of the office. As Dana opened it, Susan recalled how fascinated she had been when she discovered there was an aircraft company located in Winnipeg. She had been debating what she wanted to do after she finished her science degree when she attended one of the many career fairs scheduled every spring on campus. Susan happened upon the session with a representative from Bristol Aerospace, and midway through realized she'd found her calling. The following day, as soon as her classes were over, she proceeded to the college library and immersed herself in the firm's intriguing history. Entering the building, she was struck by the strange coincidence that she should encounter Robert Wharton on the premises.

Dana had quickly determined that this beautiful girl with the sensational red hair and emerald eyes could be the key to the mystery that had surrounded Robert's whereabouts during his lapse from the firm. She glanced at the wall clock as she ushered Susan inside and unobtrusively slipped the sign from "open" to "closed." It was approaching two o'clock, and soon her day would officially be over. Besides, Robert was the last staff person on site, and Dana did not think he would venture anywhere near her, just in case she was still with the enigmatic visitor.

"While you're gathering your necessary forms, would you care for another coffee? Or I have cold soda in the fridge. You could not have chosen to come on a better day, because Friday is often a quiet afternoon, with most of the executives and engineers having already left for the day. So, I'm at your disposal, and we can complete those papers in the staff lounge."

Dana did not have the slightest notion of focusing on any mundane documents. As soon as they were comfortably seated, she planned to put the diffident girl at ease, and then she fully intended to find out everything she could about her. Although Dana had never been blessed with children of her own, not a single young person, male or female, had come through the doors of Bristol Aerospace who and not benefited from her solicitude and attention. However, she was surprised, given how upsetting Susan's presence had been to Robert, that she was motivated to offer either to this apparent interloper. Still, Dana's instincts told her that there was much more here than what first met the eye, and few could unravel a riddle as capably as her. Her first clue was how seemingly lacking in confidence Susan was for a woman with her exquisite appearance and presumed intelligence. Dana had a niggling feeling there was something vaguely familiar about her, but she could not grasp what it was. However, if she could establish rapport, she might be able to encourage Susan to confide in her.

What started with a simple question, "Tell me again about meeting Robert?", developed into a subdued conversation and eventually into a heartbreaking disclosure of the time Susan had known Robert, until, two hours later, Dana was ensconcing Susan in her arms as the young woman wept. All the while, at the back of her mind, Dana could not stop thinking, *How could two young people experience so much tragedy in their lives, and how strikingly similar were their circumstances?*

Finally, when it was nearly more than she could bear, Dana managed to alleviate Susan's distress enough to take her to the washroom and wash her face with cold water. "I'm sorry, Mrs. Andrews. I thought I had moved beyond my despair, but seeing Robert today brought all these feelings back. And I completely forget my therapist's directions about how to get a grip on my emotions. I'm so sorry."

"Don't be, my girl. Sometimes even the best psychologist doesn't understand that there's nothing like a good wailing to rid the heart and soul of its sorrow. Are you feeling better?"

"Yes, thank you. Oh, what time is it? I've taken up such a lot of your day. I'm very sorry."

It was late afternoon. The traffic along Portage Avenue would be horrendous with Winnipeggers vying to leave for their weekend getaways. By the time Susan reached the city's outskirts, the brilliant prairie sun would be on its descent, and she would be driving the entire way with it glaring off her windshield.

"Please, Susan, stop apologizing. Instead, tell me your plans. Presumably, that's your car in the parking lot. Where are you planning to go?"

"I'll pick up a teen burger and drive back to my godparents' farm. I should be home before dark."

"Good heavens, from what you've said, they're more than two hours away on that busy highway. No, we'll telephone to let them know you're staying over with my husband and me here in Winnipeg and that you'll arrive home tomorrow." Even as she was about to extend her offer, Dana knew there was a great deal of unfinished business between Robert and Susan, and she was the one person who could assist them to find a path to completion.

✳

Alex and Francine were well past Headingley before he uttered a single word. When they started on their way back to Winnipeg, she had expected and tried to make conversation, but her husband was as silent as a stone. She was astounded. How could a person be so outgoing and effervescent for five days and then become as reticent as a cloistered monk the next? Not for the first time, and far from the last, Francine was convinced she must be the reason for Alex's fluctuating moods.

When Alex finally spoke, it was fortunate that she was driving the speed limit of twenty-five miles per hour, or she may not have been able to avoid veering into the ditch. "Could you please drive me to Wellington Crescent, and do you mind staying over at the dorm tonight? I need to have it out with my parents, and I'd rather you weren't on the premises for the ugly scene that I know our news will cause."

"I don't have a room at the dormitory anymore. For obvious reasons, I didn't renew it as Mrs. Alexander Winston the Third."

"Well then, could you bunk in with one of your friends for the night? I promise we'll be together in my suite tomorrow." Francine had come to a stop for a red light, and she turned to glance at Alex. She was on the verge of saying, "How can you possibly call that two-room cottage on the edge of the riverbank, overshadowed by the grandeur of your parents' mansion, a suite?" when she decided to maintain their tentative peace.

When Francine began the ascent up the circular driveway, Alex let out a groan. He had forgotten that it was Sunday, and, sure enough, as they approached, he spotted his wimpy brother-in-law's Mercedes by the front entrance of the impressive edifice. Just what he needed. It was unnerving enough his mother would hear every word, never mind that Leigh and his sister would bear witness to the full extent of his father's tirade.

✳

"Where the hell have you been? I was just on the way to my study to telephone the police chief and ask him to activate the Missing Persons Unit that he's so eager to launch. You couldn't have called, if not to wish your family Merry Christmas, at least to tell us what was happening to you?" Alexander II roared as he caught a glimpse of his son coming through the heavy oak door as if he was a fugitive. "Have you eaten? You may as well join us in the dining room. Dinner is still on the table, not that any of us had much of an appetite worrying about the prodigal son and sole heir to the family fortune."

"Oh, thank you, Father. I always suspected you wouldn't leave me much in your will," Priscilla said with rancour. "It's just as well Leigh and I don't need handouts from you, not like your precious son will undoubtedly always require.”

“Stay out of this, Prissy. At the moment, I don't have the slightest interest in your inheritance, although if your brother doesn't come up with a convincing reason for his extended absence, you might be the recipient of all my wealth.”

While Penelope glared at her husband, her years of marital experience prohibited her from retorting. “That's what you think? I intend to spend most of it after you're gone.”

Alex slide into his customary chair. Reaching for the piece of roast beef that his father had likely, sliced for him out of habit, he hoped his sister would prolong the debate. He suddenly realized he was starving, and he knew he might be able to defend himself more effectively if he had some sustenance.

“Stand up and be a man. I'm waiting. What have you been up to for the past ten days?”

“For your information, Dad, I got married. As it happens, Francine comes from a warm, loving family, and I had the most enjoyable wedding and the best Christmas holiday of my life,” Alex said, taking another bite of meat.

Alexander II stared at his progeny as if he had suddenly sprouted another head. “What in God's name are you nattering about? We spent the better part of Boxing Day at your fiancé's, and Shannon was at home, unlike some people's children, to graciously help her parents host their open house.”

“Well, then you have proof positive that she didn't become my wife.” To his surprise, Alex was actually beginning to enjoy his father's reaction. His face was turning bright red, and his neck was straining his collar until he looked as if he might have what his sister used to call a “hissy fit.” Remembering his mother had mentioned that his father recently started on medication for high blood pressure, Alex felt a momentary pang of guilt, but it was short-lived.

"Just who the hell did you marry?"

"Actually, Father, you met my wife once when I invited her to join my welcoming family for Sunday dinner. Fortunately, I spared her from your hearty congratulations for our memorable occasion. Francine is staying at the university dormitory for tonight."

"Are you *stupid*? Surely you didn't marry that rustic peasant who couldn't even decide which fork to use for her salad! Do you need your head examined, or should I arrange to have you admitted to the Brandon Hospital for Mental Diseases? For God's sake, tell me you're just trying to give me a heart attack, so you can have my money now."

"I'll be bringing Mrs. Francine Winston to my cottage. You know that historical abode for the past maids of the manor you so kindly bequeathed to me, although as soon as I graduate with my degree, we'll be looking for a house in which to raise our impending family."

"Are you saying the girl is pregnant? For heaven's sake, is that the reason you married her?" Before his son could respond, a light went on in Alexander's head, and he knew he had found the loophole to release Alex from this unsavoury marriage.

✻

"Get into my office now." Startled by the sudden order, Alex stood staring at his father. "Right this minute!" Alexander said as he pointed to the ornate entrance of the study as if his son had no previous knowledge of its whereabouts. Alex had experienced more than his share of disconcerting encounters, especially over these past few years with the patriarch of the family behind that door, and his instincts were clamouring that the worst had yet to come.

"My first action tomorrow morning will be to contact the office of the Roman Catholic Archdiocese of Winnipeg and request a meeting with Archbishop Paul Morell at his earliest convenience. I intend to request an annulment of your ridiculous marriage to that Francine

Stoneboat, and I want the proceedings to begin at once."

"Her name was Stonehenge, not 'boat!' And, there is no way you can annul our marriage. We were wed in a proper church with a minister officiating and had the required number of witnesses when we signed all the necessary documents. For your information, everything was perfectly legitimate."

"Almost four years of university, and you're still so naïve about the ways of the world! You don't have the faintest idea that you have just said the operative word, which fits one of the well-defined canonical grounds for marriage annulment. Furthermore, in the dining room, it was you who identified the specific canon."

"You don't know what the hell you're talking about. How much 'ceremonial' wine did you drink for dinner?"

"Well, big shot, instead of wasting your time in a classroom, you would have been better off listening to me. Not only am I very cognizant about what I'm saying, I've also seen a recent application successfully enacted on precisely the same grounds." Opening a drawer on his massive walnut credenza, Alexander pulled out an official document, and read it out loud. "Total wilful exclusion of marriage (Canon 1101, sec.2.) You or your spouse did not intend to contract marriage, as the law of the Catholic Church understands marriage. Rather, the ceremony was observed solely as a means of obtaining something other than marriage itself, e.g., to obtain legal status in the country or to legitimize a child." He looked up at Alex. "As I recall, it only took Paddy Riley a little more than three years to get rid of that gold-digging Italian Shannon married during her summer sojourn in his country."

"That can't possibly be true," Alex finally managed to say. He was dumbfounded by what his father had read, never mind that it was Shannon's marriage that had been annulled. "I don't believe you for one second. For my entire life, you have boasted about all the things you've seen, said, and done, but I'm no longer that little boy who clings to your every word. I've questioned your credibility for years, and I concluded long ago that you were full of blarney, no doubt inherited from your Irish mother."

No sooner were the words were out of his mouth than Alex recognized that he had committed a critical mistake. Alexander Winston II was opinionated, overbearing, and vociferous in all aspects of his life, but he was absolutely intolerant of anyone expressing anything even slightly unfavourable about his revered dead mother. Everyone who knew him was well aware of the overwhelming sacrifices she had made in her marriage to his father and had the sound sense to never even skirt any reference to her.

"You think I need your belief or approval? I'm the lord and master of my own estate. I have immense wealth with all of the influence and power that accrues to money and position, and I would worry about what my useless son thinks of me?" Alexander bellowed.

Knowing he had awakened a sleeping lion, Alex decided to fight back for a change rather than acquiesce to the oppression of his dictatorial father. He would be damned if he was going to allow his old man to behave toward his wife like she was some outcast! Was that not the very reason why he was so sensitive about what Alex's grandfather had done to his grandmother? This was the same man who had spurned "Lord" Winston's wealth, because he had treated his mother as if she were displaced from the leper colony on the Greek island of Chios.

"I don't give a damn what you do. I married Francine, I'm the father of her baby, and tomorrow, I'm bringing her to live with me."

Even with the solid door of the study securely closed, he was certain the others in the dining room could hear his father's uproarious laughter. Alex decided he'd had more than enough of his father's derision and started toward the door.

Although he did not get very far, at least it spelled the end of his father's laughter. "Get your ass back here. There is no way on God's green earth you'll ever walk out on me. I don't give a damn what you do with your 'wife' now, but when the annulment is finalized, you'll sign the papers. Furthermore, not one word of our conversation leaves this room, got it?"

"Why the bloody hell would I ever say anything? You'll be a grandfather before the Catholic Church will succeed in nullifying my bona fide marriage in St. Andrew's Anglican Church in Hartney."

"Terrific! Thanks for saving me a long-drawn-out hassle. There is another way, and with a much shorter waiting list. I know damn well that you didn't seek the required exemption, so it'll be considerably quicker for Archbishop Morell to enact Canon 1108, sec.1." He quoted again from the document. "'Catholics have to marry in a Catholic wedding ceremony which is celebrated by either the bishop, the parish priest, or another cleric delegated by either of them. If they fail to do so and marry in a non-Catholic wedding without obtaining a dispensation from the bishop in advance, the marriage is invalid in the eyes of the Catholic Church.'"

"Do you make up stories as you blab your way throughout the day? You've told me ad nauseam about the arranged nuptials between Shannon Riley and me, and now you glibly state that my betrothed has already been married. What made you think that I would accept 'used goods?' At least Francine was a virgin when I first took her."

"Well, you sure as hell weren't! At any rate, none of it matters, because as I just read, your wedding is invalid, so the only document you'll be signing is the marriage certificate to Shannon Riley. Then our respective family fortunes will be secured for generations to come."

"I've just said that I'll honour my marriage to Francine and take responsibility for my child. You know, old man, you better get your hearing checked."

"I've had enough of your lip and even more of your stupidity. Of course, you will sign every paper I set in front of you, Alexander

Winston III, or I shall cut you off without one red cent. You don't have the balls or the hunger to amass your own riches, as I did. What will you do? You'll be out on the street—no monthly allowance, no Porsche, and I'll even make it impossible for you to get a job within the Winnipeg business community. But worst of all will be no inheritance. So, who wields the power? Now get out. I want to enjoy my brandy in peace."

*

After a delicious breakfast of whole wheat pancakes topped with fresh blueberries and leftover honey-glazed ham, Dana convinced Susan to follow her to the Bristol Aerospace office before returning home. She knew Robert would be waiting for their morning coffee, and even though she had yet to figure out the best approach to ensure that he and Susan at least talked to each other, she had a vivid picture in her mind not only of the academic advantages for Susan but also of the potential personal benefits for both of them.

Ever since John Glenn Jr. a United States Marine Corps aviator, engineer, and astronaut had orbited the Earth, circling it three times in 1962 in his Mercury capsule *Friendship 7*, the competition to enrol in the aeronautical engineering degree at the University of Manitoba had been fierce. Since Susan was about to begin her junior year for her bachelor of science, she might be well advised to consider changing some of her courses, if possible, in preparation for the associate in science in aeronautics degree, currently offered on the Winnipeg campus.

Still, Dana had her qualms regarding Susan's chances about being accepted even into the associate degree program, unless she had some help. Without Susan mentioning her grade point average, Dana had little doubt but that she would be near the top of her class. More than likely, her chosen field of science and her subsequent specific courses would create the real challenges, not Susan's academic capabilities.

Following dinner on the Friday evening, the women had left Joel on kitchen cleanup while they went for a leisurely stroll about the grounds of the well-treed acreage. Contrary to her expectations, Dana was quite drawn to the soft-spoken, self-effacing youth, although, given the desolate events of her life, Susan had ample reason for her serious demeanour. How had she ever been able to survive and recover enough to pursue the new direction of attending university?

But then Dana had often wondered the same about Robert. Surely if Robert and Susan had each found the strength to overcome the tragic deaths of their respective parents, they could find a way to rebuild their relationship. She knew Robert well enough to believe he would neither have taken his feelings for Susan nor their marriage lightly, and when it ended, he must have experienced severe angst and despair. Nonetheless, Dana knew that if she asked him, he would readily help Susan to complete her application and, furthermore, provide a letter of recommendation.

The question was how she could ensure that Susan would be willing to accept his help and advocacy. The last thing Dana wanted was to recreate any animosity between Robert and Susan. She had been considered the diplomat of Bristol Aerospace for as long as anyone in the firm could remember, but on this occasion, she was stymied because of her limited knowledge of Susan. If only she had more time to familiarize herself with the woman walking by her side, but both were approaching their respective vehicle.

At that moment, the brilliant morning sun happened to shine on Susan's crimson hair, highlighting auburn flecks interspersed through-out its deep red colour. Looking at her in the resplendent light, Dana uttered, "My, God, you are beautiful. No wonder Robert fell head over heels in love with you!"

"What did you say? Did Robert tell you that?"

"No, but Robert wouldn't have married you unless he loved you.

During the week, he seldom takes a break, but when he returned to the company, Saturday mornings became our time. I've come to know him very well, and I believe he'll do whatever he can to promote your acceptance into the aeronautical program at the University of Manitoba."

"What could he do? Oh, how I wish he had been able to talk to me when I needed him the most. He just shut me out, as if I didn't exist. Why couldn't he have been honest with me from the beginning?"

"My dear child, pardon the cliché, but hindsight is twenty-twenty. Let's drive to the office, where Robert is waiting, and you can speak to each other now."

"I'm so sorry, Mrs. Andrews, but I don't have the courage to face him today. Thank you for your warm hospitality and your willingness to seek his assistance, but I'm just going to drive home. I'll look at the application again on my own, and maybe I'll come back at a later time."

∗

Following a restless sleep, Francine awoke shortly after nine. The first thought that flashed through her mind was whether she would hear anything from Alex. Fortunately, the guest room at the dormitory had been vacant, but it was booked for the remainder of the week. Had she known she was going to be abandoned the minute they reached the city, she might have kept the bed-sitter she had managed to rent in the fall. At the same time, it occurred to her that maintaining an option would have been a smart idea regardless of Alex, likely more so because of her pending reception by his family.

She was becoming agitated, and after a light breakfast, she decided to venture out for a stroll around the nearby park. The wind had stopped gusting, and the sun had chased away the low-lying clouds, offering an invitation of warmth. Francine was intent on having a healthy pregnancy, and she planned to embark upon an invigorating daily walk for her health and that of her baby. She had just exited the door and was on her way down the stairs when she was nearly bowled over by Alex bounding up the steps two at a time.

"Oh, thank God, you're still here. I was afraid I would miss you. My father issued an ultimatum last night, and I must have been awake until four this morning. I have to say that some vigorous lovemaking would have calmed me down. But for now, why don't you grab your luggage, and we'll drive both cars to the Salisbury House on Pembina for brunch. We'll have the rest of the day to get settled at our place and catch up on our marital relations after we've eaten. What a lucky break that classes don't start until tomorrow!"

"Didn't you say your father gave you an ultimatum? Do you still have a home to go to, or are we looking for a place to live?"

"My cottage was not the topic of his demands, but let's talk about it over some food. I'm starving, and I've only had one cup of coffee."

When they were seated at a table near the window, Alex persisted in engaging Francine in any and every possible subject of conversation. He'd recognized his error in mentioning the previous evening's encounter with his father. He did not intend to breathe a word about the invalidity of his marriage to any living person, and certainly never to Francine. Not for one moment did Alex believe it would ever come to pass.

By the end of their first week back in Winnipeg, Francine and Alex had established a routine that was tactfully facilitated by Hazel. At every opportune time, she discreetly filled the refrigerator, and close to the dinner hour, the oven, with food, so the young couple would not be burdened with the onerous tasks of shopping and preparing meals. While she was in the cottage, it took precious little time to tidy and clean, and it was just as easy to gather their soiled clothing and add the items to the household laundry as it was for them to waste essential hours at the laundromat on Portage Avenue. After all, both had very busy schedules at the university.

The second trimester of Francine's pregnancy was heavenly. She could not recall ever having felt so healthy and exuberant. Her friends and classmates chided her she was blossoming and that she should seriously consider birthing a houseful of children. Furthermore, she and Alex were enjoying a honeymoon period of marital bliss. Francine never went near the big house, nor did Alex's parents ever deign to walk across the sloping grounds to welcome her into the Winston family.

Still, Francine could not believe her lucky stars. They were very cozy in Alex's cottage, which appeared much more spacious than it was, because Hazel maintained impeccable orderliness and cleanliness. A small mahogany desk and a comfortable chair were situated in front of the bay window overlooking the Assiniboine River and made an ideal location for her writing assignments. As she became heavier during the final months of gestation, Francine found coming home a pleasing alternative to studying at the university library.

In the middle of April, when Mother Pat and Uncle Daniel decided to spend Easter with them in Winnipeg, they booked into the Viscount Gort Hotel on Portage Avenue. During the first three days of their week-long visit, Alex joined Francine and her parents for meals and sightseeing. However, on the fourth morning, when they had a full day of activities planned, beginning with a tour of the Manitoba legislative building, followed by an early afternoon stroll through Assiniboine Park, and culminating with dinner before attending a Winnipeg Symphony concert, Alex begged off. "I'm tired. I can't keep up with the pace you and your folks maintain. I just want to have a little lie in and laze around here for the day. I'll join you at the restaurant for the evening, okay?"

They waited as long as possible before ordering, but Alex did not arrive. Francine had telephoned the cottage, but after the seventh ring, she placed the receiver into its cradle and pensively made her way back to the dining room. Neither was Alex home when she had returned. Following her busy day, Francine was asleep the moment her head hit the pillow.

Alex was in deep repose beside her when she awakened the next morning, but Francine knew better than to disturb him. Where had he been, and what time had he come in?

Aside from being weary from all her visiting, Francine had a niggling feeling that something was amiss about Alex's vanishing act. In her heart, she felt there was more to it than just the possibility her husband was overwhelmed by the intensity of her parents' assiduousness. She had begun to notice Alex was changing ever so slightly toward her. As her pregnancy progressed, and she became heavier with child, Francine detected his insidious aversion to her.

Whereas their lovemaking had been almost a daily occurrence since their marriage, Alex had not made any attempt at being amorous during the past two or three weeks. At first, Francine felt relieved. She was starting to feel cumbersome with the more than twenty pounds she had gained. Her doctor had cautioned her about her weight, but she seemed to be hungry all the time. It neither helped that Hazel had increased their meal portions, nor that the Winstons' cook had commendable culinary skills. Then there was the upsetting fact that Alex was home for dinner less and less often, so she tended to nibble all evening. Francine had tried to lengthen her daily walks, but she was becoming increasingly tired with her advancing pregnancy and the demands of her academic year-end requirements.

Why was it that when you need someone the most, the person is the least available? Francine wondered as she spent yet another evening waiting for Alex to return home. Or perhaps she had just become more aware of his frequent absences after Mother Pat and Uncle Daniel had continued on their journey to Kenora to visit Pat's dying sister. Alex had grudgingly arisen to have breakfast with them on the morning of their departure and then stayed out late that evening. Did it have something to do with the confrontation he'd had with his father at the beginning of the year? Francine had repeatedly queried him about Alexander II's ultimatum, but Alex had skirted the issue so many times that, finally, he had yelled at her to stop asking. As the time for their baby's arrival drew nearer, instead of joy and anticipation, Francine could not help experiencing a strange sensation of loss with regard to her husband, even though they had only just begun their marriage.

✳

When the taxi delivered Hope to JFK, she realized she had arrived at least forty-five minutes too early. She had been so anxious to meet Jessica and Edward's airplane and escort them to the New York Hudson Hotel before taking them to Central Park that she had not checked her watch. She was not convinced that it had been as much an oversight as it was her excitement about seeing them again. It had been too long since she had experienced a good chinwag and a hearty laugh with her friends, with anyone.

On the morning Jessica telephoned to invite her to Francine's sudden wedding, Hope had wanted to attend more than anything she could recall for some time, but she had already accepted bookings for three seasonal recitals. Had she not flown back to Manitoba one short month after visiting her grandparents for Thanksgiving in Canada to attend her grandfather's funeral, she might have put her performing schedule in jeopardy and opted for another trip out of the country. It would have been wonderful to meet Francine's husband and see the other two members of the foursome, and she had no doubt they would have provided a much-needed boast to her sagging spirits.

On neither occasion when Hope returned to Brandon had she even tried to contact Francine or Cassandra. On her first visit, she had been home less than four days, and given such a short period, she felt she could not spend time away from her grandparents. Her grandfather was terminally ill, and Grans needed every moment of Hope's support and love. When he died sooner than either expected, the week she had been permitted for her bereavement leave was mercilessly inadequate. It seemed as if she had scarcely been able to assist Grans with his funeral arrangements and the interment before she was on her way back to New York. Hope had tried to comfort her grandmother with a proposal that she visit her again in the Big Apple come spring, but the faraway look in her beloved Gran's eyes belied its likelihood.

Minutes before Jessica or Edward spotted her in the throng of people waiting for their loved ones to deplane, Hope watched them come through customs. She always appreciated Edward's solicitousness toward Jessica, and she was suddenly reminded of the day the two girls had become friends. Her memories were as vivid as if it was yesterday, but she felt like a lifetime had passed since the last time they had been together.

"Hey, Jess and Edward, I'm over here." When they reached her, Hope threw her arms around Jessica and held her for a long ensconcing hug.

"What about me? Don't I get at least a small embrace, since I'm the one who travelled all the way to bring her to you?"

"Sorry, Edward, and no brief cuddle for you either! You won't believe how long I've been waiting to see you two. I feel like it's been ages since I've seen or touched someone who cares about me."

Jessica detected the pathos in Hope's voice and peered at her with a quizzical look. Was this the same woman who could hardly wait to begin studying at the great Juilliard School of Music, the one who had left the love of her life without so much as a backward glance, never mind a proper farewell? What had happened during the intervening months?

Hope observed Jessica's perplexity, and not wanting to engage in any inquisitive conversations in the airport, said, "Let's get out of here and hail a cab to take you to your hotel. It's gorgeous, and after we've had something to eat, it's only steps from Central Park. I thought I'd have a substantial meal now, so a snack would suffice before my final practice at seven o'clock for my recital tomorrow. The day is ours, and then the two of you can enjoy a romantic dinner and evening."

"That's sounds terrific. When do you want to visit the Metropolitan Museum of Art, Edward? I know I'd far rather have one of our in-depth tête-à-têtes than spend hours at the Met. What's your availability tomorrow, Hope?"

Once timelines were established, the three friends embarked upon a hectic but satisfying schedule that fulfilled each of their expectations.

✳

Hope was in the hotel lobby before nine the next morning, and when the receptionist rang, Jessica suggested she come to her room for coffee instead of meeting in the café. Edward had left early. Their room was breathtakingly beautiful, with a view of the Hudson River, and the food service was prompt and comprehensive. Soon the friends were comfortably seated in the two high-backed armchairs on either side of the ornate fireplace engrossed in catching up with the highlights of their respective lives.

Not surprisingly, the first topic of conversation was Francine's wedding. Jessica regaled Hope with every detail of the five days spent getting to know her beau, celebrating family and friends, reliving past experiences, remembering the fun times, and even recalling some of the not-so-amusing episodes of their youth. The more Jessica chatted, the more engaging she became, until Hope was transported back to her days in Souris, the delicious dinners at the Lingnan, the strolls to the knoll overlooking the blue hills on the sheep farm, the sleepovers in Francine's loft, and suddenly, she realized how homesick she was.

After a while, Jessica began to notice that Hope was uncharacter-istically quiet. As a rule, she was the one who carried many of their discussions, but this morning, it was as if she was mesmerized. "Well, listen to me. I'm doing all the talking without letting you get a word in edgewise. Tell me, what's going on with you?"

"Please don't stop, Jessica. You have no idea how much I'm enjoy-ing listening to you and recapturing all those memories. It's balm to my soul to hear what everyone is doing. Since I have come to New York, I've been so lonely. I can't begin to tell you how much I miss all of you." To Jessica's astonishment, Hope burst into tears. In between sobs, she uttered, "I haven't felt so abandoned since my mother died."

Jessica moved to Hope's chair and gently took her into her arms. She would never forget Hope's devastation when her mother had died so young and how her new chum's distress had motivated Jessica to embark upon her career path. "Remember how none of us could wait to grow up and become adults? Now, we're all so busy in our lives that we no longer have time for one another. Still, I thought that each of us was pursuing and succeeding in our chosen fields. Have you lost your passion for music, my beloved friend?"

Hope roused herself from Jessica's embrace. "Thank you for being here for me. No, it's not my desire to play the violin, nor will it ever be. Rather, it's the arduous road I must travel to live my dream. Juilliard may be recognized as one of the world's leading music schools with its prestigious programs, but the sacrifices students, especially those on scholarship, are expected to make are beyond imagining. The compe-tition is so fierce that no one trusts anyone, nor is any time wasted on developing camaraderie, and God help anyone who becomes the top performer. If I thought I'd been ostracized before, I was sadly mistaken."

With a flash, Jessica understood the isolation that Hope was no doubt experiencing. She knew that her childhood friend would strive and achieve the pinnacle of success and must suffer the consequences throughout her tenure at the famed school.

∗

Hope's performance of Mendelssohn's "Violin Concerto in E Minor" for the recital that evening at the Lincoln Center for the Performing Arts was otherworldly. As she had played the last note, the full house rose as one, as if together they had transcended the confines of the concert hall. When they came down to earth, they could not let her leave. Finally, after three encores, with the last being Hope's signature piece, the curtain descended.

Before departing for the airport the following morning, Jessica gathered Hope into her arms. "You have been blessed with the most incredible gift. Promise me that you'll always endure to share your virtuosity with the world."

∗

Convocation was fast approaching. Alex had not said a word about which day he was graduating, and it was nearly impossible to ask him. During the last month of the semester, they had become like ships passing in the night. The majority of Francine's final examinations were take-home written compositions, which she preferred to complete at the desk in front of the window. She subsequently rose early and drove to the university in the morning, when she was most energetic to access the library for her research. Then by midafternoon, when she returned to the cottage, Alex had departed for the day. Francine was finding the third trimester of her pregnancy exhausting and most often retired in the evening before whatever hour Alex returned home.

It was not until she had handed in all of her assignments that Francine realized she had not seen Alex, except for short periods on Saturdays and Sundays, for the past two or three weeks. On the last morning of April, she waited until after ten o'clock to make a fresh pot of coffee and then roused Alex from a deep slumber. "Hey, sleepyhead, it's time to get out of bed. Since exams are finished, and we haven't spent any time together for ages, let's plan to do something today."

"Why the hell are you waking me up at such an ungodly hour? I only got to sleep, and besides, I have a splitting headache."

"It's little wonder. You smell like a brewery. Where were you last evening, and when did you get in?"

"What is this, twenty questions? Why can't you bloody well let me have some peace and quiet? Shouldn't you be on your way some-where?" Alex muttered as he turned toward the wall and pulled the covers over his head.

"Enough already. I have the right to speak with my husband occa-sionally. Besides, we need to do some serious planning about where we're going to live when this baby arrives in little more than a month," Francine said, pulling the duvet off the bed.

"Hey, just what the hell do you think you're doing? We're perfectly okay right where we are, so give me back that damn blanket."

"Don't tell me you've already forgotten that we were going to buy our own home as soon as you graduated. If we don't start looking, we won't have time to get moved in before my delivery."

"Are you thick or something?" Alex said, sitting up and glaring at Francine. "I'm not graduating. I already told you that I dropped two of my courses and have to redo them in the summer semester."

"This is the first I've heard anything about you failing, not that you ever bother to speak to me. So, what will we do? We can hardly stay here with a baby. There's barely enough room for the two of us, not to mention all the necessities for raising a child, and for which we've yet to do any shopping."

"Well, unless you have a better idea, this is it, babe. And, we're bloody lucky my parents provide a roof over our heads and put food on the table. I haven't seen any offers from yours."

"This isn't about my folks, and it has even less to do with your parents, who still haven't had the decency to acknowledge my presence on their grand property. If it wasn't for Hazel, we would have, or at least I would have, starved these past four months, since you eat here less and less. You can stay in that damn bed. I'm not spending today, never mind the summer, in your precious hovel with you. I'm going home to be with my family, who love and care about me."

✳

Within fifteen minutes, Francine had thrown her few personal belongings in her suitcase and was on her way. She had scarcely reached the outskirts of the city before she was flooded with an overwhelming sense of relief. Driving west on Highway 1, she spotted the historic White Horse Monument in the rural municipality of St. Francois Xavier. She pulled over and was soon reading the information on the three nearby plaques about the Fort Ellice Trail, White Horse Plain, and the Assiniboine River.

On the beautiful spring morning, the grass was greening, the Manitoba maples were in full bud, and the pure white cumulus clouds contrasted vividly with the ocean-blue sky. As she continued to walk, Francine became aware that she was taking deep breaths to ease the residual tension from her body. She was just beginning to realize how oppressed she had felt during her self-imposed hours in the cottage writing the comprehensive essays required for her graduate degree.

Suddenly, she was free and going home, where she longed to be more than anywhere. She had not stopped to telephone that she was coming, and now all she wanted was to cover the distance as soon as possible. Francine returned to her car, which she still considered the best gift she had ever received, especially that morning, because it gave her the autonomy to leave her disreputable husband behind.

Now that Francine had the time to think about Alex's errant

behaviour over the past two months, she wondered what he had been doing. With characteristic naïveté, she assumed he had been studying at the university library because she always needed the desk. Neither for the first time nor far from the last, she chastised herself for being too trustful of others. Alex had only been taking four courses, and if he had failed two of them, he certainly could not have been spending his time poring over his books.

As the miles sped by, Francine's suspicions about Alex's activities tended more and more to the possibility that he had been with another woman. Suddenly, he'd lost interest in her and had not made any amorous advances since around the time he had started staying out late at night. She did wonder if her husband was no longer attracted to her because of her steadily increasing girth. To be truthful, she'd not minded, because of her level of fatigue and her concern that their lovemaking might harm the baby. By the time Francine was turning onto the gravel road toward her uncles' farm, she was convinced that her husband had become unfaithful to her.

✳

Patricia was gazing out the kitchen window when she observed the dust from an approaching vehicle. It was too soon for Daniel and Darrin to be returning from Brandon, and she instantly intuited that it would be Francine. In her heart and soul, she had been hoping and praying that Francine would come home to have the baby, but she had not expected her to arrive so early. She knew that one of Francine's final assignments was the preliminary proposal for her master's thesis, and she doubted she could have completed the requirements so readily.

The minute Francine stopped the car, Pat was outside waiting for her to open the door. After a warm motherly hug, she said, "Welcome home, darling. It's wonderful to see you. Let me get your bag while you go inside. I'm sure you're tired after all your hectic end-of-the-year activities."

"Thank you, Mother Pat. I'm glad you're at home, since I didn't bother to call. I left the city on the spur of the moment."

Before climbing the stairs into the house, Francine paused to peer about as if seeing everything for the first time. Observing her, the qualms Pat had kept at bay since their visit during Easter crept back into her mind. She placed her arm around Francine's shoulder. "Come in the house, my girl. We'll go through to the patio, where you can sit while I bring you a drink and a bite to eat. Then you'd best tell me everything."

Tucking into the delicious cheese rolls and chef's salad that Pat had produced within minutes, Francine realized, in her haste to get away from Alex, she had not eaten any breakfast. "How did you prepare all this food in such a short time? It's exactly what I need, and you're precisely who I want to be with. I'll never be able to put anything over on you, will I, Mother Pat?"

"Nor would I ever want you to, my darling. There's a reason why the fridge is full of salads and baked goods, but we'll get into that once you've brought me up to date."

"Oh, Mummy Pat, this time I've really made a mess of everything. I can't believe that, at twenty-three, I didn't take contraceptive measures and then thought the answer was to marry the father of my baby, a man I hardly knew. And what I've learned over these past four months only serves to prove the stupidity of my choice."

"Just a minute. I refuse to sit here and allow you to beat up yourself. It takes two to tango, and I have more than a strong hunch that it's a very good thing that your husband is not within my field of vision right now."

Patricia listened without saying a word as Francine summarized the essence of her short married life. Pat could hardly believe her ears, but it took more restraint than she thought she possessed not to interrupt when Francine revealed that Alex's parents had never once acknowledged her. What kind of people could live on the same property and not walk a hundred yards to welcome their daughter-in-law and soon-to-be mother of their grandchild into their family?

By the time Francine had expressed that they would be raising the baby in the cottage, Patricia was seated on the edge of the lounge chair, barely able to control her anger. "Well, that does it. Nobody is going to treat my daughter and grandchild like second-class citizens. Good for you for deciding to come home. You and your baby will live on the farm with us, and all our family and friends will rejoice in God's blessing of a new life."

*

The cars pulled into the Bristol Aerospace parking lot within minutes of each other, and together, the two women walked the short distance to the office. It had taken Susan ten months to consider seeking Robert's assistance, and she had driven to the city to spend Friday evening with Dana and Joel. The aroma of fresh coffee invited them into the building. With neither speaking, Susan, still wondering what had possessed her to come after her tense encounter with Robert the previous autumn, followed Dana as they approached the open door of the staff lounge.

Without raising his head, so intent was he on the newspaper he was reading, Robert responded to Dana's salutation. "It is a beautiful morning, isn't it? The Winnipeg Free Press has an interesting feature article in the business section, but I'll be finished in a minute."

The confident tone of Robert's voice was so different from their brief, tense conversation the previous year. Susan gazed at him from the doorway and could hardly believe it was the same man to whom she had been married. What happened to his scrawny build and those dark-rimmed glasses he had worn from morning to night, which Carole invariably had to say made him look like such a geek? Although, when they were courting, Susan had thought Robert looked sophisticated and handsome compared to any of the boys at high school.

Dressed in a light-blue T-shirt, revealing his well-developed shoulders and muscular arms, it became obvious to her that, some time ago, Robert had begun to work out regularly at a gym. The thick glasses were nowhere in sight, so he must have been wearing contact lenses, which had suddenly become popular by 1971, when the mass production of the soft corneal corrective lens made them affordable. His appearance was so altered, Susan realized that, in her distress the previous year, she had not really looked at him.

As if suddenly becoming aware of the silence in the room, Robert glanced up from his paper. At that moment, knowing that he was seldom rude, Dana chose to speak. "Robert, I knew I would need your assistance in completing Miss Smith's application, so I convinced her to join us for our Saturday tête-à-tête. I hope you don't mind, but many of these technical questions are beyond my capability. Susan and I have stayed in touch, and she's visiting Joel and me this weekend."

A smile began to form around the corners of Robert's mouth. He knew full well how it would have occurred that Dana had become friends with Susan. After all, he had long ago lost track of the number of times he had sat in the Andrews' kitchen enjoying the warmth and comfort of Dana and Joel's company, as much as her delicious meals. "If you're willing to accept my help, Susan, I would be more than happy to assist in any way that I can."

Parts of the application were indeed complicated, and after they drained the coffee pot, Dana excused herself on the pretext of catching up on her correspondence. When Dana and Susan sat down, they had chosen chairs across the oval Mahoney table from Robert. Whether she was being shy or did not want to be an intruder during Dana and Robert's customary Saturday morning conversation, Susan said very little.

However, as Robert and Susan prepared to work, it was apparent that the task would be facilitated by side-by-side proximity. Remembering his manners, Robert rose and asked, "May I please come sit beside you, so we can read and answer the application together?"

"That would make it easier," Susan said as, possibly for the first time since their breakup, she looked directly into Robert's gentle brown eyes. She was surprised by the discernible affection she saw, and when he claimed the chair on her right, his nearness electrified her body in a way she had not experienced for what seemed like a lifetime. In a flash, Susan was taken back to that resplendent autumn day when she encountered Robert in his shiny red convertible, and he had asked her to show him the surrounding countryside.

"We'd better get started," Robert said several moments later in a husky voice, "because, as I recall, these forms can be very detailed." He dared not look at Susan and kept his eyes focused on the document in front of him. Fortunately, she had completed the vital statistical information, including her previous education and related experience, of which, to his surprise she had none. In fact, her three years of university science courses had limited transferability to any degree in aeronautics. If Susan was choosing to change her major this late in her program, she would need to take several additional courses, and Robert had grave doubts that she would even qualify for the associate degree, never mind the bachelor of science in aeronautics.

Robert quickly grasped the reason for Dana's notion that the complexity of Susan's request was beyond her. Still, he was not about to dishearten Susan so early in the process. He could hardly believe she was sitting beside him, and he was almost certain he was not alone in having felt the sudden galvanism between them. After graduating on the dean's honour list, Robert had maintained excellent rapport with the aeronautics faculty, and now that he was teaching an introductory course and working with third-year students at Bristol Aerospace, he was not without a sphere of influence.

✳

In the outer office, Dana listened with half an ear as, rather than type reports, she proceeded with catching up on her filing. She overheard their hushed tones but not what they were saying. Still, she was optimistic, since she knew the situation was much different from the distressing scene she had happened upon almost a year earlier. Furthermore, Dana had seen how Susan looked at Robert when she entered the room.

Every fibre of Dana's being told her that the young man and woman in the next room still harboured positive feelings for each other. She appreciated that their path to healing and reconciliation would be a long, slow, arduous road, but for Dana, a firm believer in the concept of only one true love, the journey was well worth the challenge. More importantly, in her heart, Dana understood that these two, who had both suffered such overwhelming tragedy, would need a sensitive mentor to provide gentle nurturing along the way, and she knew just the person.

✳

The day following her return to the farm, Francine and Pat were on their way to Brandon as soon as they had eaten lunch. While Francine was still sleeping, Patricia, knowing that Dr. Jamison started the day in his office before going to the hospital for rounds, telephoned to determine his availability during the afternoon.

"Good morning, George. How was your weekend at the lake? As I remember, it's always a lot of work opening up the cottage for the summer."

"Right you are, Pat. Actually, I'd forgotten that Lindsay and you usually rallied our girls when they were younger to help you, with the promise of them setting the first bonfire of the season. My, time does fly, doesn't it? Now, what can I help you with at this early hour?"

Patricia had scarcely begun to explain about Francine's unexpected arrival when George said, "I'll be delighted to see her after my last patient for the day. Why don't you bring her to the office around five o'clock, and since you're coming to the city, as soon as I have a minute, I'll call Lindsay and Cassandra. Bring Daniel and Darrin, if you can convince him to leave his sheep, and we'll go out for supper. It's been too long since we've had a chance to get together."

"Thank you, George, that'll be great. From what I've been able to ascertain, Francine has little, if any, of the basic necessities she'll require when her baby arrives, so we have considerable shopping to occupy our time until we meet you. Bye for now, and thanks again for fitting Francine into your busy schedule."

*

Placing the receiver back into its cradle and grabbing his light jacket, George departed for the hospital. The majority of days as he strolled the four blocks along McTavish Avenue, he tended to let his mind wander and enjoy the scenery, especially now as the trees were budding and the grass was greening. But today he was preoccupied.

Not unlike the majority of her family and friends in attendance for Francine's wedding, George had enjoyed meeting her young man. He too had found Alexander Winston III to be a charismatic and winsome fellow who, throughout their gatherings had not only charmed, but at times had come close to mesmerizing the guests.

On two or three occasions when George stepped outside for a breath of fresh air, he observed Alex, who had apparently excused himself from the social activities for a cigarette. It was, therefore, with surprise that George noticed an unmistakable shadow of darkness flitting across Alex's handsome countenance before he became aware of the older man's presence. Although George could not have had any frame of reference to begin to comprehend what he clearly saw as a contradiction, he did wonder how someone could change so quickly.

What did they really know about Alex? It had all been so sudden. He suspected that Pat and the twin brothers did not have much more information. George tried to remember when he had learned about Francine's beau, and after searching his memory, he could only conclude that his first awareness had come with the family's invitation to her impromptu wedding. Furthermore, if Cassandra, who had been protective of Francine since her uncles had brought her to Manitoba, had known that Francine was planning to get married, she would have shared the news with her parents.

The more George thought about the precipitate marriage, the more he realized that, as much as he disliked the term, Francine's was a "shotgun wedding." Regardless, he was delighted that she was choosing to raise the baby rather than attempt to terminate the pregnancy or give the infant up for adoption. He knew for certain that Pat and the uncles would embrace the child into heart and home, and it would be exciting to finally welcome a newborn into their circle of friends. George and Lindsay were beginning to speculate that each of the foursome was so intent upon a successful career that none of their parents would ever hear the pitter patter of their grandchildren's little feet.

George had always been an astute observer of the human condition, a skill that was considerably enhanced during his years of being married to Lindsay, even more so as she was completing her PhD in psychology. Since his morning conversation with Patricia, his unspoken doubts about Alex had grown from investigative questions into serious misgivings. How supportive was her husband when Francine returned to her ancestral home just four to six weeks before the arrival of her offspring? George could not have been happier when he realized that now he would be the physician to deliver her baby, but his daughter did not hold the monopoly on safeguarding her. If Alexander Winston III were to so much as to harm a hair on Francine's or her child's head, he would first answer to their doctor, and then Cassandra would take deft action in court.

*

The ploy was working perfectly. As Carole had intuited, Aileen was not at all interested in walking three blocks every week to cash a cheque, especially while the city was still in the grip of winter. Furthermore, by the second week, Jimmy was so besotted with her granddaughter that if Carole were to ask him to stand on his head and spit wooden nickels, he would have tried to comply.

On Wednesday on the third week, Aileen handled Carole an envelope and told her not to open it until she arrived home. Although it practically burnt a hole in her pocket on the bus ride to the YMCA, she did wait, and she was not surprised in the slightest to find a cheque for $500 inside. For the life of her, Carole could not understand what an elderly woman spent such a generous amount of money on during a week, but she planned to take full advantage of Aileen's extravagance.

The moment Carole saw the cheque, she knew, she found the way to withdraw extra money from the senior's trust account. For whatever reason, Aileen had chosen to leave a space before the numerical amount as well as on the written line. Within a matter of seconds, Carole added a two in front of the five hundred and wrote the word "twenty" on the next line before the five. She had already decided she would go to the bank late in the afternoon on Thursday, when Jimmy was tired from a busy day, rather than on Friday morning, when, presumably, he would be bright and alert.

Tomorrow would be the definitive test. If Jimmy placed $2,500 in the envelope he always provided, Carole planned to walk straight to the nearest stop and catch the 3:30 bus to Osborne Street. Over the past three weeks, she had done her homework and had completed her plan by opening a chequing account, in addition to paying for a large safety deposit box at the Toronto Dominion Bank. She would arrive just before closing, and once within the private confines of the storage vault, she would lock $2,000 in her box, ensuring that Aileen's five hundred was secure in the sealed envelope.

If Jimmy noticed the difference in the amount of the cheque on Thursday afternoon, he did not comment. In fact, he was so happy that Carole had come without Aileen that he scarcely took his eyes from her beautiful face as he counted the one hundred-dollar banknotes. Had Jimmy asked, she was ready to explain that Aileen was planning an excursion to Toronto for a long weekend, but Carole was content to retain this reason, should the topic arise in the future.

Week after week, her approach was the same. At first, she could not believe the ease with which she was compounding her stockpile of cash. Then she began to worry that since she had no idea about the amount of money that was actually in Aileen's trust fund, she might soon delete the resource. Subsequently, she decided to pre-empt this occurrence by seeking precise information from Jimmy before he brought it to her attention. Also, Carole realized that she would be well-advised to query when the year-end statement would be sent to Mrs. Riley.

The following Thursday, she wore a new floral summer dress that accentuated her blue eyes and which she knew Jimmy would find irresistible. When she was seated across from him, she leaned close and whispered, "I have a special request from my grandmother, and she assured me you would gladly look into it for us. As you know, Jimmy, she doesn't like to be bothered with too many details, but she thought it wise to have me ask you."

"Most certainly, Shannon. Please, tell me what she wants, and I'll get on to it as soon as possible."

"Oh, she said that since you're such a bright young man, it would only take you minutes to obtain the information. All she needs is for you to confirm the current balance in her fund and the date for the end of her financial year. If you could please write it on a piece of paper and slip in into the money envelope, I'll make sure she receives the information first thing tomorrow morning."

✳

Aileen could not have been happier about their arrangement. "Sandra" was such a presentable and intelligent young woman that she was fully confident she would readily be accepted as her granddaughter. In addition, she had been accurate in her estimation that Jimmy would be receptive not only to her but also to their scheme. Finally, Aileen had been able to outwit her overbearing son and gain access to the money that Joseph had so generously set aside to satisfy her whims.

At last, she could look forward to her weekends, which hitherto she had spent languishing in her cottage waiting for her negligent granddaughter to visit or Paddy to invite his mother to attend the lavish dinners and parties staged within the grand house. Before Joseph passed away, Aileen had been the lady of the manor and was the hostess of all the social events and gatherings with the many Riley friends and business associates. But that had all changed. Joseph had scarcely been laid to rest when Aileen was relegated to the historic maid's quarters, as if she had suddenly become a crone.

More and more, Aileen was convinced that one of Sandra's most appealing characteristics was the respect with which she consistently treated her. Aside from that one unsavoury evening when Sandra had seemed distressed just because Aileen was enjoying her champagne before they were to attend the opera, she had always been congenial and affable. Indeed, she had become even more attentive and sweet-tempered toward her ever since they had initiated their banking strategy.

Not once in the months she'd known her had Aileen ever given a moment's thought to how Sandra acquired the finances to support herself. Furthermore, it never occurred to her to question what the young woman did with her time on the days when she was not with her at the Crestwood. Aileen had been quick though to realize the folly of seeking her companionship for social outings and subsequently made arrangements with her few remaining longstanding friends. Now that Aileen could spend the money that Joseph had promised her, every Friday morning before leaving for the seniors' centre, she packed a small overnight bag. At the end of the afternoon, instead of returning to her lonely abode on the riverbank, she took a taxicab to the Fort Garry. If only Elise Hathaway had not died, she would have been equally delighted with the prospect of weekend excursions to the iconic hotel. If Elise had been able to join her, during the course of their conversations, the two women, who had been friends for over fifty years, might have eventually uncovered some striking similarities between Sandra James and Kate Stone.

✳

Since becoming Alex's wife, Francine had steadily been slipping back into the throes of oppression, except this time, it was real. Her husband's family, and then Alex himself, had contributed to her feelings of mental distress and subservience, not by any harsh or prolonged treatment but rather by their complete estrangement. As far as Alex's parents were concerned, Francine's existence had never been acknowledged. As her pregnancy had advanced, Alex had progressively withdrawn from her as well.

As she had done throughout her life, Francine buried her emotions in work and survived by focusing on finishing the expected requirements for her academic year. Two weeks passed, but regardless of how long she slept, she could not overcome her fatigue. It was once again Pat who came to her rescue. "Francine, I suspect that the third trimester of pregnancy must be tiring for every woman, but I know you, my girl, and you have more than physical weariness weighing you down. How do you feel about calling Dr. Donahue and going for a few sessions before your baby arrives?"

"Thank you, Mother Pat, but after reviewing Dr. Donahue's notes, I've started to practice her exercises again and have almost worked things out. Mostly, I was so busy this last semester that I didn't identify or express my feelings, and now that I'm back home with you and my uncles, I realize how lonely and isolated I was after returning to Winnipeg since Christmas. Maybe if I'd been more insistent with Alex, we might have spent some time with his family."

A flash of anger gripped Pat, and she was on the verge of uttering, "There you go again, Francine, trying to take responsibility for someone else and then, no doubt feeling overwhelmed with guilt. The way those people have treated you is unconscionable." Knowing that she would not help her beloved daughter with her appraisal, she replied, "Well, my darling, that's all behind you now. You've returned to the haven of your family's home." Under her breath, Pat said, "And, never more will you or your child be made to feel so ostracized."

The candid discussion seemed to trigger a release for Francine, and during the last month of her pregnancy, she gradually recovered her buoyancy. With the return of her spirits, Francine regained her interest in what was happening with her friends in the Hartney district, and following an afternoon nap, she often accompanied Pat on a round of visiting.

Late one Monday afternoon, subsequent to a trip to Souris to pick up the fixings for a quick supper, they decided to have tea with Margaret. When they drove into her yard, although an unfamiliar vehicle was parked in the driveway, it hardly served as a deterrent. It was not unusual for former students or past colleagues to make an impromptu visit to the Devonshire farm, and more often than not, Patricia would be acquainted with the unexpected guest.

As it happened, on this occasion both Pat and Francine knew the identity of Margaret's surprising caller. What could possibly have brought him to the home of the principal he had so surreptitiously usurped? Nonetheless, rather than any tension in the air, there was a feeling of camaraderie between the two individuals seated on the front veranda. Francine had not seen Michael for years, but still her heart fluttered, and her face flushed.

"Good afternoon, Mrs. McGregor and Francine. It's been a long time since our paths have crossed. You're looking well, Francine. Like most people in the community, I hear all the updates, and I was aware that my congratulations are in order. How are you feeling? I know your baby is due before long."

"I'm very happy to be home among family and friends, especially as my delivery draws nearer. Thank you for asking, Mr. Griffin."

"Oh, please, call me, Michael. It's wonderful to see you, and perhaps you can bring me abreast of all the changes in your life."

Patricia was about to ask him to drop his formality regarding her name when she noticed the slight nod of Margaret's head gesturing her into the house. As soon as they were in the kitchen, Margaret said, "Why don't we let the young people get reacquainted while we have our refreshments on the back deck?"

"You old schemer, I know what you're up to, although I had no idea that I would ever encounter Michael Griffin having tea with you in the comfort of your home."

"He's a fine young man, and we've become great friends. Monday afternoons are our time for tête-à-têtes. You're the one who is out of synch, since Friday is customarily your day, my dear. And, yes, I'm not above being a matchmaker. For a while, I thought I might bring Susan and Michael together, but wait, in a minute I'll share her remarkable news. Now, as I recollect, Francine was always smitten with Michael, who is very lonely, and would love to have his own children rather than just teaching those of others. So, tell me what kind of husband sends his wife to her ancestral home to go through labour and delivery on her own? It must be almost six weeks since Francine arrived on your doorstep, and when has she last heard from the father of her baby? If you ask me, it doesn't bode well for Francine or her child, and why not consider future possibilities?"

"Okay, I hear you, and although extremely premature, I can't say I would be unhappy with such an outcome. I have had more than my share of doubts regarding the prognosis of Francine's marriage. However, as you have so accurately identified, only time will tell what might happen. Since we have some privacy why don't you fill me in about Susan's news? When did you find out about it?"

*

"Margaret, Mrs. McGregor, come quickly! If I learned anything while working on Mr. Russell's farm during calving season, it was that when the water breaks, the birth is imminent."

Both women leapt out of their lounge chairs and bounded around the side of the house to find Francine in the throes of a strong contraction. Although neither had given birth, both had been present during their respective mothers' labours and deliveries.

Pat glanced at Margaret. "I don't recall much about when my two much younger sisters were born, but it does seem that at the beginning, my mother's pains were not so sudden and overwhelming as Francine's appear to be. Something must be wrong. I'm going to take her to Brandon right now. Please telephone George and ask him to meet us at the hospital in forty-five minutes."

"I'll drive, Mrs. McGregor, while you sit in the backseat to be with Francine."

"That's very kind, Michael. Thank you, and for heaven's sake, please call me Pat. Let me help you into the car, my darling. In no time at all, you'll be in Dr. Jamison's capable hands."

As luck would have it, George was still in his office catching up on his paperwork when Margaret telephoned. As soon as they hung up, he called the hospital to expect Francine's arrival within the hour. Following a brief conversation with Lindsay, he completed the patient's file he had been recording and then left for the maternity ward at Brandon General Hospital. Lindsay and Cassandra joined George in Admissions a short time later. Facing at least a twenty-minute wait, the Jamison family decided to grab a snack in the hospital coffee shop just around the corner.

Dr. Jamison had been surprised by the urgency in Margaret's voice and advised the nurses in the labour room to be prepared for a possible precipitate delivery. The affable doctor smiled to himself, thinking that if indeed this was the case, his daughter's closest friend seemed to have a propensity for haste. George had long ago lost track of how many babies he had delivered throughout the course of his medical career, but under controlled circumstances, and with a young, strong primipara, he had come to consider a quick labour and delivery a godsend for the woman.

Lindsay and Cassandra were engrossed in conversation when Patricia joined them in the waiting room on the second floor. After exchanging hugs, they continued chatting until, a few moments later, Michael hesitantly approached the door. "Oh, hi, Pat. I guess this is where we stay until Francine has her baby?"

"Didn't I mention that you could drive home, Michael? I've called my men to let them know we're at the hospital, and I'll spend the night with my friends here in Brandon. You can leave my car at Margaret's, and we'll pick it up when time permits."

"Not a chance, Pat. I didn't risk life and limb speeding to get Francine to this hospital to go home before I have news for Margaret. And don't think for one moment that I'm not as eager to see and hold her baby as are you three women!"

✳

Mark Christopher Winston made his boisterous arrival at 9:02 p.m. on Monday, June 17, 1974. Despite the fact that Francine had not heard a word from his father since her abrupt departure from the city, she did not have the slightest qualm about proceeding with the name and registration of her son. Not for a second would Francine have considered that her child receive the unoriginal appellation of Alexander Winston IV.

Not until that Monday, when Mother Pat had taken her to Brandon to start shopping for her newborn, and later, when Dr. Jamison had confirmed he would be in attendance during her confinement, did Francine feel she could breathe again. At first, she thought she had been holding herself in control since her fight with Alex, but as the days passed, she realized it had been for much longer than from the moment of her outburst. It was only when she was cocooning in the affection and safety of her parents' embrace that Francine started to grasp the full impact of her alienation within the Winston family environment.

✳

By the end of four weeks, when Carole had squirreled away $8,000 in her safety deposit box at the bank, she began to realize the potential of her implemented strategy. At the same time, she knew she would need to be ready to flee at a moment's notice. Still, she planned to bide her time to maximize her earnings, while cautioning herself to be aware of any warning signs to indicate that her scheme had been detected.

Weeks passed, the season changed from spring to summer, her reserve grew, and still the arrangement continued without a hitch. During the months Carole lived at the YMCA, she made it a policy to be friendly but distant with the other young people in the residence. Now she became even more guarded. Knowing that she had to maintain her edge, during the days she was not at the Crestwood, she left right after breakfast and did not return until early evening.

Every day Carole chose a different route to walk around Winnipeg's downtown, putting in time until the William Avenue Library opened its doors. Once inside the building, which combined elements ·of classic Greek and Roman styles, she intensified her research for a suitable destination when she was ready to make her escape. The more she studied, the more she was leaning toward settling in either Tofino or Ucluelet. Both of the small relaxed isolated towns on Vancouver Island in the Pacific Rim National Park Reserve off Canada's west coast in British Columbia offered a plethora of advantages for someone on the run. Furthermore, the pictures of the unbridled natural scenery, ancient rainforests, lakes, sandy beaches, and year-round surfing looked incredibly appealing, never having seen the ocean.

The next step was to determine the means by which to arrive at this haven, which was far removed from any of her past travels and likely inaccessible by bus. Also, she wanted to veer away from public transportation, because she would be travelling with a large suitcase to hold all her personal possessions and, more importantly, the oversized attaché case she had found at Eaton's on a shopping expedition. She had searched for just the right case, one that would be sufficiently secure and of ample size to hold all her money. In a rare moment of extravagance, Carole had purchased the black leather bag, made in Italy, because it had two locks that could be programmed with three corresponding numbers. The beautiful briefcase did, however, have the singular drawback of being ostentatious enough to attract others' attention.

Following considerable reflection, Carole decided to purchase a car. She would have loved to buy one of the new Camaros she had seen in the windows of the Chevrolet dealership in St. James, but after chiding herself for worrying that her new briefcase would be too conspicuous, she could hardly risk driving a flashy automobile.

One day while in the library, Carole was reading the *Winnipeg Free Press* when she came across an advertisement for Select Auto Sales Inc., which had opened its doors in 1970. She liked the fact that the dealership was a private company, but it was located some distance away on Dawson Road.

Before mapping out the bus route to reach the site, she decided to call the office. The owner answered the telephone, and after an amiable chat, with Carole being very convincing that she would be prepared to pay cash, he arranged for his son to meet her. By the end of the week, she was not only the proud owner of a blue 1968 Chevrolet Chevy II/ Nova, she also had been referred to a nearby family member of one of the company's employees, where she could store her purchase in a garage at a reasonable monthly rate.

As Carole continued with her planning, she was becoming increasingly excited about what was turning into a grand adventure. She had never been farther west than her parents' farm, and the prospect of seeing the Rocky Mountains and the North Pacific Ocean was exhilarating. Tempted though she was, she had parked her car in the garage, and aside from starting it on a regular basis to ensure it was operational when she needed it, she did not drive around the city. Of course, before making the final purchase, she confirmed that her vehicle was roadworthy and capable of negotiating majestic mountainous passes, when she chose to venture beyond the confines of Manitoba.

The more time passed, the more meticulous she became about the finer points of her elaborate plan, so determined was she to address even the minutest details of her stratagem to circumvent anything going wrong. She studied maps in the library and learned that she could follow the Trans-Canada Highway all the way to Vancouver. She also purchased a roadmap of British Columbia. She even guesstimated the approximate number of hours, inclusive of day and overnight breaks, to travel the distance of 1,612.5 miles from Winnipeg to Tofino.

The wait was interminable. The routine at the bank had become so well-established that the process was almost too easy. Each Thursday, by the time Carole arrived, Jimmy had twenty-five crisp new one-hundred-dollar bills ready in a sealed envelope, presumably so he could take advantage of their visit to plead yet again for a date. Since she trusted him to provide an accurate accounting of her money, he reasoned that soon she would appreciate his reliability, and he became more insistent every week. Carole always received his advances with good humour but never committed. Then she thanked him and made her measured departure.

One day when Carole was adding her share to the safety deposit box, she reviewed the statements Jimmy had previously provided. Time was marching on, and even if her scheme continued to go undiscovered, she knew that the necessity of confirming a specific date to bring the contrivance to its natural end was becoming urgent. Furthermore, she was finding that the waiting was a tricky balancing act, and she was becoming increasingly edgy. The last thing she wanted to do was cut and run too soon. On the other hand, with each passing week, she was pointedly aware of the escalating jeopardy of being caught.

Subsequently, that afternoon following her departure from the bank, she stopped at a drugstore to buy a 1974 calendar before heading to the library. She was on a first name basis with the head librarian, and when she arrived, she requested the temporary loan of an adding machine.

Then, sequestered in a little-used section of the building, Carole began her calculations, ready at last to make her critical decision.

She circled Friday, March 8, on her calendar, since it was the first day that Aileen had introduced her to Jimmy at her bank and then withdrawn the sum of $500. The next Friday, Aileen had accompanied Carole, but for the last two Thursdays of March, she had gone alone and presented Jimmy with the cheque for $2,500. She figured that if she could continue until the last Thursday before the Thanksgiving weekend, she would have collected $2,000 for thirty weeks, for a total of $60,000. It was nearly two-thirds of the marginally over $90,000 that had been in Mrs. Riley's trust fund when the two women had initiated their existing arrangement.

When Carole added the $500 that Aileen had been withdrawing for thirty-two weeks on October 10, the fund would have been depleted by a grand total of $76,000, leaving a balance of $14,000, give or take a few hundred dollars. On occasion, Carole paused to wonder about Mrs. Riley's reaction when she received her year-end statement in early January, although she had a strong hunch that it would be Aileen's son who reviewed the bank document before his mother would see it.

Several times, Carole even speculated about what would happen to Jimmy when Paddy Riley brought the missing funds to the bank manager's attention. Once the truth was revealed, it would definitely have a deleterious impact upon Jimmy's future career in any financial institution. But he was always complaining that he had never found his job to be very satisfying. Carole suspected though that the most critical consequence for him was that Jimmy would be held criminally culpable for the fraudulent activity.

Nonetheless, she could not waver or deviate from her well-executed plan. For her, $60,000 was a small fortune, and it could set her up for life. After all, what were her options? She had not even completed grade ten, and she had precious few employment skills. She realized the importance of keeping her mind focused on the task at hand and returned to the library day after day in her latest pursuit of studying the intricacies of financial investment, with a discerning eye to the Tofino real estate market.

＊

As the clock neared eleven, Dana telephoned the Pizza Place and ordered two medium pizzas—pepperoni and mushroom and ham and pineapple—to be delivered to the office just before noon. It was not uncommon for her to be asked to arrange for a pizza delivery during the week when late-afternoon meetings ran into the evening, and she was well acquainted with Dave, the delivery man.

"Thanks for being so prompt. Would you mind carrying them into the boardroom, while I follow with this tray of drinks? It will be okay, since it's just Robert and a friend this morning."

"Happy to oblige, Mrs. Andrews. Anything for you and Mr. Wharton." However, when Susan and Robert simultaneously glanced up at the sound of voices, Dave had to tighten his grip on the boxes to avoid dropping them on the floor. During his brief conversations with Robert, he'd often got the impression that the chief engineer was something of a loner, so where had he been hiding this red-headed beauty?

In typical fashion, Dana took charge of the situation with a quick introduction. "Susan, meet Dave who could drive to Bristol with his eyes closed, we're such regular patrons of this delicious pizza. When I noticed the hour, Robert, I decided that your customary light breakfast would be doing little to keep your blood sugar up, and if you wanted to show Susan around our establishment later, both of you would require some sustenance. Thanks very much, Dave. I've got your payment ready on my desk."

Dana had observed Dave's reaction to Susan, but she had no intention of letting the gregarious young man engage Susan in conversation.

She would join Robert and Susan for a couple of pieces of pizza, and then she planned to leave the two of them to carry on with this second encounter, which was turning out to be far more favourable than the first. Dana caught the flicker of gratitude in Robert's gentle eyes in response to her overt suggestion, and she would wait to follow-up with him on Monday morning regarding how their afternoon unfolded.

As she was departing the office with the remaining pizza for Joel's lunch, and long before she arrived home, her budding ray of hope was well on its way to blossoming into subtle optimism.

✳

From the moment Mark Christopher was placed into her arms, Francine knew that giving birth to her son was the most creative activity she would ever engage in throughout her entire life. When he latched on to her breast and began to suckle, she transcended the confines of the bed, the hospital, the world surrounding her, and all those within its sphere.

It was not until her third attempt that the nurse was able to reach Francine. "I'm sorry, Mrs. Winston, to intrude upon your bonding with your baby, but you have a number of visitors wanting to meet him. If I may take him, we'll make him presentable for his eager admirers. Also, another nurse will check you into a room on the maternity floor, since you were ushered straight to delivery."

"Oh, thank you. I just can't believe this perfect little being belongs to me. Please, don't be long. I can't bear to be separated from him."

Even after Francine was transferred to her hospital room and had received a sponge bath, she was still in a trance when Mother Pat came through the door. "Congratulations, my darling. I'm very impatient to meet my first grandchild. George has assured us that he's a handsome and healthy specimen, although, with your second, he did mention that you better leave home earlier if you plan to deliver within the walls of a hospital."

"As soon as Uncle George entered the labour room, he started to tease me about not wasting any time. On the other hand, I'm quite happy that Mark Christopher didn't dally in making his entrance into this world. Regardless of what I'd read about contractions, I wasn't prepared for the process of labour being so appropriately named. However, the moment the nurse placed him in my arms, all memory of the pain disappeared."

When the bassinet was wheeled into her room, an entourage followed in its wake, led by Cassandra, who threw her arms around her dearest friend. "Congrats, Francine. He's beautiful, and, of course he looks just like you. I can hardly wait to hold him, but I'll get in line behind the grandmas. My mum has already worked it out that since I'm to be his godmother, she'll quite naturally become his god-grandmother."

Basking in the glow of her loving mother and friends' attention, Francine was at first surprised, and then pleased to see Michael bringing up the rear. She had been astounded to encounter him that afternoon—was it only four hours earlier?—and was very appreciative he had driven them to Brandon, so Mother Pat could comfort her during the harrowing ride in the backseat. Still, Francine hardly expected him to stay or to be interested in seeing her baby. A vivid memory of her schoolgirl infatuation flashed through her mind, bringing with it faint stirrings of her heart.

*

At her insistence, Francine and Mark were discharged within a mere thirty-six hours to Pat's and half of the Hartney district's capable care. Alice and Malcolm were driving into the McGregor farmyard just as Margaret and Susan arrived with fresh-baked muffins. It was as if they were setting a precedent, as over the course of the next few weeks, one friend or another arrived at the homestead, bringing enough food to not only feed the new mother but also every member of her family.

The majority of the young people born and raised in the community had left for greener pastures in Brandon or Winnipeg, where the opportunities and enticements of city life resulted in many forsaking their country roots. Subsequently, Mark Winston was the first baby born in the district in a long time, so he began to warm the hearts of the grandmothers, who seldom saw their offspring's children, and they came bearing gifts for the infant and his mother.

The warm and unexpected reception was the antithesis of Francine's experience during the past several months in Winnipeg, and before long, she was lingering in her attempts to reach Alex. To her credit, she had called the cottage late in the evening of Mark's birth but had been unsuccessful in conveying the news to her husband. During her one-day stay in the hospital, she had telephoned morning, noon, and night, to no avail. Where could Alex be, or was he simply not allowing the noisy instrument to intrude upon his privacy? In desperation, when her baby was almost a week old, Francine left a message on the answering machine at the big house requesting that either of the senior members advise Alex that he was the father of a son, Mark Christopher Winston.

When days passed, and Francine still had not heard a word from her absentee husband, she became less and less inclined to ever see him again. In truth, she was very possessive of her baby, and aside from sharing him briefly with doting grandmothers, especially Pat, she relished the requirements and joys of motherhood. Whenever she was nursing Mark, she communed so thoroughly with him that the world could have fallen down around mother and babe with neither having any awareness.

One Monday afternoon, Michael accompanied Margaret to the McGregor homestead. He stayed back by the car until she greeted her hosts and cuddled Mark before approaching Francine. "I hope you don't consider my tagging along presumptive. If you think I'm overstepping the bounds of propriety, please tell me, and I'll leave."

"Oh, no, Mr. Griffin. Thank you for coming to see how well Mark is faring, although I can't imagine how he couldn't, given all the tender loving care he's receiving. I believe you haven't yet had a chance to hold him."

"Thank you, Francine, and please call me Michael. I'd love to have a turn, but I'll warn you that, with my inexperience, he'll probably start crying."

To his delight, when Michael cradled Mark in his sturdy arms, the baby gazed at him with his grey-blue eyes full of confidence before drifting off to sleep. Pat motioned him to a lounge chair on the deck with a small table to his right, where she placed a glass of iced tea. He soon joined in the conversation when he realized that Mark was perfectly contented, instead of wailing his head off as Michael had anticipated. It was certainly not from any lack of longing that Michael had seldom found himself in the company of babies, and as the minutes ticked by, he became increasingly relaxed and serene with the new undertaking.

The following Monday, he returned, and when he was once again received as if he was part of the family, Michael eagerly awaited his turn to hold Mark. Soon, he could hardly bide his time until another week had come and gone, and it was his day to visit with Margaret before they paid a visit to the McGregor household.

No one within that loving home, whether family member or visiting friend, who had observed the look of tranquility that graced Michael's handsome face the minute Mark was nestled in his arms could ever have questioned the budding bond between man and baby. Still, it was Michael himself, although he suspected he was not alone, who, before long, began to wonder if his fondness was limited to the child or if indeed his affection was not also blossoming toward Mark's mother.

*

The hours had passed much too quickly, and when Susan glanced at her watch, she realized it was even later than she'd thought. After Dana took her leave, Robert continued to assist Susan with the completion of the decidedly complicated application. As they were gathering their Coke bottles and glasses, which he proceeded to wash in the kitchen sink, Robert said, "Susan, would you be interested in having a tour through Bristol Aerospace before you get on your way?"

"I would like that very much. Actually, I remember when I first attended the career fair and continued my research at the college library, I was fascinated there was an aircraft company in Winnipeg and that it had such a long and impressive history. I hadn't finished reading the information about the degrees in aeronautics before I knew what career path I wanted to follow."

"You've made a great choice, because air and space travel are the wave of the future. Bristol Aerospace has built on its experience in precision sheet metal to become a major supplier of accessories to jet engines as well as an important repair and overhaul centre for the Royal Canadian Air Force. In the late nineteen fifties, when the company was selected to build several test rocket airframes for ongoing research into high-power solid-fuel propellants, it was so successful that it partnered with Aerojet General to become Bristol Aerojet. It recently opened the Rockwood Manufacturing Propellant Plant in Stony Mountain, north of Winnipeg, to produce motors to be used for the United States standard rocket launchers."

"I can certainly understand why you're the chief mechanical engineer, Robert. You really are aware of what's happening with the company."

The sound of his name on Susan's lips was as refreshing as dew glistening on grass on a hazy Manitoba morning in mid-July. It had not happened for more years than Robert cared to remember, and he never thought he would hear it again. How he wished he had not failed her so miserably. If only he had been honest with her, they might still be together as husband and wife and living in Winnipeg.

"Oh, Susan, I'm so sorry I was not there for you when you desperately needed me. Maybe if I hadn't been running away and pretending to be someone I wasn't, I might have been able to give you some support. But I want you to know that, for all my shortcomings, I really did believe our marriage ceremony was authentic."

Susan was silent for several moments before she replied. "Thanks for saying that, but I don't know that you or anyone would have been able to reach me. I felt so responsible for my parents' deaths that guilt overwhelmed me until I suffered such a profound depression that I wanted my life to be over. If it hadn't been for Margaret Devonshire and later her husband, James, I might have put an end to it all. Then, when Margaret accused you, even contacting that lawyer to ascertain that we weren't married and later convincing me that you were to blame, I became angry enough to come out of my depths of despair."

It was Robert's turn to be quiet. At last, he said, "I guess it was all my fault, but at least I was able to help you, even if my assistance was somewhat oblique."

"I'm not sure there's any point in fault-finding now, and if there was, it would still be Carole who I would hold accountable. However, I chose to trust her, instead of leaving the note for my parents. Furthermore, you didn't exactly kidnap me. I decided to run away with you at my own volition."

They had reached the front entrance of the Bristol office. Robert would have given his right arm to stop the afternoon from ended. He did not have the courage to ask Susan about seeing her, and he realized it could be years before their paths might cross again. Dare he ask for her number? Even if they did not get together, perhaps he could just call her from time to time and ascertain how the faculty of aeronautics was progressing with her application. A sudden idea seized him. "I teach an evening class at the university on Monday, and I could hand-deliver your papers right to the department head, if you would prefer, rather than putting them in the mail."

"That would be very kind. Thank you, Robert, and now I must be on my way. Margaret and James will be wondering what has happened to me. Thanks for all your help."

Before he could say another word, Susan had hastened to her car. She had sensed Robert's hesitation about letting her go, and if she was honest, she had also wanted to linger, but she needed time to think. He had been part of her life during such a painful period that she did not know whether she could ever trust him again. Or herself. She had to keep taking one step at a time. She could not allow anyone or anything take her back to that catastrophic ordeal. And what about Robert? Had he completely recovered from his own personal tragedy?

Still, Susan had to admit that he seemed so different from the man she thought she had known and loved in her youth, and the changes far exceeded his physical appearance. Now Robert presented as responsible, gentle, and sensitive, not as a flamboyant suitor sweeping her off her feet. But then, she too had grown and developed from a smart aleck adolescent impressed by his flashy red convertible to a mature woman. Throughout the day, Susan had experienced faint stirrings of her previous feelings for Robert, and when she let her guard down, to her surprise, she was drawn to him again. Moreover, she sensed the attraction was mutual. Could they have any possible chance of starting over?

✳

Saturday, August 24, began as a splendid morning with a gentle westerly breeze lowering the scorching temperatures they had been experiencing since the beginning of July and portending an early autumn. With her hand pushing open the screen door, where she was about to join her family on the veranda for a late-morning coffee, Francine froze, seized by a sudden foreboding.

"No, you're too late," she muttered as she stood like a statue until Patricia emerged from her chair, on the verge of inquiring if Francine was all right, when they all turned to the clangourous noise of a vehicle roaring down the lane.

The twin brothers rose simultaneously, realizing the unfamiliar sound had to be emanating from a stranger's truck. Daniel was glad that Darrin, who was usually in the pasture attending to his sheep by that time of the day, had remained to have a turn bathing Mark. Whether it was because of the stricken look that flashed across Francine's face or the sinking feeling in the pit of his stomach, Daniel understood that his wariness could be mitigated by the presence of his protective no-nonsense brother.

✳

How much farther before he arrived at the house? God, he could not believe he was driving this old rattletrap, but then Alex was even more dubious about what kind of reception he would encounter when he reached his destination. If he had the slightest awareness of how the day was going to begin, he would have stayed at Shannon's beach cottage on Lake Winnipeg when she had pleaded with him the previous evening.

His father's imperious voice was still ringing in his ears as he negotiated the driveway to the McGregor homestead. Alexander issued his edict when his son arrived outside the garage expecting to jump into his Porsche and enjoy a late breakfast at the Salisbury. Alex was even contemplating a return to the resort, concerned that the sudden cooler weather could herald the end of summer. To his consternation, when he tried to open the door, it was locked.

"You will be driving that Chevy Shortbed Stepside until you have returned from the farm in the middle of nowhere to bring your son and his mother home."

"You must be kidding. I can't drive that piece of junk. Even if I wanted to go, I could hardly bring them back in that. You bought that truck when I was ten years old."

"You'll do precisely what I say. Not that you would be aware, but as it happens, babies come with a lot of paraphernalia, and you're going to need it. And that truck will be your only means of transportation until you get your family home."

"What the hell do you care where they are? I hardly think for one moment that you want to make the acquaintance of your grandchild, especially since you never once acknowledged his mother when she lived on your property for over four months."

"You really are as thick as a post. I'm going to have to check with your mother again to ascertain whether you were switched in the nursery at that damn hospital. Surely, even you don't think that the Holy Roman Catholic Church would enact a canon to invalidate a nonexistent marriage. Then you'll be stuck with that woman for life. On the other hand, if you're so afraid of that country mouse, I must have seriously failed you when trying to teach you about the sheer power of position and money. I warn you, Alex, that whatever you do, don't prove to me that all my efforts have been wasted on you. Thank heavens, your sister and her husband recognize the conferred social status of being a Winston."

Sitting at the wheel trying to muster enough courage to open the door, the only thought racing through his mind was, *Talk about jumping out of the frying pan into the fire*. Alex could imagine what Francine would say to him, since he had not even telephoned after the birth of his son. By now, their kid had to be almost two months, if not older. And then there was that one uncle, the sheep farmer who had made no bones about disliking him.

It was not until he had climbed out of the truck that Alex realized they were all standing and gaping at him. He remained beside his vehicle for protection, half expecting to hear the boom of a shotgun. As his anxiety heightened, he became giddy and nearly burst out laughing, thinking the uncles actually did have a use for that particular firearm when he brought Francine home at Christmas.

The ensuing silence deepened until finally Daniel broke it. "Well, young man, you can't stand there all day, so you better come and state your business. If you've decided to meet your son, you'll have to wait until he awakens from his morning nap."

"Thank you. Hello, Francine, you look great. Motherhood certainly agrees with you. I'm really sorry it took me so long to come, but I had to pass those two summer courses. Now, as you can see, I've borrowed my father's truck to bring back the necessary accessories that accompany a baby. Maybe after he gets up, I can start loading them."

If Francine had been staring at Alex before, now she was glaring at him as if he had suddenly landed from Pluto. "You don't honestly expect Mark and me to go back with you, do you?"

"Why do you think I've come? As far as I remember, we both agreed that you would spend the summer with your folks, and then I would have peace and quiet to study for my courses to graduate this fall. Of course, I can understand how you might have forgotten, being so busy giving birth and taking care of Mark, but you're my wife. Surely, you always planned to come home to your husband."

Patricia dare not glance at any of her family, because the reality of what was about to transpire was abundantly clear, and she would have started to wail. The snippet of a long-ago conversation with Darrin came as a flash of memory, and now she fully understood what he meant when he said that Francine's husband was dangerous, because he was not only glib-tongued, but he was also swift on the uptake.

As he approached the veranda, he looked apprehensive, and then, quick as a wink, he found all the correct legal, moral, and guilt-inducing words to justify his coming to take Francine and Mark back to Winnipeg. It mattered not one iota that he had been absent during labour, delivery, and the more than two subsequent months after his son's birth. It counted even less that he had not contributed one cent toward the necessities of life during that period. Francine was his lawful wedded wife, Mark was his child, and unless she chose to change their marital status, she was obliged to share his domicile with their son.

Following a strained dinner, during which the only person able to consume any food was Alex, the twin brothers grudgingly helped him load Mark and Francine's personal belongings into the ancient truck. Francine sobbed uncontrollably in Pat's arms even as Pat's heart was breaking, wondering how the McGregor home could ever recover from the abrupt exodus of a beloved daughter and only grandchild.

Patricia spent the first of many sleepless nights hearing the silence, no longer interrupted by Mark's welcome cries, as she tried in vain to get rid of her ominous feeling that, in less than three hours of Alexander Winston III's unannounced encounter, he would succeed in crushing the spirit of those who resided within the walls of the old farmstead.

✳

Seth MacDonald, the elder grandson of one of the three brothers who had founded the company in 1930 and the current president and CEO could hardly believe the droves that attended the open house at Bristol Aerospace on the Saturday and Sunday of the final weekend of August. Although in the early morning, rain had threatened, by the afternoon, the weather cooperated for their outdoor displays and barbeque, with people coming and staying on both days, until they closed the gates at six o'clock.

When Dana approached him about the possibility of organizing the event, she had to convince Seth about the relative merits of such an undertaking. It had never been done before, and the company had always managed successfully without any need for "marketing," as she called it. Still, Dana had been around the firm much longer than him, had shown him the ropes when he was promoted, and since then had proven to be an invaluable asset with the myriad tasks expected of him.

"That's an interesting proposal, Dana. I'm really curious about how you came up with it," Seth said when, on the third consecutive morning, she had persisted in getting his approval to begin the arrangements.

"The seed was actually planted last autumn when a bachelor of science student from Brandon College appeared at my desk. She was very interested in aviation and needed assistance with the completion of the application for the aeronautical degree program at the University of Manitoba. Susan Smith did not make her comment to me but rather to Robert Wharton, whose help, for obvious reasons, I solicited. He later shared her remark with me, and the essence of it was that she had no idea there was a thriving aerospace company in Winnipeg. The more I thought about it, the more I wondered how many other people had never heard of us, even though we've been around for over forty years. Then, one evening when I was at the library I came across an article, 'The Marketing Revolution,' published in nineteen sixty by a man named Robert Keith, and the idea struck me."

"Mrs. Andrews, you never cease to amaze me. I suspect the day will come when you'll be the president of this company. Let's do it. And by the way, you wouldn't happen to have an ulterior motive, would you? The rumour mill is rampant regarding your matchmaking expertise."

✳

From the moment Dana mentioned the upcoming event to Robert, he was ready to assist her. He too had been reflecting upon Susan's observation about Bristol and wondered if they needed to consider making others more aware of the company's existence. "What can I do to help you, Mrs. Andrews?"

"How many times must I ask you to call me Dana? And, yes there is something I need you to do, Robert, the sooner the better. Could you please call Susan and check if she's available on August twenty-fourth and twenty-fifth and also if she would be agreeable to having an article in the newspaper?"

"You know I would gladly do anything for you, Mrs. . . . . Dana, but I don't even have her number, much less the confidence to call her. What would I say to her in the unlikely event she would talk to me?"

Following Robert's favourable account of how his afternoon with Susan had wrapped up, Dana was certain they were on the path to starting anew. Clearly, she had been wrong. Within a week, he had resumed the diffidence that had characterized his interactions with women his age since his return to Bristol. Regardless of whether Robert challenged every skill she possessed for bringing couples together, Dana was determined she would persist, so convinced was she that Susan and Robert belonged with each other.

"Susan gave me her number, and I could call her if it's all right with you. I'll also need your permission to be included in the publicity with the Winnipeg Free Press. We want to request a feature article not only on Bristol Aerospace but also on its chief engineer and how the idea for an inaugural open house originated."

By the time Robert left the reception area, the wheels in Dana's head were whirling at top speed, and she immediately called the Devonshire number. She was fortunate enough to reach Susan at home and following a dose of gentle persuasion Susan agreed to come to Winnipeg as soon as the newspaper requested her presence for an in-depth interview.

Dana had always been blessed with an intuitive mind, which she considered a sacred present, and subsequently felt honour bound to achieve the ultimate with her God-given gift. She could already visualize Susan spending one or two days with her and Joel in preparation for the article and then for the open house. Given the expectations and demands of the August weekend, she would be expected to stay at least three or four days at the Andrews' home, of course, with Robert also being a guest for dinner.

Although Dana had the foresight to ask Susan if she could pass on her telephone number to Robert, he would hardly need that information with the frequency of invitations she was planning. Respecting that Susan would want to be part of the upcoming statutory holidays with her godparents, Dana would stagger her visitations with Joel and her on either the days before or after Thanksgiving and Christmas.

✳

The Bristol Aerospace Inaugural Open House was an immense success. The feature article in the business section of the Saturday edition of the *Winnipeg Free Press* the previous week was the very antithesis of its customary publications, and it would have been a wonder if many could have overlooked it. In the event the title, "Aspiring Aeronautical Student Spurs First Open House at Winnipeg's Aerospace Firm," had not garnered more than the usual morning readers, the picture on the front page of the exquisitely beautiful redhead standing beside an Avro CF-100 Canuck no doubt did.

The readership on that particular Saturday morning attracted at least two improbable individuals. As a weekend respite from their two sets of energetic twins, Derek and Tiffany were spending Friday afternoon until early Sunday evening in Winnipeg. Prior to a wonderful dinner at the Fort Garry Hotel, they had enjoyed the bottle of Alfred Gratien Brut Classique champagne he had ordered while sharing the hot tub in their suite. The next morning, Derek had arisen long before Tiffany and was partaking of his coffee as he perused the paper. The photo of Susan could hardly escape his attention, and the memory of his desire for her in his distant past came flooding back. Fortunately, within minutes, so did all his bygone reservations, and he would never have forsaken his wife, family, or career for any woman on earth.

The other unlikely reader was Carole. She was amazed that her former school chum had made the front page of the *Winnipeg Free Press*, not to mention the Saturday morning feature article in the business section, but she was astounded by her appearance. Nonetheless, she knew she could still reduce Susan to a quivering mass of rubble simply by taunting her about the deaths of her parents. Carole was sorely tempted to attend the open house to do just that, but she dared not risk her impending flight from the city in a little more than six weeks hence.

Not one word was spoken in the more than two hours of travel between the sheep farm and the ornate portal at 393 Wellington Crescent. Francine sat in a snivelling stupor while nursing Mark for the entire distance. Alex had glanced at them on several occasions and was on the verge of asking her how long it took to feed their son. If this were the usual required time, he would have little need to wonder what the three of them would do in the limited confines of the cottage. But he decided to bite his tongue.

While Alex was punching in a code, Francine suddenly broke the uneasy silence. "So, when did you install this fancy gate? Is it locked to keep people in or out?"

"I have no idea. I returned one evening to find it in place and then had a hell of a time trying to get into my own driveway. My father is becoming weirder with each passing year."

"Well, at least we won't have to put up with the gate, or him, for long. Tomorrow, as soon as I've fed and bathed Mark, let's go house hunting and burn our bridges with your 'hospitable' family."

Alex could not believe how quickly Francine had recovered from her apparent apathy, but he chose to wait before answering her until Hazel helped them unload Mark's accessories and position his crib, bath table, carriage, and stroller in the cottage with the organizational skill only she seemed to possess. Even so, there was hardly any space left to move around, and it was fortunate that Hazel would spare Francine the necessity of using the kitchen other than for their morning coffee.

No sooner had Hazel left than Francine said, "It's abundantly obvious that we can't stay here for long. Have you any idea what part of the city you want to live in? Hopefully you've already met with a real estate agent."

"When the hell would I have had time to look for a place to live? Oh, what the bloody hell, you're going to learn the truth anyway, so it might just as well be sooner than later. I didn't pass my exams, I don't have access to my trust account, and we have to live here until I get those last two courses."

As Alex had expected, Francine was furious. It was fortuitous that Hazel had asked if she could take Mark for a short ride around the grounds in the carriage, and they were out of earshot. Now, completely out of her daze, Francine yelled, "What are you playing at? You were so busy all summer you couldn't come to be with me during my labour and delivery, you couldn't come to the hospital to meet your own flesh and blood, we didn't hear a word from you for over two months, and then you arrive on my family's doorstep to haul us back to this tiny dwelling behind a gate that can only be opened with a code I don't know. Not that Mark and I have any means of escape, since there wasn't any time for me to make arrangements to have my uncles drive my car to Winnipeg. Why in God's name did you bother to disrupt our lives and bring us back here?"

"I'm sorry, Francine. My father has been riding roughshod over me all summer, and I could barely think straight anymore, much less study. I thought that if you were here with me, I could settle down this next semester, so we can finally be out from under his domination."

How did Alex always manage to find the words to succeed in making others feel sorry for him, as well as ensure that his handsome face would invariably reflect sincerity? On the other hand, her one brief encounter with Alexander Winston II would suffice for Francine's lifetime. In all fairness, Alex did have the right to get to know his own son, and since they were now in Winnipeg, she ought to try to make the best of their circumstances.

✳

The honeymoon period for Alex's enthusiasm of being a father lasted less than four weeks. To his credit, during the initial ten or twelve days, he made a first-rate effort, but every time he reached out to hold Mark, his son started to cry. At first, Alex decided it was because Francine was in the room, but when she stepped outside the cottage, Mark wailed even louder, until she had to rescue him. Alex attempted to rock him to sleep, to gather him up from his nap, to bathe him, burp him, and take him outdoors for a carriage ride, and still the moment Mark set eyes on his father, he started to scream.

As it was, Francine was having difficulty getting Mark to breastfeed. Whereas he had been eager to nurse from the time she had put him to her breast in the delivery room, suddenly, he had become fussy and would only latch on to feed if she was lying down. Francine did not have the slightest idea what was causing the change, and other than asking Hazel, who had become the only other person in Winnipeg with whom she communicated, she was at a loss. She hesitated to telephone Patricia, because she had never been a mother and, understandably, would have limited knowledge about breastfeeding.

But, it went far deeper than that. Francine had only called home once, on the evening she had left the farm. She knew her family would desperately want to hear from her. In fact, they would be worried sick about Mark and her, and yet inexplicably, she did not pick up the telephone. The longer she waited, the less she could bear to tell her family about what was unfolding for Mark and her since they had forsaken hearth and home.

Rather than force Mark to nurse sitting up, Francine took him to bed. Ensconced within her loving arms, he resumed being an avid feeder, and often they were so comfortable that both fell asleep with her infant continuing to suckle. Alex could not recall how many times he found them together in bed, but one evening when he came home early to engage in marital relations with his wife, he went berserk.

"What the hell is this? Every time I want to screw my wife, that kid is attached to your boob like a permanent fixture."

Francine had heard Alex come in and was already rising from the bed. "As it happens, I was just putting Mark in his crib." She detected the scent of alcohol emanating from Alex as she walked past him. "While I'm busy, why don't you find a condom, and I'll be right with you."

"Why would I wear a rubber when you're breastfeeding him every hour? Don't you know it's a natural form of contraception?"

"That's nothing but an old wives' tale, and I'm not on the pill, so you'll use a condom unless you want to conceive another baby before Mark is a year old."

"No damn way! Are you intent on destroying any pleasure I might get from your grossly out-of-shape body?"

"Well, pardon me! You try carrying and delivering the next one, and we'll see what you look like less than three months after giving birth."

"What are you going on about? You're really losing it! You're so out of synch, you don't have a clue about anything, certainly not what it feels like for a man to wear a damn sheath. Now come here if you want me to make love to you."

"I'm not the person in this relationship who has lost touch, the one who comes and goes like a shadow in the night. How about you tell me where you spend your time and with whom?"

"That's none of your bloody business. Don't ever think you'll tell me what to do or where I can go, or I'm out of here this minute."

"I'm your wife, and I have every right to know. If you don't like it, you can get the hell out now! Why didn't you leave us with my family, where Mark and I were loved and had a life?"

Without another word, Alex threw a few pieces of clothing into a duffel bag and strode out the door, slamming it behind him.

✳

Had it not been for Hazel, Francine would neither have seen nor spoken to another person other than Mark during the balance of September. When she thought about her situation, it occurred to her that the peace and contentment of caring for her son were more than enough to make her happy. She became more and more absorbed in Mark, until she no longer felt guilty about not communicating with her family and friends. The truth was, with the exception of Hazel, who spent her every spare minute with them, Francine did not have to share him with anyone.

When they were on the farm, so many people had been coming to visit them that many days the only time Francine could cuddle her son was when she was feeding him. Mother Pat and her uncles wanted to do everything else for Mark and would take turns bathing, singing, strolling, and rocking him to sleep until she decided to let him suckle for long periods, as if she was his human soother. Francine did pause to wonder now if it was because Mark was growing and becoming stronger that he had started to refuse her breast when she was in a sitting position. Of course, she would never know, but true to form, Francine began to analyze and to obsess about her son.

On the afternoon of Sunday, September 29, Penelope was searching the grounds for Hazel, who was disappearing for longer periods every day, when Penelope found herself drawn to the cottage. She had not so much as gone near her son's haunt in years, and when she arrived, she discovered her maid standing in the doorway. Hazel gestured for Penelope to be quiet, and both women stood listening to the sweet sound of Mark's laughter.

The request for silence had been unnecessary. Penelope stood spellbound. She had yet to see her grandson's face, but the mirth emanating from the baby took her back to Alex's happy infancy, and she heard the wonder and joy reminiscent of her son so long ago. Suddenly, Francine became aware that she was no longer alone, and when she turned to look, all she could do was gape.

"No, this will never do!" Penelope said. "My grandson and his mother cannot live in this hovel. Come, Hazel, we'll start right now to move them to the suite on the upper floor of the main house."

*

By October 1, Carole had discreetly moved all of her personal belongings except what she needed for the next nine days to the rented garage, placing everything in the trunk of her car. September had been interminable, with Carole becoming increasingly jittery with each passing hour. She could scarcely eat, and when she finally did fall asleep, she often awoke early in the morning. To make sure no one observed how edgy she was, she left the YMCA before breakfast and grabbed a coffee and muffin in the library café. She patted herself on the back for having the foresight to pay her October resident fee in advance, thus eliminating any need to approach the office, while making it appear that she was still in Winnipeg.

Prior to cashing Aileen's cheque on the second Thursday of October, Carole thought about getting Jimmy a small gift for his undying loyalty but quickly realized the folly of such an action. Instead, when he invariably asked Carole for a date, she said, "What about the first Saturday evening following Thanksgiving?"

"Do you really mean it? Give me a minute while I write it in my day timer. Where will I meet you?"

"Right here in front of your bank, Jimmy. See you then."

As soon as the bus dropped her off at the YMCA, Carole walked to the garage, retrieved her attaché case, and proceeded to her own bank to empty her safety deposit box. She loved the bank's policy of not allowing anyone in the vault while she was attending to her business, not that she tarried. She could hardly wait to exit the building and lock her money in the truck of her car.

*

Friday, October 11, dawned bright and clear with every indication of a beautiful Indian summer day. Lady Luck was with Carole when she arrived at Crestwood Centre. She had no sooner removed her light jacket than Aileen motioned for her to meet in the lavatory.

"Good morning, dear. I'm glad you've arrived early, because I have such a busy weekend organized that I'm leaving before noon today, so, if you have plans, you may go now."

"Thank you, Aileen. Have an enjoyable Thanksgiving with your family." Carole gave her patron a hasty hug and was gone.

Originally, Carole had hoped to reach Moosomin before nightfall, but her chance of getting as far as Regina in the daylight had just increased significantly. She was in her car and on the outskirts of Winnipeg by 10:30 a.m. She decided to buy gasoline and grab a sandwich at a service station along the highway, not wanting to risk running into anyone she might know in Brandon or Virden. Once she left Manitoba, she expected she would be home free, and although she drove right by the turnoff to her parents' farm, she never considered the possibility of stopping to see them.

As she travelled along the Trans-Canada Highway, she began to experience the freedom and joy of the open road. It occurred to her that it was easy and so rewarding to take advantage of others, although she certainly had earned her due with Aileen Riley. Following her weekend binges, the elderly woman had become decidedly more difficult to be around, more demanding, and more irritable. No doubt, there might be those who would consider Carole's actions criminal, but to her credit, she had always given freely of her time and attention to please Aileen. Besides, it was not her fault that she was much smarter than anyone she had ever met. Now, at long last, she could dispense with every one of her aliases and arrive in Tofino as Carole Martin.

✳

They waited. Family, friends, and neighbours were all eager for Francine and Mark to come home. It had never been proclaimed, and yet the district had the collective perception that there were issues about Francine's urbane husband. Whether it was because he was not one of them, or if it was owing to the fact Alexander Winston III came from a position of wealth and power would be debated time and time again, but it seemed unlikely that a clear decision would ever be reached.

Following two weeks without hearing from Francine, it dawned on Pat that her hands were tied, since she had neither a telephone number nor an address for Alex's family, other than that they lived on Wellington Crescent. How could she have allowed that to happen? Why had so much about Alex and Francine's relationship been shrouded in mystery? The situation became far more complicated when Pat could not find the number for Alexander Winston II or III in the telephone book or the address in the Henderson's Directory of their home or business.

When he realized that Patricia was becoming unduly worried, Daniel said, "I know you're concerned, my darling, but can't you imagine the adjustments all three of them are making as they begin to coalesce as a family? They need time, and we must be patient. Have faith in Francine. She'll call."

"Thank you, my dearest. No doubt, you're right, as usual." Pat sincerely appreciated her husband's calming nature, yet she had an eerie feeling that all was not right with Francine and Mark. She might have let it go if she had not decided on the spur of the moment to drop in on Margaret one Monday afternoon. She arrived as Michael was getting into his car. "Oh, how nice to see you, Patricia. What have you heard from Francine, and is she bringing Mark home for Thanksgiving?"

Hesitating as she decided how to answer, Patricia said, "Thank you for asking. We certainly hope so, since we miss both of them very much."

"I know what you mean. I do too."

Later on the way home, Pat reflected on Michael's candid response and wondered which one he was most anxious to see. Since he had become the principal of Hartney School, he had added extracurricular activities and made several significant changes that had endeared him to students and parents alike, with the board singing his praises. Michael had to be the most eligible bachelor in the district, and yet the only woman to spark his interest since Hope's departure was Francine. For some time, she and Alice had attempted to arrange a match between him and her granddaughter, to no avail. That was it. Patricia would ask Cassandra to use her legal expertise and contacts to track down the Winston's telephone number and exact address.

Before leaving the Andrews' home, where he and Susan had been invited for Sunday dinner after the open house, Robert asked if he could call her now and then to chat. "I would like that," she replied, "but please give me a chance to apprise my godparents about meeting you again."

Early the next morning, he telephoned her as she was about to depart. "Hi, I hope you had a restful sleep. Have you seen the front page of the newspaper this morning? You might want to talk to Margaret and James as soon as you return to the farm."

"Dana and I were relaxing with our coffee, enjoying the chance to chat about mundane things. Let me fetch it from the veranda, where Joel likes to read it before leaving for work."

The press had been everywhere throughout the weekend of the Bristol Aerospace Open House. Susan remembered the cameras flashing when Robert introduced her to Dr. Zachary, but she was unprepared for the caption under the photo, "Faculty chair guarantees aspiring student a seat in aeronautics program" on the front page of the *Winnipeg Free Press*.

After perusing the article, Dana said, "Take this paper with you, Susan. We'll get our hands on lots of copies. Goodbye, my dear, and drive safely."

✱

All the way home, instead of wondering how she was going to tell her godparents about Robert, Susan kept thinking about what the article had said. It was not until she was turning into the driveway that she became nervous.

Margaret had just finished trimming the hedge and walked over to the car to welcome Susan home. "You look lovely, darling. I take it your event was a success."

"You could say that. Do you have time to join me for a coffee? I need to bring you up to date on a most unexpected occurrence that actually began last August."

Once the women were seated on the deck, Margaret listened intently as Susan disclosed all that had transpired over the past year. Following her narration, she unfolded the newspaper on the coffee table for her godmother to read.

"What a stunning picture of you, Susan, in your mint-green linen suit, but is the younger fellow really Robert? I would think that Dr. Zachary is the older man on your left."

"As I said, he's an entirely different person in every aspect, not only physically. And the best thing is that now we can talk to each other. Of course, we've both changed considerably since we were together."

"I feel as if you're seeking my approval, Susan. I admit that I'm surprised, but how you proceed is your choice. However, I request that you allow me to tell James. I know when he'll be most amenable to hearing your news, and then we'll ask Robert if he would like to join us for Thanksgiving dinner."

✳

It had not taken Cassandra long to track down two telephone numbers for the Alexander Winston II residence at 393 Wellington Crescent in Winnipeg. Immediately, Pat tried each of them in turn, letting them ring off the hook. At last, early in the evening, one number was answered, and when she asked to speak to Francine, a male voice replied, "I'm sorry, this is the telephone for the main house. Please ring her on the cottage line."

Before Pat could identify that she was having difficulty reaching anyone, the line went dead. Placing the telephone back into its cradle, she reflected that now at least she had confirmed which number she would persist in calling. And ring she did, for the next three days, every hour morning, afternoon, and evening, but never with success. Daniel tried to reassure her that maybe they were on a family vacation and again made a plea for patience.

However, early on the Wednesday morning following Thanksgiving, Pat said, "Where is it written that we have to wait for Francine to come home? On this glorious Indian summer day, we'll drive to Winnipeg and visit with our family." With considerable misgivings, Daniel agreed, and within the hour, they were on their way.

Patricia was so eager that they did not stop for lunch, driving until they arrived at 393 Wellington Crescent. The mansion on the extensive, impeccably groomed treed property was breathtaking, with a gate sturdy enough to guard a fortress. But inputting the number for a code box securely fastened to one of the adjacent brick posts was the only apparent means of entry. Before Daniel could stop her, Pat pressed on the horn.

Then, noticing the sign with the unusual disclaimer, "No Trespassing. Violators Will Be Shot. If You Survive, You Will Be Shot Again," Daniel urged, "Please, Pat, let's just back away from the gate, to wait until someone comes along, going in or coming out, and opens it."

They parked near the property for over an hour. Finally, Daniel convinced Pat to leave and search for a restaurant, promising they would return when family members might be returning from work.

Shortly after four o'clock, they resumed their watch, remaining several feet away from the entrance to one side. The minutes ticked by, becoming an hour, and still there was no traffic arriving at 393 Wellington Crescent, which continued to be as quiet as a mausoleum.

Neither spoke. Daniel could not help wondering why someone would spend so much money to build such a huge house to spend so little time in it, but he kept his speculation to himself. When he could no longer bear to see the despondency on Pat's face, he gently said, "My darling, I'm going to start the car, and we're going to the Viscount

Gort to book a room for tonight rather than drive home in the dark. Rest assured, Patricia, Francine will call us before long, because she'll want her car with winter coming."

As the weeks passed, Pat's solicitude changed to anger. Fortunately, Indian summer lasted until the end of October, and she found solace in her garden. One warm day as she was gathering the last of the root vegetables, her bitterness resurfaced, and she shouted out to the prevailing westerly wind, "How could my beloved daughter abandon me without a word?" No sooner were her words out of her mouth than she stopped dead in her tracks. Is that not what she had done? She'd left one fall day and had not gone home for decades. Was history repeating itself? "Oh, please, God," Patricia prayed, "don't let Francine and Mark stay away as long."

✳

When Sandra had not arrived by eleven o'clock on Wednesday, October 16, Aileen's annoyance shifted to worry. Where was that girl? Her head was aching, and she was desperate for one of Sandra's soothing neck massages. It did occur to Aileen that she might want to consider cutting down on her weekend drinking, especially if she ever stayed at the Fort Garry Hotel for three nights again. No doubt though, her consumption had more to do with meeting Walter Whitmore and enjoying a couple of gin and tonics in the bar before they shared a bottle of champagne with dinner.

Since Aileen had left the senior centre at noon on Friday, she arrived at the hotel earlier than usual. After she had checked in and read for over an hour, she became restless. The sun's rays shining through her window on the second floor were warm and inviting, so she put on her walking shoes for a short stroll around the block. It was a gorgeous Indian summer day, and after walking longer than she anticipated, Aileen decided to stop in the lounge to quench her thirst before dressing for dinner.

She noticed the dapper gentleman on her way to the small table by a window. She was about to order when he appeared at her side. "Good afternoon, Madame. May I join you? Please don't think me forward, but I was wondering if I might buy you a drink?"

Walter was charming, and by invitation had accompanied her to the Palm Lounge for dinner that evening. Aileen liked him from the start, preferring to dine with a man rather than eat alone. And Joseph would have been so pleased for her.

Aileen ate and drank more than was her custom, but she always had the good sense to know when she'd had enough. Furthermore, she wanted to leave Walter with a favourable impression, so before signalling for the girl to take her to her room, she said, "I have thoroughly enjoyed your company, Walter, but I must leave you. Perhaps if you're available tomorrow, we may meet again."

They met around the same time on Saturday and Sunday, enjoying their aperitifs before progressing to the dining room. It was not until Aileen was checking out on Monday morning that, to her surprise everything the two of them had consumed over the course of the three days had been added to her bill. She had scarcely enough cash to cover the full amount, and was quite miffed, but then she decided she had so enjoyed Wally's companionship, and after all, it was only money.

✳

When Sandra did not come on Friday, October 18, Aileen was beside herself. If only she had thought to get her telephone number, but she supposed she could call the downtown branch of the YMCA. Should she reach her, Aileen was ready to take a taxi and pick her up before the two of them went off to the bank. On the other hand, rather than waste precious time, why not go directly to the bank alone and convince Jimmy to accept her cheque with one signature?

The minute Jimmy noticed Mrs. Riley enter the bank, he motioned her to the sit-down wicket. Before she had a chance to say a word, Jimmy said, "Oh, Mrs. Riley, I'm so glad to see you. Shannon didn't come yesterday, and I know you can get a message to her. We planned to meet for a date tomorrow, but she didn't mention what time."

"I'm here, because I haven't seen Shannon this week. Now, I have a special favour to ask. Since she didn't come to the centre, I need you to cash my cheque with only my signature."

"What do you mean, Mrs. Riley? I thought Shannon lived at home with you and her parents. And you know I can't accept your cheque without both signatures."

Aileen realized her slip a moment too late, but she glossed over Jimmy's question. "Oh, be a dear, just take my cheque and give me my money. I have an important engagement."

"I'm very sorry, Mrs. Riley, but I must follow the bank's policy, or I'll jeopardize my job. I wonder though if you would mind giving me Shannon's telephone number."

"Well, aren't you sweet? You won't cooperate with me, but you expect me to help you. No money, no number. Goodbye, Jimmy." With that, Aileen stormed out of the bank.

For the first weekend in months, Aileen did not check into the hotel. She attended mass with her son and daughter-in-law before joining them for Sunday brunch at Paddy's club. When they were ready to depart, Aileen remained, visiting with friends until past four in the afternoon. By the time the taxi delivered her home, she was fatigued and asked the maid to advise her family that she would not be dressing for dinner. Instead, Mabel brought her a light meal of soup and scones, and Aileen retired early.

Sometime during the night, Aileen awoke with a hacking dry cough and a sore throat. By morning, she was congested and soon developed the worst head cold and bronchitis she had experienced in years. Her symptoms lingered for ten days, with her recovery not occurring until just before Halloween. As invariably happened in Winnipeg, when the witches and goblins were preparing to go trick-or-treating, the snow started to fly. Aileen did not return to the Fort Garry Hotel, preferring instead the comforts of her own home, although the irony that her one-weekend of abstinence had resulted in a lengthy respiratory illness did not escape her.

✳

By late afternoon, Francine and Hazel, while Cook dismantled the crib, had moved her and Mark's belongings to the upper floor of the house. The entire time, Penelope had remained seated in a leather recliner holding her grandson. It was not until Mark awoke and began nuzzling her bosom that she relinquished him to his mother. Approaching the door to leave, Penelope said, "Make yourself at home. Hazel will continue to bring your meals to you."

The apartment was luxurious, spacious, and beautifully decorated, with an enormous master bedroom and ensuite, another full bath off a second bedroom, a fully equipped kitchen, and a sunken living room leading to a balcony facing the river. After nursing and changing Mark, she laid him on a blanket on the carpet and went exploring in search of the telephone. Francine had a sudden urge to call home, wanting to enlighten her family about her new and improved accommodations.

Strangely, she could not locate a telephone, in the living room, bedrooms, or kitchen, and she vaguely wondered who had previously dwelled in the posh suite. Deciding she would ask Hazel when she arrived with dinner, Francine carried all the crib components from the second bedroom to the larger one, where she began to reassemble it. She would make use of the well-equipped room for Mark's clothing and diapers and during playtimes, but she would never sleep a wink if she were separated from her son by a five-inch wall.

By the time Hazel arrived with a supper tray, Francine was almost too tired to eat. She had just bathed and settled Mark when she heard a light knock on the door. When she opened it, Penelope asked, "May I please talk to you for a few minutes? I've just come from apprising Alex that you and Mark will now be residing with me, but he'll remain in the cottage. I'm aware that he comes and goes at all hours of the day and night, so now he'll no longer be disturbing his family's sleep." What Penelope did not tell Francine was that she also knew he was having an affair with Shannon Riley, and for reasons she did not yet appreciate, she would not tolerate her grandson being tainted in any way by his philandering father.

Curiosity had carried Penelope to the cottage, certainly not any anticipation of caring about her only grandchild. Nonetheless, from the moment she set eyes upon him, something stirred in her heart, and within the month, she developed an intense bond with Mark. In the beginning, she treated her daughter-in-law with kindness and respect. In fact, Penelope's affronts and restrictions had begun so insidiously that, for a long time, Francine was not even aware they were happening. As her love for her grandson deepened though, Penelope became increasingly straightforward in her criticism and expectations.

One afternoon when Penelope let herself into the suite, she found Francine feeding Mark with both of them sound asleep in the rocking chair in the nursery. Penelope was appalled that Francine was always disappearing into the bedroom and lying down to nurse him, which prompted her to purchase the rocker. Lo and behold, the moment Francine sat in the chair rocking Mark, he had begun to feed again in a sitting position.

Keeping her voice low to avoid waking Mark, Penelope tersely uttered, "How long have you been sleeping with him using you like a soother? Put him down in his crib, so he can have a restful nap. At any rate, it's high time you stopped nursing Mark. He's becoming a big boy and is old enough to manage with a cup and table foods, not languishing at your breast day and night for his sustenance. We have the wherewithal to provide our grandson with proper nutrition. And when he awakens, we'll move his crib here to the nursery, where it should have been set up in the first place. Besides, you're never going to lose all that extra weight if you keep eating for two."

Francine was groggy from her abrupt awakening but had the presence of mind to be glad that Penelope was whispering. If she had not been concerned about disturbing Mark, Francine thought Penelope might be yelling at her, which was as surprising as her sudden directives. Penelope had always been good-hearted and amiable with her, so rather than upset her further, Francine did as she was told. Truthfully, she was becoming quite fond of Alex's mother and had begun to wonder why he always made reference to her histrionic fits.

Mark stayed asleep when placed in his crib, and Penelope curtly said, "I'll come back later to take him for his stroll around the grounds."

The more Francine considered Penelope's comment about weaning Mark, the more she began to speculate that her mother-in-law might be jealous she could not feed her grandson. Surely Penelope could appreciate the continued benefits of an infant receiving his mother's milk, and Francine involved Penelope in all other aspects of his care. Regardless of how covetous Penelope became, Francine had every intention of nursing Mark until he decided to wean himself from her breast.

The following day, when the portion of every meal on her tray had been downsized by half, Francine realized that Penelope's restrictions were not nearly so subtle. When she began to focus on some of her other elusive limitations since she had been moved into the main house, the extent of her confinement dawned on her. Mark's baby carriage and stroller were kept in the rear veranda, with Penelope advising her that she was to use the servant's entrance and the back set of stairs when leaving and returning to the house. Her query regarding a telephone was met with the instant response that one was available in the cottage. She was informed that she was not to access the main floor of the house at any time, and it occurred to her to wonder if Alexander Winston II was even aware that Francine was now residing on the upper level of his immense home.

Still, Francine had never experienced such security and contentment, as if she and her child were being cocooned during the critical formative period of Mark's infancy. She was free to devote all of her time and energy to her son, as she developed the skills to be a capable mother. But she had heart-rending qualms about not going home for Christmas, and she wrestled with her conscience until she finally decided to write an explanatory letter to her family and friends. She gave Hazel money to procure the loveliest cards she could find and included her epistle with her holiday greetings. Then, when Penelope offered to take the cards to the post office, Francine's initial misgivings were alleviated. As the festive season drew nearer, however, Francine could feel especially Mother Pat and her uncles' profound umbrage at not seeing Mark for his first Christmas, and she began to vacillate.

*

On the Friday evening of the second week in January, which had been more hectic than usual, Paddy was pouring a scotch in his study as he absentmindedly perused the day's mail. He had noticed the bank statement for his mother's trust fund and was eager to confirm its performance with the increasing interest rate. Holding the paper in his left hand, Paddy just about dropped the crystal decanter from his right when he read the bottom line. "What the hell?"

Steadying himself, Paddy set the liquor container on the bar, and with his drink and the paper in hand, sat down in his favourite recliner. He put on his reading glasses and studied the document in detail, but the balance remained the same. Slightly more than $14,000, although he vividly recalled that it had been over ninety thousand when he had reinvested it the previous December. How could this have happened?

His mother must have succeeded in bribing her granddaughter to accompany her to the bank to co-sign. Paddy was quick to observe they had started in the spring and continued to withdraw money every week until Thursday, October 10. But that could not have been the case. Shannon had stayed at the cottage on Winnipeg Beach for the entire summer. The longer Paddy stared at the statement, the more uneasy he became, his instincts screaming that much more was going on than met the eye.

As he was contemplating, his private telephone rang. "Good evening, Gerry," Paddy said. "You do have an uncanny facility for knowing when something is amiss." After Paddy apprised his cousin of the reason for his unusual remark, he went on to say, "If Shannon did indeed go with Aileen, I can't imagine she would not bring her grandmother's excessive spending to my attention. I know that Dad left the money for her enjoyment, but I can't for the life of me figure out what she did with twenty-five hundred a week. Other than on the weekend, my mother doesn't go anywhere."

As his cousin replied, the memory of a conversation with a colleague on the bench in Brandon flashed through Judge O'Meara's mind. Derek Barclay had telephoned him some time ago with as much an inquiry as a warning in regard to a young female fraudster who had bankrupted a number of senior women before suddenly disappearing. Could she have relocated where there would be considerably more quarry upon which to prey?

"So, Paddy, here's what I'd like you to consider. Don't say a word to anyone over the weekend, clear your calendar, and meet me in my chambers on Wednesday at three o'clock with all the possible players. That is, the bank manager, the teller, your mother, and your daughter.

If anyone balks, mention that I shall issue a subpoena."

✳

Before the clock struck three, everyone was waiting in the ante-chamber, some more nervous than others, but with Jimmy the leading candidate. His apprehension was not helped by the bank manager, Mr. Norton, who drove Jimmy to the meeting while prodding about whether he had been observing all the bank's policies. By the time they arrived, Jimmy was so flustered that he kept his eyes pasted to the floor, even when they were called into the judge's office.

He did raise his head during the introductions when he heard the name "Shannon Riley." Before Jimmy could stop himself, he blurted, "You're not Shannon Riley!"

"What do you mean, Jimmy?" Judge O'Meara asked gently, believing that the situation was about to be resolved quickly.

"She's not Mrs. Riley's granddaughter. I've never seen this woman before in my life, even though Shannon came to cash Mrs. Riley's cheque every week after she came to the bank with her grandmother to meet me."

"Well, Paddy and Fred, it would appear there are three accomplices, one willing, one unknowing, and the other not present. Now, I could argue that Mr. Reeves be charged with fraud, even though he was likely an innocent bystander trying to please his client and whose head might have been turned by a pretty woman. I could debate that Mrs. Riley be accused of being an accessory, but the real perpetrator has disappeared scot-free and probably will remain so unless we decide to cooperate. I have no doubt that both of you gentlemen want Jimmy behind bars, but I suspect, Paddy, you might have some reservations about your mother spending the rest of her life in prison. Yet, they are both guilty of the crime."

"How can Mrs. Riley be considered culpable when it's her money?"

Fred Norton demanded.

"The teller would hardly have set up the scheme, and how much did you keep for you each week, Jimmy?

"I never touched a penny of Mrs. Riley's money. She and her grand-daughter were so nice to me. I liked Shannon, and we were supposed to go out on a date. I really need my job. I look after my mother, and if I go to jail, she'll be left alone. I only did what they asked me to do."

"My question was rhetorical, Jimmy. You might be considered legally negligent for not questioning the increased amount, but then, that's not your job. On the other hand, you could be implicated, Fred, if your head office starts making inquiries when your branch is smeared in the papers. So, we can sit here and argue the criminality of this situation, call the police, have Jimmy and Aileen arrested, and create nasty publicity, or we can work together to capture the real criminal."

Once Aileen grasped that she could be held legally accountable for her actions, she provided every piece of information she had gleaned about Sandra James. She and Jimmy would work with the police sketch artist to come up with a reasonable facsimile of the imposter to be circulated to police stations throughout the country. Mr. Norton finally agreed Jimmy could keep his position with the bank but that he would be transferred to a smaller branch with fewer investment portfolios.

During a silent ride home, aside from glancing at his daughter and wondering why she could not have accompanied her grandmother, Paddy never said a word. After he dropped Shannon off at the door of the main house, he drove his mother to her dwelling. His only comment was, "Tomorrow I'll transfer what little is left in your trust fund to your checking account. You may as well spend dad's hard-earned money on yourself as throw it away on some swindler."

Enough was enough. Margaret could no longer allow her dearest friend to wallow in misery, and pine away for her ungrateful daughter, who did not even have the grace to communicate for her son's first Christmas. And she certainly was not going to let the McGregors spend the day alone in the vain hope that Francine and Mark might arrive at the last minute. When she and James stopped for dinner at the Lingnan and Trin told her that they were flying to Toronto for ten days during the festive season, Margaret knew she had to take action.

For the past several years, Cassandra had journeyed to Hartney to drive her grandparents to Brandon for the holidays. Lindsay decided it was too much to expect her mother to prepare the turkey dinner, and George was invariably on call at some point between Christmas and New Year's, if not for most of it. Alice and Malcolm were still spry enough to enjoy many of the seasonal celebrations the city had to offer while also delighting in their family gatherings. Their only wish was to see Cassandra married and having children of her own instead of spending so many hours at that law firm.

On Wednesday morning, two weeks before Christmas, Margaret dropped in on Pat. She had decided that if Patricia had still not heard from Francine, she was going to insist they come to the Devonshires. When she had a mug of coffee in hand, Margaret said, "Do you recall me mentioning that James and I had driven to Winnipeg for the Remembrance Day long weekend to visit Dana and Joel Andrews, Robert's surrogate parents? At any rate, all three are coming from the city over the holidays, and not only James but also Susan and I want the McGregors to join us. She's eager for you to meet the real Robert Wharton."

"This is sounding serious. I'm pleased for Susan. I really admire her for moving forward with her life. Maybe they would have stayed together if not for her parents' tragic circumstances, but at least they have found each other again. And from what you've said, they are developing a much more mature lasting relationship."

"I have a hunch that one of Susan's reasons for asking you to come is that Robert is going to propose."

"Let's hope Francine makes it home for Christmas. She would be very happy for Susan. During their years at Brandon College, they became good friends."

"Yes, Susan has hinted that she would like Francine to be her maid of honour."

"I know she would be delighted. Thanks for your invitation, Margaret. If Francine arrives in time, we'll be happy to join you."

"And if she doesn't, we still expect you and the twins, and please come early, so we can visit."

"Oh, we couldn't leave before Francine arrives. We wouldn't want her coming home to an empty house."

"Please, stop it, Pat. Tape a note to the door, and tell her to come to us, in the unlikely event she appears. As your closest friend, I'm going to be candid. It's high time you took your life back instead of blaming yourself for Francine's abandonment."

"It's my fault. I don't deny it. Life is cyclic and often cruel, and our mistakes come around to haunt us. History does repeat itself."

"I don't believe that for one second! I think we may only have the present moment and a choice to endure or to enjoy. So, I'll take pleasure in setting three additional plates on my dining room table for Christmas dinner."

✳

Not one person answered Francine's letter or sent a Christmas card. She was so overcome with self-pity that she could hardly muster the energy to care for Mark. She could not imagine how she would have managed without Penelope. She came every morning and afternoon, and aside from periodically harassing or intimidating her about continuing to nurse, especially if she found the two of them asleep after a feeding, she was a godsend.

On Christmas Day, Penelope came bearing gifts for both of them, and Hazel delivered a generous tray of a turkey dinner with all the trimmings, followed by a hearty serving of plum pudding topped with caramelized sauce. Penelope spent several hours with them, playing with Mark and visiting with Francine before departing to entertain her dinner guests. When she left, and Francine decided to listen to one of her gifts, a recording of Mozart's "Requiem in D minor, K. 626," with Herbert von Karajan conducting the Berlin Philharmonic, her sense of gratitude became mingled with feelings of affection for her mother-in-law.

*

Time marched on. The weeks turned into months, the months became years, and soon Mark would celebrate his third birthday. He had grown by leaps and bounds and was a robust child. He was as energetic whether exploring the substantial grounds surrounding his home or indoors listening to stories and playing imaginary games with either his mother or grandmother.

With each passing year, Penelope doted more and more on her grandson. Francine was alarmed by her increasing possessiveness but attempted to foil her mother-in-law's domination by continuing to nurse Mark, if only at bedtime. Francine knew that breastfeeding was her undisputed realm, and regardless of how much Penelope threatened and verbally abused her, she would not be deterred from this sphere of influence.

The extent of Francine's bonding with Penelope became more apparent one Thursday afternoon when her mother-in-law was away at her customary bridge game. Francine and Mark were playing hide-and-seek outdoors when he saw Alex coming from the cottage. Mark stopped and stared until Francine realized that her son would have no recollection of his father. Furthermore, it dawned on her that he had never been in the company of any man, and with little surprise, Mark ran up to her and clung to her leg.

"What have you done to my boy? You're making him into a sissy! Just what the hell are you and my mother doing in that house? How can you allow her to control you so completely?" Alex yelled.

"Penelope takes care of Mark and me, giving us everything we need instead of treating us like pariahs. Maybe if you weren't so busy gallivanting, you might remember that you have a son. And stop shouting; he's not accustomed to such behaviour."

"Your benefactor has banned me from even entering her precious home, so how could I get to know my son? Just how long do you intend to be confined under her house rules? Do you ever get to go anywhere?"

"Until you're ready to assume your responsibilities and provide us with a proper home. In the meantime, if you want to see Mark, we play outside mornings and afternoons, unless the weather is bad."

Sporadically over the summer months, Alex did join them for their outdoor activities, always on a Thursday afternoon. Before long, Mark looked forward to seeing him, particularly enjoying their roughhousing and feeding the birds along the riverbank. Francine maintained her distance to permit father and son to get to know each other, except when Alex enticed Mark to play near the fast-flowing river. Then she hovered like a hawk, ever fearful that harm might befall her reason for being.

*

In short order, Dana understood that Margaret was a kindred soul. Both women were of the same mind that Susan and Robert were meant for each other, but by tacit agreement, they proceeded with only the gentlest of persuasion. Dana and Joel were invited to the Devonshires' gatherings, which expanded to include most of their closest friends. Before long, Patricia, Alice, and Lindsay concurred, and the respective families were optimistic, there might soon be a wedding in the district.

Heaven knows this circle of women needed something positive to anticipate. They had done their best to console Pat over the years, making sure she attended all the community functions, although they always felt as if they were walking on eggshells around her. Her friends saw the bleakness in her eyes, felt the pain in her heart, and wondered whether Patricia would ever truly come return the detachment that had claimed her.

Fortunately, the one person who could rekindle the light in Pat's eyes was Michael. In recent years, Marika and Jonathon had started travelling to Europe, and whenever they were away, the coterie of friends ensured that Michael received his share of dinner invitations. He had been invited to the Devonshires one Easter, and as the guests were relaxing in the living room before dinner, Michael was telling Pat that his parents had telephoned the previous evening from Cornwall.

Robert had been standing nearby, and when he heard mention of the English county, he visibly paled. At that moment, Michael glanced up and noticed his ashen color. "Are you all right? Why don't you sit in this chair, and I'll get you a drink of water."

"No, I'm fine, thanks. I don't believe we've met. I'm Robert Wharton."

"Oh, I'm sorry, Robert," Pat said. "I didn't realize you hadn't been introduced to Michael Griffin. His tea time with Margaret is Mondays, so, of course, he's known Susan for years." By the time they were called to the table, which was laden with baked ham, scalloped potatoes, savoury salads, and vegetables, the two young men had enlivened Pat with their animated conversation about the relative merits of flight, whether by air or in space.

✳

May 1977 proved to be a memorable month for Susan. Following the successful Bristol Aerospace open house, when the *Winnipeg Free Press* acclaimed Susan, she had been fast-tracked into the associate in science in aeronautics degree at the University of Manitoba. She would graduate at the top of her class on the Friday before Mother's Day, and three weeks later, on the last Sunday of the same month, Susan and Robert would be joined in holy matrimony.

Even when Susan had started her final year, and convocation was the subsequent spring, no wedding plans had been set in motion. Margaret and Dana were convinced that, after their first fiasco, Robert and Susan were gun-shy. The two women decided that the time for mild inducement had come and gone, and Dana hosted an impromptu dinner. While they were eating, Margaret, seemingly on the spur of the moment, proposed that she and James host a small garden wedding at the end of May as the apple and cherry trees were blossoming, and the engaged couple blithely agreed.

✳

The morning of May 29 dawned bright and clear with dew sparkling in the grass and the buds on the fruit trees opening with the rising sun. Before two o'clock, when Reverend Walmseley arrived to officiate, the guests were seated on the three rows of dining chairs in the Devonshires' living room. With Robert and Michael, his best man, standing at the makeshift altar that Darrin had so capably constructed, Pat began to play the bridal chorus processional.

Susan was resplendent in an emerald silk gown. It was the exact colour of her eyes, and it contrasted exquisitely with the crimson tints of her hair. Robert turned to glance at his bride and thought he might stop breathing, scarcely able to believe that this day had actually come. During the ceremony, the love between Susan and Robert was palpable, and if any of the wedding guests had any qualms about the second union between these two young people, their doubts were dispelled by the time Patricia played Felix Mendelssohn's "Wedding March."

As pleased as Margaret was for her goddaughter, the necessity for her to be in that role was still bittersweet. She dared not think about June or Bert or even glance at James for fear of inducing her interminable sorrow. Then, when Margaret noticed that pain had returned to haunt Pat's eyes, she realized there were too many ghosts within this small gathering of people, and she was glad she had a multitude of tasks to occupy her mind.

Toward the end of the evening when Margaret was thanking Cassandra for being Susan's maid of honour, Cassandra said, "You're welcome, Margaret, but I would have given anything for Francine to have stood up for Susan. I can't say that I've ever seen two such sad people at a celebratory event as Patricia and Michael."

✳

If Susan's wedding had been the catalyst in her quest to bring Francine home, the gold-embossed invitation addressed to Ms. Cassandra Jamison, which she received a month later, catapulted her to the brink. It said, "You are cordially invited to Miss Hope Harding's debut at Carnegie Hall in Midtown Manhattan in New York City, United States, located at 881 Seventh Avenue the evening of Saturday, September 3, 1977 at 8:00 p.m. Miss Harding will perform Johannes Brahms' 'Violin Concerto in D major, Op. 77.' Sir Georg Solti, music director of the Chicago Symphony Orchestra conducting."

She'd been heartsick since Francine had forsaken her family and friends to live with her affluent husband in Winnipeg. Cassandra had long ago lost track of how many times she had called the telephone number, which Pat had provided, and then given up. One weekend while in the city, she drove to 393 Wellington Crescent. Seeing the wrought-iron gate, she sat in her car across the street with her eyes peeled for hours. Cassandra had even been on the verge of asking Judge Barclay to subpoena the residents of that address, but she knew it was neither his jurisdiction, nor were there any grounds for the court order.

The moment Cassandra entered the front door, Lindsay knew there had been a paradigm shift. "Do you want something to eat, Cass, before you tell me what's happened?"

"Thanks, Mum, but I don't think I could swallow if I was hungry. This time I'm not going to quit until I've found Francine." Handing the invitation to her mother, she continued. "I could never live with myself if she missed Hope's inaugural performance at one of the most prestigious musical venues in the world. Where is Francine? God, you'd think she was being held hostage somewhere!"

"Just a minute, Cassandra! You've triggered my memory about a recent psychological phenomenon that I read a while ago, which sounded most unusual. Let me grab my DSM. Here it is. It's called Stockholm Syndrome or capture bonding, and it was only described in 1973. It's a condition whereby hostages begin to express empathy and sympathy and may even come to love their captors. The peculiar thing is that the traumatic bonding does not necessarily need a captive scenario but can describe 'strong emotional ties that develop between two persons where one of them intermittently harasses, beats, threatens, abuses, or intimidates the other.'"

"That's bizarre. Why in heaven's name would Francine ever allow herself to be treated like a prisoner?"

"Ah, my darling, there is no one quite as vulnerable as a new mother. And Francine, with her long history of traumatic loss, overwhelming feelings of oppression and guilt, and frightful nightmares has always been much more susceptible to the expectations and control of others than most people I know."

"But who could be imprisoning her? I didn't get the impression

Alex was that kind of guy. Footloose and fancy-free, yes, but not mean. On the other hand, what do we know about his family? Francine told me that he didn't even bother to invite them to their wedding, so if she's trapped in this strange captive situation, what can we do? Have you ever treated a patient with this disorder?"

"I haven't, but once the condition was identified, Eleanor thought she might have helped a woman come to realize that it had happened to her. It may be tricky though, because even if you do find Francine, chances are she will not see herself as a victim."

"Thanks for that information, Mum. I'm planning to take Thursday off before the Dominion Day weekend, and I'll telephone the number that Pat said was for the cottage every hour of the day and night, starting at six in the morning until I talk to someone. Come hell or high water, I'm going to bring Francine and Mark home!"

Who would have considered that she would run into someone she knew, and Adele Perkins of all people? If Carole had recognized her when a family of four walked into the Sugar Shack, she would have asked her co-worker, Barbara, to serve them. Adele had packed on so much weight that Carole did not recognize her until she heard her whiney voice. "Well, I can't believe it's you, Carole Martin. It's been years since I've seen you."

Thinking that her cover was about to be blown, Carole blurted, "What are you doing here?"

"We're here on a summer holiday. This is my husband, Myril Hanson, and these are our children, Marie and Carl. What are you doing here?" No sooner were the words out of her mouth than Adele realized she had gone back to an old habit of parroting her former classmate, one of the many mannerisms that Carole had always hated. But she had been so surprised by her abrupt reaction that she could not stop herself.

Suddenly, Adele realized she no longer needed to be on the defensive with Carole. "It looks like you never did find a man to take care of you, so you have to work at the only job you would ever get. But then, you weren't much of a woman, or daughter, for that matter. You were always about you. Your father is dying, and you haven't been home to see him. You probably don't even know that Myril and I bought your dad's farm to save your parents from bankruptcy when he was held legally accountable for his mother's debts. Apparently, your grandmother was scammed out of her home and every penny of her life savings by a con artist, but they were too embarrassed to call the police. At any rate, if you decide to go back, your folks now rent a little shack in Hartney, and your mother was lucky enough to be hired as the secretary at the Anglican church."

When Carole walked to her tiny two-room home, she took a circuitous route and kept glancing behind to determine that she was not being followed. As soon as she had served Adele, she had spoken to the owner of the ice cream parlour and begged off with a splitting headache. She recalled that Adele was cheap and told Barbara she was welcome to keep her tip, if any was forthcoming.

Fortunately, Carole was off work for the next two days. She decided to lie low rather than chance encountering Adele and her pudgy family again. Damn the luck that she'd run into her in the first place. She only worked at the dessert shop, so she had something to do and could make enough money to cover her daily expenses. Adele had a big mouth, and no doubt the minute she returned to Manitoba, she would broadcast that she had visited with Carole Martin in Tofino, that well-known hippie haven on the west coast.

Before long, Carole had come to enjoy the free-spirited, kindly, young people with their unconventional appearances, tolerance, and advocacy of free love and peace, although she did not have the slightest interest in becoming one of them or in experimenting with drugs. She had distanced herself so much over the past several years that she was not only self-sufficient but also wary that she might let it slip that she had sizeable investments in trust funds and real estate.

Finally, Carole had everything she'd ever coveted in life, and she had no intention of leaving Tofino. Still, she was concerned about her father, and she began debating whether she could trust Adele's assessment of his state of health. If she had mentioned that it was her mother who was at death's door, she would not have considered making the long journey. She and Betty had been at odds throughout her adolescence, although Carole had fond memories of her dad. As she had over the course of her life, Carole kept her own counsel, resolving that she would let Adele's rumours die down and wait until spring before driving to Hartney.

✳

As soon as her alarm rang at 6:00 a.m. on Thursday morning, Cassandra placed her first call. On her twelfth attempt, at five in the afternoon, someone answered. "Hello. It's a beautiful day at Alex's hideaway."

"Please stay on the line, Alex. This is Cassandra, and we need to talk."

"Ah, a voice from the past. I'd love to chat with you. I've just been playing outdoors for hours with my son, and it's always an exhilarating experience."

"Then Francine and Mark are with you. That's precisely why I'm so glad that at last I've reached you."

"Well, in a manner of speaking, they're with me. However, Francine and I have not cohabitated for years, not since my mother moved my family into her grand house and locked me out. I have no idea what it's all about, except that my domineering mother has total control over my wife and child. The only time I can freely play with Mark is Thursday afternoons when Mother is at her bridge game."

"Listen to me carefully, Alex. It is very important that you understand everything I say if we're going to be able to release Francine and Mark."

When Cassandra began to explain what might be transpiring at 393 Wellington Crescent, the silence became ominous, until she feared she was speaking into dead space. "Alex, are you still on the line?"

"Could that be possible? My mother has always been a control freak. Actually, I don't know how many times I've wondered why Francine would allow herself to be so totally under her thumb. You're telling me it's an illness? Holy hell, if Francine doesn't believe us, is there anything we can do? Nonetheless, I'll help with whatever you ask, on one condition."

"You are hardly in a position to bargain, Alex. You will do precisely what I say, or I'll have Judge O'Meara issue a subpoena."

"Oh, God. My father knows him from his country club. I'm not asking for any favours, Cassandra. I just want to be able to spend time with my wife and child."

"Look, don't think you're going to pick up where you left off and expect Francine to be ready to jump back into bed with you. She's been in a traumatic situation for almost three years, and she'll need time and counselling to recover."

"Please, Cassandra, she is not the only one who has suffered. Do you think I haven't missed Francine and Mark? Give me a break; they're my family!"

"Okay, Alex, what's your condition?"

"You take me too."

"Really, you'll give up your lifestyle, your Porsche, and your wealth, with all its privileges, to live on a sheep farm? Know this: Francine and Mark are never going back to your parents' home."

"Neither am I. If Francine has been traumatized in three years, think about how I feel after being raised by a controlling histrionic mother and a tyrannical father! During those few days on the farm, I received more love than I experienced in a lifetime with my parents."

"I hear you, Alex. You can come as long as you promise not to have any expectations of Francine. In fact, I can already envision several ways that you can enhance my escape plan. First and foremost, you must not give Francine the slightest indication of what is about to occur. When I arrive in the afternoon on July seventh at three o'clock, walk with Francine and Mark to the gate, and quickly help them into the backseat of my blue two-door nineteen seventy-six Ford Granada. Other than what you have on your person, don't pack anything to tip Francine off that you're fleeing with her and Mark. Very likely, she has become loyal, even devoted, to your mother, and if she senses what's happening, she'll resist. Is that perfectly clear?"

"Wow, Francine really has been brainwashed! What else can I do before next Thursday?"

"Since you're serious about not returning to Winnipeg, visit your bank tomorrow, and consolidate all your money into a private fund that only you can access. Then, at a travel agency, book two flights to New York City for Wednesday, August thirty-first, for Hope's debut. Of course, bring the tickets, but leave part of the stub, obviously without the date, lying somewhere in the cottage. It might throw your mother off our scent momentarily, to give Francine much-needed time with her family and Dr. Donahue to begin to decompress from the trauma and stress of her captivity."

As soon as Cassandra hung up, she drove to her mother's office to consult with her. Lindsay agreed that resuming counselling with Dr. Donahue would help Francine reclaim her equanimity, and she telephoned her colleague to arrange an appointment.

"Also, I think the Jamisons need to plan a visit to the McGregor farm over the weekend. I know Patricia kept everything in Francine's loft just as it was the day she left with Mark, but her baby is now a toddler."

"How right you are. I threatened Alex within an inch of his life not to bring anything with him other than what he could carry. How soon can you wrap up? Shall we start by making a list of some of the items we'll purchase tomorrow before we drive to the country?"

"We'll have a much more significant task once we've conveyed our heartfelt news. Quite naturally, everyone will be overjoyed, and it will be our job to prepare Pat and Francine's uncles about how changed she might be. Under no circumstances must they rush to her and show their love and enthusiasm. We all need to remember that Francine has been proselytized and will probably remain loyal to the memory of her captor for some time."

✳

They were belted into the comfortable first-class seats of the Boeing 707 jet aircraft waiting for the red-eye flight to New York via Toronto. Francine could barely contain her excitement as she anticipated the thrill and freedom of soaring through the firmament for the first time. Although Cassandra had flown before, she was grateful for the extra amenities and larger seat, which would make for a more restful night. She had been stunned by Alex's generosity when, on the day of their successful escape, he had presented her with the airplane ticket.

"How did you know I didn't have a chance to make my booking? Although I never would have sprang for first class? What do I owe you?"

"No, Cassandra, I'm the one indebted to you. I purchased three tickets to authenticate for Penelope that Francine, Mark, and I left together. She wouldn't have the slightest inking that a child flies free with his parents, and I wanted to validate that the three of us departed as a family. I did have to fabricate your birthdate, telling the agent you were my sister-in-law and would be bitterly disappointed with my memory loss if she would not issue your ticket. Please accept it as a token of my gratitude for helping me to break away from the bonds of my overbearing parents."

✻

Over the eight weeks since coming home, Francine had made remarkable strides in recovering from the effects of her traumatic bonding. From the moment Cassandra helped Alex coax her into the car, she seemed to have gone numb, and she appeared dazed during the drive to the farm. Fortunately, Mark fell asleep before they reached the city limits. Cassandra kept glancing in her rear-view mirror, wondering if Francine was also sleeping, but Francine stared straight ahead, eyes wide open, for the entire trip.

When they arrived, Francine went into Mother Pat's open arms with a homing instinct. They remained locked in each other's embrace for until Daniel and then Darrin held their niece in ensconcing hugs. Not one word was spoken. At last, Mark broke the healing silence by asking about the sound of a lamb bleating from a nearby pen. Alex took his son's right hand while Darrin reached for his left, and together, they strolled toward the source.

Patricia and Daniel took a similar stance with Francine. They led her into the house and up the stairs to her loft. As soon as she saw her bed, she walked toward it, slipped off her shoes, and crawled under the eiderdown quilt. Within seconds, Francine was sound asleep. She never moved a muscle until the following morning at eleven o'clock, when she awakened as if from the sleep of the dead. Francine had reached the bottom step when Mark came running to her with Patricia in tow, "Mummy, Mummy, this is my grandmummy, and she let me sleep with her last night."

"Yes, my darling. She is my mummy, and we're going to stay with her, Granddaddy, and your uncle forever."

As soon as Francine began to understand, with the help of Dr. Donahue's weekly counselling sessions and the resumption of her breathing exercises and self-affirmation techniques, how insidiously her mother-in-law had controlled her, she began to recover. Francine realized she had become so confused about what she was feeling, that she had suppressed her emotions and identified with Penelope, mistaking her intermittent abuse for acts of kindness.

One day when Cassandra was visiting, Francine, unable to contain her lingering feelings of resentment and mistrust any longer, blurted, "Why didn't you answer my letters? I wrote to both of you every week starting the first year after Mark and I left. I sent cards to all my family and friends every Christmas, and not one person even bothered to respond. I was so hurt it was little wonder that Penelope became my only friend in the world."

The glance between Patricia and Cassandra summed up what must have occurred at 393 Wellington Crescent. Francine was incredulous. "Neither of you received any of my letters or cards? For years, Hazel brought me stationary, envelopes, the most beautiful selection of cards, and stamps, always promising me that they were posted. Did no one ever get my mail?" As reality dawned upon Francine, any remnant of loyalty for Penelope dissipated into thin air, replaced with justifiable rage.

✳

No one could have been more relieved when the wheels finally touched down on the tarmac of LaGuardia Airport than Francine. Regardless of the oversized seats, neither she nor Cassandra could do little more than doze for short periods. Alex, on the other hand, was lost to the world from the minute they departed from Toronto. When at last Francine could plant her feet firmly on the ground, she conceded that as much as she appreciated the speed with which they had arrived at their destination, she would far rather travel by car.

All thoughts of weariness disappeared, however, when they spotted Jessica and Edward waving frantically as they came down the escalator at the arrivals gate. Years had passed since the foursome had been together, and the anticipation of five days in each other's company was enough of an adrenaline rush to propel them into a flurry of activities.

The three girlfriends wrapped their arms around each other in a circle of enthusiastic hugging. Edward and Alex exchanged handshakes before moving the luggage outside to a taxi stand. Soon, they were on their way to the historic New York Buckingham Hotel on the corner of 57th Street and 6th Avenue. They had followed Hope's recommendation to register at the hotel on one of Manhattan's choicest corners. At the intersection of art, music, and fashion, the privileged Midtown location provided effortless access to Central Park, the Metropolitan Museum of Modern Art, Lincoln Center, and Fifth Avenue couture.

＊

One Sunday afternoon at the farm, Cassandra had been lamenting that she could never afford the cost of the Buckingham when Alex said, "Oh, sorry, Cass. I must have forgotten to mention that I've booked a two-bedroom suite for the three of us. I hope you don't mind my presumption, but I've stayed there before, and I'm aware of its proximity to all the touristy sites and for Hope's recital."

Cassandra could not help staring at Alex as she thought, *So, this is how the rich and powerful do things!* As the only child of a physician, she had certainly never lacked for any of life's necessities or material possessions, but her family had always planned and budgeted for major purchases and travel expenditures. The notion of booking an extra international airline ticket and a suite in one of New York City's most elegant hotels was foreign to her. Once she recovered, she said, "Thanks, again, Alex, for including me in your travel arrangements."

"You're welcome, Cass. By the time I finally graduated with my degree, Penelope had already moved Francine and Mark into her grand house. When at last I could access my trust fund, I discovered that my grandmother had left me the bulk of my grandfather's fortune. Money comes with benefits as well as pitfalls, and I'll never be able to thank you enough for bringing me with you. True to my promise, I'll sleep in the spare room, and you and Francine can share the master bedroom."

Even Darrin had glanced up from his newspaper at Alex. He had been full of surprises since he had returned to the McGregor farm. Possibly for the first time in his life, Alex was earning his keep by becoming Darrin's right-hand man with his burgeoning flock of sheep, rising as soon as the aging farmer left for the pasture. Since Alex could spend hours with Mark during the day and at mealtimes, he had not once complained about bunking in with the hired man in his lodgings.

Eventually, all the McGregors' friends and neighbours came to visit Francine and Mark, with the exception of Michael. Everyone was pleased to become reacquainted with Alex, welcoming him back to the district. True to form though, Pat made sure that Michael was reunited with her daughter and grandson by taking them to join Margaret on Monday afternoons for tea.

As the date to fly to New York drew nearer, Francine began to prepare Mark that he would be staying with Grandmummy and Granddaddy. He had become so besotted with his grandparents and the wide-open spaces of their farm that his only concern was whether he could sleep with them during his mother's absence. When Mark said, "Mummy, I have to stay and look after the two baby lambs Uncle Darrin gave me," Francine became overwhelmed with fond memories of her welcome to the McGregor sheep farm so many years earlier.

No sooner had the five friends sat down in the Buckingham café than Jessica said, "So, can I tell you our news, and no, we are not about to start a family. On Monday morning, as you are flying back to Canada, Edward and I'll be on our way to the oldest medical school in the Western United States, the Stanford University School of Medicine near Palo Alto, California. Both of us have been awarded postdoctoral fellowships, Edward for internal medicine, and mine, of course, for oncology. I'm especially excited, because the medical school has a long history of pioneering innovations in the diagnosis and treatment of cancer."

"Wow, congratulations!" Francine said. "You both are going to become famous doctors, but then Cassandra and I always told you that, Jessica. We just never predicted that you would marry a man as smart as you."

In the midst of the friends' felicitations, Alex ordered the best champagne the hotel had to offer. After enhancing everyone's orange juice, he made a toast to Jessica and Edward.

"Thank you to the best friends anyone could ever wish for. We're so glad that we can all be together this weekend." Jessica paused, glanced toward Francine, and then continued. "Our only disappointment might be that none of us can see Hope until after her performance at her debut party. If you thought Hope was perfectionistic when she was studying music in Brandon, you will never believe how uncompromising she has become. After my folks visited for ten days in Toronto, they flew with us to New York to see Hope before returning home. She lamented that she only had time to join us for a quick pre-curtain dinner at the Grand Tier before we left for our concert, and within the hour, she was gone. However, New York is a fascinating city, and rest assured, we'll all be too enthralled to miss Hope."

The greatest artists of classical music since the time Carnegie Hall was built in 1891 had performed in the Main Hall, known as the most prestigious concert stage in the United States, and Hope Harding was no exception. Her guests were ushered to a second-tier box with six seats.

When Hope glided across the stage on the right of the seated musicians in the orchestra pit toward Sir Georg Solti, she appeared diminutive. Attired in an exquisite long azure silk gown, which the guests fortunate to be included in her celebratory party observed enhanced the colour of her eyes, she looked more ethereal than earthly. By the "Adagio (F major)" of Brahms' only violin concerto, known for its lyrical melodies and rich orchestration, the great hall stilled to the plaintive sounds of the Stradivarius as the virtuoso seized their collective souls, transporting them to a realm far beyond their temporal being.

The silence persisted after the completion of the "Allegro giocoso, ma non troppo vivace (D major)." When the audience at last descended to earth, realizing that forty minutes had passed, they erupted in a soaring melding of "Brava!" and "Encore!" Nonetheless, Hope's debut at Carnegie Hall would long be remembered for her unprecedented encore of the grandeur Beethoven's "Violin Concerto in D Major, Op. 61" in its entirety. Hope's impromptu performance was followed by her signature piece before she left the auditorium. No one would ever know if the orchestra had had an opportunity to rehearse the second concerto, but all were cognizant that a heavenly spirit had touched their souls.

＊

Hope's champagne flute was being replaced when she glanced into his admiring eyes. "You are gorgeous."

His response was instant. "And you are divine."

Too much time had elapsed before she could partake in the long-awaited reunion of the foursome. Hope was ecstatic that all three had arrived and were looking festive dressed in their finery. She was on the verge of hailing her friends to where she was standing when the dashing gentleman in the white tuxedo and sky-blue cummerbund had approached her. "I'm Alexander Winston the Third."

"Really!" In a flash the cells of her body began to tingle as she remembered how she had soared with Michael. But before Hope could articulate another word, she was enveloped in an enormous hug within the circle of her three lifelong friends. Following the usual salutations and updating comments, conversation faltered as Hope could not keep her eyes off Alex. He was equally mesmerized, and soon the two drifted away in search of another glass of champagne.

Jessica was quick to raise the alarm. "Francine, if I were you, I'd get my husband out of Hope's clutches this minute. Those two have eyes for none other, and the expressions I saw are sensual."

Even if Francine had any inclination to intercede, her opportunity was short-lived. When she looked around for them, they were nowhere to be seen. As the hours passed, she and Cassandra decided to walk back to the Buckingham. Neither had completely recovered from their red-eye flight or their extensive touring, and they wanted to enjoy their last day with Jessica and Edward, who had to leave early.

Alexander was neither seen nor heard from for the balance of their sojourn in New York. On Monday morning, when it came time to check out of the Buckingham Hotel, the two women gathered their belongings, leaving Alex's possessions where they lay, and departed on the premise that he would settle the bill. Cassandra suspected it would only be a matter of time before she would be filing Francine's divorce papers, which she would provide as a personal favour for her childhood friend. Deep in her heart, Cassandra felt that Michael would be a loving husband and father, and she would most certainly expedite his coming to call on Francine.

On the flight home, Cassandra doubted whether Alex could ever be true to anyone. She surmised it was not so much that he could never be free from his parental bonds as it was that he needed the accoutrements of wealth and position. Still, the first-class seat was a nice touch.

*

It arrived out of the blue on April 21, the first warm day of spring in 1978. The irony that the subpoena ordering Francine Winston, an "unfit mother," to appear at the Brandon Court of Queen's Bench on Monday, May 15, the day after Mother's Day, was not lost on her lawyer. In fact, Cassandra wondered if she had precipitated its arrival by serving Francine's divorce papers to 393 Wellington Crescent.

However, alerting his parents to the impending termination of their son's marriage had become inescapable. It was as if Alex had disappeared off the face of the earth. Eventually, Cassandra determined that, following her spectacular debut at Carnegie Hall, Hope had been invited for inaugural performances to the great music halls of London, Paris, Rome, and West Berlin. Conceivably, Alex had accompanied her, but the itinerary for her international tour was not available.

The grounds for Penelope's claim that Francine was incompetent to provide for Mark's care stemmed from allegations that, for the first three years of her son's life, Francine had been clinically depressed, and dependent upon her mother-in-law's intervention and generosity. Her decision to relocate to her parents' farm in Hartney amounted to little more than displacement of her maternal responsibilities, proven by the rapidity with which she relinquished the boy to his grandparents to facilitate her travel out of the country.

By the time Cassandra had read that Penelope was suing for the permanent custody of her grandson, Francine had all but become undone. For possibly the first time, Cassandra decided to take a tough stance with her friend. "Come on, now, Francine, have some faith in my legal expertise. Do you think for one second that I'm not going to fight tooth and nail for you and Mark?"

On Monday, April 24, Cassandra set up a temporary law office in the loft, and together the two women began to gather declarations from the residents of the District of Hartney to affirm that Francine was competent, caring, and entitled to raise her child. They happened to arrive at the Lingnan on the Wednesday afternoon, as Trin was serving none other than Carole Martin.

"Well, well, if it's not my birdbrained classmate from days of old, Francine Stonehenge. Oh, no, that's right. You think you got married and changed your name. So, where did you leave your bastard son?"

Without a backward glance, Cassandra left Francine to cope with Carole's belligerence, striding straight into the kitchen. She asked Trin to allow her into her living quarters and to tell her the location of the telephone before she said, "Please go to Francine, and make sure you keep Carole in the restaurant, even if the two of you are forced to sit on her. Whatever you do, don't let her leave."

As it transpired, her words of warning were unnecessary. Carole was having too much fun berating Francine, who stood frozen in amazement that Cassandra had walked out on her. At last, she uttered, "I'll have you know that my child is not illegitimate. I'm married to his father."

Carole's derisive laughter struck a chord in Francine, her nemesis reducing her to the same inadequate feelings she had experienced during their school days. When she stopped her chortling enough to speak, Carole said, "You always were so clueless about what was going on around you, although I don't suppose anyone would have bothered to tell you that there's no record of your marriage to Alexander Winston the Third."

"You're the one who has taken leave of your senses. We were

married in the Anglican church in Hartney."

"Well, smartass, why don't you explain that to the Holy Roman Catholic Church? My mother told me that not long ago, two representatives from the Archdiocese of Winnipeg made an official visit to the St. Andrew's Anglican Parish in Hartney. The young and inexperienced minister handed over your documentation, as they requested, and it has since been expunged. Then, when the new pastor realized his glaring mistake, he contacted Manitoba Vital Statistics, but it seems the good Reverend Walmseley, in his haste to start his vacation, neglected to register your marriage. Voila, no marriage certificate, and your kid is a bastard, like I said!"

At that moment, Cassandra returned to the restaurant and, overhearing Carole, it was all she could do not to cheer.

Within ten minutes, two RCMP from the Souris detachment arrived at the front door, with another officer covering the back to circumvent any attempt at flight. As the sergeant handcuffed her, he said, "Carole Martin, you are under arrest for alleged fraudulent activity in the Province of Manitoba." Then he read Carole her rights before leading her to the door and protecting her head as he positioned her in the backseat of the police cruiser.

✳

As soon as they arrived back to the McGregor farm, Cassandra enlightened Francine's family regarding the legal implications of all that had occurred during their eventful afternoon. "The minister's blunder and Reverend Walmseley's oversight render a divorce superfluous. In court tomorrow morning, I'll file for Mark's surname to be changed to Stonehenge."

Prior to their return, the friends had stopped at the St. Andrew's Parish in time to observe an elderly woman locking up the old English church. Francine was still digesting the fact that she was legally free from her marriage. However, as she admired the exceptional architecture of the historic house of worship, with its spacious grounds and well-kept trees, she realized she would have no qualms about another wedding in that beautiful place and briefly allowed herself to daydream about Michael.

Meanwhile, Cassandra was introducing herself to Betty and inquiring if she had a few minutes to spare. "Mrs. Martin, could you join Francine and me for a cup of tea at the café? I have a piece of information that I need to convey to you."

"If you don't mind, I'd rather that you came to my humble home, but please excuse the mess."

When they were seated in Betty's small parlour, Cassandra said, "Mrs. Martin, I'll come straight to the point. Before you hear it through the grapevine, I'm sorry to tell you that I've just had your daughter, Carole, arrested for alleged fraud."

Betty slumped even lower in her threadbare chair. "I'm glad. You can think me a terrible mother if you like, but it's what she deserves. She ruined our family and then showed up here driving a new car after her father died. She all but killed him. Oh, I know the doctor said Fred had cancer, but Carole caused enough worry and grief to put both of us in our graves. We had to sell the farm, which was supposed to go our son, Randy, to pay off Fred's mother's debts after Carole bilked her out of every dime she had, and more. Our other children all scattered, they were so embarrassed, and Fred and I were forced to rent this hovel. I was lucky the minister took pity and gave me a job, or we would have had to go on welfare."

Neither Cassandra nor Francine dared to move while Betty vented her anguish. After Betty paused and breathed a deep sigh, Cassandra asked, "Mrs. Martin, did you ever report Carole's actions to the police?"

"I would have, but Fred wouldn't let me. He didn't want the whole district knowing our dirty little secrets. Even so, in no time, all kinds of nasty rumours spread. That's why the other kids left."

"Mrs. Martin, I'm a lawyer. I'll not ask you to appear in court, but would you consider making a written statement of what you have told us? We have evidence from several other elderly women who Carole deceived, but the impact on her own family could send her to jail for a long time."

While Betty made a list of the events, beginning with the day Fred received the call from his mother saying she was going to be evicted, Cassandra telephoned the Souris RCMP station and asked them to impound Carole's car. There was little she could do to compensate the senior citizen, but she intended to appeal for Betty to be awarded the automobile.

Later, with Francine continuing to answer Pat and Daniel's questions, Cassandra placed a telephone call to Judge Barclay. "I'm sorry, your honour, to reach you so late in the day. Do you have any availability to meet in your chambers tomorrow? I need to apprise you of critical developments in two significant cases."

"And, Ms. Jamison, you expect to keep me in suspense for nigh on to twenty-four hours? I thought you knew me better than that! We'll attend to the paperwork tomorrow, but give me your verbal update now, please."

*

Derek Barclay vividly remembered his telephone conversation with Judge O'Meara and the police sketch he had received in the mail several years earlier. He'd had such an inkling of familiarity with the woman's face outlined in the drawing that it bothered him for days. The more he studied the picture, the more convinced he became that he knew her, but his memory of her identity continued to elude him.

One afternoon when Cassandra had been in his chambers, on an offhand chance that she might help him in his perplexity, Derek said,

"Ms. Jamison, please do me a favour, and look at this sketch."

He had scarcely given her the image when she proclaimed, "Why, that's Carole Martin from Hartney, Manitoba!"

In a less formal circumstance, Derek would have hugged her. "Thank you. I was certain she'd crossed my path, but do you think I could put a finger on her name?"

They alerted the police immediately to her identity, but although a nationwide search warrant had been issued, Carole had vanished. That is, until Cassandra's quick thinking and subsequent actions culminated in the alleged perpetrator being arrested by the RCMP detachment in Souris and subsequently transferred to the Brandon Correctional Centre.

"Ms. Jamison, I applaud you," Derek said. "I'll dispose Carole Martin's arraignment for Monday, May fifteenth, immediately following Mrs. Winston the Second's suit seeking custody of her grandson. And tomorrow morning, I'll sign a name change court order, and have the court issue Ms. Francine Stonehenge a certified copy of her son's name change from Winston to her maiden surname."

The Court of Queen's Bench in the Old Law Courts Building, made from Manitoba limestone and brick marble from Quebec, on Princess Street in Brandon filled to capacity as soon as the majestic oak doors opened at 9:00 a.m. on Monday, May 15, 1978. They all came from the District of Hartney, with the exception of eight adults and one small boy. Neither Francine nor any of her family or Betty Martin or any of her other three children appeared on the Monday, which, over time Judge Barclay would refer to as "Hartney's Day in Court."

When court was called to order, the plaintiff and her high-priced Winnipeg lawyer were at their table, but the attorney for the defendant was seated alone. Vincent McGee, Q.C., could not believe Francine had not arrived, but then he would never have imagined that, as the top-paid criminal lawyer in the province, he would be the counsellor in a custody suit. He had only made the concession to Alexander Winston II, because he was Paddy Riley's friend and business partner. Rumours abounded that Paddy's cousin, Judge O'Meara was on the cusp of retirement. Vincent would capitulate to almost anyone, even the man who referred to himself as "Lord" Winston, to facilitate his appointment to the bench. And his reimbursement was exorbitant.

The Winnipeg lawyer was brought back to reality sharply when he heard the defendant's attorney say, "Your honour, may I make a motion for dismissal? After due diligence with the Vital Statistics Agency within every provincial and territorial jurisdiction, neither a record of the birth or marriage for Francine Winston, nor of the birth of Mark Christopher Winston, exists. I hereby submit the written documentation from each of the agencies throughout Canada."

Counsellor McGee could not believe his utterance. "Jesus, Mary, and Joseph! What the hell are you saying?"

With a resounding thud, Judge Barclay's gavel came down. "Order in the court. One more outburst from you, Mr. McGee, and I'll cite you for contempt. Ms. Jamison, approach the bench."

Within minutes, Judge Barclay proclaimed, "All rise. I declare the charges of Mrs. Penelope Winston the Second against the unfit mother, the non-existent Francine Winston, and the lawsuit seeking permanent custody of the non-existent child, Mark Christopher Winston, null and void. Case dismissed. Court is in recess and will resume at ten o'clock. Clear the court."

✳

Before leaving, Judge Barclay passed a note to the court clerk requesting Ms. Jamison to meet him in chambers in ten minutes.

"Please come in," he said when she arrived, "and find a comfortable chair. I have a fresh pot of coffee, and you take sugar and cream, if I'm not mistaken."

"Thank you, your honour. My nerves would appreciate something to calm them."

"Let's drop formalities within the confines of these walls. If you were nervous, no one would have known it, least of all Vincent McGee. You were brilliant, Cassandra. That had to be the shortest lawsuit in my career on the bench, and the fact you left the famed Winnipeg counsellor sputtering in my courtroom was delightful. I'm tremendously relieved that you're not representing Carole Martin, although after essentially making a citizen's arrest, I'll see you in court." Taking a drink of coffee, he continued. "However, another reason I've asked to speak with you is because my father is dying, and he has proposed that you be given first refusal to purchase Barclay & Barclay. Over the years, he has done his share of philandering, but he always did know the law and the first-rate lawyers, as did his father. My grandfather would not only have approved of how quickly you became senior partner but also of you owning his firm, regardless of what you may choose to name it. Please, think about it, Cassandra, when you have a chance. Now, we're due to return."

Once Judge Barclay had asked the audience in the full courthouse to be seated, he allowed for several moments of silence. He had intended to study the defendant, but instead he was captivated by Susan Smith's stunning beauty. She was accompanied by a man who resembled her professed husband of years ago. When he averted his eyes to the accused, although she looked defiantly at him, she gave no indication that she recognized him.

As the proceedings progressed, with the alleged fraudster pleading "not guilty" and choosing trial by judge, Judge Barclay believed beyond a doubt that Carole must not have any recollection of her previous encounters with him.

Following a quick perusal of his court dates, he asked her court-appointed lawyer and the Crown attorney to approach the bench. With both in agreement, when they returned to their respective counsel tables, Judge Barclay struck his table lightly with his gavel. "This court is adjourned until the morning of Monday, June nineteenth, nineteen seventy-eight at nine o'clock, when the criminal trial of R v. Martin will commence."

*

It was shortly after 11:00 a.m., and with any luck, Derek would reach Tiffany by telephone before she started to prepare her lunch. Both sets of twins were in school all day, and if his wife were available, he would suggest they go to their golf and country club for a spontaneous outing.

"Hi, hon. How's your morning going? I've wrapped up here with record speed, and I would like to take one of my favourite girls out for the afternoon. We can have a bite to eat, and if we manage a tee time, we might fit in nine holes before the kids arrive home."

"What a lovely surprise on such a beautiful day. If we don't have time for golf, I would enjoy a leisurely walk along the Assiniboine Riverbank trails. I'll be ready and waiting when you come."

When Derek drove into the driveway, Tiffany met him with their walking shoes. "How do you feel about going to the Royal Oak Inn before our stroll in the Park? It's such a rarity to have my husband all to myself on a weekday that I don't feel like sharing him with our friends at the club."

They were seated in the elegant restaurant, and after placing their order, Tiffany said, "You look as smug as the cat that swallowed the canary. Do you want to tell me about it, my darling?"

As Derek narrated the morning's events, a smile of growing gratification heightened his handsome features. "You would not believe the number of people from Hartney who were in the courthouse. I was especially pleased to see a woman I represented years ago at an inquest into the deaths of her parents. Susan Smith was understandably devastated by their loss. From what I observed this morning though, she has taken back her life and is with the man who had presumed to have married her in a fake ceremony in Hawaii, and they're expecting a baby. I've heard so many horrific stories during my years on the bench that it warmed my heart to see them still together under much happier circumstances. And I'll never forget the adroitness with which Cassandra Jamison dispensed with the wealthy Penelope Winston the Second and her pretentious lawyer in their claim to take custody of Cass's godchild. Now to be seated here with you, seeing the love in your beautiful eyes, all in all, it is a most soul-satisfying day."

✳

The surprises began the moment court was in session. When he was seated behind the bench, Judge Barclay raised his head to peruse his courtroom and observed Carole Martin seated alone at the defendant's table. She was staring directly at him and grinning from ear to ear. It was then he realized his mistake, understanding that the accused not only recognized him but also considered that she could get the best of him during her trial.

Suddenly, memories of the audacious adolescent assailed him, but Derek restored his calm with several steady intakes of breath. It was rare for him to underestimate anyone, and now that the defendant had decided to represent herself, he would be unrelenting with the rules of evidence, objections, and observation of courtroom protocol. Even though Derek anticipated that she could be challenging, he had full confidence in his extensive legal education, training, and experience.

Carole did not stand a chance. Allyson Wright, the Crown attorney, was superb in her presentation of evidence, calling forth key eyewitnesses and plaintiffs, seniors all, several now destitute after being scammed of their life savings by the accused. Nonetheless, it was Cassandra Jamison, when she was called to the witness stand to read Betty Martin's impact statement, who provided the crowning touch.

On Thursday, June 29, 1978, Judge Derek Barclay handed down his fair and impartial decision. He found the defendant guilty as charged of fraud and sentenced her to four years at the Federal Penitentiary for Women in Kingston, Ontario, and he attached five years of probation supervision after release, along with an order for restitution. Any application for the granting of parole would be contingent upon Carole's demonstration of repayment to her multiple victims.

*

On the Monday evening, one week following Francine's return from New York City, Michael called on her. He had his afternoon tea with Margaret, who was quick to apprise him that, due to two fateful errors, the marriage between Francine and Alex did not exist. Michael grabbed a bite to eat and showered before driving to the McGregors' farmstead.

He had scarcely climbed the steps to the veranda when Mark came flying out the front door. "Michael, Michael, you've finally come. You have to see my two lambs before they grow into sheep."

Francine arrived on the heels of her son, and although trying not to be as enthusiastic in her welcome, she was nonetheless overjoyed with his arrival. With Mark holding Francine's left hand and Michael's right, the trio headed toward the pasture. When the rays of the setting sun glimmered through the heart-shaped leaves of the majestic poplars, Michael had a bounce in his step that he had not experienced for years.

*

Michael seldom repeated the same mistake twice. Following the fiasco of returning Hope's ring, he was hesitant about making a similar purchase. It was only the timing that perplexed him. Should he wait until after he asked Francine or have an engagement ring in hand to present to her if she consented to marry him?

With every other matter of his heart, Michael did not have the slightest doubt. During the agonizing three years of Francine's absence, he had missed her beyond measure, thinking of her whenever his mind was otherwise not occupied with the demands of his principalship. Falling asleep at night had been nerve-wracking as he fretted about what had happened to Francine and her baby.

Bide his time he did though. Perhaps it was his European mother's influence, but in many ways, Michael was old school. Although he was a frequent visitor to the McGregors' home, it was not until he had heard the blissful news that she was free that he approached her uncles and Mother Pat to inquire if he could court Francine. He was patient when they began to talk about their future, and Francine shared that she still needed time to recover from her ordeal in Winnipeg, as well as to become accustomed to the idea that Alex was no longer in the picture.

On Christmas morning, he had been invited to join the McGregors for brunch before all their many close friends gathered at the Griffins' log home for a festive potluck dinner. When they had consumed until they were satiated and the presents had all been exchanged, Michael said, "It's such a beautiful crisp day, would you care to join me for a walk, Francine?"

Patricia sensed that Michael might have an ulterior motive, and knowing her grandson, she immediately distracted Mark by offering to help put together the train set he had received for Christmas.

They soon reached the edge of the garden, where Michael brushed the snow off the bench overlooking the hillside. "I've kept a present for you until now," he said once they were seated. Then he lowered himself onto his right knee in front of her. "Francine, will you marry me?"

She had barely breathed "Yes" when Michael presented her with a small jewellery box, in which a delicate shared-prong one-carat princess-cut diamond in a gold setting was waiting to be placed upon her willing finger.

✳

With all the windows and doors open, the old English church was not overly hot on the summer morning of Saturday, July 21, 1979. The ceremony was scheduled to commence at ten o'clock, but people had been gathering on the spacious well-treed grounds since shortly after nine. Those who were not on the guest list came anyway; the Hartney district had undergone a much-needed coalescing transition following the days in the Brandon Court of Queen's Bench.

Francine was demure in a two-piece light-blue linen ensemble, while Cassandra, her maid of honour, and Susan, her bridesmaid, were apparelled in pale pink. Michael was attired in a dark blue suit, as was his best man, Robert. To the sheer delight of everyone, so was Mark, in his dual role as groomsman and ring bearer. Mark Christopher had learned to sign his name, and he became the youngest person ever in the annals of the historic church to witness a wedding record.

Coffee and cake were served outdoors before the bridal party and invited guests departed for the Devonshire's colourful floral garden for a sit-down luncheon catered by the women of the community. Michael and Francine were planning to leave early in the afternoon to begin their journey to the west coast. They tussled with the notion of taking Mark with them until it was settled by the boy himself, when he said, "Mummy and Michael, I can't come with you. I now have four lambs of my own to care for, and Uncle Darrin needs my help with all his sheep."

Neither Francine nor Michael had ever seen the Rocky Mountains. By the time they motored through the gradual incline of the foothills in Alberta, they were wonderstruck by the majesty of the approaching peaks. Once they reached Banff, both were amazed at how the mountains dominated the skyline. They enjoyed touring and walking around the resort town before travelling to the picturesque Lake Louise, its glacier-fed turquoise water ringed by high mountain summits. After staying two nights in the stately chateau overlooking one of the most scenic sites in Canada, which was beyond what either could have imagined, they hiked to the Lake Agnes Tea House for a bird's-eye view.

Still, for all the magnificent scenes, it was along their leisurely drive through the awe-inspiring Kootenay National Park on the Banff-Windermere Highway that Michael and Francine were most enamoured, especially with the village of Radium Hot Springs. They disembarked from their vehicle at the sign that promised "The Mountains Shall Bring Peace to the People."

Two days later, on a hike about a half a mile above the Radium Hot Springs Pools, in a grove of towering red cedars along the Redstreak Campground trail, they came to a special place. No sound could be heard. Holding hands, Francine and Michael sat on a large flat rock listening to the silence and feeling the peace.

Printed in Canada